W9-BTH-474

Dr Whittle reviews the latest archaeological evidence on Neolithic Europe from 7000 to 2500 BC. Describing important areas, sites and problems, he addresses the major themes that have engaged the attention of scholars: the transition from a forager lifestyle; the rate and dynamics of change; and the nature of Neolithic society. He challenges conventional views, arguing that Neolithic society was rooted in the values and practices of its forager predecessors right across the continent. The processes of settling down and adopting farming were piecemeal and slow. Only gradually did new attitudes emerge, to time and the past, to the sacred realms of ancestors and the dead, to nature and to the concept of community.

Unique in its broad and up-to-date coverage of long-term processes of change on a continental scale, this completely rewritten and revised version of Whittle's *Neolithic Europe: a survey* reflects radical changes in the evidence and in interpretative approaches over the past decade.

CAMBRIDGE WORLD ARCHAEOLOGY

EUROPE IN THE NEOLITHIC

The Cambridge World Archaeology series is addressed to students and professional archaeologists, and to academics in related disciplines. Each volume presents a survey of the archaeology of a region of the world, providing an up-to-date account of research and integrating recent findings with new concerns of interpretation. While the focus is on a specific region, broader cultural trends are discussed and the implications of regional findings for cross-cultural interpretations considered. The authors also bring anthropological and historical expertise to bear on archaeological problems, and show how both new data and changing intellectual trends in archaeology shape inferences about the past.

Books in the series

RAYMOND ALLCHIN AND BRIDGET ALLCHIN, *The rise of civilization in India and Pakistan* (1982)

DAVID PHILLIPSON, *African archaeology* (1985)

ALASDAIR WHITTLE, *Neolithic Europe: a survey* (1985)

CLIVE GAMBLE, *The palaeolithic settlement of Europe* (1986)

CHARLES HIGHAM, *Archaeology of mainland South East Asia* (1989)

SARAH MILLEDGE NELSON, *The archaeology of Korea* (1993)

DAVID PHILLIPSON, *African archaeology* (second revised edition) (1993)

OLIVER DICKINSON, *The Aegean Bronze Age* (1994)

KAREN OLSEN BRUHNS, *Ancient South America* (1994)

SE

CAMBRIDGE WORLD ARCHAEOLOGY

EUROPE IN THE NEOLITHIC

THE CREATION OF NEW WORLDS

ALASDAIR WHITTLE

School of History and Archaeology
University of Wales, Cardiff

CAMBRIDGE
UNIVERSITY PRESS

Published by the Press Syndicate of the University of Cambridge
The Pitt Building, Trumpington Street, Cambridge CB2 1RP
40 West 20th Street, New York, NY 10011-4211, USA
10 Stamford Road, Oakleigh, Melbourne 3166, Australia

First published 1996

Printed in Great Britain at the University Press, Cambridge

A catalogue record for this book is available from the British Library

Library of Congress cataloguing in publication data
Whittle, A. W. R.
    Europe in the Neolithic: the creation of new worlds / Alasdair
Whittle.
        p.   cm. – (Cambridge world archaeology)
    Rev. edn of Neolithic Europe, 1985.
    ISBN 0 521 44476 4 (hardcover). – ISBN 0 521 44920 0 (pbk)
    1. Neolithic period–Europe.   2. Man, Prehistoric–Europe.
    3. Europe–Antiquities.   I. Whittle, A. W. R. Neolithic Europe.
    II. Title.   III. Series.
    GN776.2.A1W45   1966
936–dc20   95-12812 CIP

ISBN 0 521 444764 hardback
ISBN 0 521 449200 paperback

Europe in the Neolithic: the creation of new worlds succeeds and replaces *Neolithic
Europe: a survey* by the same author (first published 1985; ISBN 0 521 24799 3
(hardback) and 0 521 28970 X (paperback))

SE

For Elisabeth

CONTENTS

ILLUSTRATIONS

PREFACE

The publishers of this series asked me for another edition of my *Neolithic Europe: a survey* (1985), and this is the result: a new book altogether. In it I try to characterise a way of life rooted in the forager past, especially in its social values of sharing and integration, but distinguishable not only by material and economic changes but by new beliefs about descent, beginnings and time: about the place of people in the scheme of things. If I give less importance than many to some of the technological changes seen in the archaeological record, I emphasise throughout the importance of long, slow, Neolithic histories.

This book is more selective than its predecessor. I say far less about research traditions and conditions, and problems of chronology, except when they directly affect my narrative, and I describe far fewer material sequences for their own sake. These matters have not become less important, but both the specialist and the student interested in them will find plenty of signposts to them in the references at the end of the book. In presenting a personal synthesis achieved through selection, I am not aiming to reflect orthodoxy or consensus, even if such existed. I try to make it clear where I diverge from other possible versions of Neolithic histories.

Where does Europe begin and end? My Europe in this book is a selection of places and regions from the wider area of modern political Europe. Some might extend Europe as far east as the Urals. I cover selected aspects of Ukraine, and the river Dniepr is my effective boundary. Though I wish I had more, I have little space for Byelorussia or the north-west part of Russia. I discuss southern Scandinavia in some depth, but not the rest of the north. In the heart of central and western Europe, I have had to choose some areas for longer treatment than others; I say little in detail about the upper Danube basin, for example, nor about the catchment of the Seine: the Paris basin. In times later – and earlier – than the Neolithic period, it would be quite arbitrary to separate the north African coast from the Iberian peninsula or the central Mediterranean; in the Neolithic I see a different kind of development in north Africa, and in this instance it is convenient to follow the political geography of modern or historical times. For lack of space, my treatment of the central and west Mediterranean is briefer than the region deserves.

Not only is this Europe geographically very varied, but it has numberless histories. In the Neolithic period, there were many Neolithics. Such diversity encourages me to select themes and problems. I offer neither a handbook nor an encyclopaedia. I try first to characterise the forager way of life, and then to examine the conditions in which new forms of belief, social relations, material culture and subsistence were adopted. In nearly all areas, I now believe that it was largely indigenous people who created Neolithic histories. Not only was this process gradual in most regions, in no one region were its consequences quite the same. That is my justification, if such is needed, for selection. I recognise the sting in Peter Levi's dictum in *The Hill of Kronos* that 'the naive and parasitical scholar with insufficient time to be thorough is like a greedy man without a tin opener'. I can only say that I have opened many cans, and hope that the reader enjoys my arrangement of the resulting heaps.

Interpretation is unavoidable, central, obligatory. There can be no retreat into description alone. I do not believe that the past exists only in the present, but the evidence from the past that is available to us is the result of choices and interpretations (where to look, what to excavate, how to record) in the first place. I make no claim that we can truly know what went on in the Neolithic period. Would there not have been innumerable contemporary ways of telling the same story, even in one region at one moment of time? The challenge is to try to think imaginatively about other lives. Any book of this kind is really a prolonged conditional sentence, an extended hypothetical argument. In the interests of readability, I have tried to reduce the number of stated qualifications, but they should be taken as read throughout.

I use calendrical chronology throughout, based on calibrated radiocarbon dates, and tree ring dates where they are available. Radiocarbon dating is not precise. That is part of the nature of a Neolithic narrative. The rich evidence also allows many other ways of telling. The reader can decide which are most successful.

ACKNOWLEDGEMENTS

My debts to others are substantial. I am grateful to my university for study leave, to my department for a travel grant to Greece, and to my colleagues for taking on routine duties in my absence. I am grateful to the British Academy and to the Polish and Hungarian Academies of Science for supporting exchange visits, and to all those Polish and Hungarian colleagues who helped me. Among many others, the following have supplied essential information: C. Perlès; K. Gallis; G. Bailey; P. Halstead; J. Bintliff; Tj. van Andel; N. Kyparissi-Apostolika; J. Chapman; L. Bartosiewicz; R. Kertész; E. Lenneis; S. Hiller; J. Lüning; J. Weiner; S. Andersen; N. Andersen; C. and D. Mordant; C.-T. Le Roux; J. L'Helgouac'h; S. Cassen; L. Louwe Kooijmans; W.-J. Hogestijn; G. Eogan; G. Cooney; R. Whitehouse; C. Scarre; and P. Dolukhanov. On my travels, the following were particularly helpful: Kostas Kotsakis; Jacek Lech; Zofia Sulgostowska; Hanna Kowalewska-Marszałek; Romuald Schild; Ryszard Grygiel; Jolanta Małecka-Kukawka and Stanisław Kukawka; Janusz Kruk; Halina Dobrzańska; Eszter Bánffy; and Nándor Kalicz. I am particularly grateful to Clive Gamble, Robin Skeates, Bob Chapman, Humphrey Case, Julian Thomas, Caroline Malone, Simon Stoddart and Lawrence Barfield, for reading draft chapters and offering constructive criticism. Douglass Bailey and Richard Bradley read more of the manuscript than was probably good for them, and offered invaluable criticism and encouragement throughout.

My university library in Cardiff and the Ashmolean Library, Oxford, provided every help, and my brother Peter and his family kept an open door for me during innumerable trips to the latter. Howard Mason did all the drawings with his customary skill.

My family kept me going throughout the process of research and writing, and I dedicate the book to my wife, Elisabeth, for her love and support.

CHAPTER 1

THE TIME OF ANCESTORS

What then is my Europe? It is in the mind . . .
Flann O'Brien, *The Best of Myles*

Some histories

This history could start in many ways and in many places.[1] In Europe as a whole, the Neolithic period begins from after 7000 BC. What we choose to label as Neolithic societies appeared in south-east Europe between 7000 and 5500 BC, in the central and west Mediterranean from before 6000 BC, and in central Europe from about 5500 BC, and finally in north-west Europe from before 4000 BC. The period can be defined as lasting till around 3000 BC in south-east Europe, and about 2500 BC elsewhere.

In one beginning – in north-west Europe, around 4500 BC, well into a wider history – the ancestors were invited to occupy stone houses, dark, quiet and difficult of access, and cajoled to remain with the hospitality of gifts of food and stone. In their honour, large upright megaliths were set up, trees of stone that resisted time and the seasons. In later generations, with the spirits firmly rooted and now taken for granted, other forms of stone shrine were built, holding the idea of ancestors but allowing easier access for the comings and goings of people. Some chambers in the stone houses of the dead were roofed with pieces of earlier standing stones, fragments of memory from a timeless past. Human ancestors were laid in the shrines of the spirits. Now there were appeals to dry bones, and fingerings of empty skulls and motionless limbs. Human descent was traced through union with the spirits, and the shrines fostered regeneration, celebrated harmony in the universe, and expiated the guilt of beginning to domesticate the natural world.

Here I invoke the early Neolithic sequence of monument building in Brittany. As we shall see in chapters 6 and 7, not everyone would agree with the order of events, let alone my imaginative interpretation of them. In a sense, this hardly matters. What it should be possible to agree on is the individuality of this coastal region and its distinctive sequence. This particular unfolding of changes was also rooted in other, wider histories. I follow many other scholars of recent years in believing that the people of coastal Brittany who built these first monuments were the descendants of foragers who had kept the land in earlier millennia. This may not have been a large population, nor did it live an existence completely isolated from a wider world. Foragers in this area had themselves honoured their dead by placing them in small cists framed by stone, symbol of permanence, and by red deer antler, symbol of fertility and regeneration, inserted in the accumulations of feasting debris which archaeologists prosaically label shell middens. The idea of the stone house

1.1 The *Grand Menhir Brisé*, the former stone row and the restored Table des Marchand at Locmariaquer, Morbihan, Brittany. Photo: Laboratoire de préhistoire armoricaine, Université de Nantes.

must have come from the timber longhouses of central and western Europe, which appeared from about 5500 BC and which are now well documented in the Paris basin as well as as far east as Hungary. The builders of timber longhouses may themselves have been the descendants of native populations, who developed new forms of mobility to colonise the dense woodlands of the valley systems of central and western Europe. They kept domesticated animals and cultivated legumes and cereals. They probably made much less use of game and native plants than their predecessors, though the contrast can be exaggerated. It is unlikely, however, that people in Brittany undertook new constructions in pursuit of or as an expression of the acquisition of a new form of subsistence. In fact, the evidence in the region, as in many others in north-west Europe, suggests that they only very gradually became farmers, a label which is probably inadequate and inappropriate right through the Neolithic period. Other ideas to do with domesticated resources and with novel ways of sharing and presenting food in clay containers may have come up to Brittany from the west Mediterranean via the central-west coast of France.

The north-west coastal region of France at the start of its Neolithic was thus linked to two other major regions. The populations of longhouse builders in central Europe, archaeologically the Linear Pottery culture or LBK, were in turn linked, by one means or another, to a world further east, in the Balkans. Most scholars have accepted that the LBK was the product of further colonisation by farming communities established in south-east Europe from about 6500–6000 BC onwards, as far north as the Hungarian plain in the Carpathian basin. In this book, in chapter 6, I argue for a different history, of the continuity and adaptation of local population. At this stage, the difference of opinion does not matter. What is important is the history around the appearance of the LBK. This takes us on to the history of south-east Europe, and beyond. In the central and west Mediterranean basin, there is likewise little agreement about the conditions in which the Neolithic period began, nor is even the date firmly established in many regions of the basin. I support, in chapter 8, a lower chronology, but again advocate a central role for indigenous population throughout the area. The reasons for the adoption, sometimes wholesale, often at first partial, of new subsistence resources and new forms of material culture were complex. They may have been rather different from those in south-east Europe, in central Europe and in parts of northern Europe. Pots and sheep may have been adopted initially as novelties, to complement existing routines of wide-ranging hunting and foraging, and to bolster already established traditions of food sharing. That the subsistence base of the Mediterranean basin became slowly agrarian tells us nothing about the circumstances of initial change. People in Brittany around 4500 BC were therefore at the end of a complex history of histories, of whose details they may hardly have been aware.

I have begun with Brittany because its evidence is both familiar and appealing to me. One has only to turn to other parts of north-west Europe to find other beginnings and other sequences, even though there are strong similarities. Offshore in Ireland, a pattern of constructions rather similar to that in Brittany can be seen, culminating in the great monuments, the so-called passage tombs, of the Boyne valley. In southern England, stone and wooden shrines became gradually more elaborate and were increasingly annexed for the expression of human concerns. By about 3500 BC, people began another kind of construction new to the region, widespread in other parts of western Europe but markedly absent so far from Brittany and barely present in Ireland. Special places were defined by circuits of ditch and bank. These enclosures were in part sacred arenas, where the ancestors, the dead and the natural world were treated with, but also the scene for an intense social negotiation, to do with the acceptance of a harmony of symbols, a working out through feasting and gift giving of matters of identity and cooperation. We do not really know why such enclosures appeared in such numbers at this time across such a wide area of western Europe, from central-west France to southern Scandinavia, but I argue in chapter 7 that they were part of the process by which new forms of community were created, rather than merely the unexplained symptom of more populous farmers. It should be unsurprising that the idea of enclosures had a longer history. Ditched circuits had first been constructed in the later part of the LBK, and were then elaborated in the Lengyel culture of central Europe. It remains fully to unravel the transmission and elaboration of the idea.

In later phases of the Neolithic, what happened was still dominated by histories of near and far. In Brittany, northern France, Britain and Ireland, the time of ancestors still counted for much. In some areas, shrines and ossuaries were still built or at least used in the old ways. Even larger enclosures were constructed, of ditches, banks and upright stones, creating formalised spaces which guided people through rituals of gathering and feasting. In Brittany people jogged the memory of ancestors with great stonelines. Many scholars have seen these later monumental constructions as expressions of social power exercised by segments of the community, but I shall argue that they were as much to do with pre-serving and celebrating the timeless world of the past.

Roughly between the Rhine and the Vistula, a different world came into being in the later part of the Neolithic. There the past was more taken for granted. In the Globular Amphora and Corded Ware cultures, burials variously celebrated the memory of particular individu-als, the importance of close kin, and the value of animals. People marked their identity by the display of material symbols appropriate to their age and gender. This has often been seen as a more warlike, perhaps male-dominated society, but I shall argue in chapter 7 that older values persisted, of hospitality, generosity and cooperation. People were not on their way to becoming better farmers. Their lives were still mobile. Herding cattle through cop-piced woodland may have been a far more common occupation than a sedentary existence tending cultivated plants. But this world was not unchanging. There was much more contact with other regions. The Corded Ware culture or complex as a material phenome-non was spread from the Rhine to far east of the Vistula, and from northern Switzerland far up into the eastern Baltic. It may have been affected by changes in the world of south-east Europe. This is the aftermath of the horizon at which many scholars introduce the speakers of Indo-European, irrupting out of the steppes to upset the stable world of settled life in the Balkans and Greece, and then spreading further west and north. One alternative approach has been to put the Indo-Europeans on a much earlier train, or to have them already in place in central or northern Europe. In chapters 5 and 7, I accept the tradi-tional linguistic arguments for a particular historical moment of language formation, but follow others in arguing for the creation and spread of new language by processes other than population movement. The history of the enculturation of steppe people may have been linked through widening contact to people far to their west.

A Neolithic world

A critique of some past models

The nineteenth-century term 'Neolithic' is redolent of novelty, but what was new in this period, and should an old label be retained? Over the successive generations of research, the Neolithic phenomenon has been approached in several different ways: as a chronology, a technology, a culture, an economy, a population, a social structure, and latterly as a con-ceptual system. In a sense the phenomenon embodies all these aspects. No one is sufficient on its own, though research has tended to emphasise one or other aspect at any one time, at the expense of others. There is also good reason to criticise the application of each succes-sive dominant model.

Chronology. In crude terms, the Neolithic period was first recognised as part of a wider chronology for prehistory. It rapidly acquired other connotations, but a concern with ordering time sequences has remained. The order of events is vital. Dendrochronology in the Alpine foreland now offers the possibility of reading the biographies of individual sites to precise calendar years, and it is also now possible to offer calendrical calibrations for radiocarbon dates right through the post-glacial period. But there is still not enough concern with the Neolithic period as history rather than as mere sequence.

Technology. On technological criteria, the Neolithic period was separated in the nineteenth century from its predecessors by the appearance of ground and polished stone tools and of pottery, innovations which were later seen to coincide with the introduction of new forms of subsistence. It is very doubtful whether we can meaningfully separate the Neolithic period from the preceding Mesolithic by such criteria. Foragers in the Mesolithic had effective technologies for heavy and light cutting, as well as for hunting, digging, and water and snow travel. They had woven and knotted nets and baskets for fishing, and they had containers. If technology is interpreted in its widest sense, Neolithic people were able to harness the pulling and lifting power of domesticated cattle, and developed use of the ard or scratch plough. But foragers must too have had effective means of tending plants and preparing soil, if they chose to do so.

Culture. Since the 1920s, if not before, the culture model has been a dominant way of organising the evidence for the Neolithic period in Europe. Some of the terminology already used in this introduction reflects the strength of the culture historical approach. One radical approach has been to dismiss the spatial patterning of material culture as an illusion created by the arbitrarily placed viewpoint of any given observer.[2] The problem lies, however, not with spatial patterning but on the one hand with its many layers ('polythetic' culture in the language of the 1960s) and on the other with its interpretation. The dominant mode of interpretation has been to read each cultural grouping as an ethnic entity, and to see the succession of cultural changes as a record of arrivals (rarely departures) of new 'people'. This is changing. Far fewer scholars in the Balkans, for example, now believe that the appearance of the Vinča culture (described in chapter 4) in the sixth millennium BC has to be explained in terms of the arrival of new population from further south, even though Vinča material culture was in many ways very different from what had preceded it. Most scholars in both Scandinavia and Britain would now see the beginnings of their Neolithics as the product of indigenous change rather than of new population arriving by colonisation. But the change of viewpoint has been selective. There is still an enormous disposition to believe in colonisation, which affects our interpretation of beginnings in south-east Europe, in central Europe and in the central and west Mediterranean, and of endings in south-east and central Europe. The development over recent years of both ethnoarchaeology and a theory of agency should allow us to see people as knowledgeable agents actively employing material culture in any number of social situations and strategies.[3] This kind of theory has still to be widely deployed with the European Neolithic evidence. One example is the late forager Ertebølle culture of southern Scandinavia (discussed in chapter 6). This is now widely seen as the indigenous predecessor of the regional early Neolithic, but the argument is often framed in economic terms, with little attention paid to the role of material culture in first maintaining and then altering a sense of identity.

Subsistence economy and settlement. Since the evolutionary characterisations of the nineteenth century (and even of the eighteenth-century Enlightenment), and reinforced by Childe's famous 1920s label of a 'Neolithic revolution', the Neolithic period has been seen again and again as an economic phenomenon. People in south-west Asia are seen to have developed control over both plants and animals, whether to solve problems of population and resource depletion or to underpin a sedentary lifestyle,[4] and the resulting spread of a new economy becomes inexorable. The inherent superiority of early agriculture over foraging has rightly been challenged, but the existence of a pre-formed agricultural 'package' is still widely accepted; discussion then centres on how long foragers could hold up the new machine. The whole concept received a further boost with the introduction some fifteen years ago of the idea of a 'secondary products revolution', in which new forms of traction and transport technology and new forms of animal exploitation, including milking and the use of wool, supplemented the initial intensive cultivation of cereals and the breeding of animals for meat.[5] In this view, whatever the undoubted merits of some aspects of the secondary products model, people hit the soils and grazing resources of Europe already as sophisticated 'farmers', programmed for a future career of relentless growth and intensification. There has been too little discussion of the social context of production.[6] In the chapters that follow I note many examples of what may be called a non-intensifying Neolithic, when people can be characterised by lives spent following cattle in woodland as much as on land cleared for cultivation, and when they defined themselves in relation to animals as subjects of social value rather than as objects of economic or dietary concern.

A recurrent and pervasive element of the economic model has been the assumption that while foragers led mobile lives, farmers were sedentary. Aspects of this have been challenged. Better knowledge of ethnography has produced many examples of more or less sedentary foragers, and a more discriminating vocabulary with which to describe different kinds of mobility. It has also raised awareness of patterns not well represented in the ethnographic record. On the other hand, the relation of sedentism to food production has been examined. It is possible to see sedentism as the cause of the adoption of food production, rather than food production as the enabler of sedentism.[7] But few scholars (including myself) have resisted the equation of 'farming' with 'settled life'. Following the lead given by a minority of scholars, this book strongly advocates a much more flexible approach to all these matters, right across the continent. I shall describe tell occupations in south-east Europe, for example, which have so often been seen as the acme of successful, sedentary Neolithic existence, as the anchors or tethers in patterns of radiating mobility.

Population. 'Economic archaeology' had its heyday in the early phase of 'processual archaeology', in the 1960s and 1970s, but both preceded that and has outlasted it. Interest in population dynamics has a similar history. Several population-led models were developed for the beginnings of domestication in south-west Asia, and in Europe the vision became one of farmers, blessed not only with an adaptable and productive subsistence base, but with powers of rapid breeding as well. In some circumstances, the adoption of agriculture was seen to lead to an unleashing of reproductive potential, after the heavy constraints of foraging existence. In one view, the Neolithic spread across Europe at a steady rate in a 'wave of advance', fuelled by a burgeoning population increasing on its frontiers.[8] Such expectations have rarely been met by the dating evidence for a much more punctuated process, or by the lower than predicted density of sites on the ground, and they bypass comparative ethnographic and historical evidence for effective means of population control. The landscapes I envisage had in them much more movement by far fewer people.

Social structure. Again since evolutionary schemes of the nineteenth century, reinforced by Childe's interests in social change, and encouraged in turn both by processual archaeology's rather rigid classifications and by the concerns of post-processual archaeology with the concepts of power and ideology, students of the Neolithic period have long assumed a steady process of social change. Different kinds of journey have been envisaged, from savagery to barbarism, from hunters to peasants to leaders, from bands to tribes to chiefdoms, from lineages to households, or from 'big men' to 'ritual authority structures' to 'prestige goods economies'.[9] But the nature of the journey has been the same whichever theoretical tour operator one travels with: farmers different ('more complex') from foragers, and later farmers more riven by concerns with power and control than early farmers. All such accounts rely to a greater or lesser account on a sense of evolution. They draw on a broad ethnography which is itself the product of very specific and much later historical conditions. They tend to reduce diversity to a limited number of stereotypes (rather like social characterisations offered by structural functionalists in the anthropology of the 1920s and 1930s). And they minimise the importance of individuals.[10] Assuming some kind of universal human nature, the divisions of the present day are projected into the past; the spark in the engine of social change is one given off by relentless conflict and competition.

I do not envisage the Neolithic period as some far-off Arcadia. There may well have been endemic bickerings, and we shall see evidence for individual killings and destructions, and the occasional more brutal massacre. The stone axes and adzes of the period, some of which were undoubtedly put to good use on wood, may also have been weapons. But there is little evidence for an increase in endemic levels of conflict during the period, except perhaps in arid parts of Iberia towards the middle of the third millennium BC, a complex issue which I discuss in chapter 9. One frequent response is to claim more subtle forms of domination or hegemony, through control of knowledge, ritual and belief.[11] This makes extravagant demands on the concept of ideology, and ignores the context of landscapes with space in them in which to avoid coercion. I prefer an emphasis on values, ideals and social sanctions, rather than on social structures. We may be dealing with a very broad range of fluid social relationships, for which a vocabulary derived from a recent ethnography is quite inadequate. Terms like lineage and household have their uses in making us think about social organisation, but it is an illusion to think that we can capture Neolithic social reality with them. So much of the Neolithic evidence seems to be to do with people coming together in shared activities and projects, that I use the term, admittedly itself vague, of community. In part, the long process of becoming Neolithic – which in some areas, for example southern Scandinavia, began in the Mesolithic – was the participation by people in new forms of social interaction. It must be legitimate therefore to canvass the relevance of ideals and values of sharing, hospitality, generosity and honour, with shame as a powerful sanction for non-participation, non-reciprocity or deviance.[12] These too are probably anachronistic, but the shift in vocabulary is fundamental. We can substitute conflict, domination and coercion, even if we deny the existence of Arcadia, with notions of rivalry and emulation.

Belief. In the 1930s, some scholars discussed the spread of monument building in north-west Europe in terms of 'megalithic missionaries'. From the 1970s monuments were associated with profaner concerns, such as the marking of territory, the display of group solidarity, or the duping of other members of society. The idea of 'megalithic missionaries' could be dismissed as just another version of the invasion hypothesis of the culture history model, but it does contain a sense of the sacred. This needs to be revived in Neolithic studies. Part of the ground has been prepared in the recent *domus:agrios* model, which demands attention to the conceptual world of the Neolithic.[13] The model proposes that a set of concepts based around the idea and practice of the house, the *domus*, was both a metaphor and the mechanism for the domestication and socialisation of people. The *domus* was defined in relation to the wild or *agrios*, which became a more important organising principle in later parts of the Neolithic. Stimulating though the model has been, it raises many questions. It relies on a simplistic binary opposition, in the style of structuralist anthropology, and it is simply implausible to consign hunters and foragers, and then the world beyond the Neolithic settlement, to a domain characterised as wild. The model makes many conventional assumptions about the nature of Neolithic society, sedentism and landscape. *Domus* and *agrios* seem to operate as substitutes for individuals. And it is, in common with other approaches since the 1970s, a very secular world that is presented.

Time and histories

If part of the process of becoming Neolithic was participation in new forms of social interaction, another part was a changing sense of belonging, of descent and of place in the scheme of things. It is vital to consider notions of time and the sacred.[14] Becoming Neolithic may have been much more a spiritual conversion than a matter of changing diets. Notions of human community may have been sanctioned by links to a divine community of sacred beings, from whom descent was derived. Sacred beings could have been seen to have offered gifts of new resources, but in so doing brought a beginning to a previously timeless world. The web of social values and social relations was underpinned by a sense of divine or ancestral intervention. Community was created to satisfy spiritual prerogatives.

This is not a covert recall of 'mother goddesses'. I shall not argue for any uniform set of beliefs about time, descent and the sacred across Neolithic Europe as a whole. Histories intervene. The sense of sacred beginnings held by monument builders in fifth-millennium BC Brittany may have been very different from that of the first generations of tell users in the Balkans. In chapters 3 and 4, I shall follow others in arguing that figurines in human and animal form may in fact be to do with human ancestors rather than a pantheon of divine beings as the late Marija Gimbutas and others have suggested. The growing bulk of tell mounds themselves was further visible proof for successive generations of the time of their ancestors. In the LBK of central and western Europe, dominant spiritual concerns may have been cattle, woodland and again the community of human forebears. The well-adapted foragers of north-west Europe, already in many ways themselves on parallel tracks, may have been converted to new ways by the transmission of a new sense of time, of beginnings and of their place in the scheme of things, derived from these long histories.

I have begun to set out some aspects of the diverse Neolithic phenomenon. We can retain the term as a useful if at times clumsy label, but its connotations are shifting rapidly. The changes we are interested in cannot be confined to the Neolithic period alone. There was no uniform process, no single history. The Neolithic period is itself a series of becomings, rather than the spread of something already formed. The ultimate consequences of settled life and agrarian subsistence, perhaps achieved only in the first millennium BC, cannot be projected back into conditions at the beginning.

I shall try to situate each region in the context of its history. There are many histories to tell, each affected by another. I shall evoke a world of woodland and rich resources, native and imported, a world not without risk but endowed also with the possibility of choice. I envisage routines of restrained mobility, people and their animals moving through landscapes, only partially tethered by the needs of cereal cultivation, which may have been as much for fodder or beer as for human food, but strongly attached to chosen places as part of their identity. The evidence for growth of population, spread of settlement, and intensification of economy is more limited than our models have predicted. For the most part, I envisage patterns of slow change, of convergence, of continuity of indigenous population. These were small-scale, face-to-face societies, held together, even when dispersed through their landscapes, by a strong sense of community. I shall argue that that sense of community and the values which underpinned it were linked to a sense of time and descent, and to a sense of the sacred. In the chapters that follow I try to show why.

CHAPTER 2

KEEPING THE LAND: INDIGENOUS FORAGERS, *c*. 9000 TO AFTER 7000 BC

A camp in northern Germany

Around 7700 BC, somebody camped on a small sand island on the edge of a shallow, reed-fringed lake. He or she cut a strip of bark from a birch tree, big enough to take a sitting or curled up adult body, and laid it on the ground; then lit a fire by the bark mat with two pine logs; and stayed long enough to burn the fire for a while, to knap some flints, leaving small spalls behind, and to have one or more snacks of hazelnuts, whose shells were smashed with an old knapping hammerstone. The weather was probably warm enough to sleep out overnight unprotected by further shelter. The bivouac seems only to have lasted for a day or two, perhaps even for a few hours. The individual was probably not alone. Some metres away a larger fire was lit, around which some flints were also knapped and hazelnuts eaten; there were traces of pine bark mat. The season may have been autumn.

This is the site of Duvensee 13, in the coastal hinterland of northern Germany between the present Baltic and the river Elbe.[1] The Duvensee lake lies in flat country, previously covered by ice at the height of the last glaciation several millennia before. In the early post-glacial period there were many other small, shallow lakes and small rivers in this area, and woodland developed, birch appearing first, then pine and hazel, and finally oak, elm, lime and alder. Several, probably successive, sites are known on the low sand elevations on the edge of or actually in the former Duvensee lake. All appear to have been small, transient camps; some were perhaps used for generalised foraging, but others had specialised tool-kits and very little animal bone, although that survives well enough in the deposits present today. Duvensee sites 5, 6 and 13 especially have been interpreted as specialised short-stay gathering camps, to exploit the late summer or autumn crop of hazelnuts, hazel being now more abundant in the changing woodlands. Other sites along the Stecknitz river a short distance to the east could have been part of a larger foraging territory.

How typical was this situation across Europe as a whole in the early post-glacial period, from roughly 9000 to after 7000 BC? Despite much variation from region to region, the Duvensee case points to recurrent aspects of the forager way of life which were important nearly everywhere, and which are fundamental for understanding the nature of subsequent changes across the continent after 7000 BC. Population was dispersed through the landscapes of Europe, and very few kinds of area were not used. Coasts, lakes and rivers were used again and again, but so also were uplands. People, however, were not necessarily everywhere, and at any one time the density of population may have been rather low. The inhabitants of the early post-glacial period were mobile, and were able to exploit a wide range of landscapes and resources within each region. The size of human groups probably fluctuated, but was never very large. Face-to-face, individuals perhaps encountered only

2.1 Hearth and birch mat at Duvensee 13. Photo: Bokelmann.

tens of other people in any one year, and the number of occupants in camps and bases may usually have been correspondingly low. The procurement of resources was based on dispersal, mobility and diversification; specialisation was seasonal. Although the strategy relied on flexibility and movement, it was based also on planned repetitions.

Foragers in early post-glacial Europe

In the cold phases of the last glaciation, the distribution of people was naturally restricted. In the warmer phases at the end of the glaciation, people moved northwards, and there is evidence for their presence in Denmark. In the post-glacial period, specialised reindeer hunters moved north along with the herds they followed. There were also foragers far north by about 7000 BC, for example in Karelia in north-west Russia, as seen at sites like Vis and Veretye, and soon after at Olenii Ostrov.[2] It has often been assumed that the successors of late-glacial hunters were their descendants, but substantial population displacements and mixing may have taken place in this process; movement up the rivers of Ukraine and Russia to the far north has been proposed as well as from central Europe.[3] During the last glaciation, most of the islands of the Mediterranean were not inhabited. Cyprus was occupied for a while around 9500 BC, though Crete seems to have been empty until the start of the Neolithic. Sardinia and Corsica were occupied from about 8000 BC. Likewise Ireland and at least some of the larger islands off north-west Scotland were occupied in the early post-glacial period.[4]

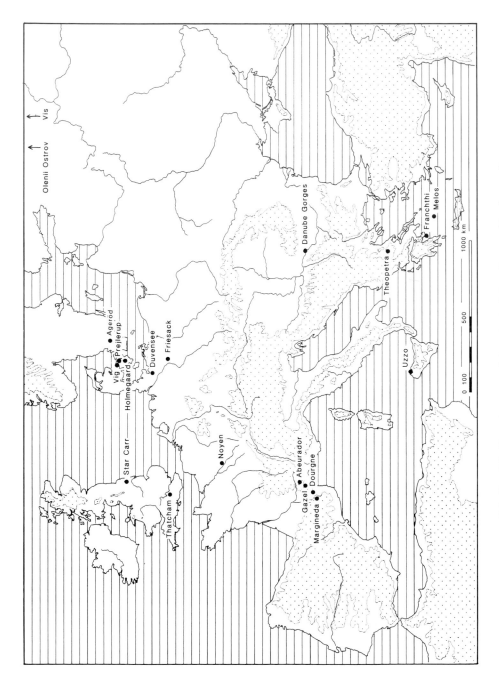

2.2 Simplified location map of the principal sites discussed in chapter 2.

Many different parts of the environment were used. We know of sites on the coasts of the Mediterranean, and submerged sites are beginning to be recognised around the south Scandinavian coastland. Particularly in the north, sites around shallow lake and marsh edges were common, as already seen at Duvensee, but also in many other examples in England, on the north European plain, east of the Baltic and up into north-west Russia. Riverside locations were also chosen. Because of rescue excavations the famous sites in the Danube Gorges between Romania and Serbia are well known, but it is surprising that there are not more. Thatcham in southern England is one case, and riverside sites in Moldavia and Ukraine are further examples. The important recent finds at Noyen-sur-Seine in the Paris basin must indicate that there are many more such discoveries to be made across the continent. Uplands were also exploited, as shown by sites in the hills above the Danube Gorges, and by a whole series of sites in central and northern Italy, southern France and the Pyrenees. Balma Margineda in Andorra (described below) is one example at about 1000 m above sea level. Although people thus used diverse parts of the environment, it is not clear that they were ubiquitous. There is relatively little evidence for their presence in large parts of central and south-east Europe. This may be a question of research bias and a failure to recognise relevant assemblages in surface contexts, but it may indicate also a reluctance to exploit large, uniform and heavily wooded lowlands, lacking the natural breaks and variation offered by lakes, marshes and rivers. At any rate, this would be one way to explain the relative invisibility of early post-glacial inhabitants in countries like Greece and Bulgaria, and the contrasts in numbers of sites known between, for example, Poland and the Czech Republic.[5]

Population density may have been overall rather low. In certain locations, there may have been larger seasonal aggregations. Some lakeside sites are quite large, such as Ageröd 1 in southern Sweden, but this like many others can be seen as the result of successive occupations over quite long periods of time; site size reflects, in part, preferred locations in planned subsistence strategies.[6] It is possible that in very favourable locations there was near-permanent aggregation; the Danube Gorges are a favourite candidate. Nonetheless, on a region by region basis, there were probably smaller rather than larger human groups. The famous site of Star Carr, for example, can now better be seen in context as a result of further survey, excavation and analysis. The site was occupied in the summer, but probably not every summer. It functioned as a hunting camp, probably in relation to other summer and winter camps on the contemporary coast. Other sites near it, on the lake and marsh edges and in the uplands around, were much smaller.[7]

To make a living, people moved around, as they had, in different ways, in the glacial period. Most of the time they walked, but they also had boats capable of both inland and maritime voyages, and skis in the far north. Mobility enabled different resources to be used at different times of the year. At Balma Margineda, for example, altitude – around 1000 m above sea level – presumably precluded winter occupation, and plant remains and fish bones suggest that the main seasons of use were early summer and autumn. Perhaps high summer took some hunters even further into the mountains, while in winter and spring other, lower-lying sites such as those in the Aude valley of neighbouring southern France would have been occupied. (The contemporary coastline is long since submerged.) Mobility, along with population dispersal and small group size, reduced risk and

2.3 The aurochs skeleton from Prejlerup. The arrow symbols indicate the positions of flints embedded in and around the bones. After Fischer.

uncertainty in resource procurement. Diversification also spread risks. There are certainly sites where there is specialisation in procuring one particular resource. Balma Margineda was geared in its earliest post-glacial levels to ibex hunting, but its use was seasonal. There are other sites where one particular resource, if not exclusively procured, probably made an above-average contribution to subsistence, such as river fish in the Danube Gorges, and perhaps tunny at Franchthi Cave in southern Greece.[8] But there are few early post-glacial sites where there is not a range of resources.

The diversity of resources used is impressive. In the nature of things hunting and meat-eating are understandably more visible, since bones are easier to recover than plant remains, and points and barbs are prominent parts of toolkits in stone, bone and antler. This bias is bolstered by instances of the skeletons of large, wounded animals, such as the wild cattle from Vig and Prejlerup in Zealand, Denmark; the excitement and the drama of the chase make it appear self-evidently important.[9] Of the larger animals people hunted wild cattle, elk, red deer, ibex, roe deer and pig. There have been some suggestions, based on a preponderance of young pig in Danube Gorges sites, of close management of animals. Hunting in woodland may have been as much by encounters as by planned intercepts, and we do not know in any detail how it was carried out. The number of wounds in the animals at Vig and Prejlerup could indicate small hunting bands rather than individuals. Also hunted were furred animals and smaller game. People caught river and sea fish, hunted sea mammals including seals and whales, and collected shellfish and land snails. There is also now, at last, better evidence for plant use. Hazelnuts have long been found, because their carbonised shells survive well; stones of wild fruits have also been found in the Mediterranean. Several excavations in the Mediterranean have produced other seeded plants, including wild oats and barley, lentil, chickpea and bitter vetch. There are claims for cereals in the Danube Gorges.[10] This is an important development. We do not know what the balance of resources was, but these new finds begin to suggest the possibility of intensive collecting, and perhaps even of plant tending. There is no clear evidence yet for plant cultivation, but we should not necessarily assume that people were ignorant of the possibilities. It has been suggested that hazel was deliberately encouraged for nut production, by clearance of other trees, around 7000 BC.[11]

There has been much debate about how best to label people with this kind of subsistence, both in the past and in the present.[12] I use the general terms 'foragers' and 'foraging', because they offer a sense of generalised and flexible procurement. Two further aspects need to be considered. I have hinted at the possibility of some measure of control over resources. Plants could have been carefully tended, for example seeded plants in the Mediterranean. Woodland could have been cleared to encourage hazel for nuts, since the species recolonises quicker than many others. Clearings would be likely to have encouraged concentrations of game, since regenerating woodland offers more nutrition. There are hints from the pollen record in eastern and northern England that clearances were made, in some cases in a sustained manner. There could even have been more direct control over the movement of deer and other animals, though archaeological evidence for this is elusive.[13] The other important aspect is storage.[14] Storage could have offered a further means of reducing risks. Its technology is basically simple; meat and fish can be dried or smoked, and many plant foods need no further treatment. But the evidence for storage is elusive in the archaeological record of this period. Hints come from cases like Balma Margineda and Star Carr, where the representation of body parts in the animal bone assemblages has been carefully studied, suggesting that not all carcasses taken to a given site were fully consumed there.[15]

Early post-glacial foragers therefore made a living by dispersal, mobility allied to planned exploitation, and diversification. They may have chosen to exercise some control over both plant and animal resources, and may have used simple storage techniques further to reduce the risks of fluctuation in the seasonal and annual supply of resources. There is no need to assume uniformity of practice across the continent, which the case studies below do not support. In all cases, however, the diversity of resources used seems to show a shared flexibility and considerable knowledgeability.

The early post-glacial setting

If foragers can be characterised as flexible, they had good cause to be. The eighty or so generations of foragers lived through considerable changes in their environments. Many scholars are now reluctant to concede that the actions of people were directly determined by their environments, but temperature, sea levels and positions, vegetation, and the abundance of animals, plants and other foods were both backdrop and foreground in the lives of early post-glacial foragers. If we conceive of these people as working with and in the natural environment, we can probably anyway sidestep that particular theoretical objection. The scale and nature of early post-glacial environmental changes have been set out many times, and the case studies below will include some specific local details. The treatment here is therefore deliberately very brief, but the setting is important, and will remain so in the period after *c.* 7000 BC.

At the end of the last glaciation, temperatures had risen dramatically, and by *c.* 7000 BC summer temperatures were probably 2–2.5° higher than at the present day. Climate, however, probably fluctuated, with the so-called Boreal period in northern Europe (very roughly *c.* 8000–7000 BC, following the Preboreal period, *c.* 9000–8000 BC) being marked by relative dryness. The rise in temperature not only banished the ice sheets further and further north, but released water back into the oceans. Sea level rise had in fact begun in the later stages of the last glaciation. By about 9000 BC sea level in the Aegean had risen to about –40–50 m, and by *c.* 7000 BC to about –25 m or less. Large areas of land were lost around the Mediterranean, and in the North Sea. The Baltic underwent a complicated series of transformations from closed to open waters, as the effect of sea level rise was offset by the rise of land freed of the weight of ice. Britain was separated from the continent by 7000 BC at the latest.[16]

Temperature rise also enabled the progressive spread of woodland. There had been some relict woodland in parts of southern Europe in the last glaciation, but the pollen diagrams from Greece, for example, show the relatively rapid extension of woodland after 9000 BC, leading to the establishment of deciduous oak woodland as the dominant lowland vegetation. This pattern is repeated in most parts of southern Europe. In the uplands there was more fir and pine. In central and northern Europe, the succession was from more or less open tundra to birch and pine woodland, followed by hazel and then the constituents of mixed oak woodland, notably oak, elm, lime and ash.[17]

Within these growing and changing woodlands, the resources available to people altered. Reindeer, bison and to large extent horse in northern Europe, ass and ibex from lowland southern Europe, disappeared, to be replaced by cattle, red deer, roe deer and pig. Fish returned to inland rivers and lakes. Woodland and woodland edges contained a range of plants exploitable as food: nuts, fruits, roots, tubers and seeds. The opportunities for flexible and knowledgeable foragers must have been considerable. Resource abundance coupled with strategies of dispersal and mobility may have made direct control of resources unnecessary. This is not to say that people were necessarily ignorant of the possibilities of resource control, but to stress that choice was available. The matter of choice brings in the question of values, and those will be discussed after the following selection of detailed case studies of early post-glacial foragers in action.

Case studies

Balma Margineda: upland and lowland in the west Mediterranean

Balma Margineda in Andorra is a large rockshelter at about 1000 m above sea level.[18] It lies at the entrance to a large upland basin, with peaks rising to 3000 m, but is not far from lower country in the valleys of the Valira and Segre rivers, the latter running eventually into the Ebro. The site was used for long periods from the end of the last glaciation through into the Neolithic. Clearly the strategic position of the site made it a preferred location to which people returned again and again as part of a planned strategy. The succession of stone tool assemblages in the stratified deposits of the shelter shows continuity from the latest Palaeolithic to the earliest Mesolithic or Azilian phase, and through the Mesolithic, and therefore presumably continuity of population. Pollen analysis and charcoals provide the local evidence for the general environmental trends to warming and the spread of woodland. In the post-glacial period, pine woodland dominated at this altitude, but the evidence shows the gradual appearance of fir and then deciduous oak, lime and alder, as temperatures increased by the end of the Mesolithic.

People came to these wooded uplands to hunt. It is always difficult to determine the season of an occupation. Here, trout bones indicate use of the site in early summer and in autumn. Perhaps Balma Margineda was some kind of hunting base on the edge of a large upland hunting range, and midsummer sites might be found further into the mountains. In the early levels the principal quarry was ibex, with very rare chamois, pig and red deer. By the early Mesolithic (site level 5 and above), there were slightly more pig and deer, reflecting no doubt the upwards expansion of deciduous woodland. From the representation of skeletal parts in the shelter, it looks as though whole animals were brought back to the site for butchery; there are many bones from the lower limbs and heads of animals. The bones also have many cut marks and long bones are frequently splintered and broken. This indicates meat processing. It is possible that meat thus processed was not all consumed on the site, but taken elsewhere.

As with so many sites of this kind, it is the animal bones which attract attention. But people used other resources as well. Trout and eel were caught. Hazelnuts were collected in some abundance, although hazel was not a common species in the environs at this time. Other fruits and nuts were collected, including *Pistacia* and blackberry. The seeds of the genus *Valerianella* were also found. The excavators deliberately searched for such material.

The site is not on its own. As conditions warmed in the latter stages of the last glaciation, people in the north of Spain and the south of France changed patterns of hunting and movement to adapt to woodland animals and resources. Diversification included the collection of plants and land snails, fishing and bird hunting. The movements of herd animals in the cold phases of the last glaciation may to some extent have conditioned the movements of people. Now, human mobility became an element of planned strategies in chosen resource zones. As conditions warmed, the mountain range was quickly exploited. Many other high sites are known along the Pyrenees and its flanks. It must be presumed that the users of Balma Margineda went elsewhere at other seasons of the year, but

2.4 Excavations at the high-altitude rockshelter, Balma Margineda. Photo: Guilaine.

regional patterns of movement are not well known. Mesolithic sites are known in parts of the Ebro valley, as well as near the Spanish coast, but it is unclear what the annual range of any one human group may have been.[19]

On the north side of the Pyrenees there has been a series of important excavations at rockshelter sites down the valley of the Aude, as far as the southern end of the Massif Central, which may give some indication of the size of an annual range. The Abri de Dourgne is quite high up the Aude on the north slopes of the Pyrenees, at about 700 m above sea level. Lower down the valley, on the edge of the Massif Central (on the Montagne Noir), the Balma Abeurador is at about 560 m above sea level, and the Grotte Gazel not far away, at about 250–300 m. The distance between Dourgne and Abeurador is over 70 km. There is no proof that these sites were all part of one unified territory, and occupation began later at Gazel (from about 7000 BC or later), but a seasonal pattern of movement up and down the valley and its environs would make sense. At Dourgne, ibex were again the principal quarry in the earlier post-glacial period (from about 8000/7600 BC), and then pig and red and roe deer were exploited as well. This trend is found also in the longer sequence at Abeurador. At Gazel from about 7000 BC, in surroundings of oak woodland, the game most hunted were deer and pig. From the early levels of Abeurador, there is evidence of plant use. Apart from hazelnuts, the excavations recovered seeds of wild legumes, *Lens, Pisum, Lathyrus cicera, Ervum ervilia, Cicer arietinum* and *Vicia*. These legumes are a valuable source of food, providing starch and protein. Since they are said not to form dense natural stands, there has been some discussion of the possibility of their cultivation. This is doubtful. The legumes may have grown abundantly enough for intensive collection to have been worthwhile, or their sparseness may indicate that they were only used as an occasional resource. The seeds have, however, been recovered from successive levels through the Mesolithic occupation of the shelter.[20]

What we lack in this region is knowledge of lowland and coastal sites. The contemporary coastlines have been submerged. It is possible that coastal lowlands could have offered sufficiently abundant and diverse resources for annual movements to have been much restricted. If this was the case, however, it is hard to explain why the specialised upland sites just described, and all the others through Iberia, southern France and Italy,[21] were occupied at all. The next case study brings in a coastal site, but there too it seems clear that other parts of the landscape were being used as well.

Grotta dell' Uzzo: coastal foragers on Sicily

Sicily was joined to Italy during the Ice Age and there is evidence of Palaeolithic occupation. As elsewhere in the Italian peninsula, the lithic assemblages show continuity from the Palaeolithic into the Epipalaeolithic or Mesolithic (when 'Epigravettian' industries are typical). The Grotta dell' Uzzo is on the east side of the promontory of S. Vito lo Campo in the hilly north-west of the island. It is a very large natural cave about 45 m high and 50 m wide and deep, perhaps chosen in part for its impressive size. It is now 65 m above sea level; when occupation of the cave began about 8500 BC, sea level would have been some 40 m lower. The cave looks east over a shelving coast, but is backed by hills behind. Charcoals

2.5 Features in the Mesolithic deposits at the Grotta dell' Uzzo. Top: human burials, in successive levels; below: animal bones in trench Q at the back of the cave. Photos: Tagliacozzo.

indicate that oak woodland was the natural vegetation from early in the post-glacial period.[22]

The site was used through the Mesolithic period and substantial archaeological deposits accumulated. It is not clear whether the stratigraphy is uninterrupted, particularly at the end of the Mesolithic, but it looks as though this was a site to which people came frequently at the very least. Red deer and pig were the animals most commonly exploited. In the later Mesolithic levels, it has been claimed that an increase in the numbers of young pig indicates domestication, but there is no other support for this idea; the pattern could just as well be explained by a changed hunting strategy or by a different season of exploitation. Less commonly hunted were roe deer, furred game, and birds. Shellfish and crabs were collected, and seafish were caught, including tunny. The evidence for marine exploitation increases towards the end of the Mesolithic period and into the beginning of the Neolithic, in the seventh millennium BC, when three species of whale were added to the list of catches. This all seems to imply the use of offshore boats (presumably skin-covered canoes). Further adding to the diversity of resources, acorns and wild grapes were collected, and at the very end of the Mesolithic or at the start of the Neolithic, wild olives and the seeds of legumes appeared (*Lathyrus* or *Pisum*).

The trenches excavated within the cave have revealed eight simple burials; given the great size of the site, the original number would have been higher. The bodies of both adults and children were covered with earth and stones, and were provided with simple grave goods of shell and bone ornaments and flint tools. Six of these skeletons had caries or tooth decay, which has been taken to show a high consumption of carbohydrates or of natural sugars.

Uzzo is not the only Mesolithic site in western Sicily, others being known around Trapani and Palermo, but it does not appear to have had immediate neighbours. Other sites are known both on the coast and inland. It is possible that the diversity of resources shown at Uzzo could have supported people at the cave for longer periods than elsewhere, and the burials certainly suggest a location of permanent significance. Whether there was anything like sedentary existence, as opposed to restricted mobility or long seasonal stays in an unusually favourable niche, is harder to tell. Even if mobility was relatively restricted, there is no evidence yet for other than scattered or dispersed communities. The next case study is also of a coastal site, but where the immediate surroundings have been better investigated. There too a large coastal cave appears to have been isolated.

Franchthi Cave, Greece: foraging by land and sea

Franchthi Cave is in the Argolid or north-east part of the Peloponnese in Greece. It is a large, long cave, the back part of which is now blocked by rock falls. Perhaps like Uzzo it too was chosen in part for its impressive size, far in excess of that needed for the shelter of its users. It is now just above sea level directly on the coast. When first occupied in the late Palaeolithic around 20,000 BC sea level was fully some 120 m lower, and the immediate coast would have been about 5 km away to the west; a large coastal plain was connected to modern Attica to the north-east. By about 8500–8000 BC the sea level was about −38 m,

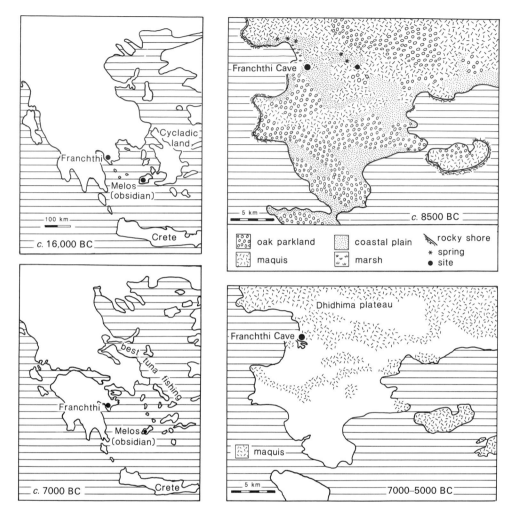

2.6 The setting of the Franchthi Cave, from the Palaeolithic into the Neolithic period. After van Andel and Runnels.

some 2 km away from the cave, and by about 7000 BC, the level had risen to about –25 m. Pollen analysis both locally and from elsewhere in Greece shows a shift from steppe-like vegetation in the late glacial period to deciduous, perhaps here rather open, oak woodland in the post-glacial period, and suggests a climatic shift from cooler and drier to warmer and moister conditions.

The Franchthi Cave has been intensively investigated, by a limited number of cuttings within and outside the cave, and a substantial survey was carried out in the areas round about.[23] At Franchthi in the late Palaeolithic period around 20,000 BC, wild cattle and ass were hunted on the coastal plain, perhaps especially around now submerged springs. Forays were also made into the hills behind the cave, where survey has found a number of small camps. The quantity of remains in the cave is small and occupation there may have been sporadic. After a probable hiatus in occupation centred around 15–16,000 BC, occupation resumed from about 12,000 BC. This coincides with climatic improvement, sea level rise and the spread of woodland. As well as large game, red deer now became an important resource. Small game, fish, shellfish and land snails were all exploited, as well as wild cereals, legumes and nuts. Obsidian, a dark, translucent volcanic glass with very fine flaking properties, was obtained from the Aegean island of Melos and first appeared at the cave about 10,000 BC. Boats must have been used in its transport, since Melos is over 100 km by sea from Franchthi. The source, the main one in the Aegean, may have been discovered earlier in the Palaeolithic when the island would have been reachable on foot because of dramatically lower sea levels.

The picture is of a fluctuating human presence, with adaptability, mobility and diversification, and long traditions of knowledge implied by the acquisition of Melian obsidian. Franchthi and its environs are not the only areas of Greece to have been investigated, but it is the only substantial, well-investigated post-glacial Mesolithic occupation in Greece. The cave or rockshelter site of Zaïmis near Megara in the Isthmus, and Ulbrich, a now unlocated site somewhere in the Argolid, had Mesolithic levels but there has been no recent research at them. A shell midden is known on Corfu at Sidari, and there is a possible site on the Aegean island of Kythnos.[24] This is puzzling, since Palaeolithic occupation of some parts of Greece is quite well documented. Recent survey along the Peneios river in Thessaly found Middle Palaeolithic sites. Research in Epirus in north-west Greece suggests a long occupation of a rich coastal lowland, with sporadic forays into the valleys and mountains of the interior, but little or no sign of the Mesolithic is so far apparent. This may in part be due to the nature and organisation of research. Recent work at the Theopetra Cave, near Kalambaka on the north edge of the Thessalian plain, has documented a Mesolithic presence in Thessaly for the first time, with stratified levels in the cave including a microlithic flint assemblage and a woman's burial.[25] With the consolidation of warmer conditions in the post-glacial period, one might expect an increase in the density of sites, but so far these have not been found in any quantity.

The Mesolithic levels at Franchthi are some 2 m thick. Occupation may not have been continuous, and there may have been less in the later Mesolithic after about 8000 BC. The deposits formed more slowly and were relatively sterile and stony; the end of the Mesolithic may be absent. Such variation could be the result of periodic abandonments or alterations in seasonal patterns of occupation.[26] Thick deposits should not automatically be equated with permanent or sedentary occupation. Mesolithic occupation was neither static nor unchanging.

After about 9000 BC people at Franchthi used a broad range of resources. They continued to hunt wild ass for a while, but switched increasingly to red deer. Cattle and pig were also a quarry, and land snails, shellfish and small seafish were exploited. Plants were used in much the same way as in the latest Palaeolithic, with pistachio, almond, pear and wild oats being predominant, but there was an increase in the use of both wild barley and oats. The plant remains suggest that the cave could have been used at least from spring to autumn. From about 8000 BC the situation changed. There is evidence for more use of the sea. The quantities of Melian obsidian increased, and the bones of large tunny fish appeared in quantity. We do not know where these fish were caught, but this was presumably offshore in boats, and it is possible that fishing grounds were far from the cave itself. Plant remains decreased in quantity in the upper Mesolithic levels, perhaps reflecting changing patterns of occupation. There was one Mesolithic burial in the cave, a simple grave in a depression covered with stones, and there was another scatter of bones. This belonged to the lower part of the Mesolithic occupation.[27] There are hints here of mobility and specialisation partly replacing diversification and restricted movement. It remains very odd that it has been so difficult to find other Mesolithic occupations in the Aegean and on the Greek mainland, even making allowance for loss of coastlines. The picture at face value is of a sparse population, at first perhaps relatively restricted to one region, and then later ranging more widely. A broad spectrum of resources was used.

There are comparisons and contrasts to be made with other parts of the eastern Mediterranean and its coastline. People crossed to Cyprus around 9500 BC and hunted out the island population of pygmy hippopotami. This might be characterised as mobile opportunism. Down the Levantine coastline people used a broad range of resources, but this diversification had long been characteristic. Plants were one important component. At Tell Abu Hureyra in Syria, up to 150 species of plants with edible seeds or fruits were identified in the Epipalaeolithic phase (c. 10,000–9500 BC). These were probably collected from the wild, rather than tended or grown deliberately. Year-round occupation at Hureyra is considered very likely, on the grounds of its well-placed location: on the edge of the Euphrates river with steppe to south and west.[28] In the Levant generally, however, in the Epipalaeolithic/Natufian phase, there are more sites, a greater range of site types, and greater evidence for diversification and experimentation than in Mediterranean Europe at the same time. From the Pre-Pottery Neolithic phase (starting about 9000 BC) there is evidence for permanent occupations, and the domestication of cereals and animals (with or without morphological changes accompanying). The consequences of these developments will emerge in the next chapter. Here it is important to see that although sites like Franchthi and Uzzo shared some characteristics common right through the Mediterranean in the Epipalaeolithic or Mesolithic, their specific local conditions were not the same as in the east Mediterranean coastlands.

The Danube Gorges: a riverine concentration

Mesolithic sites are still at present very thin on the ground not only in Greece but also in many parts of the Balkans. In part, this may simply reflect the history and nature of research, and there are signs, as in Greece, that fresh search will produce more evidence. In Bulgaria, for example, large surface assemblages have been found in the Pobiti Kamuni area west of Varna. A scatter of sites is reported from Romania, including several in the Dobrogea, and from around the Sea of Marmara, in European Turkey. Fresh research has begun to locate Mesolithic sites in tributaries of the Tisza valley on the north-west side of the Hungarian plain, near Szolnok, significantly in zones not affected by sedimentation.[29] Despite this growing evidence, it may still be the case that foragers were both thin on the ground in some areas and absent from others. On ecological grounds, extensive, uniform

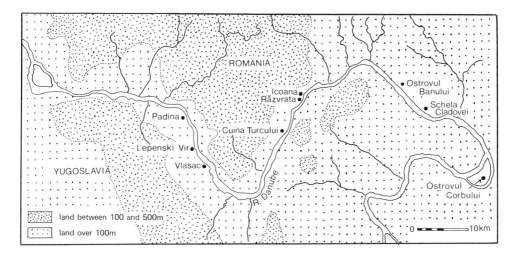

2.7 Simplified location map of the principal sites in the Danube Gorges. After Srejović and Letica.

woodlands may not have offered a high density or concentrated variety of resources. The discovery of sites might be predicted in more varied parts of the landscape, in river valleys, estuaries (especially that of the Danube) and on coasts.

One notable exception to the dearth of sites is the concentration in the Danube Gorges between Romania and Serbia. Here the river runs for over 100 km between the hills. The topography, the micro-climate of the Gorges and the nature of the river may all have combined to offer foragers an exceptionally favourable niche, but so much is known about these sites because of the rescue excavations in advance of damming for hydro-electric schemes from the 1960s onwards. The depositional history of the rest of the Balkan Danube and of its major tributaries is little known. One clue to the likelihood of other discoveries in the future is that known sites are not confined to the Gorges themselves, some being below the Gorges where the river meanders through a more open plain, such as Velesnica and Ostrovul Corbului.

Concentrated within the Danube Gorges and their immediate environs there is a series of famous Mesolithic sites, including Schela Cladovei and Icoana on the Romanian side, and Lepenski Vir, Padina and Vlasac on the Serbian side.[30] Their occupants exploited deer and pigs in deciduous woodland, perhaps collected wild plants, and caught large fish. The sites contain various structures, including well-built stone hearths. Lepenski Vir, the best-preserved site, has a whole series of larger and smaller trapezoidal structures incorporating hearths at their broader ends facing the river. Burials have been found quite commonly, both within these structures and on their own. It is widely claimed that these sites have a long history within the pre-Neolithic occupation of the region; that a sedentary or near-sedentary lifestyle was achieved, with some control over both plants and animals, specifically pigs; and that the structures can be seen as domestic dwellings, and the sites containing them therefore as villages of some kind. One recent account has evoked the drama of the taming of the 'wild', including death and its attendant mysteries, as part of the

2.8 North-eastern part of Lepenski Vir I. The individual structures range from phase
Ib to Ie. Photo: Srejović.

process of people settling down.[31] There is reason to question all three propositions. I shall
argue that there was still much mobility in this area, and little or any direct control over
resources, and that several of the sites were sacred points in the landscape rather than
permanent bases.

There is no doubt of a long history of human presence in the Gorges area. There are
late-glacial and earliest post-glacial occupations, for example, at Cuina Turcului and
Ostrovul Banului on the river and at Băile Herculane rockshelter some 20 km up a side tributary. There is likewise no doubt of stratified sequences and rebuildings at some of the
sites. Lepenski Vir has two major phases before the character of the site changed radically,
and phase I has at least five sub-phases. Padina, Vlasac and Schela Cladovei likewise have
two main phases. The chronological problem has been a series of inconsistent radiocarbon
dates. Lepenski Vir I–II has a seemingly coherent run of dates beginning about 6400 BC
and carrying down to about 5600 BC. This is not, however, much earlier than the first
Neolithic in the more northerly part of the Balkans. Vlasac I has dates beginning around
6800–6900 BC, but Vlasac II, which should of course be later, has dates from about
7000–6500 BC. Dates for Padina A range from 8300 to 6800 BC, but Padina B has dates little
before 6000 BC. Romanian, Serbian and other specialists prefer the earlier dates, and it has
been claimed that at Schela Cladovei a late occupation is overlain by a structure with artefacts in the earliest local Neolithic style. But at Padina B, trapezoidal structures in the local
style are definitely associated with early Neolithic, Starčevo pottery. Another argument has

been that those dates which are seen as out of sequence have been contaminated by rises and falls in the waters of the Danube. This is unconvincing, since all dates should have been affected, not just some.[32] Taking the most coherent series from the deepest stratigraphy at the best-preserved and investigated site – Lepenski Vir – it is at least as likely that the main phase of structures and burials in the Gorges area dates to the period of the first Neolithic in the region.

All the sites close to the river in the Gorges would have been subject to annual or periodic flooding. As elsewhere in Mesolithic Europe, a broad spectrum of resources was used. Deer, cattle, pig, chamois, other game, several species of river fish, birds, molluscs, and perhaps large-seeded grasses were used. There were domesticated dogs. The ages of animals at Vlasac are consistent with occupation in different seasons of the year, and the supply of large river fish could have been constant. Whether this shows year-round occupation is another matter. It has been claimed that pigs at Icoana were being brought under direct human control. Many of them were under a year old, and were killed at different times of the year. There was, however, no sign of change in their dentition, the usual criterion of pig domestication, and there was no sign of a similar age pattern at Vlasac, where there was a very big animal bone assemblage.[33] It is at least as likely that variations in the season or duration of occupation are being reflected. It has also been claimed that large grass pollens in coprolites (preserved human faeces) at both Icoana and Vlasac are in fact from domesticated plants.[34] A supporting claim is that perforated antler artefacts at Icoana and other sites were hoes or digging sticks. But the pollen argument is weak. The number of large grains is small, and some size variation is likely in a grass population. No carbonised plant remains were systematically recovered from the rescue excavations of these sites. Digging sticks for plant extraction or even for tending would be plausible, but the artefacts themselves cannot prove cultivation. The worn teeth of the many human skeletons in these sites also suggest that plant foods were important, but irregularities in enamel growth indicate periods of malnutrition.[35] This is not easily reconcilable with the model of completely successful, near-sedentary existence.

An alternative model would be to envisage a pattern of settlement based on the river, but with movement along it and into the hills behind, and beyond. From an early date in the post-glacial period raw materials of distant origin, such as Hungarian obsidian, were used in the Gorges area; later, graphite was obtained from north-west Bulgaria.[36] Such movement might have been due to a series of exchanges, but is also compatible with people being on the move over broad areas.

Not all the sites were of the same character. Some have less regular structures, such as hollows and circular arrangements of stakes, perhaps huts, and hearths which lack formal or very regular edging. These include Vlasac 2, Icoana 1, Padina A and perhaps Schela Cladovei. One or two are distinguished by the more formal character of the structures and their internal fittings. The difference may not just be the result of differential preservation or of different excavation conditions. Lepenski Vir remains the prime example. It has signs of sequence, from less regular structures in its basal, 'proto-Lepenski Vir' level, in which rectangular hearths are the main feature, to the well-known trapezoidal structures of phases I and II (described below). In phases Ia–e there were never less than twenty structures, laid out to a common plan and nearly all facing the river; the phase II structures were more disturbed, but appear to continue the same sort of pattern. Vlasac also has some variation in its sequence, with the structures of phase 2 being less well defined than in phase 1. In phase 1 some of the surface structures were trapezoidal but others were less regular and dug into the subsoil, and there were hearths around which no formal structure was defined.

Burials were another component of some of these sites. Some human bones were deposited with little formality. This is the case in the basal level and then phases 1a–b at Lepenski Vir. In the basal layer, only adult crania (skulls minus lower jaws) were found. From the latter part of phase Ib, there were much more formal and complete inhumations within the trapezoidal structures. There was often more than one burial per structure, up to a maximum of five, but not every structure contained burials. Other sites like Vlasac 1, Padina A and Schela Cladovei also have many burials. At Vlasac 1, the burials far out-number the structures, and here and at Padina they are found both within and between structures. I conclude that some sites may better be seen as regularly used base camps, which were regarded as places of permanent significance, while others can be interpreted as burial grounds or sacred exposure areas.

The structures of Lepenski Vir I–II were varied in size. There was usually at least one larger structure per level, normally with a central position. There were also on occasion very small structures (structure 49 in Ic and 55 in Id), which mimicked the others in internal detail. Usually the broader end faced the river. Going in centrally from the broader end was a linear arrangement of stone platform, lined rectangular hearth and then further stone settings, some with uncarved or carved boulders. When they occurred, burials were usually across the zone at the back of the hearth. The space taken by this formal arrangement was consider-able, leaving little room for the practical business of living in the smaller structures. There are other odd features. There seem to have been remarkably few stake or post holes, though it is usually assumed that the structures were roofed. The finds seem largely to have been confined to the structures themselves, though this appears not to have been the case at other sites in the Gorges. Structures both large and small have been described as possessing only a modest inventory of finds. The character of the flint industry is firmly within the local 'Epigravettian' tradition going back into the end of the Palaeolithic.[37] Had there been a radical move to sedentary existence, one might reasonably have expected to see more change. Within the structures, the deposition of animal bone seems to have been very formalised. Fish remains were left on the west side of hearths, and stone clubs on the east side. Parts of red deer (skull fragments, antlers or shoulder blades) were frequent finds on the stone 'tables' at the back of the hearths.[38] An alternative interpretation is to see the struc-tures as unroofed shrines or altars, their edges lined with stones and their floors carefully laid.

Burial practices at Lepenski Vir were varied. There was a tradition of partial burial. The first disposals were of adult crania, and in later phases there were occurrences of leg bones on their own, and of skeletons lacking feet and hands. There were child burials in phase Ic beneath the structures. Adult burials were more common; numbers fluctuated and seem to have declined in later levels in phase I. The normal rite was extended single inhumation, the body either laid directly over the zone at the back of the hearth or set in a shallow simple grave dug into underlying levels. Grave goods were few and simple, though antlers were often placed over the body. One example from phase Id shows the most complex sort of arrangement. An adult man was laid out with the cranium of a woman on his left shoulder, an aurochs skull on his right shoulder, and a deer skull by his right hand with antlers nearby.

Extended inhumations were common at other sites, as at Vlasac, Schela Cladovei and Padina, and there were probably contracted inhumations at Padina as well.[39] Most graves were single, and personal grave goods were simple and few. Red ochre was sprinkled on many graves, and at Vlasac some graves had fish teeth apparently strewn over them. At Vlasac there were also some cremations and some partial burials; a greater percentage of the female burials in phase I may have been complete than of the male burials. The treatment of the dead varied through the Vlasac sequence. In phase II, both men and women received extended and contracted burial, while there was also some disposal of male skulls on their own and children were represented only by long bones. Likewise, in phase I, artefacts, food remains and raw materials were found with burials, but only food remains and raw materials in phase II. The numbers of burials are significant: fifty-seven in Vlasac I, eighteen in Vlasac II (with a number that are not assigned to a specific phase), over forty at Schela Cladovei, and so on. If these sites were occupied periodically or episodically over generations, the burials may have accumulated only gradually.

The model of sedentary settlement and a degree of resource control in the Gorges is flawed. Instead, there was a rather varied range of sites, subject to periodic flooding and mostly without very formal layout or well-defined structures. These could be seen as base camps, perhaps for longer seasonal occupations than elsewhere, but within a pattern of movement up and down and beyond the river. Some locations were regarded as special and had permanent significance marked by offerings, objects of worship and burials, but that enduring sense of place can be distinguished from fixed settlement. If the chronology proposed here is correct, many of these developments belonged to the period of the first Neolithic in the wider region, and I will consider further aspects of the symbolic system at Lepenski Vir in that context in the next chapter.

Noyen-sur-Seine, northern France: further evidence for riverine settlement

Extensive excavations of Neolithic enclosures beside the river at Noyen from the 1970s onwards led on to a deliberate search for organic material in former river channels. As well as locating the probable channel of the Neolithic period, this planned research found a former channel from the Mesolithic period. Beside this channel there had been a series of occupations, dated to around 7000 BC.[40]

The valley of the Seine is here comparatively broad, about 6–7 km across. To north and south there were low plateaux. Pollen analysis at the site itself has shown the regular vegetational succession for the post-glacial period: first pine woodland, and then the spread of hazel, oak and elm, and later lime. In the early part of the post-glacial period the river had wide, slow channels. Tangled side channels and a still back channel also developed, which gradually became a swampy pond and eventually marshy grassland. The occupation around 7000 BC coincided with still active but quite varied channels. It is not yet established

2.9 Mesolithic features at Noyen-sur-Seine. Top left: general view of gravel pit and old channel; top right: excavation of the peaty base of a Boreal period channel; centre: pinewood dugout canoe; below: woven fishtrap. Photos: C. and D. Mordant.

whether there were other, braided channels in the valley bottom, creating a broad wetland. Whatever the case, this was a very different setting from that of the Danube Gorges.

People used the site as a base camp or hunting camp, from spring to autumn. They hunted large woodland game and small riverine creatures, and fished. They used a large dugout canoe. There were a few human bones. The preserved material is all from the sides of channels and deposits, so that the nature of activities and structures on the contemporary surface above the river is not known. The remains in the channel are spread out over tens of metres, so that a succession of occupations is likely. There is no specific evidence for their size in any one season.

Red deer and pig were the most common quarry. Roe deer and wild cattle were also taken, along with wolf, fox, lynx or *Felis*, otter, beaver, and small aquatic turtles (otherwise known as pond tortoises). Kills were made from spring to autumn, though this need not imply continuous occupation over that period in any one year. The animals were mostly butchered or quartered elsewhere, and there is plenty of evidence for on-site consumption. Cone-shaped fish traps of twisted willow fronds were set in side channels to catch eels, predominantly through the summer months. Many of the eel vertebrae have traces of burning, which could be from smoking for preservation. The dugout canoe, made from a pine trunk, hollowed out by fire and finished by flint axe, was at least 5 m long. No flint axes were found on the site itself. The excavators have suggested that winter camps need not have been far away on the terraces and surrounding plateaux. Many more plateau sites are known, either open sites or occasional rockshelters.[41] Most of these sites are relatively small, and it is possible that there were bigger aggregations of people during the summer months.

Even in the present state of research, a few other valley-bottom sites are known elsewhere in northern France, and many more must be predicted.

Friesack and Star Carr: inland water-edge hunting camps in northern Europe

The final case study also shows the liking of foragers for locations beside water, and contributes important information about the frequency of visits and the possible density of settlement.

Superficially it appears that there are even more sites as one moves north on to the varied landscapes of the north European plain and the Baltic/south Scandinavian coastlines. Compared with the Balkans, there are more Mesolithic sites known in central Europe. A recent study of Bohemia has shown the relative density of sites compared with earlier periods, and demonstrated how new survey can quickly add many more sites. A recent survey of the Polish Mesolithic has shown that sites are known across the country, but that many more are to be found in the central river valleys and to the north than in the southern uplands.[42] This brings us back to the kind of landscape with which the chapter began at Duvensee. Across the north European plain there were major and minor rivers running from south to north, and also many shallow west–east valleys formed as a result of the diversion of watercourses during the advances and retreats of ice sheets. In the early postglacial period there were many shallow lakes in such settings. Pollen analysis has shown

2.10 Excavation of the stratified lake-edge deposits at Friesack. Photo: Gramsch.

again and again the vegetational succession through pine and birch woodland to oak wood-land. This wooded but broken inland was used by foragers, but probably rather less often than the contemporary coasts.

The Friesack site, Kr. Nauen (north-west of Berlin and about 150 km inland from the Baltic), is on a low sandridge beside a small lake, part of a series of similar settings along former glacial tunnel valleys.[43] The flat, sandy valleys had many small lakes and ponds, probably connected by meandering streams. These shallow waters were reed-fringed, and backed by woodland. The lakes held fish, and the woodland edge and the water itself would have been attractive to game. People came here off and on over a very long period through the Mesolithic, and to at least one other site in the locality some 500 m away. Other sites are known in the valley further afield.

As at Noyen, nothing survives of the actual contemporary surface of the occupation; the excavated part of the site consists of the zone where rubbish and residues were tipped or eroded down the side slope of the sandridge towards the lake. The range of materials which survived is impressive because of the waterlogged conditions. People came here to hunt large game (red and roe deer and pig principally, with some elk in the early occupations, and some wild cattle), small game (mainly beaver and pond tortoise, but also hare, wolf, wild cat and lynx) and birds, and to fish (pike and catfish). There is no specific evidence for the use of plants for food, though plant fibres were used for nets and baskets; these might have been used for gathering plant material. In the period down to just before 7000 BC, antler evidence suggests spring occupations; later, as oak woodland became more important, the evidence suggests autumn occupations. It is difficult to estimate the duration of any one visit to the site, or the size of the group involved. The density of finds increases after the earliest occupations, so that the location perhaps became more established in a regional cycle of mobility. A wide range of activities was carried out at the site. There were finds of hunting weapons (spears, arrows, a bow), extraction tools (axes, a possible digging stick), carrying equipment (twisted nets or baskets) and a range of flint and other tools for cutting and scraping. This does not look like the inventory appropriate to a short-stay camp, but whether it implies days or weeks at a time is not clear.

The spreads of occupation material down the side of the sandridge are interleaved with lenses of eroded sand and with peat layers. The whole deposit is over a metre deep. This fine stratigraphy, combined with radiocarbon dating, has allowed estimates of the frequency of occupation. The site was used episodically, perhaps on average about once a generation, with a range of intervals from about ten years to a century. Usage varied through time. From about 8700 to 8450 BC there were some fifteen occupations; five between around 8350 and 8150 BC; and another fifteen from about 8050 to 7800 BC. Other occupations are known in the vicinity, but it does not appear that there would have been many groups in the locality, and perhaps not more than one, in any one season.

There were many other inland occupations in the early post-glacial period across the north European plain into south Scandinavia and into England. Among many other well-known sites, Hohen Viecheln, a little to the east of Duvensee in northern Germany, was in a glacial valley similar to Friesack. Duvensee, Holmegaard and Svaerdborg in the southern part of what is now the island of Zealand, Denmark, and Ageröd in southern Sweden were beside lakes. Ulkestrup and Mullerup were part of a string of sites along a marshy watercourse stretching some 40 km from inland to the coast; this incorporated some areas of shallow open water.[44] These were probably all summer occupations.

Star Carr, in northern England, was another summer occupation, in the ninth millennium BC, a few kilometres inland from its contemporary coast, beside shallow, open water, part of a series of irregular, shallow lakes.[45] People hunted large and small game including birds, but it is not known whether they fished. The bone suggests that this was a hunting camp, a local base from which hunting was carried out, to which partially butchered kills were brought, and from which processed meat was taken for use elsewhere. There are other sites along the lake edges nearby, but none as large as Star Carr, nor with its range of equipment. These were probably hunting or other task-specific stations, and small sites on the hills to the north and west were presumably used in summer only. Isotopic analysis of their bones at the contemporary, neighbouring site of Seamer Carr suggests that domesticated dogs had a predominantly marine diet.[46]

This finding begins to link inland and coast. Some at least of these people spent time on the coast. At Svaerdborg, in inland Zealand, there is a bone of grey seal, perhaps from a seal skin. Underwater exploration around the Danish coasts is now beginning to find sites on the Mesolithic coastline. Several sites have been located dating to the middle of the Mesolithic period after 7000 BC, in sufficient quantity to suggest quite intense coastal habitation. These have been located south of Zealand and between Lolland and Falster in south-east Denmark, at depths of 4 to 6 m. One site on the west of Zealand, Musholm Bay, has remains at a depth of 8 to 9 m, and probably dates to soon after 7000 BC. It contains, among other residues, hazelnuts, fish bone and the bones of woodland game. The location was originally on a small bay, close to the mouth of a river. On the east side of Zealand, in the narrow inlet later to be Öresund, sites have been found at depths of 6 to 20 m. It looks as though use of the coasts was general.[47] Down to about 7500 BC the Baltic was effectively a lake, with a narrow inlet through what is now the Store Baelt; after that date, the continuing rise of sea level began to outstrip the effects of land uplift and the south Scandinavian coast began to assume something like its present form. But there is no reason to suppose that coastal settlement began only as the Baltic opened and filled.

A way of life as a system of values

My account has highlighted several important aspects of the way of life of early post-glacial foragers: dispersal of population, low density of population and small group size; mobility; diversification of resource use; and planned, seasonal patterns of exploitation. Coast and hinterland in both the Mediterranean and northern Europe were part of inter-linked territories. The scale of movement by any one group is not known, though there were long-distance movements of raw materials, and there is no sign in the distribution of common artefact styles of restricted territories.[48] There are hints from the details of meat and fish processing of the storage of foodstuffs, and some favourable locations may have enabled a reduction in the extent of mobility seen elsewhere. I have so far discussed mobility in rather general terms, though hinting at variations in kinds of movement. The distinction has been proposed between circulating or residential mobility and radiating or logistical mobility.[49] This is a useful working vocabulary, which I will adopt for the rest of the book, without necessarily envisaging that the differences are absolute. In circulating mobility, people changed their residences more or less frequently, according to seasonal resource abundance or other choices. In radiating mobility, they maintained a particular base or bases for longer periods (*not* necessarily permanently) and made forays from it or them for specific tasks. In the early post-glacial period, foragers might better be characterised as using circulating rather than radiating mobility.

All the evidence considered so far must reflect social choices. Social values were not derived from and determined by the technological and economic practicalities of making a living. It is at least as likely that daily practice was guided by shared social values and goals. What was eaten and how and by whom, where people lived, with whom and when, how place and the dead were regarded, are all social and conceptual as much as economic or practical questions. How are such issues to be addressed? Specialists of this period have often considered both practical and social issues by means of analogy, using the ethnographic record of recent and present-day foragers as a source of models for interpreting those in the past. This raises, however, two basic problems. Recent and present-day foragers are very varied, and they are the product of specific historical circumstances.

While some modern foragers are relentlessly mobile, some in the recent past achieved a sedentary existence. Opposed to examples of assertively egalitarian groups are societies with intensive procurement, embedded storage capacity, ranked social and occupational differences, leadership and property.[50] Clearly the absence of so-called food production does not entail particular or restricted sets of social relations. Secondly, there has recently been a vigorous debate about hunter-gatherers or foragers in southern Africa, centred on the issue of the relationship between foragers and their agro-pastoral neighbours.[51] The question is whether foragers can be seen as an independent system or whether they must be regarded as a specific creation of a wider historical system including herders and farmers. We should not suppose that there is a timeless, ahistorical forager way of life.

Can any analogies be retained as useful points of departure? Some forager groups in India and southern Africa have recently been characterised as knowledgeable, and flexible, and as skilled procurers of resources from very varied sources. These people use pooled knowledge within shared value systems. In their particular situations, they not only hunt and gather, but herd and cultivate from time to time as opportunities or necessities arise; they nonetheless remain essentially foragers.[52] This has encouraging resemblance, at a general level, to the characterisations above of early post-glacial foragers as based on flexibility and diversification. Another useful generalisation has come from study of recent hunters in Lappland in the far north of Europe. What distinguishes herders from hunters is not a body of technical knowledge, for the hunters seem perfectly well aware of alternative subsistence procedures, but their respective common values. Hunter life is based on an ethic of sharing, herder life on an ethic of acquisition.[53] One complication evident in the ethnographic record is that ideal and practice are not always the same. An expressed ethic of sharing may be counteracted by much more individualistic practice.[54] There is probably no such thing as a completely egalitarian society. One account of what are described as 'assertively egalitarian' societies is in fact restricted to the social life of adult males.[55]

Assertively egalitarian societies have economies based on immediate rather than delayed returns. That is to say, they lack investment in facilities which produce returns at a later date, storage of food or materials, and assets held in the form of rights (usually by men). They have positive and active sanctions against saving and accumulation, and positively encourage sharing. Goods circulate by exchange (and by gambling). People are separated from property, and leadership is discouraged and refused. There is equal and immediate access to the means of getting food, and to the means of coercion. Economic and social activity is orientated to the present, rather than to the past or to the future. By contrast, delayed-return systems are orientated to the past and future as well as to the present, and depend on a different set of values and structured or differentiated relationships. Those foraging people with immediate-return systems have no difficulty with the technical aspects of agriculture and pastoralism, but are inhibited from such changes by the rules governing sharing, ownership and association.

The foragers of early post-glacial Europe cannot be characterised in terms of immediate-return economic systems. They had fixed facilities such as fish traps and there was investment in the means of transport such as canoes. There are hints of storage. The whole pattern of mobility and planned seasonal exploitation could imply an acceptance of ordered relationships and adherence to group codes. On the other hand, given the conditions of population density, dispersal and mobility, it is hard to see what could have prevented equal access to the means of food or to weapons. There was simply too much space for coercion easily to be applied. The distribution and mobility of the population could have been more than demographic fact or a strategy to avoid the risk of depleting resources. They may themselves express an ethic of integration and cooperation, through which people bound themselves to participate in the ordered round of seasonal exploitation. There is no need to choose between the options indicated by the ethnographic record. The foragers of early post-glacial Europe emerge as distinctive in their own right.

In this light, initial characterisations can be broadened. Early post-glacial foragers practised a range of residential strategies, based largely on dispersal and circulating mobility. There was planning and repetition, and favoured sites were long in use; there was regard for the past. There was also innovation through the generations; foragers were takers of opportunities rather than opportunistic.[56] Dispersal and mobility served to reduce the risk of resource depletion, but also expressed an ethic of cooperation and integration, by which all group members were bound. There was probably some measure of direct control over some resources, and there was some storage, but there was no significant accumulation of foods or goods. There were no obvious differences between generations (between elders and younger people) or between the sexes, in so far as this can be judged from those burials that occur. (Those in the Danube Gorges may well be late, as argued above, but the same generalisations hold true.) Membership of social groups probably fluctuated. The stratigraphy of a site like Friesack or the fluctuations in burial treatment through the sequence at Vlasac may be testimony to variations in group size and composition. The broad cultural groupings suggest open membership at a wider scale, perhaps connected with open breeding networks.[57] There was a sense of past, present and future. This can be seen in the economic system, as argued above, and is expressed in the presence of the human dead on the sites of the living. The useful distinction can be made between funerals and rites of ancestral veneration.[58] Human remains have turned up in small quantities at sites other than formal burial grounds (as in the Danube Gorges), for example in submerged sites off the present Danish coast, at Noyen-sur-Seine, at Uzzo and at Franchthi. At Noyen, there were pieces of head and long bone, suggesting that selected parts of the dead were carried around by the living; several had cut marks on them. The dead of a group could have had a continuous presence amongst the living. A practical ethic of sharing and cooperation may have been reinforced by a conceptual order which united people and nature, the living and the dead.

CHAPTER 3

THE FIRST GENERATIONS: SOUTH-EAST EUROPE, *c.* 7000/6500–5500 BC

A settlement in central-southern Bulgaria

Some time around 6000 BC in a Balkan lowland a community rebuilt one of its settlements on the low mound created by the remains and debris of its predecessor. Continuity in style of layout went with continuity of occupation. Rectangular houses were built with mud or daub over a frame of small wall posts, and were set in ordered rows, quite close together, with wider lanes between. There were tens of such buildings. Standing at the doorway of one of them, a visitor would have had an impression of considerable architectural uniformity, relieved by varied patterns of red and white decoration on the outside walls. Past the pitched roofs would have been seen a still well-wooded landscape, but with fields or plots closer to the settlement and small clearances kept open by grazing animals. Other settlements and occupations would have been visible in the distance. Turning from the view of the world outside, on which the settlement had already made some impact, and through which its occupants at other times moved, to the domestic world inside the house, the observer would have faced a darkened but large rectangular room, perhaps with several other people in it. At the far end a clay oven was the source of heat and food, with pots on the ground around it. Clay figurines, perhaps to do with ancestors or mythic figures, were firmly linked to the domestic world, and served to unite people in a set of common beliefs. Beneath some houses there were burials of former inhabitants. This was a long-established point in the landscape. At the time of its rebuilding, this construction was already centuries old, and it was to be rebuilt several times more but to endure – with interruptions in occupation – for another two and a half thousand years.

This is the settlement mound or *tell* of Karanovo in the valley of the river Azmak near Nova Zagora in central-southern Bulgaria, in the second of its seven major phases of occupation. The mound rises 12 m, and covers over 4 ha. A massive programme of excavation has uncovered only part of the site, leaving impressive sections through millennia of Neolithic life.[1] There are many tells, probably thousands in Greece and the Balkans, as far north as the Hungarian plain.

How are Karanovo and other tells to be regarded? How did they come into being, and how were they used? How did they relate to a wider landscape? Their interpretation should not be taken for granted. These and other sites from the first generations of the Neolithic can be taken to represent a series of profound changes, compared with the previous foraging life, since they show larger communities, a new sense of place and identity, a novel subsistence base involving new resources brought from outside Europe, diverse material culture which could signal complex messages, and increased reverence of the dead as

3.1 The Karanovo tell. Top: general view of the accumulated mound; below: house IV and other features revealed in recent excavations, Karanovo I. Photos: Hiller.

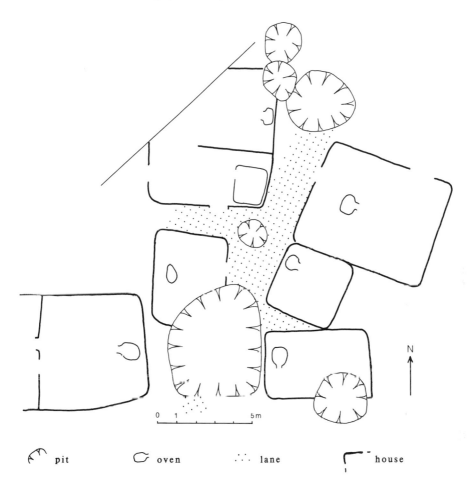

3.2 Houses and other features in building phase III, Karanovo II. After Hiller.

ancestors and as a principle for descent. Not only have these changes over the first thousand or more years of the Neolithic appeared profound, but they have usually been taken to indicate a break with previous forager populations. But both the process and rate of transformation are problematic. The Neolithic was a long time in the making, and its makers may have had much to do with earlier generations of foragers. The tell can be seen as the slow-growing symptom of gradual, internal change rather than as the stamp of rapid, external innovation.

The colonisation hypothesis

In the first thousand years or more of the Neolithic period in south-east Europe, people lived in small communities. Some sites, like Karanovo or Sesklo in Thessaly, appear to have been in and out of use, while others were used for demonstrably shorter periods. There are clear signs of more people in the landscape than before. River and stream valleys and the edges of old lake basins were favourite locations for occupation. The rather uniform houses within settlements and the ordered nature of the layout of the unenclosed, undefended settlements, suggest cohesive, successful communities. Well-fired pottery, often painted, was used in abundance for the preparation and presentation, though perhaps not often the cooking, of food. There was an increased flow of raw materials for stone tools. Clay figurines in human and animal form were firmly centred in house and community, and probably accessible to all community members. Increased diversity of material culture extended to beads and bracelets in stone and shell, clay seals, and stone and other studs, all perhaps to do with personal appearance, decoration and identity. Wild animals were still hunted, but at most sites the bones of sheep and goats, cattle and pig are far more numerous, and of these – with variations and exceptions – sheep and goats were usually most common. These had often been killed quite young, suggesting their use for meat. People grew crops of cereals and legumes: wheats and barleys, peas, lentils and vetches.

All these general characteristics can be found in the Neolithic of adjacent south-west Asia, from Turkey to Iran if not further east, south to Israel and north to beyond the Iranian mountains into Turkmenia.[2] There the period from roughly 9000 to 7000 BC saw the culmination of the twin processes of settling down and the domestication of plant and animal resources, though this was not at a uniform rate in each region. Some of the first sedentary communities may not yet have had fully domesticated resources, and not all the users of domesticated resources need have been sedentary. Wheats, barleys and legumes, and sheep and goats were the dominant resources; cattle and pigs may have been domesticated a little later. People lived in mudbrick and post-framed houses, often very closely set together in nucleated hamlets or villages. Change may have come slower in many parts of Turkey, to the west of core areas of transformation in the Levant, Mesopotamia and its eastern fringes, but by 7000 BC there were established Neolithic communities like Haçilar and Çatal Hüyük.[3] Pottery making spread through this whole region from about 7000 BC.[4]

The evidence was set out in the last chapter for the relative sparseness of forager populations in south-east Europe. As part of the expansion of the Neolithic, there were movements of people by sea to both Cyprus and Crete. At the start of the Neolithic, both islands appear to have been empty, though Cyprus had had an earlier episode of occupation, noted above.[5] This is indicative of purposeful colonisation. The lowest level of the settlement at Knossos on Crete, though probably lacking pottery and perhaps formal house structures, shares many other characteristics of the early Neolithic.[6] It is therefore often assumed that there was a movement of people from Turkey or other parts of south-west Asia, either by sea or by land through Thrace. The most popular reason given for this movement is population increase. (Future research into DNA patterns might help to trace the descent of specific populations.) Another model recently formulated proposes that the practice of agriculture was in large part to generate goods for exchange, in order to accumulate prestige; according to this, favourable land could have been very purposefully sought out.[7] Radiocarbon dates suggest a Neolithic presence in Macedonia and Crete from soon after 7000 BC, and in Thessaly by 6500 BC. There were sites like Karanovo in central-southern Bulgaria by 6000 BC, and other sites to the north as far as the Hungarian plain date from around that time onwards.[8] This pattern indicates some kind of south–north movement,

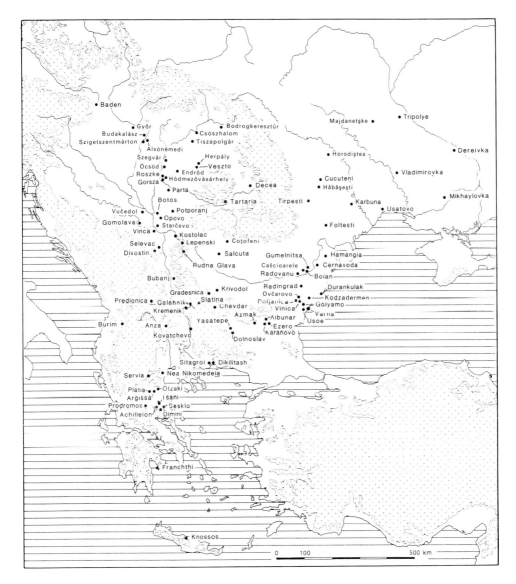

3.3 Simplified location map of the principal sites discussed in chapters 3–5.

and suggests the continuation of colonisation fuelled by population increase. Even at a previously well-used site like the Franchthi Cave, the evidence for change appears considerable. There was a rapid shift there in the use of cereals, from wild barley and oats, to emmer, einkorn and barley, and in the exploitation of animals, from red deer, pigs and tunny, to sheep and goats. The style and range of stone tools changed little, but soon after the beginning of the Neolithic there were greater quantities of obsidian from Melos, brought in as pre-formed cores, and large flint blades were also imported. Plain pottery was soon in use. Occupation extended beyond the cave, perhaps connected with cultivation by spring-fed

3.4 Simplified outline chronology for the areas discussed in chapters 3–5.

BC — 3000 · 3500 · 4000 · 4500 · 5000 · 5500 · 6000 · 6500 · 7000

E HUNGARY
BADEN · TISZAPOLGÁR BODROG-KERESZTÚR · TISZA · Szakálhát · ALFÖLD LINEAR · KÖRÖS

MOLDAVIA & UKRAINE
Yamnaya · Foltesti-Usatovo · TRIPOLYE · CUCUTENI · pre-Cucuteni–Tripolye A · Sredny Stog · Dniepr-Donets · Bug-Dniestr · E. LBK · CRIŞ

LOWER DANUBE
Cotofeni–Cernavoda III · Cernavoda I · GUMELNITSA · BOIAN · Dudesti · CRIŞ

W BALKANS
Baden · Bodrogkeresztúr · BUBANJ HUM · Tiszapolgár · Plocnik · Tordos · VINCA · D · C · B · A · STARČEVO

N-E BULGARIA
Cernavoda III – Ezerovo · Cernavoda I · Kodzadermen–Varna · Sava–Poljanica · Usoe II · Usoe I–Samovedene · Chonevo–Ovcharovo · Hamangia

C-S BULGARIA
Ezero · (transition or hiatus period) · KARANOVO · VI · V–Maritsa · IV · III · I–II

GREECE
EBA · Sitagroi IV · FN · Sitagroi III · LN II · Dimini · LN I · MN · Sesklo · EN · early Sesklo · early ceramic

BC — 3000 · 3500 · 4000 · 4500 · 5000 · 5500 · 6000 · 6500 · 7000 streams in the now flooded plain below the site. It can be argued either that the inhabitants of the cave were newcomers or that they were rapidly and decisively influenced by newcomers and new practices around them.[9]

The acculturation hypothesis

There are at least three models of indigenous change to set against the colonisation hypothesis. The first has proposed that there was independent development in south-east Europe of the domestication of both cereals and sheep and goats.[10] This is unlikely. The cereals which came to prominence in the Neolithic were wheats and barleys, and the record of plant use at the Franchthi Cave shows a complete shift away from the wild oats and wild barleys used in the late Mesolithic. There is no evidence that sheep and goats were part of the early post-glacial fauna of south-east Europe. There is no sign of them at Franchthi Cave, nor earlier in the late-glacial cave and rockshelter sites of north-west Greece.[11] The second model proposes increasing complexity in the indigenous foraging population of the region, with moves, before the Neolithic, to sedentism, resource control (including of plants) and social differentiation. This draws especially on the evidence of the Danube Gorges, reviewed in the previous chapter, and could be supported by the ethnography of complex forager societies from various parts of the world.[12] This too is unconvincing, not through weakness of the analogies, but because of difficulties with the chronology and interpretation of the Danube Gorges evidence. The last chapter set out a rather different view of change in the Gorges, involving a still partially mobile settlement pattern, and the emergence of sacred sites more or less parallel to the introduction of the Neolithic in the region as a whole. We will return to this below.

A third model can be proposed. This features foragers of the kind characterised in the previous chapter: mobile, adaptable, flexible, knowledgeable, and perhaps with an ethic of sharing. These people were takers of opportunities, and could have got wind of changes in settlement, subsistence and other aspects of life, on voyages by sea for tunny fishing and the acquisition of obsidian. The motivation for adopting the use of herded animals and cultivated plants could have been initially to support the existing social ethic as much as to broaden further the spectrum of resources already exploited. Both animals and plants could have been seen to be compatible with a mobile lifestyle, and would have offered secure resources to share and to store. In this way, we can envisage the transition as an enhancement of the existing social sytem, rather than as the kind of radical break which is so often proposed. It is a crucial point, because the interpretation of so much else that follows is affected by the nature of the beginning.

What the south-east European Neolithic became over forty or more generations does not reveal what it was at the beginning. Even after forty generations, the Neolithic of the region was diverse in its presence and character. Whether or not a 'preceramic' or 'aceramic' phase is accepted in Thessaly, there is evidence (presented below) to show a gradual development of settlement. It is therefore false immediately to contrast sparse populations of foragers with a densely packed Neolithic settlement pattern. Further, the Neolithic presence in Turkey, both in western Anatolia and in European Turkey, is itself so far very weak.

Nor was there marked increase in settlement density over the succeeding millennia, for example in the reasonably well-surveyed Konya basin in west-central Turkey.[13] This weakens the case for a Neolithic expansion fuelled by population increase, and proponents of the colonisation hypothesis must then posit the existence of Neolithic sites in western Turkey buried and concealed in river valleys, or very long-range movement of colonists by sea from further away in the east Mediterranean.[14]

Some of the earliest radiocarbon dates may not be reliable. The three from Knossos level X, for example, have large standard deviations, and the earlier two were from oak stakes. The wood dated might be older than the occupation. This is important, since it is usually assumed that Crete was colonised right at the very beginning of the Neolithic. This is not to deny its colonisation, but that could be seen as part of a secondary process of infill once the Neolithic was underway. Knossos remained a relatively small and isolated site for much of the Neolithic period.[15]

At the Franchthi Cave, there seems to be continuity in the style and range of stone tools, though it remains uncertain how continuous the stratigraphy is through the Mesolithic–Neolithic transition. Though the range of lithic sources used increased substantially in the Neolithic, and the manner in which they were used changed, there was continuity of use of obsidian. A particular shell, *Cerithium vulgatum*, also continued to be collected from the shore, an odd coincidence if there had been a complete change of population at the cave.[16] It is also important to reconsider the active role of material culture in the early part of the Neolithic. It is too simple to assume that this was just part of the cultural baggage of incoming population. Pottery itself was a recent innovation. Its production, forms and use changed considerably through the first thousand years of use. This may be the result of development among an incoming population, but it is also legitimate to envisage the active acquisition of novelties by an indigenous population.

If the third acculturation model which I advocate here cannot be accepted, a compromise solution would be to envisage some limited colonisation, perhaps by sea, into what later became relatively densely settled areas, such as Thessaly and central-southern Bulgaria, with continuity of population in most areas around: in southern Greece, Greek Thrace, Albania, north-east Bulgaria and perhaps parts of north-west Bulgaria, much of the Danube valley and into the Tisza–Körös river network in south-east Hungary. There are plenty of recent cases of mutually beneficial contact and exchange (of foodstuffs – proteins for carbohydrates – and of know-how) between foragers and farmers, and it has been suggested that marriage partners could have been exchanged across a 'porous frontier' between two such populations.[17] In that case, it is doubtful whether future DNA-based research will pick up clear patterns of genetic descent. Incoming population would have had to explore a new landscape. That would have taken time, and it is doubtful if it was achieved entirely without the assistance of the existing, knowledgeable inhabitants.

The Danube Gorges: indigenous resistance?

I argued in the last chapter that the most spectacular developments in the Danube Gorges were late, to judge by the chronology of Lepenski Vir itself. In this case, the emergence of a

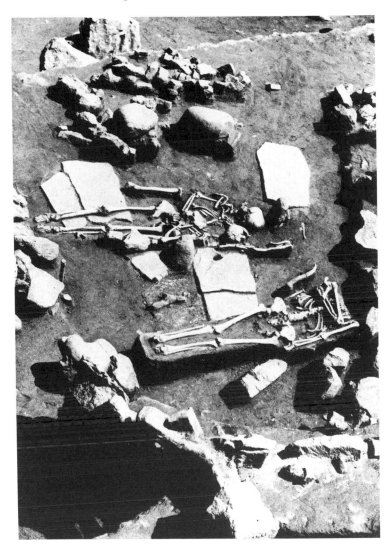

3.5 Structure 65 of Lepenski Vir Ib. The burial in the foreground belongs to structure 36 of Lepenski Vir II. Photo: Srejović.

sacred centre could be seen not as a symptom of a complex foraging society prefiguring the Neolithic, but as some kind of reaction to changes in the region as a whole. It has been suggested that the reaction was to incoming Neolithic populations,[18] but it could as well have been to the process of indigenous acculturation.

Lepenski Vir is in a dramatic setting, on a large terrace, faced by a whirlpool in the river and a spectacular trapezoidal rock on the opposite bank. The shrines could have been periodically visited for special depositions. The burial of the dead would have strengthened the ties of the population to this particular spot. Plain and decorated stones ('altars' and 'sculptures')[19] enhanced the rear space of the shrines. The combination of setting, tradition, offerings, ancestors, spirits and the special knowledge required to communicate with them, must have made the place potent. In the early part of phase II, many of the sculptures were placed in front of the structures, and these included the largest and most striking of the whole sequence.[20] It has been suggested that the layout of the site betrays internal social differentiation and the emergence of a dominant lineage in charge of the central space of the site (where the largest structures are to be found), and that the sculptures represent lineage leaders, living and dead.[21] It is hard to see how one can test either proposition, and the former is only plausible if the site is seen as a direct mirror of social relations to the exclusion of other dimensions, which is doubtful.

A more general interpretation may be more satisfactory. The site stands out in the local context. It was special in many dimensions. It emphasised the links of a population to local place, to the past through the dead, and to a natural and spirit world. It was to do with identity. It could therefore have offered a point of conceptual resistance, either to incoming Neolithic population, or to a leaking away of old loyalties and affiliations in the process of acculturation. In the end this was unsuccessful and the site was abandoned, to be re-occupied after an interval in phase III with obvious dislocation of the tradition.[22]

The areas of Neolithic settlement

People were widespread throughout the regions of south-east Europe but were by no means everywhere. Patterns of distribution can only have formed gradually, over generations and centuries. There were many sites in Thessaly[23] and in parts of the Maritsa valley of central-southern Bulgaria.[24] There was a scatter of sites up the Struma and Vardar valleys, and down the Morava and into the Danube valley. Starčevo, the classic site for central Serbia, is on the left bank of the Danube near Belgrade.[25] There is a further scatter of sites up into southern Hungary, some west of the Danube in the *Dunántúl* or Transdanubia, but many in the Tisza–Körös–Criş river network of the *Nagyalföld* or Great Hungarian plain.[26] There are also sites in the main Danube valley between Bulgaria and Romania, and around the edges of the Carpathians. To the east of the Carpathians, the distinction must be made between the forest-steppe zone, across the middle stretches of valleys like the Bug, Dniestr and Dniepr, and the more southerly, drier, steppe zone. Initial Neolithic settlement involved the forest-steppe zone.[27]

Fewer sites are known in central and southern Greece. In northern Greece, while there are settlements at Nea Nikomedeia on the southern edge of the Aliakmon basin and at Servia higher up the Aliakmon valley, there are no known Early Neolithic sites (down to about 6000 BC) eastwards in the rest of coastal Macedonia and Thrace, as far as the Turkish border. There are likewise few early sites in European Turkey. Sitagroi, a tell on the plain of Drama, was first occupied from about 5500 BC.[28] There were no Neolithic sites of this period in the lowest Danube and they appear sparse in northern Bulgaria south of the Danube. There were few sites east of the Carpathians, and few in the hillier, inland parts of Bosnia and Adriatic Croatia. These patterns are of course in part a reflection of the distribution and intensity of research. Recent work has shown the existence of sites in areas previously more or less blank, for example in both central Albania and its eastern, mountainous part, and in north-east Bulgaria, both inland and on the coast.[29]

Not only was the Neolithic presence thus rather varied, but the density and character of sites varied from region to region. In Thessaly there are in total probably some hundreds of tells, though estimates vary and thorough survey is likely to change the figures. In eastern Thessaly, recent survey shows nearly 120 Early Neolithic sites (roughly down to 6000 BC), and as many for the Middle Neolithic (roughly 6000–5500 BC).[30] But each period is some five centuries or more. The pottery sequence allows some (perhaps crude) general phasing within the Early Neolithic period. Around twenty sites of Early Neolithic date have been excavated, but not all were occupied from the beginning of the regional sequence. There are a few candidates for an early, 'preceramic' phase, such as Sesklo, Argissa and others, though the validity of this characterisation and its chronological priority have both been doubted.[31] These continue into the EN I phase. Others, such as Otzaki and Prodromos, appear to begin in the EN II phase. In southern Macedonia, though there may be problems in accurately correlating regional pottery sequences, the known sites also appear a little later, Nea Nikomedeia from the EN I/II transition and Servia from EN II/III. Achilleion in southern Thessaly began, in these terms, in EN I (earlier test excavations had suggested, falsely, the existence of a preceramic phase at the site), and occupation lasted from about 6400 to 5600 BC. Survey of other sites in the local area suggests that Achilleion was the earliest, most others belonging after 6000 BC. Slightly further afield to west and east the tells of Tsani and Tsangli began some time around or after 6000 BC.[32] The raw figure for site spacing in both the Early and Middle Neolithic phases in Thessaly is around 5 km,[33] but this density may in fact have been rare in any one generation. There were also gaps in the occupation of many tells, and the questions of their permanence, duration and independence must further be considered below.

Another area of sustained occupation was the Maritsa basin. In the Nova Zagora region of the Azmak river, a tributary of the Maritsa, it has been estimated that there were some twelve early sites in a 30 by 10 km area. This is the region to which Karanovo belongs. Here too there may be variation through time and space. There have been references to pre-Karanovo sites, and the tell of Azmak, some 25 km to the west of Karanovo, could be seen as the focus of another settlement area. There are further nuclei in the upper Maritsa valley, for example near Pazardzik.[34] There is further variation not far away. To the west and north of the Maritsa valley, Chevdar is an early tell site in the upper Topolnitsa valley, and Kazanluk an early settlement mound in the upper Tundsa valley. Kazanluk appears to be on its own in its immediate locality, while there are only two other low tells within a few kilometres of Chevdar, neither in the main valley like Chevdar.[35] There has been quite a lot of recent research in the middle and upper Struma valley, which has found a number of early settlement mounds. In the upper valley, there were successive occupations at sites including Kremenik, Kraïnitsi, Galabnik and Pernik. In the middle valley Kovatchevo appears to be the only early site, despite intensive survey in the early 1980s. It is doubtful if many of these occupations began much before about 6000 BC, and the character of some occupations, for example at Kremenik, remains to be established.[36] Though the build-up of a mound may not reflect permanence of occupation, these varied tells can be contrasted strongly with small sites in coastal and inland north-east Bulgaria, for example at Tsonevo and

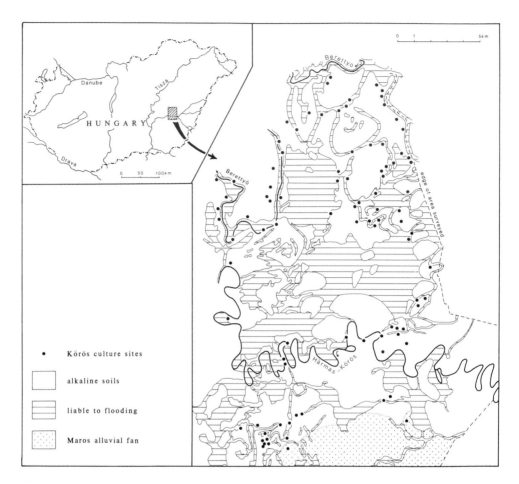

3.6 The distribution of Körös culture sites in part of the Hungarian plain. After Magyarország Régészeti Topográfiája.

Ovčarovo, which are characterised by thin occupation layers, a rarity of formal house structures and the presence of so-called pit-dwellings.

In a former lake basin connected by tributaries to the Vardar river, Anza is a low settlement mound with three phases of occupation before about 5300 BC, beginning about 6100 BC. There was a break between phases I and II at the site. The site appears to have no immediate neighbours, though Vrsnik lies in a similar location some kilometres to the east and Rug Bair a little into the hills to the north-west.[37] Classically, sites in the Starčevo and Körös–Criş areas have rather thin layers, very often from a single occupation. Starčevo itself was situated on the left side of the Danube, above the floodplain on the terrace edge, with the river probably much closer than at the present day. Most Starčevo–Körös sites have rather poorly defined structures on them. So-called pit-dwellings are recurrent in the Starčevo area, and are often assumed to be the principal form of habitation. At Divostin I, however, there were traces of rectangular post buildings as well. In the area around

Divostin a wide variety of site locations was chosen, though the overall density of sites at any one moment was probably low.[38]

In the Tisza–Körös–Criş river network of the southern part of the Hungarian plain, there are some areas where early settlements appear to have been numerous. There are spreads of occupation along the edges of terraces and islands above the floodplains, but the occupation layer at any one place is characteristically thin, and these ribbon sites are probably the result of repeated, shifting occupations over long periods of time. The most recurrent features are pits, often large and with substantial inventories of food remains and artefacts. Some above-ground structures are considered to have been built in this area.[39] The possibilities of movement, impermanence and seasonal shifts in settlements are perhaps at their clearest in this area, but they should not be ignored elsewhere in the region. Even in favoured areas like Thessaly and the Maritsa valley, the density of sites may only have slowly increased, and people may still have moved on a seasonal basis. This argument will be developed below.

The location of settlements

The small pit-dwelling sites of north-east Bulgaria were mostly situated on windy plateaux. The sites of Burim and Podgori in Albania were well into mountainous regions.[40] These kinds of location are unusual. Most Neolithic sites in this period were lowland rather than upland, and many were close to water, on the edges of rivers, streams and sometimes marshes. Most of the examples already cited conform to this pattern, though their locations varied considerably in detail. Starčevo was fronted by a broad floodplain, probably both wooded and marshy, with a meandering or braided river system running through it. Karanovo was close to a much smaller flow. It is harder there to reconstruct the contemporary pattern of soil and vegetation, but the site may have been close to areas of periodically flooded land or backswamp. Galabnik in the upper Struma was sited in an active floodplain.[41] Nea Nikomedeia now lies well inland, in the orchards of the southern part of the Aliakmon/Axios delta. At the time of occupation, the sea was probably much closer, perhaps some 5 km. The site is on a low rise. The immediate setting was one of oak forest, with marsh and meadows, both freshwater and saline, closer to the sea.[42] Selected sites from Thessaly will provide a further detailed case study of diversity.

Locations in Thessaly

'I feel that I am really in Thessaly', wrote Edward Lear in 1849, 'for width and breadth now constitute the soul and essence of all the landscape.' Over a century later Milojčić, the director of the German excavations in the 1950s, wrote (my translation) that 'Thessaly is one of the most distinctive landscapes of Greece – a seemingly endless, fertile plain, where the brooding summer heat knocks the traveller's breath away and the icy winter wind makes those without shelter tremble . . . Thessaly was and still is today the grainstore of Greece.'[43] These are pervasive images, but they have to be modified in the reconstruction of the Neolithic setting.

Thessaly has a diverse landscape. The east coast is shut off by the Ossa–Pelion range, and the main, easily accessible shoreline was in the bay of Volos. As elsewhere the sea originally came further in, later alluviation having pushed the shoreline out.[44] Thessaly consists of two main basins, east and west, divided north–south by a range of hills. The Peneios runs from west to east through the northern parts, with the Enipeios and other tributaries branching out in the western basin. In the southern part of the east basin there was formerly a large lake. No major river empties into the bay of Volos. Pollen diagrams suggest that the basic vegetation was oak woodland and that the climate was perhaps similar to that of today – hot in summer and cold in winter – but more moist. It has been suggested that the east plain and the southern coastal zone were 'semi-arid', but this remains to be established.[45]

There were many tells, except in the southern part of the east plain, and most were near permanent water. One or two are known on the coast, such as Pyrasos. Many are found in the low foothills of the southern parts of the area and on the eastern side of the central ridge. Others are on the plains proper, beside or near larger and smaller watercourses.

This diversity of location probably existed from the beginning. Of the preceramic occupations, Argissa lay beside the Peneios itself in the north part of the east plain, Soufli on the other bank of the river several kilometres to the east, Gendiki in the foothills of the Ossa range in the north-east of the east basin, and Sesklo on the edge of low hills a little inland from the coast of the bay of Volos. Sesklo sits above a small stream valley. Achilleion, another early site, lies above the south-east part of the west basin proper, above the valley of a tributary of the Enipeios, in rolling country rising to a range of low hills. This is dissected by small streams; Achilleion lies close to one of them, at 200–300 m above sea level.[46] Many early sites may have had locations similar to those of Sesklo and Achilleion, and many of the tells in the plains proper may belong to more developed phases. Undoubtedly, however, there were early low-lying sites, such as Argissa, or Prodromos in the west basin. It is often assumed that there was a dense distribution of substantial settlements from the beginning of the sequence, that sites were more or less permanently occupied, and that the Neolithic basins were essentially the same as today in terms of topography and hydrology.[47] I have already suggested that the first proposition is doubtful, and there is important new evidence which casts doubt on the other two assumptions.

Platia Magoula Zarkou is a substantial tell beside the Peneios in the extreme north-east of the west basin of Thessaly.[48] It has occupation levels throughout the Neolithic sequence (and into the Early Bronze Age), the first dating to the late Early Neolithic, perhaps a little before 6000 BC. Like most other tells on the plains proper, it rises above the present floodplain. Recent soil studies have suggested, however, that the rivers of the region were not incised into their present levels (when the floodplains are perhaps 3–15 m lower than in the Neolithic) until about 5000 BC. Detailed coring at the tell, which has not been carried out elsewhere, showed that its base was up to 4–5 m below the present surface around the tell, and at least 1–2 m below river sediments of Neolithic date. The Early and Middle Neolithic occupations at the site (the period covered in this chapter) were contemporary with the deposition of several metres of fluviatile loam and silty clay.

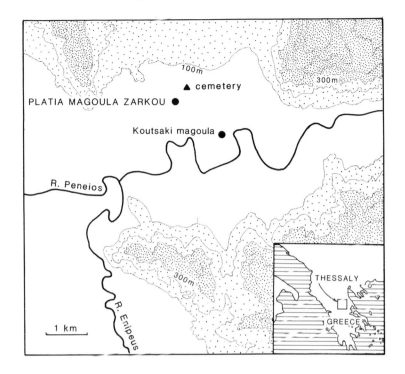

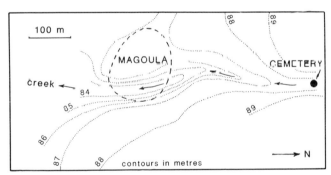

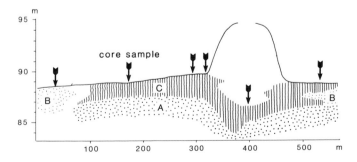

3.7 The setting and stratigraphy of Platia Magoula Zarkou. A: sand and gravel subsoil; B, C: loams. After van Andel *et al.*

The Middle Neolithic occupation may have begun to rise above this, but the Early Neolithic occupation seems to have begun on the bank of a creek in the active floodplain of the Peneios. It seems unlikely that occupation can have been permanent at this locale in the early stages. That leaves open how far people shifted in the flood season of the first months of the year, but crucially it frees us from the shackles of a model of full sedentism from the beginning of the sequence. To anticipate, people may have chosen locations where they could exploit fresh floodwater deposits for cultivation, as part of a wider annual cycle of procurement and movement. The dominant animal species throughout the Neolithic sequence was sheep/goats. If people moved, be it only short distances, then perhaps not all known sites in a given phase can be regarded as independent. It is time to examine the structure and history of settlements themselves.

The creation of place

For either foragers or colonisers, mobility would have been a sensible strategy for reducing risks, and for foragers it would have been part of the pre-existing way of life, deeply embedded in shared values. Some people may have become fully sedentary from an early stage, but the evidence from the region as a whole suggests that 'settling down' was a gradual process. Mobility was retained in varying degrees throughout the Neolithic. In ways that may not have been fully envisaged at the beginning, people were gradually defined by their attachment to chosen areas and places, in this way creating a network of regional and local identities on a scale that had not existed in the forager period. New resources could have been adopted by foragers to take advantage of new opportunities for resource procurement, but it would be limiting to envisage the Neolithic as simply a reaction to subsistence change. Another fundamental motive may have been to enhance the existing social ethic, to extend the bonds of group and community. As in the forager period, there was still plenty of space, and it is hard to see how people could have been coerced into change. A wider community was gradually constructed. One of the principal means by which this was achieved was by the creation of place.

In the more northerly parts of the region (the Starčevo–Körös areas) and in other areas like north-east Bulgaria, many occupations were relatively brief. In the Körös region, while particular zones of the landscape were favoured – the junction between terrace/island and floodplain – the place of occupation wandered. Though there is animal bone evidence for occupation at all the major seasons of the year,[49] it is unclear how precisely this can be applied to the situation in any given year or any one generation. Even if people were on a particular terrace continuously for a few years, the attachment was to a landscape zone, not a particular place. The structural evidence (described further below) supports this impression of impermanence. Huts, houses or pit-dwellings may have been appropriate for a lifestyle with considerable mobility, without either a practical or a social need for greater investment in structures more solid or more enduring. The evidence from Divostin I of above-ground houses is rare for the Starčevo area. Coming further south, the lower levels of sites like Kremenik in the Struma valley had uncertain evidence for structures (though this clearly does not apply to the post-framed structures of Galabnik).[50] Was there a patterned difference between the north and south of the region? After all, the sequence at Anza begins in phase I with interconnected mudbrick buildings and at Karanovo I with rows of rectangular post-framed houses,[51] and it is easy to assume that the settlement mound was an inevitable part of the Neolithic lifestyle, especially if the colonisation hypothesis is favoured. But there is other evidence for more gradual development in southern parts as well, and the tell can be seen as the product of distinctive relationships.

There are two issues to consider: the choice of a place for repeated occupation, and the permanence and continuity of that occupation. Enough has been shown of the situation at Platia Magoula Zarkou to doubt year-round occupation in all cases. The preceramic levels of Argissa and Sesklo were thin, with no definite structures other than ditches and pits, though in both cases admittedly the area of excavation was very limited.[52] Thin levels characterise the early occupations at most other excavated Thessalian sites, and Theocharis referred to the 'variety' of Early Neolithic occupations compared to the 'stabilisation and improvement' of Middle Neolithic ones (after about 6000 BC).[53] At Gendiki, there was a sterile layer above the thin preceramic level. At Soufli, there were three distinct preceramic layers with separations in between. The evidence for structures generally in the Early Neolithic is poor.[54] At Sesklo, the first definite evidence from the 'acropolis' of the site comes in EN III, where there are signs of walled and roofed mudbrick and *pisé* (compacted mud) structures. At Achilleion, the bottom level Ia was only 20 cm thick and not present in all the test squares (of an admittedly small excavation). Extrapolation from the radiocarbon dates has suggested a maximum duration of 100–150 years. The discernible structures were 'pit-dwellings'. By contrast, layer IVa later in the sequence was estimated to have lasted only 75–150 years, but was characterised now by substantial buildings and was well over 1 m thick in some places.[55]

Excavations have usually been confined to the tells themselves, and because of their size usually to small portions of the mounds. At Sesklo, unusually, there were excavations outside the mound, in selected areas upslope.[56] In Area B, the main occupation was Middle Neolithic, but there were signs of thin, stratified occupations of EN I–III, and partial remains of stone-walled structures. In Area C, there was a preceramic occupation with a 'pit-dwelling' and there were signs of three stone-footed structures of some kind, of EN I date. The Middle Neolithic occupation in Area B consisted of an area of close-set, stone-footed buildings. But this was not part of the tell proper. By the Middle Neolithic on the 'acropolis' of the site a pattern of close-set buildings can be recognised (some described further below), and the distinctive nature of the site may have been reinforced by walls which both defined and retained this special place.

In central-southern Bulgaria few early sites have been published in detail. At Karanovo there were three building levels in phase I, and two in phase II, with 0.6–1 m and 1.75–2 m of build-up respectively. Post-framed buildings were a feature from an early stage. Renewed excavations at Karanovo have so far reached Karanovo II levels. It has been suggested recently that tells like Karanovo were seasonally occupied.[57] At Anza further west, there were also regular buildings from the outset. It might be possible to envisage slower, longer development further to the south.

The sum of the Greek and southern Balkan evidence suggests that the density of early settlement was lower than in later phases, that there were frequent interruptions in the occupation of chosen places, that the intensity of occupation in early stages may have been less than later in site sequences, that occupation of some sites at least could only have been possible on a seasonal basis, and that the creation of a mound may have been the result of very deliberate and conscious action structuring the placement of buildings and the accumulation of their debris.

The use of settlement space

Dispersed and single-level settlements

Settlements varied enormously in size, duration and internal layout. A useful basic distinction is between those with a dispersed layout, often with less regular structures and without repeated occupations, and those with an ordered layout, with uniform structures, continuity of place in rebuildings, and repeated occupations. Crudely speaking, this is the difference between 'flat' or thin sites and tells or settlement mounds. It may be tempting to ascribe greater sedentism to the way of life bound up with tells, but this assumption must be critically examined.

Rather little is known about the size or layout of 'flat' sites. Some in the Starčevo and Körös areas are of considerable linear extent, some stretching along terrace edges for hundreds of metres, but that does not convey their size at any one phase of occupation. Excavation has usually been of restricted extent, though at Divostin I it was possible to see early structures spread over an area at least 80 by 60 m. Endrőd 119 in the lower Körös valley was a small occupation by comparison with neighbouring sites, covering some 75 by 50 m.[58] A 'site' may therefore be the result of repeated and shifting occupations. Information about structures is poor. So-called pit-dwellings are rather varied, circular to oval depressions with hearths within them, and sometimes with post or stake holes around suggesting some sort of roof or cover. There are well-excavated examples from Divostin I, and from as far afield as Transylvania and Ukrainian Moldavia. They do not appear to have particular orientation or spacing. Ridged, tent-like structures have been claimed on Körös sites, but there were probably also some framed structures, like the two rather ill-defined rectangular affairs at Endrőd 119. At Divostin I, up to six more regular structures were found, rectilinear in layout and framed by earth-sunk posts and shallow wall slots, and with laid floors. The plans are incomplete and it is not clear how large these structures were. They too were dispersed, though they may have shared a common orientation.

The early layers of sites that became settlement mounds also share some of these features. The first phase of Anza contained interconnected rectangular houses (some 12 by 6 m) with mudbrick walls. The total extent of the settlement in phase I was estimated as up to 4.75 ha, but it seems unlikely that the whole area was simultaneously in use at any one time. Although seen in small excavated areas only, the first phases at Argissa and Sesklo also show irregular structures and thin layers. At Sesklo, the areas outside the 'acropolis' or mound proper are of the greatest interest.[59] Structures have been found over a wide area, perhaps at least 10 ha in extent. As in the mound proper, all the phases of the Early and Middle Neolithic are represented, but outside the mound the complete sequence is not to be found in any one excavated trench.

Development through time: Achilleion

Although the excavations there were of very limited extent, Achilleion is one of the best examples to show the development of the use of settlement space.[60] In phase Ia, there was a possible pit-dwelling ('pit house' in the report), followed in Ib by reuse of the pit and the appearance of plaster floors with artefacts of assorted kinds, including food preparation equipment. The earliest structure dated to late phase Ib, lying immediately above the features just described. The structure had a rectangular end, formed of compact *pisé* above a stone footing set in a bedding trench. It had a plaster floor, with a food preparation area and a work area, with artefacts of various kinds and two clay figurines. In phase II the layout of the area was further elaborated. There was a small post-framed house (little more than 4 by 2 m). Inside at its east end there was a pebble-lined firepit, with a horseshoe-shaped super-structure around one side. It contained many bones. There were two figurines and a frag-ment of an anthropomorphic vessel nearby, as well as various tools and animal bones. Just outside the northwest corner of the structure there was a hearth, with around it a quern, a grinding stone, a ladle, a scraper and blades, an axe and two figurines, as well as pots. Next to that was a bigger pit, with discarded bone. Further to the east, there was a probable yard, belonging to the post structure just described or another. Its plastered surface was bor-dered by small clusters of stones. On it lay a wide variety of artefacts, including blades, antler tools, pottery and figurines. It had a domed clay oven next to an area with food pro-cessing equipment and animal bones; a figurine lay on the bench or front platform of the oven. There was a pit next to the oven.

This phase might only have lasted as little as twenty-five years. In the succeeding phase IIb, there is information from a bigger area. Continuity of style of layout was maintained, but another small post-framed house was built to the south of the former structure. This too had hearths outside it (including another clay domed oven) and work and food prepara-tion areas beyond, with various artefacts. The work areas were littered with stone, antler and bone tools. Where the former house had stood there was now a large circular hearth with a hardened surface adjacent, with food preparation equipment on it.

In phase IIIa, there were no structures in the excavated area, but deposits continued to accumulate. There were large burning areas, pits and few artefacts. In phase IIIb there was a resumption of the style of layout seen in phase II, with post house, external hearths and pits, and a yard area with domed clay oven, 'fire platform' or raised rectangular hearth, plas-tered floor and pit. There were many artefacts and several figurines in the latter area.

After rearrangements in phase IIIb (showing among other things a longer post house), two-roomed houses appeared in phase IV, with stone footings set again in bedding or foundation trenches. Inside, these had plaster floors, hearths and probable raised benches. Outside, other features continued, including hearths, pits and work areas. In this phase, a ditch was dug around the excavated settlement area, perhaps more to demarcate than to

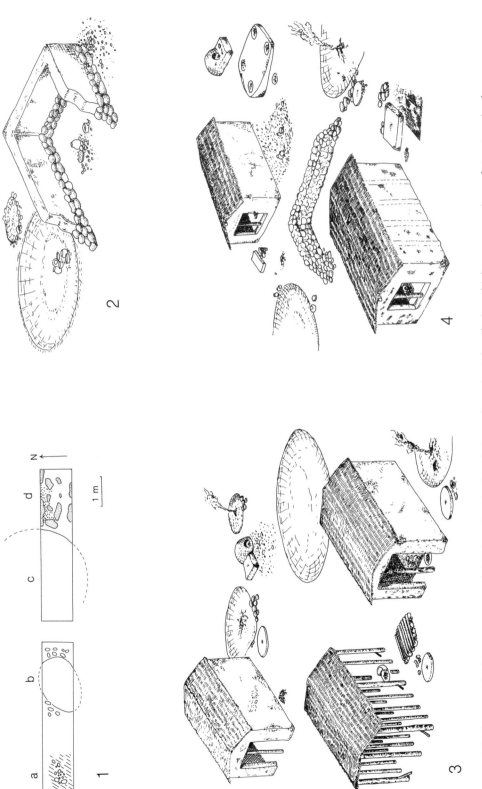

3.8 Houses and other structures at Achilleion. 1: early Ib. a, d: floors; b, c: pits; 2: late Ib; 3: multiple reconstructions of structures in phase II; 4: early IIIb. After Gimbutas.

enclose it. In phase IVb, stone-footed (perhaps stone-walled) buildings continued, but were now set on a different alignment.

Although the excavation area was small and the descriptions may seem repetitive, the unusual and important Achilleion detail shows that one cannot simply assume a given, universal model of settlement from the mere existence of a mound, which may have changed much during a long history. There was considerable continuity through the sequence, but there were also disruptions and changes. The eventual accumulation of a mound is compatible with shorter or longer abandonments, and with relocations within the total area of the mound. The distribution of artefacts and other residues around the settlement is also suggestive of abandonments. Tools, vessels and figurines in work areas and by ovens and hearths may indicate an intention to return. There is no specific evidence from Achilleion for the seasonality of occupation. The artefact evidence would be compatible with periodic, perhaps seasonal leavings of the site, perhaps not even by the whole community, and the impression from the architectural sequence is of a trend through time to larger and more solid buildings. Combined with a more intensive rate of mound accumulation, this too could suggest that permanent occupation became gradually more established.

A final important point concerns the use of space. It is conventional to date the appearance of sedentary settlement from the appearance of well-built structures. Those from phase II onwards at Achilleion would probably qualify, though those from phase II itself were of modest size. But if one changes the terminology from 'house' to the more neutral 'structure' or 'building', different possibilities are retained. And in the Achilleion detail, the activity outside and between the structures is at least as striking as the structures themselves. Activity could be characterised as formalised and ordered, in that there were set areas for certain tasks, and most tasks including tool use and food preparation took place in the open, rather than within the structures themselves. This kind of use of space need not entail permanent occupation.

Tells

Achilleion shows development through a mound sequence. It also introduces the notable range of excavated settlement mounds, whose layouts were ordered, often with considerable continuity over long spans of time, where rebuildings and reoccupations were frequent, and where the buildings themselves were rather uniform. The classic examples of these come from central-southern Bulgaria and Thessaly. Some sites were large. An average area of 0.5–1 ha is quoted for tells in Thessaly, with the number of inhabitants between 50 and 300.[61] The mound proper at Sesklo is less than 1 ha in area, and Argissa, partly eaten away by the Peneios, some 1.5 ha.[62] It is unlikely that such sizes were the norm from the beginning of site sequences. In Bulgaria, Karanovo was eventually 12 m high by the Early Bronze Age, and covered an area about 250 by 150 m, around 4 ha. Yasatepe is 4 m high and Azmak 8 m; their diameters at the base are 150 m and 80 m respectively.[63] At Karanovo, earlier excavations showed considerable build-up in phases I and II, and the prominent features were one-roomed, post-framed houses. In phase I these were about 7 by 7 m and less. There was an oven on the side or back wall of each house. In phases I and II the houses were closely spaced on a common orientation, and were arranged on either side of wood- or sand-covered lanes. There is little other information on the spaces between houses. We do not know the extent of the early settlements here, and estimates have varied from 15–30 to over 60 houses.[64] The more recent excavations show buildings from phases II (and III) on the very edge of the mound, and it may be that the higher figures will be more appropriate.[65] These could give a figure for Karanovo of 300 or more inhabitants, but it would be unwise to assume such a number throughout every stage of the sequence or at every other settlement mound. Nonetheless, some locally high populations are possible by the end of the period covered here.

A large house from Slatina in Sofia, Bulgaria, was burnt down at the end of its life, which has preserved many unusual details.[66] It belonged to a large settlement area (over 8 ha), though its size at any one time has not been established, and to the first of four early levels, dated to around 5800–5600 BC. (It is probably therefore not the earliest kind of site in its area.) About 12.5 by 9.5 m, the building had light post or stake walls over 2 m high covered with wattle and daub. Its pitched roof rested on the walls and central posts. A wooden floor substructure rested on narrow planks and clay and was pinned into the subsoil. The floor was clay-lined, renewed some fifty times. This is assumed to have been an annual event. The interior was arranged into one main room, entered by a doorway in the short south end wall, with a narrow compartment at the far end entered by another doorway slightly off-centre. There was a hearth just inside the main doorway, and two wooden structures that could have been beds. Opposite the central roof posts there was a raised platform on one side and a loom on the other. A small pit was next to the posts. Towards the rear of the main compartment and on either side, there were clay-lined containers (mostly unfired) which held grain and legumes. A large clay oven, originally domed, occupied the centre of the rear of the main compartment. Next to it was a grinder and an ash pit. The rear compartment had stone and bone tools, and a large clay rectangular box, with pierced lid and four feet, interpreted as a house model or sanctuary for a household spirit.

Might the Slatina building have been special, because of its size and long history? Not enough is yet known of the rest of the site, which has been excavated over a number of years on a rescue basis. Elsewhere, uniformity of buildings is recurrent, though there is plenty of variety between sites. Thus there are varied clay models, showing pitched roofs and smoke holes. At Prodromos, parts of a wooden roof of roughly trimmed trunks and branches were preserved. There are close-set Middle Neolithic houses at Otzaki in Thessaly, which have shared, buttressed walls. At Anza in phases II and III, there was a shift to free-standing post-framed houses. The stone-footed buildings within the Middle Neolithic layers on the mound itself at Sesklo were free-standing, while contemporary ones outside had shared walls. Here and elsewhere there is evidence for two-storeyed buildings, for example in the so-called 'potter's house', but this is not markedly larger in ground plan than others.[67]

One marked exception to this picture of internal uniformity is Nea Nikomedeia.[68] The site consists of two main occupation levels of rectangular, post-framed houses, some with an internal partition. These were renewed from time to time, with overlapping plans in successive layers. In the first level, there was a larger building, some 10 by 10 m, apparently sur-

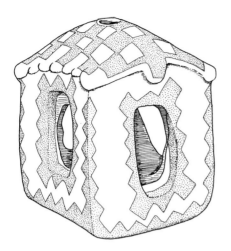
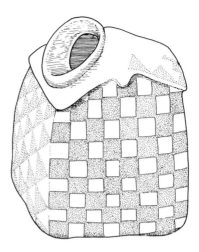

3.9 Red-painted clay models of structures from (left) Crannon and (right) Myrrini, Karditsa, Thessaly. Heights about 9 cm. After Theocharis.

rounded by smaller neighbours. This had two internal partitions, and amongst its artefacts were two unusually large stone axes, two caches of hundreds of unused flint blades, several hundred clay discs and five female figurines. It has been suggested as a shrine. One of the larger buildings in phase IVa at Achilleion has also been claimed as a shrine on the basis of figurines. In both examples, the case is unproven. A more marked kind of difference is the spatial variation seen at Sesklo, between buildings outside the mound proper, with shared walls and without such a long history of continuous occupation, and those on the mound, demarcated in the Middle Neolithic by encircling retaining walls, free-standing and with very long histories of occupation underneath them. It has been suggested that this marks some kind of social differentiation.[69] It could be, however, that it was the site itself or the community of its users that was being highlighted in various ways.

Burials

A final aspect of virtually all the kinds of site surveyed here is the recurrent but irregular presence of the dead within the settlement area. No separate, formal burial grounds have been identified, and only a fraction of the original populations can be represented. Most bodies were inhumed, though some cremations are known in Thessaly, and there are some signs of secondary, disarticulated burials, as at Prodromos. The dead were mostly placed in simple graves within the settlement area. Some were next to houses and some under them; in Körös sites, like Endrőd 119, graves seem to have been placed close to large pit complexes as well as next to houses. Most burials were single, though collective examples are known, as of women and children at Nea Nikomedeia. All ages and both sexes are represented. Infants as well as adults can be found buried on their own, for example in the Franchthi Cave, and at Anza, in one case in phase I there inside a pottery jar. Grave goods were mostly few and simple. The best explanation is that the dead were deliberately

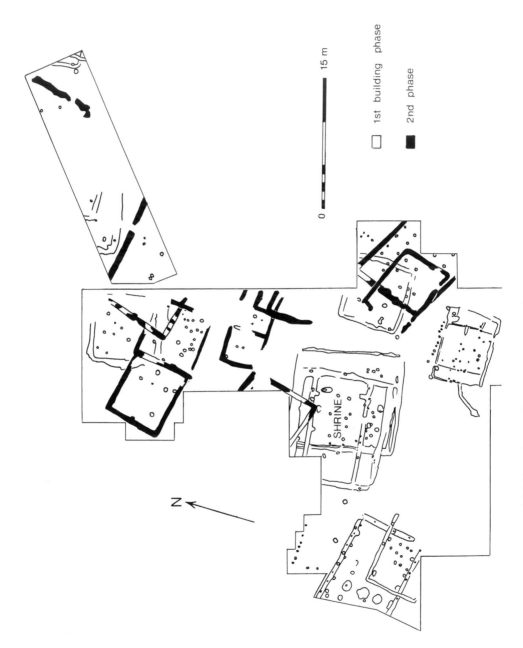

3.10 Two phases of structures at Nea Nikomedeia. After Theocharis.

15 m

1st building phase

2nd phase

N

SHRINE

included in the sphere of the living, to maintain close links between past and present members of the community.[70]

Material culture

The people in these kinds of settlement had a wide range of material culture, from stone tools to pottery vessels and clay figurines. Although the generalisation is risky, because we do not know how many organic materials have been lost, there was a greater range of portable material in this period compared to the preceding forager period. Often this has been treated as merely the result of increased technical knowledge or as the inevitable accompaniment of a supposedly sedentary way of life. Paradoxically, however, the volume of long-range procurement of stone tools increased, and there is considerable variety in pottery vessels. In line with changed theoretical perspectives on material culture, it is more challenging to consider the range of artefacts as items actively used in the construction of Neolithic communities.

Stone tools

Some of the best investigated evidence comes from northern Greece. There, people used a variety of lithic materials, such as flint, chert and obsidian, for tasks such as scraping and cutting. They had a range of mainly simple, small, blade-based tools. They also had rather small stone axes. Many of these from sites like Achilleion and Anza were under 10 cm long.[71] It is perhaps little surprise that the pollen diagrams do not show a major human impact on woodlands in this phase. Few of these sorts of tool were distinctive in style, though it is suggested that the technicalities of production were different in preceramic Thessalian sites compared to the Franchthi Cave.[72] The quantities of lithic material in use were usually relatively restrained. The inventories of finds from work areas and floors at Achilleion, for example, are mostly quite short. The hundreds of unused flint blades in the large house at Nea Nikomedeia were exceptional.

More striking are the range of materials in use and the distances over which they were procured.[73] In the preceramic level at Argissa, for example, four categories of material were used. Locally available jasper (a kind of chert) was simply worked for flakes and irregular blades. Brown-grey flint, perhaps from the mountains to the west, was used for blades, probably struck from carefully prepared cores. Honey-coloured flint was used almost exclusively for very regular blades. The source is not known, but is probably not local, and it appears that it was the already struck blades which were imported. Finally, obsidian, presumably from Melos in the Aegean, was used for blades and bladelets, carefully struck from cores imported in an already prepared state. It was the most abundant material. The range of knowledge implied is surprising if an incoming population was involved. Achilleion has small quantities of obsidian from its early contexts, first appearing in late phase Ib. It was never more abundant than local jaspers throughout the sequence; there were twenty-seven pieces from the excavated areas of phase I. Working areas were in the yards and on the surfaces between houses. Obsidian was moved north as far as Thessaly. So far, no obvious decrease in quantity as distance from source increases has been observed. Rival explanations for its procurement have been direct acquisition, starting originally in tunny fishing expeditions in the Mesolithic, and production and transport by specialists.[74] The former model can be better aligned with other indications of mobility, but the distances covered are surprising. The practical logic of movement over such a range is unclear, when local materials were available. It is as though the system had other motives, overriding the practical, and serving to connect scattered communities in a single practice. Further afield, Hungarian obsidian continued to be moved into the northern Balkans.[75]

Pottery

At Achilleion, pottery was found in the houses, beside hearths and ovens, in food preparation areas in yards, and discarded in pits.[76] In the earliest level, only simple open and globular bowls were found, but from phase Ib on there were bowls with ring bases and some fine wares, including the first painted pot from the site. A number of vessels had thickened walls and globular forms, but nearly all the pottery throughout the sequence was burnished, and many were covered with a slip. Later in the sequence there was more varied painted pottery in greater quantities and there were some new shapes and a greater range of vessel sizes.

The pottery from Divostin fared rather worse after abandonment of the site, because the deposit was then heavily weathered before subsequent reoccupation took place in the Vinča period.[77] There were bowls, of finer ware, some decorated, and more globular jars, often of coarser fabric. As at Achilleion, a number of vessels were poorly fired.

The quantities of sherds recovered in even a small excavation can be staggering; there were some 100,000 from the 1973 season at Achilleion alone. It is much harder to convert this into numbers of vessels but in crude terms it would appear that pottery was abundant. However, in any one context there may only have been a certain quantity in use. At the Franchthi Cave, the patterns left by firing suggest that pots were not stacked during firing but were treated individually; a low rate of production is implied.[78] Whether this applies also to tell settlements further north remains to be seen.

What was pottery used for? It has of course a potential range of practical uses, including storage, food preparation, cooking, and eating and drinking. Few early pots were capacious. At Slatina, cereals and legumes were mostly stored in unfired clay containers, and there may have been containers in other materials for seed corn and food. At Servia, large quantities of einkorn, lentils and *Lathyrus sativus* were found on the floor of the basement or lower room of a house. (This was in a fire destruction level, and the location of the remains might only reflect the stage in processing reached when fire broke out.) Rather few pots may actually have been used for cooking, since there is comparatively little variation in form and fabrics, though this begs the question of how food was cooked anyway. The good finish of vessels from Achilleion and many other sites and the absence of blackening do not, however, suggest that cooking was a primary role. Pots may have been used more often for the preparation, and especially for the presentation of finished food and drink. The ring bases on a range of pottery from Thessaly and Bulgaria suggest that pots were designed to be set on level surfaces. We do not know where meals were eaten. It is not certain that they

3.11 Painted red-on-white wares from Thessaly and central Greece. 1–2: early painted style from Thessaly; 3: solid style from Tsani, 4–5: Sesklo phase, Thessaly; 6: Chaeronea. After Theocharis.

were taken indoors. The Achilleion evidence suggests the possibility of food sharing in communal contexts between the houses. The 'tulip jars' of sites like Karanovo in Bulgaria, and related shapes in Thessaly, strongly suggest that these vessels were for liquids. It is possible (as discussed further below) that cereals were used in part for brewing weak beers.[79]

Far too little analysis has been done, but probably most pottery was produced locally. This does not preclude variation. One example comes from the end of the Middle Neolithic phase at Sesklo. Painted pottery from the mound proper is made from finer fabrics than vessels in the settlement area beyond (though the sample from the latter was rather limited), and appears more abundant. This may indicate differential access to clay sources and potting skills, and thereby some kind of social differentiation.[80] If the distributional differences are genuine, however, it may be again the context of the mound which is important, the best pots being used in meals and gatherings in the heart of the community.

As well as being recognised as significant in local contexts, pottery was probably emblematic of identity and allegiance over broader areas. There are very broad regional patterns of ceramic style.[81] Very briefly and crudely, there are traditions of fine pottery including much painted ware, in Greece and central-southern Bulgaria. These are the pre-Sesklo to Sesklo and Karanovo I–II traditions respectively. Red-on-white designs predominate in the former, white-on-red in the latter (though there was much less painted pot in Karanovo II). Further north, in the Starčevo–Körös–Criş complex, painted pottery is rarer, black-on-red and white, and there is a wide range of incised, impressed and roughened decoration. It is clear that these broad distributions were not static. The phase I pottery at Anza, for example, included fine painted white-on-red vessels, recalling sites to the south and east. In phases II and III, the pottery was in Starčevo style.

There were differences within regional sequences too. There was an earlier 'proto-Starčevo' phase, with simple impressed decoration before a main Starčevo phase with a fuller range of decoration and forms. This parallels the kind of development proposed in Greece, from an Early Neolithic phase of widespread, simple forms (with or without an early unpainted horizon) to a Middle Neolithic phase of greater variety of decoration and form, and greater regional variation, with western Macedonia, Thessaly, Boeotia and the Peloponnese emerging as ceramically distinct zones.[82] Identical decorated fired clay stamp seals from four widely separated sites in Thessaly – Nessonis in the north-east, Pyrasos in the south-east, Tsangli in the centre-south, and Filia in the south-west – also show wide contacts.[83] There may be further variation within each of these regions, since it has proved difficult exactly to match the ceramic sequences of sites like Argissa in the north of Thessaly with those of sites like Sesklo and Achilleion in the south. Likewise sites in the upper and middle Struma, in western Bulgaria, share aspects of the painted pottery tradition of Thrace, but diverge from it as well.[84]

Figurines

On many settlement sites of this period there are fired clay figurines, and some in stone and bone.[85] These are mostly rather small, stylised figures in human form, and there are some animal figures. The body can be represented standing, squatting and sometimes sitting. Parts of the body are delineated, though arms are often close to the trunk or folded across it. Faces are usually schematic (though some seem to show more individual character and expression), and it has been suggested that some are portrayed as wearing masks. The head can project prominently. Where gender is indicated, more figurines are female, and sexual features often appear exaggerated. Through modelling, painting and incision there is also representation on some of hats, hair and dress, and there are abstract decorative designs on others. Animal figurines are mostly stylised four-footed creatures, but tails and horns are represented on some. Rather similar simple forms can be found over the whole area, and there are also specific inter-regional types, such as the widely distributed rod-headed figurines. There are regional types, with those of Thessaly for example distinguishable from those of central-southern Bulgaria. Further variation might exist within regions or between sites. There is certainly variation through time, as in the appearance in the Sesklo sequence of 'corn-eye' figurines in the Middle Neolithic.[86]

Such figurines have been found over and over again within settlements. Very often little detailed information about their context has been recovered, and many are fragmentary or broken. Those from Divostin I were very weathered, like the pottery. In some cases, however, there is better information, and it seems that figurines were used throughout the settlement area. At Nea Nikomedeia, the context of five figurines in a larger, central house has already been described. At Achilleion, figurines were found on house floors, beside hearths and ovens, and in yards with food preparation equipment, from late phase Ib onwards. In phase IIa, there were two figurines and a fragment of anthropomorphic vessel

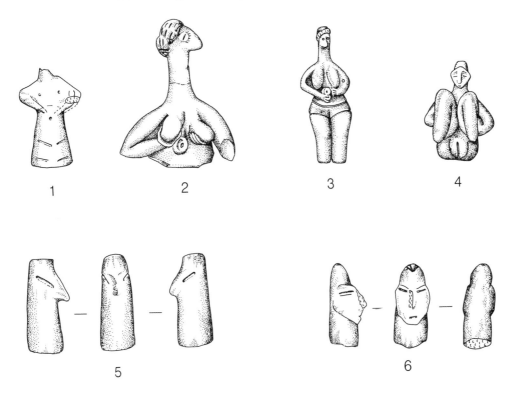

3.12 Clay figurines from Achilleion (mainly phases II and III). Various scales. After Gimbutas.

near the firepit within the post house. There were two figurines in the area around the external hearth, a 'pregnant' figurine on the footing of the domed clay oven outside the house, and a further female figurine and an animal figurine on the adjacent plaster floor. In phase IVa, a two-roomed house has been described as a 'house-shrine', but in view of the ubiquity described above, this is disputable. The larger of the two rooms had a bench running along one end, on and around which there were figurine fragments (as well as spindle whorls, a spool, a needle and pottery discs). The other room, apparently not connected, had a hearth. The replacement of this building in the next subphase of phase IVa has also been described as a 'two-room cult place', but it seems more satisfactory to see a continued presence for figurines throughout the settlement. By a hearth in one of the rooms there were several figurines as well as tools, but in a pit outside the house there were broken painted pots, tools and 'cultic equipment', and around a domed clay oven in the yard outside there were also several figurines and painted pots. Finally, at Divostin I, small numbers of figurines were recovered from pits, pit-dwellings and one of the above-ground structures or houses, as well as in less defined contexts.[87] Here too these artefacts appear to have been in constant use within the settlement.

The dominant interpretation of figurines has been that they are representations of goddesses, gods, spirits and other mythical figures.[88] The recurrent female figure has given rise to the idea of a mother goddess concerned with fertility and reproduction. The great variety of figurines at a site like Achilleion is accommodated within a pantheon of versions of the mother goddess, each with specific roles, for example a bird goddess, a snake goddess, a pregnant goddess, a frog goddess, and so on.[89] Such an approach can be traced back to nineteenth-century views of social development and to the early influence of psychoanalysis. Much of the interpretation rests on later historical analogy from very wide areas and long spans of time, and there are internal inconsistencies of approach. Thus, rather less is made of animal figurines, and male figurines are characterised as representations of a single male god.

One alternative is to retain figurines in the realm of the sacred and the mythic, but to retreat from specific interpretations of role and *persona*. An attractive recent suggestion is that figurines are representations of ancestral figures, serving both to affirm descent and ancestral ties and to appease and manage the souls of the departed whose presence might still have been felt among the living. This is the approach favoured here. Another alternative is to follow recent suggestions that figurines are symbolic tokens or even representations of human and animal individuals. Identical broken, decorated figurine legs from a scatter of sites in the Peloponnese were taken to be tokens of a range of possible contacts between individuals, kin or alliance groups, including trading and marriage relationships.[90] A still more specific suggestion, developed first with reference to a later phase, the Copper Age or Chalcolithic, in north-east Bulgaria, has been that figurines were not mythic or ancestral paraphernalia but indicators of individual identity.[91] Specific contexts for use by individuals could have included initiation or birthing rituals, though the ubiquity noted above seems to demand some more general role.

Figurines can be seen as one of a series of ways in which people were defined and encouraged to take specific roles within the emerging tradition of settlement, with its round of seasonal movements and gradual formalisation of place. At their most general, the figurines could be seen to reflect a consciousness of identity and of origins, a concern with categorisation, and a recognition of differences between people, and between people and animals, and perhaps between people and a spirit or mythic world, which were all important in the creation and maintenance of a Neolithic way of life.

A range of other material equipment can also be seen as to do with identity and appearance. These items include stone and clay studs and beads, clay spoons, clay stamp seals and bracelets of Aegean *Spondylus* shell. *Spondylus* was transported much further north in the next period to be considered, but occurs in early levels as far north as Anza.[92]

Subsistence

People grew wheats, barleys and legumes, collected wild fruits and nuts, herded sheep and goats, cattle and pigs, and hunted wild game. Of this range of resources, the dominant ones were the plant and animal domesticates. The relative use of these is not known, nor the scale of production. It is sometimes argued that more reliance was placed on plant cultivation than on animal herding. The recurrent assemblages of cereals, legumes and animal domesticates occur widely over the area, with only a few exceptions, and occur in the 'preceramic' levels of sites like Argissa. Must this economy, which undoubtedly used imported resources, have been brought in by colonists, and was it operated in a stable fashion from the beginning, involving sedentary settlement?[93] Several of the usual assumptions should be challenged.

Of the domesticated animals, sheep and goat do not seem to have been part of the indigenous fauna of south-east Europe.[94] Nonetheless they are normally the most abundant species in bone assemblages, and their ages at death, the majority rather young, indicate that they were kept especially for their meat. The bones of young animals are probably under-represented in excavated assemblages because of greater attrition through scavenging, erosion, chemical decay and so on.[95] However, not all sheep and goats died young, and some may have been kept not only for breeding but for other products and for a reserve of protein, and they may have been valued for reasons other than the purely economic or dietary. They could have been moved around in cycles of still mobile settlement. The representation of skeletal parts from Prodromos in western Thessaly suggested that some joints had probably not been consumed there, but were moved elsewhere into the settlement network. Pollen diagrams in Greece do not show much perceptible impact on woodlands by clearance or grazing. This might indicate that greater reliance was placed on plant cultivation and collecting than on animal herding and hunting, but it may only indicate the continuation of mobile settlement by small populations for many generations after the beginning of the Neolithic.[96]

Local domestication of cattle and pigs is likely throughout the area, evidence coming from sites like Achilleion, Anza and Endrőd 119.[97] An incoming human population could have domesticated local stock, but equally the indigenous population could have begun to use local resources in new ways, applying knowledge learnt from the outside or not previously applied. Cattle could have been herded around the landscape, but it is less plausible that pigs were moved to any extent. Both species were usually slaughtered at young ages, indicating their use for meat, but there are variations. In the surviving bones at Achilleion, more calves were slaughtered than lambs and kids, and at Anza there were significant numbers of mature cattle. In the outlying small Neolithic sites of north-east Bulgaria, cattle were the most numerous species and many animals were kept until maturity.[98] At Thessalian sites like Achilleion very large numbers of pigs were killed while juvenile. This is consistent with their rearing for meat, but it might also be seen as a seasonal indication. There is no distinctive sign in the architecture, layout or perimeters of settlements of facilities connected with animal stalling or control.

People exploited wild game, birds, fish and molluscs at sites in Thessaly such as Argissa, Sesklo and Prodromos. At Starčevo, and at other more northerly sites, there were larger quantities of wild game, birds and fish; an impressive spectrum of forest and floodplain resources was used. At Starčevo itself, as well as the domesticates, there were red and roe deer, wild cattle, horse and boar; beaver, fox, wolf, bear, badger, otter and wild cat; wild ducks, geese, swans and birds of prey; and pike, catfish, bream and carp. At the Körös site of Röszke-Ludvár, close to the junction of Tisza and Maros, fish appear to have been cleaned and dried on a large scale. At Endrőd 119 in the Körös valley, fish species included carp, pike and pike perch but were dominated by catfish, which could have been trapped in pools shallowing after floods. At this site, the best studied in the Körös area, there were also many birds of different species. But domesticated animals predominated over wild.[99]

People grew wheats, barleys and legumes. These included emmer, einkorn, bread and club wheat; 2–row and 6–row barley; and lentils, chickpeas and bitter vetch. They sometimes grew oats and millet. They also used figs, pears, acorns, grapes, almonds and pistachio, probably all in wild form.[100] We know very little about the detailed practice, scale or location of cultivation. The carbonised plant assemblages at Chevdar and Kazanluk suggest that individual species were grown as separate crops, in a simple rotation.[101] Since wheats and barleys have different soil preferences and growing characteristics, this is plausible enough, though wheat species and barley species may have been intermingled. Whether carbonised residues from floor and pit deposits would be sufficiently unmixed or from single episodes of plant processing is another matter. The unfired clay containers in the Slatina house mostly had mixtures of grain (wheat and barley) and legumes, though one had grain alone.[102] Scale can only be estimated by analogy. Yields of many fold can be obtained and maintained experimentally with similar crop species on good soils; legumes are nitrogen-fixers, and animals could have provided manure.[103] There was the potential for high-yielding cereal cultivation, but that is not to say that this was achieved or practised from the beginning. The evidence of the pollen diagrams, used by some to argue for limited flocks, is also compatible with rather limited cultivation of plots, perhaps hoe-cultivated and sporadically used.

The location of plots is also critical. The reasonable general assumption is that plots or fields were close to settlements. Throughout the region as a whole, therefore, many were close to water and seasonally flooded areas. The location of sites like Argissa, Nea Nikomedeia, Karanovo, Chevdar, Galabnik, Anza and Starčevo allows the possibility of cultivation of floodwater deposits, and the specific evidence of Platia Magoula Zarkou reviewed above strongly supports it.[104] This would imply intensive, seasonal cultivations, with spring sowing, in naturally open parts of the environment. It also weakens the link between cereal cultivation and fully sedentary settlement. This model does not apply to all sites. Presumably little cultivation around sites like Sesklo and Achilleion could have been flood-based, unless plots were much further from settlements, and rain-fed plots in artificial clearings are a far better model. Some locations in the river network of the Hungarian plain may have been subject to early summer flooding, due to meltwater from the Alps, which would presumably have been unfavourable for floodplain cultivation. This may have favoured the Tisza and its tributaries over the Danube. It is easy to assume that each settlement mound was an independent unit, its inhabitants practising total self-sufficiency. Might it not also be the case that people at sites like Achilleion used cereals grown elsewhere, further from the settlement or near other settlements?

If people subsisted mainly on cereals, they would have had a dull diet, the species used being most appropriate for making biscuits, unleavened bread and gruel. Emmer and einkorn, for example, lack gluten in their flour and cannot be baked into anything lighter than biscuits. The genetically more complex, hexaploid bread and club wheat were better suited for baking.[105] Both barley and wheat could have been used to make weak beer.[106] There is no specific evidence from plant remains to support this, but the techniques of fermentation are simple, and there is a wealth of closed pottery containers suitable for both fermentation and drinking. (The exposure of cereals and water to wild yeast naturally present in the air will lead to fermentation, and the addition of sprouted grain acts to convert starches to sugar which the yeast uses to turn into alcohol.)

Should we envisage cereals and legumes as staples, with the diet enlivened by meat and alcohol on special occasions, and supplemented by fish, small game, molluscs and wild plants? In many ways this would be an odd development, given the breadth of the forager diet and the range of tastes it offered. Or did people in fact retain a broad diet? The evidence could be read to show consumption of a lot of meat from young animals, and perhaps milk and blood as well, supplemented by wild plants, fruits for sweetness, and by porridges and gruels, washed down by quantities of weak beer. The main shift may have been in the animals kept. These show a trade-off of diversity for reliability and predictability. This kind of shift does not have to favour the colonisation hypothesis; it is just as plausible that flexible, knowledgeable foragers who were, in Bird-David's terms, resource-oriented rather than technique-biased,[107] should have made a calculated shift of this kind.

Sedentism is not inevitably entailed by the adoption of animal husbandry and plant cultivation. There may have been considerable early variation, since the patterns which were eventually dominant had to be learnt and accepted. Some settlement mounds appear to be the only sites in their vicinity, such as Kazanluk or Kovatchevo. But in other instances, as at Anza, there are other sites in neighbouring parts of the landscape which could have offered complementary resources. Quite close to Anza, but further into the hills, Rug Bair is one such site. Its users exploited the same range of domesticated animals supplemented by game as at Anza.[108]

The making of community

To the contemporary mind, the house is a powerful icon of stability and permanence. The tell house of later generations in the Copper Age has been characterised as in a real sense living, an active participant in society, reborn with fresh layers of memory and association each time a rebuilding took place.[109] It is attractive to apply this idea to earlier generations of the Neolithic. The tell itself has been characterised as 'the fixed point of human existence, the location of hearth and home, where life had its beginning and end'.[110] The major challenge, however, is to put both house and tell into context and sequence.

One powerful recent model proposes that the house was the physical location for the concept of the *domus*, which acted as both metaphor and mechanism for domestication, or the acceptance by people of the restraints of settled life and the practice of agriculture.[111] In the idea of *domus*, according to the model, were rooted ideas of identity and values of nurturing, continuity and fertility. In this way the constraints of settled life were given positive values in opposition to the ideas of the 'wild' and the physically and conceptually dangerous and unstructured aspects of nature. The house and domestic symbolism constructed the fabric of society and maintained social order.

This model can be both criticised and developed. It entails a particular view of the predecessors of the Neolithic, which is at odds with that argued here. It seems implausible that we should confine foragers to a state of passive ignorance, living in the 'wild'. The early house in fact makes no explicit symbolic reference to the 'wild', and it appears from food residues that people were well aware of the advantages of non-domesticated resources when they chose to exploit them. Moreover, the house appears largely out of context, with little reference to neighbours and a wider field of social interaction (perhaps acting as a theoretical substitute for individuals).[112] Perhaps the model is still rooted in a modern, Western conception of the autonomy of the household. Another general account of the development of social relations through time has also stressed the consequences for social action of the emergence of the autonomous house, which is argued to provide privacy and the possibility of individualisation.[113] This and the *domus* model take the existence of sedentism from the beginning of the Neolithic for granted.

We know nothing of the composition of households. The general assumption is of some kind of family unit, present in each house. This assumption must be questioned as a universally applicable model. Forager ethnography shows both rather uniform shelters and a fluctuating membership of camps, together with fluctuating composition of the small social unit in individual shelters.[114] Early forms of Neolithic settlement were fluid. Within settlements, shared space between houses and structures, in yards and open areas, was at least as important as the domestic interior.

Interpretation needs therefore to be broadened from the house alone, to the whole community in which the living house resided. People may not have spent all their lives rooted to one location. They may have come gradually to accept or value locations of fixed importance, though this need not have been entailed or envisaged in the initial shift to domesticated resources, as embodying both the history and practice of community. Continued use of fixed locations imposed formalised, structured, rule-bound behaviour, the more so perhaps the older and the more continuous the occupation of a particular settlement mound became. The mound gradually became the focus of group identity. I suggest that other possible social allegiances, for example to family or kin group, were subsumed in a growing sense of community. Houses, the burial of some of the dead within or under them, and figurines (if seen as markers of personal identity), can all be taken to suggest the actions of individual members within a community. But there was no real privacy. Cooperation was routine within the settlement, and may have been so outside it. We know nothing of how cultivation was organised, nor of the ownership of flocks and herds. Could anyone have been denied open access to the means of subsistence? The procurement of distant raw materials might have been in the hands of specialists, but there seems to have been open access to the fruits of this procurement. Styles of pottery and figurines imply shared identities, at first broader and then perhaps more regionalised. There may have been no conceptual separation of ancestors from the world of the living. The community existed as much in outlook and shared concept as in action. In Gellner's words: 'A concept is, of course, far more than a "mere" concept: it encapsulates and communicates and authorizes a shared way of classifying, valuing, a shared range of social and natural expectations and obligations.'[115]

It is unlikely that a sense of community needed to be given positive values in opposition to concepts of the wild, since it enhanced pre-existing values of sharing and cooperation.

The aim of this chapter has been to argue continuity and to show that it took time for most aspects of the Neolithic to develop, from a sense of place and shared identity to fixed-place settlement and cultivation; there was still plenty of variation from region to region by 5500 BC. The Neolithic community did not spring to life fully formed. It was created gradually and unevenly over the first generations.

CHAPTER 4

OLD AND NEW HISTORIES: SOUTH-EAST EUROPE, *c.* 5500–4000 BC

A burial ground on the Hungarian plain

Towards 4000 BC, a young girl died aged only 5 or 6 years and was laid to rest in the burial ground of her forebears on the Hungarian plain. She was interred in a simple earth-dug grave, lain on her left side with her legs flexed. She was probably clothed, and was decked with a necklace of limestone beads, a string of beads around her hips, and further strings hanging down from her waist. On the fifth finger of her left hand she wore a copper ring, and another on the third finger of the same hand, and she had copper rings on her fore-arms or wrists. Behind her body in the grave were 6 pottery vessels, and there was one in front of her.

This is grave 24 in the burial ground of Tiszapolgár–Basatanya, near the Tisza river in the northern part of the Hungarian plain.[1] The girl was treated in death very similarly to older women. In grave 33 a woman 25–30 years old was buried on her left side, with neck-lace, beads around the hips, pots at hands and feet, and a copper ring on the fifth finger of her right hand. In grave 27 there was a woman aged 55–60, with beads around her hips, several pots by her head and around the upper part of the body, a fragment of a grindstone, and a copper ring on the third finger of her left hand. The girl may have had an equal social position to these adults, perhaps by virtue of belonging to a particular family, lineage or other social grouping linked by descent, or she may have been presented in her burial rites as a future member of more than one adult female age set, of grown and older women respectively, as the necklaces, strings of beads and finger rings suggest. In death, she may have been conceived as joining a timeless community of ancestors.

Women and children were buried as often as men in this burial ground, though if one counts the graves of boys, there may have been slightly more male graves. Males were dis-tinguished by being placed on their right sides, usually partly flexed. The same sorts of grave goods as in adult men's graves could be found in boys' graves, but generally in lesser quanti-ties. The man in grave 52, aged perhaps about 25, was one of the most abundantly provided in the whole burial ground. He wore a copper bracelet on his left arm. By his neck was a long flint blade, and there were three more of these in front of his chest. Without listing every grave good, around his head were a portion of red deer antler, the shoulder blade of a wild ox, cattle feet bones, a pendant split from a wild boar tusk, the lower jaw of a wild boar, and three pots. In front of his face there was an antler hammer-axe and two pots. Behind his legs there was a dog, and at his feet two large jars (one with sheep bones) and a pedestalled bowl. It might be tempting to infer greater social position for males from this abundance, but the con-cerns of the mourners may have been more to celebrate aspects of concern to all in the com-munity: the ability to provide hospitality with food and drink, familiarity with the surroundings of the plain, participation in networks of exchange and alliance stretching to the edge of the plain and beyond, and the promotion of distinctive identity.

Those who had gone before were not forgotten. There were some sixty burials in the Tiszapolgár culture phase of the cemetery. They took place over many generations, perhaps over centuries (and more were to follow in the Bodrogkeresztúr culture phase, covered in the next chapter), but the overall plan of the cemetery is orderly. The graves were set in rows, which spread gradually from west to east, and each row was probably formed from south to north. The graves, which shared a common orientation, must have been marked in some permanent fashion, since there were very few cut into each other, and the exceptions may have been deliberate, to mark special relationships between the deceased. In this way the community of the living and the world of the dead were presented as ordered, enduring and timeless.

Although to any one individual growing up on the northern part of the Hungarian plain at this time the social world must have seemed without beginning or end, the Tiszapolgár phase came at the end of a very long phase of development.[2] In the previous chapter, we saw scattered communities of the Körös culture in the river networks of the more southerly parts of the plain. In the succeeding Linear Pottery culture from about 5500 BC, settlement spread right across the plain to its northern margins, though it was still generally dispersed. From the Szakálhát phase and then in the Tisza–Herpály culture phase after 5000 BC, there were still many scattered, 'flat' sites, but certain locations were used for repeated settlement, leading to the creation of settlement mounds. Excavations have shown substantial houses, rich inventories including decorated pottery and figurines, and small burial grounds within unoccupied parts of the mounds. The subsistence base was varied, fish, fowl and game being used alongside crops and domesticated animals (including locally domesticated cattle). Tells may not have been occupied continuously by all their inhabitants or users, and more traditional sorts of sites were in contemporary use.[3] In this region as in others, the Neolithic community as a set of shared concepts had to be created, and as elsewhere the creation was fragile. In the succeeding Tiszapolgár phase, from after 4500 BC, we know very little about the details of settlement apart from what can be inferred from the cemeteries. Some tells were occupied on a reduced scale, but probably the bulk of the population was again scattered in small groups. The Tiszapolgár–Basatanya cemetery is the largest of the Tiszapolgár phase, but even this was the product of many generations and was perhaps used by people from a wide area around.

Old and new histories

The inhabitants of the northern part of the Hungarian plain in the later fifth millennium BC belonged to a diverse wider world of old and new histories. In south-east Europe as a whole there were many changes in this long period. There was an increase in the density of settlement in many areas and an expansion of settlement in others. Some existing tells continued to grow, and there are limited signs of architectural differentiation within them. Some new foundations were densely occupied with close-set houses. Cemeteries appeared beside these, with individual burials variously furnished with grave goods. Domesticated cattle

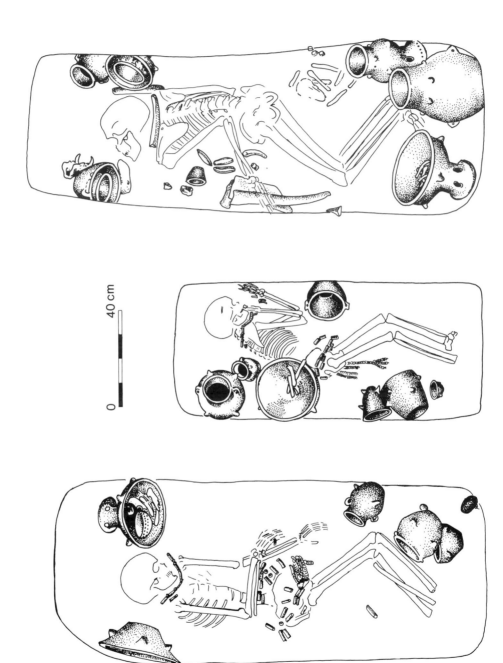

4.1 Tiszapolgár graves in the cemetery at Tiszapolgár-Basatanya. From left to right: nos. 33, 24, 52. After Bognár-Kutzián.

40 cm

0

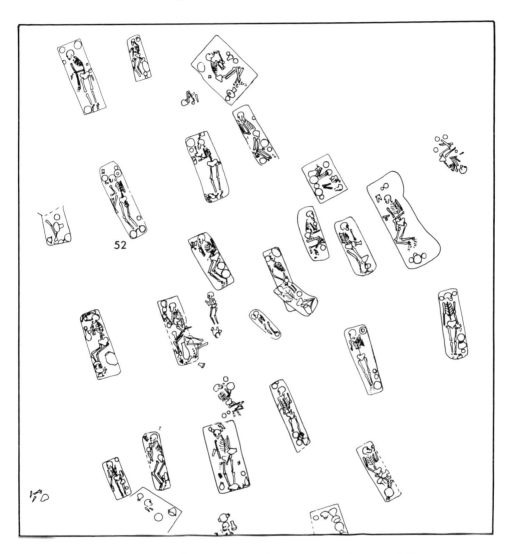

4.2 Part of the Tiszapolgár phase area of the cemetery at Tiszapolgár-Basatanya.
Graves 33 and 24 are in rows to the north of 52. After Bognár-Kutzián.

appear to have become rather more numerous than before. Copper metallurgy was developed and other crafts were intensified, along with an expansion of long-range exchange.

There have been far-reaching claims about the nature of change in both individual aspects and in society as a whole. According to one hypothesis, for example, more settlements may have become more permanently occupied, and from increased sedentism flowed other changes, including craft specialisation, possibilities for accumulation and opportunities for social differentiation.[4] One analysis of the use of space within tells in north-east Bulgaria claimed to unravel the playing out of strong inter-lineage competition in the changing configurations of buildings.[5] Some have seen certain buildings as shrines or temples, and it has been asserted that in some areas at least, for example in the Vinča culture of Serbia and surrounding regions, cult practice was centralised in certain powerful locales.[6] The varying inventories of grave goods, especially in the spectacular cemetery of Varna on the Black Sea coast, have been seen as expressions of considerable differences in social position and power.[7] Society as a whole has been seen as riven with internal competition, and there have been suggestions of domination by priests, chiefs or other leaders, and even of a state-like character to society as a whole.[8] The supposed dynamism of the period is partly reflected in the terminology employed (though that is also confusingly varied from region to region). Since the fifth millennium sees the widespread adoption of copper working, that chronological period is widely known as the Copper Age,[9] which in turn has acquired connotations of its own to do with change and social differentiation.

In contrast, this chapter will attempt to put change into context, and build less generalised models of development. It covers a very long period of time, and wide areas of space. Change was probably very slow from generation to generation, as we have already seen on the Hungarian plain. There were still small populations, though locally there were greater numbers and some substantial settlements are known. This was a landscape with still many spaces in it. In this perspective, a different sort of Neolithic/Copper Age emerges, in which endless histories are enacted in some areas, with repetition of ancestral ways of doing things in the effort to build and rebuild concepts of community and place, and newer histories in others, with attempts to create a sense of antiquity through the use of planned settlement mounds and burial grounds. Virtually everywhere the past was important to create a sense of timeless belonging, and exchange linked individual communities to a wider network of kin and allies with similar values. Regional histories are all-important, and in this perspective the local scale of social action is at least as important as broader process.

In broad terms, a contrast can be drawn between the regions where continuity was strong – the old histories – and those where a Neolithic/Copper Age way of life was only developed during the period from roughly 5500 to 4000 BC – the new histories.

In Greece, tell settlement continued in Thessaly, with probable increase in the number of sites in parts of the plain. The first tells appeared in northern Greece, as at Sitagroi and Dikilitash, though large, 'flat' sites are known as well. There were more settlements in the islands of the Aegean. Some architectural variation appeared at Sesklo and one or two other sites in the form of large, three-roomed buildings (*megara*); multiple encircling walls at Dimini were probably for spatial demarcation of separate work areas or living areas rather than for defence. One or two separate burial grounds are known, and there was only a little copper in use in the fifth millennium BC, possibly but not certainly from Greek ore sources. Continuity is symbolised in the height of tells like Argissa or Platia Magoula Zarkou.[10]

Similarly in central-southern Bulgaria, existing tells like Karanovo and Azmak continued to build up, though each individual site has interruptions in the sequence of occupation, and the Karanovo IV phase of the late sixth millennium BC may have been partially characterised by non-tell settlement. Buildings were still closely spaced, but many were now regularly two-roomed, and on the whole larger than in earlier generations. Individual buildings have been claimed as shrines, and a whole collection of buildings at Dolnoslav has

4.3 Section through the tell at Karanovo. Photo: Hiller.

been characterised as a cult centre, though generally the strong impression is still of uniformity and regularity. No separate burial grounds are known beside established tells. A wide repertoire of painted pottery and figurines in clay, bone, antler and stone was accompanied by developed metallurgy in the fifth millennium BC. After the first simple beaten products of the later sixth millennium BC, the inventories include cast rings, chisels, and shaft-hole hammer-axes of various forms. Copper was obtained from veins in the hills behind Nova Zagora at Ai Bunar. By contrast, in eastern coastal Bulgaria and in inland north-east Bulgaria northward into the lower Danube valley, the first tells appeared in the fifth millennium BC, replacing earlier more sporadic occupations of pit-dwellings. Relatively small, bounded or enclosed settlements were founded, like Poljanica in north-east Bulgaria or Căscioarele in the Danube valley. Within these were set closely spaced houses, to be replaced many times in more or less the same configuration. Small burial grounds were formed outside several of these tells. Larger burial grounds are known at Varna, and to the north in the Dobrudja/Dobrogea, as at Durankulak and Cernavoda. By the second half of the fifth millennium BC, there were many elements of material culture shared between these two broad areas, as implied by the label 'Karanovo VI–Kodzadermen–Gumelnitsa'.[11]

Over much of former Yugoslavia with extensions into south-west Romania, the Vinča culture succeeded the Starčevo–Körös complex, from the mid sixth millennium BC. Settlements were more numerous. In some areas they were also more widely spread across the landscape. The forms of settlement were varied. The Vinča tell continued to be occupied, forming a considerable mound. There were new tell foundations, like the large site of Gomolava in the Sava valley. There were also large flat sites, like Selevac and Potporanj, the focus of repeated occupation but where vertical superimposition of new buildings was not so important as elsewhere, and there were many smaller, shorter occupations. Already by the mid fifth millennium BC if not earlier, the settlement pattern had reverted to one of dispersed, smaller units, in the late Vinča and Krivodol–Bubanj Hum horizons. Only two instances of burial grounds are known, one within and one outside a settlement, at Gomolava and Botoš. There was a wide range of finely made but plain, dark pottery. Copper was obtained from ores in Serbia, at Rudna Glava and other sources, and the range of products was similar to that in the southern Balkans. [12]

As already sketched, developments northwards on the Hungarian plain were quite similar to those in the Vinča culture area. In the post-Starčevo–Körös horizon, settlement spread northwards right across the plain. (The Linear Pottery culture also took settlement beyond the Danube, into central and western Europe far beyond the Carpathian basin. This process is followed in chapter 6.) After changes in the Szakálhát phase, some nucleation followed in the Tisza–Herpály phase of the earlier fifth millennium BC, with quite widely separated settlement mounds forming as well as open or flat sites of varying size. By the Tiszapolgár phase of the later fifth millennium BC, few tells remained in use. Largely on negative evidence, settlement was dispersed in small units across the riverine landscape of the plain. Burial grounds, which had formed in the previous phase within unoccupied parts of settlement mounds or areas, now appeared as places in their own right, as already described at Tiszapolgár–Basatanya. Elaborate pottery of the Tisza phase was replaced by plain pottery in the Tiszapolgár phase, and figurines, so prominent in the former, dropped out of use in the latter. Copper was obtained by exchange, as also fine flint and obsidian, and the quantities at Tiszapolgár–Basatanya, out on the plain, were modest indeed, compared with sites both on the edge of the plain, and further afield in the central and southern Balkans.[13]

There had been scattered Criş settlements both west of the Carpathians in Transylvania and to the east in the more southern part of Moldavia. As settlement began to infill in the lower Danube and Dobrogea, Linear Pottery culture sites appeared around the northern fringe of the Carpathians and into northern Moldavia, as at Tîrpeşti. From the early fifth millennium BC, Neolithic settlement spread progressively eastwards into the forest-steppe zone of southern Ukraine. This brought Neolithic communities of the Cucuteni–Tripolye culture into contact with local riverine communities, first in the Bug–Dniestr zone, and then in the Dniepr zone. Cucuteni–Tripolye communities shared many characteristics with those of the Balkans, but were also distinctive. They combined cultivation and animal husbandry, but also used game and fish. They may have become aware of horses managed or domesticated by their steppe neighbours of the Sredny Stog culture in the middle–lower

Dniepr zone. They acquired copper by long-range exchange from Balkan sources, but not Caucasian gold. There were repeatedly occupied sites of various sizes, some of the largest probably belonging to the later fifth millennium BC. Substantial houses mirrored Balkan forms, as did exuberant painted pottery and figurines. As an exception to the pattern of burial grounds appearing in newly settled areas, only one separate cemetery is known, though burial grounds are characteristic of the Sredny Stog culture.[14]

Regional patterns of settlement

In Thessaly the pattern of settlement continued to be dominated by occupation of tells. Overall the number of sites appears to have increased. Many sites in use earlier were abandoned and new foundations, dating to the earlier part of the period covered here, were located especially on the plains, shifting from the foothills so favoured in earlier generations. According to the evidence from Platia Magoula Zarkou, the mound there was by now free of the direct effects of seasonal flooding, but sites on the plain would generally still have been close to water. New, relatively small sites appeared in the southern, probably dry part of the eastern plain, but their occupation appears to have been short-lived.[15] These broad patterns are largely the result of surface surveys. We know rather little in any detail about the early structural history of new foundations, and it is all too easy to assume that more sites in the landscape reflected more sedentary occupation. The pattern may rather reflect the continuing effort to maintain a sense of community and place. In this light, sites which continued in use like Sesklo could be considered the most successful, acquiring an aura simply through their antiquity. One apparently new foundation from this period, the Thessalian Late Neolithic, is Dimini, set on a low hill above what would have been then an embayment of the sea. According to excavations so far, it developed rapidly with a coherent site layout (described further below).[16]

This period saw the establishment of settlement in areas previously avoided or little used, such as large parts of Macedonia and Thrace. In the relatively small plain of Drama in Thrace, several sites appeared from the beginning of this period, including Sitagroi. The first three main phases of the Sitagroi mound approximately cover the period. In the first two phases, Sitagroi and other sites occupy what could be considered prime positions close to water in the bottom of the plain, and some expansion is detectable within the second phase. This was followed in the third phase by fewer sites, which could reflect a more stable pattern of long-established sites. The pollen diagrams from the plain do not show any substantial human impact on the wooded surroundings, as in earlier generations in Thessaly, and although the excavations at Sitagroi were of rather limited extent, the structural and stratigraphic evidence suggests a staccato early biography for the site. Floors and middens were found, but no certain walls or post holes.[17]

Surveys in central and eastern Macedonia have found large, flat sites like Vassilika, Arethoussa and Thermi, which have many analogues to the north but do not seem to be part of the Thessalian pattern. Limited excavations have shown limited vertical build-up of occupation deposits, with gaps in the respective sequences. Well over a thousand years after the start of the Neolithic in the region as a whole, much settlement was still mobile.[18]

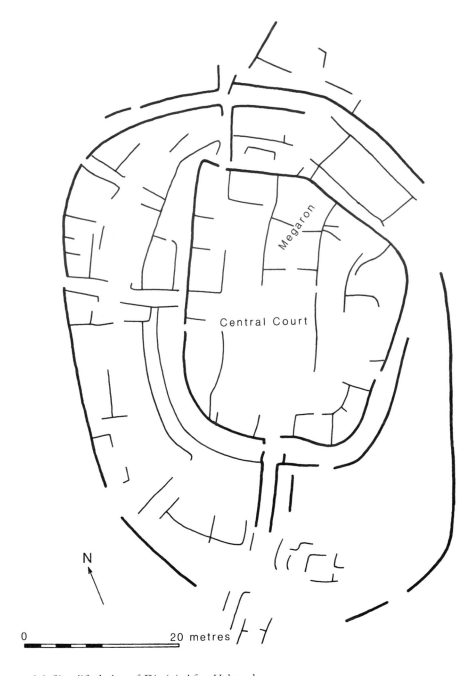

Central Court

Megaron

N

0   20 metres

4.4 Simplified plan of Dimini. After Halstead.

In the islands, the earliest well-documented occupation was at Ayios Petros on Kyra Panayia in the northern Sporades off the south-east tip of Thessaly, dating perhaps to the beginning of the sixth millennium BC. The island is a small one, and the occupation might be considered seasonal, but there is a broad range of artefacts including pottery, figurines and Melian obsidian, and there were domesticated animals and child burials. All this may indicate at least a major seasonal base.[19] More sites appeared in the islands, including Saliagos in the Cyclades, from the end of the sixth millennium BC. Other sites were started in the Cyclades, Sporades, Dodecanese, Chios, Samos, Limnos, Lesbos, Samothrace and Thasos in the fifth millennium BC.[20]

In central-southern Bulgaria, the pattern of tell occupation continued. By the end of this period, long-used mounds such as Azmak and Karanovo had reached heights of several metres. Probably no one mound was continuously occupied, since excavation has shown each to have breaks in the sequence of occupation. (One possibility is that occupation shifted around within and on the mounds, so that a break in one part need not have signalled complete abandonment of the tell.) Karanovo, for long considered as the yardstick for the period in the region as a whole, is now seen to have had significant breaks between the Karanovo IV and V phases and between V and VI. Azmak too is seen to have breaks, being unoccupied in the Karanovo IV phase, occupied from site phases 8–5, abandoned in the phase equivalent to Karanovo V, and then occupied in site phases 4–1.[21] If these detailed site chronologies are reliable, they have considerable implications for the density of settlement and the status of individual sites. In the Nova Zagora region around Karanovo, there were some twenty investigated sites in use in this phase, compared with twelve in earlier generations. This is a crude estimate, since there are many more uninvestigated sites, and in the Karanovo IV horizon as a whole there may have been a general phase of open settlement away from the tells.[22] As in Thessaly, it is tempting now to assume that the increase in sites and the existence of new foundations like Ezero in the Nova Zagora region reflect more sedentary occupation, but this may still not be the case. A clay bank was found around the foot of the Azmak mound in the Karanovo V phase,[23] which could be seen as protection against seasonal flooding. The pattern may have continued to be one of seasonal mobility combined with flux in the choice of locations for the major phases of occupation. It is important to consider the status of abandoned mounds. They can hardly have been disregarded, since both their substantial physical presence and the long associations with ancestral place must have fixed them in both the eyes and minds of the inhabitants of a region. Perhaps the most successful communities had a number of such sacred places within their overall territory, to be reused – reconsecrated? – according to the rhythm of ritual cycles of which we know virtually nothing. Around Karanovo, sites were spaced at intervals up to 5 km.[24] In a recently investigated example, the neighbouring tells of Drama and Krumovo were set over a kilometre apart in a small basin in the Katnica valley, a tributary of the Tundza. Drama had occupation levels of the fifth millennium BC.[25]

As in Macedonia and Thrace, so in coastal eastern Bulgaria and north-east Bulgaria inland settlement was expanded and established in this period. Neither area had been empty in earlier generations. The first phase of occupation at Golyamo Delčevo near Dalgopol in the lower Kamchiya valley some 30 km from the Black Sea coast, for example, consisted of pit-dwellings probably of the later seventh or earlier sixth millennium BC. There are several other known early occupations, for example at Usoe and Sava in the coastal region, and at Poljanica, Kodzadermen and Samovodene inland. Above-ground structures are known in the area at Ovčarovo-gorata. After a long break in occupation, a palisaded enclosure was established at Golyamo Delčevo in the Sava phase of the earlier fifth millennium BC. After another break, the site was re-formed as a tight arrangement of some twelve structures, bounded by a palisade. That arrangement lasted for only two occupation levels, whereupon there was another break. But after that the plan of the site was re-established on very similar lines, and was maintained through another thirteen levels.[26] Despite the spectacular presence of the Varna cemetery, rather little is known of contemporary settlements on the coast itself. 'Pile-dwellings' have been found in several locations on what would have been an inlet of the sea in the fifth millennium BC, close to the Varna cemetery.[27] Further up the coast on the southern edge of the Dobrudja/Dobrogea, a tell some 3 m high was formed at Durankulak through the fifth millennium BC. This was set by the sea, with a lagoon behind, and the burial ground beside the tell had over 1000 graves. The first occupation at the site consisted of pit-dwellings.[28] Neolithic occupation of the Dobrogea proper seems to have begun with the Hamangia culture in the later sixth millennium BC. It is characterised above all by large cemeteries, but there were again occupations defined by pit-dwellings.[29]

There was a similar pattern of infill inland. Several closely spaced small tells have been investigated near Targoviste. They were placed at intervals of a few kilometres, some on the edge of the Vrana valley (a tributary of the Goljama Kamcija) with hills behind, others out in the valley on raised locations. Poljanica, Ovčarovo, Vinica and Targoviste have long sequences through the fifth millennium BC, with few breaks in occupation. As at Golyamo Delčevo, the sites are characterised by closely set houses within bounded perimeters, palisaded or ditched. There is another example at Radingrad, near Razgrad on the Danube side of the Ludo hills.[30]

Similar sites occur in the lower Danube in the fifth millennium BC as part of the range of settlement forms. There were close-set houses in rows within sites like Radovanu and Căscioarele, the latter set on a small island in a lake, which was part of the lowest valley. Other sites from the fifth millennium BC include tells, like Gumelnitsa itself, rarely more than 2–3 m high.[31] Considerable numbers of these sites are known through the lower Danube valley, but they have been little studied as a pattern. Many seem to occupy positions on the edge of terraces, but there is much more to learn about site spacing, duration of occupation and variation. Much earlier, there had been a scatter of Criş sites but more sites appeared from the later sixth millennium BC, notably with the Dudeşti culture in the lower Danube valley in southeast Romania. The stratified levels of subsequent sites like Boian and Gumelnitsa therefore represent consolidation of the settlement of the area.[32] But only a little to the west, in northwest Bulgaria, settlement was rather more dispersed throughout this period. There appear to be relatively few sites with significant stratigraphic build-up, and by the later fifth millennium BC, the pattern includes sites like Zaminets, a small site set on a spur, in a commanding if not defensible position.[33] In this development, the area had more in common with the Vinča culture area than with the rest of the lower Danube valley.

The Vinča culture covered a large area, centred on Serbia and parts of Bosnia, Croatia and western Romania, and taking in a great range of landscape, from wetlands in valley bottoms to rolling foothills. It lasted for a millennium or more, from the mid sixth to the mid fifth millennium BC or later. In simple terms it can be divided into an earlier and a later phase (with many subdivisions added by the regional specialists), and there are many local variants. It is only to be expected therefore that there should be considerable variation, but some important generalisations can be made. In many areas, there were substantially more sites than in the preceding Starčevo phase, which were also more widely spread across the landscape, for example in the central-southern Sumadija region, the northern Sumadija (roughly the triangle between lower Sava, the Danube and the lower Morava) and the Srem or middle Sava region.[34] In central-southern Sumadija there was a scatter of Starčevo sites, including Divostin, discussed in the previous chapter. In the earlier Vinča phase, more sites appeared, widely spread across the landscape from valley to foothills, and encompassing a range of sizes. Selevac, for example, was a very large site, over 50 ha in all, which was occupied from *c.* 5100–4400 BC. The maximum depth of stratigraphic build-up was about 3 m, though in places much less, and though the site was in use for a long time, clearly different rules governed the tenure of space and the relocation of successive buildings. In this area, sites occurred every few kilometres, but Selevac stands out as the only very large site in its region. In the later Vinča period, the pattern seems to have reverted to one of generally smaller sites, well dispersed.[35] From the mouth of the Morava to the Mlava to the east, there had been a scatter of Starčevo sites along the Danube. In the earlier Vinča period low tells formed in low-lying, marshy areas, while in the later Vinča period, there were shorter-lived sites in more elevated locations, perhaps chosen for their greater security.[36] Vinča itself, on the right bank of the Danube just south of Belgrade, was a substantial tell, some 6 ha in extent and with some 7 m of Vinča period deposits, but its main phase of use was in the earlier Vinča period.[37] In the middle Sava there was a dramatic increase in the number of sites, both in the low-lying wetlands of the river basin and in the surrounding country. Many sites were small and may have been seasonally occupied, but there were larger sites as well, notably the large tell of Gomolava, which was occupied through much of the Vinča period (and later).[38] As with areas discussed further south in the Balkans, we should not automatically assume that the tells that do occur were permanently occupied, the more so given the range of other sites in the surrounding landscapes. As a final example of expansion, one can note sites of the Butmir culture in inland Bosnia (Butmir itself lying just outside Sarajevo), beyond the main range of Starčevo occupation.[39]

Such increase cannot be documented everywhere. In the middle Morava valley, there hardly appears to be any expansion of the area or density of settlement compared with the Starčevo period, and in the later Vinča period there were fewer sites than before. Further south, the occupation of Anza continued in the Vinča period, but only to *c.* 5000 BC, and it does not seem to have acquired more close neighbours than before, though it increased in extent in its final, Vinča phase.[40] Likewise in the Banat (encompassing the lower Tisa and its tributaries in north-east Serbia and westernmost Romania), in the wetlands of the Tisa basin, there is little obvious increase in numbers or a spread of settlement. The site of Opovo, in the basin of the Tamis, a tributary of the Danube, belonged to a pattern of dispersed wetland sites little changed from the Starčevo period. The connections between sites, however, may have altered. Opovo may have been seasonally occupied, perhaps by a larger community than would have been normal in the Starčevo period. Some distance to its north in the Banat there was another of the very large, 'flat', earlier Vinča sites, Potporanj.[41] We shall return to questions of site occupation and community composition below. The later Vinča culture was succeeded by the Krivodol–Bubanj Hum horizon in the late fifth millennium BC. This has not been well characterised, but settlement appears to have continued the trend to dispersal, with some quite small, remote sites in potentially defensible locations.[42]

From the same date that saw the expansion of Vinča settlement in many areas, the Linear Pottery culture took settlement right across the Hungarian plain to the hills round its northern fringes (where the Bükk culture emerged at the end of the phase), and thus considerably beyond the limits of Körös occupation. Sites were still relatively small, with various small post structures and pit-dwellings, and dispersed along the edges of terraces above the floodplains. Occupation levels were thin, as in the Körös phase.[43] By the Tisza–Herpály phase of the earlier fifth millennium BC, after beginnings in the Szakálhát phase, the pattern of occupation had changed.[44] There were still smaller sites with generally single occupation layers dispersed through the wetlands, but larger sites also now appeared. Some were 'flat' or very low tells, with build-up rarely exceeding 2 m, but of considerable size, up to several hectares, like Gorsza near the Tisza–Maros confluence in southern Hungary or Öcsöd–Kováshalom in the lower Körös valley near Kunszentmárton a little further north. The latter covered 21 ha in all, with two main occupation levels. It actually consisted of at least five foci of habitation, none of which need have been permanent. There were also low tells, with deposits up to 4 m deep. These are found especially in the southern and eastern parts of the plain (most distinctively in the Herpály area of the Berettyó valley in the eastern plain), but occur as far north as Csőszhalom near Tiszaújváros in the northern part of the plain.

Recent excavations have shown how the tenure of a particular location could change through time, dispersed, short-lived nuclei of occupation gradually coalescing to form larger tells, as at Berettyóújfalu–Herpály in the Berettyó valley of the eastern plain. Nearly all sites were close to water, on terrace edges above larger and smaller floodplains and wetlands. In many areas the largest sites appear to have been spaced at intervals of several kilometres, but it is clear from recent survey and excavation that they were not isolated. In one or two areas, like the Tisza–Maros triangle, there are several large sites close together, Hódmezővásárhely–Kökénydomb and Tápé–Lebő being neighbours of Gorsza; it is not clear whether these sites were in use at the same time.[45]

This pattern changed in the succeeding Tiszapolgár phase, but the change was relative rather than absolute. Few tells remained in occupation, and the relevant levels are thin. The dispersed cemeteries and few known occupation traces suggest an emphasis on dispersal, or the ending of conditions which favoured varying degrees of aggregation.[46] Place was now marked by the timeless community of the dead rather than by periodic large gatherings of the living. This period overlaps with the later Vinča/Krivodol–Bubanj Hum phases further south, suggesting a widespread trend, and indicating once again that the Neolithic lifestyle did not entail immutable patterns of settlement.

The expansion of Neolithic settlement out into the forest-steppe region of Ukraine, beyond the zone of Criş settlement in Romanian Moldavia and the westernmost Ukraine (former Soviet Moldavia), began with the Linear Pottery culture north of the Carpathians and continued through the Pre-Cucuteni and Cucuteni–Tripolye sequence of the fifth millennium BC.[47] More is known about the details of individual sites and their placings than pattern and densities as a whole. Tîrpeşti in northern Moldavia, occupied from the Linear Pottery phase through the Pre-Cucuteni phase to a developed Cucuteni stage (A/B and B in conventional cultural terms), lay on a terrace of a tributary of a tributary of the Siret river, in the foothills of the north-eastern Carpathians.[48] The first, Linear Pottery, occupation consisted of pit-dwellings, the site becoming better defined from the Pre-Cucuteni phase by an encircling ditch and substantial rectangular buildings. Many other Cucuteni–Tripolye sites were placed on high terraces or on the interfluves between the major valleys of the region. Concentrations of buildings appear to be characteristic, as at Hăbăşeşti and Truşeşti. The largest sites occur in the Tripolye area to the east, like Vladimirovka, Varvarovka VIII and Starye Badrazhi, and the concentrically arranged Majdanets'ke between the Southern Bug and the Dniepr. These cover up to 70 ha, and contain up to 200 houses, but it is not clear whether these were all in contemporary use. Such sites may belong late in the Tripolye sequence, nucleated according to some for defence (discussed further in chapter 5). There were extensive post-war excavations in both Romania and the former USSR but few sites have been fully published, and military and political sensitivities have precluded detailed studies of sites in the landscape.[49]

Colonisation and acculturation

The settlement evidence shows not just infill but also expansion of the areas of Neolithic settlement. Was this due to continued colonisation, fuelled by growing populations, or was it the result of further acculturation of native populations in the areas surrounding the primary Neolithic zones? Curiously, this aspect – part of the newer history of the area – has not been much examined as a general process, despite the enormous interest taken in the initial Mesolithic/Neolithic transition. Providing answers is as difficult as before, since the evidence for the existence of native populations in the seventh and sixth millennia BC remains as elusive as in earlier millennia.

Both colonisation and acculturation may be involved, one or other process dominating in different areas. The coincidence of Vinča infill and expansion with the intake of the rest of the Hungarian plain by the Linear Pottery culture could suggest that some population growth was a dominant factor in both areas. (Older ideas of wholesale movement of the Vinča population from unspecified points to the south can be set aside.)[50] But we have seen that people were not everywhere in the central Balkans in the Vinča phase, and the processes of cultural transformation and their relation to population dynamics are hardly understood at all. It is possible that early Linear Pottery groups in the Hungarian plain – such as Szatmár II – emerged in the north by acculturation while Körös groups still continued to the south. The Bükk culture in the hills around the northern fringes of the Hungarian plain might be a candidate for having native origins, though there is little evidence locally for the pre-Neolithic phase. But its distinctive cultural identity, compared to the Linear Pottery culture of the plain, and the familiarity with local obsidian sources are suggestive. Likewise, it might be possible to link the intake of Thrace and central and eastern Macedonia with continued settlement growth in both Thessaly and central-southern Bulgaria.

Whether such a model can be applied to the area of the Black Sea coast and north-east Bulgaria/south-east Romania is uncertain. Since the Dobrudja/Dobrogea is one of the few areas of south-east Europe where a Mesolithic is at all reasonably documented, there is a *prima facie* case that acculturation was involved in the formation of the Hamangia culture.[51] In the forest-steppe zone, there is firmer evidence for a native presence. The best model may be of a rolling, 'porous' frontier, on which river-based communities of native people of the Bug–Dniestr culture maintained independence for a time while partially adopting subsistence practices from the Linear Pottery and Pre-Cucuteni culture, before being absorbed into the developed Cucuteni–Tripolye complex.[52] Interaction then took place with native steppe people much further east, a process which is followed in more detail in the next chapter.

Communities of the living and of the dead: houses, settlements, burial grounds

There were very varied histories over south-east Europe as a whole. By 5000 BC, a Neolithic lifestyle had endured in some areas for a long time, but in others it was a recent development. Despite the varied changes of the later sixth and the fifth millennia BC, I shall argue that there was continuity, of essential concepts of community, place, descent and identity. This was enacted in different ways in different areas, partly in accord with the antiquity of regional history. Communities in newly settled areas had a shorter past, but were in contact through exchange and other mechanisms with communities with older traditions, and the resulting interaction with long-valued concepts may be responsible for some of the variations in the archaeological record. There is hardly space to treat every region in comparable detail, but the following selected case studies serve to illustrate most of the major themes.

Northern Greece

Contrasted with the wealth of information from earlier generations, the evidence for the layout of settlements in this period is disappointingly sparse. One striking change in the area of older settlement in Thessaly was the appearance at a handful of sites of large, centrally placed buildings. Sesklo provides one example, and there are others at Visviki and Agia Sofia, and perhaps Dimini.[53] That at Agia Sofia was set on some kind of mud platform, separated from other buildings by a ditch. The building at Sesklo was some 20 by 9 m, divided into three parts, with laid clay floors and a large rectangular hearth in one room and raised circular platforms in another; it was more or less centrally placed on the acropolis or main mound. With reference to Bronze Age buildings, such structures have acquired the tag of *megaron*. That is probably unhelpful, since it carries connotations of special status and power, which may well be anachronistic. The Sesklo building was accompanied by other, smaller structures, and there were retaining walls around the mound. It is not at all clear that this need be regarded as the building of a dominant social group or individual.[54] It could be regarded as a cult house or a village meeting house, in a tradition which goes back to Nea Nikomedeia. But the apparent increase in the formalisation of space may be significant. As the mound became ever more venerable through its inexorable antiquity, so the space within it may have been treated in increasingly special ways, and reserved for unusual meetings and ceremonies. The previous main phase of Middle Neolithic occupation had ended with burnings and destructions, and it is attractive to regard these as either deliberate or as having been accorded special significance in the history of the place, as a contrived or adventitious event serving to mark out a special point in the development of the site.[55] No such formalisation appears to accompany the much younger settlement mounds or 'flat' sites of Macedonia and Thrace. The early development of Sitagroi and Dikilitash is strikingly reminiscent of the case of Achilleion discussed in the last chapter.

Dimini was a new foundation in this period.[56] It lay on a prominent low hill above the coast, a few kilometres from Sesklo and other older tells. It consists of several concentric retaining walls, between which there were buildings and work areas, with the innermost defining a broad central space empty except for some buildings around the outer part. The walls are not now seen as defensive, and there are several entrances through all the circuits. The central area recalls the yards and communal spaces seen in earlier generations at sites like Achilleion, but is much larger, some 28–34 m across. The individual buildings appear to contain their own hearths, and the residues both of food processing, in the form of animal bones, and of craft production, in the form of *Spondylus* shell artefacts and pieces, were similarly found in concentrations over the site. One building within the central yard has superficially the form of a *megaron*, but the most recent excavator has suggested that this was a Bronze Age refurbishment of a much simpler construction of the Neolithic. Here perhaps the layout harks back to older traditions of shared space, but reflects also the formalisation of space in a long-settled area. The users of Dimini can hardly have been ignorant of regional tradition.

Although houses of more or less equal size and layout remained the basic architectural unit, we do not know much about the composition of households. A clay model from beneath a house floor at Platia Magoula Zarkou was presumably a foundation offering, and may also have represented an idealised or mythical scene as lived social existence. The excavations at the mound were very restricted, though deep. The model was found in a pit dug into the debris of the previous occupation level, which had been covered by the clay floor of the next. It consists of a single room or house, unroofed, with a single door, a partial internal division, and a raised platform and an oven on the back wall. It contained eight figurines in human form. The biggest two may represent a couple, one female, the other, four-legged, perhaps male. There is another female and male pair, with a smaller figurine, and there are three smaller and schematic figurines in one corner. There is also an elongated, decorated clay object with the smaller figurines.[57] It may be more plausible to see this group as representing either ancestor figures or actual occupants than goddesses and gods, as discussed in the last chapter.[58] The range of figures could represent three

4.5 House model and figurines from Platia Magoula Zarkou. Photo: Gallis.

generations of a family, or may personify a more general idea of descent bound up with household continuity and embedded, literally and metaphorically, in the fabric of the mound, by this date (the Tsangli phase) ancient. The figurines of this model were quite carefully executed, but many others from this period were more summary.[59]

Separate burial grounds rarely occurred in northern Greece, judging by negative evidence and the pattern of excavation so far. An older tradition of selective deposition within the settlement zone may have been followed. At Platia Magoula Zarkou, a cemetery of cremations in pottery jars was found some 300 m from the mound itself (few other investigations have ranged this far), and later at Kephala on Kea there was another separate burial ground,[60] but generally one may deduce that the dead and the ancestors were bound in with the living into a timeless community centred on the settlement mound.

As earlier, the pattern (though not the style) of settlement was not immutable, and there were relocations and new foundations in this period. The apparent shift in emphasis to the plains may suggest increased importance for flood-fed cultivations, even though individual mounds like Platia Magoula Zarkou were probably by now not themselves directly inundated.[61] Older patterns of mobility may therefore have been maintained, and in such a context the ideas of place and renewable community would have been no less important.

The evidence for subsistence is, like that for the settlements themselves, patchy. The inhab-itants of Dimini cultivated cereals, and used sheep, goats and pigs, perhaps principally for meat, and cattle for other purposes, since they were generally killed at greater ages. The data might reflect a mainly winter occupation.[62] There may have been more use in general of cattle and pigs, and in the fourth millennium BC sediment began to silt up the bay below Dimini.[63] Both factors might reflect greater woodland clearance, though there is little in the pollen diagrams to support this.[64] Patterns of mobility and the scale of subsistence produc-tion may have remained much the same as in earlier generations.

Central-southern Bulgaria

At Karanovo and Azmak, the layout of closely spaced buildings in ordered rows was main-tained over very long periods, right into the late fifth millennium BC in the Karanovo VI phase.[65] The more recent excavations at Karanovo have shown rows of structures from the Karanovo III and IV periods, on the edge of the settlement mound, which was therefore potentially densely occupied. But only outer parts of the Karanovo mound have been exca-vated. Azmak was completely excavated, but disappointingly remains unpublished, and few details of its layout are available. At both these sites, and at others in the region, the trend through time is for larger buildings with an internal division. In the Karanovo VI levels at Karanovo houses were some 8–12 by 5–6 m, generally with a smaller front compartment, entered by the only external door on the short south side. They remained, as in earlier generations, more or less uniform in size and layout, each with a grinding platform and closed clay oven on or near the back inner wall. At Azmak in the Karanovo VI levels, there were two larger buildings, a two-roomed structure 19 by 9 m and a three-roomed structure 18.4 by 6.3 m. We do not know yet whether there are any other distinguishing features of these buildings, and the detail of their setting within other buildings is not known.

In recent years the upper levels of a 6 m high tell at Dolnoslav, south of Plovdiv in the Maritsa valley, have been completely excavated.[66] Occupation must have begun earlier. The fifth millennium BC layout contained, according to preliminary accounts, several closely spaced buildings. Several on the south side of the mound were distinguished by the number of elaborate hearths within them, by the quantities and variety of figurines and other arte-facts, and by life-size human figures painted on their walls. This zone of the site was further demarcated on the ground by three lines of coloured matter, and was approached by a coloured path. This exciting discovery has been hailed as a group of shrines which formed a cult centre, perhaps with significance for very wide areas around. It has also been linked to a cave sanctuary in the hills to the south.[67] But its real significance lies in the complete excavation of one level of a long-established location. Other long-lived mounds could have had parts given over to ancestral cult and highly formalised behaviour, as suggested for Thessaly by the large building at Sesklo. Dolnoslav does not appear to lie in a major settlement concentration, and it is hard to envisage the circumstances in which it and it alone could have contained cult facilities revered for hundreds of kilometres around. So far, no separate cemeteries beside or near settlement mounds have been discovered in this part of Bulgaria.[68]

The Black Sea coast and north-east Bulgaria

There were few settlements in earlier generations in this area, and very few locations with renewed occupations. That situation changed radically in the fifth millennium BC.[69] New foundations contained generally closely set rows or blocks of houses, with little variation in size or style, and were often bounded by palisades, ditches and banks. There was massive continuity through the generations of the fifth millennium BC, with few stratigraphic breaks and repeated rebuildings which mirrored the levels below. We know from one area that such sites were spaced at intervals of only a few kilometres. Outside such sites there were separate burial grounds, which contained mostly single burials, of men, women and children, variously furnished with grave goods. At Varna on the Black Sea coast, the richness of the goods in some graves, including a few without human remains, was remarkable. The number of graves in these cemeteries ranged from a few tens to hundreds. This kind of settlement pattern has been best investigated in Bulgaria, but could have been typical of a wider area including the Dobrogea and the lower Danube valley.

Golyamo Delčevo in the lower Kamchiya valley has already been described in this chapter.[70] Around Targovište, there are the notable excavated sites of Poljanica, Ovčarovo and Targovište, along with other unexcavated mounds. All three seem to show a similar kind of development to Golyamo Delčevo. Poljanica was laid out in its first phase as four blocks of more or less contiguous houses, divided by four lanes intersecting at the centre, aligned on the cardinal points, and each leading to an entrance in the perimeter of 2–3 palisade lines, formed by stout posts.[71] The houses were rectangular, 9–10 by 5–6 m; nearly every one had an oven within. Renewals of the houses in the second and third phases were accompanied by modification of the perimeter by the addition of ditching and embankment. By phase IV, the number of houses had expanded considerably. These were now mainly free standing, with very narrow alleys between them, though the old layout of central lanes more or less survived. Some buildings consisted of conjoined compartments, but there was now more size variation. There were two large structures in the centre, about 11 by 9 m, but there were other large structures in other parts. Again there was an oven in most buildings. The perimeter appears to have been more flimsy in this phase, with one main palisade line. This kind of expanded layout then persisted into later levels, with further redefinition of the palisade perimeter in late phases. There were no major stratigraphic breaks between the building levels.

Ovčarovo also shows expansion through its sequence.[72] In phase I six free-standing rectangular buildings were set in two rows, within a perimeter of up to three palisades. In the second level, the site was still bounded, but now only by a single palisade, within which there were two rows of nine, rather larger, rectangular buildings. By the middle phase, perhaps after a short stratigraphic break, the perimeter was redefined by a shallow ditch which held multi-post palisade lines, and the interior was covered by a less regular layout of varied buildings, some free-standing, some conjoining. In the last two phases the settlement shrank in size to only five or six buildings, partially enclosed by a single palisade. At Targovište, there were three spaced rows of independent houses within an encircling shallow ditch.[73] The rows of houses became more confused in the second and third phases,

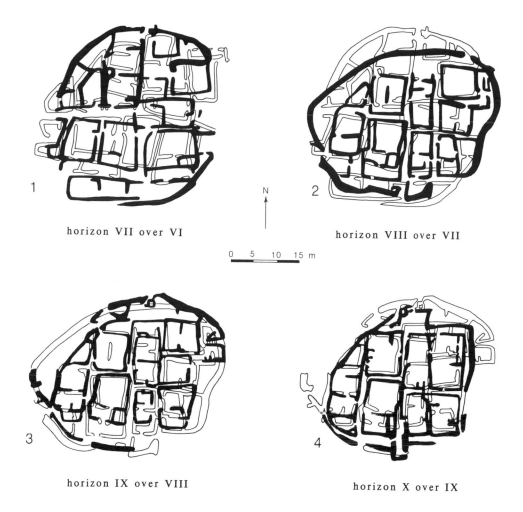

1 horizon VII over VI

2 horizon VIII over VII

N

0 5 10 15 m

3 horizon IX over VIII

4 horizon X over IX

4.6 Successive levels and rebuildings at Ovčarovo. After Bailey.

and some buildings were conjoining. In the fourth phase, apparently without a stratigraphic break, the layout of houses was redefined into two or three rows with a different orientation from that of the earlier levels.

A similar style of settlement layout was found at Vinica, between Targovište and Golyamo Delčevo in the middle Kamchiya valley, and at Radingrad near Razgrad and Hotnica near Veliko Turnovo on the outer rim of the lower Danube valley.[74] At Durankulak on the Black Sea coast on the southern edge of the Dobrudja, there were several levels of occupation through the fifth millennium BC, characterised again by ordered rows of closely spaced buildings. There is no certain evidence here for a defined perimeter. In the fourth level there were at least four rows of rectangular or slightly trapezoidal buildings.[75] Several of these were stone-footed, but had internal post walls, and most were divided into two compartments. Building IX was centrally placed within the site, and

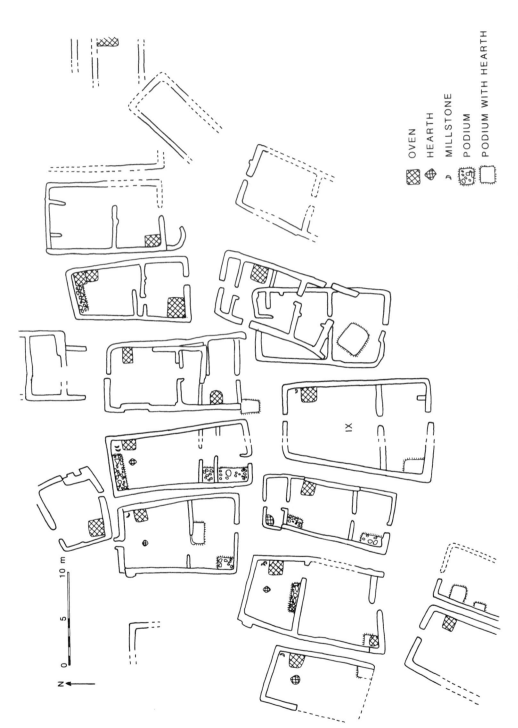

4.7 Simplified plan of level 4 at Durankulak. After Todorova.

OVEN

HEARTH

MILLSTONE

PODIUM

PODIUM WITH HEARTH

IX

N

0   5   10 m

was slightly larger than the others. As at Dolnoslav, this has been characterised as a special cult building, but the available details do not suggest different internal fittings or special demarcation. We have too little information about settlement layout in the rest of the Dobrogea, but sites already mentioned in the lower Danube valley like Radovanu and Căscioarele in south-east Romania suggest that relatively small, densely packed and usually ordered sites were common over a wider area than north-east Bulgaria.[76]

The inhabitants of such sites grew crops and kept domesticated animals, in the case of Golyamo Delčevo sheep and goats, cattle and pigs in almost equal quantities; they also hunted a lot of wild game.[77] A little further afield in the lower Danube valley, wear on cattle limb bones has been taken to suggest the use of cattle for traction.[78] Since animals were probably not kept within settlements, communal ownership and husbandry could be envisaged. A pollen diagram from the lagoon next to Durankulak does not show much human impact on the vegetation.[79] It is no more certain in north-east Bulgaria than in central-southern Bulgaria or Thessaly that such sites were occupied year-round. The well-defined perimeters of most of these sites could be an important clue to conditions of land intake and settlement mobility. It seems unlikely that the palisades and ditches were for defence against other humans. There are no other clear indications of endemic warfare, and as the settlements increased in size, suggesting perhaps gradual population growth, so in some cases, as at Poljanica, did perimeters become slighter. The layout of the interior of these sites would have left little room for animals, unless rather small numbers of animals were kept in the houses along with people. It therefore seems unlikely that perimeters were to protect flocks and herds. The role of the perimeter may have been to signal the existence and identity of a newly chosen settlement location, especially in the initial phase of settlement expansion, when no one of these sites would yet have formed a mound. The perimeter may have served both to limit the number of occupants and to provide symbolic protection during periods or seasons when some, most or all inhabitants were elsewhere. In this way, chosen places without the benefit of deeply stratified and visible antiquity could have been made special from the beginning of their use.

One point of view, on the basis principally of analysis of variations in house size and in paths of access to houses, is that such sites were riven with internal competition along lineage lines.[80] Thus enlarged house sizes at Poljanica were taken to show the emergence of dominant lineages. There is little reason to accept such claims without much further evidence of internal social difference. What is striking in all these cases is the continuity of the style of layout. Each house could have been regarded as a living being, with an identity and a renewable tradition of memories associated with its history. In this scheme, each 'living house' would have been part of a 'living settlement', the ideology behind which it would have been very hard to subvert. We are uncertain anyway about the details of residence.[81] It seems rather naive to envisage a lineage, however that is to be defined for these purposes, confined to single buildings or even distinct settlement zones, though the layout of a site like Poljanica could suggest four founding groups. Most houses or groups of compartments had an oven, but we do not know whether conjoining buildings reflect agglomerations of generations, separate residence for men and women, spouses and partners, or some other factor altogether.

4.8 Objects from the 'cult scene' in level IX, Ovčarovo. Photo: Fol and Lichardus.

Cult was integrated into daily practice. There are no obvious separate shrines within Poljanica and the other sites. At Ovčarovo, one unremarkable building in level IX had a miniature 'cult scene' in the form of figurines and model furniture and other paraphernalia, found on its floor.[82] There were four small figurines, several tables (more tendentiously, 'altars'), small round objects perhaps representing pots, and three small clay cylinders or elongated drums. All the figurines and three tables were decorated with painted curvilinear and rectilinear motifs. The concentric designs on the furniture have been seen as sun and moon motifs. Those on the figurines also incorporate spirals and concentric arrangements, and a clay house model from beside the oven of the same house also has painted designs on its outer walls, of chevrons and other motifs.[83] If figurines represent ancestors, there were strong links between the living and the dead, and between the houses and their occupants. These continuities seem far more important than barely discernible internal differentiation.

Other evidence for internal differentiation from this general area is ambiguous. A number of other structures within settlements have been claimed as shrines, for example at the Hissarluka tell, Razgrad, at the Ruse tell on the lower Danube, and at Hotnica.[84] At the latter, gold and other objects (discussed further below) were found in a pit within a house, but which was otherwise similar to its immediate neighbours. At Căscioarele on the lower Danube, a large two-roomed building in a late Boian level (about 5000 BC) had one room painted in cream-on-red with curvilinear, spiral and angular designs, and there were remains of two painted clay pillars rising from the floor. There was also a crouched burial by one of the pillars, seemingly from the same occupation level.[85] From a later, Gumelnitsa level a restored clay model appears to show buildings on a raised platform, which have been interpreted as temples or shrines.[86] From the area of the fifth-millennium BC Gradesnica culture of north-west Bulgaria (with some examples in north-east Bulgaria too) there are small clay plaques inscribed with complex rectilinear motifs. Similar motifs appear on pot bases, spindle whorls and other small fired-clay objects. Since each motif is unique, this inscription may have served to mark personal property. But even if this explanation is preferred to that of religious or other symbolism, it remains unclear whose property is so marked. Goods may have been held and inherited by families, lineages or other groupings, rather than by individuals, just as I have suggested that animal husbandry remained a matter for collective action.[87] There have also been claims for specialised workshops, which could have implications for the organisation of craft production. The evidence consists of buildings within settlements with concentrations of particular objects or methods of manufacture, for example of bone figurines at Hotnica and of *Spondylus* ornaments at Hîrşova, in the lower Danube valley.[88] It is doubtful if such activity was genuinely restricted, because excavations have regularly been of limited extent and because other signs of craft activity occur widely. Conversely, it is possible that some craft activities were carried out beyond the confines of tightly spaced settlement interiors.

Separate cemeteries were a striking development from the late sixth millennium BC onwards in north-east Bulgaria and the lower Danube area. In north-east Bulgaria, such burial grounds were placed close to bounded, ordered settlements.[89] There were some thirty graves at Golyamo Delčevo, about forty-five at Vinica, and about twenty-five at Devnya, inland from Varna in the lower Kamenica valley (where the adjacent settlement has not been investigated). There were also small cemeteries beside Ovčarovo, Poljanica, Targovište and Radingrad, but these are still unpublished. Despite some claims to the contrary,[90] such burial grounds show few signs of marked differences in social position.

Set against the long continuities of occupation, the burial grounds can only hold a very small percentage of the people of the adjacent settlements. Graves were added gradually at intervals, but earlier graves must have been marked, as on the Hungarian plain, since so few graves intersect. Formal, public disposal of this kind might have been reserved for members of particular groupings within communities, but the context suggests otherwise. Men, women and children were buried in simple, earth-cut graves, which varied little in size, depth or other treatment. Most people were provided with some grave goods, principally pots, but also tools and ornaments. There are slightly more graves of adult men, who tended to have slightly more grave goods, but the differences are not marked. There were also some empty graves, provided in the usual manner with grave goods, but without human remains. The communities of the dead do not therefore seem to have been internally differentiated, and this seems to match the situation within the communities of the living. The inhumation of people in public rites and the durable marking of their graves imply that individuals were remembered, but the burial grounds as a whole could have come to be regarded as the ancestral home of the forebears of the living community, permanently occupied even when the living were elsewhere. It would be useful to establish how many of these graves belong to an early part of the settlement sequences. According to rather scanty published information, the graves at Vinica were contemporary with the earlier period of occupation of the settlement mound, but at Golyamo Delčevo they dated to the latter stages of occupation.[91]

Some larger burial grounds are known on the Black Sea coast and in the lower Danube valley. Varna, the most spectacular example of all, had nearly 300 graves. Next to the settlement mound at Durankulak there were over 1000 graves,[92] presumably here reflecting both a greater percentage of the inhabitants and a longer sequence of burial through the life of the settlement; approximately half the burials belonged to the Neolithic occupation before the fifth-millennium Copper Age phase. Most of the Copper Age graves, which overlapped the area of their predecessors, shared a common orientation, and many were marked with stone slabs. Men were usually buried in extended position, women crouched, on their right sides. Children were also buried in the cemetery. The dead were provided with grave goods, including pottery, tools and ornaments. The quantities varied. Grave 732 belonged to an adult, and was one of the most abundantly provided. It contained several pots, flint tools, a string of beads (principally greenstone but including three gold and one *Spondylus* beads), two copper bracelets, three bone ornaments and a bone idol. There were also abundantly furnished graves of adult women, children or juveniles, and empty graves. Graves 447 and 558, of adult women, had several copper and *Spondylus* rings and bracelets, and gold beads. Further north, there were some graves within the Ruse tell, presumably within a temporarily unoccupied part, some 300 graves in the Hamangia phase cemetery at Cernavoda above the lower Danube, and over 100 in the late Boian cemetery at Cernica in the lower Danube valley south of Bucharest.[93] Neither Cernavoda nor Cernica can be related to a settlement history, but once again all ages and both sexes are represented in the graves. Most were provided with grave goods, which while varying in quantity do not seem to form the basis for presentation of marked social difference. Each repetition of a basically uniform grave rite must have served to reinforce the links between the living and the dead, and the concept of communal solidarity in both life and death.

The Varna cemetery

In the fifth millennium BC, there was a narrow estuary connected to the sea on the Black Sea coast at Varna. Around this are known several 'pile-dwellings', though none has been fully investigated. A little above the former estuary, a large burial ground was discovered by chance in 1972. In the meticulous excavations which followed, some 281 graves were discovered up to 1986, belonging to the mid–later fifth millennium BC.[94] In many respects, this cemetery is similar to others in the Black Sea/lower Danube area. It is large, and appears to have been in use for some time. It contains the graves of men, women and children, which show some gender differentiation, and has some empty graves or cenotaphs. But the abundance and nature of the goods in some graves and cenotaphs, and the treatment of some of the cenotaphs, have prompted speculation that this burial ground both reflected a markedly divided society and served a very wide area around, suggesting extensive social or political control.[95] Can this kind of interpretation, which is at odds with the rest of the evidence presented so far, be sustained, and if not, how is the Varna cemetery to be seen?

The limits of the cemetery have not so far been determined; it extends over an area at least 120 by 60 m. Graves of the various kinds were distributed across the whole area, though there may have been proportionately more empty graves in the southern portion. There appear to be roughly defined groups or concentrations of graves within the overall layout. Graves were not set in rows, but were spaced at intervals, generally shared a common orientation, and were presumably marked, once again, since there are very few intersections. They were simple rectangular pits, cut to varying depths into the subsoil, up to 2.5 m, but there is no obvious correlation between grave treatment and contents. Each grave was backfilled, but never included topsoil, indicating again the rule-bound nature of the proceedings.

About seventy graves were disturbed and their character could not be accurately determined. There were some 155 inhumations, ninety in extended position and sixty-five in tightly contracted position, mostly on the right side. For the most part, these graves were provided with rather similar sets of grave goods, though it appears that men were generally buried in the extended position and women in crouched position. Grave 7 belonged to a young man, about 20 years old. There was a pot by his head, and a perforated stone hammer-axe by his right shoulder. His arms were folded across his chest, and there was a flint blade by his right upper arm, and another pot on the left side of his upper body. Grave 6 belonged to a man, estimated as 30–35 years old. He too was extended, with arms folded across the chest. He was provided with a pot by his head, and with another and flints by his hip. He was wearing a copper earring, and had a copper hammer-axe at his right shoulder, and a copper needle or awl and a flint blade by his right upper arm. (Details of a crouched burial have not yet been published.) There were other graves in this series with fewer goods, but pots, tools and ornaments were common grave goods, and so far only some twenty burials certainly lacked grave goods completely. These rites could be taken to emphasise differences between the genders (though it is fruitless to attempt to quantify this in terms of 'wealth' or 'status'), and to celebrate on behalf of the communities of both the living and the dead the ability to provide food, drink and hospitality, to engage in exchange and to behave in communally sanctioned and valued ways.

Out of this series there is one example of an extended burial which had an exceptional abundance and variety of grave goods. Grave 43 contained the extended body of a man, estimated as 40–50 years old. Like others, he had been carefully placed in his grave, head to the north, with his right arm by his side and his left on his chest, and his right foot lying over the left. By his head and chest there were several pots. By his right arm there were a copper axe and a 'sceptre', a stone perforated hammer-axe with a beaten gold shaft. On both upper arms there were heavy gold rings, and from the head down to the lower legs there was a profusion of other gold ornaments: small gold discs around the head, gold beads and discs down the body, perhaps originally attached to clothing. A beaten gold tube, best interpreted as a penis cover, was found by the right hip. This had small perforations for attachment at its thicker end, and might best be seen as having been attached to outer clothing, enabling it to end by the hip, rather than to the body itself. There were gold discs by the knees, together with a hammer-axe, an axe, a chisel, an awl and a needle, all in copper, as well as a stone axe. In all there were 990 gold objects in the grave, weighing over 1500 g. There were also bone and *Spondylus* ornaments.

This astonishing assemblage was more abundant and more varied than any other accompanying a burial in the cemetery. It might therefore be seen as the burial of a socially pre-eminent person, perhaps a lineage head at a moment of intense internal competition.[96] In support of this, grave 43 lies close to a number of other notable burials, including graves 6 and 7, and of cenotaphs. Against this interpretation is the scale of difference between grave 43 and the rest of the series. In other men's graves a hammer-axe is found at the right shoulder, perhaps as a badge of maleness as much as a token of social position; in grave 43 there are six hammer-axes/axes. The great quantity of gold was used principally to adorn the clothed body, and in the case of the penis cover to emphasise its maleness. Although it is easy to assume that gold had the same value for these people as for ourselves, the material is not difficult to work (as described below) and its very abundance may rather suggest that it had a different value. However, the details of its occurrence in the Varna graves do suggest that it had some special significance. It was found in only sixty-one graves, thirty-four of which were cenotaphs (described below) yet which had 60 per cent of the gold. Gold does occur in some twenty-two other burials, in the form of beads and appliqués, but only in grave 43 in the manner described above. A different interpretation therefore begins to emerge for grave 43. The man in it could have had religious or symbolic importance, either in life or in death, for the whole community which used the Varna cemetery. It is easy to assume that grave goods were personal possessions. Rather, they can be seen as the gifts of the living,[97] in the case of grave 43 provided by a wider group than simply the man's family or lineage. Mediation with the ancestors at a moment of particular interest could have been the concern of the whole community.

This impression is reinforced when the remaining fifty-six graves are considered. These are empty: cenotaphs or symbolic graves. Ten of these in fact had some human bones. They were all rather deep graves. Grave goods included bone figurines. Another forty were well-provided empty graves, with goods including gold and copper ornaments and tools, flint blades and *Spondylus* ornaments, and pottery, of a kind and range seen in the rest of the Varna cemetery and in others like Durankulak. These graves had been carefully made. At the base of number 5, for example, there were traces of red ochre and black organic matter. At the north end (normally the head end in the burial series) there were three pots and flints, and a copper hammer-axe and chisel. In the centre of the grave there were three gold rings and a gold bead, and throughout there were thousands (2200) of *Dentalium* shells; 30 cm above the base in the fill of the grave there were a pot, a copper needle and a bone figurine, and 60 cm above, red colouring and more *Dentalium* shells. A similar kind of patterning has been described for graves 41 and 97. These two series can be seen as closely connected to the main burial tradition. The ten partial bone assemblages could be secondary burials, and the more numerous others could be substitute burials, since the style of placing of goods is so similar. Some might be for people who had died elsewhere, but others could have been part of ancestral rites bound up with the dead already in the cemetery. The remaining cenotaphs support the idea of ancestral veneration.[98]

Graves 2, 3 and 15 were mask graves, graves 1, 4 and 36 exceptionally provided empty graves; all lay close together in the southern part of the cemetery and graves 6, 7 and 43 were not far away. All had been carefully made. In grave 2, there were again traces of red

4.9 Cenotaphs or empty graves at Varna, during excavation. Top: grave 4; below: grave 36. Photos: Fol and Lichardus.

ochre and black organic matter at the base of the grave. Above this were three distinct groups of grave goods. At the north end there were again several pots. A little to the south there was a clay mask of human form and at natural size, probably fired though poorly preserved at the time of excavation. The mask or face showed ears, nose and brow. Gold ornaments picked out features of the face, a strip diadem across the brow, rings in the ears, discs for the eyes and a strip across the mouth; there were two gold amulets below the face. In the southern part of the grave there was a further group of goods or offerings, including a convex bone figurine, a flint blade, a spindle whorl and *Dentalium* shells. Graves 3 and 15 were rather similar. The excavator has suggested that these were female-associated, because of the gold neck amulets. There were no convex bone figurines in the series with burials.[99]

Graves 1, 4 and 36 were richly furnished with a range of tools, ornaments and pots. They were notable for the quantity and weight of gold objects: 216 (about 1090 g) in 1, 33 (1500 g) in 4 and 857 (790 g) in 36. These included beads, rings, discs and appliqués, including in the form of horned animals, a solid model astragalus (or animal heel bone) and hollow, tubular shafts (perhaps cast) for hammer-axes and 'sceptres'. Grave 1 was partly disturbed but graves 4 and 36 suggest again that goods or offerings had been placed carefully with reference to imaginary bodies. Most of the goods in grave 4 were at the base of the grave, which was strewn with red ochre and black organic matter. At the north ('head') end there were a stone axe and a pot on a great pottery dish or shallow bowl decorated with gold paint. Beneath this were two copper chisels and a hammer-axe, a bone figurine, and other gold ornaments. On the west side (where the right side of an extended body would have been) there were a pot and a perforated stone axe with gold shaft mounts, and in the middle of the grave there were another copper axe, an antler axe, and gold beads, rings and other objects. From grave 36 there was a greater quantity of gold including beads, rings, the astragalus and animal figures, a miniature diadem and a cross-headed sceptre.

These might be regarded as the graves of people who had died away from their home region, but it is striking that the most abundant assemblages should be reserved for such a category. It is more plausible to suppose that these graves were in fact connected with ancestor worship. If, as time went by, the dead already in the cemetery were regarded as founding ancestors as well as or rather than known, remembered individuals, their importance would have been enhanced. It could have become important to mediate with such ancestors or placate them by further rites, acts of ancestral veneration which borrowed the form of burial rites to emphasise the close bonds between the living and the dead. Ancestors were treated with a material exuberance denied to the ordinary dead, the man in grave 43 having already been argued to have been of unusual status. Their offering pits could have remained open for long periods, and the details of the fills certainly suggest a phased, ritualised backfilling, with further offerings. On this analysis, the Varna cemetery stands more as testament to the spiritual world of its users than to their secular wealth or internal social divisions. There were cenotaphs in the other cemeteries of the region, though none was so strikingly furnished as at Varna. We cannot tell from the cemeteries alone what notions there may have been of cycles of ancestral comings and goings, but such an idea is as plausible as social crisis caused by inter-lineage competition, to explain the most abundant assemblages. We can refer again both to the shorter history of the region, in which memories of beginnings and the tracing and retracing of descent would have been important, and to the likely cycle of settlement occupation. Varna may have served a very wide area roundabout, but it is equally striking that its immediate region had few known settlements. The more people moved, the more important it was for the ancestors to be tied to particular locations. The Varna cemetery can be regarded either as the key to a scale of social difference not otherwise suggested by the evidence, or, as argued here, as an extreme form of a wider pattern, with its roots in both historical circumstance and ancestral veneration.

Serbia, Bosnia, Croatia, western Romania: the Vinča culture

Settlement mounds were an important feature of denser and more varied settlement through many parts of this region, but detailed information about them is scarce. Recent excavations at Gomolava and renewed excavations at Vinča are not yet fully published. Gomolava was in use throughout the Vinča phase, though Vinča itself was abandoned in the later Vinča period, some time after 5000 BC.[100] There were close-set rows of houses at Gomolava, the inhabitants of which husbanded cattle, including probably recently domesticated stock, and cultivated a range of cereals.[101] The pattern is familiar from further south, but marks significant change in this region. It has been claimed that there were more figurines at such sites than in smaller or shorter-lived sites,[102] but it is very hard to quantify their occurrence. Vinča culture figurines are distinctive, with mask-like triangular faces and large eyes, body decoration and often indications of dress; many are seated. Their principal context was domestic, since only two Vinča cemeteries are known, one from Botoš in the Banat of northern Serbia, separate from any settlement, and the other within a temporarily unoccupied part of Gomolava.[103] In the southern part of the area, some very large figurines are known from settlement contexts, for example two heads about 17 cm high from Predionica, near Pristina. These might have been from figures originally 50 cm high. Another seated figure from the same site is 18 cm high.[104] There have been few claims for separate shrines in this area. One unusual find came from the Transylvanian settlement mound at Tărtăria. In a pit dug into an earlier Vinča level there were 26 clay figurines, two alabaster figurines, a clay 'anchor', a *Spondylus* bracelet, and three unbaked clay tablets, accompanied by the burnt, broken and disarticulated bones of an adult man.[105] All the tablets have inscribed signs, some in the form of schematic representations. Two of the tablets are rectangular, and the third is circular. One has an animal, another figure and a branch or tree. One view is that this represents a cow pulling a plough ahead of a person.[106] The other rectangular tablet and the circular tablet are perforated. Both have mainly abstract signs. It has been suggested that this was the burial of a shaman or spirit-medium.[107] It might also be seen as another foundation offering, like that in Platia Magoula Zarkou in Thessaly, connected to ancestor worship. Similar inscribed signs appear on the bases of some Vinča pottery, for example from Divostin in the Sumadija.[108]

Some of the most informative recent research has been carried out on low tells or 'flat' sites. To the south, Anza was occupied in the earlier Vinča period.[109] The specific cause of

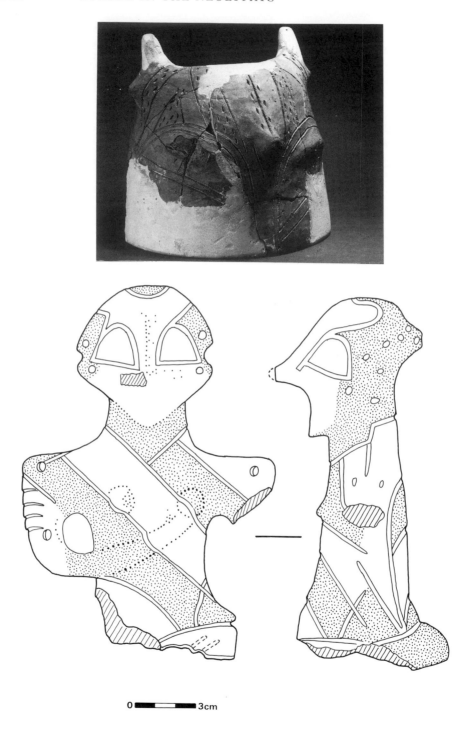

0 ▰▰▰▱▱ 3cm

4.10 Figurines from Vinča. Top: early Vinča animal lid. Photo: Gimbutas. Below: late Vinča red-painted figurine. After Tringham.

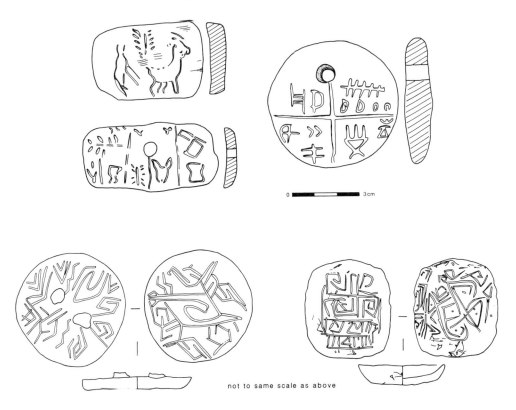

0 ▬▬▬ 3cm

not to same scale as above

4.11 Inscribed clay discs. Top: Tărtăria; below: Kurilo and Gradesnica. After Vlassa and Todorova.

its abandonment *c.* 5000 BC is not known, but this site history fits a broader pattern of change in the later Vinča horizon. The Vinča occupation covered some 9–10 ha, though it is unlikely that the whole area was in use at one time. Details of the buildings have yet to be published, and more information on these has become available from two sites further north, Selevac and Opovo.

Selevac is a large site, some 50 ha in total extent, in the Vrbica valley in the foothills to the west of the Morava in the Sumadija.[110] The deposits of the site are up to 2.5–3 m thick, but the site probably consisted of series of shifting smaller foci, perhaps 3–15 ha in extent. It was occupied in the early and probably at least part of the late Vinča period, from the later sixth into the earlier fifth millennium BC.[111] Clearly this was an occupation on a scale and of a duration unprecedented in the preceding Starčevo phase; the regional setting has been described above. The inhabitants used subsistence resources much like those of their predecessors, with increasing emphasis on cattle, and were able to procure raw materials including a little copper from varying distances beyond the site. It has been suggested from the horizontal displacement of building plots in the later phases of occupation that plough cultivation over bigger fields succeeded hoe cultivation of gardens close to houses,[112] but the evidence is circumstantial.

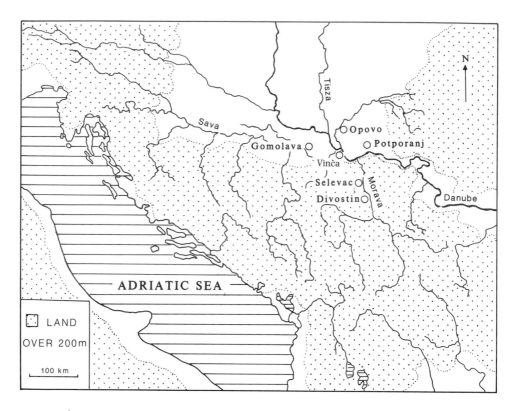

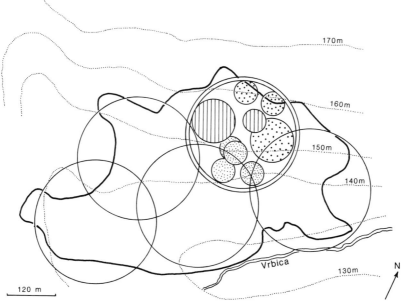

4.12 The setting and possible structure of Selevac. The model shows one zone in use, with hypothetical household or lineage groups, within the overall area of the site. After Tringham.

The sequence of structures at Selevac site is important. Four building phases were found, representing the varying replacement of rectangular, post-and-daub buildings, in many cases perhaps following their deliberate destruction by burning. With the passage of time, the structures became more solidly built and perhaps lasted longer. This process of gradual site establishment is familiar from further south. In the earlier levels replacements were made vertically above their predecessors, but in the later levels there were horizontal displacements. This may only reflect short-term shifts within particular residence foci, but may also be tied up with a failure or reluctance to establish a long-term commitment to fixed place. Within and around the buildings there were plentiful finds of pottery and lithics. It has been claimed that the whole process of raw material procurement, craft production and consumption was more complex in the Vinča phase, as a consequence of increased sedentism.[113] It is unlikely that the relationship is a simple causal one. Here as elsewhere, it is not clear that the whole of the site or any of its individual foci was in continuous occupation. The abundance of material culture may have been part of a series of social relationships and transactions, involving exchange, gift-giving and the provision of hospitality, designed to consolidate a sense of community. The very large sites such as Selevac may have drawn occupants from a wide area around, who also had allegiances elsewhere.

This is a rather different model to the claim that Selevac and other sites like it were composed of autonomous households, which acted as independent units of production, generally in competition with one another.[114] One weakness of this claim is the equation of house with household, even when the definition of household is broadened to something as inclusive as 'co-resident domestic group', probably kin based. The household model envisages that when competition reached unacceptable levels, communities fissioned, to produce the later Vinča settlement pattern. Another weakness of the model, though it successfully demands attention to the process of change, is that it is no easier to see the existence of autonomous households in the later Vinča horizon. Divostin also in the Sumadija about 50 km from Selevac, for example, was occupied in the later Vinča period, after *c.* 5000 BC.[115] The settlement as a whole may have covered an area at least 60 by 40 m, considerably smaller than Selevac. It consisted of spaced rectangular houses, rebuilt at least once. These were freestanding, at distances of 5–15 m, but shared common style and orientation. This is not to deny the possibility of individual action or of varying interests within such a settlement, but to stress that the sense of ordered community remained, even though the patterns of residence changed.

Opovo lies in the Banat north of Belgrade, in the wetlands of the Danube–Tisza basin, near a tributary of the Danube, the Tamis.[116] This zone had already been settled in the Starčevo phase. The site is a large (about 200 m in diameter), low mound, with three main occupation levels, which was used over two or more centuries in the later Vinča period, *c.* 4700–4500 BC. The repeated use of the site shows a fixed pattern of occupation, but the site is very different from many seen further south in the Balkans. The settlement area perhaps consisted of a series of shifting residential foci, since there were no certain house remains in the excavated area in the middle phase. However, the houses of the third phase copied the orientation of those of the first, and occupied almost the same plots. Rather

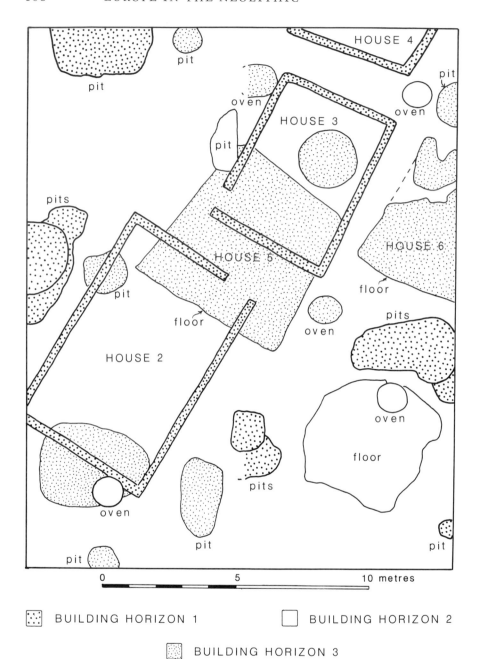

HOUSE 4

pit

pit

pit

oven

oven

HOUSE 3

pit

pits

HOUSE 6

HOUSE 5

pit

floor

floor

pits

pit

oven

HOUSE 2

oven

floor

pits

oven

pit

pit

pit

0   5   10 metres

⬚ BUILDING HORIZON 1   ☐ BUILDING HORIZON 2

⬚ BUILDING HORIZON 3

4.13 Structures and other features from three successive levels at Opovo. After Tringham.

than individual ownership or tenure of building plots this may indicate a strong conformity to communal practice. The rectangular houses were simply built, with small poles and daub, and lacked partitions. Those of the first phase lacked clay floors. One building in phase 3 was two-storeyed, careful excavation showing the upper floor and its contents directly superimposed on the ground-floor level. Most of the houses had been burned, perhaps deliberately. As at Selevac, this has been seen as the action of autonomous households, marking the end of individual cycles or generations, but given the close spacing of the houses and the risk of fire it is unlikely that this practice was not communally sanctioned and scheduled.

The inhabitants of Opovo husbanded domesticated animals and used cereals, perhaps cultivated on flood deposits, but they also exploited a lot of wild game. They used raw materials brought in from varying distances, including a little copper, but many of the flint tools appear to have been made elsewhere than on the site. Included in the midden deposits were stray human remains. This could have been a seasonally occupied site, but more generally it may also reflect the less stable social conditions, characterised by settlement dispersal and by lack of settlement continuity, which were seemingly widespread in the later Vinča period and subsequently. The Opovo excavations were concentrated on a 16 by 20 m cutting, and the post-Vinča Krivodol–Bubanj Hum horizon is not well characterised over broad areas in Serbia and surrounds. The process of change in the more northern part of the Balkans may also be followed by returning to the Hungarian plain.

The Hungarian plain

Why then did people go through cycles of aggregation and dispersal, if not owing to the emergence of autonomous, competitive households and their subsequent fissioning? I have suggested so far that one explanation for this area could lie in a reluctance in the first place to make a long-term commitment to fixed places. Smaller communities with a tradition of independence may have engaged in aggregation to take advantage of its short-term benefits, but unlike further south may have preferred then to disengage. Another explanation could be that the phase of aggregation was necessary to integrate a population, more widely dispersed and more numerous than before, but this once achieved, the impetus for centralised gatherings weakened. Of interest for this model is the fact that throughout the Vinča sequence and that of the Hungarian plain from the late sixth into the fifth millennium BC there were many more smaller sites in the landscape than larger ones.

Developments on the Hungarian plain ran parallel to those of the Danube basin to the south, if a little later. As the early Vinča expansion began, so the Linear Pottery culture expansion across the plain took place. Linear Pottery sites on the plain were small and dispersed, at a time when large early Vinča aggregations were beginning. Some of the aggregations which began c. 5000 BC in the Szakálhát phase and continued into the Tisza–Herpály phase were complex. At Berettyóújfalu–Herpály in the Berettyó valley on the eastern plain, the nature of the site changed throughout five phases of occupation.[117] It began as a series of small nuclei with fenced enclosures delimited by a ditch, which were succeeded by a planned layout of large, tripartite, two-storeyed houses, closely spaced and conjoining, in

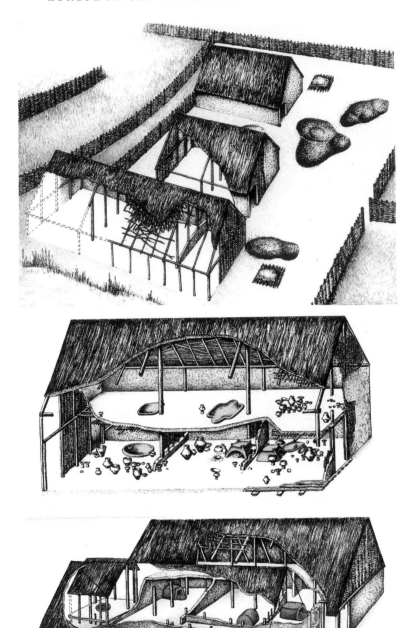

4.14 Houses from Tisza and Herpály culture sites. Top: Öcsöd–Kováshalom (Tisza); centre: Berettyóújfalu–Herpály, level 11 (Herpály); below: Hódmezővásárhely–Gorsza, house 2, level 10 (Tisza). After Kalicz, Raczky and Horváth.

an area also delimited by a ditch. In the upper levels the layout of buildings was looser, and there was also late occupation beside the mound, which had grown up to 3 m high. The houses themselves were carefully built with clay and clay/wood floors, several times renewed. They had closed clay ovens and open hearths within, as well as clay storage bins and clay tables. There were incised and painted pots and stone tools in abundance, and some *Spondylus* beads and copper rings, pendants and beads. Rather simple anthropomorphic figurines occurred only in the early levels, and no building has been classed as a shrine or has unusual concentrations of cult paraphernalia. Some foundation burials and deposits were placed under houses, and there were some other formal burials in unoccupied parts of the site in the middle of the sequence.

There were other large buildings both in tells and in low-mounded sites. At the tell at Vésztő–Mágor, a house 13 by 5.5 m had two rooms with plastered floors.[118] In one room, there were a sitting female figurine, clay tables and anthropomorphic pots in a group on the floor. The context for such cult equipment appears domestic, since in this and the other room there were pots, clay bins, stone and bone tools, and loom weights. Many fish scales were found here. This was probably therefore the sort of context in which other notable figurines were found, especially in southern parts of the plain, including the seated male figure from Szegvár–Tűzköves or the so-called Venuses (seated female figures) of Kökénydomb, from the tell at Hódmezővásárhely–Kökénydomb.[119] Szegvár–Tűzköves has both a tell and an adjacent horizontal, single-layer occupation.[120] Substantial buildings also occur in low tells (and perhaps also in single-layer occupations). At Öcsöd–Kováshalom houses ranged in length from 7 to 18 m. Up to half a dozen were set in small fenced compounds, several of which were scattered over a broad area. At Gorsza a low tell formed, beginning with occupation defined only by pits and a ditch. In the second phase there were substantial buildings, including the exceptional six-roomed house 2.[121] This had six rooms and an end annexe, laid out in the form of a U, with a narrow central passage. There were also upper floors or lofts. Each room had an oven, and there were looms and clay bins, and many pots on the floors. The internal walls were decorated with incision and red paint. The innermost room had two decorated rectangular clay bins, which have been suggested as cultic equipment, but the context again appears firmly to be domestic.

On the south-east edge of the plain in Romania, an unusual building has been discovered in a low tell at Parţa (Parác), south of Timişoara, in a level equivalent to the Szakálhát phase.[122] This was some 12.5 by 7 m, somewhat larger than the other buildings around it, which shared a common orientation and close spacing. At the east end, a large double doorway gave on to a hearth and raised clay platform. At the base of this there were cattle skulls, and on the platform two large linked clay figures (perhaps 1 m high), which have been reconstructed as having a human and an animal head respectively. The inner part of the building was divided symmetrically into four compartments, provided with further clay benches and ornamented with clay animal heads. The western end was entered by one doorway, further highlighted by clay animal heads on the outside wall. This exciting find is a rare example for the region of a structure which can be considered as a shrine of some kind in its own right, rather than as a building with a 'cult corner' or cult equipment contained within it. The building was renewed in the succeeding level, and ended its life by being burned.

4.15 Details of excavated structures. Top: Berettyóújfalu–Herpály, levels 11–12;
bottom: Hódmezővásárhely–Gorsza. Photos: Kalicz and Horváth.

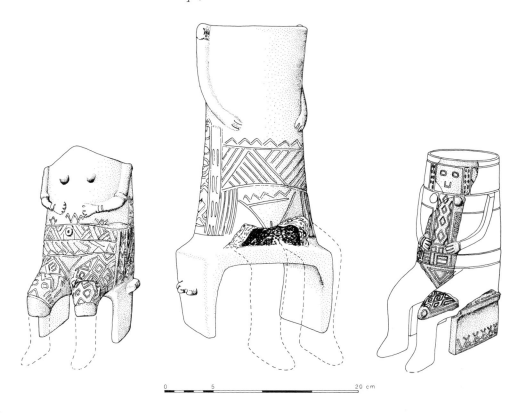

0   5   20 cm

4.16 Tisza culture seated figurines from Hódmezővásárhely–Kökénydomb. After Kalicz and Raczky.

In both the tells and the low-mounded sites there were groups of individual burials in small clusters, in temporarily unoccupied parts.[123] There were around fifty in total at Gorzsa and Öcsöd–Kováshalom, and over seventy at Szegvár–Tűzköves. Most of the burials were of adults, usually contracted, with men lying on their right side and women on the left. At Vésztő–Mágor burials had been placed in coffins. Grave goods were generally simple, restricted to personal ornaments including copper and *Spondylus* arm rings.

These people kept domesticated animals, especially cattle, of which many were recently domesticated. They cultivated emmer and einkorn, barley, millet and peas, perhaps on flood deposits like their predecessors, and perhaps with the help of ploughs.[124] They also hunted wild animals, in some cases on a considerable scale, as at Berettyóújfalu–Herpály, and fished. Surprisingly, the careful excavations at Herpály itself produced hardly any fish bones. Might this reflect the season of occupation, or a taboo on fishing? Obsidian, flint, *Spondylus* and a little copper were obtained by exchange from sources fringing and beyond the plain.[125] It has been suggested that nucleation and centralisation of population took place in this phase, as a defence strategy to protect valuable herds of cattle which were a vital medium of exchange for raw materials from beyond the plain.[126] With a better knowledge of the overall range of settlement and of the development of individual tells and low mounds, such an explanation looks less plausible. Although individual houses were often burned, there is no clear evidence for warfare or conflict. There were still small communities dispersed through the landscape (itself probably a better defence mechanism had one been needed), and at locations which became chosen places the beginning of the occupation sequence regularly involves separate small nuclei, formed usually by at least a handful of houses. As in the Starčevo–Vinča contrast, there may have been an increase in population over the Linear Pottery culture. Even the repeatedly used sites may not have been permanently occupied by all or part of their inhabitants. The mounds did not begin as such but were gradually created as places of fixed permanence. These places were the focus for ritual, exchange and burial. The settings for such negotiations with neighbours, kin, ancestors and others were groups of buildings, carefully built and colourfully decorated, themselves probably redolent with meaning as embodiments of identity and value. Foundation deposits of bull horns, antlers, dog skulls, axes and infant burials have been found.[127] The motifs and colours used on house walls probably unite with those on pots and figurines in a single symbolic scheme. Through domestic cult and burials close to the settlement, people mediated with their ancestors and traced descent, an important concern for a growing population with a comparatively recent history. Through the provision of hospitality and by gift-giving, the living negotiated a wider sense of community which could incorporate previously more independent groups.

The process was similar to that begun further south at least a millennium and a half earlier. On the Hungarian plain the process ended differently, in renewed dispersal in the Tiszapolgár phase, with which this chapter began. Perhaps in the end, as postulated in the household model, aggregation fuelled rivalries which led to fission.[128] But unlike the household model, the hypothesis here is of larger basic social groupings than autonomous households. The girl in grave 24 at Tiszapolgár–Basatanya seems to have belonged to a wider descent group than that. In this northern part of the Balkans, the ideology of the residential collective was not permanently accepted as it had been in many areas further south, and it was perhaps values of independence and competitive equality which prevented this.

Material dimensions

Much of what archaeologists dig up in south-east Europe consists of rich assemblages of artefacts – pots, tools, and ornaments in various materials – and traditionally much effort has been devoted by scholars to ordering this abundant material into time- and space-frames. My account has so far taken only selective account of this material dimension. This was a pervasive part of everyday life, as ever present as the buildings and their layouts or the graves of ancestors and their contents, and it was charged with meaning.[129] Nor were patterns of material culture stable through time.

The Hungarian plain

In the Linear Pottery phase, rather similar styles of pottery were in use. Pots could have signalled a broad sense of identity appropriate to the conditions of dispersed, expansive settlement. Raw materials from beyond the plain were obtained and were probably in general circulation, though some processing may have been in the hands of specialists, as at Boldogkőváralja on the edge of the Zemplén hills to the north of the plain, north-east of Miskolc, where 500 flint blades were found in a pot within a small settlement.[130]

In the Tisza–Herpály–Csőszhalom phase, there was greater regionalisation of pottery styles, forming distributions roughly in the south (Tisza), east (Herpály) and north (Csőszhalom). These coincide with the appearance of perhaps more numerous and certainly more varied sites in the landscape. Decorated pots and figurines were prominent in many buildings. Pots were not just containers. They must have carried associations from the activities with which they were connected, the preparation and especially the presentation of food and drink. Their forms and decorations may have signalled general concepts of identity. Specific pots could, by ethnographic analogy, have stood for particular people, spirits or ancestors,[131] including those with human faces on them and others. Pots were not usually deposited as grave goods. There was a considerable flow of materials from outside the plain, including obsidian and flint from the Zemplén hills, flint from Poland and perhaps the Bug–Dniestr region, *Spondylus* ultimately from the Aegean, and copper perhaps from central Serbia or Transylvania.[132] There is no obvious specialisation in processing within settlements.

In the Tiszapolgár phase, plain pottery was used and there were no figurines. Regional pot styles have been discerned, but the variations are not great.[133] Pots perhaps again signalled integration into broad patterns of kinship and alliance, rather than allegiance to chosen locales. Though plain, pots were clearly still important. As we have seen, they were regularly placed in graves at Tiszapolgár–Basatanya and other sites. In grave 3 at Öszentiván VIII, just south of Szeged in the southern plain, an adult man was buried with both food remains and pots.[134] There were two front legs and one hind leg from a calf, the brisket and rib of a cow, and all four legs of a sheep and a pig. There were four pots: a simple bowl, two necked jars (one 20 cm high) and a pedestalled bowl over 30 cm high. The tradition of ritualised hospitality was maintained. The flow of raw materials into the plain continued, perhaps now with some more signs of specialised involvement. No heavy copper implements have been found in the middle of the plain. Any one of the heavier shaft-hole hammer-axes found on the edge of the plain, for example, would have provided enough copper for all the ornaments in the Tiszapolgár–Basatanya cemetery, and metal-working was restricted to the Lucska group on the northern edge of the plain (Lucska or Lúčky is across the Ukrainian border in the upper Tisza valley).[135]

There is not the space to treat every other region exhaustively. I offer selective discussion of pottery and copper and gold from some other regions to underline the importance of the material dimension.

Pottery

Pottery was abundant, and was used in both domestic and sepulchral contexts. Vessels were very varied in form and size, from cups, bowls and dishes to large, closed, necked jars. In many areas the tradition of painted pottery continued, reaching exuberant heights with the

4.17 Vinča pottery from Anza. After Gimbutas.

bichrome and trichrome wares of the developed Cucuteni–Tripolye culture or graphite-painted wares of the Karanovo VI–Kodzadermen–Gumelnitsa complex. But it would be misleading to claim that the significance of pots resided in their decoration alone, and that plainer vessels, as in Thessaly in the fifth millennium BC, reflect less importance for hospitality and social interaction based on the taking of food and drink.[136] Many pots were well finished, even when plain, as in the Vinča culture where black, burnished vessels predominated. There was a considerable range of Vinča forms, well documented in sites like Anza, Selevac and Divostin. Paint, often red, was used on figurines, as on the Predionica heads.[137]

Many pots were probably used for the display and consumption of food and drink, but others were used for both storage (of dry foods and liquids) and food preparation. We do not know how many pots were actually used for cooking. In the houses of the Tisza-Herpály culture, there were sophisticated two-piece closed, clay ovens, with a firing compartment and a cooking or baking compartment.[138] Pots in the same contexts seem to be largely either bowls and dishes, perhaps for serving, and jars of various forms, perhaps for storage or preparation. Hearths and work places were also found in the spaces between houses.

One example shows the close links between pottery, hearth and house. House 14 at Divostin was a substantial, two-roomed structure with carefully laid floor and two hearths in the smaller room and three in the larger.[139] Pots were found in both rooms, tending to be near the hearths. Varied forms were classified as storage vessels for dry foods and liquids, food preparation vessels and food consumption vessels. There were proportionately more preparation vessels and fewer consumption vessels in the outer compartment than in the inner, even though the largest hearth and another were sited on the back wall of the inner compartment. Was food more publicly prepared than it was consumed? Or was food taken outside the house altogether, to be shared with all those entitled to it?

Pots in graves attest the significance and associations attached to clay vessels. For the most part, pottery from graves is similar to that from settlements, though in the case of the Tiszapolgár culture much more is known of burials than of settlements. Pots no less than figurines or houses may have been closely associated with individual people, both living and dead, and we may invoke again the ethnographic evidence referred to above.[140] Given that pots were in nearly every structure within settlements and carried a range of possible connotations or meanings, they were an important medium for the expression of people's identity. However, it is easier to appreciate such communication at the level of the individual site or cemetery, than over the broad areas defined by shared ceramic styles which many archaeologists have taken to indicate common cultural identities.

We do not know much about pottery production. There is no clear evidence within houses for manufacture, and the risk of fire would have encouraged firings to be made beyond settlements. Pyrotechnic skills, however, presumably drew on the long tradition of the domestic fire, and perhaps here again there was another metaphoric link, between the cooking of food and the firing of pots. Pottery nearly everywhere was well made, and creatively decorated with a vast array of motifs. Special skills were needed in some areas to obtain certain results, like the graphite decoration fixed at high temperatures on to some Karanovo VI–Gumelnitsa pottery.[141] Another example of unusual skill is the great gold-painted dish in grave 43 at Varna, described above. How the gold paint was applied and fixed is unknown, though this was possibly as a dust in a matrix of glue.[142] Despite these examples, pot making was probably not a restricted or specialised craft. Most pots were probably made near where they were used, according to regional styles. There are some cases of long-range movement of pots. Examples include the Cucuteni pots at Gumelnitsa and Căscioarele in the lower Danube valley; central Greek or Thessalian sherds at Corinth; a north Greek bowl in the Cucuteni level at Tîrpeşti; Hungarian plain vessels at Vinča; and Bükk vessels both far to the south and far to the north of their point of origin on the fringes of the Hungarian plain.[143] Such pots could have been exchanged in their own right or for their contents, or could have accompanied individuals on the move.[144] But these exceptions underline the general pattern of consistent regional styles, probably the sum of a considerable number of places of local production. What is harder to understand is the significance of these regional styles.

The regional ceramic distributions were varied in time and space. The sequence on the Hungarian plain ran from Linear Pottery uniformity through Tisza–Herpály–Csőszhalom regionalisation to renewed Tiszapolgár uniformity. The Vinča style extended over hundreds of kilometres, but it can be broken down into a number of smaller style zones about 100 km or more across. There may have been greater stylistic unity in earlier phases.[145] As the lower Danube was infilled from the later sixth millennium BC there were at first a number of more or less distinct regional styles there and in surrounding areas: for example at the beginning of the fifth millennium BC (the early Copper Age in Bulgarian terminology) Hamangia in the Dobrogea, Boian in the lower Danube north of the river, Poljanica in north-east Bulgaria, Gradesnica in north-west Bulgaria, Sava on the Black Sea coast, and

Maritsa (Karanovo IV/V) in central-south Bulgaria, while the large Vinča area lay to the west/north-west. By the late Copper Age of the later fifth millennium BC, the patterns had changed, with the Varna group on the Black Sea coast, a large Karanovo VI–Kodzadermen–Gumelnitsa area from central-south Bulgaria up into the lower Danube, and a fragmented later Vinča/Krivodol–Bubanj–Salcutsa IV area to the west/north-west.[146] It is possible, however, that the unity of the Karanovo VI–Kodzadermen–Gumelnitsa complex has been exaggerated. In Thessaly, generally plainer styles of pottery predominated in the Late and Final Neolithic, giving the impression of uniformity, but there were also more regionalised styles of fine painted pottery, largely restricted to eastern Thessaly.[147]

The conventional assumption has been that ceramic style expressed cultural unity, the distributions showing the existence of tribes or something similar.[148] A contrary view is that the variations were essentially continuous and without meaningful boundaries.[149] That does not seem to do justice to the evidence, but it is equally difficult to accept the equation between ceramic style and political organisation. Perhaps a better way to think of these distributions is in terms of shared ideas of identity, but without connotations of political unity. A sense of regional identity may have been less important than personal and local allegiances, and goods certainly crossed cultural boundaries, as shown by movements of stone, shell, pottery and copper. But it may have been part of the fabric of identity and of the sense of belonging and descent. It has been suggested, on the basis of figurine decoration, that there were distinctive regional dress styles.[150] Pottery may have been another way in which people were tied into a wider world and fixed to place.

Copper and gold

While pottery was generally made locally, copper usually had to be extracted from sources distant from the zones of settlement. Clay could be directly shaped into vessel forms, but copper had to be transformed by smelting from its ores, red or bronze-coloured metal coming from green and blue carbonate and oxide ores. The high temperatures used for firing pots were directed to melting copper for casting, to produce further transformations of the original raw material. Some copper artefacts were of practical use, from small hooks and needles to chisels, but many were decorative, such as rings and beads. The uses of heavy copper items like shaft-hole hammer-axes are uncertain. They may have been used as heavy-duty tools, they could have been weapons, or they may have had symbolic use only. Ornaments, tools and display items would have been in regular use and would have been seen, like pottery, but rather little copper has been found in settlements or in the occasional hoards. More occurs in graves. The supply of copper was not constant. It probably increased through time, from beginnings in the sixth millennium BC, into the fifth millennium BC. The example of the Hungarian plain has shown how an area without its own sources could obtain copper, but people furthest from the supply were liable to acquire the least. On the other hand, graves and offerings in the Varna cemetery on the Black Sea coast, an area without its own copper source, were plentifully supplied with copper from central-southern Bulgaria.

We usually regard copper artefacts in this period in the same way as we consider valuable material items today: as personal possessions, as things to accumulate, as objects of desire. Ethnographic evidence seems to reinforce and universalise this kind of value for copper, which in Africa was regarded as 'red gold'.[151] Not for nothing then is the label 'Copper Age' so often used, since copper seems to evoke and characterise changes in society by the fifth millennium BC. In one recent scheme, copper is seen as one means by which lineages compete for social position, through manipulation of production, exchange and display.[152] In another, copper belongs to the *agrios,* a set of concepts based on an idea of the wild, which was opposed to the nurturing associations of the house-centred *domus.*[153] I propose, instead, that copper in this period should be seen, like other craft products, as one more part of the shared material web in which the lives of people and their communities were enmeshed.

Copper production probably began independently of metallurgy in south-west Asia, where copper had been known in Anatolia and further east since at least the seventh millennium BC.[154] Even if the original idea of metalworking came from further east, subsequent development appears to follow its own path, and by the fifth millennium BC, metallurgy was probably more sophisticated in south-east Europe than in south-west Asia.[155] The beginnings of copper working in south-east Europe were both early and slow. Very simple copper objects, like hooks and rolled beads, have been found in sixth-millennium BC contexts. There have been claims for copper objects in Starčevo–Criş contexts, but in some cases at least it is likely that the items originated in later levels, as at Cuina Turcului and Balomir in Romania.[156] Other finds are more securely dated to the late sixth millennium BC, for example beads at Vinča, Selevac and Coka, and a fishhook at Gornea, in early Vinča contexts, beads from a Dudeşti or early Boian context at Cernica, and fragments (perhaps from beads) from Ovčarovo I and Usoe.[157] Such simple objects could have been beaten from native copper (naturally occurring in pure form) or smelted at modest temperatures (around 700–800°C) from the brightly coloured oxide and carbonate ores available on the surface. A fragment of copper slag from Anza IV seems to confirm copper smelting from about 5000 BC.

These early beginnings are important because they show that copper had been known about for a long time before the expansion of its production in the fifth millennium BC. Two copper extraction sites have been investigated, at Ai Bunar in central-southern Bulgaria and Rudna Glava in north-east Serbia, and another is known at Prljusa–Mali Sturac in the Rudnik range of central Serbia.[158] There could be many more to be discovered, including in Transylvania, because of the wide distribution of copper ores through the old rocks of the Balkan peninsula. These were places distant from contemporary settlement, far up remote hills in the Serbian cases. Activity at Ai Bunar dates to the Karanovo VI and possibly Karanovo V phases, while later Vinča pottery was found at Rudna Glava. At both sites several seams of oxide ore were followed through the parent rock, at Rudna Glava producing irregular channels, hollows and fissures, rather than regular shafts. Some thirty points of extraction were recorded at Rudna Glava along an exposure about 60 m long, and the potential scale of ore production appears to be large, but we do not know how much metal was actually extracted, and the source was exploited for a considerable period.

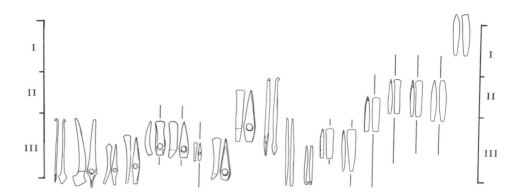

4.18 The development of heavy copper tools through the phases of the Copper Age in Bulgaria. After Todorova.

The known extraction sites coincide more or less both with the appearance of more metal in graves, often in the form of ornaments, and the development of heavy forms. These required casting (after melting at temperatures over 1000°C), at first in one-piece moulds to produce chisels and simple axes, and then in two-piece moulds to produce various shaft-hole hammer-axes, some with curved blades.[159] Presumably metal was smelted from its ores near the point of extraction, though neither Ai Bunar nor Rudna Glava has given such evidence. Some metal may have circulated as raw material, to be formed locally, as in the Varna area and in the lower Danube, and of course metal could be recycled if required. Like pottery, it was presumably worked outside settlements.

Despite the evidence of the extraction sites, it is very hard to estimate the scale of copper use. In Greece, there were local copper sources available but it is not certain that they were used, and there are few copper finds. There was a little copper at Sitagroi in phase II.[160] Only a few trinkets were imported into the Hungarian plain in the Tisza–Herpály phase. The supply increased somewhat in the Tiszapolgár phase, but was restricted in the central part of the plain, as we have seen. Copper was known in the Cucuteni–Tripolye culture of the forest-steppe/steppe zone.[161] There were copper sources in the western Ukraine, but according to metal analyses much raw material was derived from Ai Bunar, or later from Transylvanian sources. There were many ornaments, such as beads, rings, bands and appliqués, and few heavy tools. Far fewer items are known than further west. At Karbuna, to the south of Kisińov between the Prut and the lower Dniestr, not far into Ukrainian Moldavia, an unusually large group found in a pot accounts for about half of the known total from the whole area. As well as shells, there were hundreds of copper beads, dozens of flat anthropomorphic appliqués, a spiral ring and two heavy tools, an axe-hammer and an adze-chisel. These had probably been produced locally, because they were hot-forged rather than cast. Much smaller quantities have turned up within settlements, such as Novye Ruseshty. There was also a trickle of copper further east, occurring as ornaments in the graves of the Sredny Stog culture of the lower Dniepr–lower Don area and of the Khvalynsk culture of the middle and lower Volga. The metal came from south-east

Europe, via the Cucuteni–Tripolye culture, but there were distinctive local hammering and casting techniques.[162]

In other areas, where metal was more locally available, the scale of use is hard to estimate because of the circumstances of discovery. Rather little copper has actually been found on Vinča settlements, and the Pločnik hoard with heavy items may belong to the Krivodol–Bubanj Hum phase rather than a late Vinča horizon.[163] There is rather little copper in the later levels of sites like Karanovo and Azmak, though Ai Bunar is in the Sredna Gora hills near Nova Zagora. Unusual amounts have been reported from Dolnoslav.[164] On the other hand, copper occurs in many graves. Despite the distance of sources, the labour required for ore or metal transport and the skills needed to work metal, finished objects were plentiful in the cemeteries of the Black Sea coast and inland north-east Bulgaria. Copper occurred in eighty-two of the known 281 graves at Varna, and in ninety-nine out of more than 1000 at Durankulak, and in ten or fewer graves in the burial grounds at Golyamo Delčevo, Vinica and Devnya.[165] It was deposited in graves with men, women and children. At Durankulak there were differences in the occurrence of ornaments. Both sexes were provided with them, men with proportionately more bracelets and women with more rings. At Varna, shaft-hole hammer-axes appear largely to occur in men's graves.

Gold may have been obtained from a variety of sources. Analysis of the Varna gold suggested two varieties, and it was claimed that one had been derived from across the Black Sea in Caucasia. There are also many potential sources of stream gold in the Balkans, including in Bulgaria itself. It has also been suggested that nuggets could have been more widely available in the Balkans at this time, and that gold could have been mined as well as panned.[166]

The basic techniques required to work gold are simple. Little smelting may be required, and the material being soft is easily beaten. One explanation for the rarity of gold compared to copper might be that it was less attractive because of this very simplicity of working. Some of the abundance of gold at Varna could be explained as substitution for copper. In fact, according to preliminary analysis, some of the gold working at Varna was more sophisticated, combining casting with beating techniques.[167]

The gold objects from Varna show the greatest range of products and forms. In other areas, generally simple items like rings and beads were the most common. Gold working begins in the fifth millennium BC. There were very few gold artefacts in Greece, central-southern Bulgaria, the Vinča area or the forest-steppe/steppe zone.[168] There were some simple gold ornaments in the graves at Durankulak, and a small cache of gold rings at Hotnica. There was a scatter of simple beads and rings through the Gumelnitsa area of the lower Danube valley, and into the Carpathians.[169] There are two larger caches, at Moigrad in Transylvania and Tiszaszöllös on the Hungarian plain some 40 km downstream from Tiszapolgár.[170] Both caches have had chequered histories, and the circumstances of their deposition are uncertain, but it has been estimated that they could originally have weighed up to 2–3 kg and 3–4 kg respectively (compared with some 6 kg in the Varna graves). But stylistically the ornaments from Moigrad and Tiszaszöllös belong to the chronological horizon after the period considered here, equivalent to the Bodrogkeresztúr culture of the early fourth millennium BC. That leaves Varna as the major findspot of the fifth millennium BC.

Copper and gold were acquired to be used, to be displayed, worn and given away, not to be accumulated. In the latter situation we could expect many more hoards outside settlements, or concealed deposits within them, like the gold objects at Hotnica noted above. The rarity of hoards may suggest that cases like Pločnik and Karbuna were interrupted parts of exchange cycles. This shifts the emphasis away from possession and ownership to use and meaning. The circumstances of settlement space described extensively above make it unlikely that private accumulation would have been tolerated. The traditions of shared space and labour within tell and other settlements would have been a powerful sanction on such an ethic of acquisition. How should we then explain the growth of metalworking, including that of gold, through the fifth millennium BC?

Metalworking was part of a range of craft production which served both practical and other needs. The transference or exchange of a range of materials, including stone, shell, pottery and metal, would have served to link communities to a wider world. In a settlement pattern still partly mobile, it was useful to have friendly neighbours and helpful allies further afield. Exchange and gift-giving would have served to cement other social transactions such as marriage. In this perspective, metal, like other artefacts, had social functions or roles. It can perhaps better be seen as a constituent of such social transactions, rather than, as in the 'social storage' model, a material token to be given away in times of plenty for exchange for help in times of need.[171] Some of the most vigorous acquisition of copper and gold was centred on those regions with newer histories in the fifth millennium BC context, in which relationships between communities had to be forged rather than accepted from ancestral tradition.

Copper, like other transported materials, such as Melian obsidian taken to Thessaly from the early Neolithic onwards, may have stood for the successful participation of the community in exchange networks, from which flowed the ability to make gifts. Things of distant origin may have had symbolic value in their own right, as a counterpoint to ideas of fixed place. Things which were exchanged could have been regarded as either impermanent or timeless, part of a cycle of existence experienced also in the lives of both individuals and settlements. The transformations of the metallurgical process could have been a metaphor for domestication and fertility, the red colour of the metal standing also as a life symbol. Copper objects acquired by exchange could have been regarded as gifts not only from neighbours or other partners but from an other-world of spirits and gods, because of their exotic, magical properties. Grave goods could be regarded as offerings to the ancestors, an appropriate gift to be taken by the recently living to the community of ancestors. None of this need exclude rivalry and emulation, but there are two important differences to the conventional interpretations. Objects were for use, not personal accumulation, and rivalry, if it existed in these exchange systems as in some ethnographically documented ones,[172] was perhaps for abstract ideals such as esteem and reputation. In honouring the ancestors, as in all but one of the 'richest' graves at Varna, one brought honour on oneself.

The nature of society

The young girl buried in grave 24 at Tiszapolgár on the Hungarian plain had belonged briefly to a complex and diverse world. Her ancestors had had a rather different lifestyle from that of her own generation. For a number of centuries they had frequented chosen places in the landscape, creating settlement mounds. These had not endured, and perhaps an older regional tradition of mobility and independence in the end dominated. We should not take the continuities of the Neolithic period for granted. That the inhabitants of Karanovo at the end of the fifth millennium BC used the same mound, with a similar pattern of houses on either side of lanes, as their predecessors in the seventh millennium BC, is remarkable.

There is no easily available label with which to characterise these communities, and to look for one in ethnography or recent history is to miss their historical distinctiveness. I have suggested that regional history is fundamental for understanding the developments of the later sixth and fifth millennia BC. There were old histories of tradition, renewal and reaffirmation, and new histories involving the creation of antiquity, ancestry and position. I have argued that the concept of community, involving shared labour and space and common identity and values, was fundamental. I see little evidence for overt lineage or other internal differentiation, or for the emergence of households as autonomous units of production. There is limited evidence for intensification of basic subsistence production, agricultural or other. People still moved around, but were tied to chosen places. A concept and practice of wider community had to be created, and were rooted in and maintained through a strong sense of the past, tradition, ancestors and origins. The progressions of individual lives were mirrored in the cycles of house and tell occupations. The ever-present material world reinforced the values of community daily, in house form and decoration, ancestor figurines, artefacts in constant use like pottery, and exotics like obsidian and copper. Fertility was celebrated through ancestral figurines, and through the metaphor of copper, which was worn, displayed, given away, and offered to the dead. People ensured the future by looking to the past.

CHAPTER 5

ACCENTS OF CHANGE: SOUTH-EAST EUROPE, *c.* 4000–3000 BC

Carts and cattle near the bend of the Danube

Around 3500 BC a woman and a man were interred together in a burial ground. The cemetery, well above the Danube at Alsónémedi to the south-east of modern Budapest, was in some respects unremarkable. It belonged to the Baden or Pécel culture, and some forty people were buried here, laid in various positions in separate graves, and provided with goods or offerings such as pots and ornaments. We do not know whether there was a settlement nearby, and although the burial ground was further on to the interfluve to the east of the Danube than earlier sites, the cemetery was firmly in a regional tradition of such burial sites, established in the Tiszapolgár phase (seen in the last chapter) and continued in the intervening Bodrogkeresztúr phase around 4000 BC. The couple buried in grave 3 at Alsónémedi, however, belonged to a changed world.

The couple were buried along with two cattle in the same large grave.[1] The two animals were laid on their sides facing each other, heads nearly touching. On the right (thus on its right side) lay a mature cow, estimated by the wear on its teeth as 8 years old. On the left was a much younger animal, perhaps under 1½ years old, and possibly male: a young bullock. The human pair lay behind the animals, their heads near the animals' feet. They too lay crouched on their sides, facing each other and heads nearly touching. On the right (thus on her right side) was a woman estimated at 30–35 years old. She was adorned with a simple copper bead, and near her feet was an internally divided bowl, with facing raised knobs on the rim. On the left (and so on his left side) was a man of 35–40 years. By his body were two high-handled jugs, one plain, one decorated on its belly with incised lines.

Another grave, no. 28, also contained a double animal burial. Two animals, one older and one younger, again lay on their sides, facing each other with heads nearly touching. In this case, the older animal, a cow about 6 years old, lay on the left, facing a 10–12 month old calf. The sex of the calf could not be determined. Immediately behind the calf, with his head near its feet, lay the crouched skeleton of a man of about 40 years. He was on his left side, mirroring the position of the cow. Apart from two stone blades, the notable grave goods sat in a small stack directly behind the man's head and partly over the rear legs of the calf. These consisted of four clay vessels, presumably a set. At the bottom was another internally divided, knobbed bowl (the partition dividing the bowl into two thirds and one third). In it sat a high-handled jug. Both it and the bowl had lightly incised linear decoration. In the jug was a plain, narrow, tall, high-handled cup, and in that a broad-handled cup or ladle. The ladle had a couple of perforations in its handle. It was painted red inside and out, and had zigzag incised decoration around its main belly.

5.1 Cattle and human burials from Alsónémedi. Top: grave 3; below: grave 28. Photos: Magyar Nemzeti Múzeum.

These remarkable finds convey important changes. Double burials had occurred before, but there is a new kind of formality to the laying out of the couple in grave 3. That formality was extended to animals, which had previously only been used in burial rites in south-east Europe either as food, or as tokens, parts of bodies representing the whole. The animals here may have had new economic importance. The cattle appear to be of stock long domesticated. They seem now to have been used in important new ways, offering what has been dubbed 'secondary products' and uses, such as milk and traction power. The combination of mature cow and young bull would have made a good traction pair.[2] The pots in grave 28 seem to form a set. It is not hard to envisage a formalised drinking ritual, with perhaps two liquids or constituents to be mixed or served with the ladle into the high-handled jug and high-handled cup. But there are other implications. The people in these graves were defined in relation to the animals, and *vice versa*. From these two examples, it seems unlikely that there were rigid rules, but it is noticeable that in each case the man lay behind the younger, perhaps male animal, though the body position of the man in no. 28 mimicked that of the cow. We could be witnessing new attitudes to ownership, but perhaps there are also concepts here which interwove human and animal fertility and regeneration. Drinking milk (or animal blood?) could have celebrated such fecundity and continuity. The position of the pots in grave 28 directly behind the calf is suggestive of the closest possible ties.

Two other sites in the vicinity are also important indicators of change. At Budakalász, on the west side of the Danube about 15 km north of Budapest, there was a much larger Baden burial ground, with around 400 graves.[3] Again most graves contained single, crouched burials, unspectacularly furnished with grave goods. No. 3 contained a pair of cattle and a human couple. Here the humans lay in front of and transverse to the animals. A man lay crouched in front of a woman, and at right angles to two cattle side by side, their heads facing him. Of these, on the left was a calf and on the right an older beast. In the same burial ground, grave 177 was in fact devoid of human remains. In it were placed, under a big dish, a footed goblet and a small clay model or vessel in the form of a four-wheeled, high-sided cart. This was painted red inside and out, and had incised zigzag decoration.

Some 20 km to the south of Budapest, on a large island (Csepel) formed by the branching of the Danube, another cart model has come from a Baden burial at Szigetszentmárton.[4] Here three burials were discovered during house building, and the extent of the burial ground is not known. The cart model came from one grave, probably with an adult, but further details were lost. The model is complete, and its handle shows that it was also a vessel. Probably the Budakalász model was the same, but its handle or yoke is broken at its base. The Szigetszentmárton cup-model is also four-wheeled and high-sided, with incised zigzag decoration. The connections between people, animals, traction, transport and drinking are heightened by the presence in the same grave of seven further vessels, reminiscent of the situation in grave 28 at Alsónémedi. There were two internally divided, knobbed bowls, a dish, a handled cup, and one small and two larger high-handled jugs.

The cart cup-models have been hailed as showing the arrival in the northern part of the Carpathian basin of the innovation of wheeled transport.[5] This seems to have been developed first in Mesopotamia. Wooden wheels are preserved in various contexts in western Europe in the earlier third millennium BC (described in chapter 7), and it seems likely that the Baden cup-models reflect contemporary local vehicles, not just imitations of something much more distant. The earliest claimed model belongs to the Boleráz phase at the beginning of the Baden culture, from a pit assemblage at Boglárlelle on the south side of Lake Balaton. This is the rectangular superstructure of a waggon minus wheels, and there is a similar find from Radošina in Slovakia, also from a Boleráz context. The tradition of the

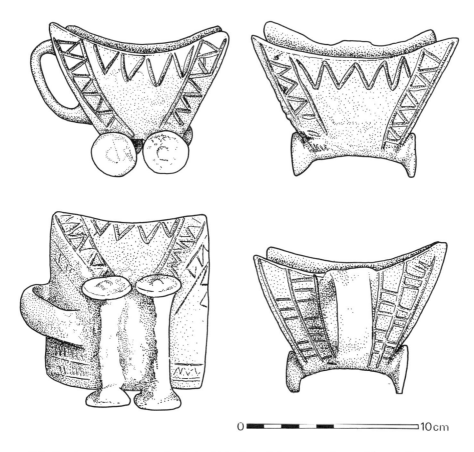

5.2 Cup in the form of a wheeled vehicle, from Szigetszentmárton. After Kalicz.

cart model continued into the Early Bronze Age in this region; many of that date have detachable wheels.

These finds indicate both new economic practices and new representations of human relationships. They are connected in part, through the appearance of wheeled vehicles, with a world to the east of the Carpathian basin. A further link with that world is provided by the nature of Baden pottery, especially the handled jugs and cups, since a wide repertoire of broadly similar shapes can be found from the Carpathian basin down into Bulgaria, northern Greece and the Aegean from about 3500 BC.[6] The details of the sequence on the Hungarian plain and its surrounds are not fully established. The Baden culture, distributed throughout Hungary and into westernmost Romania, eastern Austria and southern Slovakia, succeeds the Bodrogkeresztúr culture and the late Hunyadi phase by about 3500 BC. In certain areas there may have been discontinuity of settlement, though settlement evidence remains poorly understood. Most Baden occupation sites are represented by pits. It is possible that this only reflects a change in house construction. At the stratified site at Győr–Szabadrétdomb in the northern part of the *Kisalföld* in northern Transdanubia Boleraz pits succeeded earlier houses (of the Balaton–Lasinja phase, equivalent to

5.3 Baden culture cremation urns in anthropomorphic form, from Center near Ózd, northern Hungary. Photo: Kalicz.

Bodrogkeresztúr). The area was regularly flooded by the Danube and tributaries. The tradition of burial grounds was already old by the Baden phase, and in this respect there seems to have been continuity. Cremation urns in the northern Center group took the form of large anthropomorphic pots, which seems to hark back to much older traditions.[7]

Elsewhere in south-east Europe, there were major changes from about 4000 BC, which radically altered the world described in the previous two chapters. The people who lived near the bend of the Danube and were buried at Alsónémedi, Budakalász and Szigetszentmárton must have been aware of these transformations.

Accents of change

From about 4000 to 3500 BC there were extensive and profound changes throughout south-east Europe.[8] Most tells were abandoned, many for good, some for re-occupation after a period marked by significant stratigraphic hiatus. Such settlements as are known seem to be smaller and more dispersed; there are hilltop and cave occupations, and perhaps some defended sites. Settlement through the islands of the Aegean became much more prominent. The rich artefact assemblages of painted pottery and copper tools were replaced with plainer vessels, many in the general style already described for Hungary, and a new metallurgy based on the alloying of copper with arsenic was gradually introduced. Some cemetery burial continued, for example in central and eastern Romania and southern Ukraine, but the cemeteries of the Black Sea coast and its hinterland by and large lapsed, along with their adjacent tell settlements. Burials marked by small mounds appeared in parts of the region, as far west as the Hungarian plain, with greater concentrations in the lower Danube and the steppe zone of southern Ukraine.

The practice of mound burial (*kurgan* in Russian) has been connected with traditions on the steppes of easternmost Europe, from the Dniepr to the Urals. Other artefacts of supposed steppe origin have been found in south-east Europe at this time, such as small stone models of horseheads.[9] One often argued explanation for the changes in south-east Europe is the incursion of horse-riding steppe people. And it is to the period of *c.* 4500–2500 BC that most linguists date the existence of a homeland of speakers of Proto-Indo-European language, which many locate in the area north of the Black Sea and east to the Caspian Sea. Since there were other, non-Indo-European languages, and since Indo-European became widely distributed both in Europe and east to the Indian subcontinent, it follows that there was a historical dispersal.[10] Many have connected Balkan changes, steppe incursions and the dispersal of Indo-European language into one explanation. Restless steppe people, speakers of Proto-Indo-European, perhaps in search of grazing for their horses, pressed upon their sedentary neighbours to the west, causing that world to change, and ushering in new kinds of society based on more warlike and mobile life, less peaceful, and perhaps male-dominated.[11]

Was this the wider scene to which Alsónémedi, Budakalász and Szigetszentmárton belonged? I shall argue in this chapter that an important but less dramatic series of changes took place in this horizon. Change was neither synchronous nor identical from region to region. Histories impinge on other histories. South-east Europe was influenced by developments beyond it, perhaps in south-west Asia as much as on the steppes to the east. The shift in the nature of settlement, which lies at the heart of many explanations, must be seen against earlier patterns of mobility and the special character of tell life. Although there were influences from outside, much change can be attributed to internal 'structural reordering'. Indo-European language may have spread *after* these changes were underway, not as their primary cause. Language shift need not only be associated with large-scale (or small-scale) population movement. Indo-European may have come to be the prime language of communication in changed societies which emphasised mobility and inter-regional connections. In a sense, this was a reorientation possible from the beginning of the Neolithic.

The first step is briefly to outline the nature, scale and date of changes from region to region.

Greece and the Aegean

The picture is varied. In Thessaly there seems to have been continuity of occupation at many well-established tells. The overall pattern of settlement both in the Final Neolithic period, down to the later fourth millennium BC, and in the succeeding Early Bronze Age period, is not well documented. There may have been some abandonments of short-lived sites, and some contraction in site numbers, already in the Final Neolithic period.[12] This is consistent with dispersal of population. The islands of the Aegean became much more prominent from the Early Bronze Age, with many more settlements established, active trade and considerable craft specialisation. This is really another story, but from this date Thessaly appears a relative backwater compared with the islands and southern Greece.[13] In neither zone, however, does there appear to have been massive disruption.

In Thrace in northern Greece the situation may have been different. The stratigraphy at the tell of Sitagroi has a disjuncture between phases III and IV.[14] Phase IV dates from the second half of the fourth millennium BC; the later levels of phase III were not radiocarbon dated, but the last dated level belonged to the late fifth or early fourth millennium BC. The stratigraphy itself did not show a major hiatus. Buildings became larger and more complex in phases IV and V. There were fewer contemporary sites in the Drama region than in earlier phases, but this is consistent with either greater nucleation or dispersal of population, rather than with absolute decline. Regional site numbers had also declined in phase III. New kinds of pottery were current in phase IV, and the dark, rather plain wares, including handled jugs and cups, have been compared to Baden and other assemblages further north in the Balkans.[15] The picture is a combination of change and continuity.

Bulgaria and southern Romania

Many if not most of the established tells of this area were abandoned, said to be marked by stratigraphic hiatus – represented in some cases by the build-up of humic layers – at those sites which were subsequently reoccupied. Bulgarian archaeologists refer to this as the transition period, which may have lasted centuries rather than merely generations.[16] This is the end of the Karanovo VI–Kodzadermen–Gumelnitsa complex. At Karanovo and other large, old tells, there is said to be a prominent humic layer.[17] However, we are largely ignorant of variation within sites like this, and of the situation at smaller sites. The best published information comes from Ezero. There the Karanovo VII or Early Bronze Age levels (some eight building horizons in up to 2.8 m of deposit) directly succeeded the Karanovo VI levels in the main part of the site. On one side of the mound there had been a hiatus, but this was between the Karanovo IV and Karanovo VII levels, producing a humic layer up to 50 cm thick, and it seems clear that this was due to rearrangement of the site layout much earlier in the sequence. The notable tells of north-east Bulgaria were not used in the 'transition period'. It is tempting to assume that all these sites, both large and small, inland and coastal, came to a similar end at the same date, and in similar circumstances. This cannot yet be documented. Some occupations end with burning episodes, as at Golyamo Delčevo and Targovište. There had been earlier burning episodes, as at the end of site phase IV at Golyamo Delčevo, some of which may have been deliberate, to mark the end of cycles of household and settlement history, rather than either accidental or the result of hostile action. Some well-established sites were already abandoned well before the 'transition period'. On the basis of the radiocarbon dates, the thirteen occupation phases at Ovčarovo ended around or soon after 4500 BC.[18] Although we lack radiocarbon dates in support, it is

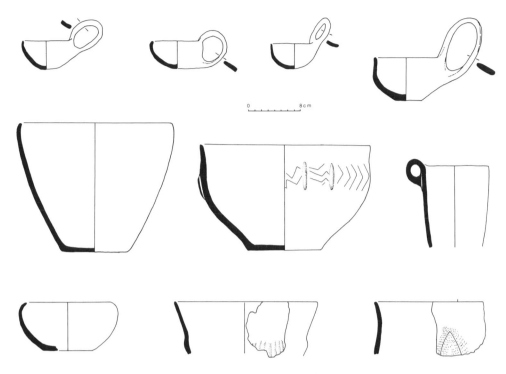

5.4 Selection of pottery from Sitagroi phase IV. After Sherratt.

possible that some of the lower Danube tells, such as Gumelnitsa itself and Căscioarele, were occupied for rather longer, into the transition period.[19] There is therefore considerable danger in mistaking gradual process for event.

In the Bulgarian sequence, constructed principally from the central-southern region, the 'transition period' is followed from the later fourth millennium BC by the Ezero–Karanovo VII phase of the Early Bronze Age. There was much change, with rather plain, dark pottery in the characteristic forms already referred to, very few figurines, and a simple range of copper artefacts including flat axes, at first made of copper alone and then alloyed with arsenic. Published detail on site layout and use is still largely restricted to Ezero itself.[20] The site had both Copper Age and Early Bronze Age levels (see above). In the Early Bronze Age levels, houses were stone-footed with apsidal ends, and not very closely spaced. There are traces of walling around the site, up to 1.5 m broad, but these were not necessarily defensive. Emmer, barley and pulses were cultivated, and sheep/goat, pigs and cattle kept. Does one emphasise the changes, or the evident continuity represented by reoccupation post-transition and the successions of rebuildings that followed?

In the lowest Danube/Dobrogea area, the suggested sequence runs Cernavoda I–Cernavoda III–Cernavoda II.[21] The situation is confusing since the various hilltop occupations at Cernavoda are not fully published, but the area is important. It takes us closer to the steppe zone, and it seems to show continuity of occupation through at least part of the 'transition period' recognised a little to the south and into the subsequent horizon. Both Cernavoda I and III have thick deposits with several occupation layers. Cernavoda can be tied to Cucuteni B to the north (discussed below). The pots of the complex are varied, and certainly rather different from those of the Gumelnitsa complex; there were plain and decorated wares, shell tempering and new shapes including again handled jugs and cups.

The middle Danube and the southern Carpathian basin

Radiocarbon dates may suggest that the widespread Vinča complex ended earlier than the Karanovo VI–Kodzadermen–Gumelnitsa complex, before 4000 BC. The succeeding group of more regional complexes is usually referred to as Salcutsa IV–Bubanj/Hum–Krivodol, and these may span the end of the Copper Age and at least the beginning of the 'transition period' further south.[22] The sites in question are varied and generally not well published. Salcutsa is a tell in south-west Romania, already occupied; Bubanj and Hum are hilltop occupations (with some depth of deposit) near Nis in eastern-southern Serbia; Krivodol is a hilltop occupation in north-west Bulgaria. The pottery assemblages include innovations like handled jugs and cups, as well as older techniques such as graphite decoration in the lower level at Bubanj.

Though imperfectly understood, these regional complexes seem to represent a continuation of the process of settlement dispersal already seen (and discussed in the last chapter) in the later Vinča culture.[23] By and large, sites were smaller, and widely distributed over the landscape, including in uplands. Occupation continued on the tell at Gomolava in the Sava valley, but in level II only hearths and artefacts were located, not formal house plans, and in level III there were Baden, Kostolac and Vučedol pits. The trend to dispersal continued in the Coţofeni culture centred on western Romania, which can be correlated with the Baden culture to its west and the Ezero culture to the south.[24] The settlement pattern is varied, with wide dispersal of sites. Pottery includes the handled forms seen already in Baden and Ezero contexts. Metalworking was on a reduced scale compared with both earlier and later periods in the area. There is evidence for local working, and the production of simple tools, ornaments and flat axes, and the novelty of triangular knife or dagger blades. One of these had a high arsenical content.

The Hungarian plain and its northern surrounds

The Baden phase, already discussed through the examples of Alsónémedi, Budakalász and Szigetszentmárton, corresponds to Ezero, Coţofeni and Cernavoda. It is also linked to developments to the north. The Baden distribution is centred on the Hungarian plain but extends into Transdanubia and north into southern Slovakia and eastern Austria. The northern connections will be followed in chapters 6 and 7.

There is one potentially intrusive element in the scene. On the Hungarian plain (as far north as Szolnok in the middle Tisza valley) and into western Romania, as already noted, there are many tumuli, which generally cover simple, single burials, very poorly furnished with grave goods, but often accompanied by red ochre.[25] These are not well dated, but many scholars equate them with the Baden and Coţofeni cultures; some at least are cut by Vučedol pits. In area surveys, for example around Dévaványa in the east-central part of the plain, the evidence suggests complementary Baden and tumuli distributions.[26]

There is little space to discuss the Bodrogkeresztúr culture, which is the major phase intervening between Tiszapolgár and Baden, and corresponds to the 'transition period' further south. This was largely a phenomenon of the plain. In general it seems to represent the continuation of a lifestyle which was established in the Tiszapolgár phase and in many respects continued into the Baden phase, though the details of the transitions are not well understood. Perhaps the most striking example of continuity comes from the continued use of the burial ground at Tiszapolgár–Basatanya itself, though burial rites changed a little in detail.[27] Settlement evidence remains sparse. A new kind of site for the plain is represented at Füzesabony on its northern edge by the three or four post rings (with an outer diameter of over 25 m) around a central deep pit containing many pots, the skeleton of a goat and the bones of a lamb, a pig, a roe deer and a hare. A related site is known at Szarvas in the lower Körös valley. Another site, which probably dates to the late Bodrogkeresztúr or Hunyadi phase, also suggests some changes. Tiszalúc–Sarkadi is up in the northern part of the plain.[28] It was over 100 m across, and surrounded by a palisade. Within there were about thirty post-framed houses, some over 10 m long, set in four rows. The inhabitants seem to have concentrated their efforts on cattle keeping, consistent with Baden practice.

The forest-steppe and the steppe regions of eastern Europe

This is the last element in what has been called the 'circum-Pontic interaction sphere'.[29] Before discussing the next horizon of changes, I shall briefly resummarise the development up to this point. The distinction between the forest-steppe zone and the steppe zone remains important.[30]

Acculturation and assimilation. In much earlier periods, there is quite abundant evidence for indigenous populations of foragers, based principally in the river valleys of the forest-steppe zone, such as the Southern Bug, Dniestr and Dniepr. The extension of a Neolithic lifestyle east of the Carpathians is associated with the Criş and then the LBK cultures, in the sixth millennium BC.[31] This may have been by a process of secondary colonisation, which is compatible with initial beginnings by acculturation in south-east Europe as a whole. That process was continued and extended in the Pre-Cucuteni phase of Moldavia, around or soon after 5000 BC, and then maintained in the fifth millennium BC by the Cucuteni–Tripolye cultures. This established Neolithic communities as far east as the middle Dniepr. Two phases and zones of native acculturation should be noted, first in the Bug–Dniestr group, neighbours of the Criş and LBK groups, and then in the Dniepr–Donets group of the early fifth millennium BC.[32] After the probable assimilation of Bug–Dniestr population, the Dniepr–Donets culture represents the indigenous population of the forest-steppe zone. These people were river-based. They hunted, fished and foraged in the river valleys, and also acquired some domesticated animals. There is a little evidence for cereal use, but we are not sure whether this was locally cultivated. Some sites of the group are found in the steppe zone, as far down as Mariupol on the Sea of Azov. A

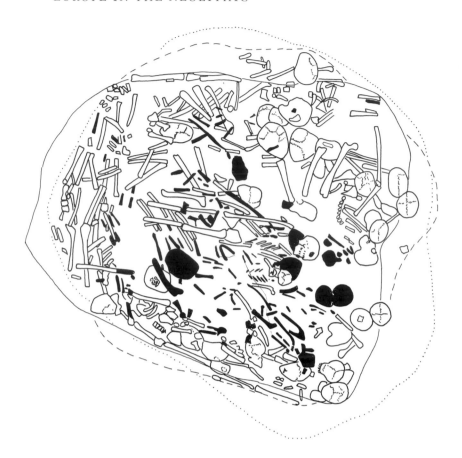

5.5 Dniepr–Donets culture collective burials in pit 3 at Nikolskoye. Burnt bones are shown black. After Telegin.

strong sense of local identity is suggested by the striking burial grounds of the group, with collective extended burials in pits and trenches. The lifestyle of these people may have been one of tethered mobility.

The Sredny Stog culture: eastern neighbours of the Cucuteni-Tripolye complex. At some stage during the fifth millennium BC the Dniepr–Donets culture is replaced by the Sredny Stog culture, which was contemporary with the major fifth-millennium phases of the Cucuteni–Tripolye complex.[33] To the east of the Sredny Stog area there were several other similar groups (notably the Khvalynsk group) in the 1500 km or more before the Ural mountains. The Sredny Stog distribution was partly in the forest-steppe and partly in the steppe zone, in the middle and lower Dniepr and lower Don valleys and surrounds. The lifestyle may still have been based on restricted mobility, and orientated to valley resources. Settlements are generally not well defined, with thin occupation layers and little good evidence for structures. Pottery was in use. Burial grounds continued, consisting largely of simple, small collective burials, with goods of pottery and tools, and with red ochre. Some late burials were marked by small circles of stones.[34]

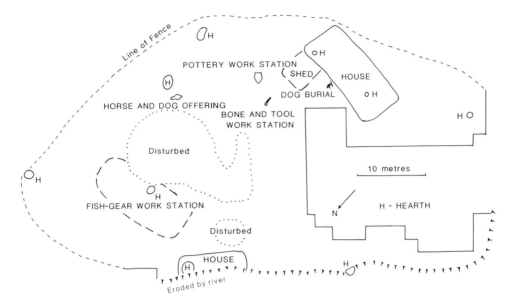

5.6 Simplified plan of the Sredny Stog occupation at Dereivka. After Telegin and Mallory.

Sredny Stog subsistence was varied. People fished, hunted small and large game including wild horse, and kept some sheep/goats, cattle and pigs (as well as dogs). They also probably herded horses and there is evidence for control of the horse by bridles, probably for riding rather than traction. This takes us to the site of Dereivka.

Dereivka: horse riding? Dereivka is on a promontory of the Omelnik river, a tributary of the middle Dniepr, between Kiev and Dniepropetrovsk.[35] An area about 60 by 40 m includes hearths, pits and two or more large rectangular structures, with slightly earth-sunk floors. Other areas seem to have been given over to specific tasks, connected with pot use, bone tool manufacture and the preparation of fishing gear and fish processing respectively. Ducks and several species of fish show the importance of riverine resources. A lot of game was hunted, including red deer, and cattle, pigs and sheep/goats were kept.

Horse bones were the most numerous remains. These could have come from both wild and managed animals. Since the horse in general shows little sign of domestication in its bone structure or size, the evidence for management is largely circumstantial. One argument is that Dereivka was on the edge of the transition from forest-steppe to steppe and therefore beyond the normal ecological range of horses in open grassland. The abundance of horse remains thus indicates herd management. It remains to be seen whether this fits detailed environmental reconstruction. Most of the horse bone could not be sexed, but the few positive identifications were all of males. Comparative study of wild horse populations in the modern USA shows that within the horse population there are harem bands and bachelor bands; a harem band contains about 30 per cent males, and bachelor groups tend to be both widely dispersed and rather unpredictable in their movements; it is thought likely that a random cull of the whole population would yield less than 50 per cent males. It has therefore been argued that the dominance of males is best seen as the product of the culling of a managed herd rather than of the hunting of a wild herd. On the other hand, the age data suggest that most of the Dereivka horses were 6–8 years old, older than might be expected in an economic cull of managed animals.

There is also evidence for riding. Perforated pieces of antler have been claimed as the cheekpieces of simple bridles. The premolar teeth of one Dereivka stallion show wear in the form of bevelling and abrasion which have been suggested, again on the basis of comparisons with modern wild and feral horses, as the result of chafing against a solid bit. If this was so, the animals must have been guided from behind and therefore probably ridden. Dereivka dates from around 4000 BC and after (and has Tripolye B2 pottery imports), earlier than known evidence for the wheel.

Rather few other jaws were available for study. The midden deposits of the site seem to have few skull fragments, though detail of skeletal representation has not yet been published. This suggests that animals were butchered offsite, and it is likely that the primary use of the horses was as a source of meat. Other Sredny Stog sites include horse bones, but no other site yet has shown the dominance of horse remains which is so striking at Dereivka, apart from Botaj near Petropavlovsk far to the east in northern Kazakhstan, east of the Urals. The Dereivka site could be seen as a station with a very broad subsistence base. Pigs and fish indicate reduced mobility, and horse exploitation may have been either incipient management or specialised, perhaps opportunistic hunting. The age and sex arguments for management are uncertain. No other jaws studied showed the same bit wear. The stallion in question may well have had unusual status, since it was part of a special deposit within the site. This consisted of the animal's head and left foreleg, along with the articulated remains of two dogs. There were also possible human bones, the two possible antler cheekpieces, and an animal clay figurine, possibly in the shape of a boar. The combination of head and feet strongly suggests a horsehide.

This detail about the Dereivka horse remains is important, since a wider argument about the emergent mobility of steppe people and their effect on their Cucuteni–Tripolye neighbours is partly based upon it.[36] The Dereivka evidence has been taken as circumstantial support for the model which sees increasing pressure from the east on Cucuteni–Tripolye population. Part of this argument concerns the nature of some late Tripolye sites, contemporary with the Sredny Stog culture. A few sites are very large, covering tens of hectares, with hundreds of structures, often concentrically arranged. Notable examples range from the 270 ha of Majdanets'ke to the 400 ha of Talljanky. These sites are found to the west of the Dniepr, in the forest-steppe zone. Some have ditches around them, and the interpretation has often been offered that these were defensive locations, protecting large agglomerations of population from the threat of marauders mounted on horses.[37]

This model is misguided. The Dereivka evidence for horse management is ambiguous, and that for riding at best limited. That is not to say that there was not experimentation going on with the horse as a mount. Rather few large Tripolye sites have been fully published, and we do not know enough about the nature of the structures concerned. An alternative model would be that these large concentrations were in part special, seasonal sites, equivalent to the tells further west. There were many other much smaller contemporary Tripolye sites, and the largest sites were spaced at more or less regular intervals among these.[38] In any case, dispersal is often a better defence against marauders than agglomeration. There was undoubtedly contact between the Cucuteni–Tripolye complex and the Sredny Stog culture, seen principally in the form of imported Tripolye pots and small quantities of copper objects in Sredny Stog contexts, usually graves. This is consistent with sporadic interaction rather than violent clashes or persistent threats.

The late Cucuteni–Tripolye horizon and the Yamnaya complex. The causal links between the developments of the previous horizon and the changes of the next are uncertain. For some, the evidence suggests the restructuring of settled populations under the strong influence of substantial incursions from the east.[39] The evidence can also be taken to show considerable continuity of development.

The late Cucuteni–Tripolye complex is succeeded in the mid to later fourth millennium BC by the complexes known as Usatovo–Gorodsk (sometimes labelled Tripolye C2) and Horodiştea–Folteşti. Gorodsk is far inland, west of the Dniepr near Zitomir (to the west of Kiev). Many of the previously occupied late Tripolye sites seem to have been abandoned in this phase. Usatovo is near Odessa on the Black Sea coast, firmly in the steppe zone which had been avoided in the Tripolye period. Horodiştea and Folteşti are both on the Prut river, in the former Cucuteni area. Seen in wider perspective, this restructuring of settlement mirrors that seen in the central Balkans about a millennium earlier. Dispersal and fragmentation were accompanied by the intake of the southern steppe zone. This might have been influenced by people to the east of the Dniepr, but there is little direct evidence for this, and we know rather little about Usatovo subsistence. Sheep/goats seem to have been more common than cattle or pigs, and horses were also used. Animal bone assemblages from Horodiştea, Folteşti, and the related sites of Stoicani and Erbiceni include horse remains, but there were far more cattle, sheep/goats and deer.[40]

There were many changes to the material culture of this horizon. Some painted pottery in the Cucuteni-Tripolye tradition continued, but most pots were plainer, some with cord decoration. There were some schematic figurines. Metal objects now included blades with central midribs and shaft-hole axes cast in two-piece moulds. Analysis shows low percentages of arsenic in the copper. The metal sources were presumably still to the west, either in Bulgaria or in the Carpathian region.[41]

Burials show further changes.[42] There were hardly any late Cucuteni-Tripolye burial grounds, whereas in this horizon there are numbers of cemeteries of mainly single graves, from Brailitsa in the Dobrogea (in a Cernavoda II context), to Decea Mureşului in Transylvania (whose date is still uncertain) and Usatovo itself. There are more isolated burials, as at Tîrpeşti. There are also many tumuli through the area of the Usatovo culture into the zone of the mouth of the Danube. Some may actually post-date this horizon, as at Stoicani, Erbiceni and Corlateni where the barrows overlie occupations of the Horodiştea–Folteşti complex. At Casimcea near Tulcea in the Danube delta an ochre-sprinkled skeleton under a large tumulus was accompanied by a stone zoomorphic head, part of the series already referred to. Some burials under tumuli were further marked by stone stelae, decorated with schematic human figures, holding hafted axes or wearing them in their belts. Tumuli are also known in Bulgaria, especially in the north. Six mounds in a group at Plačidol, near Tolbuchin, were of varied sizes; the biggest appear to have been enlarged in the process of successive interments. Thus in mound 1, some 7 m high and 55 m in diameter, grave 1 was not the primary feature. It contained the crouched, ochre-sprinkled skeleton of an adult in a rectangular grave pit nearly 5 m deep. The skeleton lay above traces of planking, and at one end of the grave pit there were the remains of two wooden wheels, 75 cm in diameter (and with a probable axle span of 1.2 m), presumably matched by another pair at the other end, now destroyed. The excavators assigned the burial to the Folteşti–Cernavoda II–Coţofeni–Ezero horizon, though like many other such finds it is probably not securely dated.

Far to the east, the Yamnaya (or pit-grave) culture represents the final element of the 'circum-Pontic interaction sphere'.[43] This was distributed from roughly the Dniepr (and perhaps a little to its west) to far east, to the Volga-Ural basin, a distance around 2000 km. The culture represents the first sustained penetration of the dry grasslands of the steppe zone. Burials and short-lived camps are the best-known kinds of sites, though there are exceptions like the walled settlement of Mikhaylovka on the lower Dniepr. The fauna from this site included cattle, sheep/goats, pigs and many horses; much game was hunted, and there was plant processing equipment. Horses were probably exploited still for meat, and it is thought that the evidence for riding is more firmly established in this horizon, though that evidence largely consists of bridle cheekpieces. Waggons are known, in the form of wheels and sometimes complete vehicles from graves. These were probably pulled by oxen rather than by horses. Different metalworking traditions emerged, for example in the Volga-Ural basin as well as in the lower Dniepr area; in the latter area deliberately alloyed arsenical bronze of Caucasian origin was predominant.

The Yamnaya complex represents an intake of the steppe zone, partly prefigured in the previous horizon (and directly descended from the Sredny Stog and Khvalynsk cultures), and based on a mobility provided by ridden horse, wheeled waggon and sheep/goats, but which – at least in some areas – was still tethered to large, more enduring bases in the major river valleys. The picture is not one of aimless wanderings by restless nomads. This characterisation is important in trying to understand changes from about 4000 BC further west in Greece and the Balkans.

Explanations of change

I have indicated, in this brief survey, that the many changes varied from region to region, and that their dates did not all coincide. Alterations in settlement pattern in the late Vinča horizon, for example, preceded those of the Usatovo–Horodiştea horizon by up to a millennium. The end of the Karanovo VI–Kodzadermen–Gumelnitsa complex may have occurred around 4000 BC while the late Cucuteni-Tripolye complex continued (Tripolye B2–C1). Very different kinds of explanation have been offered. By and large, explanations which rely on external stimuli are based on seeing a narrow horizon of successive and interrelated events, while explanations which emphasise internal factors are compatible with more gradual transformations, or at least of varying rate.

Changes in the natural environment: climate and sea level

Some scholars attribute change to alterations in the natural environment which had supported the previous generations of Neolithic and Copper Age life.[44] We know from tree ring and other evidence in the Alpine zone that periodically there were colder phases, including at intervals during the fourth millennium BC, and these might have been accompanied by drier conditions further south, which in turn could have affected the subsistence practices which supported tells and other sites, and could have encouraged greater mobility. In Greece, this could have made the Aegean more attractive than the plains of Thessaly. One might predict therefore that there would be more coastal settlement on the Black Sea coast, compared with areas inland, but here another kind of evidence comes into play. The history of post-glacial sea level rise in the Black Sea is not as well studied as in the Mediterranean. Recently, submerged Copper Age settlements have been found in south-east Bulgaria on the Black Sea coast, and it has been estimated that sea level there at the end of the fifth millennium BC was 6–7 m below the present one. Sites in the Varna estuary were seriously affected, and part of the Durankulak cemetery is also below present sea level.[45]

It would be unwise to discount such basic changes, but the evidence is very incomplete. We do not know the climatic record of south-east Europe in any detail for this period. It looks inconsistent to argue for tell abandonment due to rainfall changes at the same time as the steppes, a naturally dry zone, begin to be purposefully colonised. And it is hard to see why sea level rise should have caused more than the relocation of individual coastal sites.

Changes from the outside: enter the Indo-Europeans

Before their recent extension into all parts of the globe, related Indo-European languages were spread from north and west Europe to the Indian subcontinent. Study of the possible history of Indo-European language – 'linguistic palaeontology' – has focused on those elements which were shared by widely dispersed early versions (or families) of Indo-European. With the important assumptions that languages are never static, but constantly evolving, and that they tend to vary across space as well as through time, and with the inference through linguistic palaeontology of an ancestral 'proto-lexicon', the deductions have long been made that there was a circumscribed historical area in which the ancestral version of Indo-European language – Proto-Indo-European – was spoken, and that there was a historical moment of dispersal from such a homeland.[46] The proto-lexicon has words and terms, which have been used more closely to define the place and date of the supposed homeland. Some are words for geographical features, but river, mountain and forest are not very specific signposts, and it would not be surprising for mobile people to have encountered them. Other words, for example for beech and salmon, have been claimed as indicating a northern European area, but the 'salmon' word may not refer to migratory Atlantic salmon.[47] Various terms indicate aspects of a perhaps patrilineal descent system and male-dominated social relations. Other, potentially more helpful terms include pottery, cattle, sheep, wool (and spinning, weaving and sewing), pig, horse, yoke, plough, wheel (and axle and nave), and metal, probably copper. Many specialists are inclined to place the homeland on the steppes north of the Black Sea and the Caspian Sea, though others favour central and northern Europe. A timeband of 4500–2500 BC is suggested by many. The upper limit is defined by technological and subsistence changes, since metals, wheels and horses were obviously not in use in much earlier periods. The lower limit is defined by the fact that the first recorded Indo-European languages appeared in Anatolia in the early second millennium BC, and the supposed dispersal must therefore have preceded their appearance in Anatolia by some time.

Some of the arguments in this chain of inference are weak, and it is no surprise that there are many disagreements among the specialists. More sophisticated versions of the dispersal hypothesis seek to emphasise the likelihood that Proto-Indo-European was itself probably a series of inter-related versions in a continuum of language change. It is easy to criticise the use made of particular elements of the proto-lexicon. Horses, for example, were found in late glacial and early post-glacial Europe; the proto-lexicon term may refer to wild as much as to managed or domesticated horses. It has been argued that neither 'horse' nor 'wheel' had single roots, and may not have been in the proto-lexicon after all. The idea of a proto-lexicon prefers indigenous tradition to external innovation, and historical linguists claim to be able to detect loan words among already differentiated languages, but the case of the wheel, which seems to have been developed in Mesopotamia, not on the steppes, is a contradiction to the normally inferred basis for shared vocabulary.[48]

In the 'kurgan hypothesis' the dispersal of Indo-European speakers from the steppes is causally linked to the decline and transformation of settled societies to the west, from west of the Dniepr right through to Bulgaria and Greece and the central Balkans.[49] It has been suggested that there were successive waves of kurgan influence, reinforcing the initial impact on Cucuteni–Tripolye neighbours, and ultimately bringing a more mobile, patriarchal, male-dominated and aggressive society into being. One motive canvassed for the expansive behaviour of steppe peoples was the search for grazing.[50]

Evaluation: the kurgan advance and Indo-European dispersal

The kurgan hypothesis brings to the archaeology of the Copper Age a vision of irresistible steppe forces, which have more to do with later historical cases like the Mongols than the very varied patterns of change outlined above. It relies on crude characterisation, on the one hand of Sredny Stog and Yamnaya lifestyles as wholly mobile, and on the other of tell-centred existence as wholly sedentary. I have tried to show that both generalisations are flawed. As one more example, while horses constituted 80 per cent of the animal bone assemblage at the Don Yamnaya site of Repin Khutor, at Mikhaylovka on the lower Dniepr the figure was 10–15 per cent.[51] The search for grazing seems a weak argument for supposed expansion, and the argument can rapidly become circular. Horses were not dominant in Horodiştea–Folteşti assemblages, as we have seen, and occurred sporadically in other contexts. On the Hungarian plain, there were some horse bones in Tiszapolgár contexts, and more in Baden contexts,[52] but these could well be from animals of local rather than steppe stock; there has been lively debate about their status. Horses were not found in

Greece till the third millennium BC or later. The kurgan hypothesis ignores the chronology of change in south-east Europe. Were the hypothesis to be more convincing, one should see the earliest signs of radical transformation on and west of the Dniepr, with subsequent shock waves radiating out to the west. In fact, the reverse seems to be the case, changes working eastwards. I have emphasised the alterations of the late Vinča and Tiszapolgár horizons, and radiocarbon dates indicate that the 'transition period' of Bulgaria was contemporary with the late part of the main Cucuteni–Tripolye sequence. Different sorts of explanation seem to be called for.

One recent solution has been to attack the whole notion of a linguistic dispersal at this date and place it much earlier, with the supposed spread by colonisation of the initial Neolithic lifestyle, from a claimed homeland in Anatolia.[53] Underlying this view is a reluctance to accept change through invasion, but the solution offered is in its way no less problematic, since it equates the spread of language with the spread of people in a given historical movement. Although the hypothesis of much earlier dispersal does rightly point out many of the archaeological difficulties with the kurgan hypothesis, it has been much criticised as linguistically implausible.[54] It assumes that, following dispersal from Anatolia in the seventh millennium BC over broad areas of Europe, a considerable uniformity of language would have been maintained over thousands of kilometres and several millennia, up to the first recorded Indo-European languages of the early second millennium BC. All other reliable observations of language histories make this very unlikely, and on that basis the Indo-European dispersal must have been more recent. The early dispersal hypothesis further assumes that the spread of the Neolithic lifestyle was the result of 'demic diffusion': the spread of new people.

There are also specific difficulties with non-Indo-European languages. If Indo-European came from Anatolia, why were there still non-Indo-European languages like Hattic and Hurrian in eastern Anatolia in the early second millennium BC? The first known language, Sumerian in Mesopotamia in the third millennium BC, has little trace of interaction with Indo-European, and the first recorded Indo-European in Anatolia seems to be a minority language within a predominantly non-Indo-European community. And if Indo-European reached Greece as early as the seventh millennium BC, why are there so many non-Indo-European words and placenames in the Greek recorded from the second millennium BC onwards?[55]

Other superficially attractive glosses have been proposed, but they too ignore the likelihood of constant language change through time. One proposal is for an initial early dispersal with incoming agricultural population from the seventh millennium BC, as far as the limits of the LBK culture in the sixth millennium, to be followed by a phase of assimilation through the further diffusion of secondary agricultural innovations in the fifth millennium, and finally extended by elite interchange in the fourth to third millennia.[56] This does not assume a uniform process of Neolithic spread, and it explores other mechanisms of language dispersal, to which we will return below, but it too assumes that the early language of south-east Europe would have remained essentially static for several millennia. Another more radical hypothesis has been to locate the Indo-European homeland in a broad band across central and northern Europe, and to date it as far back as the Mesolithic or even

Palaeolithic.[57] This avoids some archaeological problems with explaining dispersal within Europe at a later date, but it creates others to do with the spread of Indo-European beyond Europe. Above all, it is thought by the historical linguists to be quite unrealistic. Proto-Indo-European of the fifth to fourth millennia BC was probably only one strand in a shifting continuum of language change. It seems most unlikely that it existed in unaltered form several millennia earlier. To posit an ancestral Pre-proto-Indo-European is to enshrine the unsatisfactory analogy of a tree of descent.[58]

Unifying archaeological and linguistic hypotheses: internal and external factors, causes and symptoms, and processes of language change

Is it possible to frame a general explanation which satisfies both archaeologists and historical linguists? Three elements are fundamental to a better account: attention to internal processes of change within south-east Europe and their differing dates and rates from region to region within the area; recognition of external factors affecting south-east Europe; and consideration of the very varied ways in which language can spread. Drawing on these three elements I suggest that the end of the fifth millennium BC was not the only horizon in which changes towards a more dispersed settlement pattern took place, but that this was the date by which the process was established over most areas. The Neolithic and Copper Age lifestyle was probably always partly mobile. Innovations such as wheeled transport and horse-riding, coming in from the outside, may have helped to reinforce tendencies to fragmentation and mobility which were already strong. Patterns of exchange may even have been affected by the emergence, further afield, of urban centres in Mesopotamia in the fourth millennium BC. Indo-European language may have spread not as the result of substantial population movement, but as a common language of communication and long-distance interaction in a world in which mobility and exchange became even more important. There may have been some movement of steppe people into Ukraine, Moldavia and the lower Danube, but this is as likely to have been opportunistic infill as primary cause of change in that area.

Processes of internal change should be visible in the sequences of individual sites like Selevac in Serbia or Gorzsa, Öcsöd–Kováshalom and Berettyóújfalu–Herpály on the Hungarian plain, in the first part of the fifth millennium BC.[59] The fluctuating patterns there of plot and house-site tenure and of population agglomeration emphasise the special nature of those long-lived tells which we have tended to take for granted as the benchmarks of the Neolithic lifestyle. On the Hungarian plain, a strong sense of community and shared identity, distinguishing criteria of the Neolithic lifestyle, were still maintained in the Tiszapolgár phase, and indeed through the subsequent Bodrogkeresztúr and Baden phases, but through the equation of the community of the dead with place rather than by the establishment of a centralised attachment by people to chosen physical and cultural locations. It is hard to say whether this really represents a fundamental shift in values. People may have preferred a lifestyle which allowed them to combine both independence and integration. It has been commonplace to infer changed patterns of ownership, economic practice, social structure and inter-group aggression in connection with such changes in residence and attitudes to place. As I have sought to show, this may be radically misguided. The secondary phase of fragmentation may have been made possible by the strong traditions of integration created by the phase of tell-orientated life.

To what extent could such suggested processes be followed in the southern Balkans and in Thessaly? It is worth remaking the point that not all tells came to an end at the same time, though that is the general impression. There was probably greater continuity in Thessaly, but even there the history of settlement was marked by a series of foundations and abandonments. It was noted above that Ovčarovo in north-east Bulgaria ceased to be occupied, after many generations of use, well before the end of the Karanovo VI–Kodzadermen–Gumelnitsa horizon. Individual site history becomes process when the biographies of different locations begin to converge. It is legitimate to scrutinise the plans and inventories of sites like Ovčarovo and its neighbours in north-east Bulgaria for signs of change during their use, and one wishes fervently that there were more published sites in other areas where similar exercises could be carried out in detail. No single style of site layout predominated, and the quantities of items like pottery, copper and shell, while varying from coast to inland, do not seem really to have altered through the long and repeated occupations.[60] While tell life was maintained, its traditions and constraints were still constantly re-enacted. The evidence of animal bones may be more promising. At sites like Ovčarovo, Golyamo Delčevo and Targovište in north-east Bulgaria a number of cattle and sheep/goats were kept well past the age at which it was economic to kill them for meat. An increase in such mature animals through the site sequence is also reported from Poljanica, with a corresponding (perhaps compensating) increase in the number of wild animals. 'Secondary' products and uses, such as milk, wool, transport and traction power may have begun to be important.[61] These were probably important elements in the fourth millennium BC, and it is significant that they can be traced earlier.

The concept of 'secondary products' has many attractions.[62] It emphasises that milk, wool, and traction for cultivation by the plough and for wheeled transport may not have been important elements of the first generations of Neolithic life. It therefore concentrates attention on sequences of change. The initial formulation of the model is not without difficulties.[63] It proposed that secondary products (a 'revolution' of equal importance to Childe's original 'Neolithic Revolution') were introduced from the Near East in a horizon of change in the later fourth millennium BC. The most convincing such innovation is that of the wheeled vehicle, for which there is pictographic evidence in the Near East from the first half of the fourth millennium BC, in the form of Sumerian pictograms from Uruk. (The Baden cart models should date between 3500 and 3300 BC; diffusion, if such it was, must have been rapid.) The evidence concerning ploughs is more complex. There are no representations in the Near East till the third millennium BC, though the cultivation of certain soils implied by site locations (*terra rosa* soils used in the Halafian period of the fifth millennium BC) may indicate the use of such technology. There have been claims for light plough or ard shares in pre-fourth-millennium BC contexts, in both south-east and central Europe, and castrated oxen can probably be documented from measurements of longbone proportions as far north as the LBK culture of the later sixth millennium BC.[64] As we shall see in chapter 7, the horizon of preserved ard marks in north-central and western Europe from the mid fourth millennium BC can be explained in part by the appearance then of monuments such as barrows which were suitable to preserve old land surfaces. There is enough variability in the age patterns of sheep/goats and cattle in earlier assemblages to allow some previous exploitation of milk and wool. (The question of whether people could tolerate milk or not – dependent on their enzymes – does not fundamentally affect issues of dating.)

The 'secondary products' horizon may really constitute a phase in which pre-existing trends were accelerated and accentuated as part of changing patterns of residence and life-style. Some innovations may have come in from the outside, such as wheeled vehicles and perhaps ridden horses. The handled pottery described at the start of this chapter suggests forms of hospitality which were held in common from the Aegean to the Hungarian plain, and therefore shows wide-ranging contact. Baden wares may imitate metal vessels of the north Aegean, as at Troy II. One hypothesis is that fermented drinks, based on milk or cereals, spread now in imitation of alcoholic Aegean or Near Eastern drink, based on the vine,[65] but I have already suggested the likelihood of fermented drinks in south-east Europe from much earlier periods (see chapters 3 and 4).

The wider world may have affected south-east Europe in other ways. In the Sredny Stog phase east of the Dniepr in the fifth millennium BC, copper seems to have been obtained from Balkan sources. By the Yamnaya horizon of the mid fourth millennium onwards, the source of copper in the lower Dniepr was probably the Caucasus. The gold of the Varna cemetery may be derived from sources within Bulgaria, but one hypothesis is that it came from across the Black Sea, from somewhere in the Caucasus area. Gold is scarce in south-east Europe in the 'transition period' and in the Early Bronze Age of Bulgaria and northern Greece. Patterns of supply and exchange seem to have been reorientated.[66] This too may be as much symptom as cause of change, but the pull of the emergent urban centres of Mesopotamia, which were developing from the fifth through the fourth millennia, may have been a factor in these reorientations.[67] I suggested earlier (see chapter 4) that copper could have been associated with regeneration, fertility and life forces. The animal burials at Alsónémedi and Budakalász show other ways in which the same sorts of idea could be expressed. A conceptual shift of this kind is at least as good a way of explaining changing patterns in the acquisition and use of copper as steppe intrusions.

Processes of language change are the last major consideration. Both the kurgan hypothesis and the hypothesis of early dispersal with the spread of agriculture equate the movement of language with the movement of a significant body of population. There are many other processes by which languages may be replaced. This has been recognised by the major proponent of the agricultural dispersal hypothesis, but the possibilities have been widened in critical reviews of that hypothesis.[68]

The possibilities are complex. A small incoming population may be absorbed by a larger body of natives, and although affecting major political and social change, come to speak the indigenous language. In a world of many languages, people would have been more often bilingual or multi-lingual than is the case in modern, industrial society. Particular languages can be adopted for communication between different groups as a *lingua franca*, or creoles and pidgins can be formed from existing languages to serve the same purpose.[69] In the context of the Bronze Age in Europe, the former case has been dubbed 'trade language'. If trade is understood here in the sense of inter-regional communication and exchange, the model is apposite to fourth-millennium BC Europe.[70] Another study suggests the ease with which a sense of identity, and with it language, can shift in small-scale societies.[71] People may shift language to counter economic, social or military disadvantages. They may seek to tame aggressors by adopting their language. They may adopt the language of people whom they admire and wish to emulate. Some social systems are more open and permeable than others, and the adoption of a different language may open new possibilities of advancement.[72] The likely background to all this is the characteristic state of language change, in which languages died out by changing into something else.[73]

Such comparative studies open the way to reconciling archaeological and historical linguistic evidence.[74] The historical linguistic evidence for a later rather than earlier Indo-European dispersal is strong; the archaeological evidence for major steppe incursions as the explanation for the decline of tell-orientated society is weak. The archaeological evidence suggests that Neolithic and Copper Age communities in south-east Europe were never wholly sedentary, and regional sequences, at varying dates and rates, show flux in the establishment of place, sometimes by the adoption of locations for occupation, sometimes by the attachment of the community of the dead to particular locales, around which the living circulated. The dispersal and fragmentation visible in the later parts of most regional sequences in south-east Europe were the realisation of possibilities inherent in the adoption of a Neolithic lifestyle, if the supposedly inevitable links between cultivation, tell life and sedentary existence can be broken.

There may have been some movement of people from the steppes and the forest-steppe zone into the Balkans, though much of this could date to *after* the major horizon of transformation. Such a spread may have been more symptom than cause, opportunistic infill rather than destructive primary shockwave. We do not know the process by which Indo-European began to be adopted, nor the limits of the original 'homeland'. Nor is it wise to envisage that its initial adoption was rapid or ubiquitous. It is possible that the transmitters of innovations such as the wheel and horse-riding were accorded considerable status, or new practices such as these may have acquired reputation in their own right in a world which was giving renewed emphasis to mobility and communication.

The cattle keepers of Alsónémedi and Budakalász may not have called to their beasts in only one language. While their predecessors may not have recognised some of the accents of change, nor would have been familiar with the wheeled vehicles of the Szigetszentmárton and Budakalász cart models, they would have been at ease with sets of drinking vessels and cemetery burial. In this part of south-east Europe, and probably in most others, change was an inflection of an existing root.

CHAPTER 6

LONGHOUSE LIVES: CENTRAL AND WESTERN EUROPE, *c.* 5500 to before 4000 BC

A stream valley between the Rhine and the Meuse

Some time after 5500 BC a small settlement of timber longhouses was built in a small stream valley in wooded country between the Rhine and the Meuse. In the first foundation, there may have been as few as three houses, but within three or four generations there were six or seven. The individual houses may have lasted about a generation, and were replaced close to their predecessors. From the beginning, the inhabitants had constructed large buildings, the centre of their social world, some about 25 m long. Each building may have housed a significant number of people, and each was set apart from its neighbours by not less than tens of metres. These people lived in a wooded environment, in which they did not make substantial clearings. They kept domesticated animals, chiefly cattle, supplemented by only small quantities of game, perhaps encountered at a distance from the settlement. In small plots on the fertile, well-watered *loess* soil of the valley, they cultivated wheats, supplemented by legumes.

After four generations or so the first longhouse settlement was joined by two or three other small groups of longhouses at intervals of a few hundred metres up the stream valley. These daughter settlements were similar in character and layout to the parent foundation, but remained smaller throughout the remaining long generations of occupation. In about the sixth generation a burial ground of simple earth-cut individual graves was begun across the valley from the parent settlement. Over seven or more generations it was to receive the remains of over 100 people. In about the thirteenth generation, towards 5000 BC, use of the burial ground seems to have lapsed. A ditched enclosure appeared on the former site of one of the daughter settlements, and then another on the site of the parent settlement as the number of longhouses dwindled. One more ditched ring or arc was dug at the head of the stream valley. The tradition of longhouse settlement did not die out after 5000 BC, but in this region the next generations of longhouses were often grouped more closely together.

This is a brief account of the Merzbachtal in north-west Germany, settled first by the site of Langweiler 8, and then by Langweiler 9, Langweiler 2, Laurenzburg and one or two others; the cemetery across the stream valley from Langweiler 8 is Niedermerz.[1] Rather confusingly, the immediate area is known as the Aldenhoven plateau, but the country is low and barely rolling. Thanks to extensive rescue and research excavations, mostly in advance of large-scale open-cast extraction of lignite or brown coal, we know that there were similar settlements in neighbouring stream valleys, tributaries of the Rur and the Erft, which in turn run into the Meuse to the north. Other similar settlement areas are known on

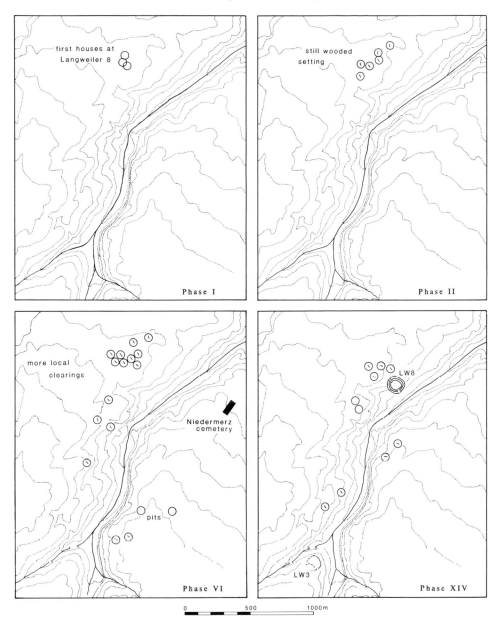

6.1 The development of settlement in the Merzbachtal, in selected phases through the sequence. After Stehli.

the edge of the Rhine valley to the east,[2] and some 30 km north-west in the southern part of Dutch Limburg, to the east of the Meuse/Maas.[3]

This seems a very different system to that represented by the inland foraging site at Friesack, discussed in chapter 2. How did this system arise? What was the scale of difference to what had gone before, and what were its consequences?

Cast in order of appearance

All these settlements belonged to the Linear Pottery culture (LBK). This chapter addresses two horizons, that of the LBK and then that of its successors down to before 4000 BC. The LBK lasted from about 5500 to after 5000 BC, in large parts of central and western Europe. It represents the further extension of a Neolithic way of life. It has usually been seen as the result of further colonisation or population movement from around the fringes of existing Neolithic settlement in the northern Balkans, but I develop the argument that it may in fact represent the acculturation (or enculturation) and transformation of indigenous inland foragers. Beyond the regions of LBK distribution there were other forager populations, notably in the areas around the Baltic. If we concentrate on diets and the technology of shelter, forest farmers and coastal foragers appear very different, but I will suggest that their lifestyles and values may have had many similarities.

In the post-LBK phase of the fifth millennium BC there were further long continuities and slow convergences. In terms of material culture, the Neolithic areas are characterised in the fifth millennium BC by new groupings, but this obscures the considerable continuity of the already established way of life. Likewise, the lives of contemporary fifth-millennium BC coastal foragers showed many patterns and rhythms already familiar from earlier periods. But there was also gradual change, seen for example in the altered structures and layouts of Neolithic settlements, and before 4000 BC, after a long period of co-existence, forager populations over broad areas – around the Baltic, on the north European plain as far west as the Rhine–Meuse delta and roughly as far east as the Vistula, in the Alpine foreland, in north-west France, and in Britain and Ireland – adopted finally more of the cultural identity of their Neolithic neighbours. Many explanations have been tried for this transition, from continued colonisation and disruption to subsistence crises facing foragers. I will argue that it represents the end of a slow process of convergence. After this, as described in the next chapter, there was still considerable continuity with what had gone before.

The Linear Pottery culture (LBK), *c.* 5500 to after 5000 BC

The Linear Pottery culture was the first Neolithic culture in central and western Europe. The name derives from the characteristic decorated pottery, *Linearbandkeramik* or *Linienbandkeramik* in German, and the acronym LBK is preferable to the more clumsy English transcription.[4] Closely related to but distinct from the Linear Pottery culture of the *Alföld* or Great Hungarian plain, the LBK culture is found from western ('Transdanubian') Hungary to the southern Netherlands, eastern Belgium and the river valleys of central-northern France, in the Paris basin. It is distributed through Slovakia and the Czech Lands, northern and eastern Austria, southern and parts of central Poland, and in Germany as far north as Braunschweig and Magdeburg. Crudely speaking, its northern limits more or less coincide with the northern limits of *loess* soils, or conversely with the southern limits of the varied sandy and clayey soils of the morainic landscape of the north European plain, but there are important outliers in Poland in Kujavia, in Chełmno-land and near Szczecin, beyond the *loess*.[5]

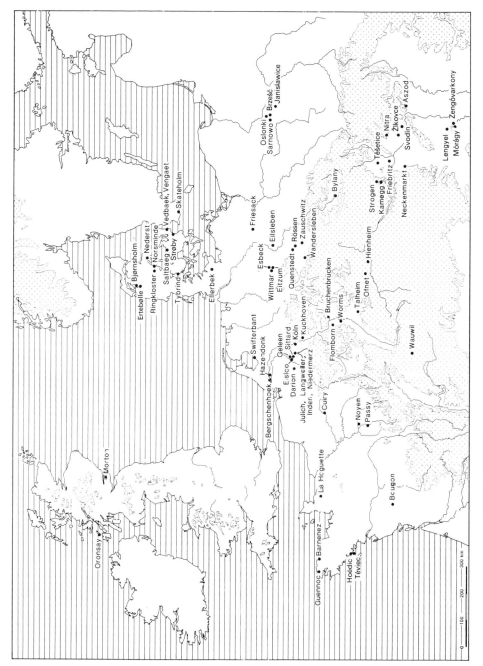

6.2 Simplified location map of the principal sites discussed in chapter 6.

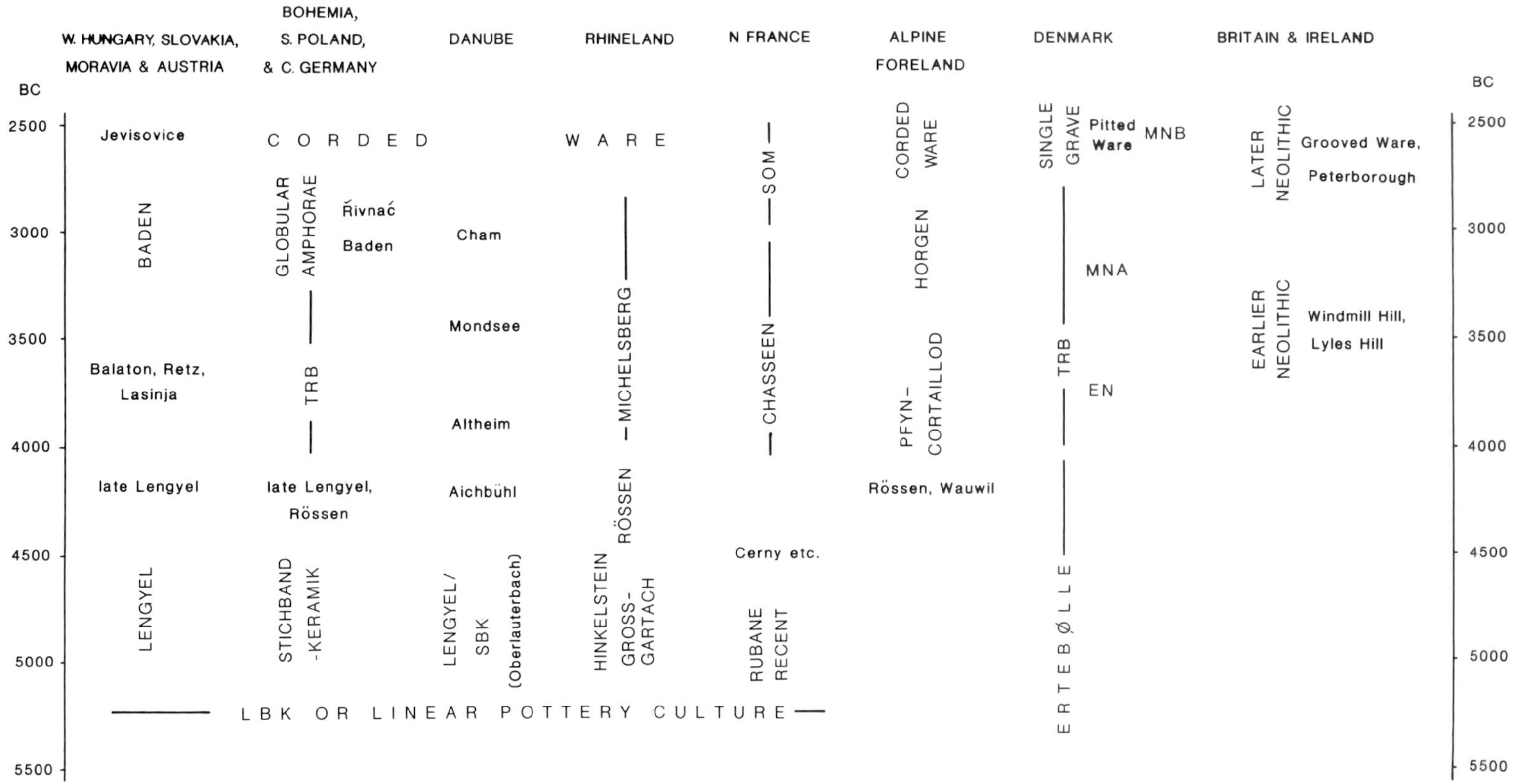

BC
— 2500
— 3000
— 3500
— 4000
— 4500
— 5000
— 5500

BRITAIN & IRELAND

LATER NEOLITHIC — Grooved Ware, Peterborough

EARLIER NEOLITHIC — Windmill Hill, Lyles Hill

DENMARK

SINGLE GRAVE — Pitted Ware — MNB

MNA

TRB — EN

ERTEBØLLE

ALPINE FORELAND

CORDED WARE

HORGEN

PFYN-CORTAILLOD

Rössen, Wauwil

N FRANCE

— SOM —

— CHASSEEN —

Cerny etc.

RUBANE RECENT

RHINELAND

W A R E

— MICHELSBERG —

RÖSSEN

HINKELSTEIN GROSS-GARTACH

DANUBE

Cham

Mondsee

Altheim

Aichbühl

(Oberlauterbach) SBK

LENGYEL/

BOHEMIA, S. POLAND, & C. GERMANY

C O R D E D

Řivnáč Baden

GLOBULAR AMPHORAE — TRB —

late Lengyel, Rössen

STICHBAND-KERAMIK

L B K   O R   L I N E A R   P O T T E R Y   C U L T U R E

W. HUNGARY, SLOVAKIA, MORAVIA & AUSTRIA

Jevisovice

BADEN

Balaton, Retz, Lasinja

late Lengyel

LENGYEL

BC
— 2500
— 3000
— 3500
— 4000
— 4500
— 5000
— 5500

6.3 Simplified outline chronology for the areas discussed in chapters 6–7.

The settlements in the north-west part of this distribution were not the earliest of the culture. Those are found from western Hungary, through northern and eastern Austria, Slovakia and the Czech Lands, to southern and parts of central Germany, as far west as the Neckar, a tributary of the middle part of the Rhine.[6] In the next phase of expansion the LBK culture reached southern Poland and the Rhine, and it is from this phase that the Aldenhoven plateau and Dutch Limburg sequences begin. Later still, LBK sites appeared in eastern Belgium and northern France. Some LBK sites are known beyond the *loess* in central and north-east Poland, but they serve to underline the general observation that the limits of distribution were reached comparatively early and then not significantly extended.[7] This process is discussed in more detail later in the chapter.

LBK settlements are typically found on fertile soils and near water in valleys or low-lying situations. Right across the distribution, the natural environment was woodland, in its climax phase of post-glacial growth. The rather scanty pollen evidence suggests that, as on the Aldenhoven plateau, limited inroads were made into these woodlands.[8] Characteristically there are clusters of settlements in preferred areas ('settlement cells') with gaps in between. The social landscape of the LBK was geographically fragmented. Over the last two decades or more, increasing support has been given to a model of more or less stable settlement, with considerable continuity from generation to generation, in terms of longhouse replacement and tenure of occupation, supported by intensive garden or fixed plot cultivation on fertile soils and by the husbandry of domesticated animals, especially cattle.[9] This contrasts strongly with the sequence of development argued for south-east Europe.

The LBK culture is characterised by a high degree of uniformity, especially in its earlier phases.[10] Across the LBK distribution, people made similar choices of locations for settlement, and built longhouses in Bohemia and Poland very similar to those in north-west Germany. Enclosures and cemeteries were widely distributed across the LBK range. Within the constructed domestic focus of longhouse and clearing, similar stone adzes and pottery were in use, especially in the early and middle phases of the culture. In some situations stone adzes and flint supplies were obtained from greater distances in earlier phases than towards the end of the culture, when pottery styles became more regionalised.[11] The scale of early uniformity can be exaggerated, however, since details of house construction and crop choice, for example, were quite varied even in early phases.[12] Such uniformity has often been linked to the question of origins and to the nature of pioneer settlement.

In sum, the LBK has usually been taken as representing a clean break with the indigenous forager population of central and western Europe. That has been seen as thin on the ground in the woodlands of inland temperate Europe, and as lacking both the social complexity and the technological knowledge perceived as necessary to become Neolithic. Somewhat by default, since the process of cultural transformation has not yet been traced in any detail, the LBK culture is normally seen as a colonisation from the fringes of south-east Europe, a demographic overflow from the Hungarian plain and points south, held together by shared material culture and practice.[13]

This chapter will explore alternative ways of approaching the LBK phenomenon, which involve the native forager population. The radical hypothesis is that the LBK culture represents a transformation of indigenous lifestyle, both in response to local factors of resource supply and in contact with Neolithic communities. I will explore the nature of LBK society, since standing at the head of the sequences of central and western Europe it is a critical baseline to understand. The radical hypothesis is that the LBK culture represents an extension of an indigenous ethic of cooperation and integration. I will challenge aspects of the now conventional model of settlement and subsistence, arguing that more attention needs to be given in this area too to the process of creating Neolithic society.

The colonisation hypothesis

Even those who have argued most vigorously against the colonisation hypothesis for both south-east and north-west Europe have accepted it for the beginnings and spread of the LBK culture.[14] The arguments are varied. The LBK culture appears at the same time as the Linear Pottery culture of the Hungarian plain and the Vinča culture further south. On the Hungarian plain the process has seemed to many people to be one of settlement expansion, and the plausibility of demographic increase gains extra weight from the (admittedly partial) process of settlement infill in the Vinča area. There were Starčevo settlements in Transdanubian Hungary as far north as Lake Balaton, and Hungarian specialists point to local groups of the later Starčevo–Körös culture as likely sources for styles of LBK pottery.[15] In the Körös area, and points south, there was knowledge of crop cultivation and animal husbandry, and above-ground houses were built, even if rather few are known in the Starčevo–Körös areas themselves. Pottery and stone tools of various kinds were in common use. Rather little is known of forager populations in northern Hungary, Slovakia, and northern or eastern Austria, though more sites have been recognised in Bohemia, and more still to the north in Poland; there are new discoveries in the region of Szolnok, in the middle Tisza valley. In the upper Danube valley, it may even be possible to document a decline in the number of later Mesolithic or forager sites.[16] There is no evidence for an early, aceramic Neolithic phase. It therefore seems plausible to argue that an expanding Neolithic population took in a series of carefully chosen, highly fertile and favourable niches through the woodland-valley environments of central and western Europe, which were relatively shunned by forager populations, because of the lower exploitable biomass of developed, closed woodland. The cultural uniformity of the LBK is conformable with a single origin in Transdanubian Hungary and its surrounds, even if the process of cultural transformation from Starčevo–Körös to LBK is not understood in detail. The details of pottery typology suggest a phased spread to the west. Radiocarbon dates suggest that the rate of spread was relatively rapid, again consistently with demographically fuelled expansion.

The case for indigenous transformation

There are many problems with the details of the colonisation hypothesis, and I set out here the case for a radical alternative. On the Hungarian plain, the picture of Linear Pottery culture settlement mirrors that of the Körös phase, with rather small, perhaps shifting, and dispersed sites. In neither case does the landscape look full, and both seem rather unlikely sources for major population infill elsewhere. Transdanubia, by comparison with the Hungarian plain, has seen much less research.[17] The overall density of LBK sites appears low, but this may only be the result of lower research activity. Only a few sites with characteristic longhouses are known. There are few finds of the earliest LBK, as at Bicske to the west of Budapest.

In many other parts of the distribution of the earliest LBK, the density of sites was low, for example in Bohemia, Lower Saxony and the Wetterau (to the east of the Rhine). The sites of Eitzum and Klein Denkte, Kr. Wolfenbüttel, in Lower Saxony, were some 14 km apart, the latter on the edge of a stream valley, the former at its head, 500 m beyond the water source. In Bohemia, only three out of seventeen micro-regions investigated in one project had traces of earliest LBK settlements. Closer to the supposed source area, a number of earliest sites like Neckenmarkt and Strögen are known in eastern and northern Austria (the Burgenland and Lower Austria, north of the Danube), but these are scattered. While some sites are on land of good agricultural potential, others are in surprising situations for supposed agricultural colonists, in narrow, sometimes hilly, side valleys. In southern Slovakia, earliest sites are quite widely dispersed through the valleys of tributaries of the Danube like the Váh, Nitra and Hron.[18] This could of course be compatible with a low-density colonisation, but if so, it becomes puzzling why it should have spread so far west so comparatively rapidly. The duration of the earliest LBK phase is thought generally to have been no more than a few generations. The sites themselves seem to be quite small. Strögen, Bezirk Horn, Austria, has four houses about 10 m apart; Bruchenbrücken, Kr. Friedberg, Germany, has at least seven houses, but the full extent of the occupation has not yet been established.[19] The current German–Austrian research project on the earliest LBK has already found some variation in crop use from area to area, and some Austrian sites at least had rather varied animal bone assemblages, which include remains not only of cattle, pigs and sheep/goats but also of red deer, aurochs, boar, wild horse, beaver, bear and lynx.[20] With the colonisation hypothesis, it has always been attractive to see the valleys and *loess* soils of central and western Europe as favourable, empty niches waiting to be filled, but there were real risks and uncertainties from climatic and resource fluctuations.[21]

It is not easy to understand the cultural transformation represented by the LBK culture, if there was continuity of population from Transdanubia and the Hungarian plain to the west, though there are other unexplained cultural re-formations, for example the appearance of the Vinča complex. The physical anthropological evidence from LBK cemeteries is compatible with continuity of indigenous population, since there is considerable variation from area to area within the LBK distribution. One analysis suggests substantial difference between LBK populations in Transdanubia and the Great Plain.[22] This is clearly an area for more research, and an obvious candidate for DNA investigations in the future, but for the present it is another weakness in the case for colonisation. The indigenous population of the area covered by the LBK culture must have been involved in the process of change, since there is no evidence for its continuation as a separate entity subsequently.[23] This is compatible with the disruption of indigenous forager communities by incoming colonists, but if the argument is for a low-density, relatively slow colonisation, that becomes less plausible. Rapid fusion is another possibility.

The basic flint toolkits of indigenous foragers and the LBK culture had much in common, being based on the controlled production of blades, often on raw material acquired from some distance and therefore economically worked. LBK flint assemblages were rather similar over broad areas.[24] LBK techniques and styles may have borrowed from indigenous production practices, seen for example in the treatment of flat retouch on LBK points. Detailed studies of this kind have been restricted to Dutch Limburg and the Wetterau, but the implication is of much wider continuity.[25] When first found, two unusual types of pottery, the Limburg style and the La Hoguette style, were taken to be Mesolithic ceramics, imported into the LBK area, and therefore support for the colonisation hypothesis.[26] As more discoveries have been made, however, it can be seen that both styles are largely confined within the LBK distribution, and so may not be 'Mesolithic' after all, even though the reason for their distinctive character is not yet understood.

Two sorts of forager situations can be explored. Inland foraging communities may have been more numerous than at first appears. They may have changed their earlier strategies of mobility, some to operate in more circumscribed areas. They must have been indirectly in contact with Neolithic communities to their south or east, through the movement of obsidian and flint. Expansion from the late Körös phase onwards may have intensified such contact, and the availability of new resources would have allowed the consolidation of indigenous ways. The construction of longhouses could have enhanced indigenous practices of aggregation and cooperation, and cattle and cereals could have been taken up to underpin these.

In coastal areas, around the Baltic, in south Scandinavia, in the Netherlands, and perhaps in Brittany and parts of Britain and Ireland, forager populations probably became more numerous. Their patterns of mobility may have altered too, with more continuous use of the coastal zone and 'logistical' use of the hinterland. By the later sixth millennium BC, forager populations of the North European plain and Baltic/Scandinavian coasts were not far from the northern limits of LBK communities. The appearance of burial grounds beside coastal forager settlements like Skateholm II in southern Sweden may be due not only to reduced mobility but also to redefinition of identity as the nature of the wider world shifted.

Inland foragers, c. 7000–5000 BC

There were forager populations inland, even though climax woodland may have reduced densities of exploitable game and plants. Foragers could clear woodland, if they so chose, as we know particularly from pollen analyses in upland areas of Britain.[27] Both fire and axes were available as the means of clearance. Foragers were not unavoidably passive agents as the natural environment changed. Foragers can be documented in many inland areas, though the evidence for their presence is weakest so far in northern Hungary, Austria and Slovakia.[28] Some areas have many known sites, like Poland and the northern half of Germany. Some sites may have been occupied only sporadically as part of continued patterns of mobility. Friesack, considered in chapter 2, is a case in point. Its occupation continued on and off till around the mid sixth millennium BC.[29] People continued to like locations by open water, which were attractive to game, though shallow ponds were infilled by natural processes of peat formation and sediment deposition. The evidence published so far suggests that visits to Friesack became less frequent in the latest phase of occupation, and shifted from spring to late summer or autumn.

In other situations, valley occupations were significant. The use of Noyen in the Seine valley, also considered in chapter 2, continued to at least the later sixth millennium BC.[30] Fishing and game hunting remained important. Here too there were shifts, with use of the site restricted to autumn, and with more pig hunting than before. A few bones of domesticated pig and cattle have been reported from late layers. In Poland, the site of Pobiel 10, near Leszno, is another large and long-used valley occupation, in a tributary of the Oder. The well-known grave at Janisławice, west of the Vistula roughly between Warsaw and Lodź, which gives its name to a late Mesolithic cultural tradition extending well to the east, also points to interesting developments. The man in question was buried with among other things a necklace of pendants made from the teeth of several aurochs and red deer, and with barely used flint blades, all made from chocolate flint, from a source north of the Holy Cross hills some 100 km to the south-east.[31]

The highly mobile foragers of earlier times considered in chapter 2 may be seen as using circulating mobility; they shifted their residences frequently.[32] On the evidence from the later occupations at Friesack and Noyen, this strategy was enhanced by late foragers as a response to changing natural conditions. Another strategy is to restrict residential moves but develop the frequency and range of forays from residential bases. This could have been advantageous in a highly wooded environment, in which desired resources of both plants and animals could have become restricted in their distribution. In the upper Danube valley, later Mesolithic sites decline in numbers, but this may reflect a shift to radiating mobility, which would leave fewer base sites in the archaeological record and more, but less visible, extraction sites.[33] There are some signs of other changes. The nests of human skulls in the rock shelter at Ofnet near Nördlingen in Bavaria have now been re-dated to the seventh millennium BC.[34] This could be seen to reflect a greater sense of group identity and territory.

If the LBK culture is to be derived from indigenous population, there is certainly evidence for the wide presence of foragers inland. Highly mobile foragers could have been disposed to adopt new patterns of existence, with mobility greatly reduced. Already less mobile foragers could have accentuated their attachment to restricted territories by investing labour in longhouse construction. In neither case need the earliest phase of LBK settlement be seen as necessarily fully permanent. In the earliest phase, and subsequently, logistical or tactical mobility could have remained important, and so as in south-east Europe, the first settlements may have been embedded in a still partly mobile lifestyle. In both cases, there seems no technological barrier to the adoption of either more substantial architecture or domesticated resources. Both may have enhanced rather than altered existing social values of cooperation and sharing, and extended the possibilities for aggregation and integration into larger social units. This would be one way to explain the cultural unity of the LBK culture. The major shift was to longhouse life, at first in rather small groups, and the shift in resources may only have been an obvious, economical subsistence adjustment, an extension of existing patterns of delayed-return practices.

Coastal foragers, c. 7000–5000 BC

Land was lost to rising sea levels in the North Sea basin. This may have led to some local increases in population density, for example in the Netherlands,[35] but the evidence of Friesack further inland does not suggest massive knock-on effects. In the Scandinavian sequence, the Kongemose phase, beginning about the mid or earlier seventh millennium BC, coincides with a greater visibility of coastal settlement.[36] One example is the site of Vaenget Nord, a little islet on the south side of the Vedbaek estuary in eastern Zealand, occupied from around 6000 BC until continued sea level rise around 5800 BC swamped it.[37] People using this site hunted game but seem to have been concerned principally with fishing in the estuary. The site may have been used repeatedly but sporadically. People carried out a range of maintenance tasks, including hide and flint working, which suggests that this was more than a short-stay camp.

Coastal settlement was not a new phenomenon, as submerged sites of earlier periods attest, newly discovered by underwater research (see chapter 2). Nonetheless a shift to radiating mobility from this date onwards is plausible, which was to be further enhanced in the Ertebølle phase of the Scandinavian sequence, from the mid sixth millennium BC.[38] There are good grounds for considering the large and numerous coastal sites of the middle and late Ertebølle phases (more or less the fifth millennium BC) as the main residential zone, supplemented by some inland sites. Evidence from coastal Scania in southern Sweden supports the possibility of this trend already being underway in the sixth millennium BC.

The settlement and burial ground of Skateholm II

From the sixth to the fifth millennium BC the Skateholm area was a shallow coastal lagoon, fronted by low ridges or barriers and containing small islands.[39] These were progressively inundated by continued sea level rise. Skateholm II, the earliest known site, was on one such small island, inundated around 5000 BC, and there are other slightly later occupations (considered later in the chapter). The Skateholm occupations show inland hunting of big and furred game and birds, combined with very wide exploitation of fish and marine mammals from the lagoon and the open sea. We do not know whether people were in the lagoon area all the year round at this date. Attachment to place was expressed in the burial ground close to the settlement. In earlier times, human bone was in circulation amongst the living, but the grouping of the dead beside the residence of the living seems to be a new development.

Over twenty graves have been uncovered at Skateholm II. Men, women, children and domesticated dogs were interred. Most were single burials, though there were two adults in grave X and two children in grave XII. One adult woman was buried with a dog, in grave VIII, and there were separate dog burials in three other graves. The burial ground covered an area about 40 by 20 m. The graves, simple, earth-cut pits, had varying orientations, but were presumably marked, since none intersect. The dead were either laid out fully extended or placed in a sitting position. They were provided with grave goods, in the form of flint and other tools for men and ornaments of various kinds for women. Other offerings

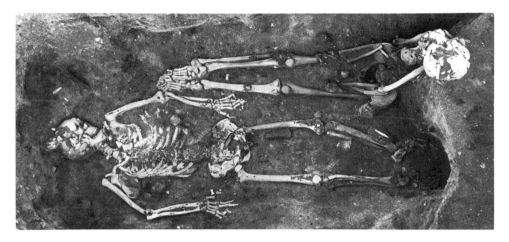

6.4 Grave X, with two adult men, one lying, one sitting, from Skateholm II. Photo: Larsson.

included red deer antlers and scatterings of red ochre. Concentrations of fish bones in the stomach area of the skeletons has suggested that the dying were given special last meals, or the deposits could be symbolic. Other food remains were put in the earth used to infill the graves. Further elaboration of the burial rite is suggested by a 4 by 4 m structure within the cemetery area, its perimeter and part of its interior defined by red ochre; it contained further deposits of flint and bone. There was also a possible cenotaph or empty grave, and some skeletons had missing bones.

It is commonplace to interpret such a burial ground as showing increased attachment to place and to the importance of group allegiance as seen especially in the burials of the young. The burial ground must also express elements of the wider world view of coastal foragers, which may well have included some reference to developments in the LBK area to the south. The circulation of bone among the living, the formal burial area and the elaborate burial rites suggest a reverence for ancestors; ochre and antlers suggest a strong interest in fertility and regeneration. The presence of dogs could indicate that there was little conceptual separation between people and animals, or in broader terms between people and nature. Perhaps these people saw themselves as working with nature, as suggested in chapter 2 for their predecessors. The wider world had, however, changed with the appearance of LBK communities to the south, whether these were colonists, acculturated native people or a fusion of both. From an early date there were burial grounds beside certain LBK settlements. It comes as little surprise therefore to find evidence of contact with the LBK world at Skateholm II in the form of a stone adze of LBK type. With the acquisition of novel exotics by exchange, if not by more direct contact, knowledge of changes to the south must have been spread rapidly northwards. Perhaps part of the explanation of the Skateholm II burial ground lies in a redefinition of local identity with reference to new developments to the south.

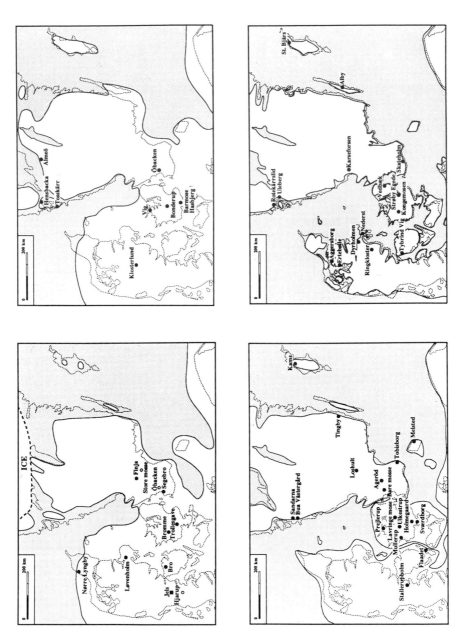

6.5 The changing coastline of the Baltic in successive phases, with significant contemporary sites. Top left: late Palaeolithic; top right: Preboreal or early post-glacial; below left: Boreal or *c.* eighth millennium BC; below right: Atlantic or *c.* sixth–fifth millennia BC. After Larsson.

The spread of LBK culture

The first phase of the LBK culture has been defined above all by a simple style of pottery, including flat-based bowls, variously tempered, and decorated with simple incised curvilinear and rectilinear motifs. This *älteste Keramik* defines a series of sites in northern Hungary, Slovakia and the Czech Lands, parts of eastern and northern Austria, and parts of Germany as far west as east of the middle Rhine and as far north as near Magdeburg. The Austrian group constitutes about 10 per cent of all known LBK sites in the country, but in other regions the percentage is lower.[40] This kind of figure reflects not only the probably low density of earliest settlement, but also the duration of the first phase. Attempts have been made to define that more precisely by radiocarbon dating, and there has been speculation that the earliest phase could start well before *c.* 5500 BC. When dates derived from old wood samples are set aside, that claim cannot yet be justified.[41] The duration of the phase is often estimated at a century or more. This would still entail a rapid, rather selective spread westwards. This is slower than that envisaged before the recent attention given to the earliest phase, when radiocarbon dates from the Netherlands were rather crudely seen as the same as those from the eastern distribution and a highly rapid colonisation inferred.[42] If the process of spread was due to acculturation of indigenous population, the ground would have been set for rapid dissemination. On the other hand, ethnographic analogy does suggest that populations can increase rapidly in certain frontier, pioneering situations.[43]

Many earliest sites are found on *loess* and other fertile soils, often but not exclusively in valleys and close to water.[44] Sites seem to have been well dispersed through the landscape within any one region, and there were large intervals between regional clusters. Settlements were small, as in the examples of Strögen and Bruchenbrücken. Some continued to be occupied in later phases, but the majority were used only in the earliest phase. Timber long houses were built from the outset, detectable in many cases by the prominent internal cross-rows of three posts, with more slender traces of the outer walls.[45] No burial grounds have yet been found belonging to the earliest phase. There was a shallow, irregular ditch around part of the settlement at Eilsleben, Kr. Magdeburg,[46] but there were no more formal enclosures. People kept cattle, pigs and sheep/goats, but they also hunted game. They grew cereals in small clearings.

Settlement was extended in the middle phase to the main limits of the *loess* and to the edge of and even on to parts of the North European plain.[47] LBK settlements were now present along much of the length of the Rhine, including the upper Rhine in Alsace and the lower Rhine north of Köln, as well as west to the Meuse/Maas. The occupation of the Aldenhoven plateau and the area of *loess* terraces beside the Maas in the Dutch Limburg, known as the Graetheide, begins from this phase. Settlement was extended into southern Poland; there were further 'islands' of LBK settlement on fertile black soils in Kujavia in central Poland, and even, as recent research has shown, in central-northern Poland in Chełmno-land in the bend of the Vistula between Toruń and Grudziądz, and in north-west Poland in the lower Oder basin near Szczecin. Within areas already occupied, settlements became more numerous. In eastern Bohemia, for example, the complex of occupations at

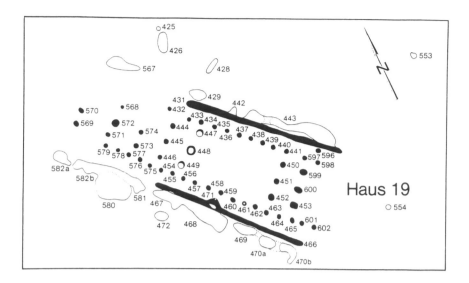

6.6 Plan of an earliest LBK house at Frankfurt–Niedereschbach. After Bernhardt and Hampel.

Bylany began in this phase.[48] It has been difficult precisely to define the date and duration of this phase (Flomborn in the west, Ačkovy in the east). The total occupation of the Graetheide has been estimated at about 350 years. One chronology for the Langweiler 8 sequence, based on the seriation of pottery decoration, yields fifteen phases. If each phase is reckoned as a generation, that gives an equivalent sort of span. The Bylany sequence, as currently reckoned, has over twenty phases.[49] The middle phase could have begun *c.* 5300 BC, therefore, and perhaps lasted two or more centuries.

In the middle phase, most of the characteristics of the LBK culture were fully developed. The settlement system, described further below, was extended into more areas, but the orientation towards fertile, well-watered soils continued. There were burial grounds, for example at Flomborn, Kr. Worms.[50] There were close similarities in material culture over broad areas, for example in pot decoration, stone adzes, often derived from distant sources, and house plans.

In the late phase, perhaps from *c.* 5100 to 5000 BC or a little later, there were further changes. Settlement was extended into parts of eastern Belgium and the Paris basin, and into selected parts of central Poland. Pot styles became more markedly regionalised, and there is some evidence for shorter-range procurement of stone adzes, and for a degree of regionalisation in house plans.[51] At the same time there may have been very long-range contacts with the Cardial complex of the central-western Mediterranean, and with the first Neolithic of western France.[52] Many of the ditched enclosures appear to belong to the late phase, although some may date to the middle phase.[53] Further cultural changes after 5000 BC bring in the post-LBK complex of the Lengyel and Stichbandkeramik cultures, to be followed in chapter 7, but there was considerable continuity of the established lifestyle into the fifth millennium BC.

6.7 LBK houses under excavation at Bylany. Photos: Pavlů.

The settlement system of the LBK culture

Subsistence: sedentism and mobility

LBK people, whatever their origin, lived in a still very wooded environment. In this they kept animals, particularly cattle, and seem to have done little hunting after the earliest phase. There is some evidence for river fishing, and simple dugout canoes of a little later date (from the Chasseen period) have been found recently in Paris.[54] Such pollen evidence as there is does not indicate large clearings of woodland. People cultivated cereals and legumes. In eastern areas they grew wheats and barleys, but with one exception in Belgium, which may show contacts with western France, barley was not grown in the west/north-west. Regional differences in crop composition are evident from the earliest phase.

This simple picture conceals real difficulties with the evidence. No longhouse has yet been found with its floor intact, owing to subsequent erosion and cultivation. Bone in many areas has been destroyed by the decalcification of *loess* soils since LBK times.[55] Bones and carbonised plant remains survive in post holes and in pits of various kinds. Some may have been deliberately deposited in pits, but many may have ended there by more indirect processes. Even when plant assemblages have been properly recovered and examined, it is difficult to identify different stages or areas of crop processing and use within settlements.[56]

Perhaps because of these basic research conditions, study of LBK subsistence has been prone to fossilise in fixed models. An older view combined inference of settlement and pottery sequence with ethnographic and historical analogy. This produced a model of shifting settlement allied to shifting cultivation. Study of the houses and pottery styles at Bylany in Bohemia suggested breaks in the sequence, and ethnographic and historical analogy suggested that yields from cultivation would rapidly decline after an initial enrichment from the burning of cleared woodland.[57] From about 1970 there was a strong reaction to this model, and its replacement is still dominant.[58] The current model envisages greater continuity of settlement occupation at nearly every site. Even if cultivation plots had to be rotated around a given settlement, there would still be plenty of land available within easy reach of each site. The combination of *loess* and proximity to water suggested very favourable conditions for prolonged cultivation, and experimental data indicate that yields can in fact be maintained at good levels; the analogy of mineral-poor tropical or northern soils is a poor guide. Wider survey emphasised how regularly the valley–water–*loess* niche was taken up by LBK communities. On largely theoretical grounds, it was assumed that crop cultivation was more important than animal husbandry, though the combination of resources as a buffer against the risk of failure was recognised as important. From these lines of argument has come the model of sedentary LBK communities, engaged in fixed, intensive cultivation of small plots or gardens: serious, settled farmers from the outset.

This issue is fundamental (though I do not wish to imply that the other characteristics of LBK society depended on subsistence practices). The time is ripe to develop another model, which incorporates elements of the previous two. Much depends on our assumptions about the degree of sedentary settlement, the balance between resources, and the

6.8 Wooden well from Erkelenz–Kückhoven. Photo: Weiner.

scale and purpose of subsistence production. Would people from a source in the Hungarian plain or its Transdanubian environs have so soon abandoned the useful strategy of mobility? Seasonal mobility is compatible with fixed bases, and the case for the development of indigenous mobility strategies has already been sketched. We can discriminate more between the settlement histories of individual sites. Some large sites in the west may have had very long sequences, perhaps unbroken, such as Elsloo and Langweiler 8. In contrast, fresh analysis of Bylany has again suggested several hiatuses in the occupation of the major complex.[59] Smaller sites have generally shorter occupations, and many have breaks in their sequences.[60]

Although most LBK sites are on *loess* or other fertile soils, it would have been very difficult to avoid such soils in most areas, once valley locations had been chosen.[61] In fact the *loess* may not have been uniformly fertile at this date. One study of soils in Belgium has suggested that at this date they were poorly developed and decalcified.[62] Not all LBK sites were close to water. The case of Eitzum in the earliest phase has already been noted. At Erkelenz–Kückhoven, in the Rhineland near Bonn, recent excavations have revealed a large LBK settlement on a dry *loess* plateau fully 3 km from the nearest watercourse, which was occupied throughout the Rhineland LBK sequence.[63] Wood-framed or -lined wells have been found (one dendrochronologically dated to 5090 BC), clearly the water source for people and animals. Perhaps here there was cultivation of rain-fed plots, but there are possibilities of seasonal occupation and mobility. Other wells are known in LBK contexts at Mohelnice in Moravia and Most in Bohemia.

Were animals kept in LBK houses? The house plans give no clear indications of such a use. There has been little application of phosphate analysis.[64] Very small herds would not have been viable, and we must envisage the herding of stock away from settlement areas. (There are surprisingly few palisades or fenced areas within LBK settlements. Short stretches have been found on sites on the Aldenhoven plateau, but in recent excavations at the less eroded site of Geleen–Janskamperveld on the Graetheide there seems to have been a palisade around the longhouse area, with fences between three or four longhouse 'yards'.)[65] This would introduce a stronger element of mobility. There have been several suggestions of seasonal herding over varying distances: over short range from bases in the Rhine valley to upland caves in Alsace, and over medium range to the Eifel hills from the Aldenhoven plateau. At an earlier stage of research, another suggestion was of long-range movement to Kujavia in central Poland, well beyond the *loess*.[66] In the last example, based in large part on the site at Brześć Kujawski, part of the argument was based on the absence of house plans in the LBK occupation. In fact LBK house plans are known from Kujavia, as well as more sites than previously. It would be possible to extend the argument now to Chełmno-land, a little further north, but that too could be another permanently used settlement region.

We do not know what foods were most important in LBK society. The diet may have consisted of cereals, supplemented by legumes and a little meat. It is just as likely that meat was more valued, as a symbol of new relationships with nature, and a desirable medium for sharing and exchange. As in south-east Europe, we know too little about what was put into LBK pots. As well as porridge, it is profitable to consider beer, milk and animal blood. Animals could have been valued in their own right. As a whole, subsistence production may have served rather than dictated the demands of the social system. Mobility may have remained an important strategy, partly bound up with the husbandry of animals, and partly in order to manage risk and uncertainty from fluctuations in resources and climate. Mobility may also have been a social strategy, to maintain fluidity and integration. Production may have satisfied the wants of hospitality and exchange as much as the basic needs of subsistence. These possible practices and values were channelled through the LBK longhouse, the basic unit in settlement after settlement.

Longhouse life

The longhouse has been taken for granted. In the context of developments in south-east Europe up to this date, especially in the more northern area of the Starčevo–Körös and *Alföld* LBK cultures, where large houses first appeared on the Great Plain in the Szakálhát phase (between the Linear Pottery and Tisza cultures), the LBK longhouse was in itself a remarkable construction. It used substantial timbers. Even the smallest were some 10 m long, and many were 20 m long and more, some reaching nearly 30 m. There were occasional examples over 30 m. Many seem to have been divided into two parts, and others into three. It is usually assumed that the longhouse was a single-storey building, but it is not impossible that some had upper floors, at least in part. Contemporary longhouses in a settlement nearly always shared a common orientation, though they were usually spaced at intervals of tens of metres from their neighbours. In some areas at least, there seem to have been recurrent arrangements of working areas outside the longhouse. Where indications of entrances survive, doors were set on the short end; down the sides were usually irregular pits originally dug for material for the walls. These were massive constructions. Investment in their building, maintenance and replacement was a commitment both to place and to social cooperation, and their use, from the manner of entrance to the probable arrangement of activities both inside and outside, was formalised and repetitive. If there was still much mobility in the lifestyle, as argued above, this would have enabled fluidity and flexibility in the composition of residential units. The longhouse should be seen as helping to create the first Neolithic communities of the woodlands of central and western Europe, rather than as just a technical response to the need of sedentary population for permanent shelter. The longhouse maintained the idea of new kinds of social relations.

Characteristically the longhouse had five rows of posts.[67] The three internal rows are usually seen as roof supports, indicating the absence of cross-tie beams. The outer rows were for walling, usually of wattle-and-daub construction; in some cases, continuous bedding trenches replaced individual posts at one end, and more rarely right around a building, and plank walls are indicated. The interior thus created, if these buildings were single-storey affairs, must have been dominated by heavy timber uprights. If so, this constructional elaboration might be seen as having symbolic properties, the qualities of wood as a natural property being centralised within the cultural setting of the house. Alternatively, some of the density of uprights might have been to support upper floors. Because of erosion and cultivation, no intact floor deposit has survived. The posts were not uniformly spaced within the interiors, since the middle parts tend to have fewer, and at least in the north-west part of the LBK distribution, earlier houses can be distinguished by a curious Y-shaped arrangement of the central posts.

Longhouses varied in length, from under 10 m to around 30 m; they were usually 6–7 m wide. In the north-west part of the LBK area, it has been suggested that there were three types of longhouse, though it is unclear how far this scheme can be followed elsewhere.[68] At sites like Elsloo and Langweiler 8, longhouses were orientated north-west to south-east. The basic unit was a middle part. Those with only this part were 8–12 m long. Many had in addition a north-west part, some defined by plank rather than post walls. These ranged from 15 to 25 m in length. Others had three parts: the middle unit, the north-west end, and a south-east part. Often the south-east part was defined by more posts, and in some three-part buildings the whole of the walls around the building were plank-framed. Such buildings were often 25–30 m long. This is probably best treated as an ideal scheme, since it is clear that there are variations, for example at Langweiler 8, but the repetition is significant. One popular hypothesis is that the middle unit was for living, and there is some evidence from charcoal in post holes for centrally placed hearths. The north-west end has been suggested as an animal stall, though there is no further evidence for this, and the south-east end as a lofted granary space, because of the extra post holes. (Analysis of some Aldenhoven plateau houses does show the presence of more chaff and weeds from crop processing in the houses with a south-east part than in those without, but the difference is relative rather than absolute.) The small, single-unit buildings appear to be comparatively rare. Some caution is necessary, since the less eroded site of Geleen–Janskamperveld suggests the

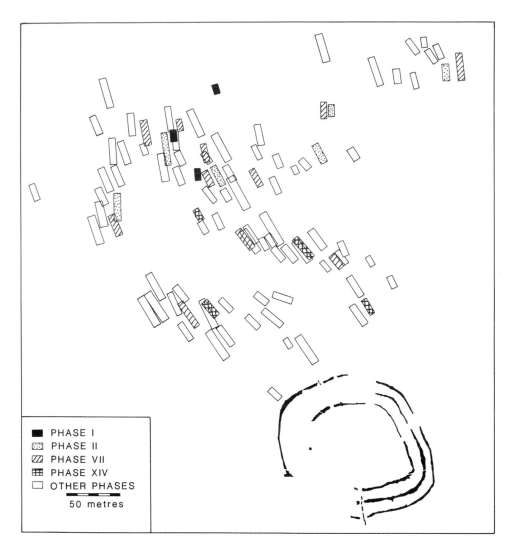

6.9 Selected phases of the settlement at Langweiler 8. The enclosure belongs to phase XIV. After Boelicke *et al.*

existence of rather more small houses than are usually preserved elsewhere. Sites on the Aldenhoven plateau are dominated by two- or three-part houses, of varying length, but with many slightly above or below 20 m. The all-plank buildings ('type 1a') are also comparatively rare, and it is unusual to find more than one on a site in a given phase of occupation. These have been regarded as of special status, but there are plenty of other buildings of more or less the same imposing length. These variations on the longhouse theme belong to the middle and late LBK phases as defined above. On the information published so far, the houses of the earliest phase were not so varied. But in this phase the basic constructional model seems to have been established, with three internal post rows, flanking borrow pits, and buildings up to 20 m in length. One at Bruchenbrücken has what appear to be plank side walls.[69]

As well as flanking daub pits alongside the long walls of the longhouses, there were usually a considerable number of smaller and larger pits round about. Analysis on the Aldenhoven plateau has suggested that there were pits in separate working areas on the west, north and east sides, in a radius of about 10 m around the longhouse.[70] According to one model, pottery was used mainly in the south part of the longhouse area, flint was worked in a northern zone, and stone rubbers and other heavy stone equipment in the north-west zone around the longhouse. It has been doubted whether this analysis can be repeated elsewhere, and at Olszanica near Kraków in southern Poland, the suggestion has been of a west–east distinction suggesting division of tasks between the sexes,[71] but the indications of formalisation and repetition are important. The longhouse imposed a pattern of action. That action was not restricted to the longhouse alone. Many settlements, including those on the Aldenhoven plateau, had areas away from and between spaced long-houses where pits are the dominant feature. These may have been shared working areas. At Olszanica, pits in one area away from the longhouses included two ovens, which was taken to indicate communal activities.[72]

Longhouses were not normally on their own. The longhouse was embedded in an idea of wider social action. The longhouse normally had neighbours, spaced at varying inter-vals, but normally not less than tens of metres.[73] Contemporary houses usually shared a common orientation. Neighbours were thus spaced within shouting distance, each long-house placed in a similar way and imposing a similar pattern of movement and use. Differences in house size may have been less perceptible than in the closer arrangements of tell settlements in south-east Europe. Large houses were not restricted to the larger settle-ments. The groupings of longhouses varied, from smaller 'hamlets' to larger 'villages'.[74] Within all sizes of sites, the individual longhouse recurs as the basic unit, though it has been suggested that there were 'wards' within settlements, such as Elsloo, composed of up to two or three houses per phase. At Langweiler 8, spatial configurations varied from phase to phase.[75] By phases III and IV, it appears that there was a greater gap between the one or two longhouses to the east of the settlement than between the five or six longhouses in a main group to the west. Other settlements appeared in the stream valley from phase V. In sub-sequent phases some east-west distinction was maintained for a while, but gradually the main grouping became the dominant configuration, without obvious 'wards' within it. So it appears that the longhouse existed not on its own but had ties or allegiances at differing levels of interaction. This integration is important.

The range of longhouse sizes can be variously interpreted. House length could directly reflect the number of occupants, but that is to assume that the composition of households remained stable through the life of a building. It has been claimed that at Elsloo and Langweiler 8 there was a trend to more smaller houses with time, which were therefore overshadowed by fewer, larger houses, but it is hard to document this trend in the pub-lished site details.[76] On ethnographic analogy, size might also reflect the particular circum-stances surrounding construction, including the size of labour group mobilised through various ties for the task. The ability to mobilise friends and allies might depend in part on length of residence in a given area.[77] In a still-mobile lifestyle, fluctuating memberships would explain some of the size variations. The largest houses could have had a role as club or meeting houses.[78] Another approach has been to suggest that house size is correlated to social position. Flint working debris shows that most longhouses were associated with basic tasks, but people may have been more involved in some longhouses than in others in the acquisition of exotics, for example of obsidian brought to the site of Olszanica, or in innovation in pottery decoration, as suggested at Elsloo.[79] Such studies have generally, however, been inconclusive, since there are weak correlations with house length (of two houses at Olszanica with the greatest adjacent density of obsidian, one was 41.5 m long but the other only 12 m long), and house length in any one plot may vary from phase to phase. If there were inequalities between longhouses in terms of access to exotics and exchange networks, they do not appear ever to have become established for long. Once again, the longhouse appears to be embedded in a bigger idea of social integration.

Longhouse settlement biographies

Individual houses were often replaced by another close by, but the plans of successive buildings rarely intersect. The plots of earlier buildings may have been carefully marked, remembered and respected. Replacement was an act of renewal. Many settlements were occupied for more than one phase, and according to conventional analyses houses in a settlement were all replaced about the same time. The place of a settlement could therefore have been conceived as having a life of its own, going through a cycle of birth, life, death and rebirth.[80] But the end of an individual building was also a moment of potential hiatus, and likewise groups of houses will have passed through similar periods of transition, some to be renewed, some to be abandoned.

There is much variation in the size, duration of occupation, and continuity of occupation of LBK settlements. It does not seem possible to fit the evidence from the whole distribution into a single model. Such diversity is probably therefore best seen as to do with a still-fluid social landscape. The Aldenhoven plateau sites which have served as such useful examples so far may not have been typical of histories elsewhere. Both the larger Langweiler 8 site and the smaller sites of Langweiler 2 and Langweiler 9 were long-lived, the latter two beginning later than the former. In the Graetheide, Elsloo and Sittard were also long-lived, but other sites round about like Stein, Geleen, Geleen–Janskamperveld and others were not in use right through the sequence.[81] In Bohemia, the large complex of occupations at Bylany can also be contrasted with smaller and shorter occupations in the region round about, but here the model of a punctuated sequence for the main site has been revived. Some 7 ha have been excavated of a total complex covering about 30 ha. In the excavated area the number of houses in contemporary use fluctuated around six.[82]

It has been tempting to ascribe greater status to larger and longer-lasting settlements, mirroring the prominence assigned to the larger houses,[83] but even this perspective may be flawed. In the light of investigations in the Graetheide, on the Aldenhoven plateau and at Bylany, the scale of difference between large and small settlement may not be as great as once imagined. Duration and continuity may be as important as size. The relevant scale of analysis may be the whole settlement cluster. The repetitions involved in longhouse life allowed people to pass from settlement to settlement, and from region to region. Rather than being the apex of social hierarchy, the larger and longer-lived sites can be seen as the focus of an unstable world. None of the larger sites were better placed than other sites in terms of soil or other resources. They are distinguished rather by a greater commitment to renewal and to place, where the idea of social cooperation and interaction was most successfully practised. Two other aspects, the treatment of the dead and portable material culture, were part of the same set of values.

The treatment of the dead in the LBK

Settlement remains

Partial human remains have been found in settlements, where the conditions of preservation are favourable.[84] Some may be from disturbed burials, others from contexts other than burials. Their presence suggests that human bone may have been in circulation among the living. A couple of examples of deliberately split and splintered human bone, from Ober-Hörgern, Wetteraukreis and Zauschwitz, Kr. Borna, Saxony, suggest ritual consumption of the remains of the dead. Further close ties between the living and the dead are suggested by burials within settlements. Their contexts are varied.[85] A few have been found in graves or pits dug for the purpose, but more seem to have been deposited in other features: in pits between the longhouses, pits alongside houses, ditches and so on. More children or juveniles are represented than adults, and more women than men. Of over twenty found near houses, all were children, as in examples beside the walls of houses as far apart as Vedrovice in Moravia and Cuiry-les-Chaudardes in the Aisne valley in northern France.[86] There may have been a conceptual link between young people and settlement continuity. At Zauschwitz, several crouched burials were found within a settlement, placed in existing large pits. In one pit, there were two crouched adult burials, together with a disordered skeleton and a separate skull, and animal bones. One child burial was rather different.[87] The child had been placed face down on the edge of a large, deep pit, and had been covered with the burnt debris of a house: ash, wood charcoal and wall daub.

Burial grounds

Children were less prominent in cemeteries. Burial grounds have been found almost right across the LBK distribution, from Nitra in Slovakia to Elsloo on the Graetheide and Niedermerz on the Aldenhoven plateau, across the stream valley from Langweiler 8.[88] They appear from the middle phase onwards, as at Flomborn, Kr. Worms. Rather large burial grounds are known at several sites; as well as the examples above, other big cemeteries include Wandersleben, Aiterhofen, Schwetzingen and Fellbach-Öffingen. Wandersleben, Kr. Gotha, Thüringen, had over 200 burials.[89] At Elsloo, the cemetery was not completely excavated; over 100 burials were found. At Niedermerz, there were about 100 burials. Many burial grounds were rather smaller, as at Wittmar, Kr. Wolfenbüttel, or

6.10 LBK artefacts from grave 83 at Elsloo. Photo: Rijksmuseum van Oudheden, Leiden.

Sondershausen, Kr. Sondershausen.[90] At Wittmar, the full extent of the burial ground was probably not uncovered, but its limits may have been reached on two or three sides; some fourteen burials are known. From the larger excavation projects on the Graetheide and the Aldenhoven plateau, it does not appear that there was a burial ground beside every settlement area, large or small. The burial ground at Elsloo is adjacent to the settlement, at Niedermerz seemingly distanced from the settlement foci of the stream valley. In both cases, the burial ground was begun some generations after the start of the settlement sequence. In other large investigations, no burial ground has yet been located, as in the Bylany complex in Bohemia. In some instances at least, it is likely that the cemetery served more than one settlement, perhaps rather a whole settlement area.

The contents and layout of cemeteries show selection and formalisation. From the numbers involved and the timespans of use, whole populations even of individual settlements were not represented. In many western areas, bone has survived poorly or not at all, but where it does there were roughly equal numbers of men and women, with children scarcer. Graves were probably marked, since there are generally very few intersections, and many burial grounds give a strong impression of spatial order, the graves of the dead, like the houses of the living, sharing a common orientation, often east–west. Graves were not dug in rigidly defined rows. Some plans give the impression of internal groups. One analysis claims reserved zones without graves adjacent to grave areas, rules for the spatial separation of men, women and children, and rules for the spacing of successive burials.[91]

The dominant burial rite was inhumation. Cremation was also practised, and some cemeteries show both rites. At Elsloo, some thirty-seven out of 117 burials were cremations, at Niedermerz six out of 102. Hollogne-aux-Pierres, prov. Liège, in Belgium is rare in probably only having cremations.[92] Graves were simple earth-cut pits. There may have been coffins at one site, Dresden–Nickern,[93] but generally the dead seem to have been lain directly in the grave. They were probably clothed. Many were placed on their left side, with the head to the east and the face looking south. This orientation could provide a link with the prevailing alignment and entrances of longhouses. Red ochre was frequently strewn on the base of the grave, and many of the dead were provided with grave goods in the form of pots, stone and flint artefacts, and ornaments. Graves were carefully backfilled, some with goods, offerings and settlement debris included at higher levels than the body.[94]

Variations in the quantity and character of grave goods have been analysed to look for differences between people. Generally, it seems as though gender and age differences were important, since there are indications that stone adzes and arrowheads were male equipment, and pots and small tools female equipment, and that older people had more grave goods. Obviously much caution is required, against both our own, modern assumptions about gender roles, and the imprecision of sex determination on imperfect skeletal material. Not all the dead were provided with grave goods or offerings, sometimes as many as a third in a cemetery. These cases include adults. Some analyses have tried to read off social differences from grave inventories. There may be some tendency for men, and older men, to receive more goods of distant origin.[95] Nitra is one example which has been interpreted in these terms.[96] More structured differences have been proposed on the basis of analysis of the cemeteries at Elsloo and Niedermerz, with the suggestion that certain individuals achieved prominent, dominant social position.[97] Unfortunately, in these cases skeletons were not preserved, and the grave goods which are the means of analysis have first to be used to determine gender differences.

Too much attention may have been given to grave goods on their own. It is easy but dangerous to assume that a grave 'good' was the possession of the individual concerned in life, since this imports Western concepts of ownership. Some analyses use the concept of status as though it had a fixed meaning. In the LBK world, the majority of the dead were disposed of in ways that are not archaeologically visible. Some may have been exposed, and others cremated. Human bones were present in settlements, and were perhaps actively circulated through the spheres of the living, important tokens of continuity with ancestors. Some burials were made in the settlement area, and child burials were a metaphor for settlement continuity and regeneration. Burial grounds grew up beside certain settlements or areas, in which selected individuals were placed, presumably at relatively infrequent intervals. Each addition to a burial ground could have been a significant event. This was an act of integration with the predecessors of a community or settlement area. Grave goods may have been linked in part to the social role of the individual in life, but they may also have been a form of communication with the ancestors, statements of enduring communal values rather than power plays among the living. It is possible that those selected were prominent people in life, but it is just as likely that the punctuated sequences of burial were bound up with particular histories and cycles of settlements and households, especially if there was fluidity in household membership and mobility of lifestyle. Continuity and integration seem more important in the realm of the dead than differences between the living.

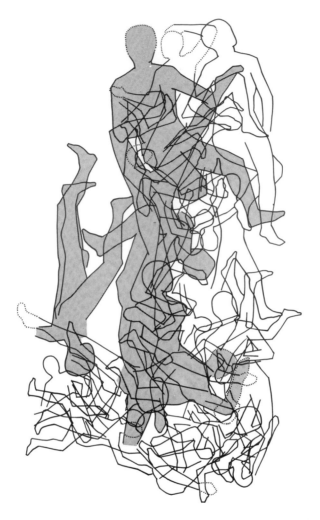

6.11 Reconstructed positions of bodies in the grave at Talheim. Men are stippled. After Wahl and König.

The Talheim burial pit

A very different kind of find was made at Talheim, Kr. Heilbronn, in the Neckar valley, a tributary of the middle Rhine. Over thirty people, men, women and children, had been put, perhaps even thrown, into a large, freshly dug pit some 3 m long.[98] The skeletons lay huddled together, in a variety of unnatural positions quite in contrast to the arranged postures seen in single graves in cemeteries. Some were sprawled face down. There were eleven men, seven women and sixteen children. Twenty of these, including children, had suffered blows to the head, probably made by stone axes and adzes, and by other unspecified blunt instruments. Two adults had also been shot in the head with flint-tipped arrows. There were very few detectable wounds elsewhere on the skeletons. Many questions are raised about the circumstances of the event. Does the lack of wounds to the body apart from the head mean that the victims were bound before meeting their fate? Did the perpetrators themselves bury the victims, or their survivors? And what sort of social group is represented?

The find has been radiocarbon dated to the end of the LBK culture. It lies near a known but unexcavated settlement. Finds elsewhere suggest that the occasional individual met his or her end by being shot, but the scale of violence here is unexpected. The LBK evidence is generally consistent with ethnographic observation of multiple ways of solving disputes without recourse to open violence.[99] It is possible that the find is symptomatic of changes in the LBK world towards its end, when enclosures and more regionalised styles appear, perhaps indicating a heightened sense of local identity, but the landscape was still very far from full, and it is hard to envisage sustained competition over land. Perhaps it is wrong to interpret the find in these sociological terms, and an alternative would be to consider some rite of expiation or punishment for religious or other transgression. But in that case the size of the group involved is surprising. Perhaps the most general inference to be drawn, consistent with the rest of the LBK evidence, is of strong norms of communally sanctioned behaviour.

LBK material culture

There was much uniformity through the LBK world. Not only were longhouses, settlements and burial grounds laid out in rather similar ways across broad areas, but the material equipment used by LBK people was similar from area to area, especially in earlier phases. Pottery forms and decoration were common over wide distances in the earliest and middle phases. Settlement analysis indicates use of pots in particular zones in and around the longhouse. Some households may have been more involved in potting innovations than others,[100] but new styles seem quickly to have been assimilated by others. It is hard to resist seeing pot decoration in this context as a system of communication. The variety and complexity of treatment of decorative bands increased from the first to the middle phases. We do not know whether particular motifs had specific meanings. Many may rather have projected a general sense of solidarity and familiarity that did not need to be actively or consciously thought about.[101] It is likely that there were many other kinds of container. The wells at Erkelenz–Kückhoven had birch-bark containers, and later (in the fourth to third millennia BC) in the Alpine zone and elsewhere there are many examples known of wooden containers. Pots may have had formalised roles in the longhouse context, connected (as in south-east Europe) with the preparation and serving of food and drink, and therefore acting as tokens of hospitality. In the late phase, pottery styles became much more regionalised. The pattern of change was varied. In the Rhineland, for example, some style zones cover areas only tens of kilometres across. Further east, the Želiezovce style is found in south-east Poland, Slovakia, western Hungary and Austria, while the Šárka style is distributed in Bohemia and Silesia.[102] But if pottery communicated a sense of identity, these changing patterns indicate a tightening of regional allegiances.

Flint tools, like pots, would have been in daily use, part of the daily social environment.[103] Flint working was carried out by most longhouses, and there appear to have been prescribed zones of activity around longhouses. Methods of tool production seem to have been very similar across broad areas. Raw material was often acquired from surprising distances. On the Graetheide, the inhabitants of sites like Elsloo were only a few kilometres from good-

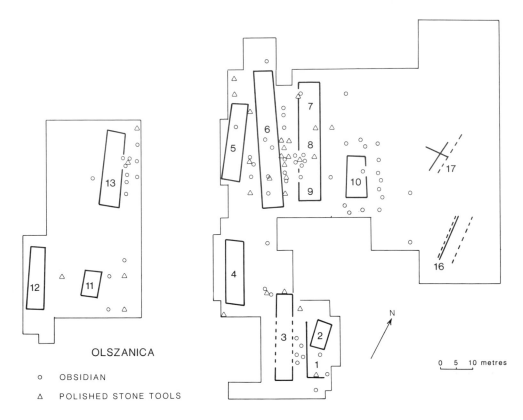

OLSZANICA

o   OBSIDIAN

△   POLISHED STONE TOOLS

6.12 The distribution of obsidian and polished stone tools around the longhouses at Olszanica. After Milisauskas.

quality flint from the chalk in the Maas valley around Rijckholt. The same source was used by the inhabitants of the Aldenhoven plateau, a further 30 km south. Many settlements may have been responsible for acquiring their own raw materials, indicating another kind of mobility within the LBK world. At the late site of Oleye in the Geer valley in eastern Belgium, very little preliminary debitage was found, suggesting to the excavators that procurement was carried out by other people.[104] This could also indicate seasonal movement.

Longer-range movement of raw material has also been documented. At the earliest phase site of Bruchenbrücken, most of the flint also came from Maas valley sources, here some 200 km away. At Bylany, the distances involved were even greater. In the first occupation, most of the flint was derived from Baltic erratics from the Elbe valley 100 km and more to the north. By the middle phases of occupation the largest percentage came from a Jurassic source north of Kraków in southern Poland, some 300 km away. The same source area supplied the nearby site of Olszanica, and it has been shown that flint was extracted from deep, open pits in the LBK period in this area, for example from the site of Sąspów. Some of the inhabitants of Olszanica had access to small quantities of obsidian from eastern Slovakia (or perhaps northern Hungary), over 150 km distant as the crow flies, with mountains in between.[105] Some of these materials may have been passed down a line of exchange, as might be envisaged for the ornaments of *Spondylus* which occur in the LBK area,[106] but for material like flint which was in regular use, an ordered pattern of acquisition is indicated. It is as though in solving a problem of daily need, LBK people chose to emphasise their contacts with a very much wider world.

The people of the LBK culture had stone axes and adzes. Axes had a symmetrical, rather flat cross-section. Adzes are the most distinctive heavy stone implement, with a plano-convex cross-section.[107] Probably both were hafted and put to general use in woodwork-ing, though much more research needs to be done on wear-traces. Some may have been weapons, and gruesome application has been seen in the case of the injuries inflicted on the Talheim victims. In some graves there were both axes and adzes, which suggests that the full heavy toolkit consisted of implements of both categories. Adzes have been found more often in graves than on settlements. At both Elsloo and Niedermerz, over thirty out of over 100 graves contained them. Usually there was one adze per grave, but some burials had more, up to four. The consensus is that the adze was associated particularly with men. In cemeteries like Elsloo and Niedermerz, where determination of sex is impossible, adzes tend to be associated with arrowheads, and where skeletons have been better preserved, as at Nitra, the main association is with men.[108] The settlement evidence from the Aldenhoven plateau and the Graetheide does not show any clear association between adzes and particular house types or sizes, nor in the case of the former area did the larger settle-ment of Langweiler 8 have any more proportionately than the smaller sites Langweiler 9 and Langweiler 2. It may be dangerous to generalise too far, however, since at Olszanica in southern Poland adzes were concentrated near the large longhouse, no. 6.[109]

The impression of open access or active circulation must be tied in with the nature of procurement of raw materials and finished tools. Axes and adzes were made of various fine-grained rocks. Many adzes were made of amphibolite, whose source has still not accu-rately been determined; a range from the Harz mountains to the Carpathians is canvassed in the literature.[110] For many areas of the LBK distribution the distances from stone source or sources to settlement use may not have been enormous, but in the north-west at least they are likely to have been considerable. There, most early adzes were made of amphibo-lite, and only later did more local basalts and sedimentary rocks come into greater use. Even in the later phases in eastern Belgium, there were still amphibolite adzes of presumably distant origin. Adzes seem to have arrived in settlements in a finished state. We do not know whether they were procured directly by the communities concerned, perhaps as part of patterns of seasonal mobility, whether they were supplied by specialists, or whether there was a general circulation by exchange from hand to hand.

Adzes have been seen as status indicators.[111] This view may be too simple. These arte-facts would certainly have been powerful symbols, perhaps carried about daily and there-fore highly visible, redolent of control over nature and suggestive of force and even violence, and imbued with an aura derived from their distant source. The question, not for the first time, is one of ownership. The status hypothesis assumes, implicitly, that a given artefact was acquired by a particular individual, and was deposited at death as a mirror of the social position of that person. Given the other formalisations of longhouse life and the wider context of cemetery burial, it may be more profitable to consider the adze as a badge, an important symbol of communal honour, continuity and full engagement with a wider social world. Such a material token may have been inheritable, passing from generation to generation to add further sanctity; only at certain moments may it have been deemed appropriate to deposit such powerful icons with the dead. The role of custodians in this sphere seems to have fallen to adult men. They may have competed among themselves for the honour of acquisition, but the evidence does not support a model of individual accumulation. These were objects which gained value by being seen, shared and transmitted, first among the living and then among the community of the dead. It is more likely, finally, that a reputation of this kind, rather than a more individualised value restricted to LBK men alone, would have made these items worth acquiring by forager communities around the LBK periphery, as seen at Skateholm II.

Ditched enclosures of the LBK: formalised communal space

Most LBK settlements were open, in the sense of lacking a defined, bounded perimeter. There are exceptions, as at Geleen–Janskamperfeld, where there was a palisade around the settlement area. Ditched enclosures are also known.[112] These were of varied size and form. Most enclosed quite a small area, rarely more than 2 ha. North-western examples illustrate diverse layouts. Langweiler 9 had a single, sub-circular ditch, punctuated by three entrances. Langweiler 8 had three concentric ditches, in a more squarish layout. There were at least two entrances through all three circuits, split by a single transverse ditch, and there are two other ordered gaps at the same points of the ditch circumference. At Langweiler 3, there were three successive arcs of ditch, none of which appears to have formed a complete circuit. Köln–Lindenthal had both ditch and palisade, laid out, perhaps in phases, to form one main ring and a minor annexe.[113] In most cases, the ditches were dug originally as a sharp, deep V, and their sections suggest rapid infill by erosion of the *loess* subsoil.

There are examples from other parts of the LBK distribution, for example the more irregular, shallow ditching at Eilsleben, and enclosures from Moravia and Lower Austria.[114] The number known continues to increase steadily, and new research conditions may bring forward others in those countries where aerial reconnaissance was formerly restricted. At the moment, more are known in the north-west. There their dates are largely late in the LBK sequence, though it has been claimed that there were examples from the middle LBK phase onwards.[115]

Two general categories suggest themselves, those with contemporary longhouses within them and those without. The former are in the minority. At Darion in the Geer valley in eastern Belgium, a discontinuous shallow ditch was set outside an oval palisade, doubled in parts. Four longhouses were grouped at one end of the interior. Parts of what appear to be similar arrangements have been found at the neighbouring sites of Oleye and Waremme. At Esbeck, Kr. Helmstedt, on the northern periphery of the LBK distribution, a double-ditched, squarish enclosure is associated with rather eroded house remains, which appear to be confined within the inner ditch.[116] At Köln–Lindenthal, arguments for and against contemporaneity of enclosure and houses can be advanced. On the Aldenhoven plateau there were no longhouses close to the Langweiler 3 arcs, and the chronological sequences suggest that the enclosure at Langweiler 9 succeeded the longhouse occupations on the

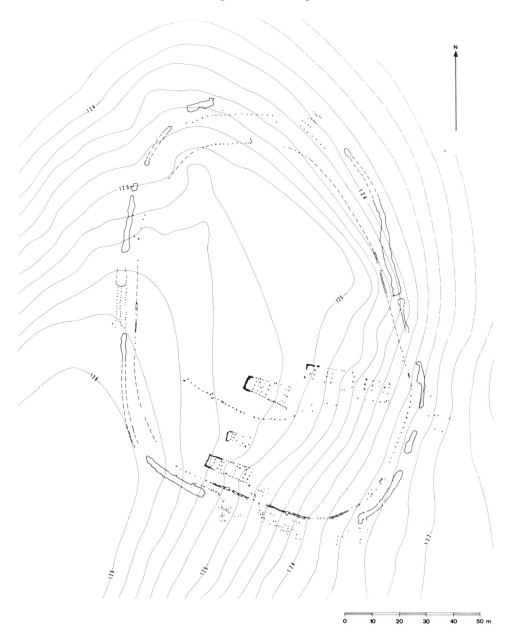

6.13 Plan of the houses and enclosure at Darion. After Cahen *et al.*

site, while at Langweiler 8 the enclosure belonged to the last phase of occupation, but was set 50 m or more from the remaining small group of dispersed longhouses. (Their remains were much eroded, but at least two appear to have been substantial, one with continuous plank walls.) There were few or no pits within the interiors, and finds in the ditches were scarce.[117]

In the cases of both the Geer valley sites and Esbeck, the excavators have suggested a defensive role. In eastern Belgium this has been connected with pioneer settlement on a hostile frontier still peopled by unfriendly forager neighbours. Esbeck might be fitted into the same sort of model. This fits the wider evidence unsatisfactorily. The presence of forager populations is not well established in eastern Belgium, though better documented in the north of the country.[118] What if, as argued earlier in the chapter, the LBK culture represents acculturated population anyway? At neither Darion nor Esbeck do the shallow ditches seem defensive. In both cases the enclosures are late in the LBK sequence. Friction on a frontier might be expected at the beginning, not the end of contact. As in north-east Bulgaria, discussed in chapter 4, bounded sites of this kind may have been part of mobile settlement patterns, with enclosure a means of defining place and establishing a routine of returns and permanence.

The Aldenhoven situation could have been rather different. Prosaic interpretations to do with stock corralling or the protection of plots are possible but unconvincing. The context of enclosure is the end of the LBK sequence. The enclosures appear to have formalised a space formerly used between longhouses (in the case of Langweiler 9) or adjacent to them (in the case of Langweiler 8). They were dug just before a restructuring of settlement into more nucleated forms (described in the next part of the chapter). They may have served to reinforce, over a very short timespan, a sense of purely local identity and independence, either by providing an arena for gatherings or simply by symbolically capturing spaces with a long tradition of communal activity. Inscribing such spaces with boundaries was akin to naming and categorising them. The consequences of the changes within the LBK world which produced such developments are followed in the next part of the chapter.

Longhouses and lagoons

The lives of foragers and farmers have often been seen as very different; the former share with and depend on nature, the latter produce from and control it. It may be fundamentally wrong in this period in central and western Europe, however, to give a determining role to the technicalities of subsistence. The adoption of crop cultivation and animal husbandry enabled people to consolidate ways of dealing with wooded, inland environments, by the strategy of radiating mobility. I have argued that this may have involved the acculturation of the indigenous population, rather than a colonisation from the fringes of the primary zone of Neolithic communities. Foragers in the coastal areas of north-western Europe were also able to shift to (or continue in, if their predecessors had already used the coastal zone intensively) patterns of radiating mobility. Foragers and forest farmers had different diets, but led rather similar lives. For coastal foragers, life was framed by use of a coastal zone with one or more bases, many of the necessities of life being derived from the rich resources of lagoon or estuary. There were periodic shifts of base, and forays inland. Contact with neighbours and with a wider world beyond was important. For forest farmers, life was framed by the longhouse settlement, set in small clearings in selected zones in the sea of woodland: artificial lagoons of productivity. There may have been seasonal forays as part of the cycle of animal husbandry, and periodic shifts of settlement bases, even of some of the largest sites. Contact with neighbours and a wider world beyond was important. Neither society appears to have been based on an ethic of accumulation or acquisition. Men and women probably had defined roles in both societies; we do not know what systems of descent were in use. Both societies emphasised attachment to place and continuity of occupation. For both the community of the dead was of basic importance. The dead were buried as known, remembered individuals, but through this treatment came to join the collectivity of the ancestors. The rites at Wittmar and Skateholm II, for example, only some 350 km apart, appear rather similar.

'Foragers' only slowly became 'farmers' around the northern and western periphery of the LBK culture, a major theme followed in the next part of the chapter. What separated them may have been a sense of identity and tradition, a style of self-definition, as much as a fundamental difference in outlook on the world. If the first forest farmers were in fact converted foragers themselves, their history of descent would explain many of the similarities to their forager neighbours. Constituent elements of self-definition, especially attitudes to culture and nature, are further explored later in the chapter.

Convergences: after 5000 to before 4000 BC

Pottery styles of the later stages of the LBK culture became more regionalised, and soon after 5000 BC different cultural groupings are recognised over the same broad area of distribution. These included the Lengyel culture (in Transdanubia, Slovakia, the Czech Lands, parts of southern and central Poland, and Bavaria and adjacent parts of Austria); the *Stichbandkeramik* culture (SBK) (as far west as the Rhine, and interleaved with or preceding Lengyel culture in Bohemia and southern Poland); the Hinkelstein and Grossgartach groups of parts of the Rhineland, with the Rössen culture succeeding all three roughly across the territory of present-day Germany; and the Villeneuve-Saint-Germain/Cerny groupings of northern France.[119]

Longhouses remained in use but their shape and construction changed. Some settlements were now perhaps more nucleated, or at least more bounded, and selected places may have become pre-eminent among local communities. In large parts of both the Lengyel and SBK distributions there were many ditched and palisaded enclosures with very formalised layouts; the number of discoveries has accelerated excitingly in the last few years. In these terms, there appears to have been substantial and significant change in the post-LBK horizon. From another perspective, however, the continuities were at least as great. Longhouse life was maintained, and the cultural environment was dominated still by decorated pots and stone adzes or axes; copper working was only very gradually introduced. The dead were disposed of in and around the settlement area, notably in cemeteries beside the zone of the living. The same sort of subsistence pattern was maintained; indeed some Lengyel sites in Transdanubia show far more use of wild game than in the LBK. The settlement system was not expansive, at either local or regional scales, even if the relationships between certain sites may have changed compared to the time of the LBK. Things that changed may have been part of a strategy to maintain and reinforce the existing Neolithic way of life.

In the same period, the coast-based life of foragers around the Baltic was continued or reinforced, enduring over several more centuries. The picture of this lifestyle has been amplified by a series of stunning discoveries over the last few years. As knowledge of the sequences around the Neolithic distribution has improved, so it has become more apparent that the final turning to what we define as a Neolithic lifestyle may have been quite rapid. Such rapidity contrasts with an apparent lack of evidence for change within the forager world in the fifth millennium BC; as among the forest cultivators and herders, the continuities were substantial.

I shall attempt to explain both the long duration of continuity and the final episode of change in terms of convergence. Both ways of life involved social relationships which had actively to be maintained. These were not the consequence of environmental conditions or subsistence practices. In both cases an idea of community may have bound people together, preventing dispersal and fragmentation, as well as accumulation and rivalry. Foragers may finally have chosen to adopt a culture which most successfully allowed them to maintain such values.

A repeated contrast: continued similarities between foragers and farmers

Woodland islands

Two sites of the mid to later fifth millennium BC in Kujavia in central Poland, Osłonki and Brześć Kujawski, can serve as examples of the continuation of longhouse lives.[120] Set about 10 km apart, each was sited in an area of fertile black soils on a low ridge partially surrounded by water. According to the results of intensive surface survey, each stands out as the major site in its vicinity, and it seems that there were no other significant sites between the two. There are signs of smaller, probably specialised camps. Each of the sites is characterised by the presence of trapezoidal longhouses, large pits, and graves dispersed through the settlement area, some beside houses, some in abandoned pits. In addition, Osłonki was encircled by a ditch, within which, according to the results of excavations so far, its houses lay. According to radiocarbon dating, the sites were in use for a long period of time, Osłonki perhaps beginning slightly earlier than Brześć Kujawski. At the latter, there were up to six superimpositions of house plans in certain plots.

Brześć Kujawski was the larger of the two. It has been subdivided into at least three subsites (3–5), perhaps a little artificially, but there are certainly variations in the density of houses across the large area (hundreds of metres across in total) in question. Speculatively, there could have been at least several houses in use at any one time in each cluster at Brześć and a similar number at Osłonki. It has been suggested that the basic and recurring social unit in these sites was the individual longhouse and its immediately surrounding space, containing large pit and work areas.[121] These structures are curious descendants of the LBK longhouse. They have broad front ends and narrow rear ends. Their walls were built from closely set posts or planks, and must also now have supported the roof, since there are no postholes within the interior.[122] These were imposing constructions up to 30 m long, set in rough rows with a regular north-south orientation. Scattered through both sites were individual burials, of men and women, and some children, variously provided with pots, stone and antler tools (usually with men), beads, pendants and in some cases copper ornaments in the form of simply made beads, sheets and diadems or head rings (usually with women). The orientation of graves generally followed that of longhouses, that is north-south, with the head of the corpse to the south mirroring the broad end of the trapezoidal longhouse.

House 56 in site 4 (the major concentration of buildings) at Brześć Kujawski has been taken to show the essential features of the individual household unit, since it lay a little apart on the north side of the site.[123] The plot was maintained over some period of time, as the house was renewed at least once. In both phases, the house was accompanied by a large irregular pit (probably for the extraction of wall loam/clay) and smaller pits, over a radius of about 20 m. Within this zone there were five burials in each phase, of mature men and women; one cranium of a child was found on its own at the bottom of a pit. In the smaller site 3, it was also possible to examine the history of an individual household, in the form of house 41, renewed as house 42. Again there was longhouse and large pit, and in the first phase a small pit with undercut sides for the live storage of tortoises and shellfish, and another irregular pit or working area where copper was smelted. House 41 ended in flames, like the first phase of house 56. Could these burnings have been deliberate? The tortoise pit became the grave for an adolescent, and there were other burials accompanying house 42.

The subsistence basis at Brześć Kujawski was very broad.[124] People kept domesticated animals and grew cereals; cattle appear to have been the most important domesticate, but pigs and sheep were also well represented. The scale of clearance is uncertain, and pollen analysis of deposits adjacent to Osłonki, currently underway, will be of considerable importance. People also hunted game and birds, and caught fish. Tortoises and shellfish were used, and there are deposits of butchered beaver bones, these animals probably being exploited not for food but for their skins. These various resources would have had periods of maximum abundance according to the rhythm of the seasons. It is a moot point how best to characterise these people in terms of their subsistence. Perhaps it is best not to choose between inadequate labels – 'farmers' versus 'foragers', for example – and more satisfactory to emphasise a broad strategy of herding, hunting, cultivation, collecting and foraging. This appears to represent a broader spectrum of resources than was evident in the LBK as a whole, but it is possible that the very good conditions of bone preservation in this region give a better picture of woodland existence than is normally possible from *loess* sites.

People did not exist solely within the confines of their longhouse plots. At Kuczyna 1 near Brześć Kujawski a semi-subterranean structure was found, which may have been connected with timber extraction from an area of poor soils. Most flint was locally available Baltic erratic, but there were also smaller quantities of both chocolate flint from over 150 km to the south-east and Jurassic flint from near Kraków in southern Poland, over 250 km to the south. (Flint distribution is discussed in further detail in the next chapter.) Copper too must have been acquired from non-local sources, presumably to the south-west or south.[125] A further complication must be mentioned. Brześć Kujawski, Osłonki and other similar sites belong culturally to the Brześć Kujawski late Lengyel group, in fact the end of the long 'Danubian' tradition begun at the start of the Neolithic. According to radiocarbon dates, this group overlaps with the beginning of the Funnel Beaker culture (TRB) in

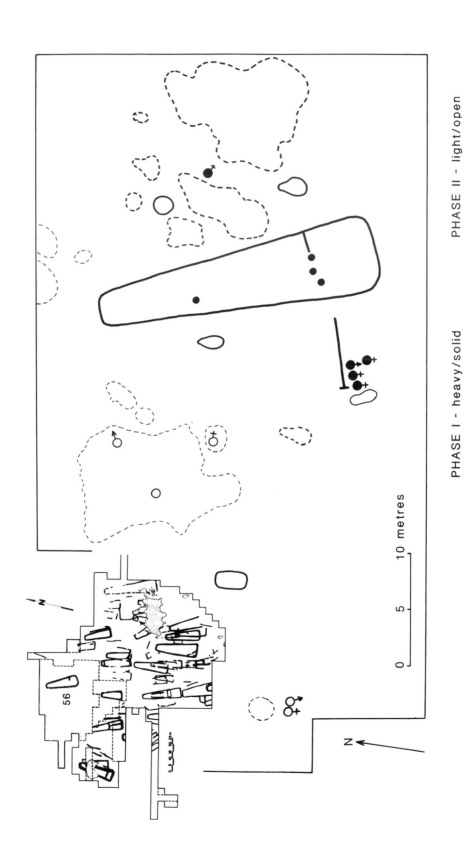

PHASE I - heavy/solid   PHASE II - light/open

6.14 Two phases of house 56, site 4, Brześć Kujawski. The overall plan of site 4 is inset, top left. After Grygiel and Bogucki.

0   5   10 metres

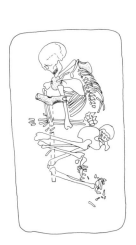
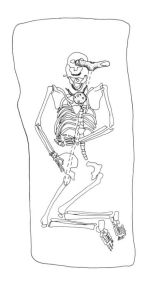
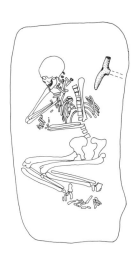

6.15 Late Lengyel culture graves from Brześć Kujawski, site 4. After Grygiel.

Kujavia. The TRB culture will be much further discussed in the next chapter.[126] A vigorous debate is taking place about TRB origins, the candidates for which are either indigenous Mesolithic people or offshoots of the 'Danubian' tradition; the argument can hardly be settled here. The relevant point, however, is that early TRB sites in Kujavia largely occupy sandy and morainic zones complementary to the black soil islands. Sarnowo is one such well-known example, some 20 km to the south-west of Brześć Kujawski.[127] This introduces another element into the wider world of Brześć Kujawski and Osłonki.

Were such sites permanently occupied? On the basis of research at other Lengyel sites in the region, especially Krusza Zamkowa near Inowrocław, one model is that residential bases were frequently relocated, to avoid soil depletion. The alternative model proposed for Brześć Kujawski and Osłonki is of stable, long-term occupation.[128] Perhaps again the concept of radiating or tethered mobility is most appropriate. Certain places became pre-eminent, in which there were the greatest aggregations of people and which were further sanctified by household burials. The link between graves and houses suggests that the long-house served in part as a metaphor for the continuity of human life. But although the long-house endured, to be perhaps on occasion deliberately destroyed before renewal, the individual occupants could have come and gone with the passage of the seasons, and the site chronologies are not sharp enough to exclude the possibility of relocations in neighbouring areas. As in the LBK, the maintenance of special places would have enabled the practice of mobility. And if the chronological overlap with early TRB sites in the region is real, the orbit of mobility may have become circumscribed.

6.16 Late Lengyel houses within a ditch and palisade at Osłonki. Photo: Grygiel.

Coastal life in the fifth millennium BC

According to traditional perceptions, life on the Baltic coastlines should have been rather different at this time, since these were inhabited by foragers, who did not build longhouses and did not cultivate cereals. The differences – as before – may have been more apparent than real. Two neighbouring sites from the south side of the Limfjord in northern Jutland, Ertebølle and Bjørnsholm–Åle, can serve as an introduction.[129]

The sites were some 8 km apart. Both were on the contemporary coastline, which then had more inlets than today, strategically placed at the head of a major inlet leading off the Limfjord. Bjørnsholm lay at the head of a side inlet, Ertebølle in a small bay on a straighter stretch of coast. Both sites consisted of large shell middens, formed by the accumulation of enormous quantities of discarded shellfish and other residues. The classic site at Ertebølle itself is a mound some 140 m or more long and 20–30 m wide (and up to 2 m high), but there are also two smaller accumulations to the south. Bjørnsholm-Åle forms a strip of similar accumulations up to 500 m long, and 30–50 m wide. Both were in use for a long period through the fifth millennium BC (pottery was made locally in the Ertebølle culture from the earlier–mid fifth millennium BC), and in fact there had been repeated occupations at Ertebølle before the shell midden began to accumulate. The composition of the middens varies. Shell was mixed with animal bones, fish bones, charcoal, ash, flints and sherds. There were hearths within the middens. Some of the accumulations at Ertebølle can be identified as the result of individual meals or quickly formed deposits (where pronounced heaps can be seen), while other areas seem to show more gradual build-up. Flint waste and other material show that the hearths within the middens were used as the locus for tool preparation, and recent excavations at both sites have also shown the use of adjacent areas, on the landward side of the mounds, for hearths and flint working. No substantial above-ground structures have so far been found. There were scattered human bones in the Ertebølle midden, according to the excavator perhaps from disturbed graves originally within the mound.

People exploited a wide range of resources. The shallow coastal waters were warm and saline. In the lower part sampled at Bjørnsholm-Åle oysters dominated, followed by cockles, mussels and periwinkles. Sea fish, eels, seals and porpoises were caught. At Ertebølle the greatest concentration of eel bone known from a Danish site was recorded; apart from that, there were fifteen or more species of seafish. Freshwater fish were also caught in nearby inland waters, including roach, rudd and pike. Both saltwater and freshwater fish may have been caught by means of fixed traps, and presumably the eels were so intercepted when they migrated from fresh water to the sea. Seabirds, ducks, swans and divers (both winter and summer migrants) are represented. The terrestrial vegetation was mixed oak woodland, in which or on the edges of which people hunted red and roe deer and wild pig. There were only a few bones of elk and aurochs at Ertebølle. Several fur-bearing species are represented, including wild cat, lynx, fox, otter, wolf and pine marten. There were domesticated dogs (as at Skateholm).

At both sites, these varied resources hint at the presence of people in each of the major seasons of the year. For example at Ertebølle, young red deer and pig indicate spring/summer; cockles were gathered in summer, when roach and garfish may also have been caught; eels were probably caught in late summer or autumn, when hazelnuts were collected; unshed red deer antler, and also furred game and ducks, may indicate winter occupation.

As was the question in Kujavia, does this indicate year-round occupation? Other smaller sites are known on the contemporary coastlines. It has been suggested that the large Ertebølle culture middens represent permanent bases, served by a network of ancillary camps, both on the coast and inland; this will be discussed further below.[130] The same ambiguities and possibilities exist as in Kujavia. The wonderfully preserved food residues can be seen as much as the by-product of gatherings of people as the reason for the existence of this kind of site. Ertebølle was already old and well known before it became a shell midden. People marked a special place by repeated visits, the physical remains of which came also to form a permanent and enduring marker on the landscape. Such a point may have had some people permanently at it, or in the surrounding zone, but it may also have articulated the circulation of people through varied zones of exploitation, within each year and from year to year. Burial grounds and material items from distant sources, discussed further below, complete the striking similarities between supposedly different farmers and foragers.

Settlement and place: the elaboration of a tradition

In most areas right across the large region under discussion Neolithic settlements were to be found in the same sorts of locations in the landscape in this phase as in the preceding LBK culture. People regularly chose *loess* and other fertile soils, generally siting their settlements near water and on the edge of small valleys. In southern Poland, for example, Lengyel–Polgar sites are found in the same tributaries of the Vistula as LBK predecessors. Similar continuity can be found in Transdanubia and Lower Austria, and in the *Stichbandkeramik* areas of Bohemia and the Elbe–Saale region, as also probably in the Rhineland and in the Paris basin.[131] This was not a universal pattern. In south-west Slovakia through the Lengyel sequence, there was a detectable shift to brown earth soils from the black earths favoured in the LBK period, and to a wider range of site locations, including some on sandy soils; on the other hand, large and self-evidently important sites were still to be found on the terraces of tributaries of the Danube.[132] In many areas, there was continuity of occupation of the same sites, though there were also hiatuses in the history of individual locations. As examples, we find SBK occupations at sites like Bylany and Hienheim. By contrast, on the Aldenhoven plateau there were only sporadic later features on the long-lived earlier sites like Langweiler 8, and Grossgartach and Rössen settlements were relocated, in the same sort of places, but on new ground.[133]

Few areas saw significant increase in the density of settlement. Kujavia may be an exception. There has been a tendency crudely to count points on maps. In some cases, for example in the Elbe–Saale region, the number of SBK points actually declines relative to those of the LBK. But what is really notable here and elsewhere is the tendency for large or nucleated sites to emerge; the overall density of settlement may not have substantially increased, but the distribution of population within a given area may often have shifted. Where pollen evidence is available, for example in the upper Vistula basin, in the upper Danube or near the Aldenhoven plateau, there is no obvious increased impact on woodland.[134] Woodland itself may have continued as a valuable resource, for timber, as noted above in Kujavia near Brześć Kujawski, or for grazing and hunting. A striking development in the animal bone assemblages from Lengyel sites in Transdanubia, for example at Aszód, is a greater percentage of wild animals (seen also at the same sort of time in Tisza assemblages on the Hungarian plain).[135] Antler was intensively worked at Aszód, but the significance of the shift may be wider than an interest in useful raw materials. Does the increase in woodland game show a reversion to forager habits, or in fact more intensive use of woodland in the catchments around large, but spaced, big sites? Could it reflect a continuation or even an extension of patterns of mobility, taking people regularly out into the landscape, as well as using their longhouse bases?

These are some of the considerable continuities to be seen in the lives of the successors of the LBK culture. Within settlements, the longhouse continued as the primary focus, and although styles changed, people used the same kind of range of material culture as before, including decorated pots and stone tools. There was the same interest in acquiring flint and stone from distant sources, supplemented in the Lengyel area by a new interest in the acquisition and production of simple copper items, but again presumably motivated by an interest in the distant and the exotic.[136] People probably had much the same sort of diet in this period, although there are some changes in the percentages of animals, as noted above, and in crop species used.[137] In western areas, new varieties of crop may have been introduced from the Mediterranean sphere.[138] As in Kujavia, the dead were still closely linked to the settlement (and in that instance closely to the longhouse). Burial grounds adjacent to settlements, serving either particular communities or a wider region, continue to be a feature. There was a SBK cemetery in the Bylany complex, with cremations as well as inhumations, and there are well known examples in the Rhineland near Worms, and later at Rössen itself, Kr. Merseburg, in the Elbe–Saale region.[139] One example of continuity comes from Wittmar, Kr. Wolfenbüttel, near the northern limits of the *loess* in the region of Braunschweig (and only some 350 km from contemporary Ertebølle burial grounds like Skateholm, Vedbaek or Strøby Egede, which I discuss further below).[140] Here Rössen graves overlapped the area of LBK burials, but were oriented at right angles to their predecessors. Whether or not there was direct continuity of use of the burial ground, there was only one instance in it of a Rössen grave actually cutting an earlier LBK one.

This world was not, however, unchanging. There were, for instance, significant hiatuses in the occupation of individual settlements and micro-regions. At Bylany, most of the SBK occupation belongs to the later stages of the proposed sequence for the *Stichbandkeramik* culture, and on the Aldenhoven plateau it is not clear what happened immediately after the end of the LBK sequence (after phase XV of the Merzbachtal sequence followed here, as described above).[141] It is possible that the extent of hiatus is exaggerated by our attachment to the culture model; as noted above, few sites in the LBK show complete continuity of occupation anyway. Another trend was towards the emergence of nucleated or large sites. On the Aldenhoven plateau, for example, there were groupings of longhouses which were prominently bounded by palisade enclosures, for example at Inden–Lamersdorf, Jülich–Welldorf and Bedburg–Kaster.[142] The concentration of houses at these sites may have been no greater than that represented by the many phases of Langweiler 8, but the style of settlement appears to have become locally more common than that of Langweiler 8 in the LBK period. These nucleations had shorter histories than had been the case at Langweiler 8; up to four phases are suggested for Inden-Lamersdorf.

In the same phase, the shape, layout, construction and to some extent the size of longhouses changed. Houses became more markedly trapezoidal. Was this to emphasise the importance of the entrance at the broad end, and the conditions under which access to and membership of a household were granted? The interior of the longhouse was now far less cluttered with internal posts, and the roof was now largely carried by the side walls, which had extra posts. These were sometimes bowed slightly outwards, producing a boat-shaped plan. Although contemporary floors continue to be frustratingly absent from the archaeological record, it is possible that in some instances more people used fewer houses. There were often clear internal cross-walls, providing two or three compartments. Some trapezoidal houses achieved spectacular lengths. At Deiringsen–Ruploh, Kr. Soest, in the Rhineland, two trapezoidal houses with continuous wall trenches were over 50 m long (a third, with spaced posts and more internal compartments or subdivisions, was a more modest 25–30 m), and three at Inden–Lamersdorf were over 40 m long.[143] A related

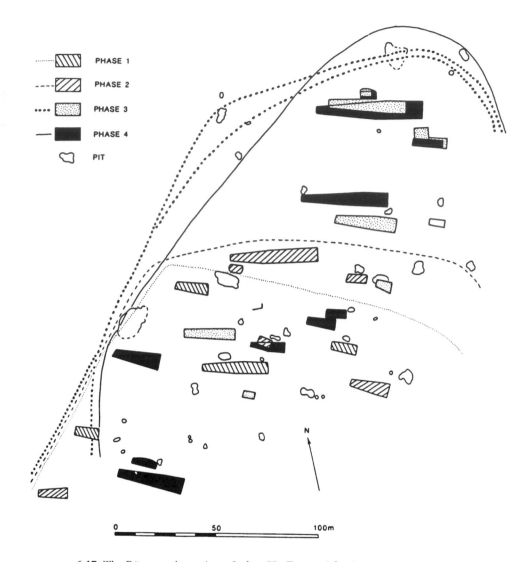

6.17 The Rössen culture site at Inden, Kr. Düren. After Lüning.

development here was the appearance of much smaller structures which seem, from the site plan, to belong to particular large longhouses.

At Bylany, the extent of SBK occupation was probably no greater than in the preceding LBK phases, and may have been smaller. Although many larger and smaller pits were recorded, only three SBK house plans were found, though these are well enough known from other Bohemian sites. It seems likely that rather more were originally present at Bylany.[144]

Large sites are notable in Hungarian Transdanubia and its surrounds at the bend of the Danube and in southern Slovakia. Probably owing to the conditions of excavation, relatively few longhouse plans are known in Transdanubia, but big open excavations at Svodín in southern Slovakia have yielded many.[145] The pattern often appears to be of one large site dominating a micro-region. Around Aszód, strategically placed east of the bend of the Danube in the Galga valley which feeds into the Tisza, there were many other Lengyel sites, but none of similar size. A very large area of occupation is characterised mostly by pits and graves; the total extent could be as much as 20–25 ha. Some small houses have been recognised. Graves have been found mainly in linear groups of around thirty, separated one from another by strips some 10–20 m wide. The total could run into hundreds or more. Men, women and many children were represented. Grave goods were very diverse, including pots, stone tools, jaws and tooth pendants of boar, and beads and armrings of imported *Spondylus*; some third of the graves had no goods, and there were empty graves or cenotaphs.[146]

Other large Lengyel sites are known in southern Transdanubia, at Lengyel itself, Zengővárkony, and Mórágy-Tűzkődomb.[147] At Mórágy, pits were again prominent. Some contained carefully placed deposits, which may be a further clue to the nature of this kind of site. One had a large handled bowl, a quern fragment, two rubbing stones, some pieces of animal bone, and a female clay figurine. Zengővárkony had some 400 graves, as at Aszód spread over a large area and arranged in clusters. At these sites single inhumations were the dominant rite, and men, women and children are again represented. There were some deposits at Mórágy of child skulls and child skeletons buried in pots, and there were also dog burials. There were many grave goods, including pots, ornaments (a few of copper) and perforated stone hammer-axes. Grave goods varied in abundance; there were probable gender-related differences; and some of the most abundant inventories appear to come from the centre of grave clusters.[148] But it does not seem legitimate to infer marked social difference from these inventories. More striking is the repeated marking or sanctification of chosen places from within the zone of settlement by association with the dead. These very large Transdanubian sites may be exceptional. We do not have to regard them as permanently occupied. At Mórágy, there are traces of a ditch system, which may unite the site with the next important development to be discussed, the Lengyel and *Stichbandkeramik* ditched enclosures.

Ditched enclosures: the formalisation of place

One of the most striking successes of Neolithic archaeology in recent years has been the discovery of more and more ditched and palisaded enclosures, belonging to the *Stichbandkeramik* and early Lengyel cultures. After extensive excavations at sites in Slovakia and Moravia, notably Svodín and Těšetice–Kyjovice, a scatter of other sites was located, including several in Bohemia; continued research at Bylany has produced two, in site areas 1 and 4.[149] Aerial photography then revealed many more sites in Lower Austria and southeast Bavaria (classed as belonging to the Oberlauterbach group), and even one or two examples further north in Sachsen and Sachsen–Anhalt. As a result the density of sites is greater outside the originally recognised area of distribution, but this can only reflect the virtual impossibility, for politico-military reasons, of sustained aerial survey up to 1989 in several of the countries in question. Apart from Sé in the extreme west (and possibly Lengyel itself), there are no known examples to date in Transdanubia, a situation which will surely change soon. Excavations at Mórágy have produced a ditch, though not yet of classic form.[150]

Svodín and Těšetice–Kyjovice serve very well to introduce these important new developments. Svodín was a large early Lengyel settlement in southern Slovakia, on a *loess*-covered terrace in the tributary system of the Danube, which runs some 16 km to the south. The settlement included both longhouses and graves over a large area (over 500 m across). The settlement had already been in existence for some time before the first of two phases of enclosure was constructed. This consisted of a circular ditch over 60 m in diameter, probably provided with four symmetrically opposed entrances, with traces of two palisade rings inside it. The ditch was some 3 m wide, and its V-shaped section reached over 3.5 m in depth. Longhouses of the continuing settlement were arranged radially outside it, but there was no sign of any structure within it. This 'roundel' was replaced in the next phase of occupation by a larger version, consisting of two great circular ditches over 140 m in diameter, furnished with four opposed entrances with out-turned terminals, and three internal palisade rings, each with a narrow in-turned entrance. The dimensions are impressive. Both ditches were up to 5 m deep, but the inner ditch was wider than the outer (6–7.5 m compared to 4 m). The distance from the outermost point of the ditch terminals to the innermost palisade entrance was fully 40 m, confronting the entrant with at least five visually graded experiences. We do not know whether there was a bank of any kind between the ditches. Behind the two outer palisade rings lay in each case a row of spaced posts, which presumably formed part of supports or even a wall-like construction. Once again there seem to have been no structures within. Outside, the use of longhouses and graves continued. Houses lay close to the edge of the ditch system, and the largest examples uncovered in fact lay close to the north-west entrance. The V-shaped ditches silted up quickly by natural erosion of the *loess*, and were recut four or five times. How long this represents is uncertain, but the primary use of the construction might only have been as long as its wooden parts endured, and there is no evidence that they were renewed. The settlement probably continued in use as the enclosure began to decay. No other such enclosures are known at present in the immediate vicinity, but there were examples at Nitriansky Hrádok and Bučany, some 30 and 70 km north-west respectively.[151]

Těšetice–Kyjovice lay on higher ground in the western part of the Morava basin. Its outer perimeter was defined by a roughly circular palisade (some 110 by 125 m), with four opposed, narrow entrances. Inside this lay a much smaller 'roundel', formed by a ditch some 60 m in diameter, pierced by four broad entrances aligned on those of the outer palisade and complemented by two inner palisade rings, also with broad, aligned entrances. The site belongs to the early Lengyel culture. It was preceded by a *Stichbandkeramik* occupation, some of whose large pits were cut by the inner palisades. There was no sign of Lengyel settlement in any part of the area within the outer palisade. Within the roundel, a few contemporary pits may have been connected with special depositions. One contained painted pottery and a human skull; another by the west entrance had many fragments of wall daub. There were a few other human remains, and some quantities of painted pottery

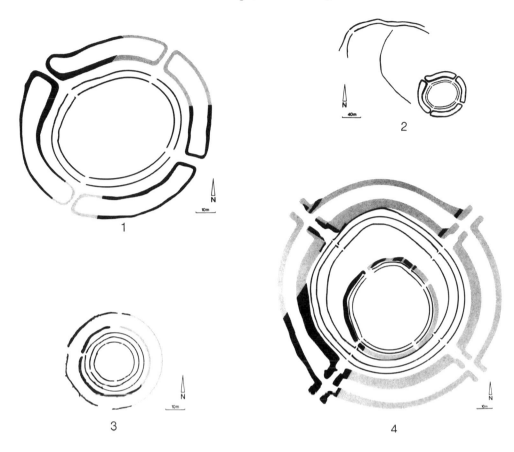

6.18 Lengyel and Stichbandkeramik enclosures. 1–2: Künzing–Unternberg, Bavaria; 3: Vochov, Bohemia; 4: Svodín 1 and 2. After Petrasch.

and figurines in the lower ditch fill. The V-shaped ditch, here up to 4 m broad and 3 m deep, had not obviously been recut, and appears quickly to have infilled by natural erosion. There were several other enclosures of similar or related type in the Morava basin, including Němčičky, Křepice, Vedrovice and Bulhary.

As aerial survey and investigation on the ground have intensified, so recognition of the extent of variation among these enclosures has increased.[152] Kamegg in Lower Austria has a well-separated outer perimeter defined by both ditch and palisade; it is possible that one replaces the other. At some sites the ditches are linked by connecting terminals, as at Friebritz 2 in Lower Austria or Künzing–Unternberg in Bavaria. There are examples of three concentric ditches, as at Osterhofen–Schmiedorf in Bavaria, and several examples in Lower Austria including Glaubendorf 2, Gauderndorf and Hornsburg 3. Many have four symmetrically opposed entrances, aligned more or less on the main cardinal points, but there are variations: only two opposed entrances piercing all three ditch rings and the two palisade rings at Osterhofen–Schmiedorf, or two non-opposed entrances through the ditches and unaligned breaks in the three inner palisade rings at Vochov, Bohemia. Some sites were bounded by extensive outer ditch works, as again at Osterhofen–Schmiedorf and Künzing–Unternberg, or at Kothingeichendorf, also in Bavaria.

A formal distinction between 'roundels' and other less formal ditched and palisaded enclosures might prove premature; context rather than classification may be the key. Quenstedt in the Elbe–Saale region is a useful example.[153] It probably belonged to the SBK culture. It had no ditches, and is therefore formally not a 'roundel' but its five concentric palisades and their three narrow entrances offered gradations of space and experience, and a predetermined ordering of movement. On the other hand, it was clearly important to many communities to dig defining ditches to a pre-set and recognisable form, even though in most cases these were destined quickly to silt up. Žlkovce in southern Slovakia is one more example of the problem of what form and formality meant.[154] This was a large and long-lived Lengyel settlement in the Váh valley, not far from the 'roundel' at Bučany. The overall area of occupation may have been as much as 30 ha. Within this was an outer palisade, some 350–400 m in diameter; longhouses and other remains were found both inside and outside it. Roughly in the centre of things was a smaller, oval palisade, over 75 m across. This was renewed up to six times. Each phase may have enclosed one substantial longhouse, but not more. In what sense should this be distinguished from the formal and ditched layouts of the 'roundels', which are themselves very varied in layout and context?

In many instances there seems to be a clear connection with large concentrations of occupation or settlement. Continued research at Bylany has produced evidence of one double-ditched, four-entranced 'roundel' (probably with another ditch a further 75 m out), and another enclosure with large outer palisade and perhaps inner ditches, as well as areas of SBK occupation and a separate SBK burial ground. None of these bounded spaces seems to have been used intensively for occupation or standing architecture. Bučany, like Žlkovce with one internal structure, stands out as an exception. The presently known distributions suggest some regularity in the spacing of such sites, in the area of the junction of the Isar and Danube in Bavaria for example at intervals of 6–8 km.[155] The ditches of these sites were prone to quick natural infilling. Some were recut, as at Svodín or Künzing–Unternberg.[156] Others appear to have been shorter-lived. In both cases, the enclosures were begun in specific circumstances, and were probably constructed rather rapidly to predetermined plans.

What were those circumstances and intentions? I discount defence and fortification. Had these been major factors, one could expect more of this kind of site right through the Neolithic/Copper Age sequence. A different approach might be to regard these sites as places of social pre-eminence, where labour could be mobilised for impressive collective undertakings. In this case it is hard to see what prevented every community or locale from having a monument of this kind, and the spacing and chronological specificity again sit uneasily with such an explanation. More promisingly, several scholars have discussed these enclosures as cult centres or meeting places, and there may have been a link with the marking of time, seen in their cardinal orientations.[157] This kind of interpretation could be taken much further, to link such sites not only with cult or ritual but with the consecration of place, the marking of time, the presence of the ancestors and the symbolic representation of communal cohesion. Much depends still on the nature of settlement. Mobility may still have been

6.19 Inner ditch sections at Künzing–Unternberg. Photo: Petrasch.

important in people's lives. Investing not only labour but also symbolic capital in chosen places could have increased attachment to territory on the one hand and enabled continued mobility on the other. The defined ways in which people must have approached, entered and experienced such monuments could be seen as a metaphor for the regularities of the comings and goings of their own lives, both from year to year and from generation to generation. People were building a tradition or idea of permanence and order.

Why now? Why did the longhouse not continue to serve a similar purpose? It is perhaps puzzling that there were not more such enclosures further to the west and north in other areas of the 'Danubian' tradition, given the numbers of late LBK ditched enclosures, discussed above. Bochum-Harpen in the Rhineland and Berry-au-Bac in the Aisne valley, belonging to the Rössen and Cerny cultures respectively, provide examples but really serve to point up the marked disparity of distribution.[158] Conventional, 'evolutionary' explanations based on increases in social strife, community differentiation or population density are superficially attractive, but they fail to account for the short-lived and regional nature of the enclosure phenomenon. This might rather be explained in religious or spiritual terms, but if a connection with other aspects of society is legitimate, the best general interpretation may be of a reaffirmation and strengthening of the idea of community. These monuments did not just reflect the stabilisation of longhouse life, they were part of its maintenance. Through reinforced attachment to specific places, chosen times for communal gathering and ritual, predetermined ways of seeing and experiencing ordered space, people were encouraged to maintain the rhythms and obligations of tethered mobility.

Burial grounds and burial monuments

To expect too much uniformity of practice may be to underestimate the diversity and creativity of Neolithic communities. A further answer to the question of the restricted distribution of formalised enclosures is that other practices may have served the same kind of ends, by different means. The varied histories of tell settlements on the Hungarian plain, of formalised ditched enclosures in the LBK and then in parts of the SBK-early Lengyel world, and of shell middens on the Baltic coasts, all begin at the same sort of time. Another continuing facet of the attachment to place was through the presence of the dead. This was clearly not exclusive of other practices, since we have seen the dead in Tisza culture tells on the Hungarian plain, and in large early Lengyel and SBK sites like Svodín and Bylany. Other examples from the Ertebølle complex are discussed below; other burial grounds came into use at Skateholm, for example. Brześć Kujawski and Osłonki have already provided examples of sites where communal identity continued to be focused through concentrations of longhouses and graves. One possibility with the large Transdanubian early Lengyel sites like Aszód or Zengővárkony is that the very large burial grounds represent some kind of equivalent to the formalised place seen in ditched enclosures. As noted above, these graves show variation in the range of grave goods and to some extent in burial rites, but more significant overall may be the multiple groupings of smaller burial grounds to make larger wholes, the presence of men, women and children together, and the lack of *extreme* differentiation in either the form of graves, the treatment of the dead, or the general nature of grave goods. These look like places of open access, where the dead of communities from a wide area around could be brought to rejoin a central, shared ancestral order.

This kind of tradition also continued strongly more to the west. The Hinkelstein burial grounds in the Rhineland, as at Worms–Rheingewann and Worms–Rheindürkheim, or Rössen cemeteries as at Rössen itself or Jechtingen, Kr. Emmendingen in Baden–Württemberg, have abundant inventories of pots, stone tools and ornaments.[159]

Frustratingly, it has proved harder to link settlements and graves in this area at this time. The Worms and Rössen finds were made long ago, Wittmar was examined in a restricted urban context, and on the Aldenhoven plateau several nucleated or bounded settlements have been found but not so far a major burial ground of this phase. More positively, this separation might be taken to suggest the continuation of a tradition of burial grounds, often placed apart, which served not just a particular settlement but a wider area, as suggested already in the LBK phase for the case of the Niedermerz cemetery in the Merzbachtal.

There is a last strand further west still: the appearance of the first megalithic cairns or barrows. These impressive, three-dimensional constructions were variously connected with ancestral spirits and the disposal of and cult of the dead, and it has often been suggested that the monuments of rectangular or trapezoidal form represent some kind of transformation of the idea of the longhouse.[160] The main distributions are westerly, from central-western France through Brittany and Normandy, Britain and Ireland, to large parts of the North European plain and southern Scandinavia. It has been claimed that there are examples from central-western France, as at Bougon, near Poitiers in Deux-Sèvres, and in northern Brittany, as at Barnenez, Côtes-du-Nord, and Île Guennoc, Finistère, which date to the earlier to mid fifth millennium BC. This is on the basis of radiocarbon dates, on both charcoal and human bone samples.[161] Bougon has circular and more elongated stone cairns, containing small chambers approached by narrow passages. The first, southern part of Barnenez was a large trapezoidal stone cairn, containing five chambers and passages, opening from one long side; Île Guennoc is a similar version of the same kind of layout, with at least four primary chambers. Another early date has come from the circular cairn at Kercado in the Morbihan.

These dates have provoked a long and vigorous debate, recently rekindled by new results from Bougon. Those who accept them argue that constructions of this kind could have resulted from a fusion of Mesolithic and Neolithic technologies, traditions and ideologies in western France. The expanding Neolithic world of the Paris basin, of the still rather uncertainly defined post-LBK or Cerny tradition, could have brought the idea and values of the longhouse to a region where small collective burials had already been made, set in stone- and antler-framed cists in late Mesolithic coastal shell middens in Brittany, as at Téviec and Hoëdic in the Morbihan. This region may also have been influenced and changed by contacts with the Mediterranean world (discussed further in chapter 8).[162] The difficulties are twofold. On the one hand, most of the radiocarbon samples have been charcoal, and the wood thus dated may have been considerably older than the archaeological events in question. On the other hand, substantial early constructions run counter to rival notions of the gradual development of cairns and chambers through a long sequence.[163]

This is a classic and important problem. I believe that a later development for western constructions, from the later part of the fifth millennium BC, better fits both the individual site and regional evidence, and the wider picture of changes being sketched here. I shall therefore examine Breton and other constructions in the next chapter.

There is some other evidence in support of gradual development, which returns us to the Paris basin and then to Kujavia in central-northern Poland. At Passy in the Yonne

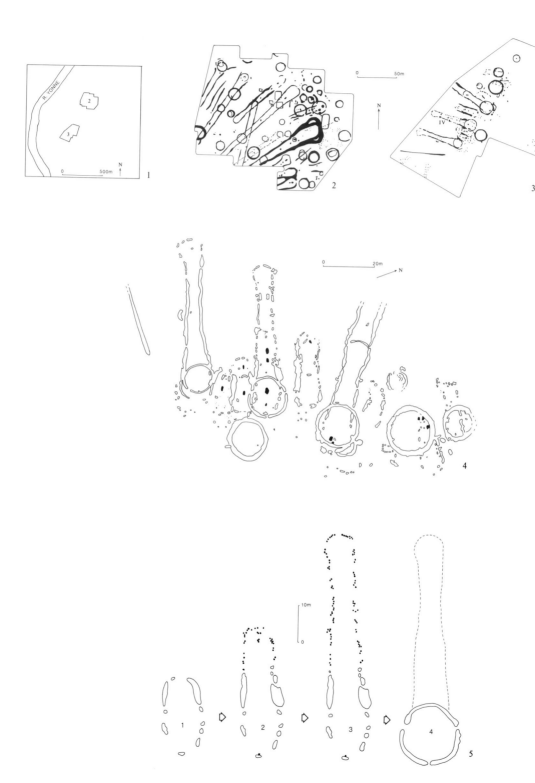

6.20 Burial structures at Passy. 1: plan; 2: area A; 3: area B; 4: detail of area B; 5: development of structure IV in area B. After Duhamel and Prestreau.

valley, a tributary which joins the Seine south of Paris, there are at least thirty elongated burial structures, sharing roughly the same orientation.[164] These were regularly 60 m long, with some shorter and one up to 300 m long. Their long sides were defined by quite narrow ditches and some stretches of post holes, and the east end often by a circular ditch. Extended single burials, of adults and children, modestly furnished with arrowheads, pots, bone tools and beads, have been found either on the central axis or in the east end of these monuments. Narrow ditches and post holes may suggest that these were enclosures rather than mounds. No. 4 in the Richebourg sub-site had gone through a process of elongation, beginning about 20 m long, and then being extended in two stages to 60 m, with four burials down the central axis. The last phase of alteration saw the addition of a circular ditched terminal. These monuments appear to belong to the Villeneuve-Saint Germain/Cerny tradition.

In Kujavia, a new view is that the Funnel-Necked Beaker or TRB culture began to emerge from the mid fifth millennium BC, overlapping chronologically with the Lengyel tradition seen at Brześć Kujawski and Osłonki, but occupying a different niche in the land-scape.[165] This view again relies on radiocarbon dates. Those from early TRB occupations at Sarnowo and Lącko overlap squarely those from Brześć Kujawski and Osłonki. At site 1a at Sarnowo, a small occupation area included scatters of artefacts, two small rectangular huts or houses and a handful of individual burials in simple earth-cut graves. It might be more consistent with the view adopted here of Breton dating and development to envisage another case of confusion spread by radiocarbon dates on charcoal samples. But if the chronological overlap is valid, a further innovation comes into the picture. At Sarnowo and at other sites in Kujavia, there are elongated trapezoidal or triangular earthen mounds, fringed by small stone kerbs, which cover at their broad ends, variously, individual burials or small numbers of individual burials generally laid in shallow simple pits, or directly on the old land surface.[166] The early date for TRB material at Sarnowo comes from an occupation beneath barrow 8, but finds with the burials and in the mounds are also of early type in barrow 8 and others. Traditionally, most scholars would have regarded these Kujavian mounds as later than the longhouses of sites like Brześć Kujawski and Osłonki. Now there is the possibility that a new cultural tradition imitated the longhouse idea and inscribed it in new form, while longhouses still existed. The Passy sites in the Paris basin, whether enclo-sures or mounds, may show a similar transformation, though within a single cultural tradi-tion. This may be a more satisfactory developmental stage to precede the major burst of constructions which accompanies the extension of the Neolithic into those parts of central, northern and western Europe occupied till the later fifth millennium BC by indige-nous forager communities.

The continuing and changing world of foragers

The Ertebølle–Ellerbek complex

Somewhere round about the middle of the fifth millennium BC people sat in the dark in a narrow dugout canoe almost 10 m long on the shallow coastal waters off the north-west shore of the present-day island of Fyn in Denmark. A small fire of charcoal glowed in the bottom of the craft, and light from it was probably used to attract fish. The people were fishing for eels, which they speared with double-headed prongs. How different such a scene, based on evidence from the coastal Ertebølle culture site, now submerged, at Tybrind Vig,[167] may seem from the business of keeping cattle and tending growing crops on the *loess* to the south. As I have already argued, the differences may be more apparent than real. There is abundant evidence from the Baltic-Scandinavian coasts for well-established forager communities, of the Ertebølle–Ellerbek–Lietzow complex; and coastal or coastal-zone sites are also well recorded in parts of the western Netherlands, Britain and Ireland, and Brittany. Inland, there is evidence for foragers in the Alpine foreland, in parts of the north European plain, and in many parts of Britain. All these communities cannot be characterised as exactly alike. Indeed the exciting evidence from the Ertebølle area has tended to colour interpretations of rather different situations elsewhere.[168] But it is hard to resist beginning with that complex.

Tybrind Vig lay on the coast, fronting shallow, warm, resource-rich waters. The site was in use for a long period through the fifth millennium BC. The total area of the site was large but how much was in use at any one time is not known, not least because what largely survive are the residues and remains in front of and immediately offshore from the site, rather than the occupation areas themselves. People used a wide variety of marine and terrestrial resources. At sea, they caught eels, small cod and spurdog, and seals, porpoises and whales. The food crust on pots indicates fish mixed with dry-land plants. People were certainly at the site in different seasons of the year, in summer, autumn and winter, though it is not clear whether they were there year-round. Their technologies of extraction and transport were effective, and to our eyes (and why not theirs too?) elegant: carefully flaked flint core axes; neatly plaited rope and fabric woven from plant fibre; skilfully carved wooden arrows and waisted bows; strong bone hooks and wooden double fishing prongs ('leisters'); and brown-patterned paddles, made of supple ash, which have justifiably attracted considerable attention.

There were many other coastal sites in other parts of the western Baltic. Some were small and seasonally occupied, and some may have been used for specialised purposes, like the swan-fowling at Aggersund in northern Jutland, or the seal-hunting at Ølby Lyng on the east coast of Jutland. Inland sites may have been scarcer, though while favourable lakeside conditions continued, as at Ageröd in central Scania in southern Sweden, they were often used. In Jutland, Ringkloster is an inland lakeside camp, from which hunting was organised, specialising in the pursuit of pig. This was possibly mainly in summer (indicated by remains of red deer calves, probably exploited for their hides), but winter exploitation is indicated by pine martens, whose fur would have then been at its best, and by unshed red deer antler. The bone remains at Ringkloster suggest that at least some of the meat was processed at the site but then taken away for use elsewhere, especially in the form of back ends. The obvious candidates for recipients were the larger coastal sites. Norsminde and Flynderhage on the Norsminde fjord, with a series of other, smaller sites, were only some 15 km from Ringkloster.[169] Many scholars have argued that at least some of the larger coastal sites, including the big shell middens, were in use more or less throughout the year.[170] A gloss on this is that shell middens may represent sites of special use, for large gatherings, feasts and rituals, which drew the coastal population together at several different times of the year. Whether or not people stayed in the same spot from month to month may hardly be demonstrable, nor in the end crucial; what does matter is the enduring stability of a system in which people may have moved around but were concentrated within the coastal zone. The special places, once again, served to anchor the shifting raft of daily and seasonal routines.

Occupation of the Skateholm lagoon in southern Sweden continued through the fifth millennium BC.[171] There were both small camps and the larger sites I and III, each of which could be regarded in turn as the major base. At Skateholm I, graves occupied a large area adjacent to the settlement. Men, women and children continued to be interred, usually separately, but there were very few child burials. Dog burials were also continued, but most were now on their own in what may have been regarded as a separate canine area. Ochre continued to indicate regeneration and fertility, but antler was no longer used. Fewer people were laid to rest stretched out than in Skateholm II, and rather more in crouched positions than was the case in the earlier burial ground. The number and quality of grave goods are said to have declined through time, while there is an apparent tendency in Skateholm I for older men and young women to receive the greatest amounts. Grave goods as well as the graves themselves could have helped to fix a collective memory of a long past. One grave of a woman (Skateholm I, no. 6) included the tooth of an elk, which would have been very rare in the area, and the find may have been very old, recalling the aurochs tooth beads of similarly venerable antiquity in some of the Skateholm II female burials. Some of the graves intersect, but most must have been marked and their positions respected. There are some variations in orientation, perhaps just reflecting the passage of time. It might be legitimate to see in the plan the existence of separate groupings. In that case, both groupings and orientations may have created or marked allegiances within the wider community of the assembled dead. This sacred ground may have served a wide area, not just the adjacent lagoon. There were at least sixty-five graves in Skateholm I (fifty-seven for people, with sixty-two represented, and eight for dogs).

Many more Ertebølle burial places are coming to light, showing varied rites and situations. The discovery of Skateholm was directly inspired by the finding of Vedbaek Henriksholm-Bøgebakken in an estuary in north-east Zealand. Here over twenty people were interred in just under twenty graves, close to one of many occupations around the estuary. It is possible that this burial ground served a smaller area than was the case at Skateholm. Most of the burials were single interments. In one triple grave, an infant lay between a man and a woman. In the chest of the man there was a sharp bone point. Other skeletons elsewhere, including at Skateholm and Tybrind Vig, bear severe injuries, and it has been suggested both that some people were killed or murdered, and that such trauma reflects an increase in societal tensions. (The last is a moot point, since we do not have enough earlier skeletons to make an adequate comparison.)[172]

Other rites are represented by the finds at Strøby Egede, not far from Ølby Lyng and other coastal sites on the east side of Zealand (further south than Vedbaek), and at Møllegabet, Ærø, to the south of Fyn.[173] At Strøby Egede there is one large grave, though

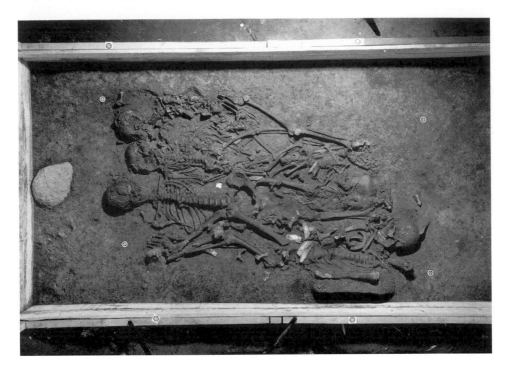

6.21 Ertebølle culture collective burial at Strøby Egede, Zealand. Photo: Lennart
Larsen, National Museum, Copenhagen.

there may originally have been others, and these probably lay close to a settlement or
occupation. In the grave eight people were interred. With their heads at one end were four
females, laid out, an infant, a child, a young woman and a mature or old woman, who was
buried first. With their heads at the other end were four males, a child, and an infant, and a
man with an infant cradled in his right arm, who appear to have been the last to be interred.
Children and the young woman were provided with beads of animal teeth and blades, the
old woman with a flint knife, and the man with five blades and an antler axe with incised
decoration. Red ochre was sprinkled on the bodies, seemingly most thickly round the children. At Møllegabet, yet another coastal occupation had traces of burials, including the
partial remains of a young man who seems to have been put in the burnt stem of a dugout
canoe, staked in place near the water, and his body covered with elm bark. This man too
had a healed wound, from a severe blow to his head. Cremations are also known from a
couple of sites, and there are late unfurnished burials from shell middens, including
Ertebølle itself. It will be very important in future research to establish which were the
modes of burial at the very end of the Ertebølle culture sequence.

These kinds of occupation are now well documented in northern and eastern Jutland,
the Danish islands, and in southern Sweden. They probably also extend along the southern
Baltic shore and the adjacent coastal zone. Ellerbek near Kiel and Lietzow on Rügen
give their names to parts of this wider complex. Several sites have been recorded on
Satruper Moor near the bay of Lübeck. Other sites are known in Pomerania

(Mecklenburg–Vorpommern), and others in Polish Pomerania as at Tanowo just to the north of Szczecin in the lower Oder, and at least as far east as Dąbki, to the west of Gdańsk. There are inland sites too, as at Chobienice south-west of Poznań, and burials have recently been found at Mszano near Brodnica to the east of the Vistula.[174] Much more research remains to be done over this broad area, but the available evidence may suggest many features classically known in the Danish–south Swedish region, and serves at any rate to keep Neolithic communities and foragers close together, as had been the situation from the LBK phase. To the east and south-east of the Baltic there were the separate forager traditions of the Kunda, Narva and Niemen cultures.[175]

People of the Ertebølle–Ellerbek complex had a rich material culture. Many artefacts of bone and antler were decorated, and at least some of wood, and there were many kinds of beads and pendants, and ornaments carved from amber. Virtually all the great range of artefacts, variously fashioned from stone, flint and organic materials, were portable or wearable; most were probably in constant use. Just as in Neolithic communities to the south, women were buried with many ornaments. At Vedbaek Bøgebakken, one young woman was buried with a new-born infant (perhaps a baby boy, from the flint blade placed with him) beside her on her right, laid on a swan's wing, with red ochre above and below the baby and beneath the woman's head. Beside her head was a mass of pendants made from red deer and pig teeth, whose deposition suggests that they had probably been in fact attached to a garment.[176] This vivid evidence shows that people wore clothes made from hide or woven fabric. No less than to the south, such rich material culture was an ever-present medium structuring people's lives. One set of values it may have expressed, consciously or unconsciously, was a close conceptual link to the natural world, from which so many materials and resources were derived. Another role may have been to indicate social *personae* and allegiances. As at Brześć Kujawski to the south (indeed the form may have been copied from the south), adult men carried antler axes or adzes, perforated centrally and presumably shafted with wood, and there were flint and stone axes as well. From the earlier to mid fifth millennium BC, pottery was in use in the Ertebølle–Ellerbek complex.[177] There may have been even earlier, though limited, traditions of pottery manufacture among forager communities on the fringes of the LBK culture. The idea of pottery, transforming natural clay into a new form by shaping and firing, was presumably adapted from the post-LBK 'Danubian' tradition. But the forms achieved and the techniques of manufacture (coil building and coarse tempers) owe nothing directly to that tradition. Forms were limited. There were S-profiled jars with pointed bases, and small shallow dishes, which have often been seen as lamps for burning oil. Neither type was decorated. The greatest quantities of such pottery come from the largest sites, including shell middens. Pots were presumably used to serve food or drink, but may also have worked as a symbol of communality, a neutral celebration of gatherings and plenty.

Other items may have been more strongly regionalised in the later Ertebølle culture, and perhaps beyond.[178] The distributions of things like antler and greenstone axes, combs, points, and harpoons, may suggest the existence of differences between Jutland on the one hand and Zealand and south Sweden on the other. This proposal of more sharply defined regional identities in the later Ertebølle culture has been much discussed, since it is not entirely certain how reliable the empirical basis is. If valid, it may be compatible with the suggested reduction of mobility of lifestyle in this region. But it should be noted that these distributions are at least some tens of kilometres across.

People must have profoundly understood and known their environment, and in that sense may be said to have controlled it. They may, rather, have regarded themselves as working with nature to obtain their living. Burials celebrate natural materials like antler, and some dogs were treated no differently in death to humans, as at Skateholm. On the other hand, the sequence of bone remains suggests that aurochs became very rare on Zealand. This might have been due to natural environmental changes, but could also be the result of over-hunting.[179] The treatment of dogs as humans could also be seen as the recognition of separations between the cultural and the natural, a difference that might have been rein-forced through the Skateholm II–Skateholm I sequence, and augmented by the adoption of pottery manufacture. Increased territoriality, if it can be accepted, and injuries to humans, if they are the result of more than endemic bickerings, would indicate that this was not an unchanging world. It was certainly not an isolated one. As noted earlier at Skateholm II, contacts had been established with the LBK culture much earlier, before or around the end of the sixth millennium BC, and the adoption of pottery indicates another form of contact. There are numerous finds of Danubian stone tools on the north European plain beyond the *loess*, and perforated axe-hammers, very like for example those in a Rössen context at Wittmar, have come from closed Ertebølle contexts in Denmark.[180] These for-agers knew of other ways of doing things in different worlds, but adopted them only selec-tively.

Another shore: Brittany

I have already referred to the shell midden sites with burials at Téviec and Hoëdic in connection with the problems of dating the appearance of megalithic cairn construc-tions. There were other late Mesolithic sites and shell middens, such as Beg an Dorchenn, near Plomeur in southern Finistère.[181] These take a late Mesolithic presence in Brittany, on the basis of radiocarbon dates, down to at least the beginning of the fifth millennium BC, and show that occupation was not confined to the Morbihan. The hunting of game, sea fishing and shellfish collection can all be documented. What is much harder to under-stand is the density of occupation. At Téviec and Hoëdic there were some nine graves each, holding respectively twenty-three and fourteen people. It is obvious that population cannot be extrapolated from selective burial rites, but these were at any rate not on the scale of Skateholm I. The major problem for the region is the effect of sea level change. At this time, the sea may have been as much as 10 m lower, and it is self-evident that many sites may have been lost. But we cannot simply transpose the conditions of the western Baltic. This was a different shore, in parts shallow and indented, but in others rocky, straight and deep. On ecological grounds alone, it may be that there was a radically smaller and more mobile population than around the Baltic. This is important, not least because this situation may have encouraged or allowed different conditions for the accep-tance of innovation.

The offshore islands

Britain has an abundant Mesolithic record, and it is possible to divide it crudely into an earlier and a later phase, but it has proved much harder to isolate the cultural elements of the latest Mesolithic. It is even possible that the use of microliths, so important for site recognition in area surveys, had gone out of use in some areas by about the end of the sixth millennium BC.[182] There may be regional traditions of flint tools. People were both on the coasts and inland, and some flint and other lithic raw materials were procured from considerable distances from their place of use and deposition. Pollen analysis from both upland and lowland situations suggests that people made some inroads into the natural woodland vegetation, to encourage browse for game or the growth of nut-bearing trees like hazel.[183]

Coast and inland could have been connected, from region to region, by seasonal cycles of circulating mobility. Contemporary south-eastern coastlines have been lost to rising sea levels and sinking land. There are no obvious equivalents to the kind of coastal sites found around the Baltic, nor yet much to match the kind of evidence recovered from the river deltas and estuaries of the western Netherlands. Coastal occupations to the west, as in south-west Wales or north-west England, seem to consist of much smaller sites, perhaps part still of mobile regional systems.[184] The situation in Ireland may have been different again, with known sites largely restricted to the coasts and to river valleys inland. Some of the coastal sites include quite large accumulations of shell midden, but the suggested model has again often been of regional cycles of mobility.[185]

Coastal sites were widespread. On the north-west coast of Scotland, people were as far offshore as the island of Rhum, south of Skye. Their presence further out in the Outer Hebrides, and to the north in the Orkney and Shetland Islands, is uncertain. On the other side of Scotland, the size of some fish from the site of Morton, Fife, also suggests offshore fishing.[186] In the Inner Hebrides and on the adjacent deeply indented coastline several late Mesolithic occupations are known. People were on the island of Jura, and further out still on the small island of Oronsay, and probably its larger neighbour Colonsay.[187] Oronsay is small and exposed. It had at least six sites, detectable as shell middens spaced along the contemporary shore, now raised beaches. As well as collecting shellfish, especially here limpets (with scallops and crabs also represented), people caught fish, especially saithe (*Pollachius virens* L.), probably in inshore waters, and hunted grey and occasionally common seals. They took seabirds. They discarded bones of deer and pigs, perhaps from meat brought from the mainland or larger islands like Jura. Grey seals calve in autumn. The earbones or otoliths of the saithe were also analysed in comparison with modern samples to suggest the season of occupation. Of the four sites investigated, each may represent a slightly different season: Cnoc Sligeach mid-summer, Cnoc Coig late summer to autumn, Priory Midden from after mid-autumn, and Caisteal nan Gillean II both summer and late autumn/winter. The middens contained hearths, and stake holes suggest flimsy shelters or drying racks, but there were no more substantial structures. Were people actually based on Oronsay for much of the year? Or did they rather, over the years, visit it repeatedly (and Colonsay intermittently), building a routine of places chosen to suit a seasonal rhythm? The rest of the evidence from the region suggests the latter, and a rather small, dispersed population may

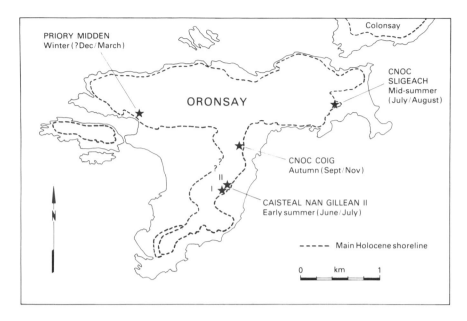

6.22 Shell middens on the island of Oronsay, with suggested principal seasons of occupation. After Mellars.

here too have circulated through its annual territory. No formal burials have been found in these middens, but there were isolated pieces of human bone, for example from Cnoc Coig teeth, feet and hand bones and pieces of skull. Did the ancestors circulate in the company of the living?

Inland: the Alpine foreland

Although the most spectacular evidence for late forager existence comes from the coasts of northern/north-west Europe, there were inland communities too. In northern Poland, some may have continued in certain areas right until the end of the Neolithic period (these are discussed in the next chapter). South of the Rhine in the Alpine foreland of northern and north-western Switzerland, there is evidence for local populations contemporary with the LBK culture and its successors. Such evidence has tended to be overshadowed by the striking survivals of Neolithic settlements in the region and in neighbouring south-west Germany. We know comparatively little about this late Mesolithic situation. Some localised areas, like the fringes of the former lake in the Wauwilermoos, in the morainic country of Kt. Lüzern in western Switzerland, show remarkable concentrations of small Mesolithic sites, perhaps the seasonal camps of another still mobile population.[188] Once again, this characterisation must be important for understanding subsequent changes.

The extension of the Neolithic way of life

Cultural geography

By the end of the fifth millennium BC, most of central and western Europe, including southern Scandinavia and Britain and Ireland, can be defined as Neolithic. It is superficially easy to define the cultural shifts, especially the adoption of pottery styles which mark out larger and smaller regions, but also new forms of flint and stone tools, and new constructions or monuments connected with ritual and the disposal and cult of the dead. In a sense this cultural transformation is merely the further extension and elaboration of the 'Danubian' tradition. Understanding what this cultural shift may have meant in human terms from region to region, and how it related to continuities or discontinuities in population, group identity, subsistence and world view, is altogether more difficult. Change may have been neither instant nor as profound as often characterised. We may rather have to take account of differences of degree, of redefinitions of the world, rather than wholly new beginnings, as the tracking through this chapter of long convergences has often hinted. The first step is some brief cultural geography.

After perhaps earlier beginnings, noted above, the Funnel-Necked Beaker or TRB culture emerged over a very broad swathe of the north European plain and southern Scandinavia. In reality this can be broken down into a series of regional traditions, which may have had rather different histories and characters.[189] But at a certain level, this new tradition united parts of the older core Danubian area and the north European plain and Baltic coasts. In the Rhineland and to its east, and partly to its west in Belgium, the Michelsberg culture and related groups were the successors of the Rössen culture and related groups.[190] At the south of the Rhine and into the Alpine foreland there emerged the Pfyn culture, with the Cortaillod culture in more westerly Switzerland, and the Altheim culture in the upper Danube area.[191] In northern France the Chasseen culture emerged, interleaved on the east and north with the Michelsberg tradition. Brittany had related but more regionalised traditions, south of the Loire and west of the Massif Central the *Néolithique moyen-Atlantique* and its antecedents could be similarly regarded.[192] Britain and Ireland, finally, have prosaically defined 'early' or 'earlier' Neolithic phases.[193]

This might all be dismissed as an unlovely choreography of pots, but at worst it provides a necessary grammar of cultural change and a usable vocabulary, and it underlines both the geographical scale and the broad contemporaneity of the transformations in question. Given also that material culture was inextricably part of the lived world, its interpretation will be important.

Transitions in action?

Despite the very broad area outlined, the varied conditions of survival, and the vigorous traditions of field research, it has proved very hard to demonstrate the actual process of transition in site sequences and stratigraphies. In Britain, for example, there are virtually no stratigraphies which show the shift from Mesolithic to Neolithic culture, and very few sites with 'contact' finds of the other tradition. It has proved difficult precisely to specify the date of the end of the Mesolithic and the beginning of the Neolithic. If native continuity is involved, we can hardly show it in individual site histories, and if colonisation of some kind is involved, we are unable clearly to point to the locations and biographies of pioneer communities.[194]

The expectation that such a capture of change in action is possible may be in part an illusion, but there is some evidence from some areas to indicate what might be found in certain forms of transition. In the western Netherlands, for example, there is ample evidence from the delta and estuary areas, when it has been searched for, for the continuation of forager traditions in the sixth and fifth millennia BC. (Much later, the Vlaardingen culture can be seen to represent the even longer history of this kind of lifestyle in these zones.) At Swifterbant in one of the polders or reclaimed lands on the east side of the present-day Ijsselmeer, it has been possible to map a system of old dunes and freshwater creeks, part of what was originally part of the inner zone of a tidal estuary, fronted by the fifth millennium BC by coastal barriers in the form of sand and other ridges.[195] Along the dunes and creeks, especially at creek junctions, have been recovered small occupations of the seventh to fifth millennia BC. By the mid to later fifth millennium BC, occupation at creek sites S2 and S3–5 was on levées beside freshwater streams, backed by marshy and wooded swamp, and easily flooded. Flooding alone makes it unlikely that people were here all year, and there were only hearths, spreads of artefacts and stake holes. On the other hand, there were burials in these sites, some eight people in site S2. People fished, fowled and hunted a wide range of game. On the evidence of site S3–5, they also had domesticated cattle (perhaps of stock long domesticated), pig, and a very few sheep and goats. There were remains of local wetland plants, some of which could have been food sources, and also of barley and wheat. These cereals might have been imported, but could also have been cultivated on floodwater deposits. Flint tools were made and used in traditional ways. People also made S-profiled pottery (more or less in Ertebølle style), and obtained perforated stone hammer-axes from Neolithic communities to the east. Further south, at Hazendonk, Brandwijk and Bergschenhoek in the Rhine–Maas estuary, occupations on sand ridges in marshes between the rivers were dated to the later fifth millennium BC (site phase 1 at Hazendonk).[196] People here too boated, fished (at the short-lived site at Bergschenhoek with astonishingly well-preserved wicker fish traps), fowled and hunted, but at Hazendonk and Brandwijk they had domesticated animals and cultivated wheat as well. Swifterbant was not an isolated phenomenon in this coastal-estuarine region.

Perhaps surprisingly, it has been difficult in the Ertebølle–Ellerbek area to find stratigraphies of transition. Earlier investigations of shell middens may not have been sensitive enough to detect rapid transformations, and the special conditions of shell midden formation do not make fine resolution easy. Recent work has not been able conclusively to demonstrate site continuities, but does suggest it strongly. At Norsminde, for example, the shell midden continued in use in the early Neolithic period. People hunted and fowled as before, and collected shellfish, though they seem to have fished less or not at all. They also had domesticated animals and used some cereals. Pots and stone tools were made in new styles. The radiocarbon dates are imprecise, and could allow either direct continuity or a brief abandonment; in either case, the transformation phase seems to have been brief. Other sorts of new locations and sites were in use in the area, as we shall see in the next chapter. Another and unusual situation is that at Löddesborg in southern Scania, where Ertebølle and TRB pots have been found in the same undisturbed layer, the former with cereal impressions on them.[197]

Survey in the Saltbaeg Vig area of north-west Zealand has shown both Ertebølle and early Neolithic sites in the same area. The Neolithic sites were more diverse in size, while some of the largest were Mesolithic. But it was not possible to isolate those sites in the phase of transition itself, however short or long that may have been here.[198] Further south, at fifth millennium BC Ellerbek sites on Satruper Moor such as Förstermoor and Röttmoor and on the coast at Rosenhof, people may have been acquainted with cereals and domesticated cattle and pig. But at the early TRB site of Siggeneben-Süd in the late fifth millennium BC the subsistence economy was still very diverse and mixed.[199]

Processes and causes

It has been customary to seek a single process and single or simple causes in understanding the Mesolithic–Neolithic transition. In the past the model of expansion by farming communities was favoured, and explanations based on demographic growth (coupled with technological superiority) prevailed. This view, rightly, has come to be regarded with suspicion over the last fifteen to twenty years, but now there is a danger of substituting a stereotyped model of forager continuity and development. Rather than a single transformation, there were many transitions.

It is important, first, briefly to examine the nature and deficiencies of the colonisation model. Earlier in this chapter I have diverged from the consensus that the LBK culture represented a colonisation of central and western Europe by outsiders of Balkan Neolithic origin. By stages, the LBK culture spread across parts of central and western Europe. It extended beyond the *loess* to islands of good soils in central and northern Poland. But the Danubian tradition went no further, and this chapter has described the long coexistence of 'farmers' and 'foragers' over the ensuing centuries of the later sixth and fifth millennia BC.[200] It is surely odd to explain the initial burst of expansion of the LBK as the result of rapid demographic growth and then to account for its standstill in terms of fastidious preferences for selected soil types. And as we shall see in the next chapter, in most zones of the secondary extension of the Neolithic way of life, the early stages can themselves hardly be characterised by rapid growth or intensive production. Given the risks of pioneer cultivation on the one hand, and the diversity of usable native resources on the other, it is a weak argument to have recourse to any idea of the inherent or self-evident superiority of the cultivation–herding economy. The characterisation of the Neolithic as a population on the move, and as a subsistence economy of irresistible attractions, has not been very successful.

The consensus has therefore swung to the view of forager continuity and indigenous transformation in the broad sweep of north-west Europe from south of the Loire to east of the lower Vistula. This shift has been aided by better understanding of modern and recent foragers, whose flexibility, resourcefulness and knowledgeability were stressed in chapter 2, and by a better understanding of the nature, use and role of material culture; resourceful and knowledgeable people can be thought of as deliberately choosing new material means of expression. But there is still a tendency, mirroring that of the colonisation–demographic growth model, to seek both simplistic and uniform explanations for such a shift. One influential general model has proposed, usefully, a sequence from the *availability* of new resources to their *substitution*, at moments determined by foragers themselves, and then to the later *consolidation* of change.[201] But this may be too focused on subsistence alone, and does it have sufficient resolution to accommodate different sorts of sequence and situation?

The cases above could show at least five different sorts of situation. In the main Ertebølle area, coexistence with cultivators must have been accompanied by considerable independence and perhaps active cultural resistance of another way of life. Change, when it came, may have been swift. It involved the adoption by indigenous people of new resources, but not at the expense of traditional resources, and some new site locations, but without a dramatic shift to longhouse life. New material media and new kinds of gatherings and ceremonies are more striking aspects of this transition. In the southern part of the Ertebølle–Ellerbek area, change may have been more gradual, involving first the partial adoption of new subsistence resources. In the western Netherlands, there appears also to have been gradual adoption of new resources (going along with the innovation of pottery and the acquisition of exotic stone artefacts), but the identity and independence of people in the distinctive environment of the deltas and estuaries may have been long maintained, even if in terms of pottery phase 2 at Hazendonk can be aligned with the Michelsberg culture. In Brittany a possibly sparse and mobile population could have fused with outsiders to have produced a distinctive new tradition. In Britain and Ireland, native communities seem largely to have been isolated both from contemporary foragers across the water and from the Danubian tradition. Their knowledge of other worlds might have been more limited than was the case in the Ertebølle complex, and their lifestyle still more mobile. But here the transition involved the transport by sea of at least seed corn and sheep and goats, neither being indigenous, so that introductions, when they came, cannot be seen as fortuitous or experimental.

Which, if any, of these models best suits the case of the Alpine foreland is open to debate, but circumstances could have been akin to that of the southern Ertebølle–Ellerbek area. From Egolzwil 3 in the Wauwilermoos there was a Rössen pot, which could be an older find (though many scholars have supposed the existence of an early Egolzwil or Wauwil group contemporary with late Rössen), and from the Mozartstrasse site in Zürich, at the head of the Zürichsee, there were sherds of Grossgartach pottery, in the earliest, Cortaillod layers: in both cases well beyond their normal distributions. There are other examples.[202] These show contacts, but more evidence is needed now of subsistence changes. All these cases together suggest that the beast of transition to be tied down was very varied, and in some cases did not take a form neatly to be netted.

Just as some scholars have favoured expansion by farmer outsiders, fuelled by demographic growth and the desire for new land, so others more recently have sought specific causes for indigenous transition, again generally of an economic or demographic nature. There have been suggestions of population growth, of social competition in part fuelled by and in part fuelling population growth, and of economic intensification (bound up with social competitiveness) leading inexorably to the perceived greater productivity of the agricultural system. One extreme view has been that the end of the Ertebølle culture came when conditions of salinity in the Baltic changed and oysters, seen as a vital late winter food, declined sharply in numbers; only a quick intake of cereals and domesticated animals could save the day.[203] The inherent improbability of this latter model has been widely pointed out: would such a system as the Ertebølle complex rely on one late winter food only? What of stored foods? What of other native resources available in late winter? How would such a decline in one shellfish lead to the adoption of cultivation and herding and not to other adaptations? But less critical attention has been given to more general socioeconomic and demographic explanations. A recurrent and basic difficulty with all the models based on economic intensification and demographic growth is that the early Neolithic situation on the north-west fringes of Europe so often seems not that different from the Mesolithic one. One suggestion framed for Britain has been that different strands of the transition can be postulated, with a primary phase of economic change and experimentation preceding a secondary stage of wholesale cultural convergence.[204] In fact this suggestion could better be reversed. People changed trains of thought, and then later gradually became enmeshed in a web of more intense subsistence practices.[205]

Another favoured model has been that social competition among foragers was the motor driving change.[206] This has usually been formulated in economic terms, with intensification of subsistence activity, including increased control over resources and territory as its prime expression. Supposedly related developments in group definition and identity, in the treatment of the dead, and indeed in injuries wrought on people in life, are seen as symptoms of the underlying trend. This kind of explanation is most attractive at a general level; so far it has not been successful in dealing with specific issues. How is intensification to be measured? People may have controlled the movement of animals like deer by making some inroads into woodland. But people had known how to clear woodland by axe, ringbarking or fire right through the post glacial period. If some domesticated animals were present in the late Ertebølle world, it is not clear in what sense this represents an *intensification*. It is equally hard to demonstrate any intensification in plant use in late forager situations, even if some cereals were present in the late Ertebølle and late British Mesolithic worlds, as detected by pollen analysis.[207] The untestable assumption is also being made, implicitly, that early forms of cereal cultivation, when and however they appeared in a given region, represent an intensification, in terms of labour for clearance, planting, tending and harvesting. Conversely, if the practice of cultivation, the building of longhouses, or the use of pottery in themselves were the result of a greater social competitiveness than experienced among collectors and fishers, one might expect more evident differences between say the Lengyel culture and the Ertebølle culture.

The social competition model normally neglects to specify the locus of competition, whether between age sets, gender sets, kin groups within communities (however those are to be defined), or between communities. If greater territoriality at a scale of tens of kilometres was the result of social competition, what form did this take at the local scale, for example from fjord to fjord? The assumptions of fixed residence and permanent allegiance which the model imports may be quite inadequate for the world of mobility which this chapter has tried to outline. Nor is it clear how social difference could be enforced in a landscape with space in it. It is possible perhaps, though it seems exaggerated, to envisage the occupation of every bay round the Baltic coasts, but such a packing model can hardly apply to the spaces of Britain and Ireland, and is not therefore successful as a general model. Also neglected are foci of competition other than economic. People may have been rivals as much for honour and reputation as for economic power, seeking those goals through hospitality, generosity, gift-giving, and the acquisition of exotic things. This need not imply dull altruism.

Other difficulties with the social competition model include its failure to deal adequately with its supposed consequences. If competition was driven by economic individualism, or indeed by attempts by people (in groupings usually unspecified) to capture ritual practice and special knowledges, why do we observe such a degree of shared culture over broad regions in the opening phases of the Neolithic? Why was there not more territoriality in both the late Mesolithic and the early Neolithic? And as we shall see over and over again in the next chapter, the history of ensuing phases of the Neolithic is not one of relentless economic intensification. Some of the most striking phases of social interaction, for example in the late fourth and early third millennia BC, coincide with periods when the evidence for both settlement and economy suggests dispersal of population and a relaxed investment of labour.

Convergences

The 'Danubian' world, itself as I have argued of indigenous origin, had many resemblances to the world of foragers to its north and west, and some indeed to the world of the inhabitants of the Hungarian plain to its south-east. The histories of tells on the Hungarian plain, of formalised enclosures in the *loess* woodlands, and of coastal shell middens run curiously parallel. They were preceded by the appearance of the longhouse across the area of the LBK culture, with examples from the Szakálhát phase (equivalent to late LBK) on the Hungarian plain. Longhouses were permanent structures which could have lasted for at least a couple of generations with only routine maintenance. They fixed a sense of place, but they did not necessarily tie the people who built and used them to permanent occupation, from season to season, year to year, or generation to generation, any more than the choice of special locations for ritualised gatherings condemned the users of shell middens to a never-ending diet of oysters or limpets. What was going on in parallel ways in both the Danubian and much of the contemporary forager world was perhaps a new form of self-definition, which operated at the broadest scale to involve whole societies. Very often, this process has been dubbed 'settling down', but the emphasis on mobility makes this an only partially appropriate label. This convergent self-definition involved changing attitudes to place, and with the passage of time to notions of sacred re-enactment, respect for ancestors and perhaps myths of origin. The ultimate shift to be sought in the long-investigated

Mesolithic–Neolithic transition of north-west Europe was perhaps in a new sense of self and belonging.[208] Foragers became 'Neolithic' when they accepted a sense of identity more tightly framed by the cultural. Nature was honoured by foragers, but could also be abused. The treatment of dogs through the sequence of burials at Skateholm may be at least as significant as the changing diets reflected in assemblages of faunal and floral remains. In those burials people had used natural symbols like ochre and antler, and often deposited goods made of organic materials, but they had also classified dogs with humans. In later burials, dogs were still treated in death like people, but were given separate space. This can suggest greater and greater classification of the world, which enabled in the end the adoption of more and new cultural media like decorated pots and polished stone axes: enculturation rather than acculturation. The material elements by which territoriality has been defined in the later Ertebølle world may also be regarded as signs of cultural classification rather than as symptoms of conflict, of reordering the world by reference to things made by people. This suggested process of convergence is more subtle than a conceptual shift from 'wild' to 'tame',[209] a dichotomy which seems far too crude to do any justice to either the knowledge or the world view of foragers.

The Mesolithic–Neolithic transition around 4000 BC in north-west Europe was less dramatic than often supposed. The key initial shift was the appearance of the LBK culture, and the rest was in many ways parallel development with slow convergence, eventually bringing unity, perhaps at a horizon of no readily explicable significance in itself, other than that this was the time when change did happen, through the longevity and weight of contact, interaction and shared history. What then of the new economic resources which have figured so large in virtually every account? These too are ripe for demythologising. If we assume that foragers were knowledgeable, flexible, and resourceful, we can envisage the logic of the choice of a seemingly narrow spectrum of domesticates in the LBK culture, though this does not necessarily characterise the earliest phase of the LBK. Different choices were made in the Lengyel culture. Enculturating foragers may have experimented with what was to hand, without committing themselves to irrevocable change. The 'availability' model needs to be reformulated. People may have been attracted by 'fertile gifts',[210] or have been interested in new ways of getting proteins and carbohydrates. In so doing, they used what was available. Such usage need not have entailed lasting or immediate commitment. Experimentation may have led to vicarious cultivation or part-time herding,[211] rather than to full-time and irreversible settling down. Given the knowledgeability of foragers, such shifts cannot simplistically be characterised as an increase in control. The fertility of different species, both animal and plant, may have been at least as important to those who made a living from and with them as the means by which they were bred.

Why should convergence have taken place? Why should people have come to merge their identity with that of another tradition? One might have recourse to the clumsy notion of contradictions between different aspects of foragers' world view: between the ideal of revering the natural world and the reality of its increasing exploitation. Another possibility is worth canvassing. I have suggested so far that we may have sought too much significance in the date at which the Mesolithic–Neolithic transition took place in north-west Europe.

Slow convergence need not have entailed a predetermined rate. It is possible to envisage unification through enculturation either earlier or later. The shift happened when it did, for identifiable reasons, but not according to a specifiable timetable. This frees us from having to scrutinise the evidence for every slightest sign of a footstep northwards by Neolithic communities, or of 'intensification' by forager communities. But another possibility to consider is whether, as the frame of explanation is shifted to the conceptual and the cultural, some kind of spiritual conversion was involved. Enculturation involved increased attention to the past, to honour ancestors and to frame lines of descent. The model of 'megalithic missionaries' used by an earlier generation of scholars has been much ridiculed, and I am not proposing to revive it in unaltered form.[212] But could not myths of origin, of shared beginnings, ways of telling the world into existence, have circulated more freely than anything else? What was talked about in eel-fishing canoes at night, as cattle were followed through woodland, while fish traps were set or crop plantings were tended? What was said before the interment in one grave of three adults and five children, during the momentous digging of great sacred spaces, or after gatherings on the ever-increasing shell middens? Through the long history of longhouse lives, could convergence of spiritual beliefs about the ways these new worlds had come into being have been the actual medium by which people enculturated themselves and came to share the same created worlds?

CHAPTER 7

UNFAIR SETTLEMENTS AND ABSTRACT FUNERALS: CENTRAL AND WESTERN EUROPE, *c.* 4000–2500 BC

People and animals by the Vistula

Over some generations around 3000 BC the remains of both people and animals were care-fully deposited according to prescribed procedures in a burial ground on a *loess*-covered bluff above the middle Vistula. Men, women and children were interred in ones, twos and threes, perhaps up to about thirty in all, but many of their skeletons were incomplete. They were accompanied by pots, small polished flint axes and ornaments, including some made of amber, and their graves contained diverse animal bones (of cattle, pigs, sheep and goats, and one or two dogs). The partial remains of people were mimicked in pits containing the partial and butchered remains of cattle, and some other animals, mostly with no skull remaining. These pits had traces of burning, and some grave goods. In addition, there were large pits with complete cattle skeletons on their own; only two had human remains, one with an adult jawbone and some bones from a child, and another with a piece of child's skull. The cattle were killed by sharp bone points, which had accompanied several to the grave. They had been put directly into their pits, without dismemberment and without accompanying fires.

There were around thirty such graves and pits over an area about 100 m across. Most were set in small groups within the burial ground, in rows of three or four. Nos. 28–31 formed one such row. No. 28 contained a scatter of partial cattle remains, parts of a human infant and parts of an adult, and a flint axe. Then the big cattle skeleton pits nos. 29 and 31, with several animals each, framed the human grave, no. 30, which contained the partial remains of a juvenile or adolescent, with pot and flint axe.

Other groups were laid out a little differently. In the group of nos. 4, 3, 1 and 6, the outer two of the row were nos. 4 and 6. Those had partial cattle remains, no. 4 with a lot of dis-membered animals and no. 6 with small dumps of bone. These outer two framed no. 3, which had several whole cattle skeletons, and a human grave, no. 1. The grave contained the partial remains of three people, from juvenile to mature in age, and several deposits of cattle bone. In the group of nos. 14, 25 and 24, the central pit no. 25 had partial cattle remains, while no. 14 was a human grave and no. 24 a grave with whole cattle.

This is the Gajowizna site at Złota, to the south of Sandomierz. It belongs to the Globular Amphora culture.[1] Death rituals here involved both the interment of the recently dead, and the circulation of remains of people already long departed. The burial ground was therefore the arena for both funerals and ancestor rites.[2] It was also witness to feasting on animal meat on a large scale, the residues of communal eating coming to resemble the partial remains of the ancestral human dead. Funerals and rites were accompanied by the

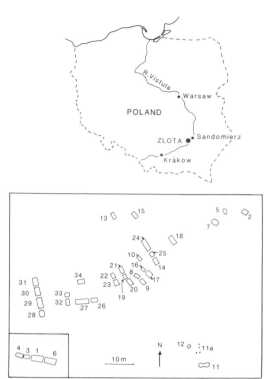

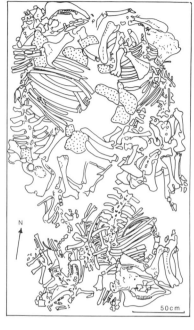

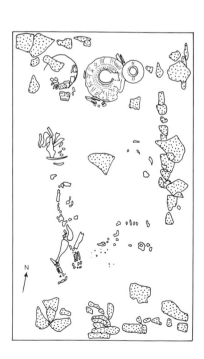

7.1 Globular Amphora human and cattle burials at Złota. After Krzak.

killing of further animals, which were honoured by not being eaten. Animals were raised not just for slaughter, but as tokens of communal life and values. The rows of graves and pits suggest protracted procedures, and as in other burial grounds, it is likely that they were marked, forming visible lines 10–15 m long: enduring monuments to the past, and markers of present and future communal concerns.

Feasts and funerals, rites and gifts

The Globular Amphora culture burial ground at Złota, although only one example from the vast area and the long timespan covered in this chapter, usefully evokes many important themes. There was considerable continuity of occupation, both at Złota itself and in the surrounding *loess* areas (rather misleadingly called 'uplands'), but remains of structures other than pits and ditches in settlement sites are regularly elusive, as seen in the well-investigated examples of Bronocice in a tributary valley of the upper Vistula to the south and at Brześć Kujawski in Kujavia to the north.[3] Most people cultivated or used cereals in this phase, and there is evidence for ard cultivation, but the scale of cereal growing is nowhere well documented. The concern with animals links this area both to the south, as at the bend of the Danube as discussed in chapter 5, and to nearly every other part of the region covered in this chapter, from Brześć Kujawski to Windmill Hill in southern England.[4]

The Globular Amphora culture, distributed roughly from the Elbe to the Vistula, represents a new formation after the big cultural phenomena like the TRB culture, whose beginnings were noted at the end of the last chapter.[5] In the northern and western areas of the TRB culture there was continuity until the Corded Ware/Single Grave culture horizon. There were other cultural shifts at a similar date to the appearance of the Globular Amphora culture, though not necessarily directly related, in other parts of central and western Europe. The Horgen culture, for example, succeeded the Pfyn culture in the north-west Alpine foreland.[6] In several parts of central and western Europe, the Globular Amphora culture was succeeded by the Corded Ware/Single Grave culture, which extended as far west as the Rhine.[7] That horizon, with which we end, has often been seen as the result of migrations, and the best moment at which to introduce Indo-European speakers to this part of Europe. I will argue that it is more satisfactory to envisage long sequences of local continuity linked to changing points of reference in the Neolithic world, some of which involved contact with far away.

Considerable energy was expended on extracting stone and flint and manufacturing from it polished or ground axes, and these were regularly moved long distances. One of the most spectacular examples is the use of the banded flint source in the Holy Cross hills at Krzemionki in central-southern Poland (to the north-west of Złota).[8] Sustained exploitation began in the TRB phase, but the greatest extraction was achieved in the Globular Amphora culture phase. Other sources were then used in the Corded Ware phase. Both Globular Amphora and Corded Ware culture graves can be seen as the beginnings of more individualised rites, but the context of nearly all of them is a collective one. Men, women and children are represented, and burial procedures do not seem markedly to stress differ-

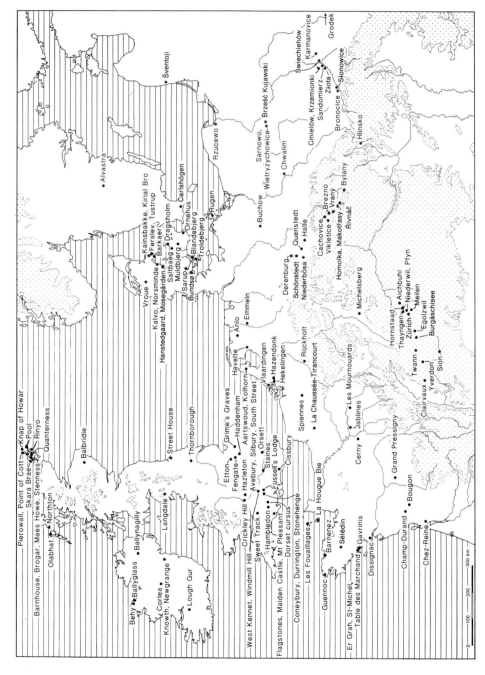

7.2 Simplified location map of the principal sites discussed in chapter 7.

ences within the community of the dead. Rites played out remembrances and the creation of social and conceptual order, reinforcing the collectivity of communal values.

Złota therefore evokes a world in which people defined themselves by reference to a collective past, to their animals, to gifts of stone from far away. People were guided by a sense of the sacred. They both separated themselves from animals and the natural world, and united with them in rites. Their values may have been based more on concepts of fertility and regeneration, of hospitality, generosity and reputation, and of shared origins and identity, than on the accumulation of differentiating status or power. Social sanctions on divergence may have been very strong. Their world changed only slowly.

What was happening in the Vistula valley cannot wholly characterise developments elsewhere. But we shall see notable similarities across wide areas. There were everywhere strong continuities with what had gone before. History had an effect in the present. People adopted the use of domesticated animals and cereals in varying ways and to varying degrees. As much concern was given to social interaction as to the routines of subsistence. Stone axes were at least as important as tokens or symbols as tools. People still moved around, and were brought together periodically by rites and gatherings in special places. To the west of Złota these are represented by both ditched enclosures and built houses of the dead of a kind barely known in its surrounding area but the practices of linking past and place, sacrifice and expiation, individual and collectivity, would have been recognisable to inhabitants of the middle Vistula valley.

Unfair settlements

In his poem 'The first kingdom', Seamus Heaney uses the phrase 'unfair settlements', referring to relations between people. I use two other connotations of the phrase in this chapter. The quality of settlement evidence across the area is very uneven. From some points of view, the best evidence comes from waterlogged sites in the Alpine foreland, from south-west Germany, through north-west and west Switzerland to the French Jura. I will take this region as the first of a selected series of examples. Here the long-known wealth of evidence – wooden floors, wall stumps, occasional roofing remains, house contents from wooden containers to nets and fabrics, food residues, animal dung and droppings – has been further enhanced by the development of dendrochronology, which is providing a series of site biographies, accurate to the calendar year. Superficially, the contrast with the stuff of the settlement record elsewhere could not be stronger: scatters of artefacts, pits, post holes, and the occasional hard-won houseplan. At first sight, the Alpine foreland evidence conforms to conventional expectations of what should constitute the Neolithic period. There are bounded, nucleated hamlets and villages, orderly in their layout, and often defined by surrounding fences or palisades. Their inhabitants did hunt and fish, but they kept domesticated animals and cultivated cereals. Sedentary existence seems the inevitable accompaniment to the adoption of agriculture. If this is the case, we are consigned, away from the Alpine foreland, to recovering the badly preserved scraps of the same sort of system.

As research both in the Alpine foreland and elsewhere in central and western Europe progresses, it appears that this view of the evidence is badly misconceived. The second connotation of Seamus Heaney's phrase applies to the Alpine foreland itself. The richness of material survivals can blind us to the special nature of the settlement adaptations in that area. Moreover, it seems increasingly unlikely that we should expect the remains of nucleated villages on the southern English chalklands, or in the coastlands of southern Scandinavia or Brittany. The values of the cattle keepers of Złota may be a better general guide to what we should be looking for.

The Alpine foreland

The process of settlement expansion can now be quite well traced.[9] The first LBK settlement was to the north of the southern end of the Rhine. Later LBK and *Stichbandkeramik* sites are found further south, up to a few kilometres of the north-west end of the Bodensee, for example. There are contact finds in Mesolithic contexts in north-west Switzerland. The first settlements around the Federsee in Oberschwaben, belonging to the Aichbühl culture, date from about 4200 BC. According to dendrochronology and radiocarbon dates, the first settlements in the Alpine foreland proper were to the north and north-west, at Hornstaad–Hörnle I (in its Hornstaad phase) on the Bodensee, at Zürich–Kleiner Hafner at the head of the Zürichsee and at Egolzwil 3 in the Wauwilermoos (both belonging to the so-called Egolzwil culture). This was either side of 4000 BC.[10] Other well-known sites in the north, such as Niederwil, Thayngen–Weier and Pfyn, probably date from after 3900 BC. The waterlogged site of Ehrenstein in the upper Danube, belonging to the Schussenried group, should belong around here. The late Pfyn culture phase at Hornstaad–Hörnle I (site phase IB), begins in 3586 BC. In western Switzerland, on Lake Neuchâtel and the Bielersee, no Cortaillod culture sites have so far been dated earlier than around 3800 BC.[11] On the west side of the French Jura, the occupation of small lakes, comparatively high up in small valleys, dates from 3700–3600 BC. Those sites may belong to the expansion of settlement from the lower-lying parts of Bourgogne to the west, rather than from western Switzerland.[12]

There then followed long continuities of population, across periodic episodes of cultural re-formation. In northern Switzerland, early Cortaillod culture was replaced by the Pfyn culture. From around 3400 BC, the Horgen culture succeeded the Pfyn culture (and related groups) in the north, and the Cortaillod culture in the west. In the west the Lüscherz culture followed about 2900 BC, succeeded by the Saône–Rhône culture.[13] Corded Ware culture occupations can be dated from before 2700 BC, a little earlier in the north on the evidence of Zürichsee sites like Zürich–Mozartstrasse and spreading gradually to the west, to mix with local traditions in the Yverdon and Auvernier phases of the Saône–Rhône culture.[14] We shall return to the wider Corded Ware phenomenon below, but in the regional context there is no good evidence for population migration or replacement.

Nearly all the investigated sites were located in originally wet or damp places, on lake shores or the edge of marshes. This was clearly a deliberate choice, and not just a reflection of research bias (though that has concentrated since the first discoveries of the mid nineteenth century on wet areas) or the accidents of survival. A particularly clear illustration of

this comes from the Bodensee, as noted above. Danubian settlements have been found within a few kilometres of the lake, but Hornstaad–Hörnle IA right on the lake shore represents a new kind of occupation. Sites by marshes or small lakes, like Thayngen–Weier or the Burgäschisee sites, were probably little affected by variations in local water levels, but sites on larger lakes, including those on small islands like Zürich–Kleiner Hafner and –Grosser Hafner, must have been affected not only by yearly meltwater floods but by longer periods of raised water levels. After literally decades of debate, it is now commonly agreed that many lakeside buildings *were* raised on stilts (even if not forming linked platforms as in the nineteenth-century reconstructions of Keller and others).[15]

Why were these wet locations so regularly chosen? There is little or no consensus. Suggested factors range from defence, proximity to fishing and grazing, ease of construction on soft subsoils, and the ease of communication provided by water.[16] No one explanation seems complete on its own. Large dugout canoes (made from lime trunks) have been found, but people in other areas were well able to get around on dry land.[17] Neither water transport nor fishing require settlements actually on the water's edge. There was a long history of dry-land construction before 4000 BC, and it may have been no easier to drive posts into lake marl than to dig post holes in *loess* or other soils. Fences and palisades around sites hardly seem defensive in character, and conflict between people could take many different forms. Waterside location by a straight lake shore would halve the amount of dry-land resources available for exploitation, including soils for cultivation. The subsistence base of these settlements, particularly in earlier phases, was very varied. These locations were unusual and distinctive, particularly in relation to what had gone before. Whatever its precise nature, this was a specialised development, not the inevitable unfurling of a typical Neolithic lifestyle in a new environment.

People were not entirely restricted to lakes and marshes. There was movement of lithic raw materials, well studied at the Bielersee site of Twann for example. In the French Jura from around 3000 BC, blades of honey-coloured flint were brought over 350 km from Grand Pressigny (of which more below) in Touraine south of the Loire. Some blades also found their way into western Switzerland soon after, in the Lüscherz phase. A little copper was in circulation in west Switzerland from the Cortaillod phase onwards, the main centres of manufacture lying further east in the areas of the Pfyn and Mondsee cultures. The high valleys were gradually penetrated. Occupation of the Valais (the Rhône above Lake Geneva) began quite early, and by the third millennium at Sion–Petit Chasseur there were burial monuments, presumably marking seasonal or more sustained use of the area.[18]

Virtually all the sites in question were nucleated, with buildings close set in smaller or larger concentrations. There is no evidence for dispersed individual houses, and little for occupation away from the lake shore or marsh edge. It is possible that some of the later occupations were larger than the earlier ones, but the picture is confused. Recent, intensive excavations have generally not been extensive in scope. Smaller sites include Zürich–Kleiner Hafner, Egolzwil 3 and La Motte-aux-Magnins V on Lake Clairvaux in the French Jura, each probably with a few houses only, and larger sites include Hornstaad–Hörnle IA and IB, Niederwil, Twann and Yverdon, each probably originally with tens of houses. At the head of the Zürichsee there were several discrete sites close

7.3 Remains of houses at Thayngen–Weier. Photo: Kanton Schaffhausen, Amt für Vorgeschichte.

together, some of which in the Pfyn and Horgen phases were probably contemporary. There may normally have been greater distance between contemporary sites. Usually houses were closely spaced in more or less ordered rows, and with little variation in size; proximity engendered uniformity. At Niederwil there were terraced rows of houses. In some cases, not all buildings may have been dwellings. At Thayngen–Weier, dung, leaf fodder and plant remains suggest the use of some structures as stalls (for cattle and goats separately) and granaries respectively. In other cases recently investigated, however, such as Hornstaad–Hörnle IA and IB, there is no sign of specialised buildings.[19]

Such settlements contained well-built, rectangular houses, generally not more than 9 or 10 m long. Construction details varied. These had post frames, plank floors, plank or wattle walls, and pitched thatched roofs. Many were single-roomed, with a central, internal hearth. In other cases, as at Aichbühl and Riedschachen on the Federsee, there were internal divisions forming two rooms. In some cases, the floor of the house was laid directly on the damp ground of the marsh edge or lake shore. In others, houses had raised floors, the post frame of the house serving as stilts. Structural timbers of this kind were generally set in a smaller or larger sill, to prevent sinkage. In perhaps the best-preserved example (because it had been burnt as well as waterlogged), at Hornstaad–Hörnle IA one building about 7 by 3.5 m actually stood as much as 5–6 m high at its central ridge, and probably had a floor raised at least a metre above the ground surface. Its timber uprights were let as sharpened points into individual wooden sills or pile-shoes.[20]

Dendrochronology has given many individual site histories. These are accurate to the year (and sometimes the season) of felling of the wood in question, though wood was not always used in the order in which it was felled. Hornstaad–Hörnle IA was built around 3910 BC and lasted not less than ten years; the dendrochronology of the early phase is still being investigated. The settlement was then consumed in a large conflagration, though there was some continued occupation after that, with further felling in 3869–3868 BC. After a long hiatus, the village was renewed (IB) in 3586 BC, with a series of five refurbishments and rebuildings through to 3507 BC. Another long, punctuated sequence comes from Zürich–Kleiner Hafner, with four major phases of occupation from before 4000 BC to after 3800 BC (layer 5: Egolzwil; layers 4A–C: early Cortaillod; layers 4D–E: earlier Cortaillod; layer 4G: Pfyn). Zürich–Mozartstrasse had an even longer sequence. Two Cortaillod and the first Pfyn layer were not precisely dated. In the first two the fir used for construction is unsuitable for tree-ring analysis, and the third was badly eroded. Layer 4A, of middle Pfyn date, had felling dates from 3745–3714 BC, with further felling episodes 3668–3600 and 3595–3539 (middle and late Pfyn), 3126–3098 (middle Horgen), 2932 and 2898–2887 (late Horgen), 2705–2700 (early Corded Ware) and finally 2625–2606, 2605–2568, and 2544–2499 BC (middle and late Corded Ware). There were layers of lake marl between the major phases, marking abandonment. Twann is another large site with a punctuated history. Dendrochronology at Clairvaux II in the French Jura has shown how the settlement lasted only some twenty years after the middle of the fourth millennium BC, beginning with one or two initial structures only.[21]

The circumscribed area of rescue investigations makes it hard to tell how big sites like Zürich–Mozartstrasse or Twann were at any one phase. But here as elsewhere, well built structures were often renewed, and the sequences of occupation were frequently punctuated. Some of the interruptions were due to fires, as at Hornstaad–Hörnle IA or at the end of the Pfyn occupation at Zürich–Mozartstrasse, but many to rises in lake levels. The inhabitants must have known of this periodicity, and it follows that absolute continuity of occupation was not a major concern. Relocation and rebuilding were part of an expected cycle.

Archaeologists have often assumed that these settlements were occupied all year round; that all had more or less the same character; and that the investment of labour in clearance and house construction bound people to full-time occupation of the spaces and places which they had created. Can these assumptions be justified? The animal and bird bones from some sites certainly suggest occupation in all the seasons of the year, such as the shed and unshed red deer antler, unshed roe deer antler, and bones of red deer calves and migrant swan from Meilen-Rohrenhaab on the Zürichsee.[22] Leaf fodder (of elm, ash, lime, and several other species), animal dung and the pupae of overwintering flies are another set of evidence often quoted in support of permanent occupation, in the belief that animals would have been stalled through the cold winter months. The fodder remains seem at least as likely to have been gathered for consumption in summer or autumn, and flies do not need the company of humans to pupate.[23] People moved around the Alpine foreland, circulating stone materials and a little copper. They may have herded animals through the woodlands, with only occasional stalling; large-scale stalling would have been very labour-

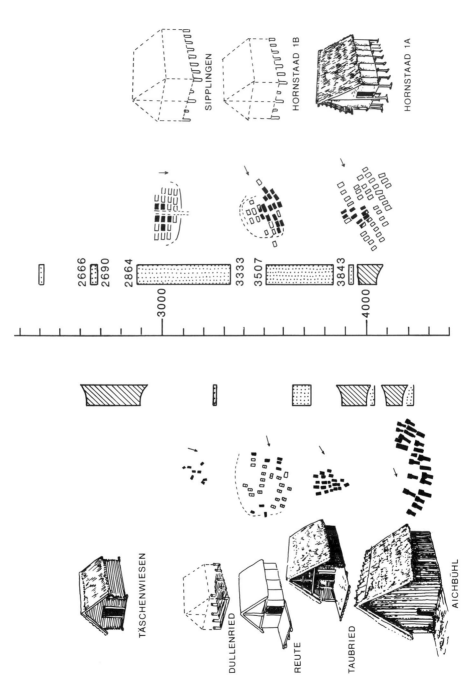

7.4 Changes in house construction in south-west Germany, on a dendrochronological scale (with radiocarbon dated phases hatched). Left: Federsee and Oberschwaben; right: Bodensee. After Schlichtherle.

intensive, and there is little sign in the environmental evidence of the local impact which it might be expected to have made. At the late site of Clairvaux III in the French Jura (from about 2650 BC onwards), it was pig droppings which were most recovered from within the settlement. There may have been some movement of animals and butchered meat between settlements. Large sites like Twann on the Bielersee, for example, had a lot of red deer bone throughout their various levels. These carcasses presumably came from a wide area around. The smaller site of Burgäschisee-Süd further into the foreland had very high proportions of red deer bone compared with cattle bone.[24] A site like that may have been used both as a hunting base, and as a grazing or breeding station, supplying larger lakeside sites. Human remains and burials are very rare within settlements, and so far no cemeteries have been found adjacent to them. There are some cist burials, some with collective deposits. One building within a Pfyn occupation at Ludwigshafen on the Überlinger See (the north-east arm of the Bodensee) was richly decorated with varied motifs in white paint, and also had female breasts modelled on the daub walls. This recent discovery, interpreted as a possible culthouse, points up the absolute rarity of such evidence. The settlement was the principal constructed point in the landscape. Settlements may have served various roles in a more mobile system, engendering the cohesion of cooperation, and articulating a flow of people through the landscape. They could have been, in this area as in others, the tethers on a pattern of mobility. People were not only accustomed to frequent rebuildings and relocations, decade on decade, but were probably also attuned to movement through the landscape from season to season.

Subsistence and environmental evidence points in the same direction. The patterns in plant and bone residues are very varied. People kept domesticated animals, especially cattle, and cultivated cereals and legumes. The scale on which they did so is unclear. Bone residues do not indicate marked intensification of cattle keeping through the Neolithic sequence, and pigs and sheep and goats became more numerous in some sites in later levels, pigs especially being a notable component of some Horgen assemblages. Cattle were raised for meat and slaughtered comparatively young, though some may have been kept for milking. From the Corded Ware horizon there is evidence for simple wheeled vehicles, for example from Zürich–Pressehaus, with slender axles and clumsy solid wheels, and presumably a rather narrow body. There is, however, little sign of a 'traction complex', in the additional form of draught animals or light ploughs.[25] People also hunted (or herded?) a lot of wild game, notably red deer. Taking the bone residues at face value, more venison was consumed than beef in the early levels of Hornstaad–Hörnle I and Zürich–Mozartstrasse. The quantity of venison eaten at Zürich–Kleiner Hafner actually increased through time, from the early to the middle levels, and pigs were more important than cattle in the earlier levels. In later levels at these sorts of site, cattle were more established as the principal animal. Throughout the sequence, woven textiles were principally made from plant fibres, not wool. The model of a 'secondary products revolution' may here be premature; the real process was a very gradual shift from red deer to cattle and other domesticates.

Although fish bone was recovered rather erratically from earlier excavations, more recent investigations have produced more, such as pike from Twann and Hornstaad-Hörnle, and from sites around the Federsee. Birds, furred game and small game were also used.[26]

People cultivated einkorn, emmer, bread wheats and barley, and legumes, probably as separate crops, since there have been finds of separately stored caches in pots. From Twann, there is a rather unappetising bun or small round loaf of unleavened wheat. There were plenty of reasonable soils, for example on outwash deposits at the head of the Zürichsee. Weeds accompanying cereals at Zürich–Mozartstrasse strongly suggest spring sowing. The weed assemblages do not suggest big open plots. Pollen analysis, both around the Bodensee and in the French Jura, does not indicate any considerable scale of early cultivation. Larger and longer-lasting clearances may only have emerged in the Horgen and Corded Ware horizons (and their equivalent in the French Jura). Until then, there may have been a cycle of shifting, short-lived clearances, and in both phases at least some of the impact on woodlands would have come from grazing animals. One suggested model is of temporary clearings with patchy crops, some mixed rather than pure, among coppiced tree stumps, and small areas of grassland. These clearings would soon be left to regenerate, and might subsequently be recleared. People also collected wild berries, nuts and fruits, and may have made use of other plants for food.[27] Cultivation, therefore, should be seen as only one component of a diverse system, based at first in large measure on relocation and mobility.

From the Elbe to the northern Bug

Gródek Nadbużny is a large TRB settlement on a low *loess* plateau above the northern Bug, near Hrubieszów in south-east Poland. Some 10 ha in extent, it has neither defining boundaries nor a clear internal plan. The main features identified were pits, possible huts, and work areas, scattered in irregular groups with spaces in between. In the animal bone assemblage, cattle were most numerous. People here had wide contacts. Their use of local Volhynian flint was supplemented by Świechiehów flint from some 150 km west near the Vistula, and by a little banded flint from Krzemionki across the Vistula in the Holy Cross hills. Copper ores were brought in from Volhynia to the east.[28] This kind of large site is not uncommon over a broad swathe of central Europe in the TRB horizon, but how much of it was in occupation at any one time, or for how long, is not known. Large sites spaced at intervals across the landscape, as in the Tripolye culture to the east, discussed in chapters 4 and 5, may have been points of reference, the venues for periodic gatherings by a more widely dispersed population. This was a different kind of formation from Danubian settlements, and what followed the TRB horizon does not represent steady expansion of either population or an agricultural economy. There was much variation from region to region.

Between the Bug and the Vistula, and north of the Vistula in southern Poland, much TRB settlement may be characterised by widely spread, often quite small occupations. In a classic study area north-east of Kraków, comprising the Dłubnia and Szreniama valleys, TRB sites were found to represent an intake of the edge of the *loess* plateaux, contrasting with the more or less exclusive valley locations of the Danubian tradition. This has been explained by expanding population and more extensive clearance and cultivation, based on use of the plough.[29] Continued use of *loess* soils and a dispersal of settlement are certainly recurrent patterns, but situations varied. The numbers of sites in the original study area are actually comparatively low, set against others surveyed in other neighbouring regions. There was some intake of the sandy basin of the Nida, north of the Vistula, as well as of the *loess* interfluves. Pollen analysis of deposits in the Vistula to the east of Kraków suggests no marked increase in clearance or in the intensity of land use in the post-Danubian horizon. Many regions had quite modest burial monuments and graves as well as small occupations, as on the *loess* plateau west of Lublin.[30] Some of the largest recognised sites were in the region of banded flint extraction, like Cmielów in the Kamienna valley, where large-scale processing of flint took place. There was a scatter of enclosure sites, like Słonowice, Kielce district, a ditched and palisaded rectangular layout in a tributary of the Vistula, or Wzgórze Zawichojskie, Sandomierz, and an unpublished example from Złota nearby, consisting also of combinations of ditch and palisade, set above the Vistula.[31]

The excavation of Bronocice on a *loess* ridge above the Nidzica, a tributary of the Vistula, has shown the existence of another major site, used through a long sequence, and standing out markedly against its smaller neighbours in all its phases.[32] Danubian sites were firmly concentrated in the Nidzica valley. In the succeeding TRB, Lublin–Volhynian (part of the so-called Lengyel–Polgar cycle or complex) and Baden phases, settlements were spread from valley to well on to the interfluves. No other sites of the size of Bronocice itself were located within a 10 km radius, and only one site of any size was within 5 km. Bronocice covers 50 ha, on a long ridge with a series of steps in it, some 1.5 km long. Extensive excavations have shown that the first TRB phase covered about 5 ha on the highest part of the ridge. An occupation about half that size in the Lublin–Volhynian phase was largely confined within an oval ditch. In subsequent TRB phases the occupation expanded on the lower part of the ridge to about 18 ha in extent, reaching some 26 ha in site phase IV, in the Baden period. There was another single-ditched enclosure. Finally occupation contracted to an area of about 17 ha in the central part of the ridge, in the final Baden phase. The features most often recovered were pits, with some graves, including a notable collective deposit from phase IV.

The Lublin–Volhynian enclosure was some 170 by 210 m across, its V-profiled ditch reaching a depth of almost 3 m.[33] The main features were pits, largely confined to the interior, where they were densely distributed. People grew cereals, and kept domesticated animals, chiefly cattle, but game including red deer still made some contribution to the diet. Here the main flint source was Jurassic flint from north of Kraków, some 30 km away, but there some quantities of Volhynian flint, from over 250 km away. A decorated pot from the last TRB phase appears to show a four-wheeled waggon, and an ox horncore from a Baden pit of the final phase suggests the obvious means of traction. The handle of a TRB pot from Krężnica Jara, near Lublin, was modelled in the form of two cattle side by side, and presumably yoked.[34] Here, closer to the Carpathian basin and more convincingly than in the Alpine foreland, is better evidence for changing uses of animals. Yet the example from Złota with which the chapter began reminds us that animals may have been raised as subjects of value as much as simply sources of protein, the means to achieving reputation, to laying on feasts in pursuit of honour, or to propitiating the ancestral dead. The largest sites like Bronocice and Gródek Nadbużny may have been where unusually large numbers of people periodically came together.

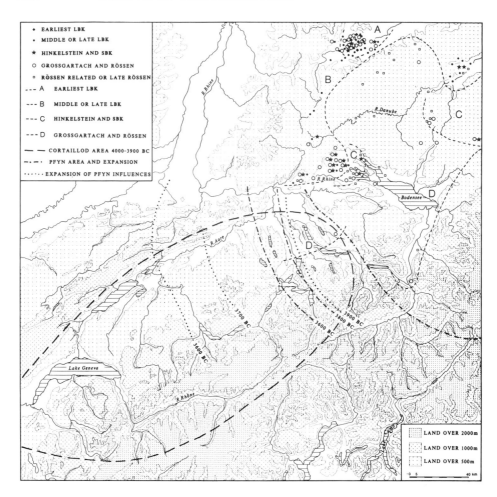

7.5 The expansion of settlement in the Alpine foreland, from the LBK to the Cortaillod–Pfyn cultures. After Schlichtherle, and Bleuer and Hardmeyer.

Elements of this pattern may be repeated in other areas.[35] In both Bohemia and Moravia and in the Elbe–Saale region, there are few known TRB houses. Sites with pits, like those overlying the palisade enclosure at Quenstedt, are more typical. It is not really clear what the overall distributions and variations of such sites are. There were some enclosures in Bohemia, as at Makotřasy, where an arc-shaped ditch some 650 m long was succeeded by a rectilinear ditch roughly 300 by 300 m, and others in the Elbe–Saale region, such as Halle–Dölauer Heide, Derenburg and Wallendorf–Hutberg. The enclosure at Halle–Dölauer Heide encompasses a maximum area of about 400 by 600 m, with ditches and palisades. Only a little interior occupation, of uncertain character, has so far been investigated. There may have been other reference points in the settlement system in the absence of very large sites, such as burial structures (discussed below) and other monuments, like the linear enclosures at Březno, Bohemia. As well as the human dead, there are

7.6 Reconstruction of the land-use cycle from evidence around Hornstaad. Top: limited clearance/coppicing and cultivation; below: grazing and regeneration. Drawings: Rösch.

also examples of cattle pairs, as in pits facing a burial structure at Buchow–Karpzow, Kr. Nauen, to the west of Berlin, belonging to the late Havelland group.[36]

Smaller enclosures appeared in some areas around 3000 BC.[37] Hlinsko near Lipnik in the upper Morava valley in Moravia was a hilltop site of the Baden culture. It had two phases of perimeter, first a palisade and ditch, and then a stone- and wood-revetted rampart and ditch. Inside there were huts, and there was plentiful production of stone and bone tools,

7.7 Continuation of the land-use cycle. Top: regeneration of woodland; below: renewed clearance. Drawings: Rösch.

pottery and textiles (seen in spindle whorls and loom weights). In Bohemia, there are a number of small enclosures of the Baden and Řivnáč cultures. Apart from Řivnáč itself, Homolka had successive systems of palisade and ditch surrounding houses terraced into a small hill, and on the Dänemark promontory at Bylany there was a small ditched and palisaded enclosure. At Vraný near Slaný a palisade and ditch were replaced by a palisade alone, both phases probably enclosing less than a hectare. There were Baden features within, characteristically in the form of pits and other ill-defined structures.

To the north, Kujavia provides another, potentially more complex set of patterns. TRB sites were more dispersed into areas of sandy and morainic soils, away from the black soil 'islands' used by the Danubian tradition.[38] Many sites were probably small, and few built domestic structures have been recovered, though there is a notable series of burial mounds and structures. Cattle bones are most numerous in the faunal assemblages. There are the well-known claimed ardmarks under barrow 8 at Sarnowo, though the spot, a series of undulating ridges on sandy soil near a small stream, is not the most obvious location for sustained cereal cultivation. In the Globular Amphora phase, there was renewed occupation of the black soil islands, for example at Brześć Kujawski, where there are pits rather than houses, some once more with cattle burials.[39] Only very irregular houses have been found in the Globular Amphora culture generally, which is otherwise often recognised by its series of burials (discussed below). In most parts of its distribution, the Globular Amphora culture is assigned to after the TRB culture or to a phase parallel to late TRB, but there is evidence in Kujavia, for example from Krusza Zamkowa near Inowrocław, to support contemporaneity throughout; in this view the Danubian tradition was represented more by the Globular Amphora culture than by the TRB. If this is accepted, a more complicated scene emerges. The overall picture is still of more dispersed and varied settlement, the abandonment of the longhouse pattern, and the framing of the landscape by burial sites and monuments, but there may have been a further internal pattern structured along cultural lines, with Globular Amphora culture sites in one part of the landscape and TRB sites in another, close together.

At the end of the sequence in several parts of this region came the Corded Ware horizon.[40] There were Corded Ware groups in southern Poland, Bohemia, the Elbe–Saale region, and northern Poland. These were not omnipresent. The excavations at Bronocice found one Corded Ware grave, though elsewhere in that area Corded Ware graves were found further on to the interfluves than earlier phases of settlement. In most areas where they occur, unlike in Switzerland, Corded Ware groups have been recognised chiefly by graves and small burial mounds (discussed below). Their considerable numbers in Bohemia and the Elbe–Saale region suggest no diminution of population. In southern Poland, some burial mounds have been found far into the mountains fringing the northern Carpathian basin. There are virtually no diagnostic sites around Sandomierz on the Vistula, but there the Złota culture (succeeding the Globular Amphora burials with which the chapter began) could be an independent group contemporary with Corded Ware culture.[41]

The Corded Ware horizon is often seen to mark the advent of a more mobile population, probably reliant on animals, but this must depend in part on how one interprets earlier phases. In Bohemia and southern Poland there was continued occupation of fertile *loess* and other soils. Much of the population may have continued to live lives structured by movement and dispersal. There is some evidence for cultivation. What may principally have changed concerned the nature of aggregation. Neither enclosures nor large occupations like Bronocice were features of the Corded Ware horizon. Nonetheless, graves and burial grounds continued to provide points in the landscape, and we can hardly be dogmatic that fewer people were involved in burial or ancestor rites in chosen places than had been brought together in earlier phases. At Halle–Dölauer Heide, for example, there were some dozen Corded Ware burial mounds, and there were Corded Ware graves at

Quenstedt, some cutting earlier TRB (Bernburg phase) pits.[42] It may even be the case that the orbit of mobility was becoming more circumscribed, perhaps through very slow population increase, with landscapes marked out now by places of more local significance, compared to the earlier points of aggregation which could have served much wider areas.

Further contrasts in this horizon can be illustrated by sites in northern Poland and in the eastern Baltic zone. Chwalim is a mid third-millennium BC occupation in the Wojnowo region south-west of Poznań.[43] It lay beside an oxbow bend of the Obra, tributary of the Oder, in a very varied landscape of river, wetlands and woodlands. It was used repeatedly, perhaps seasonally, as a base for fishing, fowling and hunting game such as deer, elk, boar and horse. The people here used pottery, which has technical resemblances to Globular Amphorae, Corded Ware and eastern 'forest' wares, but their flint tools suggest Mesolithic rather than Neolithic traditions. These could have been foragers of Mesolithic descent, in many ways unaffected by millennia of change in wider regions around.

In the region of Gdańsk, the Rzucewo group had pottery with close affinities to Corded Ware, but the lifestyle was distinctive.[44] People lived in small wooden houses, near coastal lagoons, Vistula delta wetlands, and on higher ground near the coast, perhaps in a seasonal cycle of occupations. They had domesticated cattle, pigs and some sheep and goats, but did little cultivation. They fished, hunted and caught seals. Short-stay camps out in the delta seem to have been for collecting and working amber, which found its way much further south. This too may have been a local population whose subsistence base had changed little over millennia, but which had become part of the mosaic of changing cultural and social relationships characteristic of the late Neolithic period.

Further to the east, both inland and around the eastern Baltic, a forager lifestyle was also long continued.[45] On the Lithuanian coast, just north of the bay formed by the deltas of the Vistula and the Nemunas (Niemen), a series of remarkable sites have been found along a string of lagoons parallel to the shore.[46] These belonged to the Narva and Bay Coast/Rzucewo cultures, but represent essentially the continuity of the same local population. Post-framed huts, for example at Šventoji 23, formed small camps or hamlets, which may have served as bases for more or less year-round occupation of the coastal zone. People hunted large and small game and fished, especially for pike, as well as catching seals. There are remarkably well-preserved organic remains, including wooden paddles with long spear-shaped blades, wooden bowls (complementing pottery), knotted nets of lime bast fabric, pronged leisters, trolling nets with boards, and a fish weir. Domesticated cattle, and a very few sheep and goats, were gradually adopted, as well as wheat and millet. By the time of the Rzucewo occupation at Šventoji 6, perhaps greater quantities of cereals were cultivated, but this was still only one element in a very broad subsistence base. Hazelnuts and water chestnuts were gathered, the latter perhaps to be made into flour. Hemp and mallow were also cultivated, for their fibre.

These were not isolated survivors of an outmoded way of life. Cultivation and herding were adopted slowly, to suit the local situation. Carved artefacts in amber, stone (such as the notable Narva stone elk head from Šventoji 3B), bone and wood are a further indication of rich material culture. Amber was probably exchanged from this area with the Globular Amphora culture to the south. It is possible that the lifestyle in the coastal region was more sedentary than inland in the Globular Amphora culture area to the south. Further interaction came in the Corded Ware horizon. Corded Ware/Boat Axe culture graves are known from the east Baltic, as far north as southern Finland.[47] These do not have to be regarded as the graves of an immigrant group, and the Rzucewo culture in the Šventoji region strongly suggests change within the same population.

Southern Scandinavia

A millennium earlier, there was continuity of population from the Ertebølle culture to early TRB or ENI in Denmark and southern Sweden. Regional distributions of early pottery styles match regional patterns of Ertebølle material culture. People still used coastal regions, as on south-west Fyn, in the Saltbaeg Vig study area on north-west Zealand, or in eastern Jutland. Many shell middens have EN occupations, as at Norsminde in eastern Jutland (as noted in the previous chapter). There were inland hunting sites, such as Muldbjerg in the Aamosen bog on Zealand, and coastal fishing and sealing camps, such as Sølager on an inlet in the north of Zealand or Hesselø on a small island north of Zealand in the Kattegat. At Hesselø, the overabundance of seal skull fragments strongly suggests the movement of large carcasses back to Zealand or the mainland. There are recent discoveries of early TRB fishing weirs on the coast. People continued to be interested in natural places, especially in wetlands, for the deposition of chosen items, in the EN phase including human bodies, pots, polished axes and amber. Isotope analysis of human bone has suggested a decisive shift to a mainly terrestrial diet compared with the largely marine diet of Ertebølle people at Vedbaek, but this preliminary result is open to suspicion. It may not adequately characterise either situation, and both more samples and more testing of the method, including investigation of post-depositional changes, are needed.[48]

In the ENI phase, occupation sites may have been largely small and dispersed. Little is known about the seasonality or duration of occupation. There is little evidence for substantial domestic structures. The remains preserved under a long barrow at Mosegården, near Horsens in eastern Jutland, consisted of post holes, a hearth and scatters of artefacts. The maximum area of the occupation was estimated as 50 by 20 m.[49] Pollen analysis generally suggests limited clearance of woodlands (many dominated by lime trees); peaks of birch pollen may indicate shifting cultivation or swiddening. Pigs are as well represented in faunal assemblages as cattle, and sheep and goats do not appear to have been important. The landscape may have been framed in a variety of ways: by old occupations including shell middens, natural places chosen for depositions, and by burial sites including the earliest long barrows. It is possible that the lifestyle became more mobile than in the Ertebølle phase. At Barkaer in southern Djursland, east Jutland, two long mounds were built in the ENII or possibly MNAI phase over earlier occupation largely of ENI date. The site had thin but quite extensive spreads of material. It lay in an area of rather poor soil, above what was at the time a saline inlet connected to the sea. Some of the classic early pollen analysis was carried out nearby. Most specialists see limited human impact on the vegetation at this date in the pollen diagrams. It does not look as though cultivation was the major concern of every occupation.[50]

In what we can call the middle phase, from ENII into the MNA of the Danish sequence, beginning in the middle to later fourth millennium BC, there were still plenty of small occupations. But the range and variety of sites and places increased.[51] The occupation at Hanstedgård, eastern Jutland, of the MNAI phase, was similar to Mosegården in terms of slight structures and thin spreads of artefacts, but covered a much bigger area, up to 4 ha, suggesting repeated returns to a favoured locality. It has been claimed that there were timber-framed longhouses up to 18 m long from the EN period, as at Ornehus on Zealand, but there are few examples. Earthen long barrows and stone-kerbed long and round mounds (dolmens or *dysser*) were built in ENII, and passage graves in great quantities from MNAIb. Two long mounds were built over the earlier occupation at Barkaer. Literally thousands of passage graves were built, often dispersed across the landscape. From the ENII Fuchsberg phase ditched and palisaded enclosures were built. Though their discovery in Denmark in recent years has been one of the great successes of Neolithic field archaeology, their numbers remain low compared to dolmens and passage graves; some thirty or less are now known in Denmark, and there are related sites in Schleswig-Holstein and southern Sweden. We shall return to examples like Sarup on south-west Fyn later. Some much larger occupation sites are found from the MN phase, such as Troldebjerg, Klintebakke and Spodsbjerg on Langeland. Some of these, like Blandebjerg, also on Langeland, Trelleborg, in western Zealand, and Bundsø, on Als, can now be seen actually to have succeeded enclosures. Little recent work has been done on these large sites, and their character is uncertain. They might better be regarded as points of aggregation rather than large settlements.

To the middle phase belonged the classic *landnam* or land taking, seen in a relative opening of woodland cover and greater quantities of light-loving herbs and grasses, with some cereals. The scale and duration of clearance episodes in this phase are still problematic. The original formulation, by Iversen, was of short-term, shifting cultivations, followed by regenerations, and this kind of interpretation is again in favour.[52] High values of hazel suggest coppicing and regeneration. Much clearance may have been to create grazings. Ardmarks under passage grave mounds may reflect short-term cultivations, and some may have had a symbolic character. The range of cereals grown matches that elsewhere in central Europe. There may also be regional variation. The classic *landnam* cycle is a feature especially of eastern Jutland and Zealand, while in western Jutland there was probably much less impact on woodlands at this date. It is hard to reconstruct the character of animal economies from the residues at sites like Troldebjerg or Blandebjerg, since their character and the nature of deposition are uncertain, but cattle were numerous. It has been suggested that the stone-packing graves of northern Jutland were stylised ox burials; if accepted, this would be another clue to the value placed on domesticated animals.[53]

After long debate about the extent of overlap between TRB culture and Corded Ware/Single Grave culture, the favoured model is of succession from one to the other. This is the MNB period in current Danish terminology, and can be taken here as the late phase. There is still debate, as in every region, whether the Corded Ware/Single Grave culture represents population movement, but among other considerations the successive chronology strongly supports a model of continuity.[54] Many small mounds were built over individual graves, especially in mid and west Jutland, but there was also much reuse of passage graves and dolmens in east and north Jutland. Settlements are much more poorly known. Survey and excavation in north and east Jutland have shown that small sites with pits and post holes can be recovered. There is a small post-framed structure south of the Limfjord at Skinderup, and a larger one, 16 m long, at Hemmed in Djursland. Evidence from the coast may be complementary. Kalvø was a small island in the Norsminde fjord, some 500 m from the shore. It had been used in the late TRB phase, and continued in use in the middle part ('Ground Grave' phase) of the Single Grave culture, probably as a seasonal camp. The actual occupation was poorly preserved but a small shell midden next to it showed the use of cattle, pigs and sheep, and also hunting, sealing, fishing for cod, and shellfish collection. No cereals were found in sieved samples, but they would hardly be expected in this offshore context. The pollen evidence generally can be taken to suggest a larger scale of clearance, but still mostly associated with the grazing of animals. The distribution of monuments suggests both continuity of land use, as around Vroue Hede in north-west Jutland, and a wider use of the landscape, with many mounds appearing on what are now the heathlands of western Jutland. But it is not clear that the Corded Ware/Single Grave phase represents a more mobile lifestyle than earlier, as is commonly supposed.

Another element in south Scandinavia was the appearance of Pitted Ware culture occupations, found on the north Jutland and Zealand coasts and into southern Sweden. This tradition seems to have arisen independently of the TRB culture, and cannot be regarded as a specialised variant of Corded Ware culture.[55] It too was perhaps of Mesolithic descent, or may represent a turning back to ways strongly reminiscent of earlier forager lifestyles. People fished, trapped, hunted and herded, and caught seals. Two sites now inland in east Jutland, Kainsbakke and Kirial Bro, were then by an inlet separating north-east Djursland from the mainland. Their occupants exploited both land and sea, hunting a wide range of large and small game, keeping domesticated animals including pigs, fishing, fowling and collecting shellfish. Of the two sites, Kainsbakke could have been used as a base for foraging and for gatherings. One very large pit (some 5.5 by 4.5 m across, and over 1 m deep) was deliberately backfilled with shells, animal and fish bone, and discarded artefacts: perhaps the residues of feasting. Inland in southern Sweden the bog site of Alvastra, Östergötland, had a large laid wooden platform. It has been regarded as an occupation, but might better be seen as some kind of ceremonial meeting place, where feasts were held and depositions of artefacts made. The platform was renewed or refurbished at intervals over four decades. Pollen analysis suggests coppiced woods around, with some cereal cultivation.[56] Whatever the social niche of Pitted Ware communities, their subsistence base alone must indicate a far from filled landscape at the end of the Neolithic period.

Britain and Ireland, Brittany and the coastal Netherlands

Eilean Domhnuill is an islet in the small Loch Olabhat, on the west, ocean side of North Uist in the Outer Hebrides. It has a series of Neolithic occupations from the fourth millen-

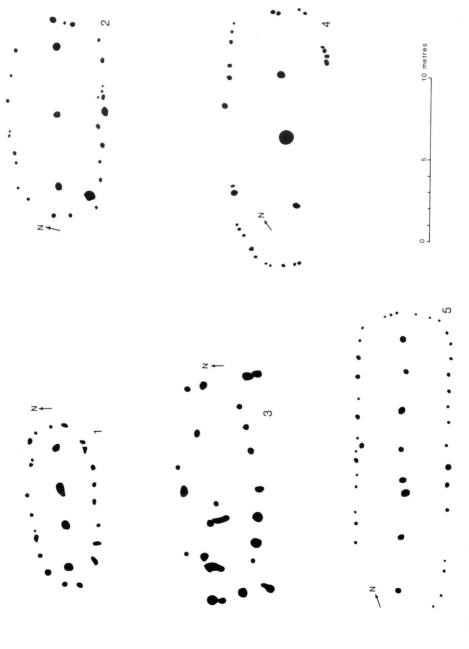

7.8 EN houses from Denmark. 1: Bygholm Nørremark; 2: Mossby; 3: Limensgård; 4: Ornehus; 5: Skraeppekaergård. After Buus Eriksen.

10 metres

5

0

nium BC.[57] The islet was defined or enhanced by palisades and low stone revetments. Within there were traces of rectangular structures, whose bases could be picked out by stone footings, but which were probably never coursed. These presumably had light super-structures. In the first phase, two structures about 6 by 4 m lay side by side. These structures were frequently modified. Their users deposited a lot of pottery and had stone querns; it does not appear that they brought animals within the enclosed space of the islet. This may have been only one of a series of occupations, others being found along the *machair* or shell-sand western coastal strip. Dispersed chambered tombs are other features of this landscape. This may not have been a sedentary population. There are still signs, for example in the site of Northton on the south end of Harris (the next island north of North Uist), of short-term coastal occupations in the later fourth and earlier third millennia BC.[58]

In the Orkneys too there is no evidence of large early occupations, and known sites like Knap of Howar, on the small island of Papa Westray, were not necessarily in permanent use. From about 3000 BC (or a little earlier), larger occupations appeared, associated with the use of Grooved Ware pottery. To famous sites like Skara Brae and Rinyo have been added more recent discoveries such as Pool on Sanday and Barnhouse in the middle of the main Orkney island. Pool was a stratified coastal site, showing sustained use of one place, but of unknown character. At Links of Noltland on Westray, the 'site' actually seems to consist of a fragment of landscape around a settlement, perhaps partially defined by boundary walls, and of non-domestic structures. It is possible that by this date in a circum-scribed island setting some occupations were indeed both larger and more permanent. Skara Brae is one indication of this, and Barnhouse another. Barnhouse had houses less closely grouped together than Skara Brae, and more varied in size. The largest was a sub stantial stone-footed affair with a surrounding stone platform and wall. The cellular interi-ors of some of the houses show close similarities to the internal layout of local tombs. The most elaborate local tomb, Maes Howe, lay close by. Rather than being the inevitable outcome of the adoption of agriculture, occupations of this kind could be seen as the result of the deliberate social integration of previously dispersed population as a strategy for taking in central and other parts of the Orkney main island. The carefully planned house interiors imposed set ways of entering, moving around and seeing. These were not 'machines for living in', but an active part of an ordered social fabric, which stressed con-formity and unity.[59]

Elsewhere in Britain and Ireland, and indeed in north-west France, traces of houses have been comparatively rare, and it has been convenient to point to the Orkney evidence in support of the argument that such a scarcity of built structures merely reflects the acci-dents and patterns of survival. After all, post structures have turned up as far apart as Fengate, Cambridgeshire, on the East Anglian fen-edge, and Balbridie, Grampian, in the Dee valley of north-east Scotland, and there have been several recent discoveries in Ireland.[60] Other recent research has made this view far less convincing. Large-scale surveys, backed up by limited excavations, and sustained regional investigations – for example around Stonehenge, around Avebury, in Cranborne Chase and around Dorchester, in the chalklands of Wiltshire and Dorset, in the upper Thames valley, the middle part of the Nene valley, and in parts of the western edge of the East Anglian fens – have not produced

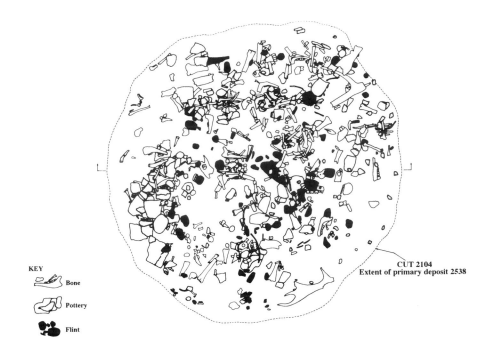

KEY

Bone

Pottery

Flint

CUT 2104
Extent of primary deposit 2538

7.9 Plan of the Coneybury 'Anomaly' pit. After Richards.

an abundant early settlement record.[61] It is hardly possible to explain this all away as the result of later erosion and destruction. In the area of chalk downland around Stonehenge, then wooded, surface survey suggests small, scattered occupations in a landscape which came gradually to be framed by long barrows and a ditched enclosure at Robin Hood's Ball. At Coneybury near Stonehenge, a large pit (the so-called Anomaly) contained the partial remains of several cattle and roe deer, and of one or two pigs and red deer. There were also a few beaver bones and some from a trout, the river Avon lying only half a kilometre away. More of the meat-bearing bones of the cattle and red deer were missing than of the roe deer. These may have been taken off for consumption elsewhere. There were also at least forty broken pots, from small cups to larger vessels usable for serving. There are no other features indicating an occupation, though the pit also contained two arrowheads, a broken polished flint axe, flint cores, flakes and scrapers, and some carbonised cereals. This feature may represent a locale used repeatedly by a still mobile population for periodic feasting in the context of important social gatherings. Those houses or structures which have been recognised elsewhere could be seen as part of a similar pattern; some may also have had non-domestic uses. Most occupations are recognised as scatters of artefacts or small concentrations of pits, some of which at least may have been deliberately dug to receive depositions of material to mark the comings and goings of settlement.

Soil, molluscan and other environmental evidence here and elsewhere suggests a mosaic of small clearances which were kept open for a while before being allowed to revert to woodland.[62] It has become simplest to regard the much discussed elm decline as the result of disease rather than of selective human interference (or selective climatic effects). Both the scale and duration of clearances remain uncertain, and both aspects may have varied from place to place. Pollen analysis of deposits receiving a localised pollen rain suggests smaller rather than larger clearances, and molluscan analysis, for example around Avebury in north Wiltshire, may also suggest a still very varied and largely wooded environment. Radiocarbon dated pollen profiles from northern Ireland and East Anglia indicate that some clearances were kept open for long periods, or at least that clearance activity in a given region was maintained for a long time. Thin turflines of buried soils under chalkland monuments may suggest rather briefer episodes of clearance maintenance. The criss-cross marks under the long barrow at South Street, near Avebury, remain one of the best indications of purposeful soil disturbance, but do not tell us how important cultivation was in the regional subsistence economy. In the deposits made in the ditches of the nearby causewayed enclosure at Windmill Hill, it is cattle along with other domesticates whose remains were prominent. Here and elsewhere there are small quantities of game. The relatively dry woodlands of the chalklands may not have been rich in game, and we have tended to frame our view of early Neolithic subsistence in terms of the positive act of clearance. Woodland and the wildscape may themselves have been important resources. Hazel had grown in the lower secondary fill of the ditch segments of the low-lying enclosure at Etton in the Welland valley, and was coppiced, harvested and intensively worked *in situ*. There is also evidence for hazel coppicing in the Somerset Levels. Chemical analysis of pots from the riverside occupation at Runnymede, Staines, in the lower Thames valley west of London, suggests that honey, pork fat and some kind of fish were put in containers.[63]

Such a landscape was framed by enduring built monuments. Other investments of labour were for impermanent creations such as clearings, and were part of a system based on cyclical movement. Even the largest built facility of the time was connected with the movement of people through the landscape. The Sweet Track in the Somerset Levels, dated to 3807/6 BC, covered some 2 km of periodically wet fen, running from the Poldens ridge out to Westhay island in the middle of the Levels.[64] Beyond Westhay island there was more fen, and perhaps some shallow open water. It is not known whether a track continued into that part. The track was a single walkway, of oak and other planks, carefully raised above a substructure of rails and diagonal cross-pegs. People could have negotiated this without difficulty, though one pot beside the track, with wooden stirrer and hazelnuts inside it, suggests an awkward moment when somebody slipped. Animals, certainly cattle, would have found the traverse harder. The wood had been harvested from both untouched primary woodland and secondary woodland (perhaps reflecting clearances in the area as early as 4000 BC or just before), and in at least one spot it was stockpiled. We do not know how many people were involved in preparing the 6000 m or more of worked timber which went into the construction. The task of building, however, may have been relatively swift, and would have been manageable by only a few people, according to experimental reconstruction. The main Sweet Track was preceded, some thirty years earlier, by a first

7.10 View and detail of the Sweet Track. Photo: Somerset Levels Project.

version, surviving in stretches. This so-called Post Track indicates that the intention was to create a lasting facility, but subject to renewal. The Sweet Track itself may have been usable for only a short time. Its timbers were little affected by beetles or fungus, and the fen may have overwhelmed it within a generation or so. It is hard to envisage that this outcome was not foreseen by people familiar with their surroundings.

People may have used this track, and other woodland paths, for different sorts of purpose. The track may have led to grazing, hunting or fowling areas. It may have been built principally to help people move around the landscape, speculatively to special places of spiritual significance in the fens, or more generally through a cycle of subsistence relocations and social interactions. A polished jadeite axe and a chipped flint axe, both in mint condition, were found in different spots beside the track. Both appear to have been deliberately placed, as axe blades without wooden hafts, which should otherwise have survived in the waterlogged conditions. The flint axe probably came from further east in southern Britain, perhaps from as far afield as Sussex, while the jadeite axe could have come ultimately from the western part of the Alps, distances of some 150 and 800 km respectively.[65]

Evidence from other regions may conform to the same kind of pattern. Pollen analyses from northern Ireland and Scotland, for example, suggest a kaleidoscope of clearings of varying durations and uses. Pollen analyses in Brittany and northern coastal Normandy indicate very little early impact on woodlands, and there may have been very little early cultivation. The Brittany interior was not much used until the later Neolithic.[66]

These were small-scale and slow-moving transformations. Recent research in the peat-lands of central Ireland has shown the existence there too of early trackways. The best-preserved early example, no. 9, at Corlea, Co. Longford, which consists of lengthways stems and brushwood with more occasional transverse pieces, is dated to around the middle of the fourth millennium BC. While the number of houses known in Ireland increases steadily, it is likely that these structures, like the examples at Ballynagilly, Co. Tyrone, and Ballyglass, Co. Mayo, were both rare and isolated. Not every area was marked by the building of permanent monuments. South-west Ireland had occupations, as at Lough Gur, Co. Limerick, but a regional early tradition of cist burials rather than mega-lithic or other tombs.[67]

While a similar story unfolded in the northern Netherlands, with clearances, monuments and probably shifting occupations, western coastal areas were still used in very traditional ways. Occupation of the old dune ridge at Hazendonk in the Rhine–Maas delta (first noted in the previous chapter) was renewed in two further phases, roughly parallel to early TRB, and the coastal Vlaardingen culture was contemporary with the later TRB of the area. Vlaardingen sites in a variety of settings within the delta were connected with fishing, fowling, hunting and herding pigs and cattle. One example is Hekelingen site III, on a Maas estuary freshwater tidal creek, surrounded by marshes and some 25 km from the contem-porary coast. People may have been there at all seasons of the year, but clearly moved around, since they caught and ate dolphins and even whales (beached on the coasts, if not harpooned offshore). Cereals were used, but were probably brought in rather than culti-vated locally.[68] Coastal and inland populations may have had a symbiotic relationship. Movement by both will have brought them into contact; the lifestyle of the coastal popula-tion might have been more static than that of people inland.

The Vlaardingen example illustrates the varied histories of subsistence and settlement continuing into the later Neolithic after 3000 BC. Overlapping with the end of the Vlaardingen culture, but succeeding the TRB culture, the Protruding Foot Beaker (PFB) culture in the Netherlands is the local variant and most westerly representative of the Corded Ware/Single Grave tradition. Inland, there is little case for population migration, and a much better one for the extension of clearance, and widening contacts seen in the import of Grand Pressigny flint blades. Solid wooden wheels have been found dating to the PFB horizon. The amount of cereal pollen increases in northern Dutch pollen diagrams in this horizon, but the palisade enclosures at Anlo, Drenthe, may suggest a primary interest in herding. PFB occupations are also known from the coastal region of the Netherlands, at sites like Kolhorn, Aartswoud, Keins and Mienakker, on the west side of the Ijssel estuary. These PFB sites could represent local movement of population or a final acculturation of the Vlaardingen population, but in either case people continued to use the diverse, wet environment of creeks, rivers, salt marshes and tidal flats. People herded cattle and used cereals (whether or not cultivated locally), but also continued to hunt, fowl, fish and forage for plant food and shellfish. A cyclical, seasonal system has been proposed of larger bases close to water, with smaller, short-stay sites further away from water. Occasional human bones in coastal PFB occupations could be from disturbed burials, or may indicate that remains of ancestors circulated with the living. The structure illustrated here, from recent

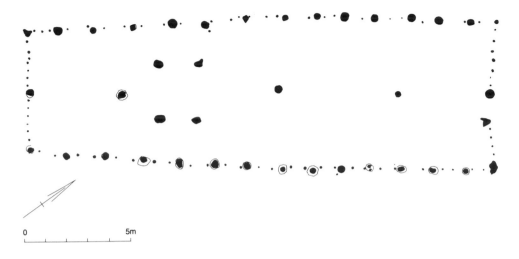

0   5m

7.11 Plan of house or communal building at Zeewijk East, West Frisia. Drawing: Hogestijn.

excavations at Zeewijk East, was kept clean of normal domestic residues, and may have served as some kind of communal centre.[69]

In parts of Britain and Ireland, the middle of the Neolithic sequence may have been characterised by less clearance and more woodland regeneration, around 3000 BC, though at this date in eastern Ireland, coastal Brittany and the Orkneys, for example, there was notable monument construction going on. Generally speaking, there appear to be none of the big occupations characteristic of the middle part of the Danish sequence, though some enclosures, such as Maiden Castle, Dorset, and Windmill Hill, Wiltshire, first used for ceremonial purposes, may later have become the focus for occupation. Bigger monuments were constructed in some areas in the later Neolithic, such as the very large circular henge enclosures of southern Britain. These are accompanied by evidence for renewed clearance. The relationship between the two aspects is crucial. Rather than see the monuments as the symptoms of an ever more sedentary and numerous population, one can envisage that renewed clearances and a more open landscape were the specific product of the circumstances surrounding monument construction. That may have been undertaken by people from wide areas around. It is not necessary to confine the builders and users of large monuments like Avebury, or Mount Pleasant, Dorset, to the immediate vicinities of the earthworks.[70]

In southern Britain, the settlement evidence remains rather meagre. More rough and ready ways of working flint ('expedient' in the technical jargon) may suggest a reduced scale of movement, but structures other than pits remain rare, even where large-scale surveys have been carried out. Many southern Grooved Ware pits were dug for the deliberate deposition of selected items, suggesting the continuation of an older tradition to do with comings and goings in the landscape.[71]

At Fengate, Cambridgeshire, on the west edge of the East Anglian fens, a modest area of ditched paddocks or enclosures was associated with a small Grooved Ware occupation. This might be taken to represent the beginnings of greater investment in fixed facilities, since a larger, co-axial field system was in use in the later third millennium BC. But the labour required for ditching would have been much less than for the earlier Sweet Track, for example, and there is no evidence of cereal cultivation. The Fengate enclosures were associated with the use of cattle, probably as a temporary holding ground in a continued pattern of movement. The remarkable and extensive system of stone boundaries preserved under peat in Co. Mayo, in western Ireland, might be seen in the same light. These were not an isolated phenomenon restricted to the locality, Behy-Glenulra, where they were first found, but occur over hundreds of metres to the east of Behy hill, and at other locations both east and west along the north Mayo coast, and probably elsewhere as well. Their precise dating remains uncertain. There is little indication of cultivation in the long strips of land, some 100 m across and bounded by low stone walls. Though only partially subdivided by cross-walls, these divisions could have served to manage cattle grazing. If they were the product of many generations of construction, the attenuated investment need not be seen as having tied the population irrevocably to this part of the landscape alone.[72]

Sacred realms of the dead

Burial grounds

In previous chapters the distinction has been followed between funeral rites and ancestor rites.[73] Here I will argue that we need to extend the concept of ancestry to include mythical and imagined forebears. It becomes very hard to maintain rigid distinctions in analysis of particular situations, and perhaps much of that ambiguity existed in Neolithic minds too.

In the last chapter we saw the presence of the dead in settlements and occupations of both the Danubian and the coastal forager traditions, and the emergence in both traditions of separate burial grounds, either close to particular occupations or serving small areas. Funeral rites changed with time through the Ertebølle sequence. Considerable further changes came in the next horizon, roughly down to about 3000 BC (and the appearance of the Globular Amphora culture). From around 4000 BC, or possibly earlier as discussed in the last chapter, monuments containing human remains were built in many parts of west, north-west and even central Europe. These megalithic and other constructions have often been taken for granted, interpreted as collective tombs, and used as sources of sociopolitical information. I shall argue, however, that renewed attention needs to be given to the structures themselves; that the significance of them and their contents lay primarily in sacred and religious realms; and that this was to do with ideas of origins, time and descent. Aside from the monuments themselves, part of the argument rests on a sense of sequence, and part on interpretation of non-monumental rites. These were the rites which provided funerals, and routinely circulated the dead among the living.

Burial rites were everywhere very varied. Following the notable Ertebølle burial grounds such as Vedbaek, Nederst and Skateholm, separate cemeteries were comparatively rare. This discontinuity should be stressed. Examples are best known from the regional groups

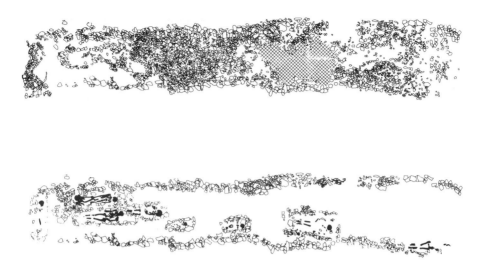

7.12 Two levels of burial structure I at Karmanovice. After Nagay–Chochaj.

of the TRB culture, such as the group of stone-lined graves at Stålmosegård, Zealand (of MNAI–III date), flat graves at Ekelberg, Drenthe, in the northern Netherlands, or Ostorf, near Schwerin, and Heek, near Borken in northern Germany.[74] There are other examples. But large sites like Bronocice or Gródek Nadbużny were not, as far as is known after extensive exavations, accompanied by large adjacent burial grounds, in the manner say of earlier Lengyel cemeteries. Nor do the settlements of the Alpine foreland have adjacent burial grounds. In that region, research and rescue have often been confined of necessity to a narrow zone of lake or marsh edge, and even the biggest recent investigations have rarely uncovered whole sites, let alone any 'off-site' areas, but there has been sufficient prospection to allow the generalisation to stand.

There were some burial grounds in these areas. North-east of Bronocice across the Vistula on the *loess* zone west of Lublin (the Nałęczów plateau), there are many small TRB occupations, and several cemeteries, consisting for the most part of separate graves, with one or two people in each, and not elaborated by any further structure. That at Karmanovice has been extensively excavated.[75] There were two areas with individual flat graves, in which people had been buried singly or in pairs, and on at least one occasion successively. The graves were laid out in more or less ordered rows. In between these two areas, there were four larger structures. The biggest was grave complex I, some 15 by 2 m, formed by low side walls of limestone. Within, and variously aligned on the long axis of the structure, there were nine graves with single and double burials, with modest grave goods. A group of three graves showed successive interments. After deposition finished, the structure was covered by more stone and clay, to an unknown height. This complex therefore became a monument. In grave complex III, there may have been a symbolic grave, and complex IV was a triangular structure (only 8 m long) without any graves at all. Rites here may therefore have come to include general veneration for the dead of the past, as well as the interment of the recently deceased. There are a few other related monuments in the Lublin area, the most easterly examples of cairns or barrows over graves, such as the trape-zoidal one at Sławinek and the triangular one at Miłocin-Kolonia, both perhaps originally about 50 m long. Large settlements and large burial grounds were not present together.

In the Alpine foreland, the burial record is meagre. None are known in Egolzwil, Cortaillod or Pfyn contexts. A number of stone cists are known, often containing the remains of several people, belonging to the Chamblandes–Lenzburg group. These occur in areas like the Swiss Valais, away from the main marsh and lake settlements. Other burials are known from the early Lutzengüetle group, in northern Switzerland.[76]

Non-monumental graves occur in the TRB area. Flat or earth graves in Denmark often appear to occur on their own, or in very small numbers, and with uncertain relation to occupations or settlement. Some were simple affairs, like the grave of a man at Dragsholm, Zealand, buried with pot, axe, battleaxe, flint arrowheads and amber pendants, close to a late Ertebølle burial of two women.[77] Others were more elaborate, variously paved or lined with stone. Some may have had wooden superstructures, like the wooden ridged affair reconstructed for Konens Høj, Jutland, though it is possible that in that case and others the main above-ground features were merely standing posts at either end of a burial area. So far, these very varied graves have not turned up in large groups, nor beside the large MNA occupations referred to earlier in the chapter. One possible but unusual exception are the rows of so-called stone-packing graves, which occur in northern and western Jutland from MNAII onwards. These take the form of paired pits, often accompanied by a larger pit or so-called mortuary house. Rows hundreds of metres long are known, up to 1700 m in the most extreme example at Vroue Hede. In fact it is not clear that we should regard these structures as directly connected with funeral rites. The 'graves' regularly are stone-packed pits, and one suggestion is that they were a symbolic representation of cattle burials.[78]

The dead among the living

Further examples of similar rites could be cited from many other regions. If the adoption of Neolithic culture did not lead automatically to an extension of the practices seen so vividly at Vedbaek and Skateholm, the dead were brought among the living in many other ways. Remains of the dead occur in occupations or settlements, on ceremonial sites, and in special deposits.

The settlement evidence is varied. Some sites have formal burials within the area of occupation. Thus at Bronocice, there was a double burial in a pit within the Lublin–Volhynian phase enclosure. In phase IV, the Baden occupation, there were seven-teen individuals in one pit, four adults and thirteen children. The oldest was an adult man (estimated at 25 years old). He lay at the centre of the pit, with two younger women on the edge, and the children roundabout. It is not excluded that this deposit was formed over a period of time, and it is a moot point whether it should be considered a normal burial at all.[79]

In a southern TRB (Baalberge–Salzmünde) context at Weissenfels, near Halle in Sachsen–Anhalt, several pits had combinations of human and animal remains.[80] Pit 7 had

7.13 Collective burials from the Baden culture (site phase IV) pit 36–B1 at Bronocice. Photo: Milisauskas.

stray human bones, six cow skulls and other bones, a pig skull and parts of three dogs. In Pit 12 the crouched skeleton of a woman lay above cattle bones and a dog skull. In pit 27, there were varied deposits through the 3.5 m of fill: cereals and animal bones in the lower part; cattle, sheep and dog remains in the middle part, including nineteen cattle skulls; and five human skeletons, adult and children, with some animal bones, in the upper part.

A few human remains only are reported from Alpine foreland settlements, for example those in the Pfyn culture layer 4 at Zürich–Mozartstrasse; these might, however, be people lost in the fire which produced a major burning horizon. Occasional human bones occur in many other occupations. There were fragments of six skulls at Bundsø on Als, from later MNA contexts. Another example already noted came from the west Dutch coastal settlements of the PFB/Corded Ware culture; this kind of practice was evidently long-lived.[81]

The remains of the dead were brought among the living in other circumstances. The most striking example is their presence in deposits at ceremonial enclosures (which I consider further below). At the causewayed enclosure at Windmill Hill, Wiltshire, in southern England, there were a few complete child skeletons. Other remains, of both adults and children, were partial. One deposit in the outer ditch circuit of the enclosure, where most human remains were concentrated, consisted of the cranium of a young child, a cattle skull, other cattle bones and horncores, and a deer bone. At Sarup on Fyn in Denmark, there were primary deposits of human bone in the ditches and interior pits of the first enclosure. In the Rhineland, the ditched site of Michelsberg-Untergrombach had many isolated human remains and some skulls in pits within its interior; there was only one complete skeleton. Elsewhere in the Michelsberg culture there were deposits of human remains in pits, ditches and rockshelters; no formal burial grounds are yet known.[82]

Some people were deliberately killed, perhaps as sacrifices. There are several notable finds from Denmark.[83] At Troldebjerg on Langeland, the split and charred bones of several cattle and pigs, a goat and a dog, were accompanied by three human skeletons. One of these, an adult woman, had been killed by a blow to the head, the fate which befell two of the cattle. At Sigersdal on Zealand, in the late EN horizon, the remains of two young women were found in a bog. The older, estimated as 18 years old, had been strangled by a cord round her neck. At Bolkilde on Als, at the same sort of date, the remains of two men were recovered from a bog, the older of the two, a cripple estimated at 40 years old, having also been strangled by a cord around his neck.

In many accounts, the above kinds of evidence have been treated as a sideshow to the action taking place in the built 'tombs', as of lesser interest or as curiosities. I believe that this is a fundamental misconception. Compared with the increasing variety of Ertebølle rites being discovered, we can hardly claim that early Neolithic rites became more diverse, but there is a sense in which they appear less formal, or dispersed into a wider range of contexts. This does not suggest less interest in the dead, but rather a widening of their significance. Formal burials may have been connected with the local importance of descent and ancestry, known individuals being revered through funeral rites and subsequent memory. In other contexts the remains of the dead could have served as talismen or tokens, to make present the realms of the dead, to remind the living of the dead and the past and at the same time to unite past and present. In a fluid social and physical landscape descent and ancestry as ordering principles among the living would have been important. There is a great danger of losing sight of the possible meanings of death and ancestral rites for the living, and of reducing this fundamental sphere to an indicator of sociopolitical trends. By making the dead present among the living, the finality of death may have been denied. It has been suggested that human sacrifices put into wet places in Denmark should be considered as part of a cult of regeneration and fertility, which found frequent expression also in the repeated depositions of pots, axes and ornaments in wet places.[84] All these practices considered so far were not merely the backdrop to other rites, but were in the centre of the spiritual and conceptual stage of early Neolithic lives. The human dead were also placed in many of the built houses of the dead, but those constructions may have had far wider meanings.

Abstract funerals

From about 4000 BC, over a very broad area of west, north-west and into parts of central Europe, as far south as near Lublin in south-east Poland and Thuringia in Germany, there were carefully built mounds, cairns and platforms, which usually contained internal chambers and other structures. Some of these constructions were modest in size and appearance, others were both large and eye-catching. Most were altered at least once, many several times, and all had the ability to endure for long periods of time. Within this elaborate, three-dimensional architecture, normally in the internal structures, remains of the dead have regularly been found. Some deposits were of individuals, but many were of tens and even occasionally hundreds of people, so that a collective burial rite is usually characterised as typical for barrows and cairns. Some of the dead are represented by whole skeletons in anatomical order, many by disarticulated and frequently incomplete remains. In some instances, it is possible that the dead had been brought to the monuments already incomplete, while in others it is likely that they were transformed *in situ*. It is then an easy step to characterising these monuments as 'collective tombs'. These were built, in various styles, for at least a millennium in some areas, and in a few areas for a millennium and a half, right through the Neolithic sequence; in nearly all areas in which they occur, they were still in use or still observed in the later part of the Neolithic sequence.

It is little wonder then that these monuments have been taken as central to Neolithic burial rites over a very broad area. Since their architecture is both impressive and costly of labour, and since only a fraction of contemporary populations, even when the deposits are multiple, could have been put into them, it has often been assumed in recent years that these monuments were the expression of differences in power and social control within and between Neolithic communities. A significant gloss on this has been that the ideology of the collective burial rite masked and naturalised a more differentiated reality.[85] The elaborate and often extended treatment of the dead, whether involving secondary burial or not, has been connected with the concept of ancestry, known individuals being transformed by the burial rite through liminal stages into anonymous ancestors, from whom descent could be claimed and through whom claims to social position and resources could be legitimated.[86] There are recurrent elements in these kinds of characterisation: the central role of burial rites; the importance given to sociopolitical interpretation; and the assumption of a common role over broad areas and long periods. I shall argue here for rather different meanings for these monuments, of a more abstract or general nature, though I shall not insist on a single interpretation. First, one western example will help both to make more concrete some of the generalisations and to introduce doubts about current interpretations.

Newgrange, Knowth and Dowth in the Bend of the Boyne in Co. Meath, in eastern Ireland, are amongst the largest constructions in the whole of western Europe.[87] These are so-called passage graves or passage tombs (in the preferred Irish terminology), characterised by round mounds, with internal chambers approached through narrow entrances and passages. Newgrange and Knowth have been extensively excavated, both inside and out. Their setting in the Boyne valley is important. The three big monuments belong to a cluster of some 40 or more monuments, over an area of about 3.5 by 1 km. We do not know in any detail the early chronology of passage tombs. It is possible that in other parts of Ireland other styles of monument began earlier. Court tombs and portal tombs are the candidates, both offering constructions three-dimensionally graded, and holding varied quantities of both cremated and unburnt remains of the dead. They tend to occur on their own, dispersed across the landscape. There are none of these in the Bend of the Boyne. The passage tomb group there, typically clustered, may therefore be relatively later, or a regional variation.

The Boyne group appears to have been structured by the big three monuments (with a possible fourth at Ballincrad), but we do not know in what order they were built. We do know that Newgrange and Knowth were accompanied by smaller monuments, so-called satellites, and in the case of Knowth some if not all of the smaller constructions, at least seventeen in number, probably preceded the large mound which they appear to encircle. Knowth itself was built, according to radiocarbon dates, around or before 3000 B C. This sequence is of fundamental importance. The smaller constructions were gradually constructed around a central space. In that space, largely now covered by the main mound, there are signs of early activity, consisting of small subcircular structures, spreads of artefacts, and an arc of double palisade, itself overlying a smaller rectangular structure. This is hard to characterise; the distinction between domestic and non-domestic occupation may be unhelpful. One interpretation can be that the smaller monuments were attracted to the edge of a sacred space, already important for rites and gatherings. The smaller monuments were all circular, up to 20 m in diameter. They were laid out in a form typical for Irish passage tombs, with the circular mound defined by encircling kerb, and the narrow passage leading to a central chamber of polygonal or cross-shaped plan. The entrances face into the central space. These monuments have been recently reconstructed as steep-sided mounds, but their passages and chambers would originally have been low: passages not more than 1.5 m high. Deposits of cremated human remains and accompanying selected artefacts were put in the chambers; successive small depositions seem likely. These could be seen as the tombs of particular individuals, or of particular social groupings, say lineages or clans, but the small deposits may rather have a symbolic character. Passages and chambers were difficult of access. The rites which were carried out in and through them seem more than funereal. The role of the cremations may have been to make present the human dead in the houses of more abstract ancestors, the mythical progenitors of the community, as acts of propiation, and of unification of the living generation with their beginnings in a timeless past: abstract funerals, in the phrase of the Scottish novelist Muriel Spark.

The construction of the main mound at Knowth could be interpreted as the expression of more centralised control over labour and ritual, but this is difficult to accept. Charcoal in the turves of the Newgrange mound, in alternating layers of earth and stone, suggests recently cleared woodland; pollen analysis at Knowth shows a variety of herbs and weeds, indicating clearings; and recent surface survey in the region, though still at a comparatively early stage of research, has not yet found dense artefact scatters.[88] This was a landscape still with plenty of space in it, even after generations of occupation and activity in the area (perhaps going back to the earlier fourth millennium B C), and it is simply difficult to envisage how close control could be exerted or maintained for long in this setting. Impressive volumes of stone and earth were shifted to create the three big mounds, river stones being brought up from the Boyne. Creation itself may have been an act of ancestral veneration, carried out to a ritually predetermined order, well before any offerings of human remains

7.14 Mound 14 at Knowth. Top: view; below: hidden decoration on the back of orthostat 8, part of the chamber. Photos: Eogan.

were made. Decorated stones were not only placed at significant visible points in the circumference of the kerbs, and in the passages and chambers, but were also hidden, as on the backs of eleven out of 123 kerbstones examined at the main Knowth mound. Some may have been decorated, and redecorated, *in situ*, but others had certainly been prepared in advance. It cannot be random that of the two chambers within Knowth (only one is known inside Newgrange) the eastern one was of cross-shaped plan, an orientation shared in other examples of this form. The mechanics of construction were certainly also effective, the structures inside both Knowth and Newgrange still being stable 5000 years later, with skilful details like provision for shedding water from the passage roofs. That skill enabled the capture of an alignment on the midwinter sunrise through a 'roofbox' or small chamber above the entrance to Newgrange. Such an orientation may have been long observed in central spaces. In Newgrange and Knowth, the passages were rather higher than in the surrounding monuments, and were presumably intended for more regular use. The passages rise as they approach their chambers. Outside Knowth standing stones and small structures mark the entrances, again presumably emphasising the importance of movement into and out of the monument. Outside the west entrance there were small stones or 'baetyls', a larger standing stone, and small circular stone settings; outside the east entrance there were seven stone settings, the largest, central one with a fallen limestone pillar, and there was a scatter of stones of exotic origin.

The chambers are carefully ordered spaces, with high corbelled vaults and side recesses in the cruciform chambers. Both Newgrange and Knowth had been disturbed in historical times, but it is certain that Knowth at least was used for a succession of cremation deposits. Among these in the east recess of the eastern chamber was a magnificently carved perforated flint macehead, but it is possible that this is a slightly later insertion.[89] If so, we may think of a series of offerings rather than a series of burial rites. These great monuments could have been shrines to mythical ancestors, houses of ancestral figures, honoured by the living, and frequently venerated by offerings which included human remains.

Newgrange and Knowth began to decay in the third millennium BC, their mounds or façades tumbling and slipping outwards. The area, however, remained significant. Large circular enclosures were built to renew the sacred tradition, as at Newgrange sites A, P and Q, and at Monknewtown a few kilometres to the north. Outside Newgrange itself, to its south-east, an arc of multiple pits was dug, probably part of a circle 90 m or more in diameter. To the west of the tomb there was a circular timber structure or setting, some 20 m in diameter. The surrounding, possibly incomplete, stone circle appears to post-date the pit enclosure. These constructions are variously associated with Grooved Ware and Beaker pottery. At Knowth a small circular timber construction outside the eastern passage grave of the main mound is associated with Grooved Ware. Also in the Beaker phase, the mounds of both Newgrange and Knowth were used as the scene for feasting and depositions.[90]

'Abstract funerals' may largely have been acts of veneration. The houses of the ancestors presented concepts of beginnings, time and sacred realms to the living. These were variously worked and reworked through time, and from area to area. It is possible that in some sequences particular social groupings annexed this cult for their own purposes, changing shrines into lineage or other ossuaries. Some regional sequences may have begun with elaborate funeral rites for particular individuals, whose monuments then acquired mythical status. The placing, building and development of these shrines are not easily to be related to or reduced to other variables of resources, cultural history or social difference. They were the central point of a cult focused on the fusion of past and present, a powerful ordering principle which fostered cohesion, integration and collectivity of action. Emerging and developing beliefs of this kind could have accelerated the process of convergence between cultivators and foragers. These monuments express a world view, not subsistence strategies. Their spiritual or religious dimension needs to be revived, without returning to the simplistic model of 'megalithic missionaries' of two generations ago. Passages, for example, may have been as much for the exits of souls and spirits as for the entrances of the living.[91] To understand these claims better, we must now consider beginnings and regional sequences.

Beginnings: houses transformed

The most likely source for the idea of these monuments was the tradition of longhouses.[92] As the longhouse changed and then largely disappeared from use in the primary areas of Neolithic settlement, so the varied monuments under discussion began to appear in the secondary as well as the primary areas of Neolithic occupation. Longhouse for the living of past generations was transformed into shrine for the ancestors of a timeless past. The long process of convergence was consolidated by the adoption of a form foreign to daily existence. That form could have been designed literally to house the spirits of imagined ancestors.

In the last chapter I reviewed claims for very early beginnings for these monuments, in Brittany and central-west France in the earlier to mid fifth millennium BC. That evidence is uncertain. It is more likely that the horizon of monument building began around or a little before 4000 BC. There may have been much variation in the early stages, but long mounds were a recurrent element. The constructions, perhaps enclosures, from the Cerny horizon at Passy in the Yonne valley in the Paris basin may indicate the date of the beginnings of monumentalisation. The earliest monuments in Brittany may not in fact have been passage graves in trapezoidal mounds, but various long mounds, shorter and longer, enclosing individual cists.[93] The first phase of the monument at Les Fouaillages on Guernsey, subsequently much altered, conforms to this pattern, and has radiocarbon dates which suggest beginnings before 4000 BC.[94] Another early monumental element may have been standing stones: free-standing megaliths. In the Morbihan area of Brittany, one large such *menhir* was subsequently broken up to serve as the capstone in at least three passage graves; two fitting pieces have been identified at the famous site of Gavrinis and La Table des Marchand. There are now other examples. This implies that in the recently excavated complex at Locmariaquer in the Morbihan, the *Grand Menhir Brisé*, other standing stones and the elongated mound of Er Grah preceded the passage grave of La Table des Marchand.[95] The early TRB mounds raised over individual burials at sites like Sarnowo and Wietrzychowice in Kujavia in central-north Poland are another important date marker. Long barrows over

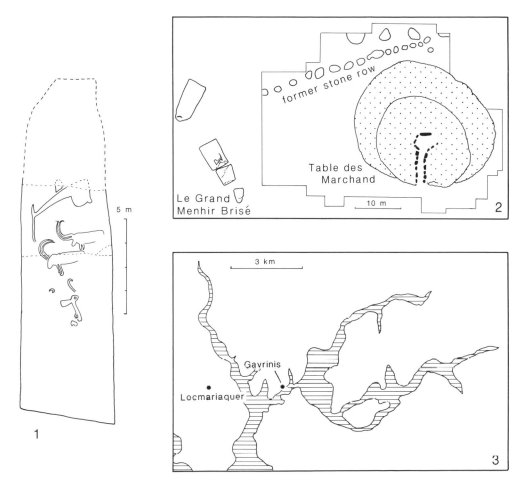

7.15 Left: reconstruction of the menhir subsequently broken up and re-used as
capstones at Gavrinis and La Table des Marchand, and perhaps elsewhere (the
Gavrinis portion sits above that from La Table des Marchand); top right: simplified
plan of La Table des Marchand, the *Grand Menhir Brisé* and the dismantled stone
row; below right: reconstruction of the coastline contemporary with Gavrinis and
La Table des Marchand. After Le Roux and L'Helgouac'h.

timber-built graves were built in some areas of Denmark from an early stage of the
Neolithic sequence, perhaps a little later than in Kujavia. Stone-chambered dolmens or
dysser were built from the ENII horizon onwards. Many were long monuments, but circular
mounds were built as well.[96] Circular forms were important in the passage grave tradition,
in Denmark, Brittany, Ireland and northern Scotland, among other areas.

It may never be possible wholly to unscramble the chronology of the early horizon of
monument building. If the dominant early form was long, we also have to accept standing
stones and some round mounds as early. These presumably had different origins. *Menhirs*
could be a reworking of the idea of sacred trees, and circular mounds the monumentalisa-

tion of round huts more characteristic of forager occupations than Danubian settlements. It is perhaps unwise to insist on single origins. Another possible source for the long mound idea could be shell middens. Most of the largest middens in southern Scandinavia came to be elongated mounds, such as Ertebølle itself, and that and other mounds in late use had had unaccompanied burials inserted into them. At Bjørnsholm in north Jutland, the Ertebølle shell midden continued in use in the EN period, and close to the midden a small long barrow was raised over a stone grave, with coffin and stone and flint axes, and a timber setting with offerings of pots.

What is important, however, is that in all these cases, whatever their precise chronology, transformations and translocations took place.[97] This could be bound up merely with imitations and emulations by foragers of their cultivator-herder neighbours, in a sort of early Neolithic cargo cult. The evidence for convergence already presented makes this an insufficient explanation. There seems here rather to be an idea of the past, a concept of time past re-presented in the present, a notion of descent, and a sense of beginnings. The meaning of early monuments need not have been the same in all regions, but the LBK/Danubian tradition would have been a powerful common element over very broad areas. We do not know the specific circumstances of transformation. Many early monuments have rather small and closed graves or cists in or under them, as at Les Fouaillages, or Sarnowo. These could be the graves of specific people rather than token offerings to ancestors.[98] But this does not explain in itself why their graves were enhanced by mounds, nor why the mounds took the form they did. The detail of the first phase of Er Grah is suggestive of more open possibilities. A primary cist or stone chamber was set in a small round cairn, with a lateral opening, subsequently blocked, which in turn was incorporated in a trapezoidal cairn about 40 m long. It is not clear what, if anything, was deposited in the primary chamber. Two cattle were buried in a pit outside, perhaps not long before the first cairn was much lengthened at both ends.[99]

At Barkaer in Jutland, there was more to the monuments than individual burial alone. The southern of the pair of mounds was lengthened twice; in each of its first two phases there was one grave at the east end of the monument, first a stone cist and then a wooden grave. Bone was not preserved in the soil conditions. The stone cist had been disturbed, and we know only of two pots and amber beads from it. The wooden grave was dug only a little into the subsoil and was framed by pits, supposedly for timber uprights. There were deposits of artefacts at each end, of pottery and amber beads, and at one end a rolled sheet-copper ornament. Should we automatically characterise these as grave goods rather than offerings? In the second phase, there was a free-standing post structure outside the east end, and the third phase comprised a further lengthening without the addition of further internal structures, and the deposition of pottery against the mound terminal.[100] These might be regarded as the graves of selected important people, say heads of households or lineages, but the goods or offerings are not otherwise remarkable. These kinds of site can rather be regarded as shrines or spirit houses, or they quickly became such. The constructions took the form of something old, important, venerable, and suitable through their familiarity to attract and retain ancestral spirits. Individual graves or token deposits served to unite the living with the ancestors past. With the spread of Neolithic culture, and perhaps enabling that spread, went the idea of a common, sacred past. The subsequent development of the monument tradition served to enhance this further.

Some regional sequences

A brief, selective survey of regional sequences will indicate how varied the monument tradition became, both from area to area and within particular areas. The idea of an ancestral past can hardly have been uniform. In most sequences, however, architecture, depositions and offerings became more elaborate through time, emphasising access and repeated venerations.

Brittany. In Brittany, the first monuments were preceded by late Mesolithic shell middens with small multiple burials inserted in simple graves or small cists, like Téviec or Hoëdic.[101] Passage graves in trapezoidal and other mounds, as at Barnenez, and Bougon in central-west France – as discussed above – could have been early constructions. I prefer a development from early long cairns covering cists, perhaps contemporary with standing *menhirs*, to the very large long mounds of the Morbihan area, covering multiple cists, and the passage grave tradition. The *grand tumulus* monuments and passage graves may have overlapped in time, but the passage grave tradition continued for longer. They represent different kinds of rite.

Grand tumulus monuments like Er Grah, Le Moustoir and Saint-Michel ended as considerable mounds, from 90 to 125 m long and in some cases several metres high. In their final form, they had no access from the outside. Primary chambers or cists could have been open for a while, but were then sealed by primary cairns and further enclosed in subsequent enlargements. Bad bone preservation hampers our knowledge of rites, as in most of north-west France, but it seems that primary use was accompanied by some deposition of animal bone. There were many depositions in primary cists of stone axes and beads. These can again be seen as offerings as much as grave goods.

Passage graves were structured around accessibility, with passages leading to and from chambers, forecourts often emphasised and visual markers in the form of façades and decorated stones. There are a host of notable monuments, from Dissignac near the mouth of the Loire and Gavrinis in the Morbihan, both in round mounds, to Barnenez on the north Breton coast, in a trapezoidal cairn, with outliers like Pornic south of the Loire and La Hougue Bie on Jersey. There were regional and probably chronological variations. Some monuments had more than one passage-and-chamber within, and in others the passage was angled. There was a complex spatial geometry of lintels, sills, passage stones and chamber corbelling and capstones. Carved motifs, schematic representations of axes and axe blades, and other more enigmatic designs, were placed in passage and chamber. Rather little bone is preserved. What evidence there is suggests small and varied depositions of human bone, perhaps as in Ireland token offerings as much as burials, though whole skeletons have been found. There were finds of artefacts both within and outside the monuments, most commonly pottery, suggesting offerings of food or drink. At Gavrinis and other monuments pots may have been placed on the stone façade of the cairn.[102]

The Table des Marchand offers a very strong contrast to the adjacent Er Grah long

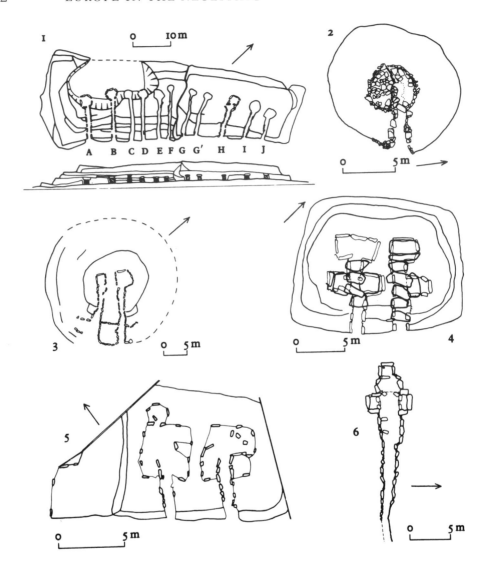

7.16 Plans of Breton, Normandy and Channel Island monuments. 1: Barnenez, Finistère (both phases); 2: Vierville, Manche; 3: Dissignac, Loire–Atlantique; 4: Les Mousseaux, Loire–Atlantique; 5: Kerleven, Finistère; 6: La Hougue Bie, Jersey. After Hibbs.

monument and the vast, fallen and broken *Grand Menhir*. Leading from it to the foot of the adjacent *Grand Menhir* is a row of eighteen stone-capped pits, which could represent dismantled standing stones. One decorated orthostat in the rear of the chamber probably came from a broken menhir, and one of the capstones comes from another menhir, a fitting part of which is to be found as the chamber capstone in Gavrinis (its decorated surface face up).[103] The passage grave here is connected with the destruction but reincorporation of old ways. The decoration of the Table des Marchand interior suggests a space that was meant to be seen by people, but the motifs may have been designed to make present aspects of ancestral beings. Passages may have been as much for the comings and goings of the spirits who inhabited these constructions as for human suppliants, and offerings of food or drink in pots contrast interestingly with the axe motif within.

The *allées couvertes* (formerly gallery graves) and the great stone rows of the Morbihan come at the end of the Breton tradition. The *allées couvertes* were more dispersed across the landscape, and are also found inland, coinciding too with more evidence in the pollen diagrams for clearance and cultivation. The stone rows may have revived the older idea of individual sacred stones, which combined together defined sacred paths for ancestral spirits to tread. The *allées couvertes* were more explicitly house-like than passage graves. As people were spread more widely across the landscape, so spirit houses went with them.

Britain and Ireland. There were many early kinds of construction. In Ireland, as we have seen, court cairns and portal dolmens were generally dispersed across the landscape, and portal dolmens occur on the east side of the Irish Sea.[104] Both had chambers rising above low cairns or platforms; some portal dolmens may have had no mound at all. In portal dolmens, the stone box-like chamber was emphasised, while in court cairns the emphasis was on transitions, from outside to court, from court to chambers, between cairn and chambers, and along the linear space of the chambers. Some monuments had double-ended courts, with chambers back-to-back, and some, perhaps later, had lateral rather than terminal court entrances. These were monuments conceived around visibility, accessibility and movement. Passage graves may have developed a little later. Linkardstown round mounds, covering closed cist graves, were another relatively early development, but more an enhancement of traditions of single burial than a variety of megalithic construction. Wedge-shaped chambers and cairns, so-called wedge graves, were probably a late form, parallel perhaps to the *allées couvertes* of northern France.

In northern Scotland, polygonal chambers with short passages in round cairns, so-called Bookan tombs, and long cairns with a prominent elongated central compartmented chamber, stalled cairns, were probably the earliest types.[105] Elaboration followed, with passages developed in both long cairns and round cairns, reaching the greatest spatial and three-dimensional complexity in constructions like Quanterness and Maes Howe on the Orkney main island. Stalled cairns were also considerably lengthened. There were monuments which do not fall neatly into categories, such as Isbister, but it is a misconception to call these hybrids. On the adjacent mainland of the far north of Scotland, the Cromarty region, there were other styles again, including long horned cairns, some of which may have developed from smaller round cairns with closed cists.

In southern England, the distribution of Severn–Cotswold monuments overlapped with portal dolmens and other constructions to the west and with earthen long barrows to the east. Laterally chambered cairns may have been the earliest Severn–Cotswold constructions. Hazleton in Gloucestershire had back-to-back chambers in a very large trapezoidal cairn.[106] Simple terminal chambers and transepted terminal chambers, as at the well-known site of West Kennet, Wiltshire, may be slightly later in date. Round cairns with closed cists were incorporated in some long cairns, and could be another early element. At Wayland's

Smithy, Oxfordshire, a transepted Severn–Cotswold monument, with megalithic façade and substantial stone kerb, directly overlay a smaller, short barrow. The first monument, like many earthen long barrows, may have been developed gradually. The primary structure was a linear stone pavement, with flanking stone piles and large post-pits at either end. This may have held a compartmented box, like the wooden structure preserved within the Haddenham long barrow, Cambridgeshire.[107] A succession of bodies were deposited in this, which I discuss below. Only later was the primary structure perhaps covered with a small, oval barrow, earth and chalk being quarried from flanking ditches. The same sort of sequence may be seen, on a larger scale, at other long barrows like Fussell's Lodge, Wiltshire.

Few, if any, of these constructions were built after 3000 BC, though many remained the focus of attention, either to receive secondary depositions, as at West Kennet, or to be incorporated into later monuments. As we shall see later, traditions of individual burial continued into this late phase.

Southern Scandinavia and the north European plain. In Denmark, the sequence seems to run from early mounds over timber and stone graves, alongside the variety of mound-less graves noted above, to stone-chambered long and round dolmens or *dysser* in ENII, with passage graves appearing with considerable flourish over a short period in the early part of MNA (beginning in MNAIb). Subsequently, rather few passage graves appear to have been built, though many were the continued focus for gatherings and depositions. 'Cult houses', usually found with other monuments as at Ferslev and Tustrup in eastern Jutland, were another slightly later development, probably more connected with ceremony and deposition than burials. So-called stone-packing graves, noted above, were made in north and west Jutland, and single burials continued in the islands.[108] There are two important trends. The long barrows and early dolmens have few, perhaps sometimes no bodies within them, whereas some of the passage graves have the remains of tens of people. In some cases the remains of the dead were carefully sorted and placed in disarticulated form (as in south Swedish cases where bone preservation is better); in others whole bodies seem to have been deposited.[109] The other trend concerns access. The long barrows and dolmens were designed to be approached in prescribed ways, as can be seen from flanking kerbs and wooden façades, as at Barkaer, but graves within them were of varied character; some were perhaps reusable, and not all were necessarily sealed by low mounds, but others appear to have been closed.[110] Passage graves, as noted in the Boyne and Brittany, allowed exits and entrances, and a plethora of pots and stone axes outside passage entrances shows the frequency of offerings. Is this a later shift to a more general, more abstract idea of ancestry, or, as I prefer, an enhancement of an already established link between past and present? Another intriguing feature is that the Scandinavian passage graves are largely housed in round mounds, and the idea of the longhouse must therefore in some sense have faded.

Over a broad area of the north European plain, the long form was dominant throughout the sequence. This might be explicable in terms of earlier cultural history, and the closer proximity of the original longhouse area. Northern Dutch *hunebedden* and north German and Polish *Grosssteingräber* show varied combinations of mound (in the latter area round as well as long), stone kerb and stone chamber, some with short entrance passages.[111] It has proved very difficult to find a clear developmental sequence, but the claimed *Urdolmen* form of north Germany, east of the Weser, with mainly closed chamber in long or round kerbed mound, could fit the pattern seen elsewhere of less access in earlier monuments. Likewise, in the exclusively elongated monuments of the northern Netherlands, it has been suggested that there was a shift from early single burials to later collective deposits. But the evidence can be ambiguous. In the Everstorfer Forst group in Mecklenburg–Vorpommern, north of Schwerin, incomplete human remains were placed in the corners of the chambers of two *Urdolmen*, at Barendorf and Naschendorf.[112]

The barrows of Kujavia, and outliers in the Lublin area of south-east Poland, clearly fit the pattern of early closed graves under sealing mounds.[113] There were other outliers. In the Saale–Elbe region of Sachsen–Anhalt, there were round and long mounds with closed cists, with complete and incomplete human remains, in the Baalberge–Salzmünde horizon, and there were some more megalithic monuments, as at Drosa and Latdorf, whose contents are virtually unknown. By the Walternienburg–Bernburg horizon, there was a very wide range of practice, including flat-grave cemeteries, cattle burials, single earth-cut graves, single cist burials and collective deposits tightly packed into small, low chambers: *Totenhütten*.[114] The latter structures were hardly monumental, and I discuss their contents below, as part of later burial practice.

The architecture of place

Monuments were not built to prescribed patterns, but there were recurrent elements which must have been deemed appropriate. Usage was as important as monumentality alone. At the Street House long barrow, Cleveland, in north-east England, there were very modest linear structures which held human remains, behind a very large curved façade of upright timbers.[115] When the mortuary structures were closed by a low, sealing cairn, the façade was burnt down. Movement is implied by the layout, but in this case the offering places were concealed behind a massive timber screen. To have any effect, this must have been approached, in prescribed ways, from the front alone. Proper treatment of the ancestors demanded careful observance of procedures and appropriate behaviour.

The architecture of most monuments can be seen to require similar progression. The front of the Hazleton cairn had a shallow concave forecourt, in which fires had been lit and some bones and sherds deposited. The cairn, over 50 m long, was flanked by very large, rather irregular quarries, and the lateral chambers could only be approached by narrow berms. The outer structures and markers at Knowth, and the collection of monuments including the 'cult houses' at sites like Tustrup, again imply a cycle of progressions. Visits and ceremonies at monuments were marked by deposition of artefacts as well as of human remains. I have already mentioned the case of Gavrinis and others in Brittany. Considerable quantities of artefacts were left outside monuments in southern Scandinavia, especially pottery, and then later stone axes and other tools. Pots were either smashed deliberately, or perhaps placed as already broken sherds. In south Swedish cases hundreds of vessels are represented. Other spectacular examples of deposition come from monuments on the north European plain. Over a thousand pots are represented at Emmeln 2,

7.17 The façade of the monument at Île Carn, Ploudalmézeau. Photo: Laboratoire de préhistoire armoricaine, Université de Nantes.

east of the Ems, and some 650 at Havelte D53 in the Netherlands.[116] Once again, it is limiting to think only in terms of human needs. These were offerings, perhaps marking the exits of human souls or ancestral spirits from within chambers.

Mythical ancestors and spirits, and the human dead offered for their company, may have been considered to inhabit other worlds, not precisely located in time or space. The distributions of monuments do not coincide directly with the settlement zones of the living, though in a mobile system the two spheres must have intersected. In some cases, the relationship may have been close. In north Wiltshire, many long barrows in the area around Avebury were placed on the edge of small clearings. But the local cluster of monuments, on the chalk downland surrounding the headwaters of the Kennet valley, may at a regional scale constitute a special or sacred area in its own right, within a much larger territory encompassing surrounding vales and the upper-middle Kennet. The Bend of the Boyne is another possible case, and in the Orkneys, the density of monuments on Rousay stands out. Monuments were not randomly placed. On Westray island, the stalled monument at Point of Cott was, like other earlier monuments, on higher ground, while the more elaborate monument at Pierowall, like others on the main island such as Quanterness and Maes Howe, was on lower ground, seemingly more in the centre of daily life. On the island of Rügen off the north German coast, there were originally so many monuments, numbering at least 250, that the island itself may have constituted an ancestral home.[117]

Despite the special character of sacred monuments and sacred areas, they were also rooted in fixed places. Many of these monuments were built in a form which endured. Repeated visits for offerings and venerations fixed a routine in the use of the surrounding landscape. The importance of monuments and their places may be measurable in the destructions that some of them suffered, as in the burnings of façades at Barkaer and Street House, or the radical remodellings of some Orkney monuments in the late

Neolithic. Another measure was the reuse of monuments for subsequent depositions. West Kennet has been one example. Many Globular Amphora and Corded Ware burials were inserted into existing monuments on the north European plain.[118] Their meaning may have been rather different, as I will discuss below, but the annexation of old features testifies to their continuing significance. It may not have been the original planned intention of monument builders to fix a sense of place, indeed that seems very implausible as a collective decision over such a vast area, but the consequence of ancestral worship in these forms would have been to attach people very closely to particular points of their landscapes.

Rites of offering

Many varied rites took place in association with these monuments. No full geographical or chronological picture is possible because of the vagaries of preservation. Little bone has survived in most Breton deposits, and there is poor preservation in many parts of Denmark. This is countered by often good survival in many parts of Britain, and some other parts of southern Scandinavia. In Ireland, cremated remains were common, which again tends to restrict information. But the difficulties of interpretation are greater still than the problems posed by uneven survivals.

Some early monuments such as Kujavian long mounds and Danish long mounds and dolmens had single graves under them, with individuals in anatomical order. These might be regarded as the burial monuments of particular individuals, whatever the reasons for their selection for special treatment. Breton long mounds might be seen in the same light. Not all stone chambers or cists were fully closed, and some may have held offerings of bones or artefacts rather than burials. Barkaer is a good example of a range of kinds of deposition. Even with these early cases, therefore, we could see rites and construction in varied ways. The burial of a particular individual could have been accompanied by elaborate construction; the fading memory of particular individuals could have become the focus for a more generalised act of ancestral veneration; or monuments could have been constructed to house and to honour ancestors from the start, with the human dead present as symbols of propiation and unity.

These possibilities make it very hard to maintain a simple distinction between burial and ancestral rites, or to restrict ancestral rites to the realms of the human dead, as the example of Wayland's Smithy illustrates.[119] The sequence of phase I of that monument probably began with a wooden compartmented box or frame, without an enclosing mound. The remains of fourteen or more individuals were deposited, male and female, young and old. Most individuals were both disarticulated and incomplete. One possibility is that this modest structure was the immediate forerunner to mound construction, and that the remains represent secondary depositions after primary exposure or burial elsewhere. The structure would then be connected with the transformation of the known dead, through a liminal phase, into members of a more anonymous community of ancestors. There is another possibility. The deposit furthest away from the eventual front of the mound was of a whole body. It is possible that rites began with complete corpses, which were gradually transformed within the mortuary structure, parts being taken away (which would account

7.18 Kujavian long mounds. Top: no. 2 at Wietrzychowice, after excavation. Photo: Archaeological and Ethnographic Museum, Łódź. Below: reconstructed mound at Sarnowo.

for anatomical incompleteness) for circulation among the living. The burial of individuals was bound into a cycle of ancestral veneration. Deposition in a mortuary structure was just the first stage in succeeding acts of propitiation and regeneration. In the case of Wayland's Smithy, the mortuary structure was probably sealed at a later stage by a small mound. At this point memories associated with the structure may have become more abstract still. Environmental evidence indicates that the spot, never much settled or cleared, was allowed to regenerate for a while before the tradition was renewed by the building of a transepted monument directly on top of its predecessor, capturing and enhancing its aura. In phase II, the chambers were continuously accessible. Unfortunately, later disturbance destroyed most of their deposits, though we do know that there were human remains in them.

At other southern English long barrows, there was a similar pattern of constructional development, but it is unlikely that there was a single style of deposition. At Fussell's Lodge, a linear mortuary area was defined originally by three spaced posts.[120] A large trapezoidal post enclosure, longhouse-like in plan, was added later, and then infilled, perhaps after an interval, by a chalk and earth mound derived from flanking ditches. Some fifty individuals are represented in the mortuary area. Most were incomplete and disarticulated. There were several groups of human bone, and offerings of pots and an ox skull. The remains of adults, juveniles and children were to some extent spatially separated in these groups, and long bones were placed on different axes in the main adult and juvenile piles respectively. The three proximal deposits were smaller. The outermost was the ox skull. Then came group D, bones from an older and a younger woman arranged to resemble a partially contracted individual. Within this lay group C, again bones from two women, with one skull and the longbones arranged diagonally across the long axis of the deposit. These may all or largely be secondary depositions. An ancestral cult house was only later transformed into a monument to the ancestors, to which internal access was no longer possible.

As time went by in many regions, larger deposits may have been formed in accessible chambers. The chronological trends are unclear. The laterally chambered Severn–Cotswold monuments, for example, may be an early type, and these have collective deposits, probably formed by successive depositions. The rather small cremation deposits in Irish passage graves are another exception. Where they do occur, the larger collective deposits may have been formed in various ways. Some may be the result of simultaneous or more often successive deposits of secondary burials, or remains already disarticulated and incomplete. In other cases, whole bodies were brought to tombs. The clearest recent example of this comes from Hazleton.[121] Its two lateral chambers and passages have disarticulated and incomplete remains, some twenty-five in the southern and fifteen or so in the northern. The north passage had been blocked by a minor structural collapse, but deposition continued in the passage alone. The last deposition at the outermost part of the north passage was the complete skeleton of an adult man. This overlay a partially complete adult skeleton, and there were other disarticulated and incomplete remains, including two skulls on a ledge. Unless this represents a change of rite towards the end of the sequence of depositions, this suggests again that there was transformation *within* the monument, and that many bones were never incorporated into chamber deposits. There are other cases

7.19 Disarticulated human remains in the south chamber at Hazleton North. Photo: Saville.

where complete as well as incomplete remains can be found, as at West Kennet, and it is possible that no one mode of deposition prevailed even at a single monument.

In several well-documented instances, there is evidence for sorting of bones by age, sex and body part. At West Kennet, the innermost chamber held male remains, adult and young; the inner pair of transepted or facing chambers held mainly adult males and females; while the outer pair contained the remains of mainly old and young people. There are signs of similar patterning in other Severn-Cotswold monuments. In the south Swedish passage graves of Carlshögen and Ramshög, there were many disarticulated remains in the chambers, and in the passage of the latter. Much of the bone was in piles. There were variations in the proportions of ribs, vertebrae, skulls and hands and feet, and in the representation of the two sides of the body. At Ramshög there were more right than left upper-limb bones and more left than right lower-limb bones; the position was roughly reversed at the later site of Carlshögen. In the case of West Kennet, there were fewer than expected skulls and long bones, and bones here too may have been abstracted and circulated in different spheres.[122]

The positioning of remains is unlikely to have been static through the use of a monument; some chambers have no remains at all. Memories and knowledge of the details of sortings may have been very patchy. The important aspects are the categorisation and repetitions represented. The human body was a powerful means of communication between the present and the past, and the significance of that link is seen in the repetitions of deposition and in subsequent offerings of artefacts outside monuments. The development of large collective deposits has been seen as representing the emergence of socially dominant groups, such as lineages or clans as known in historical and recent ethnography, but this ignores both the context and history of these practices. These monuments were only partly to do with the burial and funerals of the dead. They had more to do with ancestral cult. I have suggested that there were notions of mythical ancestors as well as of actual human ancestors and specific lines of descent. Just as the longhouse had anchored the comings and goings of earlier woodland populations, so these monuments may have fixed an abode for the spirits of the mythical ancestors. Human dead were deposited as offerings, to unite the living with their beginnings. Perhaps distinctions between real and imagined ancestors were regularly blurred. These monuments were a record of people's past. A sense of sacred beginnings made time seem endless.[123] The burials of late foragers had stressed regeneration and fertility, and partially involved a collective memory, but those rites were concerned with the burials of particular individuals. In Neolithic rites at monuments, a broader universe was introduced. Regeneration was implied in the circulation of human remains. The living and the dead were linked in a collectivity of shared existence. This kind of belief may lie at the heart of what we choose to call the Neolithic way of life.

The ancestors at rest: later forms of burial

A contrast is often drawn between the collective, past-looking rites of the middle part of the Neolithic sequence in western Europe and more individualised burials of the late phase, focused on an immediate past and the present. This is then seen as further proof of sociopolitical change, variously glossed (sometimes in contradictory fashion): as the rise of 'the individual'; as the emergence of households as a major unit of social action; as the decline of the *domus* concept; as the secondary development and intensification of agricultural production; or as the appearance of Indo-European-speaking, warlike, male-dominated society.[124] Most of these interpretations exaggerate the novelty of later burial rites, and in so doing fail properly to account for the phase of collective deposition just explored.

Individual burials had been made since the LBK–late forager horizon. They were an important feature of non-monumental mortuary rites. Fleshed individuals were put in some monuments. Individual burial therefore never went away. In the late phase of the Neolithic, equivalent to the Globular Amphora and Corded Ware horizons, we can distinguish three main areas: where monuments had never been a major feature, as in southern Poland and west along the upper Danube; where monuments had been a major feature, but were then complemented by new constructions, as in the areas of Globular Amphora and Corded Ware distribution from the lower Vistula through to the Rhine–Maas delta; and where monument use and some monument construction continued, in areas beyond the

Corded Ware distribution, as in northern and north-western France, and in Britain and Ireland.

The Globular Amphora burial ground at Złota, examined at the beginning of this chapter, showed the elaborate burial of selected individuals, but also the continued circulation of other human remains and the establishment of close links between people and animals. In this sense, the Złota burials are like all those depositions just considered, in being to do with far more than simply laying the dead to rest. Many other Globular Amphora burials were simpler.[125] There were stone-lined and wooden cists as well as earth-dug graves, typically in small groups, and usually with more than one skeleton in each grave, furnished with pots, flint axes and ornaments including amber, and the bones of cow and pig, the remains of funereal feasts. The link with animals is continued in the separate cattle burials, along with human graves, at Brześć Kujawski. These had both single and double animal burials.[126]

Corded Ware burials continued the tradition of single burial. These too were basically simple, with individuals of all ages and both sexes laid, generally crouched, in earth-graves or cists. Grave goods often distinguish male from female, though such a gender distinction is hardly an innovation of this horizon. Some graves were enhanced by small mounds, which were occasionally enlarged with successive burials. Some of these graves occur singly, as at Bronocice, but normally there are flat-grave or mound burial grounds. In Bohemia, there are some large Corded Ware burial grounds, as at the well-known site of Vikletice, which had over 160 burials. A more recent example comes from Čachovice, also in north-west Bohemia.[127] Here there were at least sixty graves, in three groups 150 m and more apart. The graves themselves were simple pits, though they may originally have been roofed in wood. Their spacing suggests that they were originally covered with small mounds, now destroyed. Bone preservation was not good, but on the basis of both bones and grave goods, there were adult and child burials, and roughly equal numbers of adult males and females. Most were single burials, provided with amphorae and beakers, and some with stone battleaxes, maceheads and axes, and copper ornaments. Ochre and animal bones continued older traditions of regeneration rites and feasting. The focus is on a recent past, a relatively small social group, and perhaps the achievements of particular individuals, though neither here nor at Vikletice are there enormous differences in the provision of grave goods from person to person.

According to many, these features represent the emergence of a new kind of society, but this is much exaggerated, as the next area shows even more clearly. Rather the situation is that the ancestors were at rest, respected but taken for granted in the established landscape, while funerals – as long before, as far back as the LBK and late forager horizon – dealt with the continuation of the living community. In the western part of the Globular Amphora distribution there were single graves and small collective graves, usually in small groups. Existing monuments were frequently reused. The structure of the mound and chambers was usually respected, though previous contents were often rather unceremoniously disturbed or thrown out, emphasising that the main concern was the house of the spirits, not the bones or offerings of human forebears.[128] Further south in the Mittelelbe–Saale area, late TRB (Walternienburg–Bernburg) burial customs included the use of low, stone-walled, rectangular structures, in which the remains of tens of people were placed.[129] There were up to ninety people in the structure at Niederbösa, Kr. Sondershausen. As well as complete skeletons in these structures there were incomplete and broken remains, and traces of fires and some cremated bone. In some structures the remains of the dead were arranged in groups or piles. Within the communities of the dead there may have been closer groupings. In Niederbösa these are indicated by groups with distinctive skeletal peculiarities. At Schönstedt, Kr. Bad Langensalza, one group within the larger deposit is distinguished by fox jaws and another by dog teeth ornaments, perhaps emblems of a more individual identity. Burials appear to have been made successively in these structures, which seem to celebrate more the collectivity of the human community than connections with ancestors. In the same region, and perhaps overlapping in time, there were many Globular Amphora burials, with graves and cists, single and multiple burials and cattle burials.[130]

Corded Ware burials continued the same tradition. At Halle–Dölauer Heide, on the same hill as but largely outside an earlier TRB enclosure, there was a small group of Corded Ware mounds, up to 25 m in diameter, covering earth-graves and stone cists. One, no. 6, enlarged an existing TRB mound, and one of its cists had wall stones decorated by pecked motifs. Some mounds had successive burials; one had been reused three times after the initial deposition. The bodies were crouched, generally west–east, with the sexes differentiated (males on their right sides with heads to the west, and the females *vice versa*). At Quenstedt there was another small Corded Ware burial ground, with over twenty earth-cut graves in four groups. These intersected late TRB (Bernburg) pits, again showing continuity of use. One model for the middle Elbe–Saale region proposes a 'big man' authority system, with older men dominating marriage exchanges and political alliances, but this owes rather more to the exuberance of Pacific ethnography than to the often rather prosaic character of Corded Ware graves in the region, in which men and women were represented in more or less equal numbers.[131]

Continuity and complementarity were features of the Single Grave horizon in Denmark.[132] In mid and west Jutland, there were many small mounds over graves dug into the subsoil, the generally single inhumations variously furnished with battleaxes, ornaments and pottery. In many instances, these extended the range of landscape in use, with Single Grave mounds at Vroue Hede for example further on to the present heathlands than earlier stone-packing graves. There was much reuse of existing monuments, especially in north and east Jutland. At Hagebrogård, for example, not far from Vroue Hede in northwest Jutland, there were two battleaxes in the upper fill of a passage grave built in MNAI. Were these grave goods, or renewed offerings?

Over the broad distribution of the Corded Ware/Single Grave culture, the concern of burial rites seems to be with themes other than a distant or ancestral past, though that was clearly respected. There was marking of gender and age difference, definition of small social groupings, some display of long-distance contacts, renewal of attachment to old places and the establishment of a presence in previously less used or unused areas. This is all rather different from the activities associated with the earlier ancestral monuments, but hardly represents a new kind of society if the ancestors were still regarded and if the practices of single burials were not in themselves innovations in this horizon. The interpreta-

7.20 Corded Ware burials at Čachovice. Top left and right are grave 44. Photos: Smrž.

tion, for a slightly later horizon, that single burials of this kind served to fix attachments to specific parts of the landscape, can be adopted here too. At Prague–Jinonice, for example, there were some sixty flat graves scattered down a kilometre of valley. Vikletice too was spread out over hundreds of metres.[133]

In the last broad area under consideration here there was greater emphasis on built monuments. Late passage graves and galleried monuments were built and used in Brittany, Ireland and Orkney. Just as *allées couvertes* were a symptom of greater inland penetration in Brittany, so wedge cairns in south-west Ireland may reflect a greater regional density of occupation. Were these more to do with local ancestors and less with an abstract past? A further connection with patterns of settlement might be seen in the *allées couvertes* and chalk-cut, underground monuments of the Seine-Oise-Marne culture of the Paris basin.[134] These were constructed in numbers as the range of landuse extended far beyond the earlier focus on valleys. These had multiple inhumations, as in the subterranean *allée couverte* at La

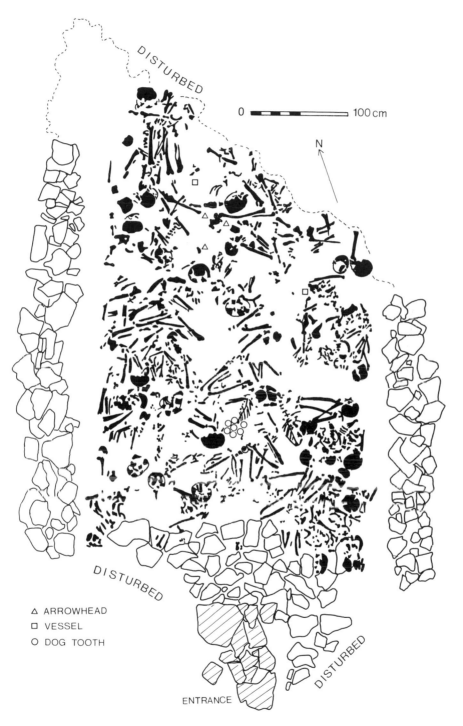

7.21 Late TRB or Walternienburg–Bernburg collective burials at Nordhausen, central Germany. After Behrens.

Chaussée-Tirancourt in the Somme, or in the *hypogées* at Les Mournouards in the Marne. Both types might be regarded more as local vaults than ancestral monuments. There were the partial remains of over 300 people in the structure at La Chaussée-Tirancourt, arranged within internal partitions. The chalk-cut *hypogées* had a narrow approach passage, often a small antechamber, and a larger, usually rectangular main chamber. They often occurred in concentrated groups, as at Razet in the Marne. Up to tens of inhumations are found. They were probably made successively, mainly as fleshed bodies, some perhaps originally in shrouds and some placed in sitting as well as lying positions. As ever, practice was very varied, and there are incomplete and disordered remains which suggest other rites including bone circulation. There were also other forms of burial in the Seine–Oise–Marne culture. A large pit at Les Maillets, Seine-et-Marne, held the largely incomplete and disarticulated remains of at least forty people, and there are other single and small collective burials elsewhere.

Some of the most elaborate Orkney monuments may have been built last, such as Quanterness and Maes Howe. These may have been used by people from a wide area around. Quanterness had multiple side chambers as well as its main chamber, and held the disarticulated remains of hundreds of people. Single large monuments may have become the focus for many communities. Some may have been used for ancestral rites and offerings, but the great numbers of bones suggest a role as ossuaries. It has even been suggested that some bones were collected from earlier monuments, both to capture the power of ancestors and to emphasise the collectivity of the living community.[135]

In most other parts of Britain, long barrow and cairn monuments were not built after 3000 BC at the latest. Existing structures were respected, and also incorporated into later monuments. The main cursus or linear monument at Stonehenge was aligned on an existing barrow, and long barrows were incorporated in the layout of the massive Dorset cursus. The chambers of the West Kennet long barrow were filled with soil and chalk, by the early Bell Beaker phase at the latest, the forecourt blocked, and a closing monumental façade constructed. There were also various pre-Beaker, later Neolithic single inhumations and cremations in certain areas of southern and northern England.[136] The tradition of single burial continued as the ancestral monuments became an immutable part of the conceptual landscape.

Ditched enclosures: social arenas

In his book on *Tribesmen*, the American anthropologist Marshall Sahlins observed that great gods and supreme beings tended to be taken for granted, while more daily concerns were with small-time spirits, witches, ghosts and local ancestors.[137] I have suggested that this was not the case in the middle phase of the Neolithic in western Europe, when considerable energy went into building houses for mythical ancestors and spirits, and keeping them happy with offerings and mortuary rites. It is possible, however, that the role of monuments was gradually changed to that of communal ossuaries, as imagined ancestors were increasingly taken for granted. We do not know the frequency of use of the first ancestral monuments. While many offerings were made outside north German and Danish monuments, the fre-

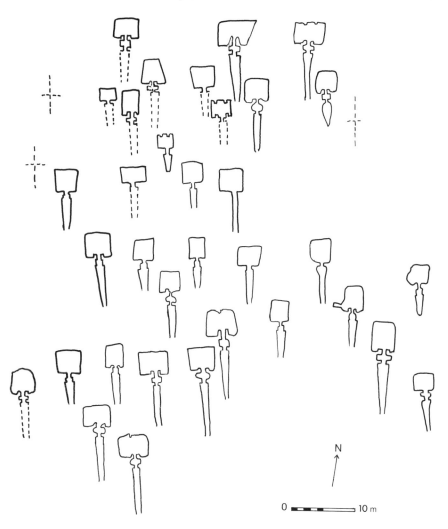

7.22 Chalk-cut tombs at Razet, Marne. After Bailloud.

quency of deposition of human remains may have been lower. Part of the mystique of these monuments may have been a relative rarity or infrequency of rites, perhaps determined according to cycles of omens and other indications of appropriateness. A different kind of gathering, a more often repeated set of rituals, and a wider range of concerns – not only with the sacred – seem enshrined in the ditched enclosures of the middle Neolithic. Both their numbers and the extent of excavation have increased dramatically in recent years. If people honoured various kinds of ancestors at the houses of the dead, they constructed another kind of image of themselves at the enclosures. In circular spaces defined by circuits of interrupted ditches, they actively negotiated many aspects of community.

Ditched enclosures are known in the middle part of the Neolithic over a broad area of western Europe, from central-west France to southern Scandinavia, and from southern

England to central Germany and Poland.[138] The distributions are far from continuous. There appear to be relatively few in the earlier centre of Lengyel culture enclosures, discussed in the previous chapter. Circuits of interrupted ditches are likewise less common further east. At present, the enclosures of the south-eastern group of the TRB are more often uninterrupted, and ditched enclosures in the upper Danube valley appear to belong mainly to the later Neolithic horizon. While common in general in the Michelsberg and TRB cultures, there are so far no enclosures in Dutch territory of the TRB western group. Distributions are not static in the present state of research. Numbers have steadily increased in southern England through aerial and other survey. Examples occur now in the valleys of the Midlands and around parts of the East Anglian fen edge, and there is an outlier in Co. Antrim, in Northern Ireland.[139] Numbers in central-west France have increased steadily, with some locally high densities. The most dramatic change has been in southern Scandinavia and Schleswig-Holstein. Around thirty are now known from Denmark, where twenty years or so ago there were none.[140] Distributions elsewhere may change, particularly as aerial survey expands where it was previously restricted for political or military reasons.[141]

The layouts of these enclosures were very varied. They range in size around a hectare to several hectares. The outer circuit of Windmill Hill was over 350 m across, and the maximum diameter of Halle–Dölauer Heide was some 500 m.[142] There were usually one to three circuits, but sometimes more. Many were circular or oval in form, while others cut off promontories or other natural features. The square-cornered examples of Makotřasy in Bohemia and Słonowice in southern Poland have already been noted earlier in the chapter. Some follow the contours of hilltops, others disregard them; Halle–Dölauer Heide and Windmill Hill are good examples of each case. Hambledon Hill, Dorset, had extensive outworks and a subsidiary enclosure. Many enclosures were in low-lying situations on valley terraces, some so close to rivers that they would have been liable to flooding. Etton, Cambridgeshire, in the lower Welland valley close to its junction with the fens, may have been flooded annually. Others such as Urmitz, Kr. Koblenz, next to the Rhine, were close to water but above regular flooding.[143]

Circuits were defined by very varied combinations of ditch, bank and palisade. Most southern English enclosures for example had interrupted ditches. Some may have been developed gradually from circuits of pits, as at Haddenham, Cambridgeshire; not all parts of a circuit need have been in use at one time. At Hambledon Hill there were continuous banks within the interrupted ditch segments, but this may not always have been the case. Hambledon Hill had wattle breastworks on the banks of its outworks, but palisades are infrequent. There are examples at Haddenham and Orsett, Essex. Some banks may have been purposeful barriers as well as boundaries – Hambledon Hill and the stone bank of the second phase at Crickley Hill, Gloucestershire, are examples – but in many other cases banks may have been low affairs or altogether irregular. Though there is evidence not only for continuous barriers, but also for attack, burning and killing, as at Hambledon Hill and Crickley Hill, I suggest that the primary role of most enclosures was formally to bound a special space, to separate inside from outside, and to invest the activities associated with the various parts of the special space with appropriate significance.[144]

Something of the same kind of sequence may be visible among the now rather numerous enclosures in central-west France. Many had discontinuous ditches and multiple circuits. At Champ-Durand, Vendée, there were three circuits of interrupted ditch. Their first phase was interpreted as ceremonial and sepulchral; finds included skeletons in the ditch segments. In a second phase, the enclosure was interpreted as being remodelled, with stone walls rising out of the substantial ditch segments. These constructions could span the Matignons and Peu-Richardien phases, beginning therefore in the Néolithique moyen-Atlantique. Other elaborate enclosures further south in Charente-Maritime, such as La Coterelle, Saint-Germain-de-Lusignan, and Chez-Reine, Sémussac, with more continuous ditches and complex entrances, may also be later in the sequence, and could be seen as more defensive.[145]

Just as layouts and settings were varied, so too were interiors. If few had a primary role for defence, few too had a primary use as places of occupation or settlement. There is little convincing evidence for permanent structures within, and rather more for pits and middens or spreads of artefacts. Bronocice and Michelsberg–Untergrombach have already been noted for their pit concentrations. Some enclosures perhaps became the focus for occupations later in their history; Maiden Castle, Dorset, is one recently investigated example of this.[146] Instead, many were arenas for a range of activities, involving the deposition of food residues, especially animal bone, artefacts and human remains, in the ditches, in interior pits and elsewhere.

Another indication of the special nature of enclosures are their numbers. Perhaps over fifty or more are known or suspected from southern England. The total of around thirty from Denmark can be set against literally thousands of dolmens and passage graves. The Sarup enclosure on south-west Fyn has tens of other monuments in the area round about. Windmill Hill has one or possibly two neighbouring enclosures a few kilometres away. These, Knap Hill and Rybury, were closer together, and it is possible that they were successive.

I have suggested so far that there was a major horizon of enclosure construction and use in the middle part of the Neolithic in western Europe, associated with the TRB, Michelsberg, northern Chasseen, Néolithique moyen-Atlantique and English earlier Neolithic cultures. The clearest regional sequence may come from Denmark, where it now seems that enclosures appeared in ENII, later than the first long barrows and perhaps a little later than the first dolmens, and a little earlier than the major burst of passage grave construction. In southern England less precise chronologies based on radiocarbon dating rather than fine pottery typology suggest the same trend, that enclosures emerged after some centuries of the Neolithic sequence. Nor may any one enclosure have existed in primary form for long. The detailed chronology from Sarup, discussed further below, shows two main phases, with an interval between, each to be measured perhaps in no more than tens of years. Crickley Hill has also yielded a punctuated history. Both these aspects of chronology are important, since they underline the special character of enclosures.

Where did the idea of enclosures come from? One answer may be the tradition of enclosure established in the later LBK horizon and elaborated in the subsequent earlier Lengyel horizon, as discussed in the previous chapter. This was suggested to enshrine an idea of shared space within longhouse occupations. It is possible that this was kept alive in succeeding centuries, but if so, its transmission is unclear. There were some enclosures in the western post-LBK area, but relatively few can be cited. Nor does this explain why an old idea should have been revived at a particular time, and put into effect across such a wide area. If this kind of approach is valid, it might indicate another form of far-reaching cultural memory, to do with how things used to be in a distant past, in the time of ancestors and long-gone forebears. There may have been other sources for the idea, such as the use of space in contemporary occupations. The circular space in the centre of things at Knowth suggests more local origins. It is clear from the descriptions so far that these sites were far from uniform. It might be fruitless to pursue a common origin, but their uses do seem to indicate a remarkable convergence at this point in the sequence. It is easiest to explain this in terms of ideas circulating about how the past and present should be treated. Two specific examples now give more focus to these generalisations.

Sarup and Windmill Hill

Sarup on the Danish island of Fyn began in the ENII Fuchsberg phase, in the later fourth millennium BC.[147] At this horizon, there are signs of more extensive clearance, and perhaps the beginnings of some larger occupations; immediately after, there was an explosion in the numbers of passage graves. The enclosure was on a low hill 2 km inland, above the junction of two streams running to the sea. It had two phases (the second in the MNAIb Klintebakke phase), probably separated by three or four generations, but each evidently rather brief. In both cases a double circuit of shallow, segmented ditches cut off part of the low promontory. In the first phase, interleaved with and immediately behind the ditches was a curious pattern of narrow entrances and closed compartments defined by continuous palisades or fences of planks, and backed by a continuous palisade line of close-set posts. Animal bone, flints, large sherds and occasional whole pots, some human bone including skulls and jaws, and charcoal, from burning or smouldering wood, were all put into the ditches. In the sandy subsoil these would have silted quickly. They had also in parts been deliberately backfilled. Some segments of the first phase had evidence of being recut and refilled three times. Material similar to that in the ditches was placed at the foot of the palisade, which would have rotted within a generation or two, and shows no sign of having been replaced. In several pits in the interior, which had also been deliberately backfilled, there were whole pots and a stone axe. The second phase was broadly similar in terms both of layout and of deposition, though the ditch segments were smaller and the palisade lines formed of slightly spaced posts. The space redefined did not exactly repeat that of the first, covering only its innermost part. The builders of the second phase would at best have been very young when the first construction was used. There were abundant deposits of artefacts and food residues in the upper fill of the second-phase ditch segments, perhaps reflecting a change in use.

Windmill Hill also dates to around 3500–3400 BC, some centuries after the first Neolithic occupations in the upper Kennet area.[148] It lay on a low chalk hill, standing on its own in front of other high chalk country. This had been used for occupation and burial

7.23 Plan of the two phases of enclosure at Sarup. Drawing: N. Andersen.

100 metres

50

0

7.24 Reconstruction view of the first phase at Sarup. Drawing: Andersen.

before the enclosure was built, but molluscan and soil evidence indicates that the setting of the site was woodland or scrub, not extensively cleared open ground. This contrasts with the more open settings of local long barrows. Recent survey and excavation indicate little contemporary occupation immediately outside the enclosure. The enclosure was defined by three circuits of interrupted ditches, the outer provided with a low bank, but the inner two not certainly with any formal bank at all. The broadest and deepest ditch segments were in the outer circuit. This disregarded the contours of the hilltop on its western side. The middle circuit was formed by alternating stretches of longer and shorter ditch segments, and the inner circuit had a marked indentation on one side. There is no way of telling for certain whether these circuits were contemporary or successive; but if the latter, they were probably added at short intervals. There is little sign of recutting of the ditches, which largely silted up by natural processes. The primary phase of use here too might only have been for a few generations, or less.

Relatively little of the interior has been excavated. Some pits are scattered across it, not all of which need be contemporary with it, and within the inner interior there are signs of former middens or occupations in the form of concentrations of struck flint. In the primary and lower secondary fill of the ditches, thus in the first generations of the site, there were abundant finds of animal bone, some plant remains, charcoal, flint artefacts, stone artefacts including rubbing stones and fragments of querns, sherds from already broken pots, and some human remains. It appears that the bulk of this material was not the result of random discards or weathering, but had been deliberately placed in varying configurations. Animal bone was the single most conspicuous category. It occurred some-

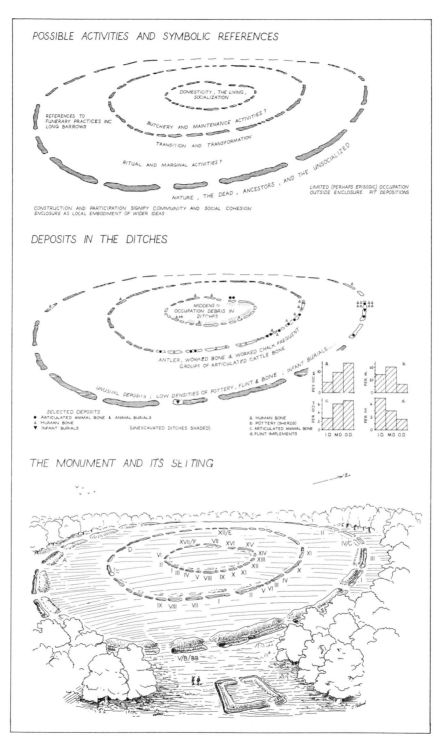

7.25 Reconstruction and interpretation of the causewayed enclosure at Windmill Hill. Drawing: Whittle and Pollard.

times as single bones, but more often as spreads and discrete groups. These typically consisted of the disarticulated and often broken or butchered remains of more than one animal and more than one species, with no more than parts of any one individual animal. These assemblages could be the residues of meals or feasts put directly into the ditches, or they may have been kept in middens or other repositories before eventual deposition. Pots included a percentage not made locally, and there were imported flint and stone axes, though largely in secondary contexts. The quantities and character of deposition varied from segment to segment, and from circuit to circuit; certain entrances were particularly marked by elaborate depositions. The stratigraphy of the ditches shows that the individual episodes of deposition must have been spread over some period of time, but the use of the site may have come to assume a map-like character, emphasising among other things human remains and more articulated animal bone in the outer circuit in contrast to greater quantities of artefacts and more disarticulated animal bone in the inner circuits.

Enclosures served to define special space, conceived as existing beyond the boundaries of normal experience. Layouts served to define a sense of identity. Their construction involved participation by a more than immediately local population, and their use a sense of movement through space and time and an ordered progression of rituals. Particular events, of feasting, offerings and gift exchange for example, could have been transformed into something timeless by inclusion within the special spaces. Depositions presented a range of concerns, from production and consumption in the form of feasting, to exchanges with neighbours, and memory of the dead. The treatment of animal bone could have served as a metaphor for the processing of human bone in other monuments. Animals may have had value and significance far beyond their role as providers of food. There is an interesting inversion between the celebration of domesticity in special arenas in out-of-the-way places, and the honouring of ancestral spirits in monuments closer to the cleared land of the living community. The physical scale of some enclosures, their spacing, feasting, gift exchange and the later history of some as more defensive works, have led some scholars to suggest that these monuments were to do with the establishment of power and differentiation through control of labour, production and ritual. Remote settings and the individuality of each act of deposition make it more likely that the monuments were the focus for intensive, participatory ceremonialism, which reworked ideas about the integration of separate communities, and brought the past into the present in more tangible ways than practised at other monuments. The enclosures are not symptoms of the differentiation of Neolithic society, but rather one of the means by which its world was consolidated.

Late enclosures in Britain and Ireland

As the Neolithic spread in western Europe, the first monuments to be built were barrows and cairns. Enclosures and further elaborations of the barrow-cairn idea followed. Subsequent tradition was very varied. In northern Europe few if any more substantial monuments were constructed in the latter part of the Neolithic. In the Paris basin, in Brittany and in Ireland, there were late styles of shrine or collective ossuary: *hypogées, allées couvertes* and wedge monuments. In Brittany, where so far ditched enclosures are only known on the fringes at the mouth of the Loire, the very old tradition of venerating large stones in their own right found new expression in the great stone rows of the Morbihan and other areas.[149] In southern and central Britain, long ditched and banked enclosures, the cursus monuments, were built in the middle part of the Neolithic.[150] These overlapped in time with causewayed enclosures. The scale of some was truly monumental, the Dorset cursus running across some 10 km of chalk downland in an area still little settled. Others, as at Dorchester-on-Thames, Oxfordshire, were shorter, but of still impressive dimensions. Many were perhaps unfinished, with open ends, and there are frequent changes of alignment. The Dorset cursus was constructed in two or three stages. Some may not have been constructed to be a single monument at all, but the pursuit of a line across the landscape, periodically and partially inscribed. The Dorset and Dorchester-on-Thames cursuses and others incorporate pre-existing mortuary structures and long barrows. Their role may have been to enhance the pathways of the ancestors and the spirits of the dead. They were rarely sited close to causewayed enclosures.

The tradition of circular enclosure was revived right across Britain and extended into Ireland, in the later part of the Neolithic, in the form of henge monuments and stone circles.[151] At Thornborough in Yorkshire the central one of three henges directly overlies a cursus monument, but in other cases there was a close link between the two forms. In the Stonehenge area, the line of the major cursus intersects the position of Woodhenge, a smaller ditched and timber structure outside the great enclosure of Durrington Walls. The first phase of Stonehenge itself and the enclosure at Flagstones, near Dorchester, Dorset, may represent transitional forms between causewayed enclosures and henges.

Henges have been much classified, but the details of this procedure are often tedious and uninformative. Their ditches usually lay within their banks, and as their circumference increased a second entrance tended to be added. Some of the very largest, like Avebury and Marden in Wiltshire and Mount Pleasant, Dorchester, Dorset, some 350–400 m across, had three or four entrances. It has been suggested that we regard these too as a series of unfinished projects, linked to what had gone before but always in the process of being modified.[152] This is important, since the great size of some henges and their more or less regular spacing across the landscape in some parts of the country, for example in a transect in central-southern England from the upper Thames valley, to the Avebury region, the Vale of Pewsey, the Stonehenge area, Cranborne Chase and finally around Dorchester, Dorset, have often been used to support models of a now structured and differentiated society, dominated by the ritual and political concerns of some kind of elite. For some, labour is seen as centrally controlled, ritual as esoteric knowledge jealously guarded, and each of the major henges and monument complexes as the focal point of a chiefdom.[153] The development of the monument complexes to which nearly all the big henges belong may have been very gradual. The bank at Avebury appears to have been built in two stages, and the monument may incorporate a pre-existing double stone row or avenue. The Durrington Walls earthwork may have been preceded by a timber palisade, and there were modifications to the entrances at Mount Pleasant. It has proved very difficult to correlate the chronology of interior structures with that of the perimeters. The stone circles within Avebury could be of varied date, the inner circles potentially earlier than the ditch and bank, and the main circle later.[154] The great circular timber setting within Mount Pleasant, site IV, could also have begun earlier than the ditched enclosure.

These were great collective enterprises, which drew people from wide areas around into feats of pooled labour, and then into active use of the sacred spaces thus created. Given the context, I find it hard to envisage a system of political coercion, and much more satisfactory to suppose a sense of sacred obligation, with shame as the sanction for failure to participate, generated by still active memories of earlier enclosures, concepts of ancestors, and notions of time. These monuments renewed the past in the present. They enhanced respect for ancestors by drawing people into public, shared rituals of a formalised nature. Henges were approached by processions, and their layouts demanded certain ways of entering, seeing, moving around, feasting and depositing.[155]

The sheer scale of Silbury Hill near Avebury tempts us to see a structured society, with social or political coercion driving the numbingly laborious and repetitive task of creating a great mound some 40 m high and 140 m across at the base.[156] But this too may have been guided by sacred rather than secular imperatives. As far as we know, there were no internal structures. It has been suggested that we take the mound literally as a platform for viewing, which served to distance the select on top from those below.[157] But in fact many people can fit on to the top and upper sides. If there was social differentiation, it is as likely to have emerged from the conditions of construction and subsequent use, as to have preceded the decision to build.

My examples so far have all been from southern Britain, but henges are found as far north as the Orkneys and related earthworks and stone settings are known in Ireland, and are now being recognised in increasing numbers. In the middle of the main Orkney island the Stones of Stenness and Ring of Brogar combine ditches, standing stones and other internal stone settings, close to the Barnhouse settlement and the Maes Howe cairn.[158] There are close similarities between motifs on stone in Irish passage graves and on clay on Grooved Ware, the major pot style primarily associated with henges. It is easier to envisage the transmission of ideas about ancestral veneration than uniform social or political process across such a wide area.

Gifts of stone, containers of plenty

It is easy to take stone and flint axes and pots for granted. They can seem an inevitable part of settled life based on agriculture, axes for clearance and other tasks, pots for the routine provision of food. That many axes were carefully finished and made of raw materials obtainable only far from their eventual place of use and deposition raises various possibilities, of craft specialisation, of elaborate and perhaps competitive means of acquisition, and of the use of artefacts as markers of status and prestige. The multitude of pot forms, decorations and assemblage styles is often seen as the basis for statements about identity, of larger and smaller social groupings. Axes and pots serve to reinforce models of a settled agricultural life, characterised in part by individual accumulation and in part by group differentiation. Here, having outlined a much more fluid social landscape and subsistence basis, I review selected aspects of axes and pots to suggest a different set of values, which expressed commonality and participation, a celebration of fertility, regeneration and plenty, and the virtues of hospitality and generosity.

That axes and pots were used for practical purposes is perfectly clear. Abundant preserved wood from the Alpine foreland, the Somerset Levels in south-west England, and elsewhere, shows cuts left by blades not only on posts but on planks trimmed down from split portions of trees.[159] There are plenty of wooden axe hafts, and in the Alpine foreland wooden or antler 'sleeves', designed both to hold the blade and to reinforce the strength and flexibility of the hafting. The technology of such hafting can be seen to have been steadily altered through the Neolithic sequence, presumably in the search for improvement.[160] But many axe blades were very finely finished by all-over grinding and polishing, a laborious and repetitive task requiring tens of hours for even the small blades mounted in sleeves.[161] Some blades were of exceptional fineness and length, such as those from cists within Breton long mounds. Elaboration was regularly far beyond the requirements of practical necessity. Nor can the scale of axe production neatly be equated with cycles of agricultural production. Phases of production of thin- and then thick-butted flint axes in southern Scandinavia, for example, run parallel, on evidence reviewed above, to fluctuating episodes of woodland management. The greatest scale of axe production from the banded flint sources in Poland fell in the Globular Amphora culture phase, when the major subsistence concern may have been mobile cattle herding, not cultivation.

One practical use of axes may have been as weapons. The Neolithic world which I am seeking to invoke was no Arcadia. Preserved bows and arrows, for example from the Somerset Levels, show a deadly killing technology, the results of which can be seen in the flint points quite frequently lodged in parts of skeletons. Examples have been found at Hambledon Hill and in earthen and chambered barrows in southern England.[162] There is also a large series of perforated stone hammeraxes or battleaxes, particularly from the broad area of the TRB and Corded Ware cultures. These do not seem day-to-day tools; many are faceted, angled and knobbed, and some decorated.[163] These too could have been weapons, though their rather narrow perforations, by which they were presumably hafted, would have restricted their strength. Once again it seems impossible to confine these artefacts to the realm of the practical everyday world. There is plenty of evidence that blades were circulated and deposited *without* hafts, as in Danish flint axe hoards from wet places, or the jadeite and flint axes from beside the Sweet Track, contexts where wooden hafts would have been preserved. Conversely, in one of the ditch segments of the causewayed enclosure at Etton, a wooden axe haft had been preserved without its stone or flint blade.[164]

Pottery was clearly used, for warming if not cooking, storage and serving. Sooting, charred residues, chemical analysis of organic residues trapped in the pot fabric, and finds of pots with contents in Alpine foreland settlements, all testify to this. But pottery is in fact probably less abundant in Alpine foreland settlements than in many other contexts of occupation. Neither category of site need have been the locus for permanent occupation. Indeed there may have been an inverse relationship between the degree of permanence and the quantities of pottery in use. Pots were present in abundance too at monuments and ceremonial enclosures. Their direct connection with the routines of settled life seems rather weak. And for all the different styles identified by archaeologists, the general character of most assemblages in any one horizon is remarkably uniform. On the face of it, pots would have been rather ineffective markers of *difference*. Their role as promoters of uniformity in a mobile lifestyle needs to be re-examined.

Banded flint and other flint and stone axes

Several different sources of flint were used and widely circulated in the Neolithic period in Poland and western Ukraine: amongst others, 'Baltic' erratic flint (brought south as far as central Poland by earlier ice sheets); Cretaceous sources in north-east Poland; Volhynian flint from western Ukraine; spotted flint from just east of the Vistula at Świechiehów in the south-east of the country; banded flint and chocolate flint from the northern fringes of the Holy Cross hills west of the Vistula; and Jurassic flint from limestone country (the Polish Jura) north of Kraków in the south.[165] We have come across some of these sources earlier. Chocolate flint had been in use since late glacial times, and was used by the most northerly LBK groups in Poland, and Jurassic flint was transported to Bylany in Bohemia in the LBK period. They continued in use in the TRB period. Other sources came into use then. At Gródek Nadbużny on the Bug, the bulk of flint was from Volhynian sources, supplemented by Świechiehów material. Both were very suitable for blade production, as well as other forms. On the *loess* plateaux west of Lublin, Świechiehów flint was dominant in the TRB phase. But in this phase, banded flint from Krzemionki and other sources in the Holy Cross hills came to prominence as the preferred material for axes.

Banded flint is distinctive and visually striking, particularly in the form of polished axes. The structure of the banding did not make it a good material for blade production. Conversely, there is no obvious technical reason why chocolate and Świechiehów flint should not have been used more extensively for axes. But banded flint came to be the preferred material for axes in the TRB and Globular Amphora culture phases, in the former over a relatively small area of the Sandomierz *loess* 'upland', but in the latter over the whole Globular Amphora distribution. Krzemionki has been explored off and on since the 1920s. Its thousands of extraction points range from simple pits to deep shafts with radiating galleries. One suggested pattern is that extraction gradually became deeper and more elaborate, following seams, and also intensified through time, with greater production in the Globular Amphora culture than in the TRB. One deep shaft and its radiating galleries alone (thought to be more typical of the Globular Amphora than the TRB phase) could have provided hundreds of flint axes.[166] Various considerations run counter to the suggestion that this was an increasingly specialised operation. The ethnography of stone extraction shows wide variations in ownership, accessibility and intensity. In both the TRB and Globular Amphora phases the settlement pattern west of the Vistula was probably one of dispersed occupations, with occasional foci provided by larger sites, monuments and enclosures. In the TRB phase, much banded flint was worked and finished at the large site of Cmielów in the Kamienna valley a little to the south, consistent with accessibility rather than control.[167] The number of shafts proposed for the Globular Amphora phase also suggests access rather than restriction, with many visits, presumably seasonal, by many different people, with 'workshops' in the area of extraction itself. The wide distribution of

7.26 Nodule, cores, flakes and axes of banded flint from Krzemionki. Photo: National Museum, Warsaw.

banded flint axes in the Globular Amphora culture, and the relative evenness of their numbers in grave contexts, may also reflect open access. Banded flint has been found up to 400 km from the source. If there was control at the point of production and the initial point of distribution, it can hardly have been maintained across such distances. The Ćmielów processing site could show a regional, communal effort in the TRB phase, with more individualised acquisition thereafter. The most plausible mechanism for long-distance movement is gift exchange. The significance of the axe could have been complex. It could have been regarded as a suitable badge of communal membership as much as of personal standing, and as a marker of the ability to participate in hospitality and gift exchange as much as to accumulate. The axe could have carried connotations of success in subsistence and independence in conflict. The material itself may have been regarded as special, a gift from the earth to circulate among both the living and the dead, and fit to link people and the natural world. The imperatives driving production at Krzemionki and other sources seem far more than mundane.

Not the least interesting feature of the history of the Krzemionki source is what happened subsequently. In the Corded Ware phase there were both flint and stone axes and stone battleaxes in circulation, but much less use was made of banded flint. One possibility is that the two cultures overlapped in time, and that banded flint was denied to Corded Ware users. It is perhaps more likely that new materials and sources were chosen to establish other values, which I explore below.

There were many other sources of flint and stone for axes in western Europe, including southern Germany, northern Denmark, eastern Belgium and Dutch Limburg, the Paris basin, Brittany, and many places in Britain and Ireland.[168] But there are frustrating contrasts between our knowledge of flint mine extractions, as at Rijckholt, Spiennes, Jablines, Cissbury or Grime's Graves, and our ignorance of the subsequent distribution of their products, and between our knowledge, through petrography, of the distributions of stone sources, such as in Brittany or western Britain, and our ignorance of production procedures at them. Despite intensive research it has proved very difficult to source flint chemically rather than visually. Some welcome progress has been made in the investigation of stone extraction. Both at Sélèdin, inland in Brittany, and high in the Langdale hills in Cumbria in north-west England, excavations have shown rather piecemeal extractions. The sequences found in the Langdales are particularly important, given the very wide distribution to both south and north of the material in question.[169] Group VI stone is a flakeable, volcanic tuff. Excavations have shown individual small points of extraction, scattered across outcrops high on the hills, almost 1000 m above sea level. The techniques of primary flaking vary, suggesting irregular and uncoordinated visits, and there are breaks in the sequences at individual points of extraction.

If we know much about the extraction, production and distribution of flint axes in Poland, most information there about the contexts of deposition is limited to settlements and burials. In southern Scandinavia and the western part of the north European plain we know far less about production and distribution but much more about deposition, not only in settlements and graves, but at passage graves and other monuments, at enclosures and in wet and dry places in the landscape. Axes and battleaxes could have been personal possessions, acquired and valued by individuals. The early grave of a man at Dragsholm contained one axe and one battleaxe among other items. Axes and battleaxes may have been of particular concern to men. But they may also have been objects of communal concern. Individual graves never have large numbers, as though it was inappropriate for an individual to accumulate more. Finds deliberately placed in wet and dry places include both single axes and groups or hoards. These were objects considered suitable both as possessions for the living and as gifts to ancestral spirits and powers of nature. A cult of fertility and regeneration has been proposed on the evidence of wet-place depositions, but there is no need to separate this from practices associated with monuments and enclosures. The dense distributions of single and multiple ('hoard') finds in some areas, for example in north-west Zealand, on both dry ground and in wet places, suggest endlessly repeated acts of deposition, each further inscribing the landscape with a set of common values. These probably continued right through the EN and MNA periods, since both thin- and thick-butted axes are well represented.[170] To repeat is to admire, to follow custom, and to honour tradition.

There were other items and materials in circulation. Copper artefacts were made in the Alpine region and in the south-east part of the TRB area, and moved from time to time, in fluctuating quantities, beyond the areas where they were produced. A copper disc was found within the settlement of the first phase at Hornstaad–Hörnle I, around 3900 BC. This was probably imported. Later, there was local manufacture of copper flat axes, simple blades and ornaments in the Pfyn culture, and further east in the Mondsee culture. There were imported copper beads in a Cortaillod context at Burgäschisee-Süd in western

7.27 Hoard of thin-butted flint axes from Hagelbjerggaard, Zealand. Photo: National Museum, Copenhagen.

Switzerland, and copper ornaments and axe blades were imported into Denmark in the ENII phase. The supply was irregular in both cases, and there is little copper in the subsequent Horgen and MNA phases respectively.[171] Copper was even rarer elsewhere. There were one or two imports into the area of the TRB western group. There was very little in Brittany or the Paris basin. Copper was not certainly worked in Ireland or western Britain in pre-Bell Beaker contexts, though that is a possibility in Ireland. Amber was circulated in the EN period within Denmark. Later, greater quantities found their way south, in the Globular Amphora culture and later. Coastal people of the Pitted Ware and Rzucewo cultures appear to have specialised in collecting and working amber. These examples may therefore introduce a different kind of production and circulation, beginning in one social context but ending in another. There may have been a role here for barter or more impersonal relations of exchange, and certainly for specialised production. There are elements of this kind of system in the last example to be treated here, that of Grand Pressigny flint.

Grand Pressigny, Indre-et-Loire, is south of the Loire in Touraine, at the centre of a flint source covering several kilometres.[172] The distinctive, honey-coloured flint – resembling untarnished copper – was probably extracted from pits on the sides of valleys and plateaux rather than shafts. It was used particularly for long blades, which were struck from carefully prepared cores. Such blades were widely circulated to the north, as far as the Netherlands, particularly in Corded Ware/PFB contexts, and to the east, as far as eastern France and western Switzerland. They may appear in the French Jura waterside sites a little before western Switzerland, from about 3000 BC onwards, and then from the Lüscherz phase of western Switzerland, both before the Corded Ware horizon.[173] Distribution was therefore again into different cultural zones. The blades might have been substitutes for copper blades, which by this date were being produced in northern Italy, as well as perhaps at the eastern end of the Alps. One striking example of this comes from the Valais at Sion-Petit Chasseur.[174] There were two early monuments, low triangular cairns with large upstanding chambers containing collective burials (or offerings of human dead), sites M XII and M VI. M XII may date before 3000 BC and M VI soon after. M VI was later altered in the Bell Beaker phase, but its primary contents included Grand Pressigny blades, and the stones at the front of the monument were decorated with schematic representations of the human torso, including dagger, belt and chest ornament. But the flint blades may also have been valued in their own right. In the Jura sites, such as Clairvaux IV, they were hafted and may have been used as general-purpose tools. In the Netherlands, they accompany burials with Corded Ware/Protruding Foot beakers, in contexts where copper was otherwise little used. In another context too, the later production of stone axes in Britain, axes of Group VI and Group I (with a source in Cornwall) were circulated far beyond the area of production.[175] There may have been a shift from items created through communal effort and circulated as gifts to the living and the dead, to objects acquired from far away, valued as desirable exotics and treated as personal possessions.

Pottery

The culture history approach has long given pots a key role in the definition of cultural identity. 'Ethnoarchaeological' studies of material culture have also sought to explore the active role of material culture in creating and maintaining social identities.[176] But I am more struck by the similarities than the differences between pottery assemblages throughout the period considered here. This is not to deny that there may have been a role for pots in the active creation and maintenance of cultural or group difference. ENI styles in Denmark, for example, were regionalised, perhaps continuing patterns of late Ertebølle material culture. In northern and western Switzerland, Pfyn and Cortaillod assemblages would surely have been visibly distinct.[177] There were varied shapes, and some Cortaillod bowls had distinctive patterns of applied birch bark, held on by resin. In the first part of the fourth millennium BC, the areas of their respective distribution changed, Pfyn assemblages gradually encroaching westwards. In Poland, one view is that Globular Amphora pots were contemporary for a long period with TRB vessels. In both cases there could have been a concern to maintain cultural boundaries or differences. In other cases, difference may be more to do with context. In the Irish passage graves, out of a probably wide contemporary ceramic repertoire, only Carrowkeel bowls (decorated with all-over impressions) were selected for deposition.[178] In most cases, however, there is little sign of selection by context. The same kinds of vessels that occur at Scandinavian passage graves or southern English causewayed enclosures, whether richly decorated or plain, also turn up on settlements or occupations. There are in fact often larger assemblages from non-domestic than

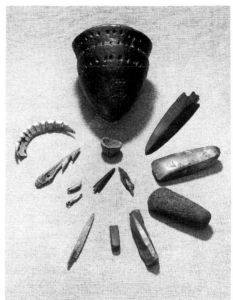

7.28 Left: TRB pots from Denmark (late EN and early MNA); right: Pitted Ware vessel and artefacts from south Sweden. Photos: National Museum, Copenhagen and State Historical Museum, Stockholm.

from domestic contexts (if such a crude distinction can be maintained for sake of argument). This alone points to the special nature of pottery. Pottery was for the provision of food and drink. Some may have been for the routines of daily life, to store and to cook or at least warm foods. But there are comparatively few repairs to pottery. Much cooked food may have been roasted or baked, and there were other containers than those of clay. People may have eaten with their hands or consumed foods as liquids. Pottery can be quickly and easily made. Some may have been transported surprisingly long distances, either for its own sake or for its associated contents. In southern England, pots made from gabbroic Cornish clay were found, in small numbers, as far away as Wiltshire, as much as 300 km from their likely point of production.[179] But most pottery was probably made for local use. There is no sign of kilns or pot-making hearths within Alpine foreland settlements. Pot making and pot use may have been part of the routine not so much of a sedentary, stable existence, but of a still mobile lifestyle, punctuated by periodic gatherings and ceremonies. On the whole, these seem to have celebrated integration and participation, not exclusion. On a wider scale, it has often proved difficult to establish the boundaries between supposedly different styles, especially in the middle part of the Neolithic, for example between Pfyn and Michelsberg at the south end of the Rhine, or Chasseen and Michelsberg in northern France. Many later Neolithic styles are visually dull, like Horgen or Seine–Oise–Marne pottery.

One medium of social communication was the provision and sharing of food and drink. The assemblages from southern English causewayed enclosures had more open-bowl forms than other contexts, which could reflect an emphasis at those sites on the presentation and consumption of foods and liquids. Assemblages in the northern TRB have a wider range of forms, from open bowls, to pedestalled bowls and necked jars. These may suggest formalised rites of mixing, presentation and serving. People were bound together, not only by physically coming together, but by the procedures of consumption, in networks and routines of familiarity. There is no reason why liquids should not have included fermented drinks, nor why at least some cultivation of cereals could not have been for this express purpose. Eating, drinking and feasting – or in some cases their symbolic representation and commemoration – were important activities not only at enclosures but at ancestral monuments. Foods and drink must have been regarded as suitable offerings to spirits and ancestors. To share them with other people was also to partake of sacred elements.

Did social values change, as often suggested, towards the end of the Neolithic period? As far as pottery is concerned, this might be reflected in the appearance of individual vessels, such as the Corded Ware beakers so often deposited with individuals in graves. Women and children were furnished with these as well as men. Whatever changes may be involved cannot be reduced in this instance to gender. Amphorae were an important element not only of Globular Amphora but also of Corded Ware grave assemblages, over much of the Corded Ware distribution. Both amphora and beaker could have had symbolic roles, respectively to project the provision of hospitality and participation in celebrations of plenty. Given all that we have seen in earlier periods, these were not innovations at all, but the maintenance of long-respected traditions.

The Corded Ware/Single Grave complex

The Corded Ware/Single Grave complex is important, since it has often been seen as the horizon for significant changes in ethnic composition and social formation and values. In it, society is often characterised as more mobile, pastoral, aggressive and male-dominated, which many scholars would explain by the arrival of new population, Indo-European speakers related to those claimed earlier in south-east Europe.[180] It is important to keep that characterisation of society and the interpretation of external origins separate, since some support the former while denying the latter. I will argue that both are misplaced. Instead, the Corded Ware phenomenon can be seen to have massive continuities with what went before. Its significance as a marker of change may have been much exaggerated.

The partial distribution of the Corded Ware culture across the areas considered so far in this book needs emphasis. There were Corded Ware groups from western Switzerland to southern Poland and the eastern Baltic, and from Bohemia and Moravia to southern Sweden. There were other groups in southern Finland and far to the east in the middle Dniepr region and beyond.[181] The absences are significant too: little or nothing west of the Rhine; little along the upper Danube despite dense distributions in the middle Rhine-Main and the middle Elbe-Saale regions; little across much of Poland; and so on. It has often been argued that the first phase represents a very broad *Einheitshorizont*, characterised by the use of B-beakers, A-amphorae and A-battleaxes. Dendrochronological dates from Switzerland suggest a start somewhere around 2800–2750 BC. But it is still not clear

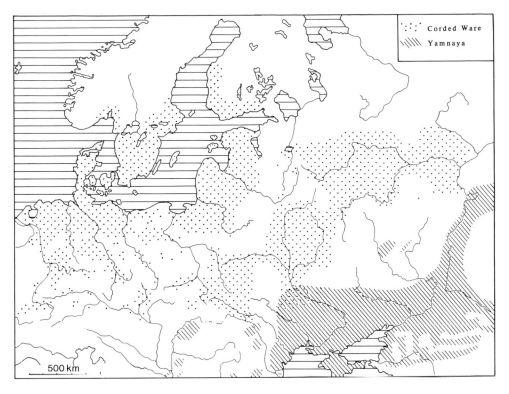

7.29 Simplified distribution map of the Corded Ware and Yamnaya complexes. After Buchvaldek.

whether the *Einheitshorizont* is an archaeological reality or a typological fiction, since its elements do not occur in exclusive association with one another. If the model of unitary origins were less favoured, this characterisation might be more critically reviewed.

Major aspects of Corded Ware settlement and burial rites have already been described above. There was no one single mode of landuse, but instead quite distinctive patterns of regionalised continuity, from the Alpine foreland, the Dutch coast, or Jutland to southern Poland and the northern Carpathians. Some of these may have been fuller landscapes, or at least more extensively cleared for grazing, on the evidence of the pollen diagrams. In this setting there may have been a more numerous but dispersed population, whose mobility (even though herds of animals were still important) could now even have been more circumscribed than before. Material culture may have taken a larger role in the maintenance of social integration than the previous aggregations of people in large-scale ceremonies at monuments and elsewhere.

Shared styles of pots and stone battleaxes may symbolise the continuation of open social relations rather than the emergence of social elites. The burial evidence does not suggest an internally differentiated society, since children and women were as likely to be furnished with potentially significant goods as men. I have already argued that pots had a symbolic role as grave goods. Battleaxes may have had the same. Since perforated stone tools or weapons go back to the horizon immediately after the LBK culture, one can hardly claim the appearance *now* of a more aggressive or warlike society, nor necessarily a more dominant role for men, with whom battleaxes are largely associated in Corded Ware graves. Rather, the battleaxe may have stood for older ideals of interaction and exchange, independence and prowess. If it was mainly associated with men, it is quite unclear that this represents innovation. Once again, as far back as the LBK, men rather than women had been buried with stone adzes and axes. If Corded Ware grave goods had a social message as well as providing for the afterlife, that communication may have reinforced traditions of integration, participation, hospitality and generosity. The message was not so much new as more concentrated, and it may have been increasingly valuable in a society more dispersed across the landscape, in groups with tighter circuits of mobility.

Many origins have been suggested for the Corded Ware complex. One recurrent and popular kind of model is that it represents some kind of ethnic unit which formed in a particular area and then spread by migration. One recent version argues for an origin in an area from the western Ukraine to south-east of the Baltic (defined by the northern Bug, the middle Dniepr and the Niemen rivers), with subsequent migration to the north-east, to the north and to the west, with Switzerland and the lower Rhine as the points last reached in the west.[182] Another recent account offers a core–periphery version of the model.[183] A broad core is proposed from the middle Rhine through central Germany to southern Scandinavia, northern Poland and south-east Poland, in which the complex formed. An equally broad periphery zone around the core is seen as the result of subsequent migration, into north-west Germany and the Netherlands, Switzerland and southern Germany, Bohemia, Moravia, the middle Dniepr and beyond in the Fatjanovo–Balanovo culture, the east Baltic and Finland. Beyond the periphery is envisaged a marginal zone, recipient of influences, imports and occasional small-scale population movement, for example in the Vlaardingen culture, the Auvernier group of the Saône–Rhône culture of western Switzerland, the Złota culture of the Sandomierz region of the Vistula, and the Narva culture of the east Baltic coast. This model breaks new ground in beginning to differentiate more critically between separate areas, rather as proposed earlier for the Bell Beaker complex.[184] It proposes processes of internal cultural and social change, leading to the selection of particular artefact assemblages and explicit differentiation between the sexes in burial. Other points in favour of migration could include the rather erratic, discontinuous distribution of the complex, and seemingly minor changes such as the use of Baltic erratic flint and the paucity of copper working in Bohemia.[185] The sequences in northern and western Switzerland are interestingly different. In the north, the cultural shift from the Horgen culture is seen as rather abrupt, while in the Auvernier group to the west, Corded Ware elements were adopted much more gradually.[186] More generally, the possibility has to be accepted of migration by 'infiltration' in landscapes far from full.[187]

I am pessimistic that a meaningful area of origin can be identified. If an area of origin is to be sought at all, it may be more sensible to look to the largest continuous or near-continuous area of distribution, roughly the middle Rhine/middle Elbe–Saale/Netherlands/north German and south Scandinavian areas. The core–periphery model envisages so wide a core that one may as well propose internal, unifying change across different cultural entities as a general model for most parts of the Corded Ware distribution. The migration hypothesis is weakest in the proposed periphery. There is simply too much continuity in Switzerland, the Netherlands including its coastal areas, and southern Scandinavia. In northern Switzerland there are still gaps in our knowledge of the Horgen–Corded Ware transition. At Zürich–Mozartstrasse this was the transition from the badly eroded late Horgen layer 2B, probably dated to 2888–2883, via a lake marl layer to the Corded Ware layer 2A, also heavily eroded, and dated to 2705–2700.[188] Since the whole style of lakeside occupation continues, it is hard to envisage wholesale population replacement. Likewise in the Netherlands and in Denmark, the preferred chronologies now have succession from the late TRB to the Corded Ware/Single Grave culture, rather than overlap, and it seems obvious that there could not have been wholesale population replacement. It is equally difficult to envisage rapid population additions which resulted in complete cultural dominance rather than symbiosis, though some much later historical parallels might be adduced. There are other, slightly earlier examples of possible cultural symbiosis in the same area, as in the middle Elbe-Saale region with the Walternienburg and Bernburg groups, or at Homolka in Bohemia, where some features of the Globular Amphora culture appeared in the *milieu* of the Řivnáč culture.[189]

In chapter 5, I followed others in suggesting that language could both form and spread by various kinds of contact as well as by population replacement and movement. It may or may not be necessary to introduce Indo-European speakers into central, northern and western Europe at this date. If so, they do not have to be the relations of a distinct ethnic group formed on the steppes. For all their novelty as assemblages, the artefacts of the Corded Ware complex have many local antecedents in the same general style. By processes we do not fully understand, particular sets were selected for widespread use, but in very varied settlement contexts. One suggestion is that drink and drugs were served from Corded Ware beakers.[190] Material culture was used to symbolise open access and communication, and language could have spread along such social pathways without significant population movement, let alone replacement.

It is easy but misleading to represent this as a process of widening contact. If one separates Corded Ware groups to the east and north-east, on the middle Dniepr and beyond and up the east side of the Baltic, perhaps as zones of acculturation or enculturation, the orbit of similarity in the Corded Ware complex is no greater than in the early and then the middle phase of the Neolithic (the LBK and post-LBK horizon and the great cultural sweep of TRB, Michelsberg, Chasseen and related groups); in fact it is rather more circumscribed. The process may rather be one of large-scale regionalisation. West of the Rhine, people may have been orientated more actively to older ways, as explored earlier in the chapter. In the Corded Ware orbit, older monuments and the spirits and ancestors who inhabited them came to be taken for granted, and greater emphasis came to be placed on maintaining social openness and recording shorter lines of descent. In a sense, these different trajectories have no predictable explanations. They were the outcome of histories which could have ended differently. The LBK culture stressed cohesion and uniformity. In the succeeding phase of the extension of the Neolithic, there was great reference to the past, in the form of imagined and actual ancestors, via collective enterprises and rites. By the end of the

Neolithic, that past was variably regarded: either still actively honoured, or taken for granted while other concerns were more immediate.

For all its unresolved puzzles, the Corded Ware phenomenon can be seen as an example of active material culture. The model of internal development within particular historical trajectories and fragmented distributions implies choice. Neolithic people did not live isolated lives. Theirs was a broad universe, with profound contacts with the otherworld and active and wide communication with other communities. A final example both provides an exception to the rule and returns us to the Vistula around Złota near Sandomierz. In southern Poland in the upper Vistula and across parts of the Sandomierz *loess* upland there was a Corded Ware group. Around Złota, further down the Vistula on the edge of the *loess* upland, there was a group, the Złota group, whose pottery and other artefacts cannot neatly be affiliated to the Corded Ware complex.[191] The choice in the literature is between regarding this as a self-contained culture or a peripheral 'variant' of the Corded Ware complex. Perhaps it was neither. There has been argument about whether to derive this group from Globular Amphora, Corded Ware or even Baden antecedents. It may be better to envisage the emergence, unusually for this part of Europe, of a strongly local identity. The descendants of the cattle slayers at Złota with whom this chapter began were themselves buried in numerous graves at Złota and elsewhere. At Złota–Nad Wawrem there was a long row of burials along the edge of the *loess* plateau. These were not in Corded Ware style. A vertical entrance shaft or pit led, via a blocking stone, to elongated niches cut into and under the ground. In these were deposited successive single inhumations, well furnished with pots, tools and ornaments. These people used Świechiehów rather than Krzemionki flint, but they still used Baltic amber. Their burials did not celebrate cattle as their forebears' had, but the creation of a collectivity in death and the continued honouring of place were in a very long Neolithic tradition.

CHAPTER 8

ONE FOOT IN SEA: THE CENTRAL AND WEST MEDITERRANEAN, *c.* 7000–5000 BC

A cave in western Sicily

A large cave on a now remote part of the north-west coast of Sicily was occupied for long periods in the post-glacial period. From it in the earlier post-glacial period its users had hunted game and birds in the surrounding oak woodlands, collected shellfish and plants, and from time to time fished. Several burials were made in the deposits accumulating within the cave, whose natural grandeur may have made it a special place in its own right. From around 7000 BC the users of the cave made many more sea fishing trips, even returning with whales. The whales may have been beached animals, but it seems likely that these forays took people offshore in boats. It may be little coincidence that at some point after this, perhaps in the later seventh millennium BC, other changes ensued in their lifestyle. Hunting continued, especially of red deer, but there were now domesticated animals, at first in small quantities: pigs, possibly indigenous stock; sheep and goats, not part of the native fauna; and cattle. In the course of time people began to cultivate emmer and einkorn wheat and lentils, and after 6000 BC also acquired the use of barley, other wheat and beans; cereals were not native. Occupation continued into the sixth millennium BC. It seems inherently unlikely that such a spot should be colonised by new population from outside, and highly probable that the same people continued their long hold on this shore and its sea. Along with new resources people began to use another novelty: containers of clay, decorated at first with impressions and some later with painted bands.

This sequence comes from the Grotta dell' Uzzo.[1] The cave has already been discussed in chapter 2 in relation to the mobile lifestyle of early post-glacial foragers. The sequence appears to be one of gradual change, of broadening of the resource base rather than of abrupt substitutions, and of indigenous continuity as new opportunities acquired by long-range contact by water were exploited to suit local circumstance.

One foot in sea

When Balthazar sings out over the Sicilian landscape in *Much Ado About Nothing* of the fickleness of men – 'one foot in sea, and one on shore/ to one thing constant never' – he might well have been describing both the broad resource base of foragers on the Mediterranean coasts and the confusing state of research into subsequent transitions.

The sequence from the Grotta dell' Uzzo can be paralleled in many other parts of the Impressed Ware complex of the central and west Mediterranean, especially in southern France and eastern Spain, and many scholars have accepted the general case for local

8.1 View of the Grotta dell' Uzzo. Photo: Tagliacozzo.

continuity. This does not so easily fit the evidence from much of southern Italy, in northern Apulia, Basilicata, Calabria and eastern Sicily, where there is much less sign of indigenous population and a large series of open occupations or settlements, including – especially on the Tavoliere plain in Apulia – many ditched enclosures, which appeared from the later seventh millennium BC onwards, if not before. The most common general model therefore has been to accept a limited measure of seaborne colonisation into southern Italy from across the Adriatic, as some kind of offshoot from seventh millennium BC developments in the Balkans and Greece, and paralleled by the colonisation of Crete and Cyprus. This is seen to establish agricultural communities in the central Mediterranean, with their novel wheats, barleys, sheep and goats, probably earlier rather than later in the seventh millennium BC.[2] In the rest of the region, indigenous communities like those of the Grotta dell' Uzzo gradually adopted elements of the Neolithic lifestyle. Possible processes of adoption run counter to general expectations. Evidence from south French sites has suggested the acquisition of sheep by native foragers from about 7000 BC or soon after, before any other changes, including the use of cereals and the use of pottery.[3] Great things could be expected of the little-explored north African shore, a potential area of transmission of innovation to the Iberian peninsula.[4]

This consensus, such as it was, has recently been challenged from all sides. There are serious problems with the reliability and representativeness of the surviving evidence. It has long been recognised that the rise in post-glacial sea levels will have flooded areas of great significance, of considerable extent in the upper Adriatic, and of lesser extent but of no less importance in parts of southern Italy, southern France and eastern Spain.[5] It is possible to suggest therefore that what went on in caves, generally in the uplands, was marginal to processes going on along the coast. Open sites in southern Italy and some in southern France and eastern Spain show that life was not restricted to caves and rockshelters.

It seems a straightforward task to peel off the stratigraphy of a cave or rockshelter, but more recently the possibilities of hiatus, erosion, intrusion and mixing have been more explicitly recognised.[6] The radiocarbon dates from such deposits may be unreliable. The bones of sheep in claimed late-forager contexts, if correctly distinguished from ibex, may in fact come from intrusive pits belonging to later occupations. The effect of this more critical approach in southern France is to begin the Neolithic Impressed Ware sequence at or soon after 6000 BC, much later than previously claimed, without a phase of late-forager experimentation. This makes a model of colonisation again attractive to some scholars.[7] A similar line has been mooted for the southern half of Portugal, a model being proposed of limited colonisation into the empty niches between the forager populations well established in the estuaries and valleys of the Tagus (the Muge area), Sado and Mira.[8] This critical approach might be more widely applicable. The sequence from the Grotta dell' Uzzo has not yet been published in detail. Much of the Neolithic occupation comes from the deposits at the front of the cave. The date of transition is extrapolated from those of samples *within* the Neolithic layers, and it might be argued that the case for continuity has yet to be demonstrated.

While there is a 'revisionist' school of thought which suppresses the date of the start of the Impressed Ware complex in southern France and eastern Spain to about 6000 BC and allows the possibility of colonisation, so there are difficulties with the colonisation model for southern Italy. The forager background is uncertain. There has been little survey which might have recognised forager occupations, a problem similar to that in Thessaly, discussed in chapter 3. Where relevant sites have been recognised and some survey carried out, as on the Salento peninsula of the heel of southern Italy, there seems to have been continuity from Mesolithic to Neolithic. The chronology of the Neolithic is far from certain. The earliest dates, around 7000 BC, come from a context of uncertain significance at Coppa Nevigata on the Apulian coast.[9] The next point of reference is a date in the late seventh millennium BC from the second level of an inland Apulian occupation, at Rendina.[10] Many of the 500 or more enclosures from the Tavoliere are associated with earlier rather than more developed styles of pottery, but these sites could nonetheless be spread over a long span of time in the late seventh and earlier sixth millenia BC.[11] There is therefore a considerable danger of taking a developed situation as typical of initial conditions.

In this state of flux, I will argue that the primary means of change throughout the central and west Mediterranean was acculturation, started through the sea-borne transmission of contacts, ideas and resources. The transformation of indigenous communities proceeded at different rates and in different ways. Subsistence change was most marked in southern Italy, but it is quite unclear whether a sedentary lifestyle was adopted even there. The process could be akin to that advocated in earlier chapters for central and western Europe in the sixth millennium BC, of the transformation of one set of foragers (into the LBK culture) and of convergence by other foragers in the areas round about. Tentatively, the sequence may begin with changes in parts of southern Italy and eastern Sicily, among indigenous foragers eager for or willing to accept new resources, somewhere in the seventh

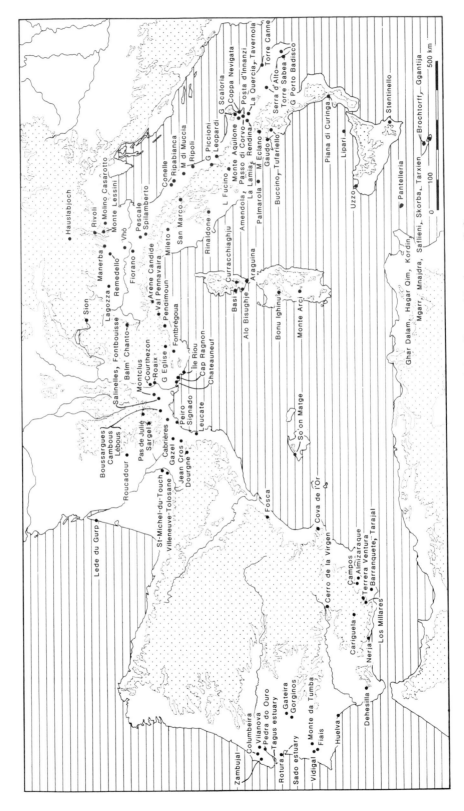

8.2 Simplified location map of the principal sites discussed in chapters 8–9.

8.3 Simplified outline chronology for the areas discussed in chapters 8–9.

millennium BC, probably later rather than earlier given the chronologies of the Balkans and Greece discussed in chapter 3. Western Sicily saw changes perhaps from the late seventh millennium BC, and central Italy from around 6000 BC onwards. At this date or soon after changes began in southern France (with influence or contact beyond into central-western France), eastern and southern Spain and southern Portugal. While there are Impressed Ware sites on the Ligurian coast of north-west Italy, probably from around 6000 BC, the Po valley did not see changes till the later sixth millennium BC, and there is a possibility that these were in part linked to developments in the Balkans and the LBK orbit.[12] Sardinia and Corsica had had pre-Neolithic occupations; elements of the Impressed Ware complex may have appeared only in the course of the sixth millennium BC. Smaller islands may have been empty for longer. The sequence on Malta begins around 5000 BC.[13] Many inland areas may have been sparsely used by the end of the sixth millennium BC, for example in central Italy, parts of southern France and inland Iberia. Although habitable, in a wetter climate than that of today, the north African coast seems largely to have been the province of foragers down to about 5000 BC.[14]

Regional sequences: beginnings and settlement

Southern Italy and eastern Sicily

'That other world, hedged in by custom and sorrow', wrote Carlo Levi in *Christ stopped at Eboli*, '. . . where the peasant lives out his motionless civilisation on barren ground in remote poverty, and in the presence of death . . .' Associated with crushing rural conditions in recent history, the southern part of Italy was prosperous enough in classical times, and it has been tempting to apply a model of successful, sedentary farmers from the outset of the Neolithic period. The lack of well-investigated forager sites had abetted the colonisation model, though there are general claims for plenty of Epipalaeolithic/Mesolithic sites in the region, which is supported by the evidence of the Salento peninsula; other relevant sites may well be on drowned coasts or in infilled valleys. Coppa Nevigata, by the former estuary or lagoon shore of the Apulian coast in the Gulf of Manfredonia, was an occupation associated with cockle collection. It may be much mixed, since there are simple lithics of possible Epipalaeolithic or Mesolithic affinity, impressed pottery and also Copper Age pottery.[15] A radiocarbon determination of the early seventh millennium BC from the site may not actually date the appearance of the Impressed Ware complex in the region. Many investigated sites in the region have domesticated animals including sheep and goats, few wild animals, and various combinations of wheats and barleys.[16] This pattern too has encouraged the colonisation hypothesis, though it is not in itself illuminating since we know comparatively little of what went on before and even less during the process of transition itself. At the Grotta dell' Uzzo, hunting of red deer continued for a long time after the introduction of domesticates, but it is possible to envisage knowledgeable foragers in less hilly situations making swifter substitutions. In the Salento peninsula – the heel of Italy – caves on the coast and inland from early Neolithic open sites were used for a broader range of established subsistence routines: hunting and gathering alongside herding.

Another strand in the colonisation hypothesis has been a misplaced belief in the unity of material culture in the Impressed Ware complex. The pottery sequence has been long debated. Some people believe that impressed wares preceded painted wares, but this has yet to be conclusively demonstrated; at a later stage before 5000 BC there were impressed, scratched and painted styles of decoration. Various schemes of regional ceramic development have been proposed, for example one on the basis of excavations at the well-known large Tavoliere enclosure of Passo di Corvo, but it may well be the case that styles were rather localised from the outset, including in the proposed phase of impressed decoration. Varied impressed styles can be found up the east side of the Adriatic as well.[17] The beginning of the LBK culture is classically associated with material uniformity, but in this instance at least the case for colonisation may be weakened by the absence of a specific common style.

Much attention has been focused on the Tavoliere enclosures, but it should be stressed that recent field research has found and investigated several open sites in the wider region. Few if any of these seem to indicate prolonged or large occupations, even allowing for the destructive effects of subsequent cultivations. In Calabria, several occupations are known in the coastal region. At Piana di Curinga, Acconia, occupation on old dunes near streams a little inland may have consisted of a series of small rectangular structures scattered over a large area.[18] One excavated structure was some 4.5 by 3.5 m, without a laid floor, but with a frame of light posts recognised from the impressions in large quantities of wall daub. This is dated to soon after 6000 BC. The excavators have claimed that this was a 'substantial and durable construction . . . a fitting material correlate for a sedentary way of life', but this remains to be demonstrated. Other occupations may rather suggest impermanence and movement. Torre Sabea in the heel of southern Italy had small pits and features connected with burning, while a little further north on the Adriatic coast Torre Canne had a large shallow pit (*fond de cabane* in the French terminology of the report). Torre Sabea and its neighbours were complemented by other coastal and inland sites (some were caves) from which a broader spectrum of resources were exploited; as well as sheep at examples like Grotta del Fico and Grotte Cipolliane there were red and roc deer, aurochs, boar, steppe ass, smaller game and shellfish. Rendina in the upper Ofanto valley on the extreme southern edge of the Tavoliere had two successive semicircular ditches, some pits and one or two possible post-framed structures. Ripa Tetta near Lucera, at 180 m above sea level to the north-west of the Tavoliere, had no obvious structures surviving. There were a hollow, a hearth and a pit, areas with burning and areas with concentrations of sherds. Daub fragments suggest shelters again. Caves on the edge of the Gargano upland to the north of the Tavoliere were also in use in this period.[19]

Some 500 or more ditched enclosures (*villaggi trincerati*) are known on the Tavoliere plain, over an area of about 70 by 50 km.[20] The plain is framed by a series of rivers running more or less parallel to each other from the Apennines to the sea. Low plateaux or interfluves lie between. Enclosures are mostly found along the edges of the valleys, and even on the larger interfluves they lie near smaller watercourses. A particularly well-studied case is the Amendola plateau framed by the Candelaro, Celone and Farano rivers. No enclosures seem to be known from the upper reaches of the valleys. They cluster in the middle reaches, but in the north-east extend to the coastal region at the mouth of the Candelaro and its tributaries. The environmental setting is not well known. The climate may have been continental and the dominant vegetation woodland; many enclosures are close to what are now light soils above limestone *crosta*. It is likely that river valleys may have infilled since the Neolithic, and it is unclear whether the coastal region was a series of closed or open lagoons and estuaries; in one model for the north-east, estuaries may have extended far back inland. Coppa Nevigata near Manfredonia had several enclosures as neighbours along or near the contemporary shore.[21]

The enclosures range in size from less than a hectare to over 30 ha; the majority are under 7 ha.[22] They consist of one to four ditches, exceptionally more, dug up to 2 m into the subsoil, which form continuous, more or less circular and oval circuits. There are generally simple breaks as entrances; some are more elaborate. Some larger sites have outer ditches some distance from inner enclosures. Most enclosures have traces of inner compounds, consisting of horseshoe or C-shaped ditches. The numbers of these vary enormously, from the many within Passo di Corvo on the Amendola plateau to only a few visible within the elaborate complex at Masseria La Quercia, between the Cervaro and Carapelle near Ordona. On the basis of surface survey and limited excavation it has been suggested both that there were more sites in the sixth than the seventh millennium BC, and that the smaller enclosures have generally earlier styles of pottery than the less common large enclosures. In other words, small enclosures may have gradually increased in numbers, until greater aggregation or nucleation took place, perhaps by the second half of the sixth millennium BC. Passo di Corvo on the Amendola plateau is one of the largest enclosures not just in its own region but on the Tavoliere as a whole.[23] It consists of a one-to three-ditched inner enclosure of some 28 ha containing some ninety compounds, and a further single ditch which encloses about another 40 ha; the maximum distance from side to side was well over 1000 m. Excavation has shown that the main layout at Passo di Corvo was preceded by two smaller enclosures about 750 m apart. Podere Fredella 8 is a single-ditched enclosure about 100 m in diameter, within the area of the main Passo di Corvo enclosure. Campo dei Fiori is a double-ditched enclosure, about 150 by 110 m, just clipped by the north outer arc of Passo di Corvo. It contained one inner C-compound. Their relative dates are unknown. It is unclear whether Passo di Corvo was laid out as one. If it grew gradually, various schemes for its development can readily be envisaged. At any rate, this one example illustrates a process of growth and aggregation. However, there is considerable variety of layout. It may be better to consider these enclosures as a series of unfinished projects, not constructed to a rigidly determined plan and often uncompleted.[24] The other large enclosures on the Amendola plateau are Posta d'Innanzi and Amendola itself. The former is a vast layout of four roughly concentric ditches, but Amendola consists of two rather smaller layouts possibly linked by a curving ditch. In other regions there are straggling layouts like Tavernola south of Foggia, on the next interfluve south from the Amendola plateau. This has at least ten discernible enclosures, each relatively small, and probably successive. At Monte Aquilone on the other side of the Candelaro from the Amendola plateau there is another interesting complex, formed by the closely spaced enclosures of Bivio S. Giovanni Rotondo, Masseria Maremorto I, Masseria Maremorto III

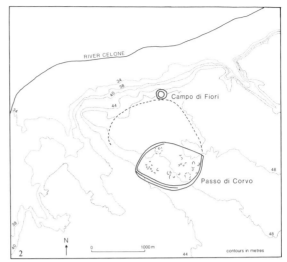

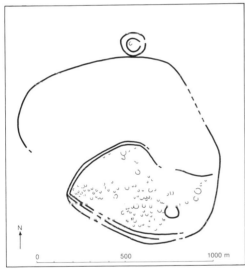

8.4 The setting and plan of the enclosure at Passo di Corvo. After Jones. Bottom right: an excavated C-compound. Photo: Tinè.

and others. Was the likely continuity of use in these cases just as important as the larger single layout of a site like Passo di Corvo?

Although first recorded by aerial photography at the end of the war, still rather little information is available about the detail of enclosures. The most extensive and prolonged excavations have been at Passo di Corvo, where several inner compounds were investigated. Other sites in the lower Candelaro have been sampled.[25] It is no disrespect to the excavators to say that results have been disappointing. These sites have been deeply ploughed since the war, and there is little clear sign of structures within compounds. More positively, one may

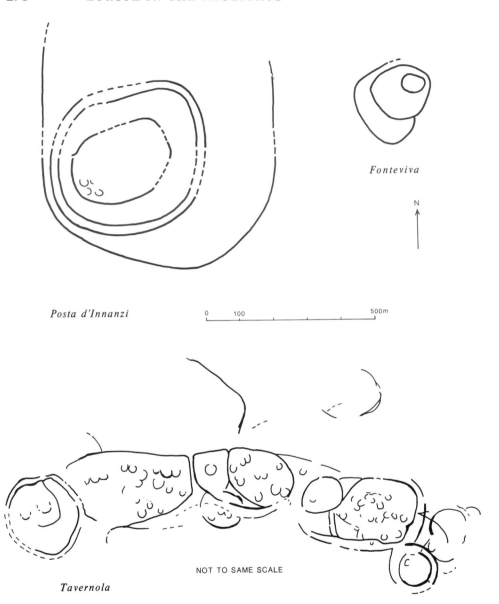

8.5 The enclosures at Posta d'Innanzi and Fonteviva, and Tavernola. After Jones.

note what seem to be modest amounts of material in the ditches of circuits and compound alike. In these terms, it seems unlikely that there was prolonged or intensive occupation within the enclosures. At Lagnano da Piede I, in a relatively high setting between the Carapelle and the Ofanto near Stornarella in the more southerly part of the Tavoliere, one C-compound was excavated within an enclosure only 200 m across but defined by four to five ditches. Preservation was here a little better. Post-framed structures were found *outside* the compound, whose interior was cobbled at a phase some time later than construction.[26]

Few if any open sites have been recognised on the Tavoliere. A concentration of C-compounds without an encircling ditch is known from La Lamia on the edge of the Cervaro valley, closer than other sites in its region to the foot of the Apennines.[27] As conditions for aerial photography have deteriorated since the war because of agricultural improvement, it is possible that other sites of this kind could have existed elsewhere. It remains to be seen whether open occupations of the kind noted earlier outside the Tavoliere can be documented within it.

The subsistence pattern at the Tavoliere sites seems consistent with that elsewhere in southern Italy. Relatively few wild animals are reported in faunal assemblages, which are dominated by sheep and goats. The range of cereals and legumes increased gradually with time.[28] We do not know in any detail whether there was variation between sites and areas in terms of crop processing and consumption. Models of seasonal transhumance to the Gargano and the Apennines have been proposed.[29] These could be extended to include the coastal region, whatever its precise configuration at this date. Drawing on the evidence of Coppa Nevigata and of the Salento peninsula further south, a broad spectrum of resources could have been exploited over the whole range of landscape used. One form of movement could have been through the Tavoliere from coast to Apennines, up and down the valleys. The label *villaggi* for the enclosures is probably unhelpful. The enclosures may mark points of coming and going, places of fixed interest in a fluid landscape. The situation could be parallel to that in the early centuries of Neolithic development in Thessaly and elsewhere in the Balkans. The scale of movement could have been greater here, and the character of place developed differently. We can only speculate at this stage whether this system was more or less mobile than that of foragers in the region, whether the whole population moved, and whether cultivation tied some people to seasonally favourable flood deposits. At any rate, it is plausible to model an indigenous development from broad-based foraging to extensive herding and foraging, with limited cultivation. If the system was mobile, it can be seen that this was hardly a regional exception.

Central and northern Italy

On either side of the Apennines there are Neolithic occupations, like Villaggio Leopardi in Abruzzo or Ripabianca di Monterado in Marche province. None is so far earlier than the middle part of the sixth millennium BC. Some kind of frontier may have existed for a while between southern Italy and late forager areas to the north; that divide once transformed, changes may have spread quickly through the lowlands of central Italy, and then more gradually inland. No one site appears to be very large, nor of long duration, nor enclosed at this date. The subsistence pattern is varied. Cereals were not found at the lowland site of Ripabianca di Monterado (9 km inland) and the inner lowland site of Maddalena di Muccia, also in Marche (60 km inland, and over 400 m above sea level); their faunas were dominated by sheep and goats, and by pigs and red deer, respectively. At the Grotta dei Piccioni and the Grotta Sant' Angelo on the border of the Abruzzo lowlands and the Apennines people exploited sheep and goats, pigs and cattle, and red deer.[30] The small Gubbio basin is well inland, on the Umbrian side of the Apennines, and at a height of some 400 m above sea level. Prospection revealed one small early Neolithic site in what was then a damp, wooded catchment. The San Marco site, on an alluvial fan, is dated to the later sixth millennium B C. It was probably small, though it was not fully excavated, being defined by a pit, a linear shallow ditch, and spreads of artefacts. Its occupants had impressed pottery akin to that in use along the Adriatic lowlands. They kept sheep and goats, cattle and pigs, and hunted deer, hare/rabbit and birds. A surprisingly wide range of cereals and legumes was in use, and wild fruits and nuts were also collected. This may have been an indigenous population shifting to new opportunities, but the position of the site in a wider world remains uncertain. It is not clear whether the upland basin was permanently occupied year-round. The situation could be compared with the Mesolithic exploitation of the inland intermontane Fucino basin in Abruzzo, whose lake and environs had offered rich resources to foragers, seen in the remains of sites like Ortucchio and Grotta Continenza.[31]

Change spread gradually northward through the heart of the peninsula. The next area to adopt new resources and material culture was northern Tuscany and the Po valley, from the end of the sixth millennium B C. The main features at Mileto near Florence were rectangular pits used for burning. People there used cattle, pigs and wild game.[32] In the Po valley at about the same date there were scattered sites in lowland situations close to water, of the Fiorano group in Emilia and the eastern Veneto and the Vhò group in Lombardy; in the Adige valley running up into the Alps there was the Gaban group.[33] In the Po valley people still relied to a considerable extent on wild game, including red and roe deer, aurochs, boar, smaller animals, and fish, tortoise and mollusca. They also had domesticated cattle and pigs, and sheep and goats, in rather smaller numbers. There is evidence for cereal cultivation, but the scale of this is uncertain. At Vhò itself, sheep were extremely rare, and only one grain of wheat was recovered.[34] Vhò and Fiorano sites seem more visible than their predecessors, and may have been larger. No certain buildings are known, but various pits have been recorded. Such sites might again best be regarded as bases in a still-mobile lifestyle. In the Adige valley, even pots were a rare novelty, as in the sequence of the Riparo Gaban rockshelter. Sheep and goats appeared somewhat later, as part of a still very broad spectrum of game.[35] People in the Po valley and its surrounds could have been influenced from various directions, from the heart of the peninsula to the south, from the Impressed Ware group on the Ligurian coast, or from the Balkan/Adriatic and LBK worlds. The first occupation of the uppermost Rhône valley in the Swiss Valais is said to date back to this horizon, a further illustration of a web of contact and change.[36]

In north-west Italy in Liguria there were Impressed Ware occupations perhaps from about 6000 B C or soon after. This must indicate that some changes spread more quickly around the coasts than inland. The relationship of Impressed Ware users to their predecessors is unclear. At Arene Candide for example, excavations have so far revealed only traces of a Mesolithic occupation. Subsequently the cave was used much more regularly, perhaps as a hunting and grazing station. A lot of wild game was still procured, including pigs, and sheep and goats were killed for their meat as much as for their milk. In the Val Pennavaira shelter sites are known further inland, such as the Arma di Nasino and the Arma dello Stefanin, respectively 150 and 500 m above sea level. Again, there is little evidence for Mesolithic occupation, and the Impressed Ware phase of the sixth millennium

BC here represents the infill of a previously marginal area. At the Arma dello Stefanin people hunted ibex, pig and other game, and herded some sheep and goats as part of a presumably mobile existence. At the nearby Grotta Pertusello sheep and goats appeared to be more numerous.[37]

What is above all unclear in such a situation is the overall system. Did people move up and down valleys, exploiting the high inland in summer, and returning to lowland bases at other times? Or were the upland shelters a peripheral or specialised part of a system based on the lowland and coast? The same questions must be faced right through the south of France and down the east side of Spain. Added to these difficulties are further uncertainties about dating and sequence, and the nature of late-forager lifestyle.

Southern France and eastern Spain

Radiocarbon dates from some south French sites, like Cap Ragnon and Île Riou on the Provence coast, had suggested that the Impressed Ware phase began in the early seventh millennium BC. Likewise there have been claims in southern and eastern Spain, based on rockshelter and cave sites in Andalucia like Cueva de la Dehesilla, Cadiz, and Cueva de Nerja, Málaga, and in Catalonia like the Cova Fosca, Castellón, for an early seventh-millennium BC horizon of impressed pottery without cockle (*Cardium*) impressions. There are now good grounds for doubting such a high dating. For the most part in southern France and eastern Spain the earliest Impressed pottery was cardial decorated, seen in Spain by the stratigraphies of Cova de l'Or in Valencia and La Carigüela del Piñar in Andalucia. This need not be universally true, since the stratigraphy of the Abri Pendimoun in eastern Provence shows a non-cardial layer (though dated to the later sixth millennium BC) below its first cardial level. But that is not far from the Ligurian Impressed Ware province, distinguished from those to its west by its non-use of cardial decoration. The early dates from southern France may be affected by the shell samples used, and there is the problem of systematic variation between the results of different dating laboratories. In southern Spain the association between samples and contexts is open to question. For these reasons, there is now a strong school of thought which dates the beginning of the southern French and eastern-southern Spanish Impressed Ware complex to soon after 6000 BC, and no earlier.[38]

Throughout these areas there were late forager communities. How numerous these were is not clear. In one recent estimate the number of southern French 'Castelnovien' sites (a name derived from the great rockshelter site of Châteauneuf-les-Martigues in the Bouches-du-Rhône west of Marseille) was in fact rather limited.[39] As seen in chapter 2, foragers ranged widely over their landscape and exploited a wide range of resources: hunting, fishing and gathering. Claims that they also acquired and incorporated sheep and goats into their mobile routines, around 7000 BC, are now to be treated with suspicion.[40] Such claims were based on rockshelter/cave stratigraphies, as at Châteauneuf-les-Martigues, and the Grotte Gazel and Abri du Roc de Dourgne in Languedoc, and on the open Provence site of Gramari, Vaucluse. It is generally accepted that there was no local post-glacial ovicaprid population; the animals had to be introduced by human agency.[41] But renewed excavations at Châteauneuf-les-Martigues found no sheep bones in the Castelnovien levels, as claimed from earlier investigations, and there are grounds for thinking that the top of the Mesolithic stratigraphy at Gazel is also disturbed by the subsequent Neolithic occupations. The possibility for contamination in the open context at Gramari is obvious.[42] Such revisionism would remove one of the most interesting potential cases of forager acculturation in the whole of Europe, but the revised scenario does better fit the wider pattern of development in the central and west Mediterranean as a whole. Some scholars have gone on to claim that this leaves open again the possibility of some kind of colonisation. One argument is that the lithic traditions of foragers and Impressed Ware users were different,[43] but I find this unconvincing. This is not to deny changes through the relevant sequences, but these can comfortably be accommodated by envisaging either cultural 'drift' or specific adaptations to changing circumstances. It may therefore be most satisfactory to accept a lower start date, but maintain the case for continuity of local population.

Where did this population reside and how did it support itself? It is most visible in caves and rockshelters, the majority both inland and upland. Relatively few sites have both Castelnovien and Impressed Ware occupations in the same stratified sequence. At many sites, hunting was the principal activity. At the Grotte Lombard in the Alpes Maritimes, for example, the faunal assemblage was dominated by red deer and other game of mature deciduous oak woodland. There were some domesticated cattle and a few sheep and goats. This is dated to the end of the sixth millennium BC. At the Abri Pendimoun, lower lying, the excavators discerned a decline in hunting and an increase in ovicaprid herding and cereal use from the impressed to the cardial level. A similar pattern of incorporation of sheep and goats into hunting and other routines is suggested by the results of rockshelter investigations in Languedoc, across a range of altitudes, from the Grotte Gazel to the Abri Jean-Cros, and the Abri Dourgne higher still. Study of the fabrics of pots from these sites suggests at least short-range movements of people. At the Baume de Montclus in the Gard, and Fontbrégoua, Var, people caught river fish.[44]

How easily hunting and herding were in fact integrated should be considered more critically. No one site has deposits sufficiently discriminated to allow detailed examination of butchery patterns among the different species at a single moment of occupation. Perhaps shelters and caves began to be used in more varied ways, by herders and hunters alternately. At a later date, herding overshadowed hunting at these upland sites. It has been claimed that this development took place within the middle part of the sixth millennium BC,[45] but the dated evidence from sites like Abri Pendimoun in Provence and Grotte Gazel, Abri Jean-Cros and the Abri Dourgne in Languedoc suggests that this happened from about 5000 BC onwards. Nonetheless, with a later start date for the Neolithic in the region as a whole, this was a relatively rapid development, and it is worth bearing in mind that in southern Italy this upland facies of the evidence may largely have been missed in research so far, as the Salento evidence strongly suggests.

Unsurprisingly, there is little sign of cereal cultivation in upland locations, in Languedoc for example. Cereals are known from the Cova de l'Or in Valencia at a height above sea level of over 650 m, and surrounded by oak, pine and juniper woodland. Presumably these represent transported foodstuffs. Cereals are documented in more lowland situations, at Fontbrégoua in inland Provence, and at Châteauneuf-les-Martigues and Peiro Signado,

Portiragnes, in Hérault, near the coast.[46] Châteauneuf-les-Martigues was originally by a coastal lagoon, and there is good evidence too for sea fishing and shellfish collection. Similar evidence is known from Cap Ragnon and Île Riou in the same region, from the submerged site of Île Corrège, Leucate, on the Languedoc coast, and from the southern Spanish Cueva de Nerja.[47] As in Balthazar's song, the Cardial resource base was clearly varied.

Some open sites are known, which shows that the pattern of settlement was probably much broader than the dominance of shelters and caves in the investigated record suggests. Le Baratin, Courthézon, Vaucluse, in Provence, had circular cobbled areas about 5 m in diameter. It is not known whether these were the floors of structures or merely work areas. Other open sites are known in the region but have not been investigated extensively. They need not have been sedentary occupations. Open sites are also documented closer to the contemporary coast, at Leucate and Portiragnes. They make it likely that many others formerly existed in the coastal lowlands. Portiragnes has not been extensively investigated, and the underwater setting of Leucate also restricted the scale of research.[48] We cannot say whether these sites were large or permanently occupied. Most investigated sites in eastern and southern Spain have been shelters and caves, but some open sites of the later Impressed Ware or Epicardial horizon, roughly the late sixth into the early fifth millennium BC, are known in Catalonia.[49] The pattern of occupation was not necessarily continuous. There are variations in the density of Cardial occupation in the different regions of southern France, which may not be to do entirely with the intensity of research. The well investigated area around Montpellier, for example, has virtually no Cardial occupation.[50] Further inland, in the southern parts of the Massif Central and the upper reaches of the valleys flowing west, there are scattered sites whose occupants used Impressed pottery but who otherwise continued as foragers. Roucadour in the Lot valley is the classic example. Its level C, from the later sixth millennium BC, has a fauna wholly dominated by wild animals, with a few possibly domesticated pigs and very rare sheep.[51] One exciting development in recent years has been the recognition of sites with impressed pottery (how uniform will be considered later) up the coastal region of central-west France between the Gironde and the Loire. La Lède du Gurp, Gironde, some 100 km north of Bordeaux on the Atlantic coast of Médoc, is one example, set on the edge of coastal marshes and surrounded by unaltered oak woodland. The resource base of such sites is still fully to be established, but there was clearly here an important potential corridor for the northward transmission of new ideas and techniques. The changes seen in Brittany in the fifth millennium BC need not all have come from the east and the Paris basin.[52]

Southern Portugal

The pattern for southern France and eastern Spain could be, on the evidence reviewed above, a late start to the Neolithic around 6000 BC, with the adoption by the indigenous population of pottery, and the addition of herding and plant cultivation to established routines of wide-ranging hunting and collecting. In southern Portugal, there is good evidence for the existence of late foraging communities in the estuaries and valleys of the Tagus,

Sado and the smaller Mira. From about the middle of the seventh millennium BC onwards, on present evidence (thus at roughly the earliest likely date for the beginning of changes in southern Italy), there were estuarine occupations, especially in the form of shell middens. These lasted to at least about 5000 BC, and perhaps longer.[53] In the Tagus and Sado especially there were numerous such middens. People collected shellfish and land snails, fished, and hunted large and small game. Chemical isotope analyses suggest that in some cases there was no significant marine content in the diet. People may have been largely tethered to the resources, marine, terrestrial or both, of the estuaries. Flint was probably collected from sources west of the Tagus, and there was an inland camp at Forno da Telho near Rio Major in the Estremadura. People may have spent much if not all of the year in the estuarine zone. It is possible that they circulated from midden to midden according to season, but the evidence from recent excavations at several locations in the Sado valley and at the Fiais midden in the Mira valley may rather suggest that larger middens acted as bases, while smaller sites were specialised camps: a pattern of radiating mobility. Both the Tagus and the Sado middens are notable for the many burials in them, another possible sign of a tethered existence, akin to that of the Ertebølle culture of the sixth to fifth millennium BC in southern Scandinavia, discussed in chapters 6 and 7. As suggested for that context, the middens may have been places for special gatherings as much as places in which to live.

As in Spain, the date of the introduction of pottery and new staples is disputed. There have been claims for early non-cardial impressed pottery, but the most likely sequence is again from cardial impressed to non-cardial impressed wares.[54] How changes took place is disputed. One model is for limited colonisation into the relatively empty niches between the three areas of the lower Tagus, Sado and Mira valleys. The inland cave of the Gruta do Caldeirão, Tomar, for example, represents a new kind of occupation, in a limestone cave on the edge of a plateau on the edge of the Tagus drainage system. Its first, Cardial layer, is dated to the late sixth millennium BC, and its occupants, some of whom were buried in the cave, hunted boar but also kept sheep. It is possible that this intake of the interior uplands was associated with the arrival of people other than those of the estuaries, perhaps from southern Spain.[55] But there is no obvious motive for such movement. The Gruta do Caldeirão site may just as well represent very occasional seasonal visits inland by the people of an indigenous system changing and expanding with the uptake of new opportunities. At Vidigal near the Mira valley, limited excavation of a coastal shell midden, dated to the sixth millennium BC and with a central shellfish dump surrounded by areas for butchery, roasting and tool maintenance, produced a handful of plain sherds. Pottery is also known from Tagus and Sado middens, presumably from upper, perhaps disturbed levels.[56] The colonisation model does not specify what the fate of midden occupants was. It is more likely that pottery and new resources like sheep were gradually adopted – for motives to be discussed further below – and that the lifestyle of indigenous population slowly changed thereafter. There is no reason why middens should not have remained an important part of subsistence strategy long after the introduction of the novelties of pottery and sheep. But as in other areas, it is possible that early Neolithic herders were more mobile than late coastal/estuarine foragers.

8.6 Shell middens of the Muge valley in the Tagus estuary. Top: Arruda (note rice paddy in the middleground); below: the section at Amoreira. Photos: Rowley–Conwy.

A pattern of islands

The larger islands of the central Mediterranean were all occupied before the Neolithic. Eastern Sicily has already been considered, as part of the south Italian zone, the ditched site of Stentinello giving its name to an Impressed Ware style found also in Calabria. The Grotta dell' Uzzo shows indigenous acculturation in the west of the island. Sardinia and Corsica had Impressed Ware occupations, in the former from around 6000 BC, as at sites in the north-west like Filiestru, near Mara, and in the latter from perhaps the later seventh millennium BC, at sites like Basi, Curacchiaghju and Araguina-Sennola in its southern part and Strette in the north.[57] The dating and stratigraphies of shelter sites are uncertain; the mid seventh-millennium BC date from the Basi rockshelter may be unreliable.

The pattern of settlement and subsistence in Sardinia and Corsica was varied. People made use of the resources of the sea, as documented at Araguina-Sennola and Strette. The evidence for seafaring from the Grotta dell' Uzzo can be extended by the evidence for the movement of obsidian (discussed further below) from Sardinia, and the smaller islands of Lipari, Palmarola and Pantelleria.[58] Supplementing and then replacing the indigenous fauna, including the rabbit-rat *Prolagus sardus* and the extinct deer *Megaceros cazioti*, people introduced to Sardinia not only cattle, pigs and sheep and goats, but also evidently red deer; on Corsica, cattle have not so far been documented in early Neolithic horizons.[59] There is little evidence for cereal cultivation. The patterns of exploitation varied. At Basi, sheep and pigs were practically the only animals, while at Araguina *Prolagus* was dominant, supplemented by fish, birds and shellfish, and only a very few domesticates. Curacchiaghju had no animal bone surviving, but its inland location, over 700 m above sea level, suggests both variety and mobility. Sicily need hardly be considered an island at all. The best case for colonisation in the whole central and western basin could be made for Sardinia and Corsica. We do not know if indigenous, pre-Neolithic occupation was continuous or dense. The islands, offshore but in easy reach, could have represented an attractive, more or less empty niche to people with seafaring skills and new resources. Alternatively, an indigenous population could itself have searched out new staples, once word of their existence got around, to supplement their insular resources. In either case, neither pottery nor lithics betray origins with any clarity.

The Balearics may have been colonised a little later, in the later sixth millennium BC. At the rockshelter of So'on Matge, Valldemossa, on Mallorca, for example, the sequence begins with evidence for the butchery of the small, endemic antelope-like ruminant *Myotragus balearicus*. Domesticates come into the sequence in the fourth or third millennium BC.[60] Perhaps the islands, which might have had some pre-Neolithic occupations, were only visited occasionally in this period.

The islands of the small Maltese archipelago may have been empty of both people and fauna before the the first, Ghar Dalam, phase of Neolithic occupation, around 5000 BC. As the later temples or shrines of the islands (discussed in the next chapter) largely face north, colonisation was probably from that direction; this also fits the picture of slow development along the western part of the north African shore, referred to above. It is unlikely that people came to Malta so late out of ignorance of its existence, since obsidian from Pantelleria to its north-west had probably already been acquired for use in Sicily.[61]

Material impressions

Pottery and food

The account of settlement and subsistence can be read as a dreary list of repetitive menus, the inevitable replacement of wild by domesticated resources. The process of change in fact is much more interesting. I have argued that the principal agents of change throughout the central and western basin, including in southern Italy, were indigenous populations. It is clear that change was instituted in differing ways and at different rates. In no one region can the label 'farmers' be really said to apply before 5000 BC; as for other regions of Neolithic Europe, we need to develop a more sensitive, less anachronistic vocabulary. Why should people have complemented established and effective routines of hunting with herding, and of collecting (and perhaps even plant tending) with cereal cultivation?

In this region even less than in others considered in this book, I can find no convincing evidence for a decline in resources or for subsistence stress. It is true that there was land loss along parts of the coastline, and the effects, especially in the upper Adriatic, may have been locally considerable. The south of France was also changed by rising sea level. It might be possible to claim that this led to such 'packing' of a previously more dispersed coastal population that as soon as new resources were available, further east in the Mediterranean basin, they were snapped up and widely adopted. In the region as a whole, however, such a stress model is unconvincing. Some areas may have had rather little or even virtually no forager occupation. We have seen one specific example from Liguria, and the adjacent Po valley, despite what was happening in the upper Adriatic, seems not to have been densely settled by late forager communities.

The process of the spread of change was gradual. Some changes perhaps spread more quickly around the coasts, as in Italy, with gradual change creeping up the peninsula, perhaps even having to pass cultural frontiers on the way. The picture is not one of instant capitulation to new ways. I have argued in chapter 2 for the knowledgeability and flexibility of foragers. The early Neolithic landscape was probably not densely settled. The Tavoliere in southern Italy might be seen as a classic early agrarian landscape, with enclosures representing concentrations of population and staking out fixed territories and resources. I have argued above for a rather more fluid, more mobile landscape. Survey in Calabria has vastly increased the number of known sites,[62] but if we take into account the timespan involved and do not assume that each located 'site' was a sedentary settlement, a rather different picture emerges here too. Whatever the overall nature of mobile systems – radiating or circulating, to use terms discussed in earlier chapters – it is clear, for example from the south French evidence, that old routines were still dominant both inland and upland. Further inland, lifestyles hardly altered at all. I noted the case of inland parts of southern France, in the upper drainage system of the Garonne basin, and one should also note the absence of early Neolithic settlement from vast areas of inland Iberia – at this date virtually the whole of the *meseta*, and the northern and north-west parts of the peninsula.[63] The argument need not be laboured; I see piecemeal and gradual adoption of new resources, community by community.

Why then were new resources adopted at all, if indigenous populations were well established and unthreatened by resource depletion, and if the maintenance of new resources implied, as it might have done, more labour? One might look to other regions of Europe for helpful comparisons, but in fact the process in each region was probably distinctive. Central and western Europe were colonised by an indigenous population (forming the LBK culture), which found new ways to exploit woodlands and valleys which had had limited previous use. In southern Scandinavia, the Ertebølle culture seems to have resisted the adoption of new resources for a considerable period of time. When those resources were finally accepted, it seems to have been the end of a long process of convergence. Neither case offers a useful model for understanding change in the central and west Mediterranean.

The spread of the Neolithic phenomenon can be seen in part as the product of its own history. In the case of the central and west Mediterranean, the spread of new resources and new forms of material culture may have been to do with the importance to indigenous populations of the values by which and the contexts in which food was shared and material culture displayed. People moved around by sea, as has been stressed more than once in the evidence from the Grotta dell' Uzzo. As changes took place gradually in Greece and the Balkans in the course of the seventh millennium BC, it is not difficult to envisage knowledge of them spreading into the central Mediterranean, and specifically to southern Italy first as the area closest to the new history of the eastern Mediterranean basin. Sheep and goats, cereals, and pots, could all initially have been adopted as novelties in their own right, associated with food and the serving and sharing of food, rather than as solutions to difficulties of population or subsistence. They could have been adopted because of their perceived compatibility with existing mobile lifestyles and values. Sheep and goats could have most easily been moved around, and cereals need only have been periodically tended. The subsequent and much later development of a more fully agrarian subsistence base can be separated from the initial adoptions.

In this model, people in the central Mediterranean basin made use of novelties because they were there, made available by another history. We know as little about the specific uses of pottery in this region as in any other. The use of pots may have been to serve foods and drink in special as much as in mundane circumstances, at least initially. Their appearance on the shell middens of southern Portugal is no surprise. In upland rockshelters like the Grotte Gazel and the Abri Dourgne in Languedoc, very probably not the scene for major gatherings, pots appeared later in the sequences than sheep and goats.[64] Bone spoons, for example from Cova de l'Or in Valencia,[65] may just be routine equipment, but could hint at formalised patterns of preparation, serving and consumption.

Although the common general label is of an 'Impressed Ware complex', the ceramic phenomenon was strongly regionalised. Working out its local sequences has induced many a migraine, as southern French scholars have confessed.[66] But the differences from, for example, the early uniformity of LBK pottery should be instructive. In broad terms, a great

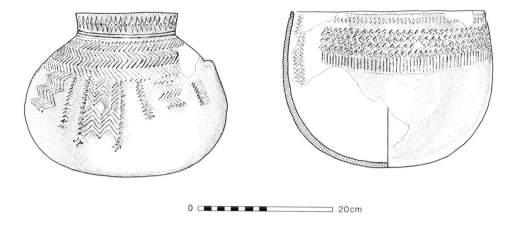

8.7 Impressed Ware pots from Piana di Curinga. After Ammerman.

variety of impressed pottery, mainly in the form of bowls and jars, stands at the head of local sequences. This was not executed to standard patterns, even within one region. The first pottery from the Grotta dell' Uzzo was different from that in eastern Sicily, for example, and pots akin to those of the Stentinello style appeared in its sequence only later. Finely decorated impressed pots from Piana di Curinga in Calabria are not matched exactly in the Tavoliere. The regional sequence proposed for southern Italy on the basis of excavations at Passo di Corvo may best fit the more limited area of the Amendola plateau. Further south in the Matera region, scratched decoration was more prominent. The development of painted decoration, reaching its climax in this period with the appearance of trichrome wares, was perhaps a feature mainly of northern Apulia, including the Tavoliere and Bari regions.[67] The elaboration of pottery in the Tavoliere seems to go hand in hand with the multiplication and elaboration of ditched enclosures. Both may have been the product of intensifying social interaction, of gatherings, feasts and social exchanges.

Decoration with *Cardium* shell was widespread but not universal. Its use distinguishes a zone from southern France to southern Spain. Perhaps the cockle shell itself had special connotations or significance. It might have signified ancestral foods even as the use of novelties spread. Pottery was therefore a medium through which to express several values. Some pots might have been exchanged over distances, especially southern Italian fine wares, as items of prestige. The spatial patterns of style (as well as limited thin-section analysis) suggest, however, that most pottery was part of the expression of local identities; the Languedoc fabric study suggested a range of about 70 km for the movement or exchange of pots. One good example is provided by the various styles current in the early stages of the Neolithic in complementary areas from the northern Apennines into the Po valley and across to its northern side. Whether the contexts of manufacture and use were in any sense competitive is quite unclear. I prefer, as elsewhere, to see pottery as a medium for the promotion of integration and cooperation, through the sharing of food and drink, ideals which presumably existed in late forager communities. Fine painted pots may have been executed for specific ceremonies, or hoarded in caves and other repositories as

8.8 Impressed Ware pot from Cova de l'Or. Photo: Martí.

communal valuables.[68] That styles were not more widely uniform is consistent with the maintenance of local identities. There appear to be few exceptions at a local level to local style. The case of Peiro Signado, Portiragnes, has often been noted for its impressed pottery which is more akin to that of sites in Liguria than of its immediate neighbours in coastal Languedoc.[69] The conventional explanation is of an outpost of people of Ligurian origin, and perhaps this can be accepted in this instance.

Obsidian and exchange

Local identities were not maintained in isolation, but in the context of contact with and knowledge of others. If few pots were transported, one of the striking features of material assemblages in this period was the movement of obsidian from offshore sources into peninsular Italy and southern France. This movement reached its peak after 5000 BC. How transport took place is not clear. The material seems normally to have been put to practical use at the end of its movement, and was not reserved for display or other purposes. But whether directly acquired from its sources by its users or cycled through a series of gift exchanges, both transport and use are notable, since in nearly all regions other lithic raw materials were available, and indeed had long histories of use in the earlier post-glacial period and back into the later Palaeolithic.

There were four sources of obsidian in the region, all in a sense remote from the main zones of settlement, though not necessarily difficult of access. These were Monte Arci on Sardinia, Lipari in the Aeolian islands off the north of Sicily, the small island of Pantelleria between Sicily and the north African coast, and the small island of Palmarola offshore from the Campanian coast.[70] Analysis has suggested that Sardinian obsidian was transported to central and northern Italy, including Liguria, Corsica and southern France. Material from Palmarola was used in Campania, and in central and northern Italy, but rarely in southern Italy and not in southern France. Obsidian from Pantelleria was taken to Sicily and northern Africa. Lipari obsidian was perhaps the most widely distributed of all: into southern Italy and Sicily, where it was the most common of the volcanic glasses used, and into northern Italy and southern France, but not to Sardinia or Corsica.

Even within Sardinia, the use of obsidian involved transport over tens of kilometres. The Grotta Filiestru was some 75 km from the Monte Arci source.[71] In Calabria, at Piana di Curinga, obsidian was the principal lithic material. At this site and others in the area, it was probably brought in as pre-formed cores. Further afield in southern Italy, there was greater use of more local flints and cherts, as at Torre Sabea in the heel. At this date, quantities in central and northern Italy were small. Two blades were found in recent excavations of the early levels at Arene Candide. In the Cardial horizon in southern France, only Caucade near Nice and Portiragnes had obsidian, the latter with the grand total of three blades (from a relatively small area of excavation).[72]

At this date therefore distance was a major constraint. We do not know how material was acquired. There is little or no information available about the extraction of material from the sources themselves. People could have travelled expressly to the sources, or passed material on when engaged in other activities, such as offshore fishing. The passage from Lipari to Calabria, for example, is easy enough. Nonetheless, there was perhaps an important element of contact with wider worlds, which was valued for its own sake. The acquisition of obsidian may have symbolised, for individuals or communities or both, both knowledge of broader horizons, which had after all brought the novelties of pottery, sheep and goats and cereals, and participation in networks of contact and exchange.

Social contexts: gatherings, cult and the dead

I have argued that the widely varying sites across the landscapes of the Mediterranean basin were part of still mobile lifestyles in the first part of the Neolithic period. We have little difficulty in seeing caves and rockshelters as places for transitory visits (of shorter and longer duration). It follows that open sites too were probably also rarely permanently occupied, either through the year or from year to year for generation after generation. Many open sites may have been, rather than anchors for a sedentary existence, those points in the landscape chosen for gatherings and aggregations of people, for social negotiation and transaction as much as for the meeting of subsistence needs. It is no surprise from this perspective that shell middens in southern Portugal, or naturally impressive rockshelters like Châteauneuf-les-Martigues in Provence, should have remained in use in the early part of the Neolithic. The social business transacted at them may have been little different to that seen in the period of their initial formation. Other enigmatic features from the early horizons of the Neolithic elsewhere in the region may be connected with the formality of gatherings: from the 'combustion' structures of sites like Torre Sabea in the heel of Italy, to the burning pits of northern Apennine and Po valley sites or the cobbled platforms of Courthézon in Provence. I have already suggested that the enclosures of the Tavoliere should be seen in this sort of light rather than as sedentary *villaggi*. The investment of labour required to construct most of them was not big, even when ditches were cut into limestone.[73] These tasks were lessened the greater the number of people involved, and the longer the period over which the changing projects were instituted. Such repetitions and plans were one way in which the social landscape was constructed and reconstructed. In this region in this period, neither were settlements sedentary nor the landscape a fixed entity.[74] Too many enclosures were abandoned or altered for them to serve as the equivalent of tells in the Balkans and Greece.

In a sense, the range of evidence from all these open sites is disappointing, in that there are few obvious signs of elaborate depositions, rituals or burials. But this is to miss the significance of gatherings in their own right. As people moved through annual cycles of mobility, so both the dead and perhaps valued items of material culture may have been extensively circulated with them. On the Amendola plateau, the excavations at Passo di Corvo produced the remains of a dozen or more people from compound ditches, and the less extensive excavations at the smaller circuits of Fonteviva, the probable predecessors to the adjacent and larger layout of Posta d'Innanzi, also found the remains of a minimum of three people. These seem to have been incomplete skeletons, with crania and major limb bones most prominent.[75] So far, there have been no discoveries of separate burial grounds associated with these enclosures. Were selected remains of the dead carried by the living on their circuits? Pots might have been made on the spot for specific gatherings. Neither they nor food remains were prominent features of ditch fills, in the manner seen in many later enclosures in north-west Europe.

The dead were present in other contexts as well as open sites. Virtually throughout the central and west Mediterranean basin, modest numbers are found in inland and upland caves and rockshelters, some of which had been in use in earlier times. This was not a new practice. There were both complete burials and partial remains, of both children and adults. Examples range from infant burials in the Grotta Pacelli in Bari province, through Arene Candide in Liguria, to La Cueva de la Dehesilla in southern Spain and the Gruta do Caldeirão in the Alentejo of Portugal. In Provence, there were separate burials of two children and a woman, and also other scattered human bones at Unang, Vaucluse. The deposits were somewhat disturbed, but not all the isolated human bone need have come from disturbed burials. At least fifteen people were represented in the depositions of the Baume Bourbon, Gard, in Languedoc. At Fontbrégoua, in the late Cardial horizon, around or just after 5000 BC, there were three deposits of human bone. In one, seven people were represented mainly by skulls, and in another the remains of six people comprised only postcranial bones; both adults and children were present. The human deposits had had very similar treatment to contemporary dumps of animal bone, having been broken and probably cooked. The skulls had scalping cuts. These details have suggested the practice of 'cannibalisme alimentaire'.[76]

Grotta Continenza in the Fucino basin inland in Abruzzo had the remains of nearly thirty people in its Impressed Ware levels, represented by complete and incomplete skeletons and by cremated remains, and by children as well as adults. In the uppermost Neolithic deposit the burnt bones of a woman were heaped over four pots. Larger numbers are not necessarily to be found at bigger and more low-lying caves and rockshelters. The rather larger Grotta dei Piccioni in lowland Abruzzo, for example, has so far produced only one

8.9 Painted scene, with human and animal figures and abstract motifs, within the Grotta di Porto Badisco. Photo: Graziosi.

child burial from its lowest level VI, while Grotta Sant' Angelo had the very partial, cremated remains of children and young adults in some of its several deliberately backfilled pits.[77]

Some of the bigger caves close to major zones of settlement did have large numbers of burials or elaborate deposits. The Grotta Scaloria, for example, on the southern edge of the Gargano limestone upland to the north-east of the Tavoliere, had many.[78] The cave forms a large complex, probably connected with the immediately adjacent Grotta di Occhiopinto, though that was probably not used till later periods. A conservative estimate is of a minimum of thirty to forty people from the upper part of the Grotta Scaloria. Some of these may have been incomplete and there may have been some removal or circulation of bone. In the lower part of the cave there was only one burial, but many deposits of painted pots beside the stalacmites and stalactites of the wet inner part, where there was an active spring. How did the rites here relate to life on the Tavoliere?

Further south still, the Grotta di Porto Badisco lies close to the sea on the east side of the heel of the peninsula (Torre Sabea is on the west side).[79] This was a complex of long narrow passages running hundreds of metres. There were occupation deposits at the eastern entrance, partially cutting into earlier, Palaeolithic layers. Some of the passages were artificially partitioned, and pots had been placed to catch the water dripping from stalactites. Many parts of the walls were decorated with abstract motifs, human and animal figures, and hand-prints, painted in red ochre or brown bat guano. Where humans and animals occur together, the human figures seem to be male and carry bows bent to the ready. These paintings are not certainly dated, but at least some are thought to belong to this period (some could precede it), and others may have been added subsequently. It is plausibly suggested that these may be in part to do with rites of initiation. No human remains were certainly deposited in the Grotta di Porto Badisco before the end of the Neolithic and the beginning of the Copper Age, but these are recorded in this horizon from two other caves nearby, Grotta Cosma and Grotta dei Diavoli, the former also with some wall paintings and the latter without any accompanying evidence for occupation. A complex circuit of sacred and mundane movement can be envisaged in this area, guided not only by the routines of herding and hunting, but by the demands of socialisation and the needs of the dead and the spirits.

CHAPTER 9

THE HEART OF THE COUNTRY: THE CENTRAL AND WEST MEDITERRANEAN, *c.* 5000–2500 BC

Death in the cold, endings in the sun

In the later fourth millennium BC, a man was caught out in the cold on the Hauslabjoch near the Tisenjoch pass in the Tyrolean Alps between Italy and Austria. This is about 3200 m above sea level, close to the main ridge of the Alps running from east to west. It is probable that the season was autumn. The man was unable to continue down or over the mountain, either because he was exhausted, or perhaps injured, or on account of weather conditions. He lay down to sleep, and despite his good clothing and equipment, never woke up.

Since his discovery in 1991, the 'Iceman' has become famous, through the combination of his sheer antiquity, and the remarkable preservation of his body and clothing.[1] Here was a man well clothed and well equipped for the high mountains. Over leather leggings and loincloth held by a belt which doubled as a pouch, he wore a deer skin coat, perhaps sleeveless, and an outer cape made of woven grasses or reeds. On his feet were calf-skin shoes with an inner filling of grass, with knotted grass strings over the instep and heel to hold the filling in place. On his head was a domed or conical cap, sewn together from different pieces of fur, and held under the chin by flaps or straps knotted together. The man had with him a wide range of portable equipment. He had an unfinished bow made of yew, a framed and closable quiver with fourteen broken or unusable arrows, a curved bone tool, spare bone points, and what seem to be spare materials for bow strings of sinew and tree bast. He also had an axe with a yew haft and a flanged copper blade; a small flint knife mounted in a wooden handle and held in a string sheath; and a retouching tool made from an antler tip lodged in a wooden handle. In his belt pouch he had a scraper, flake and awl of flint, and material that was probably a fungus usable as tinder for lighting fires. In addition he had two sewn birch-bark containers, one probably used for carrying embers of fire, and a backpack made of an outer hazel frame, larch cross-boards, and skins.

This lonely demise also illustrates other themes relevant to the wider world of the Mediterranean basin in the latter part of the Neolithic period. Different occupations and different circumstances leading to the iceman's death can be suggested. The man might have been a trader, a hunter or a shaman; one scenario has him as a refugee from an attack on a lowland settlement (he had cracked ribs perhaps incompletely healed at the time of death). Much research is still to be completed, but I prefer the simpler explanations for this individual. This was probably a shepherd, equipped for high pastures or grazings, who was making a hunting bow as he herded his flock; small pieces of ibex bone were found near the body, a species which would have been encountered in the mountains. If the man was a

9.1 Reconstruction of the man in the ice. After Thews.

shepherd, it is very interesting that he had a copper axe, since this helps to demystify this technology. The production, circulation and possession of copper artefacts have often been associated with a process of social differentiation. On this line of argument, the Iceman should have been someone special, engaged in unusual activity or driven by unusual circumstances. The other details of the find allow the argument to be reversed. The circumstances of movement were regular and expected (though of course not the outcome); copper could be acquired, perhaps routinely, by someone in this sort of geographically peripheral milieu.

Here then was a knowledgeable individual, carrying out routine movement high into the mountains. Such individual traverses may have been anchored on a stabler pattern of settlement in the lowlands below, on either side of the Alps, in the upper Adige valley on the Italian side (the Vinschgau),[2] or in the Ötztal and upper Inn valley on the Austrian side. In fact, in neither upper valley are there abundant signs of contemporary occupation, and the Iceman thus neatly illustrates the continuing theme of mobility which has been stressed throughout this book. I presume that the identity of the Iceman would have been recognisable to contemporaries, since his appearance, clothing and equipment were distinctive; in addition to characteristics and features already described, his body carried small linear tattoos, he wore two pieces of birch fungus on strips of fur on his left wrist, and there was a tassel of fur strips with a small perforated marble disc. In other ways his allegiances may have been more ambiguous. In the central and west Mediterranean as a whole, and indeed north of the Alps at this time, a series of rather regionalised cultural groupings can be defined. The copper axe of the Iceman can be paralleled in the Remedello cemetery in the Po valley south of Brescia, some 150 km to the south of the upper Adige valley. That cemetery with its single graves and copper artefacts has been taken as typical of the whole of northern Italy at this time, but it is clear that there were in fact other traditions of burial in this horizon. The Civate group along the Lombardy Alpine edge, closer to the upper Adige valley, was characterised by collective burials.[3] As settlement extended in northern Italy from the fifth millennium BC onwards, identities may have become more regionalised, but would perhaps have remained fluid and liable to change. An individual like a mountain shepherd could have seen himself as belonging to and in contact with several different worlds. Though popularly famous for his lonely death, the Iceman best illustrates the routine flux of life in the later Neolithic.

There were other circumstances and other endings in the central and west Mediterranean basin in this period. The example of the Maltese islands shows what could happen in circumstances of relative isolation. Malta and Gozo were colonised around the end of the sixth millennium BC, presumably from Sicily or southern Italy.[4] For some 1500 years we know only of small occupations, for example in the pre-temple levels at Skorba in the northerly part of Malta island, and from about 4000 BC of small rock-cut tombs used for collective burial, for example at Zebbug, Xemxija and the Brochtorff Circle. Around 3500 BC, in the Ggantija phase, and then on in the Tarxien phase from about 3000 BC, a series of remarkable constructions were made, in clusters spaced across both islands. These were stone-built temples, in the conventional terminology, or monumental shrines, accompanied in two instances by underground mausolea or shrines.[5]

The shrines were built to common principles, though the details often differed. They were basically symmetrical constructions, fronted by a concave, high, stone façade, from which a more or less narrow entrance led into a series of lobed inner spaces on either side of the axial line; some had a terminal zone. This created four-, five- and six-lobed interiors. These were further provided with built internal divisions, 'altars' and occasionally large statuary. In the south-east of Malta, one cluster consists of shrines at Tarxien, shrines at Kordin and the underground 'hypogeum' at Hal Saflieni. The constructions were cumulative. At Kordin there were three buildings. At Tarxien, there were at least four constructions, perhaps the most elaborate complex in the islands. From west to east, there were a five-lobed shrine, a six-lobed shrine, a four-lobed version, and a less usual rectangular arrangement which may have been as much an ordered space as a three-dimensional construction. The central six-lobed building may in fact have been built last of the three certain shrines here. It did not so much replace or supplant the others, though it jostles their edges, as adds to them, each new construction adding to the mounting religiosity of the chosen place by incorporating its predecessors. The Hal Saflieni hypogeum was created from the limestone rock underground, incorporating some 70 different compartments and areas on 11 different levels. Doorways mimic the treatment of above-ground construc-

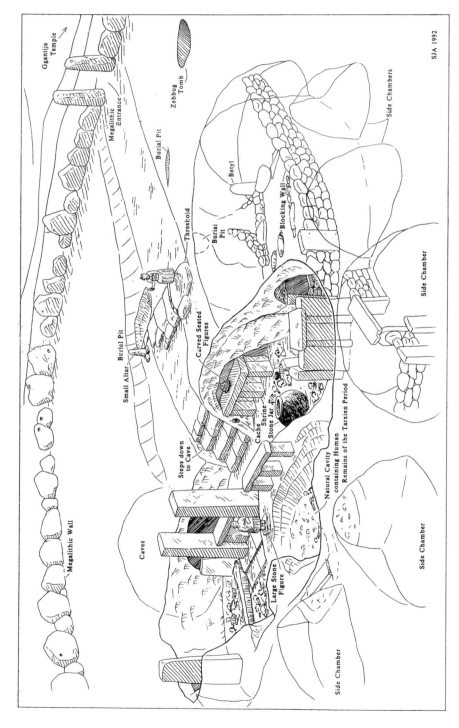

Ggantija Temple

Megalithic Entrance

Burial Pit

Zebbug Tomb

Threshold

Betyl

Blocking Wall

Burial Pit

Small Altar   Burial Pit

Carved Seated Figures

Side Chambers

Cache
Shrine
Stone Jar

Steps down to Cave

Natural Cavity containing Human Remains of the Tarxien Period

Side Chamber

Megalithic Wall

Caves

Large Stone Figure

Side Chamber

Side Chamber

Side Chamber

SJA 1992

9.2 Reconstruction and interpretation of the Brochtorff Circle. Drawing: Malone and Stoddart.

9.3 Cell in the monumental shrine or temple at Mnajdra South. Photo: Trump.

tions. The compartments held thousands of burials, though little is known in detail of their arrangement because of disturbance early this century. Another important example is the cluster more or less in the middle of Gozo. Next to the double shrine at Ggantija (probably two successive structures), an underground complex developed at the Brochtorff Circle. A megalithic circle enclosed a group of caverns close to the surface. These had been used for collective burial before the 'temple' phase, and in the Tarxien phase were further elaborated by the construction of a megalithic threshold and small shrines formed by slabs and uprights of limestone, one placed in front of a large pit used for collective burials. There were other megalithic settings nearby, as at Vella's Farm, and material cleared out from the Ggantija shrines was placed in caves such as North Cave and Ghar ta Ghejzu. There were other significant clusters on Malta, including in the south at Mnajdra/Hagar Qim and in the north at Skorba/Mgarr. For the shrine-building phase, very little occupation has been recorded. Rescue excavations and survey on Gozo suggest that more can be found, but that the major constructions did not belong to the sphere of domestic existence.[6]

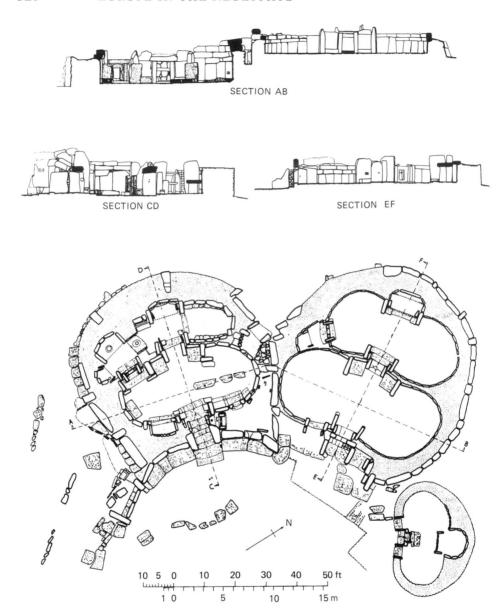

SECTION AB

SECTION CD

SECTION EF

N

10 5 0   10   20   30   40   50 ft

1 0   5   10   15 m

9.4 Plan and sections of the shrines at Mnajdra. After Evans.

After 2500 BC, constructions were largely discontinued, though the easterly building at Tarxien may date to this period, and the area of the shrines was still frequented, as again at Tarxien itself, or even used for burials, as at the Brochtorff Circle. How are these shrines and their endings to be interpreted? In the first place, their construction and use seem to mark that increasing attachment to place which can be traced in other areas of Europe through the various regional sequences, albeit here in extreme form, since Gozo is only 14 km long and Malta 28 km. Various other constructions connected with ritual and burial, gatherings and display, can be found in southern and central Italy, southern France, and around much of the perimeter of Iberia, notably in south-east Spain and southern Portugal. Closer to the area of the Iceman in northern Italy, there were varied styles of burial, and scattered stone stelae or carved standing stones.[7] In southern and central Italy the earlier tradition continued of using caves for ritual, deposition and burial hidden from normal gaze underground, into the fourth and even the third millennium BC.[8]

The particular form of the Maltese constructions is often explained as the result of geographical isolation. Before the 'temple' period, pottery styles on the islands were similar to those on Sicily and in southern Italy, and there was movement into the islands of obsidian and stone axes. Such external contacts seem to have waned after about 3500 BC. There is no obvious external reason why this should have been so, and anyway from about the same date, the start of the Copper Age in conventional terminology on the mainland, older systems of inter-regional exchange also disappeared. In the earlier third millennium BC there were various different traditions of burial and pottery manufacture in adjacent regions in the Po valley, while in south-east Spain there were sharp regional contrasts in the presence, density and style of burial monuments and other constructions. The famous complex at Los Millares, in lowland Almería, for example, stands out in the region as a whole.[9] The concentration there of tombs and walled enclosures is not an accident of differential survival, but a genuine regional difference. The Maltese phenomenon cannot therefore be the result entirely of isolation.

In the island setting, cult and religious fervour attained great intensity. There is a play between the concealment of death underground and the celebration of rites above ground, partially concealed in the shrines and perhaps not accessible to all of an audience simultaneously. The statuary in some of the shrines suggests corpulent deities.[10] Perhaps spirits of fertility were opposed, conceptually, to the agents of death. This situation, whatever its content, has often been explained in both sociological and environmental terms, and this is quite typical of explanations given of parallel phenomena in the central and west Mediterranean basin at this time. The frequency and intensity of shrine construction are seen as the result of competition between families or lineages (or some other social grouping), and the existence of competition is explained by reference to the aridity and poor soils of the islands. Rather similar explanations are given for the Millaran phenomenon in south-east Spain.[11] I will discuss the wider context much more fully below. Two kinds of stress model have been proposed for the Maltese case. In the first, some 1500 years of occupation led to environmental crisis and social competition, which was managed and mediated through ritual for another thousand years before eventual collapse. In the second, shrine building reflected a long period of stability, which was eventally replaced by a period of stress during which traditional authority was subverted. Contrary to the first model, the shrines and other constructions can rather be seen as the expression of successful adaptation to the island setting; religious fervour in this form was sustainable. Its explanation may partly lie in the field of social relations, but perhaps largely in the realms of the spirit. If the islands were relatively isolated, a particular way of envisaging the universe may have taken particular hold there. Here too, as elsewhere and at other times in Neolithic Europe, a timeless world was created, framed by a sense of place and of beginnings, maintained by repetition and tradition, and nurtured by strong belief in spirits and moral values. The end of the affair, finally, does not have to be explained by purely insular events or developments (though they need not be excluded), but may have owed much to a changing wider world beyond.

The heart of the country

When Robert Louis Stevenson goaded poor Modestine, his hired donkey, across the Cévennes in 1878, it only took him a few late September days to pass southwards from near Le Puy in Haute Loire, across 'the heart of the country', to Saint-Jean-du-Gard, within reach of lowland Languedoc west of the Rhône. The process by which Neolithic communities came to fill their landscapes was a much longer one, still in progress at the end of the period covered here.

The Cévennes are part of the crystalline geology of the southern end of the Massif Central. There is little sign of Neolithic penetration into them. The focus of Neolithic settlement extended from the coast and the lowland plains, to the limestone garrigues and the higher Grands Causses, also limestone. The initial Neolithic presence, discussed in the last chapter, was scattered. With the appearance of the Chasseen culture in the earlier fifth millennium BC, more sites including open ones not in caves or rockshelters appeared.[12] There were sites on the coast and on the coastal plain. There were abundant sites in the upper Garonne valley. Though some are known, far fewer sites have been found on the garrigues, for example near Montpellier. There were many cave occupations in the Grands Causses. In the Copper Age, beginning in the mid to later fourth millennium BC, both the garrigues and the Grands Causses were more prominent zones of use.[13] Numerous *dolmens*, perhaps as many as a thousand, were built in these areas: varied though simple arrangements of megalithic cist, chamber and cairn. Conversely there was far less visible settlement in the upper Garonne. Open settlements became more visible on the garrigues, for example in the Ferrières group, and in the succeeding Fontbouisse group, which appears from the radiocarbon evidence to be coeval with the Bell Beaker culture, there was a wide range of enclosed sites on the garrigues. These encompass larger and smaller walled enclosures, with circular cells built into the walls and with long buildings within, such as Lébous, Cambous and Boussargues, and other more irregular enclosures more recently discovered, such as Le Grand Devois de Figaret in Hérault.[14]

Sites like Lébous and Boussargues have been seen as defensive. As such they might be used to evoke a much more populous and settled population, whose competing communities were increasingly coming into conflict with each other. As elsewhere in Neolithic Europe, some of the dead in the collective burial deposits in caves and built tombs have injuries and wounds, and the alleged case of the 'couche de guerre' in the upper deposit of the rock-cut tomb at Roaix, Vaucluse, just across the Rhône, seems to add force to this kind of interpretation. Here there were over one hundred skulls, and at least fifty complete skeletons, laid stretched out, one on top of the other (probably of Fontbouisse date). Several had flint arrowheads lodged in them.[15]

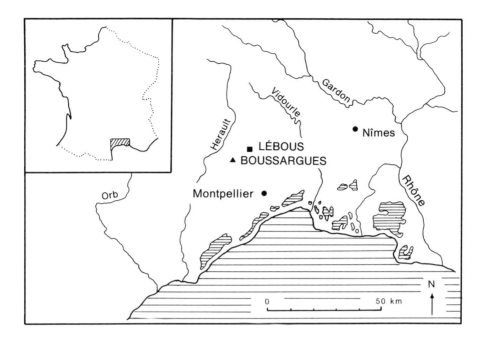

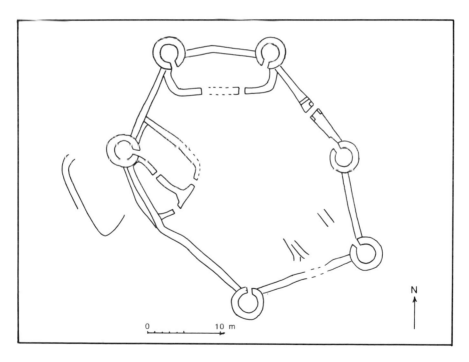

9.5 Setting and plan of the enclosure at Boussargues. After Colomer *et al.*

Another view is possible. The walls of Lébous and other related sites hardly look as though they were originally built to any great height. The cells built into them may be individual shelters rather than the bastions of 'forts' or 'fortlets'; as so often, much depends on our choice of descriptive language. The buildings inside, as studied in detail at La Conquette and Boussargues, were used in formalised, repetitive ways, with a hearth at one end and pots down the sides.[16] But there is no certain evidence for prolonged or permanent occupation. The settlement pattern may still have been based on mobility, even though the population was probably rather more numerous by the end of the period than at earlier stages. As for Roaix, there may be other explanations. Men, women and children were buried together, some probably in shrouds. Some had been partially cremated after deposition. These look like ordered mortuary rites, perhaps resulting in successive or cumulative deposits. And there were even larger collective deposits elsewhere in the region, for example of over 300 people in the cave at Pas-de-Julié, Gard, in the Grands Causses.[17]

A similar picture of gradual expansion can be traced in many other areas. The general pattern is much the same in Provence as in Languedoc, with a surge in known site numbers, including open ones, in the Chasseen period, though we do not know so far of enclosed late Copper Age sites equivalent to Lébous and others.[18] In northern Italy, as discussed in the last chapter, there was early coastal Impressed Ware settlement, for example in Liguria, and gradual expansion too up the east side of the Apennines. Neolithic groups like Vhò and Fiorano appeared in selected parts of the Po valley around the end of the sixth millennium and the beginning of the fifth millennium BC. In the fifth millennium BC into the earlier fourth millennium BC there were more numerous settlements, of the Square-Mouthed Pottery (*Vasi a Bocca Quadrata*, or VBQ) culture and then the Lagozza culture (related to developed Chasseen culture in southern France).[19] Here too it would be a mistake to think of every site on the map as a settled village or hamlet based on mixed agriculture. There are some larger aggregations, as at Pescale, Isolino or Lagozza. But at Molino Casarotto, Fimon, near Vicenza, there were small occupations, probably seasonal and successive, along the shore of a lake. People built wooden platforms on the lake edge, on which they lit fires. Their diet was still very varied, and included shellfish, freshwater turtle and pike, wild plants including water chestnuts, red deer and boar or pig, as well as sheep and cattle and wheat. In the Adige valley, closer to the later territory of the Iceman, the hilltop site of Rivoli was used in the VBQ phase as much for red deer hunting as for the herding of cattle and pig.[20] In the Late Neolithic and Copper Age of the third millennium BC, the settlement pattern may still have been based on mobility. Large aggregation sites seem to disappear from the Po valley. The Remedello and other groups are known more from burials than from occupations. There was penetration of the edge of the Alps, as seen in the burials of the Civate group. One marker of Copper Age presence are the stone stelae, some bearing representations of daggers similar to those at Remedello; another early context for stelae is the first phases of monuments XII and VI at Sion in the Swiss Valais. Stelae are found fringing the Po valley, including in southern Liguria. There were probably wooden versions in the Po valley itself. To the north, they occur sporadically, both at lower altitudes, as in the Vinschgau of the upper Adige valley, and high up. One example is the Ossimo-Borno plateau in the Lombardy Alpine fringe, at about 900 m above sea

9.6 Detail of wooden platform and hearth at Molino Casarotto. Photo: Barfield.

level; this has some seventeen stelae. Further west in the Piedmontese Alps, the rockshelter of Balm' Chanto in the Chisone valley was at 1450 m above sea level. It was used in the third millennium BC for hunting and herding; neither activity resulted in extensive clearance of the local woodland cover.[21] At the time of the Iceman's death, there would have been many other herders and hunters in high parts of the landscape.

In Spain and Portugal, patterns of settlement varied, often quite sharply, from region to region. In overall terms, it appears that here too there was a gradual increase in the numbers of sites. Beginning perhaps in the early fourth millennium BC (see below), a great range of burial cists and tombs was built. The overall distribution of megalithic constructions shows a fringe around most of the circumference of Iberia, with the exception of parts of Catalonia in north-east Spain where pit-graves were the norm. There appears to have been little penetration of the inland mesetas and sierras, either for occupation or for the placing of monuments, though some presence on the edge of the mesetas can probably be documented from the fourth millennium BC onwards.[22] By the earlier to mid third millennium BC in southern Portugal, roughly from the Tagus basin southwards, there are numerous

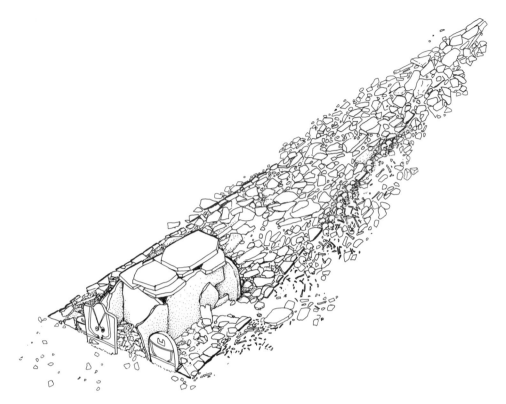

9.7 Reconstruction of the second phase of monument MVI at Sion, in the upper
Rhône valley. Note the decorated façade stones, and the long bones and skulls
discarded along the side of the monument. After Bocksberger.

sites, including both various kinds of tombs, open sites, and a series of small but elabo-
rately walled enclosures such as Vila Nova de São Pedro and Zambujal. These too have
been seen as defensive centres, like the slightly later Fontbouisse examples of southern
France. I discuss alternative interpretations below.[23] There are scattered clusters of settlement and monuments in southern Spain. The most notable, and best studied, area is south-
east Spain.[24] This is today the most arid part of the peninsula. From the fifth millennium BC
onwards, there appear to have been more sites in the landscape than in the first millennium
of Neolithic occupation, for example in Granada and Murcia, including in inland basins. In
the Copper Age of the later fourth to the earlier/mid third millennium BC, parts of the
today very arid landscape of Almería were occupied, notably in the Andarax valley at Los
Millares. Here there were some eighty tombs, walled enclosures and several smaller, walled
'fortlets'. There are related sites in north-east Almería, southern Murcia and eastern
Granada, but there is no set or repeating pattern. I discuss the significance of this development below, in relation to the vexed question of the Neolithic/Copper Age climate.

There are more sites too in the smaller islands of the central-west Mediterranean, for
example on the Balearic islands, or in various different regions of Corsica by the third millennium BC.[25]

The only region where settlement cannot be shown to have expanded is the Tavoliere in south-east Italy. By the Copper Age, though there are some rock-cut and other tombs in the region, there is very little evidence of settlement on the Tavoliere plain, so prominent in the last chapter, but considered by most specialists to have been deserted by the later Neolithic and Copper Age.[26] If true, this is an odd development, since Neolithic and Copper Age occupations, burials, and tombs of various kinds are known from central Italy on both sides of the Apennines, and there are signs of Copper Age activity in the interior and uplands of the south-east. In the region as a whole there may be a gradual process of expansion. There were aggregation sites like Ripoli, in Abruzzo, with many pits and burials in elongated ditch-like features, and later Conelle, in Marche, set on a promontory cut off by a ditch, which were rather different from the occupations of the first Neolithic generations discussed in the previous chapter. Small complexes of this kind extend in the Copper Age Gaudo phase into southern Campania, as around Buccino and Tufariello, where there are collective burials in rock-cut tombs and a small settlement.[27] If parts of south-east Italy were deserted at this date, the climate can be invoked as one agent, and soil degradation as another. The issue is discussed below. Alternatively, this too may have been a region marked by continued mobility. Even in the heyday of the ditched enclosures of the Tavoliere, few if any open sites are known, though they have been recorded from the coast. Perhaps the major development was the end of the tradition of places chosen for gatherings and marked by the digging of enclosures, rather than complete abandonment.

Subsistence and settlements: slow change?

Conventional models and an alternative

How did people make a living in these settings and in what sense were landscapes filled? How can sites like Los Millares and Vila Nova de São Pedro be interpreted? There is abundant evidence for the widespread adoption of cereal agriculture as well as animal husbandry. Such evidence has been used to support a network of hypotheses. One common view is that a sedentary existence based on mixed farming became the norm, and even that overuse of fragile soils in arid locations like the Tavoliere or the Maltese islands led to either abandonment or 'stress' and eventual 'collapse'.[28] Another view is that there was gradual intensification and specialisation of animal husbandry, a process that was to produce a Mediterranean version of the 'secondary products revolution' after 2500 BC, for example in Iberia.[29] In the south-east of Spain, the assumption is often made that the climate was as arid in the Copper Age of the earlier third millennium BC as it is today. Since there was an intake of lowland south-east Spain, and since communities are assumed to have practised mixed agriculture and led a sedentary existence, the argument runs that they must have developed techniques of water control, diversion and storage. Such circumstances would have demanded a pooling of labour and effort, reduced the opportunities for fission or independence, and made it relatively easy for self-appointed 'elites' to dominate local society. The walled enclosures, 'forts' and tombs, some with abundant and even exotic contents, are then read as the expression of either ranked or stratified society.[30] While south-east Spain represents the extreme case in the region, other evidence from southern France, and northern, central and southern Italy, can be taken to suggest the same kind of developing, differentiating, competitive society by the third millennium BC.

I will evoke a different kind of world, however, characterised by varied patterns of subsistence and settlement, with animal husbandry important, continued mobility, and little permanent difference between communities. There is no certain evidence yet for either extreme aridity or environmental stress. There were few long-term permanent settlements, though certain chosen places were used for gatherings and rituals – aggregation points – often in the earlier stages of the exploitation of a particular landscape. Tombs and burials also served to attach people to place, though I will discuss these separately below.

Subsistence: staples and use

The staples of subsistence are not in dispute, and there is not space to rehearse the details area by area. In upland situations, bone remains from caves and rockshelters still show the hunting of game, but often also the herding of stock, usually sheep and goats, but also some cattle and pigs. In southern Languedoc, for example, the later levels of sites like the Grotte de Gazel and the Abri Jean Cros show such a shift, and even at the higher-lying Dourgne rockshelter sheep and goats came largely to replace wild game. In Chasseen levels in the Grotte de l'Eglise in the upper Verdon valley in inland Provence, people both hunted rabbit, boar, red deer and ibex (the latter presumably far into the hills), and herded cattle and sheep. Arene Candide in Liguria was used in its Middle Neolithic levels as a base for seasonal herding as well as hunting, and there are plenty of examples from either side of the Apennines in central Italy.[31] It is thought likely that the Iceman was herding sheep. He also carried scraps of ibex bone and was preparing for hunting.[32]

In some more lowland occupations a broad spectrum of resources was also used. Molino Casarotto has already been cited, from the VBQ phase of Neolithic expansion across the Po valley as a whole. Large Chasseen aggregation sites in the upper Garonne valley like Villeneuve-Tolosane and Saint-Michel-du-Touch had very little game, in strong contrast to earlier generations of southern French occupations. Cattle were the most dominant animal. Bone hooks at Saint-Michel-du-Touch suggest river fishing, and we know little about cereal cultivation. As will be seen below, these were unusual sites. There were many features apparently connected with cooking. The selection of food for special gatherings may not characterise the diet through the year. Disappointingly few remains have come from sites like Boussargues: in that one case, scraps of sheep or goat bone and a few cereal grains.[33] In south-east Spain, there are still too few well-studied assemblages, but the pattern from what has been recovered at sites like Los Millares, its near neighbour Terrera Ventura, or Cerro de la Virgen, inland in the Orce valley, a tributary of the upper Guadalquivir basin in eastern Granada, is of many sheep and goats, and varying numbers of cattle and pigs. But in Copper Age levels at Terrera Ventura and Cerro de la Virgen, there were still reasonable numbers of game, fluctuating between 20 and 30 per cent of the assemblages. These are crude figures, but the continued diversity is important.[34] Some horse bones are present, but it is likely that horse was not domesti-

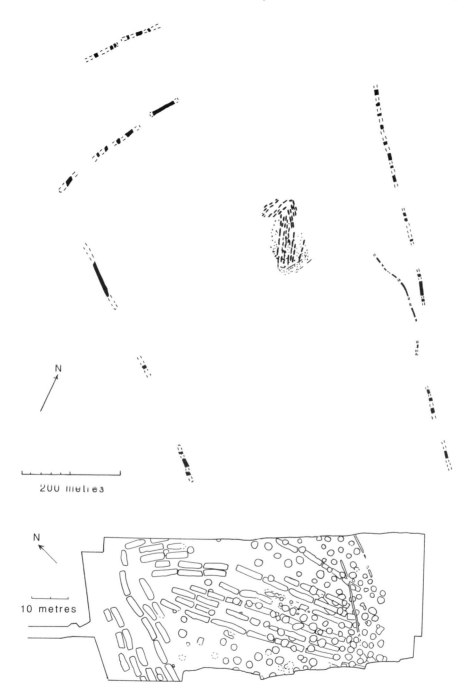

N

200 metres

N

10 metres

9.8 Chasseen enclosure at Villeneuve–Tolosane. Top: overall plan of ditches and palisade, but without the many settings of heated stones; below: circular and elongated settings of heated stones in area SXII. After Vaquer.

cated in the region until the Bell Beaker horizon or subsequently.[35] The picture is of a long continuity.

The clothes and equipment of the Iceman had trapped some cereal fragments from an area of lowland settlement. It is common to find cereal remains on sites and occupations after 5000 BC. In some cases, cereals had presumably been transported as food, for example to the Balm' Chanto at considerable altitude in the Chisone valley in the Piedmontese Alps.[36] Cereals have been documented in a wide range of other situations, from Chasseen sites in Provence, to Lagozza in northern Italy, and again Copper Age sites in south-east Spain. Recovery of this evidence has often left much to be desired, but at Lagozza we know of wheat, barley, lentils and flax.[37] We know too little of other plant use, apart from isolated examples like the water chestnuts from Molino Casarotto, and some finds of acorns in south-east Spain; grinding equipment from Late Neolithic and Copper Age sites in Corsica, which are more numerous than in earlier periods, could have been for acorn rather than cereal processing.[38] There is one suggestion of the introduction of those later typically Mediterranean staples, the domesticated olive and vine, from a late Copper Age or Early Bronze Age horizon at Tufariello in southern Campania, but the details of the context have not yet been published, and the claim is usually treated with suspicion.[39] The picture is again of a long continuity.

Such evidence has often been used to support a model of sedentary existence based on mixed farming. This is uncertain. We know very little about the scale of either animal husbandry or cereal cultivation: recurrent problems in the study of Neolithic Europe. One relevant debate concerns the environmental history of the garrigues of southern France. Some have proposed that the state of vegetational cover and soils was similar in prehistory to that of today; the implication is of a considerable impact on a fragile environment (whether by or for grazing or for cultivation, or both). Others maintain that there is evidence for clearance and change in later periods. The charcoals from a site like Boussargues show a wide range of tree and shrub species, including deciduous oak. Evergreen oak was also present, and the wider trend in the central and west Mediterranean is for the expansion of evergreen oak in later prehistory, perhaps reflecting the effects of clearance.[40] At Los Millares, the charcoals have been taken to suggest that scrub of olive, pistachio, terebinth, cistus and other species was already widespread, but that deciduous oak still fringed the rivers; in late levels, in the Bell Beaker horizon, the quantity of oak declined, the result, so it is claimed, of increasing aridity.[41] One difficulty is that charcoals may reflect human selection rather than a representative picture of contemporary vegetation. By contrast, pollen analysis from the south-west coast near Huelva – admittedly from an area today slightly less arid than lowland Almería – shows open oak woodland in the period from 4000–2500 BC.[42]

The Huelva pollen evidence has been used to suggest the management of oak woodland for grazing, as what was later known as a *dehesa*. Peaks at one stage of *Vitis* pollen could suggest protection of wild vine for its fruit, and at another stage a peak of oak and weed pollen could suggest the clearance of understorey to enhance grazing. This kind of land-use fits well with a more general suggestion of extensive woodland exploitation in the Neolithic Mediterranean.[43]

The issue of aridity is important. Broad climatic projections, now about a generation old, suggested little shift in climatic patterns over the last 5000 years. This is at odds now with the evidence from further north around the Alps, where there are fluctuations in lake levels, and from further east in the Levant, where there may indeed be signs of greater aridity from the fourth millennium BC onwards.[44] We still lack specific or sensitive data for south-east Spain, the Maltese islands and south-east Italy themselves. A buried soil from Los Millares was characterised as a xerorendsina, that is a thin soil formed in dry conditions, but much more information should be demanded about its context, formation and variation.[45] The assumption of later Neolithic and Copper Age aridity in southern zones is still unsupported. The chain of argument becomes circular. Aridity determines the nature of subsistence and the character of settlement, which can only be explained in the conceived form by reference to aridity.[46] Although studied as support for the aridity hypothesis, site locations in fact show considerable diversity and a weak link with water to the exclusion of other variables or to a greater extent than would normally be expected. Because of the aridity hypothesis, water control and diversion are predicted. The nineteenth-century investigations at Los Millares found what is described as a small aquifer leading into Los Millares. There are some pits here and elsewhere which could reasonably be seen as water cisterns. But very little evidence has emerged for irrigation. A ditch at the foot of the Cerro de la Virgen site was quickly silted up, and its later replacement was much smaller. The primary deep ditch could even have been to divert floodwater from the site.[47] I discuss alternative interpretations of the character of Los Millares below. It is simpler, however, to suppose that the contemporary climate was benign enough to enable colonisation of the south-east Spanish lowlands. We do not have to suppose permanent occupation of sites like Los Millares. Their existence cannot be attributed to extreme aridity alone, since there were the related – though not identical – phenomena of Vila Nova de São Pedro, Zambujal and others in the central-southern part of Portugal, where the climate today is less arid than in Almería. And if communities in Malta, even further south, were under environmental stress, they managed to hang on for about a millennium. Again, the assumptions can be reversed; we can suppose that conditions were benign and stable enough to enable major constructions over forty or so generations of island life.

It is inadequate to advocate one model for such a region as this over such a long period. But I propose that the basic and recurrent elements of subsistence were animal husbandry and hunting, associated with continuing patterns of mobility and in large part with the extensive exploitation of woodland, combined with a limited scale of cereal cultivation in plots and gardens of varied duration and stability. In further support of this kind of model, it is important to examine the occupations and aggregations which have often been taken to suggest a more stable and more agrarian existence.

Settlement: occupations and aggregations

I have already indicated something of the range of occupations in this period, from caves and rockshelters and open sites to ditched and walled enclosures. There is little evidence for structures within caves and rockshelters, other than those connected with burials or special depositions (discussed below). We know all too little about the structure of open sites, often represented in the archaeological record by combinations of spreads of artefacts, pits, and post or stake holes. There are very few known houses or other structures from this period. One exception are the elongated walled buildings within stone enclosures at the very end of the sequence, on the garrigues of southern Languedoc, such as Lébous and Boussargues. I have already suggested that these may not have been permanent habitations. Presumably there were roofed shelters elsewhere, but the evidence is hard to pin down. One hard-won recent discovery comes from Gozo in the Maltese islands, where at the Ghajnsielem Road site an oval hollow some 8 by 5 m was discovered, belonging to the 'temple' period.[48] This had a central mudbrick pillar, presumably for a roof, and three successive floors of crushed limestone.

In other contexts, many pits were large and often irregular. These are often dubbed 'fonds de cabane' or 'capanne', but it is doubtful whether many were actually substitutes for built structures, rather than work areas, hearths, or for disposal. One interesting concentration of such features is at Ripoli, Abruzzo, in east-central Italy. A little inland and on a terrace above the Vibrata river, there were over 100 such pits.[49] These were often irregular in plan and varied in depth, and frequently the larger ones seem to be formed of intersecting smaller ones. They contained varying amounts of pottery, including painted trichrome wares, animal bone and other material, and occasional human bone. Also on the site was a straight stretch of eleven shorter and longer ditch-like segments. These were deep and steep-sided, but narrow, and they formed no barrier in relation to the topography of the site. They did contain tens of burials.

Ripoli is the kind of site I have in mind when I have referred to 'aggregation' sites or points: larger than usual concentrations of features, used for a range of activities including the deposition of significant artefacts (in this case, painted pottery), the consumption of food, and the burial of the dead or the handling of ancestral remains. As elsewhere in Europe, the elusiveness of houses is significant. Too much research has been done to believe that this is just the unhappy result of poor survival. Settlement still involved movement and mobility, impermanence and fluidity. There is one other important implication of this view. Even when suitable data have been collected at a regional scale, we cannot easily read off from maps of settlements the density of occupation at any one time. In the upper Garonne in the Chasseen period, for example, several sites of varying size are known along the upper Garonne and neighbouring valleys.[50] I discuss Villeneuve-Tolosane and Saint-Michel-du-Touch in more detail below. But the Chasseen period lasted here for hundreds of years, perhaps longer,[51] and if individual sites were short-lived or only seasonally occupied, the density of settlement at any one time may still have been rather low. There may be some exceptions to this kind of situation. On the garrigue north of Montpellier in Languedoc, some nine Fontbouisse sites have been recorded in the Viols-le-Fort region, over an area about 8 by 4 km, and seemingly grouped around a small basin of good soils. These include Cambous and Boussargues. There is no guarantee that these were all contemporary, and it is likely that most of these sites were seasonally occupied. But the shorter chronology of the Fontbouisse phase begins to make it possible to get closer to estimates of site density.[52]

Places

I therefore interpret the settlement record of the central and west Mediterranean in this period, in generalising terms, in the same sort of way as that of other parts of Europe. As in many other parts of Europe, the process of settling down was long and slow. If people did not immediately adopt sedentary existence, they were gradually bound into a network of routines and places. In south-east Italy, that process had already begun in the sixth millennium BC with the creation and endless re-inscribing of ditched enclosures. Routines of coming and going would have been important elsewhere, in a variety of settings, though the most visible component are the caves and rockshelters. Their use, significantly and unsurprisingly, continued into the fifth millennium BC and later; in some areas it may even have intensified.[53] Perhaps artificially, I discuss these separately below, along with graves and tombs. Here I describe two further examples of aggregation points, which illustrate the continuing process of attachment to place, in the context of a still fluid pattern of settlement.

The upper Garonne valley: Villeneuve-Tolosane and Saint-Michel-du-Touch

The Impressed Ware or Cardial presence in the region was slight, and the much more numerous Chasseen sites of the region, from about the mid fifth millennium BC onwards, mark a significant infilling. One model has been of a big increase in cereal agriculture on good valley soils, supporting and encouraging a growing population.[54] I have already suggested an alternative model of considerable mobility, linked to animal husbandry – here of cattle – and limited cultivation in short-term plots. It is difficult to estimate the size of many of the upper Garonne sites, since they have often been investigated in rescue conditions. Many appear to be quite small. Some have features like pits and hollows filled with stones. At Villeneuve-Tolosane, a very early feature was a deep pit containing many land snails.

Three larger sites stand out. Saint-Geniès, Tarn-et-Garonne, was unfortunately much disturbed. Saint-Michel-du-Touch, Toulouse, was at the junction of the Garonne and the Touch. On the low triangular promontory formed by the meeting of the rivers, there were Chasseen features over hundreds of metres. One set consisted of stretches of palisade and interrupted ditches, all seemingly laid out to define the promontory. Two major lengths of interrupted ditch have been recorded, but there are traces of another four at least. It may be a mistake to look for coherence of plan. Within the zone of interrupted ditches, there were stretches of stout palisade, and there were lighter fences or palisades over the area as a whole. The ditch segments appear to have been backfilled, and various artefacts and deposits had been placed in them. In addition, there were over 300 shallow pits or hollows filled with stones. The stones had been heated, and these can be seen as formalised cooking places (of a style seen earlier in Provence at Courthézon). Some of these stone features were very large. Human remains were not prominent, but two burials were found in a large pit over 7 by 4 m in extent.

La Terrasse, Villeneuve-Tolosane, was slightly higher up the valley, near the junction of the Garonne and the Ariège, but this time on the far side of the Garonne. Its investigation took place through a housing development, and unsurprisingly many details of a site covering hundreds of metres are not known. Stretches of ditch (whether continuous or not is unclear) define a very large roughly rectangular space, at least 300 by 400 m. On one side there is a curving length of palisade, within the ditch line, and at one end another stretch of ditch, roughly 90 m outside the main layout. This again may be a series of uncompleted projects, rather than a unitary plan. The ditches had a rather uniform fill. In the lower parts there was much artefactual material and little sign of prolonged erosion, while the upper parts appear to have been backfilled, again with much material and charcoal. Over a wider area still than the ditches, at least about 500 by 500 m, there were hundreds of variously shaped stone-filled hollows: 'structures à galets chauffés'. These appear to form clusters, some overlapping with stretches of ditch, but these may be only the product of the rescue conditions. One very deep pit, over 7.5 m, lay on the known edge of the site, and is considered to be a well. Near the centre of the known site there was an area (sector SX II) of both round and elongated stone-filled features. For the most part, the round and other features cut the elongated ones. The latter are up to 10 m long and 2–3 m wide. They are laid in lines, rather like fallen dominoes. In the area excavated, some sixty or more of these were uncovered, forming a curious, roughly triangular plan. Again the overall plan may be deceptive. They may have been laid in smaller units; short, parallel rows of three or four features each may have been set out in sequence. Human remains were scarce, as at Saint-Michel-du-Touch.

Like the excavator of Villeneuve-Tolosane, I do not believe that the stone structures represent 'fonds de cabane'. Both sites may represent repeated visits to chosen places, over very long periods of time. The sites were used for the definition of place, by the repeated and varying definition and redefinition of boundaries. People gathered here, presumably in numbers, and the heated stones and cattle bones suggest that feasting was on the agenda. The stone features could be seen both as formalising the routine of such gatherings and as a deliberately inscribed memory of such events. Since there were few human remains, these were presumably arenas for social interaction, from season to season or from year to year. The dead were set in other contexts, which I discuss below.

South-east Spain and central-southern Portugal: Millaran and Vilanovan enclosures

At Los Millares in Almería, the promontory between the R. Andarax and the smaller Rambla de Huéchar was defined and cut off by three lines of walling, the outer provided with small, external circular cells and an elaborate entrance, both out-turned and in-turned. There was also an innermost walled area.[55] Further out on the plateau between the two watercourses there are four much smaller circular stone structures or enclosures, and a further five such structures along the far side of the Rambla de Huéchar. No. 1, on the Los Millares side, is about 35 m in diameter. It has two concentric rings of narrow walls, attached to both of which are circular stone cells, and central sub-circular structure. Outside the area defined by the three enclosure walls, and overlooked by the line of smaller structures, is a concentration of some eighty passage grave tombs. The site, including the

9.9 The enclosure at Los Millares. Top: view showing the promontory between the R. Andarax and the Rambla de Huéchar, and passage graves in the foreground; below: the outer, middle and inner lines of walling. Photos: Chapman.

tombs, continued to be used in the Bell Beaker horizon, but began in the Copper Age, perhaps around 3000 BC. The language used to describe this site, and others related to it in south-east Spain and central-southern Portugal, is usually military: 'citadel' for the innermost walled area, 'fortification' or 'defences' for enclosure wall, 'bastion' for circular cell, 'barbican' for elaborate entrance, and 'fort' or 'fortlet' for smaller circular structures.[56] I believe that this kind of characterisation is misleading, and that it is more profitable to examine Los Millares and other sites of this kind as part of a wider process of creating place. I have already examined those arguments to do with setting, climate and aridity, which have served to give further support to the language of defence and fortification.

Los Millares stands out, so far, both in its immediate locality and its region, and in south-east Spain as a whole. It is possible that more sites like it will be discovered, perhaps in the form of smaller circular structures. If attack or its threat affected this society, it was curiously concentrated on one site. Terrera Ventura, for example, was unenclosed through a longer history of occupation. Walling is known at other south-eastern Millaran sites, but the examples seem to be dispersed, with possibly only one per region where they occur: as at Cerro de la Virgen in the upper Guadalquivir basin in eastern Granada, Campos in the lower Almanzora basin in north-east Almería, and Tarajal in the Campo de Nijár in south-east Almería.[57] Their complete plans are uncertain. Few other sites are known in the region of Cerro de la Virgen, but there are several others in the Almanzora basin including Almizaraque, and the unenclosed El Barranquete passage grave group lies close to Tarajal.[58] Further north in La Mancha, inland in the upper Guadiana basin in Ciudad Real, an important series of *motillas* or circular stone structures have been found in recent years, but these have proved to be of Early Bronze Age date, significantly in an area with few traces of Copper Age settlement.[59]

Vila Nova de São Pedro, near Santarém, had three lines of walling: an inner more or less circular structure some 30–35 m in diameter, and two outer arcs, the middle one with external cells.[60] To its north-west in the Estremadura is Columbeira, a double-banked or -walled promontory enclosure; and to its south Pedra do Ouro, with a single-walled circuit with two or three cells, about 60 by 25 m in extent. In the lower Ribatejo there is Rotura, and others have been discovered in the Alentejo, such as Castelo de Santa Justa and Monte da Tumba. The latter, near Torrão, is only about 30 m in diameter but has an elaborate perimeter. Its wall is double, even triple in places, with a confusion of cells and other small accretions.[61]

Zambujal, 10 km inland from the Estremadura coast near Torres Vedras, is one of the most interesting and best investigated of these 'Vilanovan' Copper Age enclosures.[62] It is much the same size as Vila Nova de São Pedro. It consists of an inner thick-walled enclosure, of basically circular form. To this were attached two outer arcs of walling, like the inner wall with external 'bastions' or cells. The plan was constantly modified, with a bewildering coming and going of minor cross-walls and cells. The central enclosure appears to become a more and more solid monument of masonry as time passes. Bell Beaker pottery came into use well into the sequence.

The setting of Zambujal has also been quite well investigated. There are earlier (fifth- and fourth-millennium BC) tombs in the vicinity. The nearby cave Cova da Moura, used in

9.10 The enclosure at Zambujal. Left: general view, including the central enclosure and outer lines of walling; right: the central enclosure during excavation. Photos: Chapman.

part for burials, has levels dating to that horizon. In the Copper Age, there were continued cave or rockshelter occupations at Carrasca, also with human remains, Cova da Moura, and Portucheira. In a radius of about 10 km there are several other Copper Age hilltop occupations, in settings similar to that of Zambujal, but probably without walling, including Fornea and Penedo; Quinta d'Alem could have walling, while the definite wall at Socorro is not certainly of Copper Age date. Unlike in the Millaran area, there is no concentration of later tombs in the vicinity, but there is a scatter of corbel-vaulted monuments, which are believed to date to this horizon.[63] As with the Millaran examples, Zambujal stands out in its local setting, and currently available information may suggest that the same holds true of other Vilanovan enclosures. As I stressed above, the Vilanovan enclosures belong, in the present climate, to less arid environments than Los Millares.

Overall, a distinction can perhaps usefully be made between outer and more extensive walling, and inner or smaller circular enclosures. The triple lines at Los Millares, for all their 'bastions' and the 'barbican' entrance, were not necessarily high walls. In places they reached a thickness of 3–4 m, largely through successive additions and refurbishments. The same qualification may apply to the outer parts of Zambujal and Vila Nova de São Pedro. There are resemblances (though I imply no connection) with the perimeters of Lébous, Cambous and Boussargues in southern France, and further afield and a little earlier, with the palisaded 'bastions' of the Sarup enclosures on Fyn, Denmark (discussed in chapter 7). These can be considered in the same way as other enclosures discussed in earlier chapters: as deliberate demarcations of space, as takings of place, as eye-catching statements of communal identity. At Los Millares, the tomb concentration and the enclosures must be considered together. Each presents a different facet of communal identity. As discussed below, there is evidence to suggest that the later tomb types were spatially more complex. It is little surprise therefore to find a strongly formalised pattern of approach and entrance to the enclosures. Within the enclosures, tens of circular huts are reported. But as with the Languedoc garrigue enclosures, there is no clear evidence yet that these were the focus of intense, prolonged or permanent occupation. Some of the Los Millares 'bastions' may have been used for metal working.

What of the Los Millares 'forts'? We do not know enough about the relative chronology of the various structures. Do the smaller enclosures form part of a single plan, or precede, or follow the main enclosures (themselves perhaps subject to development through time)? No. 1 has narrow walls, which do not look as though they were ever built to a great height. One cellular structure lies a few metres outside. This was clearly not a self-standing bastion or tower. These structures could have belonged perhaps to a rather smaller social unit. They might have a mundane function to do with stock coralling. They might have served as refuges for small social groups, if the level of inter-personal conflict increased in this phase.

The same view may be advocated for the Vilanovan enclosures. They may be more to do with display and the formalisation of movement in chosen places. It is significant that the plan of Zambujal changes so often. This recalls the modifications frequently made at other kinds of monuments and enclosures, rather than evokes a never-ending succession of attacks and hasty responses. The central enclosures could again have served as refuges. There may be other structures elsewhere in the west Mediterranean, which could be similarly interpreted, including small enclosures on Corsica, such as Alo Bisughje near Sartène in the south-west of the island, probably of Copper Age date, or the earliest *talayots* of the Balearic islands.[64] The distinction between different kinds and scales of conflict is important. Even if we concede them, without conviction, a limited role as refuges for small groups, the small enclosures remain poor support for the model of centralised, ranked or stratified society in an extreme, arid environment.

Burials: the place of the dead

The Italian peninsula

The Iceman was alone at the time of his death (or at least there is no evidence that he was accompanied by others who survived), but he belonged to a community which honoured its dead and ancestors. Had he survived to die in his community, and had he been selected for appropriate treatment, his remains would probably have come to join collective burials in caves or rockshelters of the Civate group. One well-documented example, from the west side of Lake Garda (at the end of the next main valley to the west of the Adige), is the Riparo Val Tenesi rockshelter at Manerba del Garda.[65] Nearby there are traces of older occupation, both of the VBQ phase and earlier. People had been in this and neighbouring

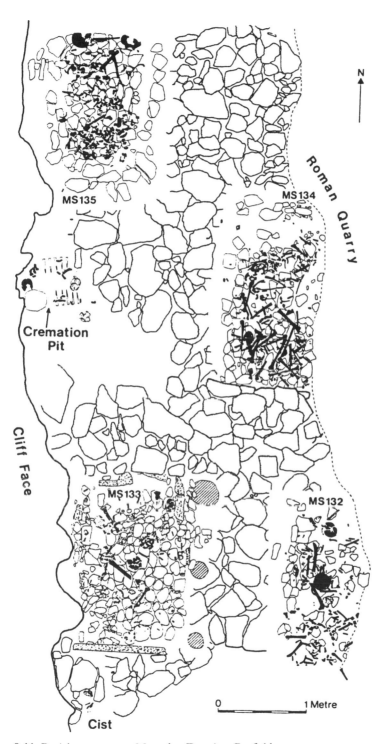

9.11 Burial structures at Manerba. Drawing: Barfield.

areas for a long time, and we know of earlier burials in caves and rockshelters.[66] The rock-shelter at Manerba extends for some 50 m, but is partially disturbed. In one better-preserved zone, following occupation horizons, a series of collective burials were made, only a little later in date than the Iceman. These were put in small rectangular chambers, about 2 by 1 m, floored with stone and probably walled in wood. One, MS 133, contained at least three skulls and other disarticulated bones. There were offerings or goods of pottery and beads of stone, shell and copper. The small structure had subsequently been filled with stone, and further offerings of four complete pots deposited. At some point in its history the structure was surrounded by a low stone platform. Outside a small cist contained the remains of an infant, and there were separate deposits of cereal grains, beans and other plants. Disarticulated bone was found in the other structures, suggesting bone circulation as well as secondary deposition, and one associated hollow had been used for burning human bone; with those bones were burnt flint arrowheads, but unburnt beads, obviously added later. Other goods or offerings included a copper awl from MS 135.

Standing stones or menhirs, some carved with human representations and usually labelled *stelae*, were also part of the Iceman's world in northern Italy.[67] Since they occur both in the western part of the Alps and in Liguria, it is plausible that there were wooden versions across the Po valley itself. They may be to do with ancestral veneration. They need not be taken to reflect anything as simple as 'the rise of the individual', given the complexity of the situation seen at Manerba and the great variety of other burial rites in the region as a whole. The context of individual stelae and menhirs was often remote; they provided the memory of an idea, perhaps of particular individuals, but as plausibly, through part for whole, of wider ideas of community and descent. On the Ossimo–Borno plateau to the west of the Adige valley, referred to above, two menhirs were put up side by side at Asinino-Anvoia. Each had an engraved side, facing east, with repeated and overlapping abstract designs. Beside them there were small stone pavings, but only a few sherds and flakes had been deposited.[68] The menhirs charted the idea of a long ancestral presence, rather than demanded large-scale ritual practice.

Collective burials were also found in the Copper Age over wider parts of north Italy, at the north end of the Apennines, in Liguria and in northern Tuscany.[69] They may be to do, in part, with the relative filling of the landscape compared to earlier generations, since fifth- and fourth-millennium BC burials, from the VBQ into the Lagozza horizons, were much less prominent.[70] But as at Manerba, the details suggest small-scale groups. In northern Tuscany and Liguria, for example, there are collective cave burials. South of the Arno, the rites of the Rinaldone group were varied. Simple individual burials, some with copper daggers (*tombe a fossa*), occur in the northern part of the distribution, while there are collective deposits in simple rock-cut tombs (*tombe a forno*), which contain both complete and disarticulated remains. In some areas, such as the Fiora valley, the known distributions are quite dense.

Apart from some of the Rinaldone burials, there are single graves in other areas of northern Italy, particularly the central and southern parts of the Po valley. There are individual cists in the hills of Monte Lessini, to the east of Lake Garda. Some 30–40 km south-west of Manerba, there were cemeteries of individual graves at Remedello (wrongly used in the past to typify the region as a whole), Volongo and Fontanella Mantovana, while individual burials

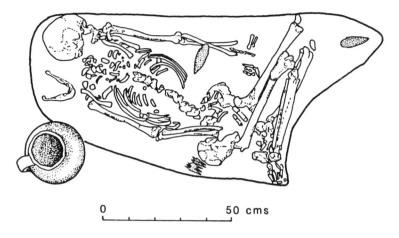

0   50 cms

9.12 Remedello grave 56. After Barfield.

on their own are known from the same sort of area, as at Cà di Marco, and to the south. Other examples of grouped burial grounds, south of the Po, include Spilamberto and Cumarola.[71]

The burial ground at Remedello di Sotto contained well over a hundred graves.[72] As in most other such cemeteries, there appear to be few intersecting graves, which were therefore presumably marked and remembered. The graves seem to be set in two main groups; in one part there are parallel rows of graves. Some contain disarticulated remains, perhaps secondary depositions. The common rite was individual inhumation of the whole corpse, often on the left side, which was accorded to men, women and children. Many of the dead were provided with goods or offerings. Children had flint knives. Adult men and women had pots and flint and copper daggers, and flint arrowheads, stone axes, copper axes, awls and a ring also occur, along with a silver hammer-headed pin. This can be compared with Corded Ware forms in central Europe. The flint daggers were made from local pre-Alpine sources (as on Monte Lessini), while one stone battle-axe was of Rinaldone type. Remedello and other cemeteries have been seen as marking the emergence of ranked or differentiated society, but this is debatable. The rite of individual burial can hardly bear such weight alone, while copper artefacts occur widely across northern Italy and Tuscany as a whole, cross-cutting the varied distributions of collective and individual burial. The burial ground represents a collectivity, a point of reference for perhaps several different communities in the area around, as suggested earlier (in chapter 4) for the burial ground, among others, at Tiszapolgár-Basatanya on the Hungarian plain. As the living came and went, their residences changing and the composition of groups perhaps shifting from year to year and generation to generation, the burial ground created a more lasting concept of community and shared descent.

Further south, in Campania, rock-cut tombs (*tombe a forno*) were used in the Gaudo group. They usually contained collective burials, of complete skeletons. The best-known examples occur in small groups: over twenty at Gaudo itself, near Salerno, thirteen at Mirabello Eclano, and nine at Buccino.[73] One of the Gaudo tombs had twenty-five skeletons. There were pots and flint daggers with these, but it is not clear that they need be

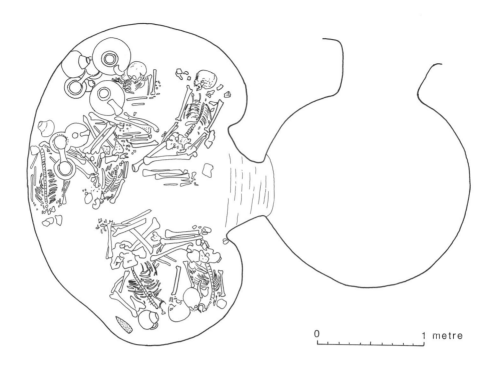

9.13 Tomb 9 at Gaudo. After Barfield.

regarded as individual possessions. The Buccino tombs contained a total of about 140 people, including about forty juveniles or children and roughly equal numbers of adult women and men. Skeletal details suggest that there could have been two main groups within this population. Some tombs were spatially more complex, with bigger chambers and access shaft or well, with a more restricted entrance or passage between. That difference might only be chronological rather than to do with differential status within the community. Some of the tombs had equal numbers of men and women. Tomb 8, architecturally simple, had two men, but seven women and twelve juveniles; tomb 4, more complex, had twelve men, but six women and seven juveniles. It is hard to say whether age and gender differences were significant in this context. The burial rite was successive. Earlier burials were swept to one side, and parts of older skeletons ended in the fill of entrance shafts. If there was some bone circulation, as in collective burials elsewhere in Europe, the final totals for each tomb cannot be given too much individual importance. The overall emphasis was on the group, probably drawn from a specific locality, and its continuity. The so-called 'Chieftain's Tomb' at Mirabello Eclano is often cited as a possible exception to this kind of context, in which only a man and a dog were buried, with seven pots, two flint daggers, a copper axe and a stone rod. But the other tombs in the group give the same sort of impression as at Gaudo and Buccino; it is the burials of a group which are being made more visible and permanent in the landscape. Rock-cut tombs are found down into south-east Italy and Sicily. Many held collective burials, though there are single deposits, as in the example from Arnesano in the Salento peninsula.[74]

Caves continued to be used for ritual, deposition and burial. In Abruzzo, large lowland caves maintained a role as places for the deposition of valuables or significant artefacts, feasting and the placement of food remains, and the interring of selected human remains, in ways that continued to contrast with the use of caves further inland and upland. They were also used for occupation. Level V in the Grotta dei Piccioni, for example, of late Neolithic date, was a thick occupation stratum.[75] At the back of the cave was a series of small, irregular circles of stone and clay. These contained sherds, tools, and bones of domesticated and especially wild animals, predominantly from meat body parts. They were at their densest at either end of the line of circles. At one end of the line, there was an infant burial in circle 1, and at the other, adjacent to circles 10–11, the skulls of two older children and other parts of a fourth child. The child remains may have been left open to view. In emphasising the young and wild animals, the performance of ritual and its enduring, visible remains may have served to celebrate continuity, fertility and regeneration. The Grotta dei Piccioni may only have been part of a set of natural, concealed places; there are preliminary reports of paintings on the walls, perhaps of the same sort of date, at the nearby Grotta Oscura.[76] As in other parts of the peninsula, there may have been a gradual shift to the presentation of human remains in other contexts. The example of the burials in the ditch-like segments at the large open lowland site of Ripoli has already been described above. In the Copper Age in Abruzzo, the use of caves also changed. More were in use, either for the routines of hunting, herding and occupation, or for the deposition of artefacts. In level III at the Grotta dei Piccioni, for example, after a stratum of sterile deposits, there were the remains of a very diverse set of wild animals, and abundant carbonised acorns.[77]

Further south, there were perhaps longer continuities, even though rock-cut and other tombs came gradually into use.[78] There is at least one example of an artificially constructed underground space, the double-lobed chambers at Ipogeo Manfredi, at Santa Barbara near the southern Apulian coast, which was used not for burials but for the deposition of animal remains, especially of deer, seashells and Serra d'Alto painted pottery. The lower part of the Grotta Scaloria had one burial dated to the fifth millennium BC, and some of the many in the upper cave could also belong to that sort of horizon. At the Grotta di Porto Badisco, many of the complex of wall paintings could belong to the later Neolithic and Copper Age. Their elaboration went on reaffirming a body of arcane knowledge, and persisted in repeating the importance of relations between people, animals and a spirit world. There were also deposits of artefacts and some burials near the entrance of the cave, dating to the fourth and earlier third millennia BC. The nearby Grotta dei Diavoli, also deep, narrow and winding, was used for the deposition of human remains, probably in the Copper Age.[79]

Southern France

In both southern France and Iberia the general trend was the same as in the Italian peninsula: a more visible and separate setting for the dead in the landscape with the passage of time. The details are different. Before 5000 BC, human remains from Impressed Ware or Cardial contexts were in caves, rockshelters and other occupations. Remains of the dead were perhaps circulated amongst the living, and were the focus of intense ritual interest, as in the unusual deposits from Fontbrégoua noted in the last chapter, which date to about 5000 BC or soon after. In the Chasseen phase, the dead began to be given a presence in separate contexts. Some burials can be found in caves, for examples in the Grands Causses, but these were relatively rare. Human remains were rarely present in large aggregation sites like Villeneuve-Tolosane or Saint-Michel-du-Touch; there was perhaps less circulation of remains. Burials in pits and cists are a new feature. Those in pits at Saint-Paul-Trois-Châteaux, La Drôme, were part of an open site; there were low numbers of people represented. There are megalithic cists, for example in the foothills of the Causses at Siran, Hérault, seemingly separate from an occupation. One of the four cists recorded in a group had three successive individual inhumations. Further north at Corent, Puy-de-Dôme, on the north side of the Massif Central, a large pit contained many disarticulated remains, predominantly of juveniles; there were some forty-four skulls.[80]

There are some 3000 dolmens in southern France. It is possible that some belong to the latter part of the Chasseen phase, around the mid fourth millennium BC. Most seem to have been constructed in the late Neolithic and Copper Age, as occupation expanded on the causses and garrigues. There are around 1000 in the Grands Causses alone.[81] There were simple constructions of chamber and short passage set in small, low circular cairns. There were variations in style from region to region, from the lower Rhône basin westwards and north-westwards, linking with the wider megalith distributions of west-central and north-west France.[82] Where human remains have survived, there are variable numbers of people; anything from ten to fifty people can be found in both Languedoc and Provence. The collective deposits appear to have been formed by successive episodes, but there were probably secondary as well as primary burials. At L'Aven de la Boucle, near Corconne, Gard, there were over forty people, but only nine skulls; many of the remains were disarticulated and incomplete. The lower level of the rock-cut tomb at Roaix presented a similar picture, and at Sargel 5 in the Grands Causses, skulls had been placed to one side of the chamber. The larger deposit of the Pas-de-Julié cave has already been noted. One hypothesis, supported by some bone pathology, is that populations were subject to outbreaks of tuberculosis, but it is clear that epidemics cannot be used to explain all collective deposits.[83] The wide and locally dense distributions of dolmens, their modest size, and the often quite low numbers of people represented in them, all tend to suggest that these were monuments belonging to small, local groups, rather as suggested for the rock-cut tombs of Campania. Their form could owe something to wider and older ideas of ancestry and spirit houses, found to the north-west, but given their late date these are just as likely to be a regional development of a tradition of cist burial. The scale was small and the focus local. As more people were present in the landscape, but still moved around, the dead of each group took on a more prominent role.

9.14 Anta Grande de Zambujeiro, Evora. Photo: Harrison.

Iberia

In earlier times, the dead had been present among the living in places significant for the routines of a mobile lifestyle: in caves and rockshelters, and notably in the later Mesolithic shell middens of central-southern Portugal.[84] In the earlier part of the Neolithic, down to about 5000 BC, and perhaps later, the dead are encountered, in ones and twos, in continued occupations in caves and rockshelters.[85] This may only reflect the dearth of open sites in the current state of research, but it does suggest the continuation of strong links between the living and the dead; both were bound into an indivisible relationship with their world.

At some point after 5000 BC, different sorts of repository emerged. The dead came to have a more separate existence. This is not obviously a symptom of more settled existence. As elsewhere, as generations passed, ideas of ancestry and descent may have come to frame people's physical and social landscape. The past was part of the creation and maintenance of a new world. The Iberian record is rich in pit graves, cists, and megalithic, dry-stone and rock-cut monuments. Their once abundant contents have not often been closely recorded, apart from the inventories of goods or offerings, and it has been difficult to achieve reliable chronologies for any one region, let alone the peninsula as a whole.[86] The sequence in the following account is still in large part speculative.

In south-east Spain there are rectangular cists and dry-walled round graves, whose contents (including pots, ornaments, flint points, stone axes and simple flat idols) suggest a pre-Copper Age date. These are part of the 'Almerian culture' as defined by earlier researchers.[87] These appear to be quite widely distributed in south-east Spain, but in relatively modest numbers. They occur in lower river basins and inland, and some are found in the now most arid parts of the region. Little has been recorded of the human remains in these structures. The dead were also still deposited in occupied caves and rockshelters. Similar structures can also be found in the Alentejo and the Algarve in Portugal. In Catalonia there was a strong tradition of individual burial in pit graves, sometimes grouped in large numbers.[88]

At some point in the sequence visible, three-dimensional monuments began to be built.[89] The final distribution is dense, fringing most of the peninsula with the partial exception of Catalonia in the north-east. There were many forms, but most consisted of some kind of chamber set in a round mound or cairn. Apart from rock-cut tombs, variations were found in chamber shape and construction, access to the chamber, and size. Many may have been used for successive, cumulative depositions, though closed chambers suggest a rather different sort of history. We know too little about the details of the human contents of most monuments. Most have inventories of artefacts, grave goods or offerings, placed within. Some have spatially complex internal layouts and three-dimensional features; few seem to emphasise forecourts or the outside, for the performance of ritual, depositions or gatherings. Many of these monuments are dispersed across the landscape, though there are some concentrations in south-east Spain which we can call cemeteries. The passage graves of Los Millares, already cited, are one clear example.

When did this phenomenon begin, and was it related to developments in north-west France and elsewhere? The rather few radiocarbon dates from south-east Spain do not suggest beginnings earlier than about 4000 BC in that region. The more elaborate passage graves, with chamber access via a passage and with corbelled vaulting in the chamber, seem to belong, on the basis of their contents, to the Copper Age of the third millennium BC. There were probably also quite marked differences in style from region to region. Around Los Millares there were predominantly passage graves of the kind briefly described. There were also a few non-corbelled, passage graves at Los Millares itself, of megalithic construction. Nearby at Alhama de Almería is another large cemetery, whose monuments were of megalithic construction, while to the north in the Almanzora basin, only some 40–50 km away, there are few of either type, but many round tombs in mounds or cairns but without passages.[90]

In central-southern Portugal, early cists were succeeded by small monuments with megalithic chamber, often of polygonal plan, and short passage. It is not clear whether all of these were enclosed in mounds or cairns; some may have been the equivalent of above-ground cists, now made more visible. The contents of some, for example in the inland region around Reguengos de Monsaraz inland in the Alentejo, suggest an early date, since they include simple stone axes, and microlithic flint points whose form can be compared with much older traditions.[91] Pottery sherds from two such monuments, at Poço de Gateira and Anta dos Gorginos 2, have yielded thermoluminescence dates of the mid fifth millennium BC.[92] I believe that these may be too early. The dates have a very large standard deviation, and they are anyway dates for the sherds not the monuments. They were obtained at a time when more scholars than today were prepared to accept the early, comparable dating of certain Breton monuments (as discussed in chapters 6 and 7). Hardly any radiocarbon

9.15 Anta do Brissos, Evora, remodelled as a chapel. Photo: Harrison.

dates in the bigger series from north-west Iberia belong this early. I would prefer to date beginnings around 4000 BC, with the subsequent accretion of bigger megalithic monuments and rock-cut tombs, some of these perhaps being built only in the Copper Age. There was a scatter of such constructions around Zambujal.[93] In north-west Spain there is now a larger series of radiocarbon dates.[94] Three monuments with simple chamber and short passage, of megalithic construction, date to about 4000 BC or after. Nine dated examples of closed megalithic chambers in mounds date from about 4300–4200 BC onwards; these were not replaced by monuments with access. Only one, Chã de Parada 4, has four dates placing it earlier, between about 4700 and 4300 BC.

In crude terms, there may therefore have been a development from burials in caves, rockshelters and shell middens, to separate below-ground cists, to closed cists or chambers in round mounds or cairns, to simple monuments with chamber access, and finally to monuments of larger size and more complex internal construction, and to rock-cut tombs. The same sequence may not be demonstrable in every region. This is a scheme of ideal stages; there are clear signs that the repertoire was cumulative as much as successive.

Two implications follow from this sort of sequence. The context for the first Iberian monuments was rather different from that in north-west Europe. There the early monuments were one of the first manifestations of a new world. In Iberia, much had already changed by the time these monuments were built. They can largely be seen as developments of local practice, but they cannot be separated entirely from a wider world. Ideas may have passed in more than one direction. The incipient monumentalisation of early Iberian monuments might have been one element in the background of ideas influencing the beginnings in north-west Europe. This is an older idea, but now made more plausible by the demonstration of connections between the Mediterranean world and central-west France (noted in chapters 6–8). In the other direction, ideas of ancestral beginnings emanating from north-west Europe might have helped to consolidate and elaborate the tradition of monument building in Iberia.

The second implication concerns the meanings of deposits at different stages in the Iberian sequence. Were the closed cists and chambers of the putatively early parts of the sequence for specific, known individuals, or could they have been to do with imagined ancestors or particular figures important in schemes of descent who came to assume a more general importance as ancestor figures? Their burials and offerings could not be touched; the architecture denied access. Later in the sequence followed here, access was built in and elaborated, and the collectivities of the dead became larger.[95] The emphasis seems to have shifted, perhaps either to a wider body of ancestor figures, or to people in various ways representative of active social groups. Renewal and repetition of mortuary deposits could have been a form of memory by which the social group from time to time reconstituted itself.

The best detail of deposits of human bone, rare though it is, comes from various southeast Spanish passage graves, with access passages and corbelled chambers, such as at Los Millares, Almizaraque and El Barranquete. We know of some 1140 individuals (said to be mainly adults) from fifty-eight of the Los Millares tombs, with the numbers per tomb varying from two to a hundred. Tomb XXI alone has detailed evidence for bone deposition; remains were disarticulated and long bones and crania were grouped.[96] At El Barranquete there were about thirty tombs in all. Eleven were excavated in the 1960s, and showed up to three levels of deposit.[97] There seem to have been some complete or near complete skeletons, while other remains were disarticulated and some grouped, defined by arrangements of stones or placement along chamber walls. The dead may have been processed, in successive rites, largely within the monuments themselves.

How are these varying later groupings to be regarded? It seems unlikely that whole populations are represented, so that there was some kind of selection for inclusion, and the details of body treatment, such as they are, suggest a concern for categorisation. From these various features, many scholars have inferred principles of exclusion and differentiation. In the later situation there were also varying assemblages of grave goods or offerings in the monuments. At Los Millares, most clearly, some of the passage graves have both more numerous and more varied goods than others, including copper artefacts, beads in various materials, flint points, decorated pottery, phalange idols, and so on.[98] Artefacts of materials such as ivory, jet, amber, callaïs and ostrich-egg shell were confined to only seventeen tombs, and of copper to thirty-two. Such abundances and scarcities were almost all contained within tombs within the inner part of the monument concentration (viewed from the triple-walled enclosure), though the tombs in question are less clearly distinguished by their size or architectural complexity. We do not know whether this reflects a chronological development or use of the monuments. The spatial differentiation is not anyway sharply demarcated.

One suggestion has been that we should regard the rarer and on occasion also the more abundant items and assemblages as 'prestigious objects' and the monuments which contain them as 'prestige tombs'; the model is of ranked, self-defining corporate groups.[99] This is problematic. The artefacts may have been deposited in the monuments, like human remains, over generations. The final tallies are not an accurate reflection of the amounts available in any one generation or at any one time. Goods, like human remains, may have circulated, both within the tombs and in contexts beyond. The circumstances in which people chose to make depositions need not have been uniform. Depositions can be characterised in different ways. 'Grave goods' imply ownership and possession; 'offerings' may suggest piety and sacrifice. I will argue below that copper artefacts were significant innovations but hardly critical in the creation of social difference, since they seem to have been widely available (as already seen in the example of the Iceman's axe). Other exotic materials such as ivory and ostrich-egg shell were presumably obtained by chains of exchange from northern Africa. This is no more striking a phenomenon than the much earlier and much wider circulation of obsidian in the central Mediterranean basin (also discussed below). The rarity of these objects or materials may suggest that they were regarded casually and were not the basis for regular rank differentiation; since they were hardly ever seen, they could have had little general significance. Goods or offerings were for the most part placed within monuments. Unreliable memories may have been maintained about which monument contained, at any one moment, which goods. The context is an implausible setting for the establishment of rank differentiation. We cannot assume that each monument was the preserve of a self-contained and self-defining social group. Some might have been inspired by particular individuals, but others by sets of specific circumstances, propitious moments, or favourable ancestral memories. Bearing in mind the wider context of environment and land-use, the composition of social groups may still have been fluid. The overall impression of a site like Los Millares is of a collectivity of action. The monuments include far more than they exclude, and artefacts may have been deposited as offerings carrying shared significance and meaning, to do with spirits, past members of society, and the social virtues of cooperation. Los Millares may have served as a place in the landscape, as an ancestral home, as a meeting point for people, groups or communities from the wider region around, but who from year to year or from generation to generation were dispersed and shifting across that region. A site like Los Millares served to create and then bond a wide sense of community.

In this rather different perspective, finally, the varying distributions and concentrations of occupations, enclosures and monuments should be seen as significant. It is unlikely that the current state of research has accurately mapped all the variation still to be recovered. But the powerful impression remains of difference both between and within regions. Other groups of monuments were smaller than at Los Millares, while some structures appear to have existed on their own. We know of comparatively little in western Andalusia. This was a world, even in the Copper Age of the third millennium BC, still coming into being, with space in the landscapes, a mobile lifestyle, fluid composition of social groups, and varying kinds of social identity from the co-residential group to the wider mutuality of community.[100]

The lives of things: histories of material culture

Pottery, obsidian and other lithic materials in Italy and southern France

The sense of wider community may have changed through time. In earlier generations, before 5000 BC, there was the broad distribution of Impressed Ware pottery, which subsumed broad regional styles. Fineware *figulina* pottery, both monochrome and painted, was widely distributed through the Italian peninsula; further research may show more regionalised patterns of painted and scratched decoration.[101] Probably at some point early in the fifth millennium, more elaborate decorated and shaped pottery styles came into use. Trichrome pottery can be divided into broad regional styles within the peninsula: broadly, Capri in the south, Scaloria in the south-east, and Ripoli in the centre on either side of the Apennines. Serra d'Alto pottery, including bowls with improbably elaborate handles and geometric and curvilinear painted decoration, may have been introduced at least as early as trichrome wares, and have outlasted them; it is largely distributed in the south and the south-east. It remains unclear whether such distributions were any more regionalised than had existed earlier. A further regional dimension is given by Square-Mouthed Pottery in the Po valley in the north. Perhaps around 4000 BC, these styles were succeeded by plain wares, of apparently considerable uniformity over the peninsula as a whole. Diana pottery is distributed from central Italy down to the south-east and Sicily. Its plain bowl forms do not appear markedly different from plain wares now current in the north, of Lagozza style, which in turn has close resemblances to the Chasseen style of southern France (and indeed more northerly as well). By the Copper Age of the later fourth millennium BC onwards, ceramic fashion had changed again. There were much more regionalised series of generally plain, dark wares, groupable into smaller distributions *within* such regions as southern France or the Po valley, and further down the Italian peninsula as well: Rinaldone, Gaudo, Laterza, Serraferlicchio.[102]

Such a genealogy of pots coincides interestingly with the history of obsidian, as several scholars have noted.[103] From the four sources, noted in chapter 8, obsidian was distributed widely through the central Mediterranean. Obsidian, probably from Sardinia, was taken to Malta, as well as Serra d'Alto and Diana pottery.[104] The broad patterns of distribution from the respective sources were also noted in chapter 8. Further analysis in northern Italy showed in fact that even that region, seemingly on the periphery of obsidian movement, received material from Sardinia, the Pontine islands and Lipari, and some came from Carpathian basin sources. The distributions and chronologies varied. Sardinian material was probably first used well before 5000 BC. Lipari material was in use by the VBQ phase, while Pontine material was confined to the Ligurian coast.[105] Some sites, such as Pescale on the southern fringe of the Po valley, seem to have accumulated or acquired more material than others. By the Copper Age, the movement of obsidian had virtually dried up, and may already have been reduced in later Lagozza phases. One piece only, for example, was found in the occupation underlying the Copper Age mortuary structures described above at Manerba on Lake Garda. As its use declined, so perhaps more intensive use was made of local flint sources, for example at Monte Lessini. The graves at Remedello have copper artefacts, locally derived flint artefacts and regionalised pottery.[106]

This kind of pattern can be found in other regions. Southern France probably received mainly Sardinian obsidian. It was present in the Cardial horizon, but in small quantities. Much larger amounts were present in Chasseen contexts. Supply may have fluctuated from area to area and through time. Despite their importance in other ways, Villeneuve-Tolosane yielded no obsidian and Saint-Michel-du-Touch only one blade. Obsidian was not the only material in circulation in this or any other region. A pale flint was extracted in Languedoc in the Chasseen horizon and circulated as far afield as Catalonia and Liguria, while there were many polished stone axes from Alpine sources.[107] Obsidian seems not to have been in circulation after the Chasseen horizon. There may have been local intensifications of flint extraction, seen for example in the shafts at Salinelles, Gard, and copper began to be produced locally (decribed below).[108] In east-central Italy, as a final example, mainly Lipari obsidian came into the Abruzzo-Marche region. In the fifth millennium BC this was still in small quantities, but the volume increased in the fourth millennium BC, along with the movement into the region of Serra d'Alto, Diana and Lagozza pottery. A little was used at the Grotta dei Piccioni, but much more was present on lowland sites like Ripoli. High-quality pink flint was extracted from Apennine sources and exported to Ripoli and other lowland sites. Again the obsidian circulation fell away in the Copper Age.[109]

For long periods of time, therefore, people were concerned with the wide circulation of lithic materials, not only obsidian, and with the continuation of broad, regional pot styles. As elsewhere, stone artefacts and clay containers had practical uses, but many other meanings besides. Obsidian and various flints must have been recognisable, and each could have been attributed distinct qualities and properties beyond the purely functional, linked to their colour, texture, source and history of use.[110] It is unlikely that such material was distributed by a single process, though the general notion of gift exchange is here, as elsewhere, the most plausible mechanism. In some cases, extraction and circulation may have been controlled by the same people; in others, people may have been able directly to procure materials from sources; and in yet others, materials may have had long histories of circulation by exchange, far from their sources. In the latter case, materials may either have formed the main substance of negotiation and interchange, or have been the by-product of other kinds of interaction. For the same reasons, it is difficult to suggest a single role for pottery. It has been suggested that Italian finewares were both exchanged over distances and should be regarded as 'prestige' items.[111] Such analysis as has been carried out suggests that much pottery was locally produced in the areas where it was used and deposited.[112] Pots were to do with food and drink, with preparation and especially serving and consumption. Even the broken pot or sherds still carried strong associations, from past participation in such activities and from the identity of past users. It is implausible that pots can be reduced to a single universal value as socially differentiating 'prestige' items. The technology required to make and decorate pots cannot have been restricted, though some potters could have been more skilful than others. As elsewhere, pots can be taken to have expressed inclusion, solidarity or some sort of common identity, far more than difference.

This web of social interaction can be linked to other aspects of lifestyle already discussed. How significant, therefore, are the changes in material exchange and ceramic style zones, seen in the late Neolithic and Copper Age? As the landscape gradually filled, it may be that patterns of radiating mobility gradually became more circumscribed, and that people became more and more attached to chosen places and areas. In many cases, the most intense social interaction may have come to be focused on more local constructions, for example the cemetery, *tomba a forno* or *dolmen*. This cannot be universally so, since it is unlikely that Remedello, for example, or further afield, the Los Millares passage grave concentration, served only their immediate neighbourhoods. The scale of change should not be exaggerated. Copper Age ceramic style zones still cover areas a hundred kilometres and more across. Nor can the possible changes in the way interaction and identity were expressed be easily linked to a process of social differentiation. I will discuss early copper metallurgy in the region as a further illustration of that claim.

Copper in context

Copper ores are to be found in several areas of the Italian peninsula, notably in west-central Italy, in parts of southern France, especially Languedoc, and in Iberia. The established use of copper artefacts and local copper working seem to appear at the same time in the region as a whole, and their appearance in separate parts of the region may have been more or less synchronous. Thus, although copper working was practised in the northern Balkans from before 5000 BC and along the northern side of the Alps from around 4000 BC, there is only limited evidence so far of earlier exchange of individual items into the Mediterranean sphere, for example in the southern Chasseen or the VBQ and Lagozza cultures. There are scattered finds of small items like awls in the late VBQ, Ripoli and Lagozza cultures. Copper working in Iberia may go back to the end of the 'Almerian' phase in the southeast.[113] This may only date to the start of the third or the end of the fourth millennium BC. The earliest finds in southern France may be those from the Grands Causses, for example in the stratified latest Neolithic–earliest Copper Age levels at the Grotte de Sargel, or within the enclosed site at Roquemengarde in the lower Hérault valley.[114] In Italy, the main horizon of introduction is generally agreed to be Remedello–Rinaldone–Gaudo, though there are some finds from the end of the Neolithic. To the north, in the west of Switzerland, there was renewed metallurgy in the Saône-Rhône culture, overlapping with Corded Ware culture.[115]

The introduction of metallurgy might have been the result of purely local development or invention; this has been suggested for both central-southern Italy and Iberia.[116] This cannot be discounted, but given the other evidence for contact between the Mediterranean world and central-western Europe, it is now at least as likely that knowledge was diffused from elsewhere. It is as though people turned to a technique of which they must have been conscious, at a time when other systems of materials distribution changed. Copper could be produced locally in many areas. It was an accessible replacement material, but was far from being the only significant material in circulation. The inventories of the Remedello graves again provide a useful reminder of what else was in use.

Little is known about the practicalities of copper extraction and working in the region. The most promising site is the group of extraction points at Cabrières, Hérault.[117] Here there were very short shafts or adits following seams of copper ore. Neither the scale of extraction nor the complexity of the operation need have been great. As much rock may have been extracted from the slightly later flint extraction shafts at Salinelles, already mentioned, or indeed from rock-cut tombs in the Rhône basin and elsewhere.

Simple forms of copper artefact were produced: pins, awls, beads, plaques, knives or daggers, and flat axes. Most could have been made in single-piece moulds or by hammering and further working. Only daggers with raised midribs, like some in southern Iberia, would have required two-piece moulds. Numbers of copper artefacts were generally low, in contexts ranging from rock-cut tombs and single graves to the passage graves of Los Millares. Most sites in Spain have produced less than a dozen objects, though there were far more – about a hundred – from the occupation at Almizaraque.[118] For this reason, it seems unwise to attach too much importance to variations in abundance in tomb or grave assemblages, since there may have been continual fluctuations in supply. On the other hand, when supplies were available, there seems to have been little restriction on access. The man in the ice was carrying a copper axe; it appears to have been a routine part of his equipment. Copper objects from closed contexts and stray finds in the metal-producing parts of west-central Italy show quite dense distributions.[119]

In some past models, copper metallurgy has been seen as one more element in the process of social differentiation, since it was seen as involving craft and labour specialisation, the production of prestige or status items, and restricted access, supply and ownership. I have given reasons to doubt most of these characterisations; and more recent models, which still claim social differentiation, have reduced the importance of the role of metallurgy.[120] How then can copper objects be regarded? They must have been esteemed for their practical properties, though perhaps no more than other materials. Probably only the blade edge of the Iceman's axe protruded from its hafting and binding; this was a tool (if not a weapon) for light chopping tasks, not for heavy woodworking. As elsewhere, copper may have been valued as a material in own right, its colour and production process carrying strong connotations of fertility and regeneration. Knife or dagger blades may have served as icons of identity, perhaps in part bound up with social roles. But they and other copper objects need not be seen only as items of individual identity. They may have served to define gender and other roles within a given social context, or have been associated with particular kin or other groups, being transmittable from generation to generation. It is debatable whether copper items should be regarded as in any way qualitatively different from other artefacts of the region. The earlier example of obsidian has already been discussed; the difference here may reside more in circulation and supply than in value, copper belonging on the whole to a world of more regionalised patterns of material culture. There were other *exotica*, such as triton shells in central Italy or carved objects made from African ivory in southern Iberian contexts, which may have been much more remarkable for their rarity and strangeness.[121]

A final example with which to put copper items into context are the plaques and 'idols' found in southern Iberian graves from the Almerian–Alentejan phases into the Millaran–Vilanovan horizon.[122] These were variously made from stone, usually schist, and bone, usually phalanges or long bones. They took varied forms, from unaltered bones and flat rectangular plaques to rods or cylinders, schematic figures and the less common anthropomorphic figures. Many are decorated, later forms probably more profusely than earlier ones. Some designs are restrained, others profuse, and some schematic or abstract, others representational or using abstract motifs to suggest human form. When sex is indicated, it is the female form which is represented. The various forms tend to have regionalised distributions: schematic figures or 'cruciform idols' and phalange 'idols' mainly in the south-east, cylinders in the west, schist plaques mainly in central-southern Portugal, but also further east, and so on. These kinds of object, which are not necessarily to be separated from other forms such as the so-called 'symbol' pottery of south-east Spain, or the numerous carved objects of central-southern Portugal, occur in varied contexts, not only in graves, shrines or tombs, but also in occupations, settlements or points of aggregation, such as Almizaraque or Vila Nova de São Pedro. Any one context generally has low numbers.

These intriguing objects raise many of the issues which the figurines of the Balkans and Greece also presented. If it now seems unlikely that they were all part of a cult of a single deity, as it appeared to earlier generations of researchers, what other kinds of interpretation are possible? Their presence both on occupations and in shrines, tombs and graves seems to bind the living and the dead together, creating connections and memories, but are they connected with varied deities or spirits, or with ancestors real and imagined, or with ideas of descent and lineage, or with the *persona* and memory of particular individuals? The ambiguities which we face in seeking understanding may have been part of the meanings of these objects in their contemporary contexts. Like copper, they do not seem to have been a means to create or enhance social differentiation. They were used to transmit ideas to do with identity and perhaps relations with a wider world including spirits and other beings. Their presence through the Iberian sequences points to a context in which such relationships needed repeated re-affirmation. We do not know quite who was signalling what to whom, but as in south-east Europe the intensity and longevity of this communication can be related to the dispersal and mobility of the population, the lack of any permanent imbalance in social relations between groups, and the centrality of identities framed by reference to the past, to descent and to a sense of the sacred.

CHAPTER 10

THE CREATION OF NEW WORLDS

Preferred histories

Generalisations

The Neolithic way of life in Europe was based above all on a set of beliefs, values and ideals, about the place of people in the scheme of things, about descent, origins and time, and about relations between people. It involved the conceptualisation of a universe peopled by spirits and ancestors as well as by the living. From spirits, ancestors and other beings came a sense of the sacred, and this, rather than anything more secular, guided people's values and ideals. Belief in relation to and descent from spirits and ancestor figures created a sense both of time and of origins. The future could be ensured by looking to and honouring the past. The values and ideals of cooperation, sharing, solidarity, mutuality, honour and esteem were central to the way of life, and were maintained even though or perhaps rather because the composition of co-residential groups fluctuated. It is possible that the composition of households or close kin groups remained stable, but the points of aggregation in Neolithic landscapes speak for a constantly shifting rollcall of those present at any one gathering. But while people moved around, the sense of community continued to be maintained, to be re-affirmed by periodic gatherings, gift exchange, sharings of food and drink, joint participation in ritual, and an ever-present web of materiality. In this sense, the Neolithic community had continually to be re-created. In line with such values and ideals, there is little sign of pronounced or established difference within any given social group. There may have been some differences within communities based on age or gender; truly egalitarian societies are rare – if they can be documented at all – in the anthropological record.[1] It is possible that there were differences between separate communities, but in landscapes with much space still in them and with a still-mobile population, much interconnected perhaps by kinship and united by shared values, this is of limited plausibility.

People did not immediately settle down from the outset of the Neolithic period. Increasing attachment to place was created, by tradition and memory, and by association with important gatherings, ritual, and the presence of the dead. Neolithic people herded domesticated animals and cultivated cereals and legumes. They still regularly hunted game, fished and collected wild plants. They did not instantly become 'mixed farmers'. Resource-orientated, flexible indigenous people shifted consciously to new staples made available by historical contingency. In this way the broad spectrum of forager resource use was maintained, though the staples changed. Cereals, perhaps anyway cultivated on a small scale, may have been as much for drink as for food. Animals, especially cattle, were valued as subjects and partners in

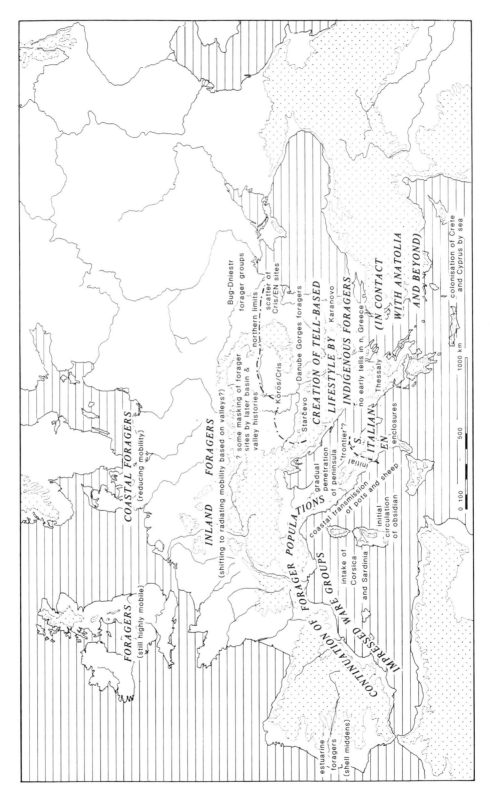

10.1 Generalising representation of selected trends, *c.* 6500–5500 BC.

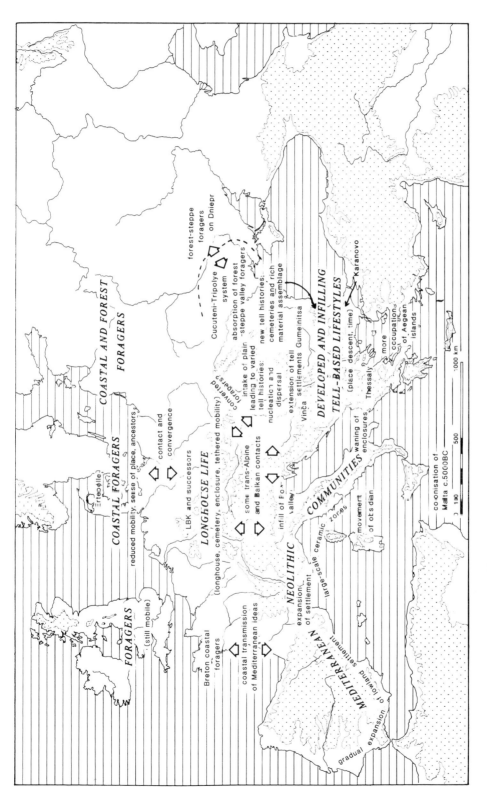

10.2 Generalising representation of selected trends, c. 5500–4500 BC.

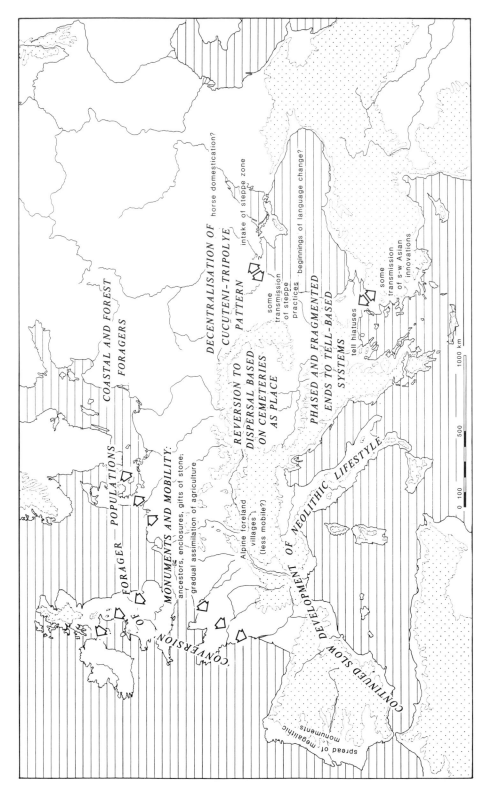

10.3 Generalising representation of selected trends, *c.* 4000–3000 BC.

Map labels:

COASTAL AND FOREST FORAGERS

DECENTRALISATION OF CUCUTENI-TRIPOLYE PATTERN

horse domestication?

intake of steppe zone

some transmission of steppe practices

beginnings of language change?

REVERSION TO DISPERSAL BASED ON CEMETERIES AS PLACE

PHASED AND FRAGMENTED ENDS TO TELL-BASED SYSTEMS

tell hiatuses

some transmission of s-w Asian innovations

FORAGER POPULATIONS

MONUMENTS AND MOBILITY: ancestors, enclosures, gifts of stone; gradual assimilation of agriculture

Alpine foreland villages (less mobile?)

DEVELOPMENT OF NEOLITHIC LIFESTYLE

CONVERSION OF

CONTINUED SLOW

spread of megalithic monuments

0 100   500   1000 km

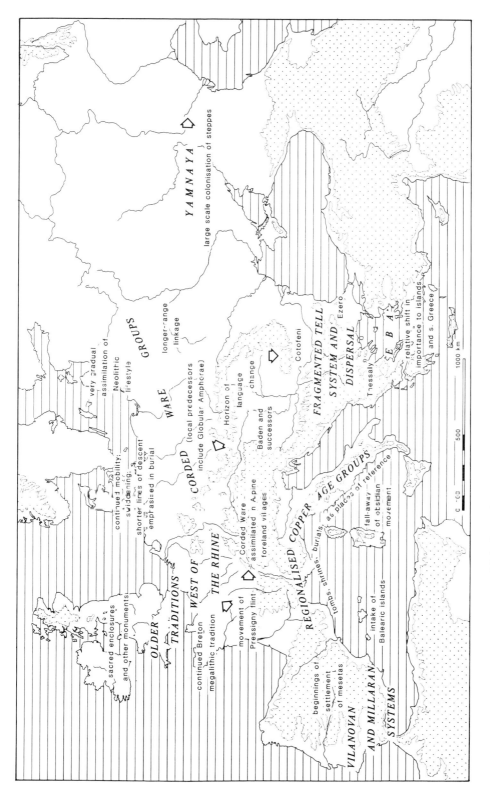

10.4 Generalising representation of selected trends, c. 3000–2500 BC.

their own right, beside or beyond their role as providers of meat and other forms of nourishment. For most of the Neolithic period, cattle were herded through woodland or partially cleared, continually regenerating woodscapes. The patterns of occupation continued to shift as chosen, fixed places were picked out by commemoration and re-use. Throughout the Neolithic period, there may have been a widely dispersed population, whose density cannot be read from the nature of points and places of episodic aggregation.

This way of life was largely the creation of indigenous people, in the run of historical circumstance. Knowledgeable foragers were not loath to adopt new resources, when they suited them, to maintain an existing social ethic. The beliefs and values of the Neolithic period are grounded in those of the Mesolithic period. The old labels are inadequate to distinguish between the two. In a sense, therefore, the Neolithic phenomenon was not so much the creation of new worlds as the prolongation of old ones. But there were fundamental differences between different conceptual orders, even though those need not neatly coincide with the chronological markers provided by a nineteenth-century system of labelling the sequence. Many earlier foragers may have seen themselves as part of an undivided, timeless world, shared by people and the animals which inhabited it: a 'cosmic economy of sharing', in one characterisation.[2] In some later forager situations and in the Neolithic way of life in general, there was categorisation and separation. A sense of time and of beginnings had intervened. Now there was a new emphasis on sharing within human society and on relationships with an otherworld. Speculatively, this shift may have been reinforced by guilt to do with the breaking of earlier bonds with nature.

Regional sequences

The above promotes a timeless sense of the Neolithic phenomenon, but of course that goes too far. It gives too little sense of change or diversity. There was no single Neolithic way of life. Histories, traditions, memories and circumstances prevented uniformity.

Foragers

In the beginning, indigenous foragers kept the land: knowledgeable, flexible people, who were resource-orientated. They made a living from a broad spectrum of resources by a strategy of mobility, and were already bound by an ethic of sharing, both among themselves and with their environment. Small groups may have been dispersed over broad areas; Friesack in northern Germany was one example of an inland site visited only episodically. Some sites and places in the landscape may have had greater significance attached to them; the caves at Franchthi in Greece and Uzzo on Sicily, with their long occupations and burials, are cases in point.

South-east Europe

In south-east Europe changes began after 7000 BC, perhaps in most parts after 6500 BC. My model is of indigenous change, of foragers in the region picking up new ways of doing things from already developed Neolithic communities in south-west Asia: herding animals, tending crops, the craft of potting, and so on. Foragers had moved about; those based at Franchthi had gone far within the Aegean to get obsidian and perhaps tunny. Not for the last time, it was mobile foragers who showed a willingness to change, and to take advantage of new opportunities, perhaps initially with the motive of supporting the existing social ethic. More evidence is gradually becoming available for the presence of foragers in different parts of south-east Europe, though their visibility in the archaeological record has been poor in the past.

The ensuing process of becoming Neolithic over the first generations was a slow one. The Neolithic phenomenon did not appear fully fledged from the beginning; beginnings in themselves need not mark a radical break. The evidence of specific sites like Achilleion in Thessaly shows buildings and structures gradually becoming more solid. Few early occupations may have been permanent, as seen in stratigraphies and the evidence for seasonal flooding at Platia Magoula Zarkou in Thessaly. Mobility, now radiating or tethered rather than circulating, was still a basic strategy. People tended crops, probably often on flood deposits but also in rain-fed clearings, and herded animals, according to seasonal cycles. They came to frame their landscapes by repeated occupations of chosen places, where accumulations of occupation debris began to form mounds. The settlement mounds contained varied groupings of houses, usually laid out in ordered fashion. Such layouts required the ordered sharing of communal space; and space between houses, as at Achilleion, was as important for basic activities as the domestic interior. People were probably not in these sites all the year round; the replasterings of the Slatina house in western Bulgaria may evoke annual re-occupations. In some parts of the region, like north-east Bulgaria and the middle Danube basin and the southern part of the Hungarian plain, built houses may have been rare features. On the sites which repeated use turned into mounds, routines of re-occupation, orderly layouts, shared space, eating together and the presence of the dead, all helped to create a sense of community. The web of materiality similarly bound people together: for example through well-made pottery for the presentation and consumption of food and drink, or obsidian and other materials obtained from considerable distances for mundane cutting tools. Figurines of anthropomorphic and human form in fired clay and other materials were part of the same web. Whether representations of deities and spirits, ancestor figures or known individuals, they evoke a world in which categorisation, conceptualisation of other worlds, memory, and consciousness of identity and origins, were all important.

By about 6000 BC, there were Neolithic communities as far north as the southern part of the Hungarian plain, and as far north-east as the east side of the Carpathians. The densest occupations may have been in areas like Thessaly and central-southern Bulgaria. Populations in the middle Danube basin and in the southern Hungarian plain may have retained an even more mobile lifestyle, and many wild resources in their pattern of subsistence. The shrines and burial places in the Danube Gorges may have belonged to the last forager populations, and may have been in use as allegiances, identities and practices were already changing in other parts of the region.

After about 5500 BC in south-east Europe there were both old and new histories. Many things stayed the same: basic patterns of occupation, subsistence and materiality. These were the old histories of tradition, renewal and re-affirmation. Some mounds continued to be enhanced by their continued occupation, their visible antiquity emphasising their special character. There may have been a gradual shift in herding preferences, towards more keeping of cattle, but the basic range of staples continued as before. People signalled identities and allegiances, and met ideals of hospitality and esteem, by their continued participation in common ways of making and using things: buildings, pots, stone tools. These show participation at different scales, local on the one hand and regional on the other. Though the configurations of archaeological cultures shifted, there was broad continuity in regional patterns: Vinča replacing Starčevo for example. The introduction and development of copper and gold working belong in part to the enduring web of materiality in these old histories. Neither the materials nor the objects produced from them may in themselves have been exceptional, but their production, circulation and use involved participation, contact and interchange, and metal objects, like other things, may have carried connotations extending far beyond the techniques of their manufacture or the practicalities of their use: in this case, metaphors of fertility, regeneration and life force.

In the new histories, people came to occupy parts of the region little or less settled in the first phase of the Neolithic: northern Greece, some of the Aegean islands, north-east Bulgaria, the Dobrogea and the lower Danube valley, Bosnia, wetlands in the middle Danube basin, the river system across the Hungarian plain as a whole, and the river valleys of the forest-steppe zone of western Ukraine. Much of this infill was the result of internally generated expansion, but the 'intake' of the forest-steppe river valleys must have involved – at the least in part – indigenous populations already long established there.

In some cases, the beginnings of new histories were a rerun of old ones. The stratigraphy of a new site like Sitagroi in the plain of Drama in northern Greece tells a similar story to those of older sites in Thessaly. In other cases, perhaps most strikingly in north-east Bulgaria, new foundations and re-foundations after about 5000 BC show the rapid establishment of very ordered occupations, signalled by layouts oriented on the cardinal points of the compass, bounded perimeters, closely built interiors, and burial grounds on adjacent space. Burial grounds are more a feature of the new than the old histories. In them, individuals were remembered as known individuals but the collectivity of these also represented a common ancestral past. Individuals – including young children – stood for the collectivity, and were honoured by appropriate treatment and gifts to take to the otherworld of ancestors and spirits. Even the astonishing assemblages of some of the Varna graves belong to this sort of context. The appearance of burial grounds may be in part connected with continued mobility, as in north-east Bulgaria, or on the Hungarian plain, where separate Tiszapolgár burial grounds, in a phase of dispersed settlement, succeed burials grouped within the occupation mounds of the Tisza phase.

Patterns of occupation were not immutable in either the old or the new histories. The sites of Selevac and Opovo in the orbit of the Vinča culture and numerous occupations on the Hungarian plain in the Tisza–Herpály–Csőszhalom orbit came to be less used and then abandoned within the fifth millennium BC. This might show a more dominant role for more independent, competitive social units, such as the 'household', but may as well indicate the success of traditions of integration. The basic mode of occupation had long involved dispersal and mobility. It was the points of aggregation which fell away or came to be replaced by other forms, such as burial grounds, rather than individual units which emerged. There are signs of resource change, such as the possible accumulation of older animals, but on the whole the evidence for either subsistence intensification or marked social differentiation is weak.

From 4000 to 3000 BC the accents of change became more pronounced. Many of the previously established cultural groupings changed radically, and the whole nature of materiality with it. Many tells were abandoned (but not all, as in Thessaly), some to be later reoccupied, like Ezero, some to be left alone. This was a gradual process, which had already begun in the fifth millennium BC. This was a shift to new ways of ordering mobility and dispersal. Far from being a collapse, the process can be seen as the successful outcome of the long creation of a sense of Neolithic community. The change carried consequences, however, and may have been influenced to some extent by outside forces. There may have been some limited movement by people from the forest-steppe and the steppe zones into some parts of south-east Europe. But if so, this may have been to take advantage of new circumstances rather than as the initial impetus causing the collapse of the established order. Identities now included greater reference to the outside, seen in widely shared pot forms and to some extent in burial custom. Further off, the emergent urban world of Mesopotamia may have caused reorientations in the flow of raw materials, which may have further helped to redefine the character of identities. It seems unlikely that the old order of south-east Europe fell to a series of shock-waves emanating from the steppes. Rather, the wider steppe zone itself began to be colonised from this horizon onwards, by developed strategies of mobility including horseriding and wheeled transport. Nonetheless, Indo-European language may have begun a process of wider dispersal into Europe from this time, as a language of communication in a world which gave renewed emphasis to long-distance contact and interchange. The Baden cattle keepers of the bend of the Danube in the later fourth millennium BC are a good example of people in touch with wider changes, as in their adoption of wheeled vehicles, but their burial grounds, their use of animals as metaphors for their own existence, and their material emphasis on hospitality, speak for the continuation of older traditions and identities rather than for the emergence of a newly structured or ranked society.

Central and western Europe

For at least a millennium and a half after 7000 BC, foragers continued to use both the interior and coasts of central and western Europe. New research suggests that foragers were already numerous on the western Baltic coastlines, and present in the river valleys of the wider region. In both situations, mobility was maintained, but probably reduced, enabled by resource abundance in favourable coastal areas, and as a strategy inland to cope with the now fully wooded environment. Contrary to its usual characterisation as the classic example of colonisation, the LBK, the first Neolithic culture of central and western Europe, beginning about or after 5500 BC, can be seen as the result of the extension of such a strategy by indigenous inland foragers. Taking advantage of new staples, but retaining mobility and initially a broad resource spectrum, they anchored a lifestyle of moving around the river valleys and woodlands on groupings of large timber longhouses and a widely shared material culture. The occupations fluctuated in size and duration; rather few were in continuous use. Longhouses varied in size. The larger ones, archaeologically more durable and visible, framed patterned routines of movement, coming together and activity, reinforced by the samenesses of pots, to do again with the provision of food and drink, and of stone tools to do with individual and group identity. Some of the dead, especially children, were placed within occupations, but across the region there were also burial grounds which generally seem to have served more than one occupation. Descent was again the focus for wider identity.

The staged spread of this system can be traced from east to west and from south to north. Eastern Belgium and the Paris basin were taken in comparatively late. And the detailed settlement histories of individual valleys can be documented, as on the Aldenhoven 'plateau' in north-west Germany or Bylany in Bohemia. Much of the distribution coincides, classically, with that of fertile *loess* soils, but from an early stage there were LBK occupations on other soils to the north, in Kujavia and even beyond in parts of north and north-west Poland. Towards 5000 BC the patterns of material culture became more regionalised, and after 5000 BC other cultural configurations emerged (*Stichbandkeramik*, Lengyel, Rössen and so on), but the basic lifestyle continued across a very broad area from western Hungary to the Paris basin. There were still longhouses and burial grounds. There were changes too. Though the longhouse was maintained, some occupations were more nucleated and some bounded by fenced perimeters. In the latter stages of the LBK, shared space between longhouses in occupations had been formalised or enhanced by the construction of ditched enclosures. After 5000 BC, these were further developed, especially in the east in the Lengyel orbit. Svodín in Slovakia and a series of other Lengyel sites show the combination of longhouse occupation and formalised, graded enclosure, defined by ditches, banks and palisades, with symmetrically laid out and often elaborate entrances, but otherwise usually empty interiors. In some cases, the enclosure may have stood alone. Here were spaces for gathering under prescribed rules, for ritual, for honouring the memory and tradition of older ways of doing things.

Around the LBK and its successors from the mid sixth into and through the fifth millennium BC, forager populations continued. To the north and in parts of the west the two populations were closely juxtaposed, and there is evidence in the north for contact. But some sort of stable frontier was maintained. The LBK did not advance inexorably, and the Ertebølle–Ellerbek culture was a long established phenomenon from the later sixth to the later fifth millennium BC. There was much convergence of lifestyle, despite one being labelled by us as Neolithic and the other as Mesolithic. Both involved tethered mobility: lagoons, coastal occupations, burial grounds and feasting places serving as anchors in the manner of longhouses and other LBK features. The technical differences in resource procurement may have mattered less to either set of practitioners than predictability, fertility and abundance; both sets of resources were exploited as means to the same end. And there may already have been a conceptual shift among Ertebølle foragers in attitudes to the natural world and the environment.

Before and around 4000 BC there was a widespread further extension of the Neolithic phenomenon, taking it into southern Scandinavia, into the Alpine foreland south of the Rhine, north-west France, and Britain and Ireland. On the east side of the Baltic an older tradition was maintained. The conditions for the extension of the Neolithic may have varied. There was convergence between the LBK and the Ertebølle–Ellerbek culture resulting in the emergence of the northern TRB. The formation of the more southerly TRB remains unclear, but seems to involve dispersed, inland foragers. There was some kind of convergence between the western LBK and a scattered coastal population in Brittany, which was also perhaps influenced from the south. In Britain and Ireland, foragers were perhaps on the whole rather more mobile, but as in south-east Europe at the beginning of it all, this need not have reduced their flexibility and adaptability: rather the reverse. Although still uncertain, the Neolithic may have begun in Britain and Ireland a little earlier than in southern Scandinavia.

Dispersed settlement, mobility through and in woodscapes, limited and transient clearances, herding, hunting and small-scale cultivations are all recurrent characteristics of the established Neolithic in central and western Europe, both in the areas of primary Neolithic presence and in the secondary areas roundabout of later occupation. There was perhaps some expansion through time of the zones of settlement, but the varying distributions were probably more to do with changing configurations of aggregation and dispersal. The evidence for substantial houses used for domestic occupation is infrequent throughout the orbit of the TRB, Michelsberg, northern Chasseen and British earlier Neolithic cultures. The contrast with the 'unfair settlements' of the Alpine foreland appears to be real, and not just a matter of differential preservation. Even in the Alpine foreland many of the hamlets may have been only seasonally occupied.

These Neolithic people were herders, small-scale cultivators and users of a still broad spectrum of resources. Their history was not one of inexorable population growth, settlement expansion or subsistence intensification. Cattle were particularly valued, to judge by deposits in the ditches of enclosures, and by animal burials in the Globular Amphorae horizon. A mobile lifestyle may have been maintained in the Corded Ware horizon too, though it is possible that the extent of mobility among a population dispersed into small units now began to be reduced.

Such a social landscape was framed, and in many senses created, by constructions of a different nature: enduring, and built upon central notions of origins and identity. The memory of the earlier great longhouses, themselves pivotal in the creation of the LBK lifestyle, was transformed into shrines for spirits and ancestors, which put into visible and durable form the idea of a common sacred past. The sense of time, beginnings and descent generated through the use of such shrines, though it need not have been a uniform experience even within a single region, was one of the central features of the Neolithic. The human dead were also united with the sacred realms of spirits and ancestors. The dead were widely present among the living, manifested not only by funerals but also by the circulation of remains in occupations and enclosures. The remains of the dead were also incorporated into shrines, perhaps to begin with as acts of offering or veneration, and perhaps in many later cases as a means of establishing and reinforcing a more particular or localised identity. These monuments provided a timeless space for ancestors, imagined and real, created and selected, but their physical presence also served to fix notions of place, inscribed by repeated use in the wider pattern of mobility.

Such constructions were joined at a slightly later horizon (generally speaking from after 3500 BC) by other social arenas: ditched enclosures. These were part of an older tradition going back into the post-LBK and especially the Lengyel horizon, and into the later LBK horizon itself. Though the nature of the tradition is not clear, the memory of older practice may again have been important. The ditched enclosures were arenas for the playing out of many social concerns. In this they overlap with the large aggregation sites characteristic of the middle part of the Neolithic sequence in many areas. The inscribing of bounded spaces on the landscape was connected with the creation of common identities. In such spaces, large gatherings took place. Feasting, the sharing of food and drink, the veneration of animals, the presentation of the human dead, the circulation of material remains harboured in special deposits and the giving of gifts can all be suggested. The placing of things in the ground united people with place, and created order in the use of bounded space. In these ways, in these arenas people celebrated domesticity, fertility, hospitality and generosity, and a shared sense of origins and belonging.

One recurrent gift was the stone axe-blade. Axes were used, to cut and trim wood, and perhaps also as weapons, but had far wider significance than their practical dimension. They were themselves gifts from the earth, serving to unite people with their surroundings. The effort required to obtain raw materials, often in remote places, to transform them into pecked, ground or polished forms, and to circulate them over considerable distances, cannot be measured in terms of practical logic alone. These were not objects of accumulation, to be hoarded as possessions, but living symbols of identity, badges of appropriate prowess and social behaviour, to be handed on to successive generations, or given away to other people, or given back as offerings to the natural surroundings. Pots too had other dimensions as containers of plenty, and were to do with the sharing of food and drink in social gatherings. It is no coincidence that the largest accumulations are to be found in enclosure and aggregation sites, and outside monumental shrines.

In time, monuments and arenas became less used, though there are many examples of modification in the later part of the Neolithic, and some regional continuations of construction (as in the Paris basin underground ossuaries or the British later enclosures). The ancestors came to be taken for granted, and the focus of individual funerals came to be on a more recent rather than a distant or timeless past. The Corded Ware phase (from about 28/2700 BC) has often been seen as a horizon marking pronounced changes in society: more warlike, male-dominated, competitive and ranked. I have argued that the changes of this horizon reflect the consolidation of a sense of Neolithic community. Shared styles of pots and stone battleaxes symbolise the continuation of open rather than differentiated social relations, through the representation of older ideals of social participation, prowess, hospitality and generosity. This was connected with the development of regionalised identities, perhaps in part in connection with language change. West of the Rhine, people were more attached still to older ways. This was the outcome of a history which could have ended differently.

The central and west Mediterranean

In this region too there were long continuities. Foragers gradually broadened their resource base, incorporating sheep and cereals, while long maintaining cycles of mobility. Those may have remained characteristic of lifestyles in most areas for much of the Neolithic sequence (including the Copper Age). As elsewhere, foragers can be seen as takers of opportunities; rather than reacting to stress or competition, new staples may have been adopted simply because they had been made available by another history, by developments in south-east Europe. Pre-Neolithic travel by sea can be seen in the colonisation of Corsica and Sardinia, the movement of obsidian and the practice of offshore fishing. Foragers were thus well placed to learn of change elsewhere.

The extension of the Neolithic into the central Mediterranean may have been by stages: at first into south-east Italy and eastern Sicily, before 6000 BC, and then subsequently further up the Italian peninsula and further west. The widespread adoption of pottery may have been as significant initially as the herding of domesticated animals or the cultivation of cereals, and may have served to reinforce existing social values of sharing and participation.

The enclosures of south-east Italy stand out as the principal monuments of the early Neolithic. Often seen as markers of the arrival of a now more sedentary existence, they may rather have been a series of unfinished projects, to do with inscribing routine in patterns of coming and going, gathering or aggregation and dispersal, and with creating, once again, a sense of place. In many areas, gatherings are otherwise reflected in the continuing use of caves and rockshelters, some used for burials and special depositions.

Coastal and inland landscapes came gradually to be more filled after 5000 BC, though there were still significant absences by the end of the Copper Age, for example in several parts of inland Iberia. Once again the phase of extension saw aggregation sites in several different landscapes: sites like Villeneuve-Tolosane in southern France or Ripoli in east-central Italy. And once again the extension of occupation was accompanied by, or perhaps enabled by, the construction of monuments: shrines, tombs and enclosures. It has often been suggested, in various models, that the environment in southern parts, such as south-east Italy, the Maltese islands and south-east Spain, determined or closely constrained the pattern and nature of settlement. Thus supposed over-use of soils in south-east Italy has been seen as responsible for the later virtual abandonment of the Tavoliere plain; aridity and impoverished soils are seen to cause stress on the Maltese islands, provoking the burst of 'temple' building, partly as a means to mediate with the forces of nature and partly as a symptom of social competition; while aridity in south-east Spain is claimed to have so concentrated settlement in areas with water that social elites emerged both to manage resources and control their communities. But there are other possibilities: of continued mobility in the Tavoliere; of successful adaptations in the Maltese islands over the thousand years of shrine building; and of enclosures and shrines in south-east Spain being part of a wider process of the creation of place in gradually infilling landscapes. The detailed climate record has still to be established; even if unvarying aridity can be demonstrated, it remains to be shown how this determined social process.

That individuals continued to be mobile is seen vividly in the Iceman himself. The life-style of most communities may also have been based on mobility, given the nature of settlement evidence, though perhaps by the Copper Age reduced or circumscribed into smaller orbits. Broad regional identities were characteristic of the middle and later Neolithic, as seen in the distributions of pot styles, and there was considerable movement of obsidian. By the Copper Age of the later fourth millennium into the third millennium BC, pots show more regionalised distributions and the movement of obsidian had fallen away. Identities may have been focused on local monuments and graves, though it may still have been easy for an individual like the Iceman to move among different peoples.

Other versions

It should be clear that my account here has often differed from the consensus view. I have supported these orthodoxies myself on other occasions.[3] It is important to highlight three aspects of such divergence in particular, because they serve to emphasise the models argued here of historical process and community in Neolithic Europe.

Beginnings

The evidence can be interpreted differently, to support an initial colonisation into south-east Europe, perhaps a fragmented infiltration by sea: what has been called the 'boat-people' model.[4] Subsequently, the spread of the LBK in central and western Europe has classically been seen as a rapid colonisation, by a whole population of expanding, purposeful farmers, on the move and filling previously empty niches. And this view, perhaps surprisingly, has been accepted even by those in the van of arguments for the role of indigenous communities in the Neolithic transition elsewhere in Europe.[5]

Settlement and subsistence

Because the Neolithic phenomenon has so often been interpreted as demographic or economic, it has been normal to see most settlements as sedentary, or the general trend through time as one towards increasing sedentism, and to envisage the practice of mixed agriculture from the beginning, with an inbuilt tendency to future expansion and intensification. Our choice of language, which I have also often supported on other occasions, does not help. Recurrent phrases like 'the first farmers', 'early agricultural communities', the Neolithic 'revolution', or the 'secondary products revolution', and even commonplace terms such as 'site' and 'settlement', predispose us to a certain reading of the evidence.

Social differentiation

The development of the Neolithic has often been read as a story of increasing social differentiation, of the playing out of imbalances in power between and within communities, preceded already in the late Mesolithic by competition for resources and position. The characterisations have been varied. Some have seen development as a shift from tribal or segmentary society to chiefdoms, others as a change from the central position of lineages to that of more individual households; another, more recent model posits a move away from the nurturing, all-embracing concept of the *domus* to the more individualising and more male-oriented world of the *agrios*.[6]

Neolithic history and Neolithic community: the creation of new worlds

In contrast to these orthodoxies, I have argued in this book for a series of histories in the hands of the participants, but framed too by contingency rather than by inevitable process. Beginnings are an important illustration of this, some being determined by the accidents of availability (as in south-east Europe or in south-east Italy), some hastened by conscious choice (as in the creation of the LBK), and others delayed by the existence of alternative traditions or by convergence (as in the Danube Gorges, in many parts of the central or west Mediterranean, or in southern Scandinavia). The history of histories affected what came after. In south-east Europe, the gradual creation of community bound the living and the dead into the same world. A sense of time and descent was experienced through reoccupations of place, the incorporation of the dead into the spaces of the living, and the veneration in figurines of ancestral figures. The LBK world turned on the ordered use of timber longhouses, themselves perhaps elaborate imitations of structures in tell sites and occupations further east. The dead were present among the living; children especially are to be found buried close to longhouses, symbols of regeneration and continuity. But in the LBK, the dead came to be put in separate burial grounds serving a dispersed population. A separate category of forebears was created (in a manner that was not previously seen in southeast Europe up to that date), composed of known, remembered individuals, whose individual graves were marked and respected, but who as a collectivity represented another dimension of time past. By the time of the further extension of the Neolithic in west Europe around 4000 BC, the longhouse had largely been abandoned as a structure, but transformations of its memory served to house ancestors and spirits, belief in which created that sense of time and descent which among other things came to distinguish Neolithic people from their predecessors.

I have argued throughout this book for continuing patterns of mobility. Before people settled down, a sense of place (in such diverse forms as tells, monuments, and cave and rockshelter occupations and deposits) had to be created by routines and by rites, framing their landscapes with points of social and spiritual significance. It is not as though there was no process, but that in minimising the differences between our own and the Neolithic world,[7] we have been too eager to see too rapid process. The Neolithic world was one of slow histories, acted out over many generations. Our own histories are usually framed by a rapid succession of events. The Neolithic sense of history might have been twofold, involving on the one hand a notion of beginnings and the creation of time past, while on the other consisting of a concept of timelessness or repetition from generation to generation.

I have also argued for varied patterns of subsistence, generally for small-scale cultivations, the products of which were used not only for food but as drink as well, and often for
large-scale herding. The case for a 'secondary products revolution' has been over-stated.
Animals should not be seen as objects or possessions alone, but as subjects of value, the
focus of veneration, and partners. People's attitudes to animals may have been ambiguous;
I have suggested more than once that guilt at the domestication of animals,[8] at their 'objec-
tification' contrasted to their earlier role in a 'cosmic economy of sharing', may have been
one element in those new senses of time, descent and beginnings, which distinguished
Neolithic people from their predecessors.

All the consensus models of society noted above have shared certain assumptions: that
the Neolithic, as a social phenomenon, arrived in each area fully formed; that change was
continuous along a predetermined evolutionary path; and that change was driven by
competition and conflict, even when channelled into ideological or spiritual realms, over
material resources, the proper substance of an essentially economic phenomenon. I have
challenged each of these assumptions. Neolithic society had to be created; development
was not uniformly linear; and there were social and spiritual dimensions at least as important as material resources.

Social values and sacred imperatives

In what ways can Mesolithic foragers be distinguished from their Neolithic successors? In
many ways there was little difference; the Mesolithic–Neolithic transition in itself was
probably less momentous than our sense of social evolution has led us to suppose. I have
argued that technological-economic factors were not in themselves of major importance,
given that knowledgeable foragers could choose between different ways of doing things.
And even later, I have given less importance to those technical innovations, such as the
plough, the wheel or copper, which have been at the heart of many an explanation of
relentless change through the Neolithic period. What mattered were the values guiding or
framing people's activities and relations with each other and the world. It seems likely that
the forager ethic of sharing and incorporation was continued in the Neolithic period.
Cultivation and herding, and elements of Neolithic material culture, were adopted as new
means to existing ends: to facilitate sharing and gatherings, and to celebrate the provision
of food and drink and the display of group identity.

This serves to emphasise the continuities between Mesolithic and Neolithic, and to give
central importance to the values of society. But what of the differences? Foragers may have
seen themselves as united with their world; Neolithic people may have been more conscious of their separate place in the scheme of things. The real significance of domestication may have lain in this sphere, rather than in productive capacity or control. Perhaps
Mesolithic foragers took animal fertility and regeneration for granted, in using bones and
antlers as symbols in mortuary rites; in venerating animals as a category separate from
themselves, Neolithic people may have become more conscious of the possibility of
failure.

In varying ways depending on regional sequences, Neolithic people may have been guided by a different sense of descent, time and the sacred. The Mesolithic world may have been a more timeless one. Though that generalisation has to be tempered by the recognition of burial grounds in areas like the Danube Gorges and southern Scandinavia, I have argued that these were mainly late phenomena, already in phases of convergence or contact. The adoption of new staples and a web of accompanying materiality, the creation of place, the incorporation of the dead actively among the living, and the cult of ancestors, all promoted a distinct sense of beginnings and time. Each gathering, shared meal or feast, each reoccupation of place, every funeral or ancestor rite carried with it a sense of how things could be otherwise.

Society has been envisaged in two main ways in recent Neolithic explanations. In the processual approach, explanations were strongly influenced by a strand of sociology and anthropology, traceable back to the functionalists and then to Durkheim, which gave prominence to an all-embracing idea of society. Society was more than the sum of its parts, and from society were derived the guiding values acted upon by individuals.[9] Other explanations, both 'Marxist' and post-processual, have paid more attention to social relations between constituent groups and individuals. Society was more or less the sum of its parts, since the different groups and individuals involved would tend to see things so differently. Both kinds of explanation have tended to focus on material resources, as the objects of management or competition and conflict, and as the prime movers of social or group change respectively. In each case, this is too limited, since beliefs and ideals are excluded.

With a new sense of beginnings, descent and time, came also sacred imperatives. The sense of the sacred was derived not from society itself, but from a sense of a world separate from and older than humans themselves. Belief in ancestors and spirits now provided sanctions and reinforcement for existing values in society. Perhaps there is no merit in choosing between the different conceptions of society noted above, since we can distinguish between ideal and practice. Neolithic ideals, divinely sanctioned, included cooperation, participation, integration, generosity, hospitality and prowess; Neolithic practice from time to time involved the resolution of conflict by violence. This contradiction was a state of affairs which existed also in forager society. A final, vivid example is the man from Porsmose, Denmark, dating from the Early Neolithic period, who had been shot directly in the face and chest.[10] In the same way, some people may have used gatherings, feasts and exchanges as occasions for the display of rivalry, contrary to or exploiting the ideals of generosity and hospitality. But ideals and values, divinely sanctioned, mediated social rivalries. The Neolithic community was a long time in the making, and then long lasting. The beliefs, ideals and values which were gradually created ensured long histories.

NOTES

1 The time of ancestors

1 Following the now extended calibration. See M. Stuiver and P. J. Reimer, 1993, 'Extended 14C data base and revised CALIB 3.0 14C age calibration', *Radiocarbon* 35, 215–30; and other papers in the same volume.

2 C. Renfrew, 1977.

3 E.g. I. Hodder, 1982, *Symbols in action*, Cambridge; J. Thomas, 1991; J. C. Barrett, 1994.

4 E.g. M. N. Cohen, 1977, *The food crisis in prehistory*, New Haven.

5 A. G. Sherratt, 1981.

6 Compare M. Sahlins, 1972, *Stone Age economics*, Chicago.

7 B. Bender, 1978.

8 A. J. Ammerman and L. L. Cavalli-Sforza, 1984.

9 E.g. C. Renfrew, 1973; J. Thomas, 1987; I. J. Thorpe and C. C. Richards, 1984.

10 J. C. Barrett, 1994; M. Shanks and C. Tilley, 1987, *Social theory and archaeology*, Cambridge.

11 See discussion in J. Thomas, 1991.

12 E. Gellner, 1988; P. J. Wilson, 1988, *The domestication of the human species*, New Haven and London.

13 I. Hodder, 1990; 1992.

14 C. Gosden, 1994. See also D. L. Carmichael, J. Hubert, B. Reeves and A. Schanche (eds.), 1994, *Sacred sites, sacred places*, London. Since they give prime attention to what people thought about otherworlds and sacred realms, I have found the following particularly suggestive: M. Eliade, 1960, *Myths, dreams and mysteries*, London; E. E. Evans-Pritchard, 1956, *Nuer religion*, Oxford; G. Lienhardt, 1961, *Divinity and experience*, Oxford.

2 Keeping the land: indigenous foragers, *c.* 9000 to after 7000 BC

1 K. Bokelmann *et al.*, 1985, 'Duvensee, Wohnplatz 13', *Offa* 42, 13–33; K. Bokelmann, 1986, 'Rast unter Bäumen', *Offa* 43, 149–63. See also K. Bokelmann, 1991, 'Duvensee, Wohnplatz 9. Ein präborealzeitlicher Lagerplatz in Schleswig-Holstein', *Offa* 48, 75–114.

2 L. Larsson, 1990; G. M. Burov, 1989, 'Some Mesolithic wooden artefacts from the site of Vis I in the European north east of the U.S.S.R.', in C. Bonsall, 1989, pp. 391–401; G. M. Burov, 1990, 'Die Holzgeräte der Siedlungsplatzes Vis I als Grundlage für die Periodisierung des Mesolithikums im Norden des Europäischen Teils der UdSSR', in P. M. Vermeersch and P. van Peer, 1990, pp. 335–44; S. V. Oshibkina, 1989, 'The material culture of the Veretye-type sites in the region to the east of Lake Onega', in C. Bonsall, 1989, pp. 402–13.

3 T. D. Price and K. Jacobs, 1989, 'Olenii Ostrov: radiocarbon dates from a major Mesolithic cemetery in Karelia', *Mesolithic Miscellany*, 10, 3–6.

4 J. F. Cherry, 1990; A. H. Simmons, 1991; C. Broodbank and T. F. Strasser, 1991; P. C. Woodman, 1986, *Excavations at Mount Sandel 1973–77*, Belfast; A. Morrison and C. Bonsall, 1989, 'The early post-glacial settlement of Scotland: a review', in C. Bonsall, 1989, pp. 134–42.

5 For general reviews across the continent see C. Bonsall, 1989, and P. M. Vermeersch and P. van Peer, 1990. For site numbers in central Europe and northwards: S. K. Kozłowski, 1991; S. Vencl,

1991, 'On the importance of spatio-temporal differences in the intensity of Palaeolithic and Mesolithic settlement in central Europe', *Antiquity* 65, 308–17.

6 L. Larsson, 1978, *Ageröd I:B – Ageröd ID*, Lund.

7 A. J. Legge and P. A. Rowley-Conwy, 1988; T. Schadla-Hall, 1989; E. W. Cloutman and A. G. Smith, 1988.

8 D. Geddes *et al.*, 1989; D. Srejović, 1972; T. W. Jacobsen, 1981; J. M. Hansen, 1991.

9 K. Aaris-Sørensen (ed.), 1984, *Uroksen fra Prejlerup*, Copenhagen; N. Hartz and H. Winge, 1906, 'Om uroxen fra Vig, saaret og draebt med Flintvaaben', *Aarboger for Nordisk Oldkyndighed og Historie* 21, 225–36. See also A. Fischer, 1989, 'Hunting with flint-tipped arrows: results and experiences from practical experiments', in C. Bonsall, 1989, pp. 29–39; and S. Mithen, 1990, *Thoughtful foragers*, Cambridge. The Vig find is Preboreal, Prejlerup Boreal.

10 A. Bolomey, 1973; M. Cârciumaru, 1973; J. M. Hansen, 1991; L. Costantini, 1989; J. Vaquer *et al.*, 1986. Were all the Abeurador seeds humanly deposited? Note also D. L. Clarke, 1976, 'Mesolithic Europe: the economic basis', in G. Sieveking, I. Longworth and K. Wilson (eds.), *Problems in social and economic archaeology*, pp. 449–82, London.

11 A. G. Smith, 1970, 'The influence of Mesolithic and Neolithic man on British vegetation: a discussion', in D. Walker and R. G. West (eds.), *Studies in the vegetational history of the British Isles*, pp. 81–96, Cambridge. The advantages of clearance are discussed by P. Mellars, 1976, 'Fire ecology, animal populations and man: a study of some ecological relationships in prehistory', *Proceedings of the Prehistoric Society* 42, 15–46. Further evidence of its practice in: A. G. Smith, A. Whittle, E. W. Cloutman and L. Morgan, 1989, 'Mesolithic and Neolithic activity and environmental impact on the south-east fen-edge in Cambridgeshire', *Proceedings of the Prehistoric Society* 55, 207–49; I. G. Simmons *et al.*, 1989, 'An application of fine-resolution pollen analysis to Later Mesolithic peats of an English upland', in C. Bonsall, 1989, pp. 206–17.

12 Among others see: L. R. Binford, 1980; T. Ingold, 1988, 'Notes on the foraging mode of production', in T. Ingold *et al.*, 1988a, pp. 269–85.

13 Earlier references, and note still E. Higgs and M. Jarman, 1969, 'The origins of agriculture: a reconsideration', *Antiquity* 43, 31–41. Further discussion of the concept of wildness in T. Ingold, 1986.

14 A. Testart, 1982; T. Ingold, 1986.

15 D. Geddes *et al.*, 1989; A. Legge and P. Rowley-Conwy, 1988.

16 For temperatures and sea levels in the north, see L. Larsson, 1990. Dates for the Preboreal and Boreal periods are extrapolated from L. Larsson, 1990, fig. 2, but usage varies from region to region, which is why I have not used these terms more. For sea levels in the Mediterranean, see T. H. van Andel and J. C. Shackleton, 1982; J. C. Shackleton and T. H. van Andel, 1985.

17 E.g. B. Huntley and H. J. B. Birks, 1983, *An atlas of past and present pollen maps for Europe: 0–13000 years ago*, Cambridge; S. Bottema, 1982.

18 D. Geddes *et al.*, 1989.

19 P. Bahn, 1989, 'The early postglacial period in the Pyrenees: some recent work', in C. Bonsall, 1989, pp. 556–60; I. Barandiarán and A. Cava, 1989, 'The evolution of the Mesolithic in the north east of the Iberian peninsula', in C. Bonsall, 1989, pp. 572–81.

20 J. Guilaine, M. Barbaza *et al.*, 1987; J.-D. Vigne, 1991, 'La grande faune mammalienne, miroir du paysage anthropé?', in J. Guilaine (ed.), *Pour une archéologie agraire*, pp. 441–90, Paris; J. Vaquer *et al.*, 1986; D. Geddes, 1980, 1983.

21 For general coverage see: C. Bonsall, 1989; J. Guilaine, J. Courtin *et al.*, 1987; G. Barker, 1981; P. Biagi *et al.*, 1989, 'Liguria: 11,000–7000 BP', in C. Bonsall, 1989, pp. 533–40

22 S. Tusa, 1985; M. Piperno, 1985, 'Some 14C dates for the palaeoeconomic evidence from the Holocene levels of Uzzo cave, Sicily', in C. Malone and S. Stoddart (eds.), *Papers in Italian archaeology IV, Part ii, Prehistory*, pp. 83–6, Oxford; S. Borgognini Tarli and E. Repetto, 1985, 'Diet, dental features and oral pathology in the Mesolithic samples from Uzzo and Molara caves (Sicily)', in C.

Malone and S. Stoddart (eds.), *Papers in Italian archaeology IV, Part ii, Prehistory*, pp. 87–100, Oxford; L. Costantini *et al.*, 1987; L. Costantini, 1989; A. Tagliacozzo, 1993.

23 T. W. Jacobsen, 1981; T. W. Jacobsen and W. R. Farrand, 1988; T. H. van Andel and C. Runnels, 1987; J. M. Hansen, 1991; C. Perlès, 1990a; S. Payne, 1975.

24 C. Perlès, 1990a, p. 120; A. Sordinas, 1969, 'Investigations of the prehistory of Corfu during 1964–1966', *Balkan Studies* 10, 393–424; K. Honea, 1975, 'Prehistoric remains on the island of Kythnos', *American Journal of Archaeology* 79, 277–9.

25 C. N. Runnels, 1988; G. Bailey, G. King and D. Sturdy, 1993, 'Active tectonics and land-use strategies: a Palaeolithic example from northwest Greece', *Antiquity* 67, 292–312; N. Kyparissi-Apostolika, 1995. Are some Mesolithic industries so firmly in an 'Epipalaeolithic' tradition that they cannot be recognised as separate? I owe this suggestion to Geoff Bailey.

26 For stratigraphic detail, see T. W. Jacobsen, 1973, 'Excavation in the Franchthi Cave, 1969–1971, Part I', *Hesperia* 42, 45–88; J. M. Hansen, 1991, pp. 161–3.

27 T. W. Jacobsen, 1969, 'Excavations at Porto Cheli and vicinity, preliminary report, II: the Franchthi Cave, 1967–68', *Hesperia* 38, 343–81; T. W. Jacobsen and T. Cullen, 1981, 'A consideration of mortuary practices in Neolithic Greece: burials from Franchthi Cave', in S. C. Humphreys and H. King (eds.), *Mortality and immortality: the anthropology and archaeology of death*, pp. 79–101, London.

28 A. H. Simmons, 1991; P. C. Edwards, 1989, 'Revising the broad spectrum revolution: and its role in the origins of southwest Asian food production', *Antiquity* 63, 225–46; D. Kaufman, 1992, 'Hunter-gatherers of the Levantine Epipalaeolithic: the sociological origins of sedentism', *Journal of Mediterranean Archaeology* 5, 165–201; G. C. Hillman, S. M. Colledge and D. R. Harris, 1989, 'Plant-food economy during the Epipalaeolithic period at Tell Abu Hureyra, Syria: dietary diversity, seasonality and modes of exploitation', in D. R. Harris and G. C. Hillman (eds.), *Foraging and farming: the evolution of plant exploitation*, pp. 240–68, London.

29 I. Gatsov, 1989, 'Early Holocene assemblages from the Bulgarian Black Sea coast', in C. Bonsall, 1989, pp. 471–4; J. Chapman, 1989; V. Dumitrescu *et al.*, 1982; E. Comşa, 1978, 'Quelques données sur le processus de la Néolithisation dans le territoire de la Roumanie', *Acta Archaeologica Carpathica* 18, 69–74; A. Păunescu, 1987; A. Păunescu, 1990, 'Scurta privire asupra Paleoliticului si Mezoliticului din Dobrogea', *Studii si Cercetari de Istorie Veche si Arheologie* 43, 35–48; M. Özdoğan, 1989; R. Kertész, 1994, 'Late mesolithic chipped stone industry from the site Jásztelek I (Hungary)', in *A kőkortól a középkorig*, pp. 23–44, Szeged.

30 None of the Gorges sites is yet fully published. D. Srejović, 1972; D. Srejović, 1989, 'The Mesolithic of Serbia and Montenegro' in C. Bonsall, 1989, pp. 481–91; D. Srejović and M. Letica, 1978, *Vlasac: a Mesolithic settlement in the Iron gates, I: Archaeology*, Belgrade; M. Garašanin (ed.), 1978, *Vlasac: a Mesolithic settlement in the Iron Gates, II: Geology, biology, anthropology*, Belgrade; B. Prinz, 1987; B. Jovanović, 1969, 'Chronological frames of the Iron Gate group of the early Neolithic period', *Archaeologica Jugoslavica* 10, 23–38; M. Ružić and N. Pavlović, 1988, 'Neolithic sites in Serbia explored and published in the period 1948–1988', in D. Srejović, 1988, pp. 51–68; V. Boroneanţ, 1973, 'Recherches archéologiques sur la culture Schela Cladovei de la zone des Portes de Fer', *Dacia* 17, 5–39; V. Boroneanţ, 1981, 'Betrachtungen über das Epipaläolithikum (Mesolithikum) in Rümanien', in B. Gramsch (ed.), *Mesolithikum in Europe*, pp. 289–94, Berlin; V. Boroneanţ, 1989, 'Thoughts on the chronological relations between the Epi-Palaeolithic and the Neolithic of the Low Danube', in C. Bonsall, 1989, pp. 475–80; V. Boroneanţ, 1990, 'Les enterrements de Schela Cladovei: nouvelles données', in P. M. Vermeersch and P. van Peer, 1990, pp. 121–5; A. Păunescu, 1990, 'Locuira mezolitică de tip Schela Cladovei de la Ostrovul Corbului (jud. Mehedinţi), *Studii şi Cercetari de Istorie Veche* 41/2, 123–47; B. A. Voytek and R. Tringham, 1989, 'Rethinking the Mesolithic: the case of south-east Europe', in C. Bonsall, 1989, pp. 492–9; J. Chapman, 1992.

31 I. Hodder, 1990.

32 Earlier references (especially J. Chapman, 1992) and R. Burleigh and S. Živanović, 1980, 'Radiocarbon dating of a Cro-Magnon population from Padina, Yugoslavia, with some general recommendations for dating human skeletons', *Zeitschrift für morphologische Anthropologie* 70, 269–74; A. Gob, 1990, *Chronologie du Mésolithique en Europe. Atlas des dates 14C*, Liège.

33 A. Bolomey, 1973; S. Bökönyi, 1978, 'The vertebrate fauna at Vlasac', in M. Garašanin (ed.), *Vlasac: a Mesolithic settlement in the Iron Gates, II: geology, biology, anthropology*, pp. 35–65, Belgrade.

34 M. Cârciumaru, 1973; B. Prinz, 1987.

35 G. J. y'Edynak, 1978, 'Culture, diet and dental reduction in Mesolithic forager-fishers of Yugoslavia', *Current Anthropology* 19, 616–8; G. J. y'Edynak and S. Fleisch, 1983, 'Microevolution and biological adaptability in the transition from food-collecting to food-producing in the Iron Gates of Yugoslavia', *Journal of Human Evolution* 12, 279–96.

36 J. Chapman, 1989.

37 J. K. Kozłowski and S. K. Kozłowski, 1982, 'Lithic industries from the multi-layer Mesolithic site Vlasac in Yugoslavia', in J. K. Kozłowski (ed.), *Origin of the chipped stone industries of the early farming cultures in the Balkans*, pp. 11–109, Warsaw; B. Prinz, 1987.

38 D. Srejović, 1972, pp. 47 and 123; J. Chapman, 1992, p. 98. Note also E. Bánffy, 1991, for a similar view of Lepenski Vir.

39 See earlier references, including J. Chapman, 1992, pp. 78–84, for more detailed analysis of the Vlasac sequence.

40 D. Mordant and C. Mordant, 1992.

41 J. Hinout, 1984, 'Les outils et armatures standards mésolithiques dans le bassin parisien par l'analyse des données', *Revue Archéologique de Picardie* 1–2, 9–30; J. G. Rozoy, 1978; R. Parent, 1971, *Le peuplement préhistorique entre la Marne et l'Aisne*, Toulouse.

42 S. K. Kozłowski, 1991.

43 B. Gramsch and K. Kloss, 1989; B. Gramsch, 1992.

44 E. Schuldt, 1961, *Hohen Viecheln: ein mittelsteinzeitlicher Wohnplatz in Mecklenburg*, Berlin; L. Larsson, 1990, and site references.

45 J. G. D. Clark, 1954; A. J. Legge and P. A. Rowley-Conwy, 1988; T. Schadla-Hall, 1989; E. W. Cloutman and A. G. Smith, 1988; P. Mellars, 1990, 'A major "plateau" in the radiocarbon time-scale at *c.* 9650 b.p.: the evidence from Star Carr (North Yorkshire)', *Antiquity* 64, 836–41; P. Day, 1993, 'Preliminary results of high-resolution palaeoecological analyses at Star Carr, Yorkshire', *Cambridge Archaeological Journal* 3, 129–40.

46 J. Clutton-Brock and N. Noe-Nygaard, 1990, 'New osteological and C-isotope evidence on Mesolithic dogs: companions to hunters and fishers at Star Carr, Seamer Carr and Kongemose', *Journal of Archaeological Science* 17, 643–53.

47 L. Larsson, 1990, p. 278; A. Fischer, 1987; A. Fischer, 1989, 'Musholm Bay. Excavation of a sub-marine settlement in a drowned forest 9 metres below present sea level', *Mesolithic Miscellany* 10 (2), 1–3; A. Fischer, 1993, *Stenalderbopladser i Smålandsfarvandet*, Copenhagen.

48 Among many other references, see J. G. D. Clark, 1975, *The earlier Stone Age settlement of Scandinavia*, Cambridge; J. G. Rozoy, 1978; S. K. Kozłowski, 1989, 'A survey of early Holocene cultures of the western part of the Russian plain', in C. Bonsall, 1989, pp. 424–41;. See also J. Chapman, 1989.

49 L. R. Binford, 1980; D. E. Lieberman, 1993.

50 E.g. A. Testart, 1982; H. Watanabe, 1984, 'Occupational differentiation and social stratification: the case of northern Pacific maritime food-gatherers', *Current Anthropology* 24, 217–19; T. Ingold *et al*, 1988a; 1988b.

51 E. N. Wilmsen and J. R. Denbow, 1990, 'Paradigmatic history of San-speaking peoples and current attempts at revision', *Current Anthropology* 31, 489–524; N. Bird-David, 1992; S. Kent, 1992.

52 N. Bird-David, 1992; N. Bird-David, 1990, 'The giving environment: another perspective on the economic system of gatherer-hunters', *Current Anthropology* 31, 183–96; S. Kent, 1992.

53 T. Ingold, 1980, *Hunters, pastoralists and ranchers*, Cambridge.

54 J. D. Speth, 1990, 'Seasonality, resource stress, and food sharing in so-called "egalitarian" foraging societies', *Journal of Anthropological Archaeology* 9, 148–88; T. Gibson, 1988, 'Meat sharing as a political ritual: forms of transaction versus modes of production', in T. Ingold *et al.*, 1988b, pp. 165–79.

55 J. Woodburn, 1982, 'Egalitarian societies', *Man* 17, 431–51; J. Woodburn, 1988, 'African hunter-gatherer social organisation: is it best understood as a product of encapsulation?', in T. Ingold *et al.*, 1988a, pp. 31–64, E. Leacock, 1978; 'Women's status in egalitarian society. Implications for social evolution', *Current Anthropology* 19, 247–55. Note also C. Meillassoux, 1973, 'On the mode of production of the hunting band', in P. Alexandre (ed.), *French perspectives in African studies*, pp. 187–203, Oxford; H. A. Feit, 1994, 'The enduring pursuit: land, time, and social relationships in anthropological models of hunter-gatherers and in sub-arctic hunters' images', in E. S. Burch and L. J. Ellanna (eds.), *Key issues in hunter-gatherer research*, pp. 223–39, Oxford.

56 N. Bird-David, 1992, p. 40.

57 J. Chapman, 1989.

58 J. C. Barrett, 1994, who distinguishes between burial rites and ancestor rites.

3   The first generations: south-east Europe, *c.* 7000/6500–5500 BC

1   G. I. Georgiev, 1961; S. Hiller and V. Nikolov, 1989; S. Hiller, 1990. *Tell* is a Near Eastern term, but it is useful as a general label since the regional names vary (e.g. *magoula* in Thessaly, *toumba* in Macedonia and Thrace, *mogila* in Bulgaria, *halom* in Hungary, and so on).

2   C. L. Redman, 1978, *The rise of civilization*, San Francisco.

3   J. Mellaart, 1970, *Excavations at Haçilar*, Edinburgh; J. Mellaart, 1967, *Catal Hüyük: a Neolithic town in Anatolia*, New York; C. Grigson, 1989, 'Size and sex – evidence for the domestication of cattle in the Near East', in A. Milles, D. Williams and N. Gardner (eds.), *The beginnings of agriculture*, pp. 77–109, Oxford.

4   C. N. Runnels and T. H. van Andel, 1988.

5   A. H. Simmons, 1991; C. Broodbank and T. F. Strasser, 1991.

6   J. D. Evans, 1964, 'Excavations in the Neolithic settlement of Knossos, 1957–60. Part 1', *Annual of the British School at Athens* 64, 132–240.

7   For the population 'wave of advance' model, see A. J. Ammerman and L. L. Cavalli-Sforza, 1984; C. N. Runnels and T. H. van Andel, 1988.

8   The most convenient listing of dates is given in M. Gimbutas, 1991.

9   J. M. Hansen, 1991; S. Payne, 1975; C. Perlès, 1990a; K. D. Vitelli, 1993. Hansen argues from the changes in plant use for changes in population; Perlès suggests continuity at Franchthi but colonisation into Thessaly and elsewhere.

10 R. Dennell, 1983, *European economic prehistory*, London.

11 J. M. Hansen, 1991; S. Payne, 1975.

12 As reviewed in chapter 2, and see D. Srejović, 1988.

13 R. Dennell, 1984; M. Özdoğan, 1989.

14 E.g. J. M. Hansen, 1991, p. 245; and C. Perlès, 1990a, p. 136 for 'déplacements maritimes' into Crete, but without source specified.

15 Knossos level X dates: BM-124 8050±180 BP, BM-278 7910±130 BP, both on 'oak stakes', BM-436 7740±130 BP on carbonised grain; level IX: BM-272 7570±150 BP on charcoal; J. D. Evans, 1968, 'Summary and conclusions. The Knossos culture', *Annual of the British School at Athens* 63, 267–76; see also T. M. Whitelaw, 1992, 'Lost in the labyrinth? Comments on Broodbank's "Social change at Knossos before the Bronze Age"', *Journal of Mediterranean Archaeology* 5, 225–38.

16 C. Perlès, 1990a; 1992a; 1992b; J. C. Shackleton, 1988, *Marine molluscan remains from Franchthi Cave*, Bloomington and Indianapolis.

17 E.g. J. T. Peterson, 1978, 'Hunter-gatherer/farmer exchange', *American Anthropologist* 80, 335–49; S. A. Gregg, 1988, *Foragers and farmers: population interaction and agricultural expansion in prehistoric Europe*, Chicago; R. Dennell, 1984. See also J. Nandris, 1972, 'Relations between the Mesolithic, the First Temperate Neolithic and the Bandkeramik: the nature of the problem', in J. Fitz (ed.), *Die aktuellen Fragen der Bandkeramik*, pp. 61–70, Székésfehervár.

18 A. Whittle, 1985, *Neolithic Europe: a survey*, p. 118, Cambridge; J. Chapman, 1992, p. 105.

19 D. Srejović, 1972; J. Chapman, 1992.

20 J. Chapman, 1992, pp. 103–5.

21 R. G. Handsman, 1991, 'Whose art was found at Lepenski Vir? Gender relations and power in archaeology', in J. M. Gero and M. W. Conkey (eds.), *Engendering archaeology: women and prehistory*, pp. 132–59, Oxford.

22 D. Srejović, 1972, p. 139.

23 D. Theocharis, 1973; M. Wijnen, 1982; P. Halstead, 1989; J.-P. Demoule and C. Perlès, 1993.

24 G. I. Georgiev, 1961; R. Dennell, 1978.

25 D. Srejović, 1988; M. Gimbutas, 1976; A. Clason, 1980.

26 N. Kalicz, 1990, *Frühneolithische Siedlungsfunde aus Südwestungarn*, Budapest; N. Kalicz, 1970; K. Kosse, 1979; A. G. Sherratt, 1983.

27 V. Dumitrescu, *et al.*, 1982; E. Comşa, 1987; V. Dergachev, 1989. See also M. Gimbutas, 1991, and R. Tringham, 1971, for general coverage.

28 M. Wijnen, 1982; J.-P. Demoule and C. Perlès, 1993; R. Rodden, 1965; M. Özdoğan, 1989; C. Renfrew *et al.*, 1986.

29 F. Prendi, 1990, 'Le Néolithique ancien en Albanie', *Germania* 68, 399–426; H. Todorova, 1981.

30 J.-P. Demoule and C. Perlès, 1993, quoting recent work by K. Gallis.

31 The preceramic phase is discussed in V. Milojčić, 1960, V. Milojčić *et al.*, 1962, and D. Theocharis, 1973. See also M. Wijnen, 1982, and most recently C. Perlès, 1990a, and J.-P. Demoule and C. Perlès, 1993.

32 M. Wijnen, 1982. Note that the radiocarbon dates for Nea Nikomedeia are rather scattered. For Achilleion, see M. Gimbutas *et al.*, 1989.

33 J.-P. Demoule and C. Perlès, 1993.

34 R. Dennell, 1984, p. 102; 1978; H. Todorova, 1981, p. 204; G. I. Georgiev, 1965; G. I. Georgiev, 1969, 'Die äneolithische Kultur in Südbulgarien im Lichte der Ausgrabungen vom Tell Azmak bei Stara Zagora', *Studijne Zvesti* 17, 141–58.

35 R. Dennell, 1978; G. I. Georgiev, 1981, 'Die neolithische Siedlung bei Cǎvdar, Bezirk Sofia', *Isvestija* 36, 63–109.

36 G.I. Georgiev *et al.*, 1986, 'Die Neolithische Siedlung Kremenik bei Sapareva Banja, Dezirk Kjustendil', *Studia Praehistorica* 8, 108–52; S. Tchodadjivev and A. Bakamska, 1990, 'Etude du site néolithique ancien de Kraïnitsi dans le département de Kustendil', *Studia Praehistorica* 10, 51–76; J. Pavúk and M. Cochadziev, 1984, 'Neolithische Tellsiedlung bei Galabnik in Westbulgarien', *Slovenská Archeológia* 32, 195–228; J. Pavúk and A. Bakamska, 1989, p. 223; L. Pernitcheva, 1990, 'Le site de Kovatchevo, Néolithique ancien, dans le département de Blagoevgrad', *Studia Praehistorica* 10, 142–96; J.-P. Demoule, M. Grembska-Kulova, R. Katincarov, J. Kulov and M. Lichardus-Itten, 1989, 'Kovacevo: fouille franco-bulgare de l'un des plus anciens villages Néolithiques de l'Europe', in C. Eluère (ed.), *Le premier or de l'humanité en Bulgarie 5ᵉ millénaire*, pp. 33–7, Paris.

37 M. Gimbutas, 1976.

38 D. Srejović, 1988; A. McPherron and D. Srejović, 1988.

39 See earlier references, especially A. G. Sherratt, 1983, and also S. Bökönyi, 1992. Note also F. Horváth, 1989, for the current view of Körös houses. Volumes 6 and 8 of the *Magyarország Régészeti Topográfiája* (Budapest, 1982 and 1989), on county Békés, give the best maps available so far of settlement location in relation to watercourses in parts of the Körös basin.

40 See earlier references.

41 A. Clason, 1980; G. Barker, 1975, 'Early Neolithic land use in Yugoslavia', *Proceedings of the Prehistoric Society* 41, 85–104; J. Pavúk and A. Bakamska, 1989.

42 R. Rodden, 1965; J. Bintliff, 1977, *Natural environment and human settlement in prehistoric Greece*, Oxford; J. Bintliff, 1992, 'Erosion in the Mediterranean lands: a reconsideration of pattern, process and methodology', in M. Bell and J. Boardman (eds.), *Past and present soil erosion*, pp. 1215–31, Oxford. I am grateful to John Bintliff for discussion of the problems of the setting.

43 E. Lear, 1851, *Journals of a landscape painter in Albania*; V. Milojčić, 1960, p. 1.

44 E. Zangger, 1991.

45 J.-P. Demoule and C. Perlès, 1993; P. Halstead, 1989.

46 M. Wijnen, 1982; M. Gimbutas *et al.*, 1989.

47 E.g. J.-P. Demoule and C. Perlès, 1993; P. Halstead, 1989. For Prodromos, see D. Theocharis, 1973, and P. Halstead and G. Jones, 1980.

48 T. H. van Andel *et al.*, 1995. Excavations at the tell were directed by K. Gallis. See also T. H. van Andel, E. Zangger and A. Demitrack, 1990, 'Land use and soil erosion in prehistoric and historical Greece', *Journal of Field Archaeology* 17, 379–96; C. Becker, 1991, 'Die Tierknochenfunde von der Platia Magoula Zarkou – neue Untersuchungen zu Haustierhaltung, Jagd und Rohstoffverwendung im neolithisch-bronzezeitlichen Thessalien', *Praehistorische Zeitschrift* 66, 14–78.

49 J. C. Chapman, 1988, 'From "space" to "place": a model of dispersed settlement and Neolithic society', in C. Burgess *et al.*, pp.21–46; S. Bökönyi, 1992; S. Bökönyi, 1972, 'Zoological evidence for seasonal or permanent occupation of prehistoric settlements', in P. J. Ucko, R. Tringham and G. W. Dimbleby (eds.), *Man, settlement and urbanism*, pp. 121–6, London.

50 See earlier references.

51 M. Gimbutas, 1976; G. I. Georgiev, 1961.

52 V. Milojčić *et al.*, 1962; D. Theocharis, 1973; M. Wijnen, 1982.

53 D. Theocharis, 1973, pp. 45 and 60.

54 D. Theocharis, 1973; M. Wijnen, 1982.

55 M. Gimbutas *et al.*, 1989, especially table 4.1, p. 33.

56 D. Theocharis, 1973; K. Kotsakis, 1981; K. Kotsakis, 1995.

57 G. Georgiev, 1961; S. Hiller, 1990; D. Bailey, 1993, p. 207.

58 D. Srejović, 1988; A. McPherron and D. Srejović, 1988; J. Makkay, 1992; N. Vlassa, 1976, *Neoliticul Transilvaniei*, Cluj-Napoca; V. Dergachev, A. Sherratt and O. Larina, 1991, 'Recent results of Neolithic research in Moldavia', *Oxford Journal of Archaeology* 10, 1–16.

59 D. Theocharis, 1973; K. Kotsakis, 1981.

60 M. Gimbutas *et al.*, 1989, especially chapter 4.

61 P. Halstead, 1989, p. 70. A slightly lower range of 0.4 to 0.8 ha is quoted in P. Halstead, 1981, 'Counting sheep in Neolithic and Bronze Age Greece', in I. Hodder, N. Hammond and G. Isaacs (eds.), *Pattern of the past*, pp. 307–39, Cambridge. Higher estimates are given in J.-P. Demoule and C. Perlès, 1993, of surface areas of 2 ha and more.

62 D. Theocharis, 1973; V. Milojčić *et al.*, 1962.

63 G. I. Georgiev, 1961; 1965.

64 G. I. Georgiev, 1961.

65 S. Hiller and V. Nikolov, 1989; S. Hiller, 1990.

66 V. Nikolov, 1989, 'Das frühneolithische Haus von Sofia-Slatina. Eine Untersuchung zur vorgeschichtlichen Bautechnik', *Germania* 67, 1–49; V. Nikolov, 1992; V. Nikolov, 1992, *Rannoneolitno selishe ot Slatina (Sofia)*, Sofia.

67 D. Theocharis, 1973; K. Kotsakis, 1995; J.-P. Demoule and C. Perlès, 1993; V. Milojčić, 1960; V. Milojčić, 1983, *Otzaki-Magula II. Das mittlere Neolithikum. Die mittelneolithische Siedlung*, Bonn.

68 R. Rodden, 1965.

69 M. Gimbutas *et al.*, 1989; K. Kotsakis, 1995.

70 D. Theocharis, 1973; R. Rodden, 1965; J.-P. Demoule and C. Perlès, 1993; M. Gimbutas, 1976; D. Bailey, 1993, p. 208; J. Makkay, 1992.

71 M. Gimbutas *et al.*, 1989; M. Gimbutas, 1976.

72 C. Perlès, 1990b.

73 C. Perlès, 1990b; C. Perlès, 1992b; M. Gimbutas *et al.*, 1989.

74 R. Torrence, 1986, *Production and exchange of stone tools: prehistoric obsidian in the Aegean*, Cambridge; C. Perlès, 1990b.

75 N. Vlassa, 1972, 'Eine frühneolithische Kultur mit bemalter Keramik der Vor-Starčevo-Körös-Zeit in Cluj-Gura Baciului, Siebenburgen', *Praehistorische Zeitschrift* 47, 174–97; J. Nandris, 1975, 'A reconsideration of the south-eastern sources of archaeological obsidian', *Bulletin of the Institute of Archaeology* 12, 71–94.

76 M. Gimbutas *et al.*, 1989.

77 A. McPherron and D. Srejović, 1988.

78 K. D. Vitelli, 1993; J.-P. Demoule and C. Perlès, 1993.

79 V. Nikolov, 1992; C. Ridley and K. A. Wardle, 1979, 'Rescue excavations at Servia 1971–1973: a preliminary report', *Annual of the British School at Athens* 74, 185–230; K. D. Vitelli, 1989, 'Were pots first made for foods? Doubts from Franchthi?', *World Archaeology* 21, 17–29; S. H. Katz and M. M. Voigt, 1990.

80 K. Kotsakis, 1995.

81 The 'culture history' literature is vast, and continues to grow. For general accounts see R. Tringham, 1971; D. Theocharis, 1973; J.-P. Demoule and C. Perlès, 1993; M. Gimbutas, 1991; G. I. Georgiev, 1961; D. Srejović, 1988: and many others!

82 D. Garašanin, 1954, *Starcevacka kultura*, Ljubljana; D. Srejović, 1988; J.-P. Demoule and C. Perlès, 1993.

83 P. Halstead, 1989.

84 See note 36.

85 M. Gimbutas, 1974; 1989; 1991; R. Tringham, 1971; D. Theocharis, 1973.

86 J. Nandris, 1970, 'The development and relationships of the earlier Greek Neolithic', *Man* 5, 191–213; D. Theocharis, 1973.

87 R. Rodden, 1965; M. Gimbutas *et al.*, 1989; A. McPherron and D. Srejović, 1988.

88 Promoted especially by Gimbutas in recent years. See note 85.

89 M. Gimbutas *et al.*, 1989, especially chapter 7.

90 L. E. Talalay, 1987, 'Rethinking the function of clay figurine legs from Neolithic Greece: an argument by analogy', *American Journal of Archaeology* 91, 161–9; L. E. Talalay, 1991; L. E. Talalay, 1993, *Deities, dolls and devices: Neolithic figurines from Franchthi Cave, Greece*, Indianapolis and Bloomington; P. J. Ucko, 1968, *Anthropomorphic figurines of predynastic Egypt and Neolithic Crete*, London; E. Bánffy, 1991.

91 D. W. Bailey, 1994; E. Bánffy, 1991.

92 See earlier general references, especially D. Theocharis, 1973; R. Tringham, 1971; and also R. Willms, 1985.

93 From a large literature see J. M. Hansen, 1991; J. M. Hansen, 1992; G. Barker, 1985, *Prehistoric European agriculture*, Cambridge; S. Bökönyi, 1974; P. Halstead, 1989; R. Dennell, 1978.

94 S. Bökönyi, 1974; S. Payne, 1975.

95 E.g. by S. Bökönyi, in M. Gimbutas *et al.*, 1989, chapter 13.

96 P. Halstead and G. Jones, 1980; P. Halstead, 1989. For pollen diagrams, see S. Bottema, 1982, and references to earlier work. Note also K. J. Willis and K. D. Bennett, 1994, 'The Neolithic transition – fact or fiction? Paleoecological evidence from the Balkans', *The Holocene* 4, 326–30.

97 M. Gimbutas *et al.*, 1989; M. Gimbutas, 1976; A. Clason, 1980, gives no specific data for Starčevo, but see S. Bökönyi, 1992, for the Körös site Endrőd 119.

 98 G. Nobis, 1988, 'Zur Fauna der frühneolithischen Siedlung Ovčarovo-gorata bei Tărgovište (NO-Bulgarien)', *Studia Praehistorica* 9, 37–53.
 99 P. Halstead, 1989; A. Clason, 1980; K. Kosse, 1979; J. Makkay, 1992; I. Takács, 1992, 'Fish remains from the Early Neolithic site of Endrőd 119', in S. Bökönyi, 1992, pp. 301–11.
100 J. M. Hansen, 1991; 1992. For a general consideration of legumes, see A. Butler, 1992, 'Pulse agronomy: traditional systems and implications for early cultivation', in P. C. Anderson (ed.), *Préhistoire de l'agriculture: nouvelles approches expérimentales et ethnographiques*, pp. 67–78, Paris.
101 R. Dennell, 1978.
102 V. Nikolov, 1992; E. Dontscheva, 1990, 'Plant macrorest research of early Neolithic dwelling in Slatina', *Studia Praehistorica* 10, 86–90.
103 For discussion of yields, see G. H. Willcox, 1992, 'Archaeobotanical significance of growing Near Eastern progenitors of domestic plants at Jalès (France)', in P. C. Anderson (ed.), *Préhistoire de l'agriculture*, pp.159–77, Paris.
104 T. H. van Andel *et al.*, 1995. For cultivation at Nea Nikomedeia, see W. van Zeist and S. Bottema, 1971, 'Plant husbandry in Early Neolithic Nea Nikomedeia, Greece', *Acta Botanica Neerlandica* 20, 524–38. I owe the point about Danube flooding to Nándor Kalicz.
105 J. M. Renfrew, 1976, 'Carbonised seeds', in M. Gimbutas, *Neolithic Macedonia as reflected by excavation at Anza*, pp. 300–12, Los Angeles.
106 S. H. Katz and M. M. Voigt, 1990. A later date for the introduction of beer drinking is suggested by A. G. Sherratt, 1987.
107 N. Bird-David, 1992.
108 R. Dennell, 1978; M. Gimbutas, 1976.
109 D. W. Bailey, 1990.
110 A. G. Sherratt, 1994.
111 I. Hodder, 1990; 1992.
112 A. Whittle, 1995, 'The scale of difference and the nature of community: reflections on Neolithic social relations', in M. Kuna and N. Venclová (eds.), *Whither archaeology? Papers in honour of Evžen Neustupný*, pp. 283–92, Prague.
113 P. J. Wilson, 1988, *The domestication of the human species*, New Haven and London.
114 E.g. J. E. Yellen, 1977, *Archaeological approaches to the present*, New York.
115 E. Gellner, 1988.

4   Old and new histories: south-east Europe, *c.* 5500–4000 BC

  1 I. Bognár-Kutzián, 1963; 1972; M. Meisenheimer, 1989.
  2 N. Kalicz, 1970; 1986; N. Kalicz and J. Makkay, 1977; K. Kosse, 1979; P. Raczky, 1986; 1987a; 1989; F. Horváth, 1989; I. Bognár-Kutzián, 1972.
  3 See especially P. Raczky, 1987a.
  4 T. Kaiser and B. Voytek, 1983.
  5 J. Chapman, 1990. Note F. E. Brown, 1990, 'Comment on Chapman: some cautionary notes on the application of spatial measures to prehistoric settlements', in R. Samson (ed.), *The social archaeology of houses*, pp. 111–24, Edinburgh.
  6 Especially M. Gimbutas, 1974, 1991. For the Vinča culture, see J. C. Chapman, 1981.
  7 I. Ivanov, 1988; C. Renfrew, 1986, 'Varna and the emergence of wealth in prehistoric Europe', in A. Appadurai (ed.), *The social life of things*, pp.141–68, Cambridge; J. Chapman, 1991.
  8 J. Chapman, 1990; 1991; I. Ivanov, 1988; A. Radunceva, 1989.
  9 Most recently by J. Lichardus, 1991, 'Kupferzeit als historische Epoche. Versuch einer Deutung', in J. Lichardus (ed.), *Die Kupferzeit als historische Epoche*, pp. 763–800, Bonn. The potential confusion is endless. In the earlier fifth millennium BC, for example, we have a Late Neolithic in Greece, Hungary and Romania but an Early Copper Age in Bulgaria; the

Hungarian Early Copper Age starts with the Tiszapolgár phase of the later fifth millennium BC, the time of the Late Copper Age in southern Balkan terminology. It is safer to refer to spans of millennia in calibrated/calendar years.

10 For these initial sketches I give only some general references; more detailed ones follow later in the chapter. For Greece, see D. Theocharis, 1973; J.-P. Demoule and C. Perlès, 1993.

11 H. Todorova, 1978; 1982; 1986. For Romania, see E. Comşa, 1987.

12 J. C. Chapman, 1981; D. Srejović, 1988; D. Srejović and N. Tasić, 1990; B. Brukner, 1988.

13 See note 2.

14 E. Comşa, 1987; V. A. Dergachev, 1986; 1989; V. Dergacev, 1993, 'Modèles d'etablissements de la culture de Tripolie', *Préhistoire Européenne* 5, 101–18; L. Ellis, 1984; M. Petrescu-Dimboviţa (ed.), 1987, *La civilisation de Cucuteni en contexte européen*, Iaşi; S. Marinescu-Bîlcu, 1991, 'Sur quelques problèmes du Néolithiques et du Enéolithique à l'Est des Carpates Orientales', *Dacia* 35, 5–59.

15 P. Halstead, 1989; T. H. van Andel *et al.*, 1995; J.-P. Demoule and C. Perlès, 1993.

16 D. Theocharis, 1973; G. Hourmouziadis, 1979; E. Zangger, 1991.

17 C. Renfrew *et al.*, 1986; J. Deshayes and R. Treuil, 1992, *Dikili Tash: village préhistorique de Macedoine orientale*, Paris and Athens.

18 J.-P. Demoule and C. Perlès, 1993.

19 N. Efstratiou, 1985.

20 J. L. Davis, 1992.

21 H. Todorova, 1986, especially chapter 4.

22 R. Dennell, 1984, p. 102; H. Todorova, 1981; 1986.

23 G. I. Georgiev, 1965.

24 R. Dennell, 1978; H. Todorova, 1986.

25 A. Fol, R. Katincarov and J. Lichardus, 1988, 'Die bulgarisch-deutschen Ausgrabungen in Drama', in A. Fol and J. Lichardus, 1988, pp. 151–80.

26 H. Todorova *et al.*, 1975; H. Todorova, 1986; I. Angelova, 1992, 'Predvaritelinshe resultati raskopok neolicheskogo poseleinya Ovcarovo-gorata', *Studia Praehistorica* 11–12, 41–50.

27 A. Margos, 1978, 'Les sites lacustres dans les lacs de Varna et la nécropole de Varna', *Studia Praehistorica* 1–2, 146–8; A. Fol and J. Lichardus, 1988.

28 H. Todorova, 1986.

29 D. Berciu, 1966; E. Comşa, 1987; H. Todorova and T. Dimov, 1989.

30 H. Todorova, 1978; 1982; 1986; H. Todorova *et al.*, 1983.

31 E. Comşa, 1987; D. Berciu, 1961; E. Comşa, 1972, 'Quelques problèmes relatives au complexe néolithique de Radovanu', *Dacia* 16, 39–51; V. Dumitrescu, 1965; 1970.

32 E. Comşa, 1987.

33 B. Nikolov, 1978; H. Todorova, 1986; B. Nikolov, 1975, *Zaminets*, Sofia.

34 J. C. Chapman, 1981; D. Srejović, 1988; D. Srejović and N. Tasić, 1990.

35 R. Tringham and D. Krstić, 1990.

36 D. Jacanovic, 1988, 'Neolithic sites in the Danubian region from the mouth of the Velika Morava to Golubac', in D. Srejović (ed.), *The Neolithic of Serbia*, pp. 111–19, Belgrade.

37 D. Srejović, 1988; D. Srejović and N. Tasić, 1990.

38 M. Ruzic and N. Pavlovic, 1988, 'Neolithic sites in Serbia explored in the period 1948–1988', in D. Srejović (ed.), *The Neolithic in Serbia*, pp. 69–110, Belgrade; B. Brukner, 1988.

39 F. Fiala and M. Hoernes, 1895, *Die neolithische Siedlung von Butmir*, Sarajevo. See also A. Benac, 1973, 'Obre II: a Neolithic settlement of the Butmir group at Gornje Polje', *Wissenschaftliche Mitteilungen des Bosnisch-Herzegowinischen Landesmuseums (Sarajevo)* 3, Heft A, 5–91.

40 J. C. Chapman, 1981; M. Gimbutas, 1976.

41 J. C. Chapman, 1981; R. Tringham, 1991; R. Tringham *et al.*, 1985; 1992.

42 P. Georgieva, 1990, 'Periodization of the Krivodol–Salcuta–Bubanj culture', in D. Srejović (ed.), *The Neolithic of Serbia*, pp. 167–73, Belgrade.

43 N. Kalicz and J. Makkay, 1977.

44 N. Kalicz and P. Raczky, 1987a. For the Szakálhát phase, see also P. Raczky, 1986, and F. Horváth, 1989.

45 F. Horváth, 1987; P. Raczky, 1987a; N. Kalicz and P. Raczky, 1987b; 1984.

46 See notes 1–2.

47 E. Comşa, 1987; V. A. Dergachev, 1986; V. Dergachev, 1989; L. Ellis, 1984.

48 S. Marinescu-Bilcu, 1981.

49 L. Ellis, 1984; V. A. Dergachev, 1986; E. Chernykh, 1992.

50 Still followed by some, for example partly in D. Srejović, 1988. But see V. Lekovic, 1990, 'The *Vinčanization* of Starčevo culture', in D. Srejović and N. Tasić, pp. 67–74; and J. Petrovic, 1990, 'A contribution to the study of autochthonous predecessors of the Vinča culture in Srem', in D. Srejović and N. Tasić, 1990, pp. 85–9. For the beginnings of the *Alföld* Linear Pottery culture, see N. Kalicz and J. Makkay, 1977; J. Makkay, 1987, 'Kontakte zwischen der Körös-Starčevo Kultur und der Linienbandkeramik', *Communicationes Archaeologicae Hungaricae* 1987, 15–24; P. Raczky, 1989.

51 D. Berciu, 1966; A. Păunescu, 1987; R. P. S. Price, 1993, 'The west Pontic "maritime interaction sphere": a long-term structure in Balkan prehistory?', *Oxford Journal of Archaeology* 12, 175–96.

52 R. Dennell, 1984; V. Dergachev, 1989; P. M. Dolukhanov, 1979, *Ecology and economy in Neolithic eastern Europe*, London; P. M. Dolukhanov, 1993, 'Foraging and farming groups in north-eastern and north-western Europe: identity and interaction', in J. Chapman and P. Dolukhanov (eds.), *Cultural transformations and interactions in eastern Europe*, pp. 122–45, Aldershot; M. Zvelebil and P. Dolukhanov, 1991.

53 D. Theocharis, 1973; V. Milojčić, A. von den Driesch, J. Milojčić-von Zumbusch and K. Kilian, 1976, *Die deutschen Ausgrabungen auf Magulen um Larisa in Thessalien 1966. Agia Sofia-Magula. Karagyös-Magula. Bunar Baschi*, Bonn; G. Hourmouziadis, 1979; J.-P. Demoule and C. Perlès, 1993.

54 D. Theocharis, 1973, p. 102, suggests a role as community house as an alternative to a leader's house.

55 See discussion below, and for the idea of deliberate destructions: D. W. Bailey, 1990; R. Tringham and D. Krstić, 1990; R. Tringham, 1991.

56 G. Hourmouziadis, 1979; P. Halstead, 1992; 1993. The history of the site might be longer; a few Early Neolithic sherds were reported by A. J. B. Wace and M. S. Thompson, 1912, *Prehistoric Thessaly*, Cambridge.

57 K. J. Gallis, 1985.

58 See chapter 3, notes 88–91, especially L. E. Talalay, 1991, and D. W. Bailey, 1994.

59 D. Theocharis, 1973; J.-P. Demoule and C. Perlès, 1993.

60 K. J. Gallis, 1985; J.-P. Demoule and C. Perlès, 1993; L. E. Talalay, 1991.

61 See again T. H. van Andel *et al.*, 1995.

62 H. Kroll, 1979, 'Kulturpflanzen aus Dimini', in U. Körber (ed.), *Festschrift Maria Hopf*, pp. 173–89, Köln; P. Halstead, 1992.

63 P. Halstead, 1989; E. Zangger, 1991.

64 S. Bottema, 1982.

65 G. I. Georgiev, 1961; S. Hiller, 1990; G. I. Georgiev, 1965.

66 A. Radunceva, 1989a; A. Radunceva, 1989b, 'Le centre cultuel chalcolithique du village de Dolnoslav, région de Plovdiv', in C. Eluère (ed.), *Le premier or de l'humanité en Bulgarie 5ᵉ millénaire*, p. 81, Paris; A. Radunceva, 1991, 'Kurzer vorläufiger Bericht über die Ausgrabungen in Dolnoslav', in J. Lichardus (ed.), *Kupferzeit als historische Epoche*, pp. 107–10, Bonn.

67 A. Radunceva, 1989a.

68 H. Todorova, 1986.

69 H. Todorova, 1986.

70 H. Todorova *et al.*, 1975.

71 H. Todorova, 1978; 1982; 1986; I. Angelova, 1982.

72 H. Todorova *et al.*, 1983; H. Todorova, 1986.

73 H. Todorova, 1982; 1986.

74 A. Radunceva, 1976; H. Todorova, 1982; 1986; N. Angelov, 1959.

75 H. Todorova, 1986; H. Todorova and T. Dimov, 1989.

76 See note 31.

77 H. Todorova *et al.*, 1975.

78 C. N. Mateescu, 1975, 'Remarks on cattle breeding and agriculture in the Middle and Late Neolithic on the lower Danube', *Dacia* 19, 13–18. Another claim in this paper is that an antler artefact from a fifth-millennium BC context at Căscioarele is an ard share.

79 G. Bozilova and M. Filipova, 1986, 'Paleoecological environment in northeastern Black Sea area during Neolithic, Eneolithic and Bronze periods', *Studia Praehistorica* 8, 160–5.

80 J. Chapman, 1990; 1991.

81 D. W. Bailey, 1990. Consider also D. R. White, 1988, 'Rethinking polygyny. Co-wives, codes and cultural systems', *Current Anthropology* 29, 529–72.

82 H. Todorova *et al.*, 1983; H. Todorova, 1986; H. Todorova, 'Kultszene und Hausmodell aus Ovcarovo, Bez. Targovishe', *Thracia* 3, 39–46.

83 Illustrated in H. Todorova, 1986, fig. 84.

84 H. Todorova, 1986; N. Angelov, 1959.

85 V. Dumitrescu, 1965; 1970.

86 M. Gimbutas, 1974. Note again the sceptical approach of E. Bánffy, 1991.

87 D. W. Bailey, 1993; B. Nikolov, 1986, 'Signes sur les ouvrages en argile de l'époque préhistorique en Bulgarie occidentale', *Studia Praehistorica* 10, 77–85; B. Nikolov, 1974, *Gradesnica*, Sofia.

88 N. Angelov, 1961, 'Rabotilnitsa za ploski kosteni idoli v selishnate mogila pri s. Hotnitsa, Turnovsko', *Arkheologiya* 3, 34–8; L. Perniceva, 1978, 'Sites et habitations du Chalcolithique en Bulgarie', *Studia Praehistorica* 1–2, 163–9; D. Galbenu, 1963, 'Neoliticeskaya masterkaya dlya obrabotki ukrasenii v Hirsove', *Dacia* 7, 501–9.

89 H. Todorova, 1978; 1986; H. Todorova *et al.*, 1975; A. Radunceva, 1976; J. Lichardus, 1988.

90 E.g. A. Radunceva, 1989; J. Chapman, 1991.

91 J. Lichardus, 1988.

92 H. Todorova and T. Dimov, 1989; M. Avramova, 1989, 'Les études archéologiques de l'époque chalcolithique en Bulgarie', in C. Eluère (ed.), *Le premier or de l'humanité en Bulgarie 5ᵉ millénaire*, pp. 25–9, Paris.

93 H. Todorova, 1986; E. Comşa, 1987; D. Berciu, 1966; G. Cantacuzino and S. Morintz, 1963, 'Die jungsteinzeitliche Funde in Cernica', *Dacia* 7, 27–89; G. Cantacuzino, 1969, 'The prehistoric necropolis of Cernica and its place in the Neolithic cultures of Romania and Europe in the light of recent discoveries', *Dacia* 13, 45–59.

94 I. Ivanov, 1988; 1989.

95 See note 90.

96 See note 90.

97 J. C. Barrett, 1994.

98 J. C. Barrett, 1994, who distinguishes between burial rites and ancestor rites.

99 I. Ivanov, 1988.

100 B. Brukner, 1988; D. Srejović, 1988.

101 B. Brukner, 1990, 'Typen und Modellen Siedlungen und Wohnobjekte der Vinča-Gruppe in der Panonnischen Tiefebene', in D. Srejović and N. Tasić, 1990, pp. 79–83. For cattle domestication, see also Vinča itself: S. Bökönyi, 1990, 'Tierknochen Funde der neuesten Ausgrabungen in Vinča', in D. Srejović and N. Tasić, 1990, pp. 49–54. See also A. T. Clason, 1979, 'The farmers of Gomolava in the Vinča and La Tène period', *Palaeohistoria* 21, 41–81; W.

van Zeist, 1975, 'Preliminary report on the botany of Gomolava', *Journal of Archaeological Science* 2, 315–25.

102 J. C. Chapman, 1981, pp. 74–5.

103 J. C. Chapman, 1981; B. Brukner, 1988.

104 R. Galovic, 1959, *Predionica: neolitisko naselje kod Pristine*, Pristina.

105 N. Vlassa, 1963, 'Chronology of the Neolithic of Transylvania in the light of the Tărtăria settlement's stratigraphy', *Dacia* 7, 485–94. Because of parallels with Jemdet Nasr in Mesopotamia, might the finds be better assigned to the Coṭofeni period? Nándor Kalicz, personal communication.

106 E. Comşa, 1987. Or is the animal a goat?

107 J. Chapman, 1983, 'Meaning and illusion in Balkan prehistory', in A. Poulter (ed.), *Ancient Bulgaria*, pp. 1–42, Nottingham.

108 A. McPherron and D. Srejović, 1988.

109 M. Gimbutas, 1976. The site architecture is to be published by the (former) Yugoslav team.

110 R. Tringham and D. Krstić, 1990.

111 Rather few radiocarbon dates were obtained, which indicate a long span. There is some Vinča-Pločnik material.

112 J. Chapman, 1990, 'The Neolithic of the Morava-Danube confluence area: a regional assessment of settlement patterns', in R. Tringham and D. Krstić, 1990, pp. 13–43.

113 T. Kaiser and B. Voytek, 1983.

114 R. Tringham and D. Krstić, 1990; R. Tringham, 1991.

115 A. McPherron and D. Srejović, 1988. The span of occupation indicated by radiocarbon dates was very long, and longer than indicated by the stratigraphy, architecture and material.

116 R. Tringham, 1991; R. Tringham *et al.*, 1985; 1992; H. J. Greenfield, 1988, 'The origins of milk and wool production in the Old World. A zooarchaeological perspective from the central Balkans', *Current Anthropology* 29, 573–93; H. J. Greenfield, 1991, 'Fauna from the Late Neolithic of the central Balkans: issues in subsistence and land use', *Journal of Field Archaeology* 18, 161–86; M. Lazic, 1988, 'Fauna of mammals from the Neolithic settlements in Serbia', in D. Srejović (ed.), *The Neolithic of Serbia*, pp.24–38, Belgrade.

117 N. Kalicz and P. Raczky, 1987b; 1984. For Szakálhát houses, see: P. Raczky, 1986, for example at Öcsöd; K. Hegedűs, 1985, 'The settlement of the Neolithic Szakálhát-group at Csanytelek-Újhalastó', *Móra Ferenc Múzeum Évkönyve* 1982–3 (1), 7–54. Note one structure as long as 38 m, at Tiszaföldvár-Téglagyár: E. Bánffy, 1991, pp. 206–7.

118 K. Hegedűs and J. Makkay, 1987.

119 J. Korek, 1987; N. Kalicz, 1970. The Kökénydomb figurines were found on the floor of a building, near an open hearth: J. Banner, 1959, 'Anthropomorphe Gefässe der Theiss-Kultur von der Siedlung Kökénydomb bei Hódmezővásárhely (Ungarn), *Germania* 37, 14–35. See also J. Csalog, 1959, 'Die anthropomorphen Gefässe und Idolplastik von Szegvár-Tűzköves', *Acta Archaeologica Academiae Scientiarum Hungaricae* 11, 7–38.

120 J. Korek, 1987.

121 P. Raczky, 1987a; F. Horváth, 1987.

122 G. Lazarovici, Z. Kalmar, F. Draşoveanu and A.S. Luca, 1985, 'Complexul neolitic de la Parţa', *Banatica* 1985, 7–71; G. Lazarovici, 1989, 'Das neolitische Heilgtum von Parţa', in S. Bökönyi (ed.), *Neolithic of southeastern Europe and its Near Eastern connections*, pp. 149–74, Budapest. For 'cult corners', see E. Bánffy, 1991.

123 K. Hegedűs and J. Makkay, 1987; J. Korek, 1987; P. Raczky, 1987a; F. Horváth, 1987; N. Kalicz and P. Raczky, 1987b.

124 N. Kalicz and P. Raczky, 1987a; S. Bökönyi, 1974; 1986. Use of the plough was suggested by J. Makkay, 1978, 'A Szegvár-tűzkövesi újkökori férfiszobor, és o "föld és ég elvásztásának" ösi mítosza', *Archaeologiai Értesítő* 105, 164–83.

125 N. Kalicz and P. Raczky, 1987a.

126 First suggested by I. Bognár-Kutzián, 1972. Elaborated by A. Sherratt, 1982; 1983.

127 N. Kalicz and P. Raczky, 1987a.

128 See again R. Tringham and D. Krstić, 1990.

129 Among many others, see J. C. Barrett, 1994. Note the denial of a universal theory of material culture by I. Hodder, 1994, 'Architecture and meaning: the example of Neolithic houses and tombs', in M. Parker Pearson and C. Richards (eds.), *Architecture and order*, pp. 73–86, London.

130 N. Kalicz, 1970; N. Kalicz and J. Makkay, 1977.

131 N. David, J. Sterner and K. Gavua, 1988, 'Why pots are decorated', *Current Anthropology* 29, 365–89; J. Sterner, 1989, 'Who is signalling whom? Ceramic style, ethnicity and taphonomy among the Sirak Bulahay', *Antiquity* 63, 451–9.

132 N. Kalicz and P. Raczky, 1987a.

133 I. Bognár-Kutzián, 1963; 1972.

134 I. Bognár-Kutzián, 1972.

135 I. Bognár-Kutzián, 1972.

136 P. Halstead, 1993, p. 608.

137 J. C. Chapman, 1981; M. Gimbutas, 1976; R. Tringham and D. Krstić, 1990; A. McPherron and D. Srejović, 1988.

138 N. Kalicz and P. Raczky, 1987a; 1987b.

139 A. McPherron and D. Srejović, 1988.

140 See note 131.

141 H. Todorova, 1978; 1986. Debate on the temperatures required to fire graphite on to pottery seems not to have continued: see E. Gardner, 1979, 'Graphite painted pottery', *Archaeology* 32, 18–23.

142 C. Eluère and C. R. Raub, 1991, 'Investigations on the gold coating technology of the great dish from Varna', in C. Eluère and J.-P. Mohen (eds.), *Découverte du métal*, pp. 13–30, Paris.

143 V. Dumitrescu, 1965, and compare Pre-Cucuteni pots to the west and south of their normal area: S. Marinescu-Bîlcu, 1981, p. 139; J. C. Lavezzi, 1978, 'Prehistoric investigations at Corinth', *Hesperia* 47, 402–51; S. Marinescu-Bîlcu, 1981, p. 61; V. Dumitrescu, 1980, *Rast*, Oxford; N. Kalicz and J. Makkay, 1977.

144 There is ethnographic evidence for long-distance pot movement, especially by water: K. Nicklin, 1971, 'Stability and innovation in pottery manufacture', *World Archaeology* 3, 13–48.

145 J. C. Chapman, 1981.

146 H. Todorova, 1986, especially maps 6–8.

147 P. Halstead, 1989; 1993; J.-P. Demoule and C. Perlès, 1993.

148 The 'culture' model, going back to Childe and earlier. For examples of the tribal interpretation, see H. Todorova, 1986; A. Radunceva, 1989; E. Comşa, 1987; D. Srejović, 1988.

149 C. Renfrew, 1977.

150 E. Comşa, 1987. See also, on footwear, E. Comşa, 1992, 'Unele date cu privire la incaltamintea din epoca neolitica de pe teritoriul Romaniei', *Studii şi Cercetari de Istorie Veche şi Arheologie* 44, 35–48.

151 E. W. Herbert, 1984, *Red gold of Africa: copper in precolonial history and culture*, Madison.

152 J. Chapman, 1991.

153 I. Hodder, 1990.

154 C. Renfrew, 1969, 'The autonomy of the south east European Copper Age', *Proceedings of the Prehistoric Society* 35, 12–47; N. H. Gale *et al.*, 1991.

155 H. Todorova, 1986; E. N. Chernykh, 1992; E. N. Černych, 1991, 'Frühestes Kupfer in den Steppen- und Waldsteppenkulturen Osteuropas', in J. Lichardus (ed.), *Kupferzeit als historische Epoche*, pp. 581–92, Bonn.

156 E. Comşa, 1991.

157 J. C. Chapman, 1981; B. Jovanovic, 1990; N. H. Gale *et al.*, 1991; E. Comşa, 1991; H. Todorova, 1986.

158 E. Cernych, 1978, 'Aibunar – a Balkan copper mine of the fourth millennium B.C.', *Proceedings of the Prehistoric Society* 44, 203–17; E. N. Chernykh, 1992; B. Jovanovic, 1979, 'The technology of primary copper mining in south-east Europe', *Proceedings of the Prehistoric Society* 45, 103–10; B. Jovanovic, 1982, *Rudna Glava: najstarije rudarstvo bakra na centralnom Balkanu*, Belgrade; B. Jovanovic, 1992, 'Les débuts de l'utilisation du métal dans les Balkans dans l'analyse archéométallurgique', *Studia Praehistorica* 11–12, 262–7.

159 H. Todorova, 1986; E. N. Chernykh, 1992.

160 V. McGeehan-Liritzis, 1983, 'The relationship between metalwork, copper sources and the evidence for settlement in the Greek Late Neolithic and Early Bronze Age', *Oxford Journal of Archaeology* 2, 147–80; C. Renfrew *et al.*, 1986; J.-P. Demoule and C. Perlès, 1993.

161 For the Hungarian plain, see earlier references; E. N. Chernykh, 1992.

162 E. N. Chernykh, 1992.

163 J. C. Chapman, 1981. Supporting a late Vinča date for the Plocnik hoard, note B. Jovanovic, 1990.

164 A. Radunceva, 1989.

165 I. Ivanov, 1988; M. Avramova, 1991, 'Gold and copper jewelry from the Chalcolithic cemeteries near the village of Durankulak, Varna district', in C. Eluère and J.-P. Mohen (eds.), *Découverte du métal*, pp. 43–8, Paris; H. Todorova, 1978; 1986.

166 A. Hartmann, 1978, 'Ergebnisse der spektralanalytischen Untersuchung äneolithischer Goldfunde aus Bulgarien', *Studia Praehistorica* 1–2, 27–45; I. Ivanov, 1988; N. H. Gale *et al.*, 1991; J. Makkay, 1991.

167 R. Echt, W. R. Thiele and I. Ivanov, 1991, 'Varna: Untersuchungen zur kupferzeitlichen Goldverarbeitung', in J. Lichardus (ed.), *Kupferzeit als historische Epoche*, pp. 633–91, Bonn.

168 See earlier references, including J.-P. Demoule and C. Perlès, 1993; H. Todorova, 1986; J. C. Chapman, 1981; E. N. Chernykh, 1992.

169 E. Comşa, 1991, 'L'utilisation de l'or pendant le néolithique dans le territoire de la Roumanie', in C. Eluère and J.-P. Mohen (eds.), *Découverte du métal*, pp. 85–92, Paris.

170 E. Comşa, 1987; J. Makkay, 1991; J. Makkay, 1989, *The Tiszaszöllös treasure*, Budapest.

171 P. Halstead and J. O'Shea (eds.), 1989, *Bad year economics: cultural responses to risk and uncertainty*, Cambridge.

172 See for example: P. Pétrequin and A.-M. Pétrequin, 1993, *Ecologie d'un outil: la hache de pierre en Irian Jaya (Indonésie)*, Valbonne.

5   Accents of change: south-east Europe, *c.* 4000–3000 BC

1 J. Korek, 1951, 'Ein Gräberfeld der Badener Kultur bei Alsónémedi', *Acta Archaeologica Academiae Scientiarum Hungaricae* 1, 35–51; J. Nemeskéri, 1951, 'Anthropologische Untersuchung der Skelettfunde von Alsónémedi', *Acta Archaeologica Academiae Scientiarum Hungaricae* 1, 55–72; S. Bökönyi, 1951, 'Untersuchung der Haustierfunde aus dem Gräberfeld von Alsónémedi', *Acta Archaeologica Academiae Scientiarum Hungaricae* 1, 72–9.

2 A. G. Sherratt, 1981. For discussion of cattle pairs I thank Lázló Bartosiewicz.

3 S. Soproni, 1954, 'A budakalászi kocsi – un char cultuel de Budakalász', *Folia Archaeologica* 6, 29–36, 198–9; J. Banner, 1956. Much of Budakalász remains unpublished.

4 N. Kalicz, 1976, 'Ein neues kupferzeitliches Wagenmodell aus der Umgebung von Budapest', in H. Mitscha-Marheim, H. Friesinger and H. Kerchler (eds.), *Festschrift für Richard Pittioni zum siebzigen Geburtstag*, pp. 186–202, Vienna.

5 A. G. Sherratt, 1981; I. Ecsedy, 1982, 'A Boglárlellei későrézkri állatcsontleletei', *Communicationes Archaeologicae Hungaricae* 1982, 15–29; V. Nemejcová-Pavuková and J. Barta, 1977, 'Äneolithische

Siedlung der Boleráz-Gruppe in Radošina', *Slovenská Archeológia* 25, 433–47; M. Bondár, 1990, 'Das frühbronzezeitliche Wagenmodell von Börzönce', *Communicationes Archaeologicae Hungaricae* 1990, 77–91.

6 See below, including C. Renfrew *et al.*, 1986.

7 J. Banner, 1956; I. Bognár-Kutzián, 1973, 'The relationship between the Bodrogkeresztúr and Baden cultures', in B. Chropovsky (ed.), *Symposium über die Entstehung und Chronologie der Badener Kultur*, pp. 31–50, Bratislava; A. G. Sherratt, 1983; N. Kalicz, 1963, *Die Péceler (Badener) Kultur und Anatolien*, Budapest; I am grateful to Dr L. Bartosiewicz for information about the Győr site (funded among others by the Hungarian National Research Fund).

8 The literature is considerable, and complex. As one authority has put it (J. P. Mallory, 1989, p. 285): 'Except for a career in politics, one seldom gets the opportunity to offend so many people at once.' For initial, general orientation (or disorientation), see J. P. Mallory, 1989; M. Gimbutas, 1991; C. Renfrew, 1987.

9 J. P. Mallory, 1989.

10 J. P. Mallory, 1989, surveying over two centuries of debate.

11 Argued prominently by Gimbutas. E.g. M. Gimbutas, 1973, and later papers.

12 J.-P. Demoule and C. Perlès, 1993; P. Halstead, 1989.

13 J. L. Davis, 1992; C. Renfrew, 1973, *The emergence of civilization*, London.

14 C. Renfrew *et al.*, 1986.

15 C. Renfrew *et al.*, 1986.

16 H. Todorova, 1986.

17 H. Todorova, 1981; G. I. Georgiev, 1961; G. I. Georgiev *et al.*, 1979.

18 H. Todorova, 1978; 1982; 1986; H. Todorova *et al.*, 1975; 1983; I. Angelova, 1982.

19 D. Berciu, 1961; V. Dumitrescu, 1965.

20 G. I. Georgiev, 1961; G. I. Georgiev *et al.*, 1979; R. W. Dennell, 1978.

21 V. Dumitrescu *et al.*, 1982.

22 J. C. Chapman, 1981; R. Tringham and D. Krstić, 1990; D. Berciu, 1961; B. Nikolov, 1978; H. Todorova, 1986; N. Tasić, 1979, 'Bubanj–Salcuţa–Krivodol Kompleks', in N. Tasić (ed.), *Praistorija jugoslavenskih zemalja, III: eneolitsko doba*, pp. 87–114, Sarajevo; M. Garašanin, 1982, 'The Stone Age in the central Balkan area; the Eneolithic period in the central Balkan area', *Cambridge Ancient History*, III, I, pp. 75–162.

23 See especially J. C. Chapman, 1981; R. Tringham and D. Krstić, 1990. For Gomolava, see B. Brukner, 1988; J. Petrović, 1988, 'Eneolithique moyen et tardif à Gomolava', in N. Tasić and J. Petrović (eds.), *Gomolava: Chronologie und Stratigraphie der vorgeschichtlichen und antiken Kulturen der Donauniederung und Südosteuropas*, pp.39–46, Novi Sad.

24 P. Roman, 1977, *The late Copper Age Coţofeni culture of south-east Europe*, Oxford.

25 I. Ecsedy, 1979, *The people of the pit-grave kurgans in eastern Hungary*, Budapest.

26 A. G. Sherratt, 1983.

27 I. Bognár-Kutzián, 1963; 1972.

28 A. Kallay, 1990, 'Die kupferzeitliche Ringanlage von Füzesabony', *Jahresschrift für Mitteldeutsche Vorgeschichte* 73, 125–30; J. Makkay, 1981, 'Eine Kultstatte der Bodrogkeresztúr-Kultur in Szarvas und Fragen der Sakralen-Hügel', *Mitteilungen des archäologischen Instituts der ungarischen Akademie der Wissenschaften* 10–11, 45–57; V. István, 1987, 'A Tiszalúc-Sarkadi rézkori település állatc-sontleletei', *Folia Archaeologica* 38, 121–7.

29 J. P. Mallory, 1989, following Merpert.

30 See chapter 4.

31 See chapters 3 and 4.

32 J. P. Mallory, 1989; D. Y. Telegin and I. D. Potekhina, 1987, *Neolithic cemeteries and populations in the Dniepr basin*, Oxford (in the preface, p. viii, J. P. Mallory comments of the burial grounds: 'In a sense the Mariupol-type cemeteries are megalithic tombs without megaliths'); D. W. Anthony, 1986.

33 J. P. Mallory, 1989; D. W. Anthony, 1986; E. N. Chernykh, 1992.

34 D. W. Anthony, 1986.

35 D. Y. Telegin, 1986; D. Anthony *et al.*, 1991; D. W. Anthony and D. R. Brown, 1991, 'The origins of horseback riding', *Antiquity* 65, 22–38. For Botaj, see S. Bökönyi, 1991.

36 E.g. D. Anthony *et al.*, 1991, p. 48A; M. Gimbutas, 1973; 1991. But note D. Y. Telegin, 1986, p. 116, and J. P. Mallory, 1989, who are far more cautious.

37 L. Ellis, 1984; D. Anthony *et al.*, 1991, p. 48A.

38 L. Ellis, 1984, especially p. 186 and fig. 26.

39 The 'kurgan hypothesis', advocated especially by Gimbutas.

40 Surveyed in J. P. Mallory, 1989; M. Gimbutas, 1991; V. Dumitrescu *et al.*, 1982. See also E. N. Chernykh, 1992. More detailed references include: H. Dumitrescu, 1945, 'La station préhistorique de Horodistea sur le Pruth', *Dacia* 9–10, 127–63; M. Petrescu-Dimbovita and D. Marin, 1974, 'Nouvelles fouilles archéologiques à Foltesti (dep. de Galati), *Dacia* 18, 19–72; M. Dinu, 1980, 'Le complexe Horodistea-Foltesti et le problème de l'indoeuropéanisation de l'éspace carpato-danubien', in R. Vulpe (ed.), *Actes du 2ᵉ congrès international de Thracologie*, pp. 35–48, Bucharest; D. Popescu, 1940, 'La tombe à ocre de Casimcea (Dobrogea)', *Dacia* 7–8, 85–91.

41 E. N. Chernykh, 1992.

42 See note 40. For Plačidol, see I. Panajatov and V. Dergačov, 1984, 'Die Ockergrabkultur in Bulgarien (Darstellung des Problems)', *Studia Praehistorica* 7, 99–111.

43 D. W. Anthony, 1986; J. P. Mallory, 1989; S. Piggott, 1983, *The earliest wheeled transport*, London; E. N. Chernykh, 1992.

44 E.g. H. Todorova, 1978; 1986; 1989; J. Rulf, 1991. For further detail on climate fluctuations recorded in the Alpine zone, see M. Magny, 1993; M. Rösch, 1993; A. Leemann and F. Niessens, 1994, 'Holocene glacial activity and climatic variations in the Swiss Alps: reconstructing a continuous record from proglacial lake sediments', *The Holocene* 4, 259–68.

45 H. Todorova, 1986; 1989.

46 The best guide to a vast literature is J. P. Mallory, 1989.

47 J. P. Mallory, 1989, p. 116.

48 J. P. Mallory, 1989, pp. 144–5 and 113; R. Coleman, 1988, 'Review of *Archaeology and language*', *Current Anthropology* 29, 449–53.

49 M. Gimbutas, 1973; 1991. Note other suggested variations in the rate of change: M. Garašanin, 1971, 'Nomades des steppes et autochtones dans le Sud-Est européen à l'époque de transition du néolithique à l'âge du bronze', in V. Georgiev (ed.), *L'ethnogénèse des peuples balkaniques*, pp. 9–14, Sofia; E. Comşa, 1980, 'Contribution à la connaissance du proccesus d'indoeuropéanisation des régions carpato-danubiennes', in R. Vulpe (ed.), *Actes du 2ᵉ congrès international de Thracologie*, pp. 29–33, Bucharest.

50 M. Gimbutas, 1977, 'The first wave of Eurasian steppe pastoralists into Copper Age Europe', *Journal of Indo-European Studies* 5, 277–331.

51 E. N. Chernykh, 1992, p. 85.

52 S. Bökönyi, 1974; 1991.

53 C. Renfrew, 1987.

54 E.g. J. P. Mallory, 1989; reviews by D. W. Anthony and B. Wailes, P. Baldi, R. Coleman and A. Sherratt, in *Current Anthropology* 29, 1988, 441–63; N. Yoffee, 1990.

55 J. P. Mallory, 1989; N. Yoffee, 1990; C. Ehret, 1988; D. W. Anthony and B. Wailes, 1988, 'Review of *Archaeology and language*', *Current Anthropology* 29, 441–5.

56 M. Zvelebil and K. V. Zvelebil, 1988, 'Agricultural transition and Indo-European dispersals', *Antiquity* 62, 574–83.

57 A. Häusler, 1985, 'Kulturbeziehungen zwischen Ost- und Mitteleuropa im Neolithikum?', *Jahresschrift für mitteldeutsche Vorgeschichte* 68, 21–74; L. Kilian, 1983, *Zum Ursprung der Indogermanen*, Bonn. Another variation has the *Alföld* Linear Pottery population as Indo-European speaking,

the Starcevo-Körös population as ancestral to Hittite-Luwian-Pelasgian, and the kurgan population as Indo-Iranian, not Indo-European: J. Makkay, 1982, *A magyarországi neolitikum kutatásának új eredméyei*, Budapest. See also J. Makkay, 1991, *Az indoeurópai népek őstörténete*, Budapest.

58 J. P. Mallory, 1989.

59 See chapter 4.

60 See chapter 4, note 5; H. Todorova, 1986.

61 D. Bailey, 1991, 'The social reality of figurines from the Chalcolithic of northeastern Bulgaria: the example of Ovcharovo', unpublished PhD, Cambridge University; S. Bökönyi, 1986.

62 A. G. Sherratt, 1981.

63 E.g. J. C. Chapman, 1982, 'The "secondary products revolution" and the limitations of the Neolithic', *Bulletin of the Institute of Archaeology, University of London* 19, 107–22.

64 See chapter 6.

65 A. G. Sherratt, 1991, p. 56; 1987.

66 See especially E. N. Chernykh, 1992.

67 A. G. Sherratt, 1994.

68 C. Renfrew, 1987, especially chapter 6.

69 J. P. Mallory, 1989.

70 A. Sherratt and S. Sherratt, 1988, 'The archaeology of Indo-European: an alternative view', *Antiquity* 62, 584–95.

71 C. Ehret, 1988.

72 J. P. Mallory, 1989, p. 261, referring especially to the social permeability of pastoralist societies compared to sedentary neighbours.

73 J. P. Mallory, 1989; J. Robb, 1993, 'A social prehistory of European languages', *Antiquity* 67, 747–60.

74 Note the claim that this is probably impossible: N. Yoffee, 1990.

6 Longhouse lives: central and western Europe, *c.* 5500 to before 4000 BC

1 J. Lüning, 1982; 1988a; P. Stehli, 1989; J. Lüning and P. Stehli, 1994; U. Boelicke *et al.*, 1988; J.-P. Farruggia *et al.*, 1973; R. Kuper *et al.*, 1977; M. Dohrn-Ihmig, 1983; W. Schwellnus, 1983.

2 M. Dohrn-Ihmig, 1979, 'Bandkeramik an Mittel- und Niederrhein', *Rheinische Ausgrabungen* 19, 191–362.

3 Also known as the Graetheide. See P. J. R. Modderman, 1970; P. J. R. Modderman, 1985, 'Die Bandkeramik im Graetheidegebiet, Niederländisch-Limburg', *Bericht der Römisch-Germanischen Kommission* 66, 26–121; P. J. R. Modderman, 1988; C. C. Bakels, 1978.

4 There are of course other terms, such as *Rubané* in French. But German has been the *lingua franca* of publication. The shorter term *Bandkeramik* is often used, and the older label 'Danubian' is also still in use as a general term. I use it later in the chapter, but without any particular geographical connotations, as a convenient way to denote the long cultural tradition begun by the LBK.

5 The best general recent accounts are P. J. R. Modderman, 1988; J. Lüning, 1988a; P. Bogucki, 1988; P. Bogucki and R. Grygiel, 1993, 'The first farmers of central Europe: a survey article', *Journal of Field Archaeology* 20, 399–426.

6 This is the phase of the *älteste Keramik*. See E. Neustupný, 1956, 'K relativní chronologii volutové keramiky', *Archeologické Rozhledy* 8, 386–406; H. Quitta, 1960, 'Zur Frage der ältesten Bandkeramik in Mitteleuropa', *Praehistorische Zeitschrift* 38, 1–38, 153–88; J. Makkay, 1978; A. M. Kreuz, 1990; E. Lenneis, 1989; J. Lüning, 1988a; J. Lüning *et al.*, 1989.

7 P. J. R. Modderman, 1988; P. Bogucki, 1988. See also the map in J. Lüning, 1988b.

8 Pollen data in J. Lüning, 1988a; P. Stehli, 1989; C. C. Bakels, 1978; J. Pavúk, 1982.

9 Started among others by P. J. R. Modderman, 1971, 'Bandkeramiker und Wandbauerntum',

Archäologisches Korrespondenzblatt 1, 7–9; J. Kruk, 1980; and J. Lüning, 1982. See also S. Milisauskas and J. Kruk, 1989, 'Neolithic economy in central Europe', *Journal of World Prehistory* 3, 403–46.

10 P. J. R. Modderman, 1988.

11 C. C. Bakels, 1987; J. Lech, 1989.

12 A. Coudart, 1989; A. M. Kreuz, 1990.

13 The list includes A. Whittle, 1985, *Neolithic Europe: a survey*, Cambridge. For a recent expression, see L. H. Keeley, 1992, 'The introduction of agriculture to the western North European plain', in A. B. Gebauer and T. D. Price (eds.), *Transitions to agriculture in prehistory*, pp. 81–95, Madison.

14 R. W. Dennell, 1984; M. Zvelebil and P. Rowley-Conwy, 1984. A. J. Ammerman and L. L. Cavalli-Sforza, 1984, point out that broad patterns of blood groups in modern Europe could reflect a Neolithic colonisation. DNA analysis of dated material is needed in the future.

15 See N. Kalicz and J. Makkay, 1977; P. Raczky, 1989; K. Kosse, 1979. The Medina group in Transdanubia and the Szatmár I group in the more northerly plain are seen as formative.

16 See chapter 2, especially note 29; M. A. Jochim, 1990.

17 J. Makkay, 1978; R. Kalicz-Schreiber and N. Kalicz, 1992, 'Die erste frühneolithische Fundstelle in Budapest', *Balcanica* 23, 47–76; N. Kalicz, 1993, 'Die Keszthely-Gruppe der Transdanubischen (Mitteleuropäischen) Linienbandkeramik im Lichte der Ausgrabung in Kustánszeg (Westungarn)', *Communicationes Archaeologicae Hungaricae* 1991, 5–32.

18 I. Pavlů, 1990, 'Early Linear Pottery culture in Bohemia', in D. Srejović and N. Tasić, pp. 133–41; A. M. Kreuz, 1990; G. Bernhardt and A. Hampel, 1992, 'Vorbericht zu einem ältestlinienbandkeramischen Siedlungsplatz in Frankfurt-Niedereschbach', *Germania* 70, 1–16; E. Lenneis, 1989; 1991; E. Lenneis and W. J. Kuijper, 1992, 'Vorbericht über die Ausgrabungen 1988–1991 der linearbandkeramischen Siedlung in Rosenburg im Kamptal, Niederösterreich', *Archaeologia Austriaca* 76, 19–37; J. Pavúk, 1980, 'Ältere Linearkeramik in der Slowakei', *Slovenská Archeológia* 28, 7–90.

19 A. M. Kreuz, 1990; E. Lenneis, 1989; J. Lüning *et al.*, 1989.

20 A. M. Kreuz, 1990; E. Pucher, 1987.

21 P. Bogucki, 1988. See also S. Milisauskas, 1986, p. 2.

22 P. J. R. Modderman, 1988, pp. 73–4; A. Bach, 1978, *Neolithische Populationen im Mittelelbe-Saale-Gebiet*, Weimar; W. Bernhard, 1978, 'Anthropologie der Bandkeramiker', in I. Schwidetzky (ed.), *Die Anfänge des Neolithikums vom Orient bis Nordeuropa, VIIIb: Anthropologie, Teil 2*, pp. 128–63, Köln; Z. K. Zoffmann, 1991, 'A középeurópai (KVK és DVK) valamint az alföldi (AVK) vonaldíszes kerámiák embertani leleteinek metrikus összehasonlítása (Metrischer Vergleich der anthropologischen Funde der mitteleuropäischen und der Alföld-Linienbandkeramik)', *A Janus Pannonius Múzeum Évkönyve* 36, 85–99.

23 P. Bogucki, 1988, p. 108.

24 M. de Grooth, 1987; J.-P. Caspar, M. Kaczanowska and J. K. Kozłowski, 1989, 'Chipped stone industries of the Linear Band Pottery culture (LBP): techniques, morphology and function of the implements in Belgian and Polish assemblages', *Helinium* 29, 157–205.

25 R. Newell, 1970, 'The flint industry of the Dutch Linearbandkeramik', *Analecta Praehistorica Leidensia* 3, 144–83; D. Gronenborn, 1990. The Dutch study has, however, been much disputed.

26 J. Lüning *et al.*, 1989; P.-L. van Berg, 1990; B. Langenbrink and J. Kneipp, 1990, 'Keramik von Typ La Hoguette aus einer ältestbandkeramischen Siedlung bei Steinfurth in Wetteraukreis', *Archäologisches Korrespondenzblatt* 20, 149–60.

27 See chapter 2.

28 See note 16.

29 B. Gramsch and K. Kloss, 1989; B. Gramsch, 1992.

30 C. Mordant and D. Mordant, 1992.

31 Z. Bagniewski, 1992, 'Untersuchungsergebnisse aus der mesolithischen Torfstation Pobiel 10 (Niederschlesien)', *Praehistorische Zeitschrift* 67, 141–62. A. J. Tomaszewski and R. Willis, 1993,

'Tool-kits and burial rites: the case of the Janisławice Mesolithic grave', *Proceedings of the Prehistoric Society* 59, 105–112. And see S. K. Kozłowski, 1991.

32 L. R. Binford, 1980; D. E. Lieberman, 1993.

33 M. A. Jochim, 1990.

34 C. Meiklejohn, 1986, 'Old bone, new dates: recent radiocarbon results from Mesolithic human skeletal remains', *Mesolithic Miscellany* 7, 9–16.

35 T. D. Price, 1987, 'The Mesolithic of western Europe', *Journal of World Prehistory* 1, 225–305.

36 L. Larsson, 1990.

37 E. Brinch Petersen, 1989, 'Vaenget Nord: excavation, documentation and interpretation of a Mesolithic site at Vedbaek, Denmark', in C. Bonsall (ed.), *The Mesolithic in Europe*, pp. 325–30, Edinburgh.

38 L. Larsson, 1990.

39 From an already big bibliography, see L. Larsson, 1993; L. Larsson, 1988, *The Skateholm project. 1. Man and environment*, Lund; L. Larsson, 1989, 'Late Mesolithic settlements and cemeteries at Skateholm, southern Sweden', in C. Bonsall, 1989, pp. 367–78; L. Larsson, 1990, 'Dogs in fraction – symbols in action', in P. M. Vermeersch and P. van Peer, 1990, pp. 153–60.

40 H. Quitta, 1960; J. Makkay, 1978; E. Lenneis, 1989; 1991; J. Lüning, 1988a; J. Lüning *et al.*, 1989.

41 J. Lüning, 1988a; A. Whittle, 1990, 'Radiocarbon dating of the Linear Pottery culture: the contribution of cereal and bone samples', *Antiquity* 64, 297–302; P. Breunig, 1987, *14–C Chronologie des Vorderasiatischen, Südost- und Mitteleuropäischen Neolithikums*, Köln.

42 By nearly everyone. See, for example, P. J. R. Modderman, 1970.

43 P. Bogucki, 1988, p. 99.

44 A. M. Kreuz, 1990; E. Lenneis, 1989.

45 A. M. Kreuz, 1990; E. Lenneis, 1989.

46 D. Kaufmann, 1983, 'Die ältestlinienbandkeramischen Funde von Eilsleben, Kr. Wanzleben, und der Beginn des Neolithikums im Mittelelbe-Saale-Gebiet', *Nachrichten aus Niedersachsens Urgeschichte* 52, 177–202.

47 P. Bogucki, 1988; P. J. R. Modderman, 1988. For Kujavia, L. Czerniak, personal communication; for Chełmno-land and near Szczecin, see T. Wiślański, 1987.

48 U. Boelicke *et al.*, 1988; P. J. R. Modderman, 1988; P. Bogucki, 1988; S. Milisauskas and J. Kruk, 1993; I. Pavlů *et al.*, 1986.

49 U. Boelicke *et al.*, 1988; M. de Grooth, 1987; I. Pavlů *et al.*, 1986.

50 U. Veit, 1993.

51 L. H. Keeley and D. Cahen, 1989; for the most westerly sites in Belgium, M. Lodewijckx, 1990, 'Les deux sites Rubanés de Wange et d'Overhespen (Belgique, prov. Brabant)', in D. Cahen and M. Otte (eds.), *Rubané et Cardial*, pp. 105–16, Liège; C. Constantin *et al.*, 1982; C. Constantin, 1985, *Fin du Rubané, céramique du Limburg et post-Rubané: le Néolithique le plus ancien en Bassin parisien et en Hainaut*, Oxford; P. Bogucki, 1988; P. Bogucki and R. Grygiel, 1993; A. Coudart, 1988, *Architecture et société néolithique: uniformité et variabilité, fonction et style de l'architecture dans l'approche des communautés du Néolithique danubien*, Oxford.

52 J. Lüning, 1988a; J. Lüning *et al.*, 1989; P.-L. van Berg, 1990.

53 J. Lüning, 1988b.

54 A. M. Kreuz, 1990; M. de Grooth and G. Verwers, 1984, *Op goede gronden: de eerste boeren in Noordwest-Europa*, Leiden; 'Un site néolithique à Paris', *Archéologia* 273, 1991, 4.

55 Only about 1000 bones survive from Bylany, one of the largest excavated areas: I. Pavlů *et al.*, 1986; P. Bogucki, 1988.

56 C. C. Bakels, 1991, 'Tracing crop processing in the Bandkeramik culture', in J. M. Renfrew (ed.), *New light on early farming*, pp. 281–8, Edinburgh. See J. Lüning, 1988a, fig. 49, for differences between house types on the Aldenhoven plateau.

57 B. Soudský, 1962; B. Soudský and I. Pavlů, 1972.

58 See note 9. There is a much more agnostic approach in J. Rulf, 1991, 'Neolithic agriculture of central Europe – review of the problems', *Památky Archeologické* 82, 376–84. See also L. Czerniak and J. Piontek, 1980.

59 C. C. Bakels, 1978; U. Boelicke *et al.*, 1988; I. Pavlů *et al.*, 1986; I. Pavlů, 1989.

60 The literature is extensive. See C. C. Bakels, 1978.

61 P. Bogucki, 1988, p. 73.

62 R. Langohr, 1990, 'The dominant soil types of the Belgian loess belt in the Early Neolithic', in D. Cahen and M. Otte (eds.), *Rubané et Cardial*, pp. 117–24, Liège.

63 J. Weiner, 1992, 'The Bandkeramik wooden well of Erkelenz-Kückhoven', *Newswarp* 12, 3–11; J. Weiner, 1993. See also J. Rulf and T. Velímský, 1993, 'A Neolithic well from Most', *Archeologické Rozhledy* 45, 545–60.

64 S. Milisauskas, 1986, on the southern Polish site of Olszanica.

65 P. Bogucki, 1988, pp. 85–8; compare P. Halstead, 1992. For Geleen-Janskamperveld, see L. P. Louwe Kooijmans, 1991.

66 R. Jeunesse, 1990, 'Habitats Rubanés en grottes et abris sous-roche', in D. Cahen and M. Otte (eds.), *Rubané et Cardial*, pp. 231–7, Liège; A. J. Kalis and A. Zimmermann, 1988, 'An integrative model for the use of different landscapes in Linearbandkeramik times', in J. Bintliff, D. Davidson and E. Grant (eds.), *Conceptual issues in environmental archaeology*, pp. 145–52, Edinburgh; P. Bogucki, 1982, *Early Neolithic subsistence and settlement in the Polish lowlands*, Oxford; P. Bogucki and R. Grygiel, 1993; L. Czerniak and J. Piontek, 1980.

67 There is a vast literature. See especially P. J. R. Modderman, 1970; 1988; U. Boelicke *et al.*, 1988; A. Coudart, 1989; J. Pavúk, 1982; J. Lüning and P. Stehli, 1994.

68 P. J. R. Modderman, 1970; 1988; U. Boelicke *et al.*, 1988; but general applicability doubted by A. Coudart, 1989.

69 A. M. Kreuz, 1990; E. Lenneis, 1989; J. Lüning, 1988a; J. Lüning *et al.*, 1989; L. P. Louwe Kooijmans, 1991.

70 U. Boelicke *et al.*, 1988; U. Boelicke, 1982, 'Gruben und Häuser: Untersuchungen zur Struktur bandkeramischer Hofplätze', in J. Pavúk, 1982, pp. 17–29.

71 S. Milisauskas and J. Kruk, 1993; S. Milisauskas, 1986.

72 S. Milisauskas and J. Kruk, 1993.

73 Synthesis in M. de Grooth, 1987; P. van de Velde, 1990.

74 J. Lüning, 1982; P. Bogucki, 1988.

75 U. Boelicke *et al.*, 1988; P. Bogucki, 1988.

76 P. van de Velde, 1990.

77 R. R. Wilk, 1983, 'Little house in the jungle: the causes of variation in house size among Kekchi Maya', *Journal of Anthropological Archaeology* 2, 99–116.

78 B. Soudsky, 1969, 'Etude de la maison néolithique', *Slovenská Archeológia* 17, 5–96.

79 S. Milisauskas, 1986; S. Milisauskas and J. Kruk, 1993; P. van de Velde, 1979.

80 See again D. Bailey, 1990.

81 C. C. Bakels, 1978; L. P. Louwe Kooijmans, 1991.

82 I. Pavlů *et al.*, 1986.

83 A. Whittle, 1988.

84 U. Veit, 1993; J. Kneipp and H. Büttner, 1988, 'Anthropophagie in der jüngsten Bandkeramik der Wetterau', *Germania* 66, 489–97; W. Coblenz, 1962, 'Kannibalismus in Zauschwitz', *Ausgrabungen und Funde* 7, 67–9.

85 U. Veit, 1993.

86 C. Constantin *et al.*, 1982; V. Ondruš, 1972, 'Dětské pohřby na neolitickém sidlišti ve Vedrovich (Kinderbestattungen auf der neolitischen Siedlung in Vedrovice)', *Časopis Moravského Musea* 57, 27–36; U. Veit, 1993.

87 W. Coblenz, 1956, 'Skelettgräber von Zauschwitz, Kreis Borna', *Arbeits- und Forschungsberichte der Sächsischen Bodendenkmalpflege* 5, 57–119.

88 U. Veit, 1993; O. Höckmann, 1982; P. J. R. Modderman, 1988; I. Zalai-Gaál, 1988.

89 U. Veit, 1993.

90 H. Rötting, 1985; H. Behrens, 1972.

91 J.-P. Farruggia, 1992, *Les outils et les armes en pierre dans le rituel funéraire du Néolithique danubien*, Oxford.

92 O. Höckmann, 1982.

93 W. Baumann, 1960, 'Körpergräber und Siedlung der Bandkeramik in Dresden-Nickern', *Arbeits- und Forschungsberichte zur Sächsischen Bodendenkmalpflege* 7, 95–138.

94 A. Whittle, 1988, pp. 153–7.

95 O. Höckmann, 1982.

96 A. G. Sherratt, 1982.

97 P. van de Velde, 1990; P. van de Velde, 1979, 'The social anthropology of a Neolithic cemetery in the Netherlands', *Current Anthropology* 20, 37–58.

98 J. Wahl and H. G. König, 1987, 'Anthropologisch-traumatologische Untersuchung der menschlichen Skelettreste aus dem bandkeramischen Massengrab bei Talheim, Kreis Heilbronn', *Fundberichte aus Baden-Würtemberg* 12, 65–186.

99 J. Haas (ed.), *The anthropology of war*, Cambridge.

100 P. van de Velde, 1979, 'The social anthropology of a Neolithic cemetery in the Netherlands', *Current Anthropology* 20, 37–58.

101 B. Soudsky and I. Pavlů, 1966, 'Interprétation historique de l'ornement linéaire', *Památky Archeologické* 57, 91–125; J. Weiner, 1993; J. Thomas, 1991.

102 E.g. W. Meier-Arendt, 1966, *Die bandkeramische Kultur im Untermaingebiet*, Bonn; J. Lüning, 1988a, figs. 15–17 and 53.

103 M. de Grooth, 1987; U. Boelicke *et al.*, 1988.

104 L. H. Keeley and D. Cahen, 1989.

105 D. Gronenborn, 1990; J. Lech, 1989; 1980; 1982; S. Milisauskas and J. Kruk, 1993.

106 C. Willms, 1985.

107 K. H. Brandt, 1967; C. C. Bakels, 1978; 1987; P. J. R. Modderman, 1988.

108 C. C. Bakels, 1987.

109 S. Milisauskas, 1986.

110 See C. C. Bakels, 1978; C. C. Bakels, 1987. The older suggestion of a source in Silesia, Poland, has been discounted.

111 Among others by P. van de Velde, 1990.

112 J. Lüning, 1988b; P. J. R. Modderman, 1988.

113 W. Buttler and G. Haberey, 1936, *Die bandkeramische Ansiedlung bei Köln-Lindenthal*, Leipzig.

114 J. Petrasch, 1990, fig. 16.

115 J. Lüning, 1988b; O. Höckmann, 1990, 'Frühneolithische Einhegungen in Europa', *Jahresschrift für mitteldeutsche Vorgeschichte* 73, 57–86.

116 L. H. Keeley and D. Cahen, 1989; D. Cahen, L. H. Keeley, I. Jadin and P.-L. van Berg, 1990, 'Trois villages fortifiés du Rubané récent en Hesbaye Liègeoise', in D. Cahen and M. Otte (eds.), *Rubané et Cardial*, pp. 125–46, Liège; M. Fansa and H. Thieme, 1983, 'Die linienbandkeramische Siedlung und Befestigungsanlage in Esbeck "Nachtwiesenberg", Stadt Schöningen, Ldkr. Helmstedt', in G. Wegner (ed.), *Frühe Bauernkulturen in Niedersachsen*, pp. 91–102, Oldenburg.

117 U. Boelicke *et al.*, 1988; R. Kuper *et al.*, 1977; P. Stehli, 1989.

118 P. M. Vermeersch, 1990, 'La transition du Mésolithique au Néolithique en basse et moyenne Belgique', in D. Cahen and M. Otte (eds.), *Rubané et Cardial*, pp. 95–103, Liège. See also L. P. Louwe Kooijmans, 1993.

119 V. Němejcová-Pavúková, 1986b; M. Zápatocká, 1986, 'Die Brandgräber von Vikletice – ein Beitrag zum chronologischen Verhältnis von Stich- und Rhein-Bandkeramik', *Archéologicke Rozhledy* 38, 623–49; U. Fischer, 1991; J.-P. Demoule and J. Guilaine, 1986.

120 P. Bogucki and R. Grygiel, 1993; R. Grygiel, 1986.

121 R. Grygiel, 1986.

122 Assuming that these structures actually were roofed buildings.

123 R. Grygiel, 1986.

124 P. Bogucki and R. Grygiel, 1993; R. Grygiel, 1986; P. Bogucki and R. Grygiel, 1981, 'Early Neolithic site at Brześć Kujawski, Poland: preliminary report on the 1976–79 excavations', *Journal of Field Archaeology* 8, 9–27.

125 R. Grygiel, 1986; B. Ottaway, 1973, 'The earliest copper ornaments in northern Europe', *Proceedings of the Prehistoric Society* 39, 294–331.

126 R. Grygiel, 1986; L. Czerniak, personal communication.

127 H. Wiklak, 1990.

128 L. Czerniak, personal communication; R. Grygiel, 1986; P. Bogucki and R. Grygiel, 1993.

129 S. H. Andersen and E. Johansen, 1986, 'Ertebølle revisited', *Journal of Danish Archaeology* 5, 31–61; I. B. Enghoff, 1986, 'Freshwater fishing from a sea-coast settlement – the Ertebølle *locus classicus* revisited', *Journal of Danish Archaeology* 5, 62–76; S. H. Andersen, 1993, 'Bjørnsholm. A stratified *køkkenmødding* on the central Limfjord, north Jutland', *Journal of Danish Archaeology* 10, 59–96; B. Bratlund, 1993, 'The bone remains of mammals and birds from the Bjørnsholm shell-mound', *Journal of Danish Archaeology* 10, 97–104; I. B. Enghoff, 1993, 'Mesolithic eel-fishing at Bjørnsholm, Denmark, spiced with exotic species', *Journal of Danish Archaeology* 10, 97–104.

130 See notes 169–70.

131 J. Kruk, 1980; J. Rulf, 1991, 'Die Umwelt zu Beginn des Äneolithikums in Mitteleuropa am Beispiel Böhmens', in J. Lichardus (ed.), *Die Kupferzeit als historische Epoche*, pp. 529–37, Bonn.

132 J. Pavúk, 1986, 'Siedlungswesen der Lengyel-Kultur in der Slovakei', *A Béri Balogh Ádám Múzeum Évkönyve* 13, 213–23.

133 J. Lüning, 1982; 1988a.

134 N. J. Starling, 1983, 'Neolithic settlement patterns in central Germany', *Oxford Journal of Archaeology* 2, 1–11; M. Godłowska, J. K. Kozłowski, L. Starkel and K. Wasylikowa, 1987, 'Neolithic settlement at Pleszów and changes in the natural environment in the Vistula valley', *Przegląd Archeologiczny* 34, 133–59; C. C. Bakels, 1978; P. Stehli, 1989.

135 S. Bökönyi, 1986; N. Kalicz, 1985.

136 V. Němejcová-Pavúková, 1986b.

137 S. Bökönyi, 1986; J. Lüning, 1988a; E. Hajnalová, 1986, 'Cultivated plants of Late Neolithic from central Europe', in V. Němejcová-Pavúková, 1986b, pp. 79–82; H. Küster, 1991, 'Jung- und endneolithischer Ackerbau im südlichen Mitteleuropa', in J. Lichardus (ed.), *Die Kupferzeit als historische Epoche*, pp. 539–47, Bonn.

138 C. Bakels, 1990, 'The crops of the Rössen culture: significantly different from their Bandkeramik predecessors – French influence?', in D. Cahen and M. Otte (eds.), *Rubané et Cardial*, pp. 83–7, Liège.

139 I. Pavlů *et al.*, 1986; W. Meier-Arendt, 1975, *Die Hinkelstein Gruppe*, Berlin; F. Niquet, 1938, *Das Gräberfeld von Rössen, Kreis Merseburg*, Halle; H. Behrens, 1972.

140 H. Rötting, 1985.

141 J. Lüning, 1988a; J. Lüning and P. Stehli, 1994.

142 J. Lüning, 1982; M. Dohrn-Ihmig, 1983, 'Ein Grossgartacher Siedlungsplatz bei Jülich-Welldorf, Kreis Düren, und der Übergang zum mittelneolithischen Hausbau', *Rheinische Ausgrabungen* 24, 233–82; M. Dohrn-Ihmig, 1983, 'Ein Rössener Siedlungsplatz bei Jülich-Welldorf, Kreis Düren', *Rheinische Ausgrabungen* 24, 287–97; M. Dohrn-Ihmig, 1983, 'Ein Rössener Siedlungsplatz von Bedburg-Kaster, Erftkreis', *Rheinische Ausgrabungen* 24, 283–6.

143 A. Hampel, 1989, *Die Hausentwicklung im Mittelneolithikum Zentraleuropas*, Bonn; K. Günther, 1976, *Die jungsteinzeitliche Siedlung Deiringsen/Ruploh in der Soester Börde*, Münster; J. Lüning, 1982.

144 I. Pavlů *et al.*, 1986.

145 I. Zalai-Gaál, 1990, 'A neolitikus körárokrendszerek kutatása a Del-Dunántúlon', *Archaeologiai Értesítő* 117, 3–23; V. Němejcová-Pavúková, 1986a.

146 N. Kalicz, 1985; I. Zalai-Gaál, 1986, 'Sozialarchäologische Forschungsmöglichkeiten aufgrund spätneolithischer Gräbergruppen in südwestlichen Ungarn', *A Béri Balogh Ádám Múzeum Évkönyve* 13, 139–54.

147 I. Zalai-Gaál, 1988, 'Kösép-európai neolitikus temetők szociálarchaeológiai elemzése', *A Béri Balogh Ádám Múzeum Évkönyve* 14, 3–178; I. Zalai-Gaál, 1991, 'Die chronologische und soziale Deutung der Mitgabe von Steinäxten in den spätneolithischen Gräbern Südtransdanubiens', in J. Lichardus (ed.), *Die Kupferzeit als historische Epoche*, pp. 389–400, Bonn; I. Zalai-Gaál, 1992, 'Neue Angaben zum Kult und sakralen Leben des Neolithikums in Transdanubien I.', *Wosinsky Mór Megyei Múzeum Évkönyve (Szekszárd)* 17, 3–20; M. Wosinsky, 1888, *Das prähistorische Schanzwerk Lengyel*, Budapest.

148 See notes 146–7.

149 The literature is burgeoning fast. See V. Němejcová-Pavúková, 1986a; 1986b; V. Podborský, 1988; I. Pavlů *et al.*, 1986; M. S. Midgley, I. Pavlů, J. Rulf and M. Zápatocká, 1993, 'Fortified settlements or ceremonial sites: new evidence from Bylany, Czechoslovakia', *Antiquity* 67, 91–6; I. Pavlů, 1986; J. Petrasch, 1990; G. Trnka, 1990 (and see the whole of *Jahresschrift für mitteldeutsche Vorgeschichte* 73, 1990, on enclosures in general); G. Trnka, 1991; J. W. Neugebauer, 1984, 'Befestigungen und Kultanlagen des Mittelneolithikums in Niederösterreich am Beispiel von Falkenstein "Schanzboden" und Friebritz', *Mitteilungen der Österreichischen Arbeitsgemeinschaft für Ur- und Frühgeschichte* 33–4, 175–87; O. Brasch, 1993, 'Im Osten endlich freie Sicht von oben', *Archäologie in Deutschland* 1993 (4), 32–5.

150 M. Károlyi, 1984, 'Ergebnisse der Ausgrabungen bis 1980 in der befestigten Ansiedlung von Sé, Westungarn', *Mitteilungen der Österreichischen Arbeitsgemeinschaft für Ur- und Frühgeschichte* 33–4, 293–307; I. Zalai-Gaál, 1990, 'Neue Daten zur Erforschung der spätneolithischen Schanzwerke im südlichen Transdanubien', *Zalai Múzeum* 2, 31–46.

151 J. Pavúk, 1991.

152 J. Petrasch, 1990; G. Trnka, 1990; 1991. Kothingeichendorf shows the chequered chronologies of some sites; it was earlier assigned to both the LBK and the post-LBK horizon. The primary reference is: R. A. Maier, 1962, 'Fragen zu neolithischen Erdwerken Südbayerns', *Jahresbericht der Bayerischen Bodendenkmalpflege* 1962, 5–21.

153 H. Behrens and E. Schröter, 1980; E. Schröter, 1990, 'Ein neolithischer Kultplatz auf der Schalkenburg bei Quenstedt', *Jahresschrift für mitteldeutsche Vorgeschichte* 73, 267–70.

154 J. Pavúk, 1991.

155 I. Pavlů, 1986; J. Pavúk, 1991; J. Petrasch, 1990.

156 V. Němejcová-Pavúková, 1986a; G. Trnka, 1990.

157 E.g. V. Podborský, 1988.

158 K. Günther, 1973, 'Die Abschlussuntersuchung am neolithischen Grabenring von Bochum-Harpen', *Archäologisches Korrespondenzblatt* 3, 181–6; M. Ilett, 1983, 'The early Neolithic of north-eastern France', in C. Scarre (ed.), *Ancient France*, pp. 6–33, Edinburgh.

159 R. Dehn, 1985, 'Ein Gräberfeld der Rössener Kultur von Jechtingen, Gemeinde Sasbach, Kreis Emmendingen', *Archäologische Nachrichten aus Baden* 34, 3–6.

160 E.g. I. Hodder, 1990, and R. Bradley, 1993, where references can be followed.

161 C. Scarre *et al.*, 1993; C. Boujot and S. Cassen, 1993; J. L'Helgouach and C.-T. Le Roux, 1986; M. Patton, 1993.

162 Conveniently summarised in M. Patton, 1993. See also J. Roussot-Larroque and C. Burnez, 1992, 'Aux sources du Néolithique atlantique: le Cardial, le "Danubien" et les autres', *Revue Archéologique de l'Ouest, Supplément 5*, 127–38.

163 E.g. C. Boujot and S. Cassen, 1993.

164 P. Duhamel and M. Prestreau, 1991, 'La nécropole monumentale néolithique de Passy dans le contexte du gigantisme-funéraire européen', *Actes du 14e Colloque Inter-régional sur le Néolithique, Blois, 1987*, pp. 91–101, Orléans.

165 E.g. L. Czerniak, personal communication. See also H. Wiklak, 1990; M. S. Midgley, 1992.

166 M. S. Midgley, 1985.

167 From many interim reports, see S. H. Andersen, 1986, 'Tybrind Vig. A preliminary report on a submerged Ertebølle settlement on the west coast of Fyn', *Journal of Danish Archaeology* 4, 52–70; S. H. Andersen, 1987, 'Mesolithic dug-outs and paddles from Tybrind Vig, Denmark', *Acta Archaeologica* 57, 87–106; T. Trolle-Lassen, 1992, 'Butchering of red deer (*Cervus elaphus* L.) – a case study from the Late Mesolithic settlement of Tybrind Vig, Denmark', *Journal of Danish Archaeology* 9, 7–37; S. H. Andersen and C. Malmros, 1985, ' "Madskorpe" på Ertebøllekar fra Tybrind Vig', *Aarbøger for Nordisk Oldkyndighed og Historie* 1984, 78–95.

168 L. Larsson, 1990; C. Bonsall, 1989; P. Vermeersch and P. van Peer, 1990. For a suggestion that the transition in one area of southern England was not like that in the Baltic, see A. Whittle, 1990, 'A model for the Mesolithic–Neolithic transition in the upper Kennet valley, north Wiltshire', *Proceedings of the Prehistoric Society* 56, 101–10.

169 S. H. Andersen, 1979, 'Aggersund. En Ertebølleboplads ved Limfjorden', *Kuml* 1978, 7–56; E. Brinch Petersen, 1970, 'Ølby Lyng: en ostjaellandsk Kystboplads med Ertebøllekultur', *Aarbøger for Nordisk Oldkyndighed og Historie*, 5–42; S. Andersen, 1975, 'Ringkloster: en jysk inland-soboplads med Ertebøllekultur', *Kuml* 1973–4, 10–108; P. Rowley-Conwy, 1981, 'Mesolithic Danish bacon: permanent and temporary sites in the Danish Mesolithic', in A. Sheridan and G. N. Bailey (eds.), *Economic archaeology*, pp. 51–6, Oxford; S. H. Andersen, 1991; I. B. Enghoff, 1991, 'Fishing from the Stone Age settlement Norsminde', *Journal of Danish Archaeology* 8, 41–50; S. Hvass and B. Storgaard, 1993.

170 E.g. P. Rowley-Conwy, 1983, 'Sedentary hunters: the Ertebølle example', in G. Bailey (ed.), *Hunter-gatherer economy in prehistory*, pp. 111–26, Cambridge.

171 L. Larsson, 1993.

172 S. E. Albrethsen and E. Brinch Petersen, 1977; S. Vencl, 1991, 'Interprétation des blessures causées par les armes au Mésolithique', *L'Anthropologie* 95, 219–28; T. D. Price and A. B. Gebauer, 1992.

173 E. Brinch Petersen, 1988, 'Ein mesolithisches Grab mit acht Personen von Strøby Egede, Seeland', *Archäologisches Korrespondenzblatt* 18, 121–5; O. Grøn and J. Skaarup, 1993, 'Møllegabet II – a submerged Mesolithic site and a "boat burial" from Ærø', *Journal of Danish Archaeology* 10, 38–50. Another cemetery at Nederst, east Jutland, is being investigated by Brinch Petersen: L. Larsson, 1990; S. Hvass and B. Storgaard, 1993.

174 H. Schwabedissen, 1967, 'Ein horizontierter "Breitkeil" aus Satrup und die manningfachen Kulturbindungen der beginnenden Neolithikums im Norden und Nordwesten', *Palaeohistoria* 12, 409–68; J. Ilkiewicz, 1989, 'From studies on cultures of the 4th millennium B C in the central part of the Polish coastal area', *Przegląd Archaeologiczny* 36, 17–55; T. Galiński, 1990, 'Zespoły typu Tanowo. Zachodniopomerski ekwiwalent vgrupowania Ertebølle-Ellerbek-Lietzow', *Materiały Zachodniopomorskie* 33, 7–47; information on Mszano from Dr Zofia Sulgostowska, and on Chobienice from Dr L. Czerniak.

175 See M. Zvelebil and P. Dolukhanov, 1991; R. Rimantienė, 1992, 'The Neolithic of the eastern Baltic', *Journal of World Prehistory* 6, 97–143.

176 S. E. Albrethsen and E. Brinch Petersen, 1977.

177 L. Larsson, 1990.

178 P. Vang Petersen, 1984.

179 L. Larsson, 1990; K. Aaris-Sørensen, 1980, 'Depauperation of the mammalian fauna of the island of Zealand during the Atlantic period', *Videnskablige Meddelelser fra dansk naturvidenskablig Forening* 142, 131–8.

180 A. Fischer, 1982, 'Trade in Danubian shaft-hole axes and the introduction of Neolithic economy in Denmark', *Journal of Danish Archaeology* 1, 7–12.

181 O. Kayser, 1992, 'Les industries lithiques de la fin du Mésolithique en Armorique', *Revue Archéologique de l'Ouest, Supplément 5*, 117–24; M. Patton, 1993.

182 C. Smith, 1992, *Late Stone Age hunters of the British Isles*, London; M. R. Edmonds, 1987, 'Rocks and risks: problems with lithic procurement strategies', in A. G. Brown and M. R. Edmonds (eds.), *Lithic analysis and later British prehistory*, pp. 155–79, Oxford.

183 See chapter 2, note 11.

184 See C. Bonsall, 1989.

185 P. C. Woodman, 1978, *The Mesolithic in Ireland: hunter-gatherers in an insular environment*, Oxford.

186 C. Wickham-Jones, *Rhum: Mesolithic and later sites at Kinloch*, Edinburgh; J. Coles, 1971, 'The early settlement of Scotland: excavations at Morton, Fife', *Proceedings of the Prehistoric Society* 37 (2), 284–366.

187 P. Mellars, 1987; P. Mellars and M. R. Wilkinson, 1980, 'Fish otoliths as indicators of seasonality in prehistoric shell middens: the evidence from Oronsay (Inner Hebrides)', *Proceedings of the Prehistoric Society* 46, 19–44; S. J. Mithen and B. Finlayson, 1991, 'Red deer hunters on Colonsay? The implications for the interpretation of the Oronsay middens', *Proceedings of the Prehistoric Society* 57 (2), 1–8.

188 R. Wyss, 1988.

189 M. S. Midgley, 1992.

190 J. Lüning, 1967; C. Jeunesse, 1990; H. Schlichtherle, 1990.

191 U. Fischer, 1991; E. Gross, 1990.

192 J.-P. Demoule and J. Guilaine, 1986.

193 I. F. Smith, 1974, 'The Neolithic', in C. Renfrew (ed.), *British prehistory: a new outline*, pp. 100–36, London; P. Harbison, 1988.

194 E. Williams, 1989, 'Dating the introduction of food production into Britain and Ireland', *Antiquity* 63, 510–21.

195 J. D. van der Waals *et. al.,* 1976–9, 'Swifterbant contributions 1–12', *Helinium* 16–19 (S3–5 in vol. 17, 3–27); J. T. Zeiler, 1991, 'Hunting and animal husbandry in Neolithic sites in the western and central Netherlands: interaction between man and environment', *Helinium* 31, 60–125.

196 L. P. Louwe Kooijmans, 1993.

197 S. H. Andersen, 1991; K. Jennbert, 1985, 'Neolithisation – a Scanian perspective', *Journal of Danish Archaeology* 4, 196–7; K. Jennbert, 1984.

198 T. D. Price and A. B. Gebauer, 1992.

199 H. Schwabedissen, 1979, 'Der Beginn des Neolithikums im nordwestlichen Deutschland', in H. Schirnig (ed.), *Grosssteingräber in Niedersachsen*, pp. 203–22, Hildesheim; H. Schwabedissen, 1981, 'Ertebølle-Ellerbek Mesolithikum oder Neolithikum?', in B. Gramsch (ed.), *Mesolithikum in Europa*, pp. 129–42, Berlin; J. Meurers-Balke, 1983, *Siggeneben-Süd: ein Fundplatz der frühen Trichterbecherkultur an der holsteinischen Ostseeküste*, Neumünster.

200 P. Rowley-Conwy, 1984, 'The laziness of the short-distance hunter: the origins of agriculture in western Denmark', *Journal of Anthropological Archaeology* 3, 300–24; M. Zvelebil and P. Rowley-Conwy, 1984, 'Transition to farming in northern Europe: a hunter-gatherer perspective', *Norwegian Archaeological Review* 17, 104–28.

201 M. Zvelebil and P. Rowley-Conwy, 1986, 'Foragers and farmers in Atlantic Europe', in M. Zvelebil (ed.), *Hunters in transition*, pp. 67–93, Cambridge.

202 R. Wyss, 1988; E. Bleuer and B. Hardmeyer, 1993. For other early contact finds, see W. E. Stöckli, 1990, 'Der Beginn des Neolithikums in der Schweiz', in M. Höneisen, 1990, I, pp. 53–60; J. Speck, 1990, 'Zur Siedlungsgeschichte des Wauwilermooses', in M. Höneisen, 1990, I, pp. 255–70; C. Jeunesse, 1990.

203 P. Rowley-Conwy, 1985, 'The origin of agriculture in Denmark: a review of some theories', *Journal of Danish Archaeology* 4, 188–95.

204 J. S. Thomas, 1988, 'Neolithic explanations revisited: the Mesolithic–Neolithic transition in Britain and south Scandinavia', *Proceedings of the Prehistoric Society* 54, 59–66.

205 See especially R. Bradley, 1993.

206 E.g. I. Hodder, 1990; M. Patton, 1993; B. Bender, 1978; B. Bender, 1981, 'Gatherer-hunter

intensification', in A. Sheridan and G. N. Bailey (eds.), *Economic archaeology*, pp. 149–57, Oxford.

207 L. Larsson, 1990, p. 294; K. J. Edwards, 1989, 'Meso-Neolithic vegetational impacts in Scotland and beyond: palynological considerations', in C. Bonsall, 1989, pp. 143–55.

208 See especially R. Bradley, 1993, and a forthcoming paper on 'Mesolithic cosmologies'.

209 I. Hodder, 1990.

210 K. Jennbert, 1984.

211 To borrow the language of S. Kent, 1992.

212 E.g. J. Hawkes, 1934, 'Aspects of the Neolithic and Chalcolithic periods in western Europe', *Antiquity* 8, 24–42.

7 Unfair settlements and abstract funerals: central and western Europe, *c.* 4000–2500 BC

1 Z. Krzak, 1977, 'Cmentarzyska na "Gajowiźnie" pod wzglédem archeologicznym', in J. Kowalczyk (ed.), *Cmentarzysko kultury amfor kulistych w Złotej sandomierskiej*, pp. 9–82, Wrocław.

2 Using the distinction made by J. C. Barrett, 1994.

3 S. Milisauskas and J. Kruk, 1993; P. Bogucki and R. Grygiel, 1993.

4 A. Whittle and J. Pollard, 1995.

5 T. Wiślański, 1970, 'The Globular Amphora culture', in T. Wiślański (ed.), *The Neolithic in Poland*, pp. 178–231, Wrocław; T. Wiślański, 1979, 'Dalszy rozwój ludów neolitycznych. Plemiona kultury amfor kulistych', in W. Hensel and T. Wiślański (eds.), *Prahistoria ziem Polskich. II. Neolit*, pp. 261–99, Wrocław; A. Cofta-Broniewska (ed.), 1990, *Kultura amfor kulistych w rejonie Kujaw*, Poznań; E. Nagel, 1985, *Die Erscheinungen der Kugelamphorenkultur im Norden der DDR*, Berlin.

6 For northern TRB continuity, see P. O. Nielsen, 1993a. For the Horgen culture, see H. Schlichtherle, 1990; E. Gross, 1990.

7 See M. Buchvaldek and C. Strahm (eds.), 1992, *Die kontinentaleuropäischen Gruppen der Kultur mit Schnurkeramik*, Prague.

8 W. Borkowski *et al.*, 1991.

9 E.g. H. Schlichtherle, 1990; E. Gross, 1990.

10 P.J. Suter, 1987.

11 See references in M. Höneisen, 1990; A. Whittle, 1988; C. Strahm and C. Wolf, 1990; B. Dieckmann, 1991, 'Zum Stand der archäologischen Untersuchungen in Hornstaad', *Bericht der Römisch-Germanischen Kommission* 71, 84–109.

12 A.-M. Pétrequin and P. Pétrequin, 1988.

13 H. Schlichtherle, 1990; P. J. Suter, 1987; C. Strahm and C. Wolf, 1990.

14 E. Gross *et al.*, 1987; C. Strahm and C. Wolf, 1990; C. Wolf, 1992, 'Schnurkeramik und Civilisation Saône-Rhône in der Westschweiz: ein Beispiel für die Auseinandersetzung zwischen einer lokalen und einer überregionalen Kulturerscheinung', in M. Buchvaldek and C. Strahm, 1992, pp. 187–98; C. Strahm, 1992.

15 See M. Höneisen, 1990; H. Schlichtherle, 1990, *Siedlungsarchäologie im Alpenvorland I. Die Sondagen 1973–1978 in den Ufersiedlungen Hornstaad-Hörnle I*, Stuttgart; A. Whittle, 1988, with references to earlier debate.

16 See for example A.-M. Pétrequin and P. Pétrequin, 1988.

17 B. Arnold, 1993, 'Logboats of the 6th millennium BC [*sic*] discovered in Switzerland', in J. Coles, V. Fenwick and G. Hutchinson (eds.), *A spirit of enquiry: essays for Ted Wright*, pp. 5–8, Exeter. The dates are fourth millennium BC!

18 W. E. Stöckli, 1990 (with references to detailed site reports); A.-M. Pétrequin and P. Pétrequin, 1988; C. Strahm and C. Wolf, 1990; B. Ottaway and C. Strahm, 1975, 'Swiss Neolithic copper beads: currency, ornament or prestige items', *World Archaeology* 6, 307–21; A. Gallay, 1990.

19 M. Höneisen, 1990; E. Gross *et al.*, 1987; H. T. Waterbolk and W. van Zeist, *Niederwil, eine Siedlung*

der Pfyner Kultur, Bern; W. U. Guyan, 1981, 'Zur Viehhaltung im Steinzeitdorf Thayngen-Weier II', *Archäologie der Schweiz* 4, 112–19.

20 B. Dieckmann, 1990 (with references).

21 A. Billamboz, 1991, 'Das Holz des Pfahlbausiedlungen Südwestdeutschlands. Jahrringanalyse aus archäodendrologischer Sicht', *Bericht der Römisch-Germanischen Kommission* 71, 187–207; A. Billamboz, B. Dieckmann, U. Maier and R. Vogt, 1992, 'Exploitation du sol et du forêt à Hornstaad-Hörnle I (RFA, Bodensee)', *Actes du 116e congrès national des sociétés savantes. Archéologie et environnement des milieux aquatiques*, pp. 119–48, Paris; P. J. Suter, 1987; E. Gross *et al.*, 1987; E. Bleuer and B. Hardmeyer, 1993; W. E. Stöckli, 1990; P. Pétrequin (ed.), 1989, *Les sites littoraux néolithiques de Clairvaux-les-lacs (Jura). II. Le Néolithique moyen*, Paris.

22 M. Sakellaridis, 1979, *The economic exploitation of the Swiss area in the Mesolithic and Neolithic periods*, Oxford.

23 P. Rasmussen, 1991, 'Leaf-foddering of livestock in the Neolithic: archaeobotanical evidence from Weier, Switzerland', *Journal of Danish Archaeology* 8, 51–71.

24 P. Pétrequin (ed.), 1986, *Les sites littoraux néolithiques de Clairvaux-les-lacs (Jura). I. Problématique générale. L'exemple de la station III*, Paris; see discussion and references in A. Whittle, 1988. H. Schlichtherle, 1993, 'Ein Kulthaus der Jungsteinzeit am Überlinger See', *Archäologische Nachrichten aus Baden* 50, 48–9.

25 S. Jacomet, C. Brombacher and M. Dick, 1991, 'Palaeoethnobotanical work on Swiss Neolithic and Bronze Age lake dwellings over the past ten years', in J. Renfrew (ed.), *New light on early farming*, pp. 257–76, Edinburgh; M. Glass, 1991, *Animal production systems in Neolithic central Europe*, Oxford; A. G. Sherratt, 1981.

26 E.g. B. Dieckmann, 1990.

27 M. Währen, 1984, 'Brote und Getreidebrei von Twann aus dem 4. Jahrtausend vor Christus', *Archäologie der Schweiz* 7, 2–6; E. Gross *et al.*, 1987; A.-M. Pétrequin and P. Pétrequin, 1988; M. Rösch, 1991, 'Veränderungen von Wirtschaft und Umwelt während Neolithikum und Bronzezeit am Bodensee', *Bericht der Römisch-Germanischen Kommission* 71, 161–86; M. Rösch, 1993.

28 W. Gumiński, 1989, *Gródek Nadbużny: osada kultury pucharów lejkowatych*, Wrocław.

29 J. Kruk, 1980.

30 M. Nowak, 1993, *Osadnictwo kultury pucharów lejkowatych we wschodniej części niecki Nidziańskiej*, Kraków; J. Nogaj-Chachaj, 1991.

31 B. Balcer, 1988; C. Tunia, 1990, 'Archäologische Untersuchungen am neolithischen Verteidigungswerk bei Słonowice, Woj. Kielce, in den Jahren 1979–1988. 2. Vorbericht', *Jahresschrift für mitteldeutsche Vorgeschichte* 73, 249–53; H. Kowalewska-Marsałek, 'Sandomierz Wzgórze Zawichojskie. Beispiel einer neolithischen befestigten Anlage in Südostpolen', *Jahresschrift für mitteldeutsche Vorgeschichte* 73, 237–47.

32 S. Milisauskas and J. Kruk, 1993 (with references).

33 J. Kruk and S. Milisauskas, 1985, *Bronocice: osiedle obronne ludności kultury lubelsko-wołyńskiej, 2800–2700 lat p.n.e.*, Wrocław. This enclosure is the most fully published part of the project so far.

34 S. Milisauskas and J. Kruk, 1991, 'Utilization of cattle for traction during the later Neolithic in southeastern Poland', *Antiquity* 65, 562–6.

35 H. Behrens and E. Schröter, 1980; E. Pleslová-Štiková, 1990, 'Umfriedungen und befestigte Siedlungen aus dem Äneolithikums Böhmens. Versuch einer kulturhistorischen Interpretation', *Jahresschrift für mitteldeutsche Vorgeschichte* 73, 191–201.

36 I. Pleinerová, 1980, 'Kultovní objekty z pozdní doby kamenné v Březné v Loun', *Památky Archeologicke* 71, 10–60; E. Kirsch and F. Plate, 1984, 'Zwei mittelneolithische Fundplätze bei Buchow-Karpzow, Kr. Nauen', *Veröffentlichungen des Museums für Ur- und Frühgeschichte Potsdam* 18, 7–61.

37 J. Pavelčík, 1981, 'The hilltop settlement of the Channelled-ware people at Hlinsko by Lipník', in J. Hrala (ed.), *Nouvelles archéologiques dans la république socialiste tchèque*, pp. 46–8, Prague; R. W. Ehrich and E. Pleslová-Štiková, 1968; E. Pleslová-Štiková, 1981, 'Chronologie und Siedlungsformen der Řivnáč-Kultur und Kugelamphorenkultur Böhmens', *Jahresschrift für mitteldeutsche Vorgeschichte* 63, 159–71.

38 L. Czerniak, personal communication.

39 M. Sobociński and D. Makowiecki, 1991, 'Current state of knowledge of archaeozoological materials of the Globular Amphorae culture in Kuiavia', in A. Cofta-Broniewska (ed.), *New tendencies in studies of Globular Amphorae culture*, pp. 145–53, Warsaw and Kraków; M. J. Dąbrowski, 1971, 'Analiza pyłkowa warstw kulturowych z Sarnowa, pow. Włocławek', *Prace i Materiały* 18, 147–64; T. Wiślański, 1979, 'Dalszy rozwój ludów neolitycznych. Plemiona kultury amfor kulistych', in W. Hensel and T. Wiślański (eds.), *Prahistoria ziem Polskich. II. Neolit*, pp. 261–99, Wrocław; A. Kośko, 1991, 'Globular Amphorae culture versus Funnel Beaker culture', in A. Cofta-Broniewska (ed.), *New tendencies in studies of Globular Amphorae culture*, pp. 87–112, Warsaw and Kraków.

40 See M. Buchvaldek and C. Strahm, 1992.

41 Z. Krzak, 1976, *The Złota culture*, Wrocław.

42 J. Kruk, 1980; M. Buchvaldek and C. Strahm, 1992; K. Kristiansen, 1991; H. Behrens and E. Schröter, 1980.

43 M. Kobusiewicz and J. Kabaciński, 1993, *Chwalim: subboreal hunter-gatherers of the Polish plain*, Poznań.

44 D. Krol, 1992, 'The elements of settlements in Rzucewo culture', in M. Buchvaldek and C. Strahm, 1992, pp. 291–9.

45 M. Zvelebil and P. Dolukhanov, 1991.

46 R. Rimantiené, 1992, 'Neolithic hunter-gatherers at Šventoji in Lithuania', *Antiquity* 66, 367–76; R. Rimantiené, 1992, 'The Neolithic of the eastern Baltic', *Journal of World Prehistory* 6, 97–143.

47 A. Butrimas, 1992, 'Corded Pottery Culture graves from Lithuania', in M. Buchvaldek and C. Strahm, 1992, pp. 307–11.

48 P. O. Nielsen, 1993a; 1993b (and full references).

49 T. Madsen, 1982; 1988; T. Madsen and J. E. Petersen, 1984, 'Tidligneolitiske anlaeg ved Mosegården i Østjylland: regionale og kronologiske forskelle i tidligneolitikum', *Kuml* 1982–3, 61–120; T. Madsen and H. Juel Jensen, 1982, 'Settlement and land use in early Neolithic Denmark', *Analecta Praehistorica Leidensia* 15, 63–86.

50 T. Madsen, 1982; S. Th. Andersen, 1993; D. Liversage, 1992. See also M. Larsson, 1985, *The early Neolithic Funnel-Beaker culture in south-west Scania*, Oxford.

51 P. O. Nielsen, 1993a; 1993b; J. Skaarup, 1993; N. H. Andersen, 1993; L. Buus Eriksen, 1992, 'Ornehus på Stevns – en tidligneolitisk hustomt', *Aarbøger for Nordisk Oldkyndighed og Historie* 1991, 7–19; F. O. Nielsen and P. O. Nielsen, 1985, 'Middle and Late Neolithic houses at Limensgård, Bornholm', *Journal of Danish Archaeology* 4, 101–14.

52 S. Th. Andersen, 1993; S. Th. Andersen, 1990, 'Pollen spectra from the double passage grave Klekkendehøj on Møn. Evidence of swidden cultivation in the Neolithic of Denmark', *Journal of Danish Archaeology* 7, 77–92. Note that the ritual nature of pre-mound ploughing has been disputed: K. Kristiansen, 1989, 'Ard marks under barrows: a response to Peter Rowley-Conwy', *Antiquity* 63, 322–7.

53 E. Jørgensen, 1993.

54 P. O. Nielsen, 1993a; M. Hansen and H. Rostholm, 1993; J. Simonsen, 1986, 'Settlements from the Single Grave culture in north-west Jutland. A preliminary survey', *Journal of Danish Archaeology* 5, 135–51; N. A. Boas, 1993, 'Late Neolithic and Bronze Age settlements at Hemmed church and Hemmed plantation', *Journal of Danish Archaeology* 10, 119–35; S. H. Andersen, 1983, 'Kalvø – a coastal site of the Single Grave culture', *Journal of Danish Archaeology*

2, 71–80; P. Rowley-Conwy, 1985, 'The Single Grave (Corded Ware) economy at Kalvø', *Journal of Danish Archaeology* 4, 79–86; E. Jørgensen, 1977.

55 L. W. Rasmussen, 1993; L. W. Rasmussen and J. Richter, 1991, *Kainsbakke*, Grenå; L. W. Rasmussen, 1984, 'Kainsbakke A47: a settlement structure from the Pitted Ware culture', *Journal of Danish Archaeology* 3, 83–98.

56 M. P. Malmer, 1984, 'On the social function of pile dwellings and megaliths', in G. Burenhult, *The archaeology of Carrowmore*, pp. 371–5, Stockholm; H. Göransson, 1988, *Neolithic man and the forest environment around Alvastra pile dwelling*, Lund.

57 I. Armit, 1992, 'The Hebridean Neolithic', in N. Sharples and A. Sheridan (eds.), *Vessels for the ancestors*, pp. 307–21, Edinburgh; I. Armit and B. Finlayson, 1992, 'Hunter-gatherers transformed: the transition to agriculture in northern and western Europe', *Antiquity* 66, 664–76.

58 D. D. A. Simpson, 1976, 'The later Neolithic and Beaker settlement at Northton, Isle of Harris', in C. Burgess and R. Miket (eds.), *Settlement and economy in the third and second millennia BC*, pp. 221–32, Oxford.

59 N. Sharples, 1992, 'Aspects of regionalisation in the Scottish Neolithic', in N. Sharples and A. Sheridan (eds.), *Vessels for the ancestors*, pp. 322–31, Edinburgh; C. Richards, 1990, 'The late Neolithic house on Orkney', in R. Samson (ed.), *The social archaeology of houses*, pp. 111–24, Edinburgh.

60 E.g. T. Darvill and J. Thomas (eds.), 1996, *Neolithic houses in northern Europe*, Oxford. Among many others, note A. D. Fairweather and I. B. M. Ralston, 1993, 'The Neolithic timber hall at Balbridie, Grampian region, Scotland: the building, the date, the plant macrofossils', *Antiquity* 67, 313–23.

61 J. Richards, 1990; A. Whittle, 1993; J. Barrett, R. Bradley and M. Green, 1991; P. Woodward, 1991, *The South Dorset ridgeway: survey and excavations 1977–84*, Dorchester; C. A. I. French, 1990, 'Neolithic soils, middens and alluvium in the lower Welland valley', *Oxford Journal of Archaeology* 9, 305–11.

62 J. Richards, 1990; A. Whittle, A. J. Rouse and J. G. Evans, 1993, 'A Neolithic downland monument in its environment: excavation at the Easton Down long barrow, Bishops Cannings, north Wiltshire', *Proceedings of the Prehistoric Society* 59, 197–239.

63 L. Moffett, M. A. Robinson and V. Straker, 1989, 'Cereals, fruit and nuts: charred plant remains from Neolithic sites in England and Wales and the Neolithic economy', in A. Milles, D. Williams and N. Gardner (eds.), *The beginnings of agriculture*, pp. 243–61, Oxford; F. Pryor, C. French and M. Taylor, 1985, 'An interim report on excavations at Etton, Maxey, Cambridgeshire, 1982–1984', *Antiquaries Journal* 65, 275–311; F. Pryor, 1988, 'Etton, near Maxey, Cambridgeshire: a causewayed enclosure on the fen-edge', in C. Burgess *et al.*, 1988, pp. 107–26; B. Coles and J. Coles, 1986; S. Needham and J. Evans, 1987, 'Honey and dripping: Neolithic food residues from Runnymede bridge', *Oxford Journal of Archaeology* 6, 21–8.

64 B. Coles and J. Coles, 1986; J. Hillam, C. M. Groves, D. M. Brown, M. G. L. Baillie, J. M. Coles and B. J. Coles, 1990, 'Dendrochronology of the English Neolithic', *Antiquity* 64, 210–20.

65 B. Coles and J. Coles, 1986.

66 E.g. K. J. Edwards, 1989, 'Meso-Neolithic vegetational impacts in Scotland and beyond: palynological considerations', in C. Bonsall, 1989, pp. 143–55; A. Gebhardt and D. Marguerie, 1993, 'La transformation du paysage armoricain sous l'influence de l'homme', *XVIe Colloque Interrégional sur le Néolithique*, 19–24; M. Clet-Pellerin, 1986, 'Analyses polliniques dans quelques sites néolithiques de Normandie', *Revue Archéologique de l'Ouest, supplément* 1, 279–84.

67 B. Raftery, 1990, *Trackways through time*, Rush, Co. Dublin; E. Grogan and G. Eogan, 1987, 'Lough Gur excavations by Seán P. Ó Ríordáin: further Neolithic and Beaker habitations on Knockadoon', *Proceedings of the Royal Irish Academy* 87C, 299–506.

68 J. A. Bakker, 1992; J. A. Bakker, 1982, 'TRB settlement patterns on the Dutch sandy soils',

Analecta Praehistorica Leidensia 15, 87–124; L. P. Louwe Kooijmans, 1993; W. Prummel, 1987, 'The faunal remains from the Neolithic site of Hekelingen III', *Helinium* 27, 190–258.

69 J. W. H. Hogestijn, 1992, 'Functional differences between some settlements of the Single Grave culture in the northwestern coastal area of the Netherlands', in M. Buchvaldek and C. Strahm, 1992, pp. 199–205. Information on Zeewijk from the excavator, W.-J. Hogestijn.

70 See note 61; N. Sharples, 1992; R. Bradley, 1993 (with references).

71 R. Bradley, 1987, 'Flint technology and the character of Neolithic settlement', in A. G. Brown and M. R. Edmonds (eds.), *Lithic analysis and later British prehistory*, pp. 181–6, Oxford; J. Thomas, 1991.

72 F. Pryor, 1978, *Excavation at Fengate, Peterborough, England: the second report*, Toronto; S. Caulfield, 1983, 'The Neolithic settlement of north Connaught', in F. Hamond and T. Reeves-Smyth (eds.), *Landscape archaeology in Ireland*, pp. 195–215, Oxford. See also G. Cooney, 1991, 'Irish Neolithic landscapes and land use systems: the implications of field systems', *Rural History* 2, 123–39.

73 J. C. Barrett, 1994.

74 M. S. Midgley, 1992, with full references.

75 J. Nogaj-Chachaj, 1991, 'The stone-packed graves of the Funnel Beaker culture in Karmanowice, site 35', *Antiquity* 65, 628–39; S. Jastrzębski and M. Ślusarska, 1982, 'Grobowce kultury pucharów lejkowatych z lublina-sławinka i miłocina-kolonii, woj. lubelskie', *Wiadomości Archeologiczne* 47, 191–229.

76 J. Winiger, 1985, *Das Neolithikum der Schweiz*, Basel.

77 M. S. Midgley, 1992; T. Madsen, 1972, 'Grave med teltformet overbygning fra tidligneolitisk tid', *Kuml* 1971, 127–49; E. Brinch Petersen, 1974, 'Gravene ved Dragsholm. Fra jaegere til bønder for 6000 år siden', *Nationalmuseets Arbejdsmark*, 112–20.

78 E. Jørgensen, 1993.

79 J. Kruk and S. Milisauskas, 1982, 'A multiple Neolithic burial at Bronocice, Poland', *Germania* 60, 211–16.

80 H. Behrens, 1953, 'Ein Siedlungs- und Begräbnisplatz der Trichterbecherkultur bei Weissenfels an der Saale', *Jahresschrift für mitteldeutsche Vorgeschichte* 37, 67–108.

81 E. Gross *et al.*, 1987; J. Hoika, 1987, *Das Mittelneolithikum zur Zeit der Trichterbecherkultur in Nordostholstein*, Neumünster.

82 A. Whittle and J. Pollard, 1995; N. H. Andersen, 1988; J. Lichardus, 1986, 'Le rituel funéraire de la culture de Michelsberg dans la région du Rhin supérieur et moyen', in J.-P. Demoule and J. Guilaine, 1986, pp. 343–58.

83 K. Ebbesen, 1993; P. Bennike and K. Ebbesen, 1987, 'The bog find from Sigersdal. Human sacrifice in the Early Neolithic', *Journal of Danish Archaeology* 5, 85–115; P. Bennike, K. Ebbesen and L. Bender Jørgensen, 'Early Neolithic skeletons from Bolkilde bog, Denmark', *Antiquity* 60, 199–209.

84 K. Ebbesen, 1993.

85 The literature is vast. There is comparatively little recent general coverage; see G. Daniel, 1958, *The megalith builders of western Europe*, London; R. Joussaume, 1988, *Dolmens for the dead*, London; J. P. Mohen, 1989, *The world of megaliths*, London. For recent approaches, see J. C. Barrett, 1994; R. Bradley, 1993; J. Thomas, 1991. Ideological masking, with English and Swedish case studies, was first discussed by M. Shanks and C. Tilley, 1982.

86 Among others, see I. J. Thorpe, 1984, 'Ritual, power and ideology: a reconstruction of Earlier Neolithic rituals in Wessex', in R. Bradley and J. Gardiner (eds.), *Neolithic studies*, pp. 41–60, Oxford. The primary reference for secondary burial is R. Hertz, 1960, *Death and the right hand*, Aberdeen (a reprint of a much older work).

87 M. J. O'Kelly, 1982; G. Eogan, 1984; 1986; F. Mitchell, 1992, 'Notes on some non-local cobbles at the entrances to the passage-graves at Newgrange and Knowth, County Meath', *Journal of the*

Royal Society of Antiquaries of Ireland 122, 128–45. Information about Ballincrad from George Eogan.

88 M. J. O'Kelly, 1982; G. Eogan, 1986; information on survey from Gabriel Cooney.

89 Information from the excavator, George Eogan.

90 See note 87, and: M. J. O'Kelly, R. M. Cleary and D. Lehane, 1983, *Newgrange, Co. Meath, Ireland: the Late Neolithic/Beaker period settlement*, Oxford; P. D. Sweetman, 1985, 'A Late Neolithic/Early Bronze Age pit circle at Newgrange, Co. Meath', *Proceedings of the Royal Irish Academy* 85C, 195–221; P. D. Sweetman, 1987, 'Excavation of a Late Neolithic/Early Bronze Age site at Newgrange, Co. Meath', *Proceedings of the Royal Irish Academy* 87C, 283–98; G. Eogan and H. Roche, 1994, 'A Grooved Ware wooden structure at Knowth, Boyne valley, Ireland', *Antiquity* 68, 322–30; P. D. Sweetman, 1976, 'An earthen enclosure at Monknewtown, Slane, Co. Meath', *Proceedings of the Royal Irish Academy* 76C, 25–72; G. Stout, 1991, 'Embanked enclosures of the Boyne region', *Proceedings of the Royal Irish Academy* 91C, 245–84.

91 E.g. B. Graslund, 'Prehistoric soul beliefs in northern Europe', *Proceedings of the Prehistoric Society* 60, 15–26.

92 An old idea, most recently discussed by I. Hodder, 1990; A. G. Sherratt, 1990, 'The genesis of megaliths: ethnicity and social complexity in Neolithic northwest Europe', *World Archaeology* 22, 147–67; R. Bradley, 1993.

93 C. Boujot and S. Cassen, 1993; M. Patton, 1993.

94 I. Kinnes, 1982, 'Les Fouaillages and megalithic origins', *Antiquity* 56, 24–30. I am grateful to Ian Kinnes for information about radiocarbon dates.

95 J. L'Helgouach and C.-T. Le Roux, 1986; information kindly supplied by C.-T. Le Roux.

96 M. Midgley, 1992; J. Skaarup, 1993.

97 S. H. Andersen and E. Johansen, 1992, 'An early Neolithic grave at Bjørnsholm, north Jutland', *Journal of Danish Archaeology* 9, 38–58; P. Ashbee, 1981, 'Reconsideration of the British Neolithic', *Antiquity* 56, 134–8.

98 A point I owe to Richard Bradley.

99 See note 95.

100 D. Liversage, 1992.

101 The literature is vast. See the survey and references in M. Patton, 1993; and other basic material in J. L'Helgouach and C.-T. Le Roux, 1986; J. L'Helgouach, 1965, *Les sépultures mégalithiques en Armorique*, Rennes.

102 M. Patton, 1993, p. 96; J. L'Helgouach and J. Lecornec, 1976, 'Le site mégalithique de Min-Goh-Ru, près de Larcuste à Colpo (Morbihan)', *Bulletin de la Société Préhistorique Française* 73, 370–97.

103 C.-T. Le Roux, 1984, 'À propos des fouilles de Gavrinis (Morbihan): nouvelles données sur l'art mégalithique armoricain', *Bulletin de la Société Préhistorique Française* 81, 240–5; C.-T. Le Roux, 1992, 'The art of Gavrinis in its Armorican context', *Journal of the Royal Society of Antiquaries of Ireland* 122, 79–108. The suggestion that the third part of the menhir could be in Er-Vinglé/Er-Grah can probably now be discounted: Serge Cassen, personal communication.

104 P. Harbison, 1988.

105 N. Sharples, 1985, 'Individual and community: the changing role of megaliths in the Orcadian Neolithic', *Proceedings of the Prehistoric Society* 51, 59–77; C. Renfrew, 1990.

106 T. Darvill, 1987, *Prehistoric Britain*, London; A. Saville, 1990.

107 A. Whittle, 1991; P. Shand and I. Hodder, 'Haddenham', *Current Archaeology* 118, 339–42.

108 J. Skaarup, 1993; E. Jørgensen, 1993; P. O. Nielsen, 1993a.

109 J. Skaarup, 1993; M. Shanks and C. Tilley, 1982. See also S. Thorsen, 1981, ' "Klokkehøj" ved Bojden. Et sydvestfynsk dyssekammer med bevaret primaergrav', *Kuml* 1980, 105–46.

110 Discussed in D. Liversage, 1992.

111 J. A. Bakker, 1992; M. S. Midgley, 1992; J. Hoika, 1990, 'Megalithic graves in the Funnel Beaker culture of Schleswig-Holstein', *Przegląd Archeologiczny* 37, 53–119.

112 M. S. Midgley, 1992. Extensive excavations in the former DDR were carried out by E. Schuldt and others.

113 M. S. Midgley, 1985.

114 H. Behrens, 1973; H. Behrens and E. Schröter, 1980. See also A. Whittle, 1988.

115 B. Vyner, 1984, 'The excavation of a Neolithic cairn at Street House, Loftus, Cleveland', *Proceedings of the Prehistoric Society* 50, 151–96.

116 C. Tilley, 1984, 'Ideology and the legitimation of power in the Middle Neolithic of southern Sweden', in D. Miller and C. Tilley (eds.), *Ideology, power and prehistory*, pp. 111–46, Cambridge; E. Schlicht, 1968, *Die Funde aus dem Megalithgrab 2 von Emmeln, Kreis Meppen*, Neumünster; J. A. Bakker, 1979.

117 A. Whittle, 1993; M. S. Midgley, 1992.

118 A. Whittle, 1988; M. S. Midgley, 1992.

119 A. Whittle, 1991.

120 P. Ashbee, 1966, 'Fussell's Lodge long barrow excavations, 1957', *Archaeologia* 100, 1–80. For discussion of the sequence, see A. Whittle, 1988; J. Thomas, 1991.

121 A. Saville, 1990.

122 S. Piggott, 1962, *The West Kennet long barrow*, London; J. Thomas and A. Whittle, 1986, 'Anatomy of a tomb: West Kennet revisited', *Oxford Journal of Archaeology* 5, 129–56; J. Barrett, 1994; J. Thomas, 1988, 'The social significance of Cotswold-Severn burial practices', *Man* 23, 540–59; M. Shanks and C. Tilley, 1982.

123 C. Gosden, 1994, *Social being and time*, Oxford. For a thoughtful version of the model of lineage glorification, see C. Brysting Damm, 1991, 'Burying the past: an example of social transformation in the Danish Neolithic', in P. Garwood, D. Jennings, R. Skeates and J. Toms (eds.), *Sacred and profane*, pp. 43–9, Oxford.

124 E.g. J. Thomas, 1987; R. Tringham and D. Krstić, 1990; I. Hodder, 1990; A. G. Sherratt, 1981; M. Gimbutas, 1991.

125 See note 5.

126 P. Bogucki and R. Grygiel, 1993.

127 M. Buchvaldek and C. Strahm, 1992; M. Buchvaldek, 1986; E. Neustupný, 1973, 'Factors affecting the variability of the Corded Ware culture', in C. Renfrew (ed.), *The explanation of culture change*, pp. 725–30, London; M. Buchvaldek and D. Koutecký, 1970, *Vikletice: ein schnurkeramisches Gräberfeld*, Prague; E. Neustupný and Z. Smrž, 1989, 'Čachovice – pohřebiště kultury se šňůrovou keramikou a zvoncovitych pohárů', *Památky Archeologické* 80, 282–383.

128 See again note 5; and E. Schuldt, 1972, *Die mecklenburgischen Megalithgräber*, Berlin.

129 H. J. Beier, 1984 (with references). See also A. Whittle, 1988.

130 H. J. Beier, 1988, *Die Kugelamphorenkultur im Mittelelbe-Saale-Gebiet und in der Altmark*, Berlin.

131 H. Behrens and E. Schröter, 1980; S. J. Shennan, 1993; P. Siemen, 1992, 'Social structure of the Elbe-Saale Corded Ware culture: a preliminary model', in M. Buchvaldek and C. Strahm, 1992, pp. 229–40.

132 M. Hansen and H. Rostholm, 1993; E. Jørgensen, 1977.

133 S. J. Shennan, 1993; J. Havel and J. Kovářík, 1992, 'Die schnurkeramischen Gräberfelder in Praha-Jinonice', in M. Buchvaldek and C. Strahm, 1992, pp. 95–8.

134 G. Bailloud, 1974, *Le Néolithique dans le bassin parisien* (second edition), Paris; A. Leroi-Gourhan, G. Bailloud and M. Brézillon, 1962, 'L'hypogée II des Mournouards', *Gallia Préhistoire* 5, 23–133; C. Masset, 1972, 'The megalithic tomb of La Chaussée-Tirancourt', *Antiquity* 46, 297–300; F. Baumann *et al.*, 1979, 'La sépulture collective des Maillets à Germigny-l'Evêque (Seine-et-Marne)', *Gallia Préhistoire* 22, 143–204. See also A. Whittle, 1988.

135 See note 105; C. C. Richards, 1988, 'Altered images: a re-examination of Neolithic mortuary practices in Orkney', in J. C. Barrett and I. A. Kinnes (eds.), *The archaeology of context in the Neolithic and Bronze Age: recent trends*, pp. 42–56, Sheffield.

136 See J. Thomas, 1991 (with references).

137 M. Sahlins, 1968, *Tribesmen*, Englewood Cliffs, New Jersey. See also E. E. Evans-Pritchard, 1956, *Nuer religion*, New York and Oxford.

138 The best general references are C. Burgess *et al.*, 1988; *Jahresschrift für mitteldeutsche Vorgeschichte* 73, 1990.

139 J. P. Mallory and B. Hartwell, 1984, 'Donegore', *Current Archaeology* 92, 271–5.

140 N. H. Andersen, 1993.

141 E.g. B. S. Ottaway, 1990, 'Eine befestigte Siedlung der Chamer Kultur in Isartal', *Jahresschrift für mitteldeutsche Vorgeschichte* 73, 415–25.

142 A. Whittle and J. Pollard, 1995; H. Behrens and E. Schröter, 1980.

143 R. Mercer, 1988, 'Hambledon Hill, Dorset, England', in C. Burgess *et al*, 1988, pp. 89–106; J. Lüning, 1967; F. Pryor, 1988, 'Etton, near Maxey, Cambridgeshire: a causewayed enclosure on the fen-edge', in C. Burgess *et al.*, 1988, pp. 107–26.

144 C. Evans, 1988, 'Excavations at Haddenham, Cambridgeshire: a "planned" enclosure and its regional affinities', in C. Burgess *et al.*, 1988, pp. 127–48; J. Hedges and D. Buckley, 1978, 'Excavations at a Neolithic causewayed enclosure, Orsett, Essex, 1975', *Proceedings of the Prehistoric Society* 44, 219–308; P. Dixon, 1988, 'The Neolithic settlements on Crickley Hill', in C. Burgess *et al.*, 1988, pp. 75–88.

145 R. Joussaume, 1988, 'Analyse structurale de la triple enceinte de fossés interrompus à Champ-Durand, Nieul-sur-l'Autize, Vendée', in C. Burgess *et al.*, 1988, pp. 275–99; S. Cassen, 1993, 'Material culture and chronology of the Middle Neolithic of western France', *Oxford Journal of Archaeology* 12, 197–208. Are there alternatives to this interpretation of the Champ-Durand ditch stratigraphy?

146 N. Sharples, 1992.

147 N. H. Andersen, 1988; N. H. Andersen, 1988, 'The Neolithic causewayed enclosures at Sarup, on south-west Funen, Denmark', in C. Burgess *et al.*, 1988, pp. 337–62; N. H. Andersen, 1990, 'Sarup. Zwei befestigte Anlagen der Trichterbecherkultur', *Jahresschrift für mitteldeutsche Vorgeschichte* 73, 427–40; N. H. Andersen, 1993; T. Madsen, 1988.

148 A. Whittle and J. Pollard, 1995; A. Whittle, 1993; I. Smith, 1965, *Windmill Hill and Avebury*, Oxford.

149 See M. Patton, 1993.

150 R. Bradley, 1993 (with references); J. Barrett, R. Bradley and M. Green, 1991; A. Whittle, R. J. C. Atkinson, R. Chambers and N. Thomas, 1992, 'Excavations in the Neolithic and Bronze Age complex at Dorchester-on-Thames, Oxfordshire, 1947–1952 and 1981', *Proceedings of the Prehistoric Society* 58, 143–201.

151 R. Bradley, 1993; G. Wainwright, 1989, *The henge monuments*, London.

152 J. C. Barrett, 1994.

153 A long list goes back to C. Renfrew, 1973. See also I. J. Thorpe and C. C. Richards, 1984.

154 M. Pitts and A. Whittle, 1992, 'The development and date of Avebury', *Proceedings of the Prehistoric Society* 58, 203–12; G. J. Wainwright and I. H. Longworth, 1971, *Durrington Walls: excavations 1966–1968*, London; G. J. Wainwright, 1979, *Mount Pleasant, Dorset: excavations 1970–1971*, London.

155 J. Thomas, 1991; J. C. Barrett, 1994.

156 A. Burl, 1979, *Prehistoric Avebury*, New Haven and London; A. Whittle, 1993. A final report on the 1968–70 excavations is in preparation by the author.

157 J. C. Barrett, 1994.

158 C. Renfrew, 1990.

159 M. Höneisen, 1990; B. Coles and J. Coles, 1986.

160 P. Pétrequin, 1993, 'North wind, south wind. Neolithic technical choices in the Jura mountains, 3700–2400 BC', in P. Lemonnier (ed.), *Technical choices: transformations in material cultures since the Neolithic*, pp. 36–76, London.

161 A-M. Pétrequin and P. Pétrequin, 1988.

162 B. Coles and J. Coles, 1986.

163 K. H. Brandt, 1967; H. Behrens, 1973; J. A. Bakker, 1979; M. S. Midgley, 1992 (among many others). M. P. Malmer points out also that battleaxes might have made poor weapons: 1992, 'The Battle-Axe and Beaker cultures from an ethno-archaeological point of view', in M. Buchvaldek and C. Strahm, 1992, pp. 241–5.

164 K. Ebbesen, 1993.

165 See J. Lech, 1980; 1982; T. Wiślański (ed.), 1970, *The Neolithic in Poland*, Wrocław.

166 W. Borkowski *et al.*, 1991.

167 M. de Grooth, 1991, 'Socio-economic aspects of Neolithic flint mining: a preliminary study', *Helinium* 31, 153–89; B. Balcer, 1988. For values ascribed to different raw materials, see P. S. C. Taçon, 1991, 'The power of stone: symbolic aspects of stone use and tool development in western Arnhem Land, Australia', *Antiquity* 65, 192–207.

168 Among many references, see J. Lech, 1980; 1982; B. Madsen, 1993, 'Flint – extraction, manufacture and distribution', in S. Hvass and B. Storgaard, 1993, pp. 126–9, Copenhagen and Aarhus; F. Bostyn and Y. Lanchon, 1992, *Jablines. Le Haut Château (Seine-et-Marne). Une minière de silex au Néolithique*, Paris; C.-T. Le Roux, 1971, 'A stone axe-factory in Brittany', *Antiquity* 45, 283–8; R. Bradley and M. Edmonds, 1993.

169 R. Bradley and M. Edmonds, 1993.

170 P. O. Nielsen, 1978, 'Die Flintbeile der Trichterbecherkulturen in Dänemark', *Acta Archaeologica* 48, 61–138; K. Ebbesen, 1993; K. Randsborg, 1975, 'Social dimensions of early Neolithic Denmark', *Proceedings of the Prehistoric Society* 41, 105–18; R. Bradley, 1990, *The passage of arms*, Cambridge; T. Mathiassen, 1959, *Nordvestsjaellands oldtidsbebyggelse*, Copenhagen.

171 See again M. Höneisen, 1990; P. O. Nielsen, 1993a; B. Dieckmann, 1987, 'Ein bemerkenswerter Kupferfund aus der jungneolithischen Seeufersiedlung Hornstaad-Hörnle I am westlichen Bodensee', *Archäologische Nachrichten aus Baden* 38/39, 28–37; C. Strahm, 1991.

172 N. Mallet, 1980 'F12 Grand Pressigny, Touraine, Dép. Indre & Loire', in G. Weisgerber (ed.), *5000 Jahre Feuersteinbergbau*, pp. 483–5, Bochum; N. Mallet, 1992, *Le Grand-Pressigny: ses relations avec la civilisation Saône-Rhône*, Grand-Pressigny; C. Verjux, 1991, 'Fouille de sauvetage d'un atelier de taille du silex dans la région du Grand-Pressigny', *Actes du 15e colloque interrégional sur le Néolithique*, pp. 173–81, Voipreux; G. Cordier, 1957, 'Le vrai visage du Grand-Pressigny', *Compte rendu de la 15e session du Congrès préhistorique de France 1956*, pp. 416–42, Paris; C. Scarre, 1983, 'The Neolithic of west-central France', in C. Scarre (ed.), *Ancient France*, pp. 223–70, Edinburgh.

173 See note 18.

174 A. Gallay, 1990; A. Winiger, 1990, 'Le Néolithique valaisan', in M. Höneisen, 1990, I, pp. 353–60; O.-J. Bocksberger, 1976, *Le site préhistorique du Petit-Chasseur (Sion, Valais): le dolmen MVI*, Lausanne.

175 A.-M. Pétrequin and P. Pétrequin, 1988; R. Bradley and M. Edmonds, 1993.

176 E.g. I. Hodder, 1982, *Symbols in action*, Cambridge.

177 See M. Höneisen, 1990.

178 M. J. O'Kelly, 1982; G. Eogan, 1986.

179 D. F. S. Peacock, 1969, 'Neolithic pottery production in Cornwall', *Antiquity* 43, 145–9.

180 Another voluminous literature. See M. Buchvaldek, 1986; M. Buchvaldek and C. Strahm, 1992; I. Hodder, 1990; M. Gimbutas, 1991; C. Renfrew, 1987.

181 M. Buchvaldek, 1986; M. Buchvaldek and C. Strahm, 1992; M. Buchvaldek, 1986, 'Die mitteleuropäische Schnurkeramik und das nördliche Schwarzmeergebiet', *Památky Archeologické* 77, 486–97; Z. Krzak, 1980, *Geneza i chronologia kultury ceramiki sznurowej w Europie*, Wrocław.

182 M. Buchvaldek, 1986.

183 C. Strahm, 1992, 'Die Dynamik der schnurkeramischen Entwicklung in der Schweiz und in Südwestdeutschland', in M. Buchvaldek and C. Strahm, 1992, pp. 163–77.

184 D. L. Clarke, 1976, 'The beaker network – social and economic models', in J. Lanting and J. D. van der Waals (eds.), *Glochenbecher Symposion*, pp. 459–77, Bussum and Haarlem.

185 M. Popelka, 1992, 'Chipped stone industry of the Bohemian Corded-ware culture', in M. Buchvaldek and C. Strahm, 1992, pp. 89–94; R. Šumberová, 1992, 'Typologie des Kupferschmucks und der Kupfergeräte in der schnurkeramischen Kultur Böhmens und Mährens', in M. Buchvaldek and C. Strahm, 1992, pp. 117–25.

186 B. Hardmeyer, 1992, 'Die Schnurkeramik in der Ostschweiz', in M. Buchvaldek and C. Strahm, 1992, pp. 179–86.

187 E. Neustupný, 1982, 'Prehistoric migrations by infiltration', *Archeologické Rozhledy* 34, 278–93; K. Kristiansen, 1991.

188 E. Gross *et al.*, 1987; E. Bleuer and B. Hardmeyer, 1993.

189 H. Behrens, 1973; H. J. Beier, 1984; R. W. Ehrich and E. Pleslová-Štiková, 1968.

190 A. G. Sherratt, 1991.

191 Z. Krzak, 1970, 'The Złota culture', in T. Wiślański (ed.), *The Neolithic in Poland*, pp. 333–355, Wrocław; Z. Krzak, 1976, *The Złota culture*, Wrocław (note footnote 1, p. 155: 'The cemetery is not a simple reflection of social relations; it rather offers a picture of the religious beliefs of its occupants').

8 One foot in sea: the central and west Mediterranean, *c.* 7000–5000 BC

1 S. Tusa, 1985; L. Costantini *et al.*, 1987; L. Costantini, 1989; A. Tagliocozzo, 1993; A. Tagliocozzo, 1992, 'Appendix. Domestic ovicaprines in the Neolithic levels of Grotta dell' Uzzo', *Journal of Anthropological Archaeology* 11, 47–102. And see note 22, chapter 2.

2 E.g. S. Tinè, 1983. Reviewed briefly in R. D. Whitehouse, 1992.

3 D. Geddes, 1985.

4 J. Lewthwaite, 1989.

5 J. C. Shackleton and T. H. van Andel, 1985; J. C. Shackleton, T. H. van Andel and C. N. Runnels, 1984, 'Coastal paleogeography of the central and western Mediterranean during the last 125,000 years and its archaeological implications', *Journal of Field Archaeology* 11, 307–14.

6 E.g. J. Zilhão, 1993; D. Binder *et al.*, 1993.

7 D. Binder, 1991; D. Binder and J. Courtin, 1987; B. Martí-Oliver, 1988. See also (without the inference of colonisation) R. E. Donahue, 1992, 'Desperately seeking Ceres: a critical examination of current models for the transition to agriculture in Mediterranean Europe', in A. B. Gebauer and T. D. Price (eds.), *Transitions to agriculture in prehistory*, pp. 73–80, Madison.

8 J. Zilhão, 1993.

9 S. M. Cassano *et al.*, 1987; S. Milliken and R. Skeates, 1989; R. Whitehouse, 1971, 'The last hunter-gatherers in southern Italy', *World Archaeology* 2, 239–54.

10 M. Cipolloni Sampò, 1982a; R. Whitehouse, 1994.

11 R. D. Whitehouse, 1992; K. A. Brown, 1991a.

12 P. Biagi and R. Nisbet, 1987.

13 J. F. Cherry, 1990; R. H. Tykot, 1994, 'Radiocarbon dating and absolute chronology in Sardinia and Corsica', in R. Skeates and R. Whitehouse (eds.), *Radiocarbon dating and Italian prehistory*, pp. 115–45, London; S. Stoddart *et al.*, 1993.

14 A. Muzzolini, 1989, 'La "néolithisation" du nord de l'Afrique et ses causes', in O. Aurenche and J. Cauvin (eds.), *Néolithisations*, pp. 145–86, Oxford; P. Sheppard, 1987, *The Capsian of north Africa*, Oxford.

15 D. Coppola and L. Costantini, 1987; S. M. Cassano *et al.*, 1987; S. Milliken and R. Skeates, 1989.

16 M. Cipolloni Sampò, 1987, 'Problèmes des débuts de l'économie de production en Italie sud-orientale', in J. Guilaine *et al.*, 1987, pp. 181–8; M. Follieri, 1987, 'L'agriculture des plus anciennes communautés rurales d'Italie', in J. Guilaine *et al.*, 1987, pp. 243–7.

17 R. D. Whitehouse, 1992; R. D. Whitehouse, 1986; S. Tinè, 1983; J. Müller, 1991, 'Die ostadriati-sche Impresso-Kultur: zeitliche Gliederung und kulturelle Bindung', *Germania* 69, 311–58.

18 A. J. Ammerman, G. D. Schaffer and N. Hartmann, 1988, 'A Neolithic household at Piana di Curinga, Italy', *Journal of Field Archaeology* 15, 121–40.

19 G. Cremonesi and J. Guilaine, 1987, 'L'habitat de Torre Sabea (Gallipoli, Puglia) dans le cadre du Néolithique ancien de l'Italie du sud-est', in J. Guilaine *et al.*, 1987, pp. 377–85; D. Coppola and L. Costantini, 1987; M. Cipolloni Sampò, 1982a; L. Costantini and C. Tozzi, 1987, 'Un gisement à céramique imprimée dans le subapennin de la Daunia (Lucera, Foggia): le village de Ripa Tetta', in J. Guilaine *et al.*, 1987, pp. 387–94; R. D. Whitehouse, 1992.

20 K. A. Brown, 1991a; 1991b; G. D. B. Jones, 1987; S. Tinè, 1983.

21 C. Delano Smith, 1987, 'The Neolithic environment of the Tavoliere', in G. D. B. Jones, 1987, pp. 1–26; A. Manfredini and S. M. Cassano, 1983.

22 K. A. Brown, 1991a; 1991b; G. D. B. Jones, 1987.

23 S. Tinè, 1983; D. H. Trump, 1987, 'Excavations in 1949–63', in G. D. B. Jones, 1987, pp. 117–36.

24 J. C. Barrett, 1994.

25 S. Tinè, 1983; A. Manfredini and S. M. Cassano, 1983.

26 J. M. Mallory, 1989, 'Lagnano da Piede I – an early Neolithic village in the Tavoliere', *Origini* 13, 193–290.

27 G. D. B. Jones, 1987.

28 See note 16, and L. Castelletti, L. Costantini and C. Tozzi, 1987, 'Considerazioni sull'economia e l'ambiente durante il Neolitico in Italia', *Atti della XXVI Riunione Scientifica dell' Istituto Italiano di Preistoria e Protostoria*, 37–54.

29 G. D. B. Jones, 1987; M. R. Jarman and D. Webley, 1975, 'Settlement and land use in Capitanata, Italy', in E. S. Higgs (ed.), *Palaeoeconomy*, pp. 177–222, Cambridge.

30 S. M. Cassano, 1985, 'Considerazioni sugli inizi dell' economia produttiva sulle sponde dell' Adriatico', in M. Liverani, A. Palmieri and R. Peroni (eds.), *Studi di paletnologia in onore di Salvatore M. Puglisi*, pp. 731–43, Rome; R. Skeates, 1994, 'Towards an absolute chronology for the Neolithic of central Italy', in R. Skeates and R. Whitehouse (eds.), *Radiocarbon dating and Italian prehistory*, pp. 61–72, London; G. Barker, 1981, *Landscape and society: prehistoric central Italy*, London.

31 C. Malone and S. Stoddart, 1992, 'The Neolithic site of San Marco, Gubbio (Perugia), Umbria: survey and excavation 1985–7', *Papers of the British School at Rome* 60, 1–69; C. Malone and S. Stoddart (eds.), 1994, *Time, territory and state*, Cambridge; R. Skeates, forthcoming, 'Unveiling inequality: social life and social change in the Mesolithic and Early Neolithic of east-central Italy', in R. H. Tykot, J. Morter and J. Robb (eds.), *Social dynamics of the prehistoric central Mediterranean*.

32 L. Sarti, C. Corridi, F. Martini and P. Pallecchi, 1991, 'Mileto: un insediamento neolitico della ceramica a linee incise', *Rivista di Scienze Preistoriche* 43, 73–154.

33 P. Biagi and R. Nisbet, 1987.

34 B. Bagolini and P. Biagi, 1975, 'Il Neolitico del Vhò di Piadena', *Preistoria Alpina* 11, 77–121; G. Barker, 1977, 'Further information on the early Neolithic economy of Vhò', *Preistoria Alpina* 13, 99–105.

35 P. Biagi and R. Nisbet, 1987; R. Clark, 1989, 'Towards the integration of social and ecological approaches to the study of early agriculture', in A. Milles, D. Williams and N. Gardner (eds.), *The beginnings of agriculture*, pp. 3–22, Oxford.

36 P. Biagi and R. Nisbet, 1987; B. Bagolini and P. Biagi, 1985, 'Balkan influences in the Neolithic of northern Italy', *Preistoria Alpina* 21, 49–57; B. Bagolini, 1990, 'Contacts entre les courants danubi-ens et méditerranéens en Italie du nord', in D. Cahen and M. Otte (eds.), *Rubané et Cardial*, pp. 73–81, Liège.

37 S. Tinè, 1986; P. Rowley-Conwy, 1992; G. Barker, P. Biagi, G. Clark, R. Maggi and R. Nisbet, 1990, 'From hunting to herding in the Val Pennavaira (Liguria – northern Italy)', in P. Biagi (ed.), *The Neolithisation of the Alpine region*, pp. 99–121, Brescia.

38 J. Guilaine, 1986, 'Le Néolithique ancien en Languedoc et Catalogne', in J.-P. Demoule and J. Guilaine, 1986, pp. 71–82; D. Binder and J. Courtin, 1987; D. Binder *et al.*, 1993; D. Binder, 1989, 'Aspects de la néolithisation dans les aires padane, provençale et ligure', in O. Aurenche and J. Cauvin (eds.), *Néolithisations*, pp. 199–225, Oxford; B. Martí-Oliver, 1988; J. Zilhão, 1993; J. Evin, 1987, 'Révision de la chronologie absolue des débuts du Néolithique en Provence et Languedoc', in J. Guilaine *et al.*, 1987, pp. 27–36; D. Asquerino Fernandez, 1987, 'El neolitico en Andalucia: estado actual de su conocimiento', *Trabajos de Preistoria* 44, 63–85.

39 D. Binder and J. Courtin, 1987.

40 D. Binder and J. Courtin, 1987; J. Zilhão, 1993; J. E. Brochier, P. Villa and M. Giacomarra, 1992, 'Shepherds and sediments: geo-ethnoarchaeology of pastoral sites', *Journal of Anthropological Archaeology* 11, 47–102. See also I. Davidson, 1989, 'Escaped domestic animals and the introduction of agriculture to Spain', in J. Clutton-Brock (ed.), *The walking larder*, pp. 59–71, London.

41 D. Geddes, 1980; 1983; 1985; J-D. Vigne and D. Geddes, 1986, 'Les premiers moutons et chèvres domestiques de France dans leur contexte européen', in J.-P. Demoule and J. Guilaine (eds.), *Le Néolithique de la France*, pp. 42–4, Paris; H-P. Uerpmann, 'The origins and relations of Neolithic sheep and goats in the western Mediterranean', in J. Guilaine *et al.* (eds.), *Premières communautés paysannes en Méditerranée occidentale*, pp. 175–9, Paris.

42 J. Courtin, J. Evin and Y. Thommeret, 1985, 'Révision de la stratigraphie et la chronologie absolue du site de Châteauneuf-les-Martigues (Bouches-du-Rhône)', *L'Anthropologie* 89, 543–6; J. Zilhão, 1993.

43 D. Binder and J. Courtin, 1987; B. Martí-Oliver, 1988; J. Juan-Cabanilles, 1990, 'Substrat epipaléolithique et néolithisation en Espagne: apport des industries lithiques à l'identification des traditions culturelles', in D. Cahen and M. Otte (eds.), *Rubané et Cardial*, pp. 417–35, Liège.

44 D. Binder, 1991; D. Binder *et al.*, 1993; D. Geddes, 1983; J. Guilaine *et al.*, 1979; J. Desse, 1987; W. K. Barnett, 1990.

45 J. Lewthwaite, 1986.

46 P. Marinval, 1992, 'Approche carpologique de la néolithisation du sud de la France', in P. C. Anderson (ed.), *Préhistoire de l'agriculture*, pp. 255–63, Paris; B. Martí, V. Pascual, M. D. Gallart, P. López, M. Pérez Ripoll, J. D. Acuña and F. Robles, 1980, *Cova de l'Or (Beniarrés – Alicante)*, Valencia; B. Martí-Oliver, 1988; M. Dupré Ollivier, 1988, *Palinología y paleoambiente: nuevos datos españoles*, Valencia; M. Hopf, 1987, 'Les débuts de l'agriculture et la diffusion des plantes cultivées dans la péninsule ibérique', in J. Guilaine *et al.*, 1987, pp. 267–74s.

47 J. Desse, 1987; J. Guilaine *et al.*, 1984; J. Lewthwaite, 1986; J. Courtin, 1975, 'À propos de la navigation et de la pêche en mer au Néolithique ancien sur les côtes méditerranéennes françaises', *Bulletin de la Société Préhistorique Française* 72, 131–2.

48 J. Courtin, 1974, 'Les habitats du plein air du Néolithique ancien cardial en Provence', *Cahiers d'Etudes Ligures* 38, 227–43; J. Guilaine *et al.*, 1984; J.-L. Roudil and J. Grimal, 1978, 'Découverte d'une nouvelle civilisation du Néolithique ancien en Languedoc', *Bulletin de la Société Préhistorique Française* 75, 101–3; J.-L. Roudil and M. Soulier, 1984, 'Le gisement néolithique ancien de Peiro Signado, Portiragnes, Hérault. Étude préliminaire', *Congrés Préhistorique de France* 21 (2), 258–79.

49 J. Lewthwaite, 1986; A. Bosch Lloret, 1994, 'El neolítico antiguo en el nordeste de Cataluña. Contribución a la problematica de la evolución de las primeras comunidades neolíticas en el Mediterraneo occidental', *Trabajos de Prehistoria* 51, 55–75.

50 J. Arnal, H. Prades and J.-L. Vernet, 1987, 'Sur l'absence de Néolithique ancien autour de Montpellier', in J. Guilaine *et al.*, 1987, pp. 537–40.

51 J. Roussot-Larroque, 1989.

52 J. Roussot-Larroque, 1989; J. Roussot-Larroque, 1990, 'Rubané et Cardial: le poids de l'ouest', in D. Cahen and M. Otte (eds.), *Rubané et Cardial*, pp. 315–60, Liège.

53 J. Zilhão, 1993; J. E. Morais Arnaud, 1989, 'The Mesolithic communities of the Sado valley, Portugal, in their ecological setting', in C. Bonsall, 1989, pp. 614–31; D. Lubell, M. Jackes and C.

Meiklejohn, 1989, 'Archaeology and human biology of the Mesolithic–Neolithic transition in southern Portugal: a preliminary report', in C. Bonsall, 1989, pp. 632–40.

54 J. Zilhão, 1993; J. Bernabeu Aubán, 1989, *La tradición cultural de las cerámicas impresas en la zona oriental de la península ibérica*, Valencia.

55 J. Zilhão, 1993. Compare P. Kalb, 1989.

56 L. G. Straus, 1991, 'The "Mesolithic–Neolithic transition" in Portugal: a view from Vidigal', *Antiquity* 65, 899–903.

57 J. F. Cherry, 1990; J. Lewthwaite, 1989.

58 H-O. Pollmann, 1993.

59 J. F. Cherry, 1990; J. Lewthwaite, 1989.

60 J. F. Cherry, 1990.

61 S. Stoddart *et al.*, 1993; H-O. Pollmann, 1993.

62 A. Ammerman, 1979, 'A study of obsidian exchange networks in Calabria', *World Archaeology* 11, 95–110; A. J. Ammerman, 1985.

63 E.g. P. Kalb, 1989.

64 See earlier references.

65 B. Martí-Oliver, 1988.

66 D. Binder and J. Courtin, 1986, 'Les styles céramiques du Néolithique ancien provençal. Nouvelles migraines taxinomiques?', in J.-P. Demoule and J. Guilaine, 1986, pp. 83–93.

67 See earlier references, including S. Tinè, 1986; R. D. Whitehouse, 1986; and now R. Whitehouse, 1994.

68 C. Malone, 1985; R. Skeates, 1991; W. K. Barnett, 1990.

69 See note 48.

70 H.-O. Pollmann, 1993.

71 D. H. Trump, 1984, 'The Bonu Ighinu project and the Sardinian Neolithic', in M. S. Balmuth and R. J. Rowland (eds.), *Studies in Sardinian archaeology*, pp. 1–22, Ann Arbor.

72 See earlier site references, including S. Tinè, 1986. For Caucade, see D. Binder and J. Courtin, 1987.

73 K. A. Brown, 1991b.

74 Note T. Ingold, 1993, 'The temporality of landscape', *World Archaeology* 25, 152–74.

75 G. D. B. Jones, 1987.

76 R. D. Whitehouse, 1992 (and primary references); S. Tinè, 1986; B. Martí-Oliver, 1988; J. Zilhão, 1993; M. Paccard, 1987, 'Sépultures du Néolithique ancien à Unang (Malemort-du-Comtat, Vaucluse) et structures associés', in J. Guilaine *et al.*, 1987, pp. 507–12; A. Coste, H. Duday, X. Gutherz and J.-L. Roudil, 1987, 'Les sépultures de la Baume Boubon à Cabrières (Gard)', in J. Guilaine *et al.*, 1987, pp. 531–5; C. Bouville, 1987, 'Les restes humains de la Baume Fontbrégoua à Salernes (Var)', in J. Guilaine *et al.*, 1987, pp. 501–5; P. Villa, J. Courtin, D. Helmer, P. Shipman, C. Bouville and E. Mahieu, 1986, 'Un cas de cannibalisme au Néolithique: boucherie et rejet de restes humains et animaux dans la grotte de Fontbrégoua à Salernes (Var)', *Gallia Préhistoire* 29, 143–71.

77 R. D. Whitehouse, 1992 (and primary references); R. Skeates, 1994.

78 R. D. Whitehouse, 1992; M. Gimbutas, 1991.

79 R. D. Whitehouse, 1992; R. Skeates, 1994.

9   The heart of the country: the central and west Mediterranean, *c.* 5000–2500 BC

1 K. Spindler, 1994; L. Barfield, 1994; F. Höpfel, W. Platzer and K. Spindler (eds.), 1992, *Der Mann im Eis,* 1, Innsbruck.

2 K. Spindler, 1994; L. Barfield, 1994. The findspot lies in the territory of the autonomous province of Bolzano/South Tyrol.

3 L. H. Barfield, 1985.

4 S. Stoddart *et al.*, 1993; J. D. Evans, 1959, *Malta*, London; D. H. Trump, 1966, *Skorba*, Oxford; J. D. Evans, 1971, *The prehistoric antiquities of the Maltese islands: a survey*, London.

5 I prefer the term 'shrine' since it carries fewer anachronistic connotations than 'temple'. Caroline Malone and Simon Stoddart have stressed the monumentality of these structures.

6 A. Bonnano, T. Gouder, C. Malone and S. Stoddart, 1990, 'Monuments in an island society: the Maltese context', *World Archaeology* 22, 190–205; C. Malone *et al.*, 1988.

7 E. Anati, 1981; F. Fedele, 1990.

8 R. D. Whitehouse, 1992.

9 L. Barfield, 1985; R. Chapman, 1990.

10 S. Stoddart *et al.*, 1993.

11 R. Chapman, 1990; A. Gilman and J. B. Thornes, 1985; and other references below.

12 N. Mills, 1983; G. Costantini, 1984; J. Vaquer, 1990; G-B. Arnal, J. Clopés and M. Sahuc, 1992, 'Le Chasséen des garrigues montpelliériennes', *Archéologie en Languedoc* 16, 35–45. Stevenson's trip is documented in *Travels with a donkey*.

13 N. Mills, 1983; G. Costantini, 1984.

14 N. Mills, 1983; J. Arnal, 1973, 'Le Lébous à Saint-Mathieu-de-Treviers (Hérault)', *Gallia Préhistoire* 16, 131–200; H. Canet and J.-L. Roudil, 1978, 'Le village chalcolithique de Cambous à Viols-en-Laval', *Gallia Préhistoire* 21, 143–88; A. Colomer *et al.*, 1990; J. Clopés, M. Sahuc and C. Sauveur, 1991, 'L'habitat de plein air du Grand Devois de Figaret (Guzargues, Hérault)', *Archéologie en Languedoc* 1990/1991, 121–31; J. Gascó, 1991, 'La chronologie absolue du Néolithique final et du Chalcolithique en Languedoc méditerranéen', *Archéologie en Languedoc* 1990/1991, 217–25.

15 J. Courtin, 1974.

16 N. Mills, 1983; G. Bailloud, 1973, 'Les habitations de Conquette (Saint-Martin-de-Londres, Hérault), in *L'homme hier et aujourd'hui. Recueil d'études en hommage à André Leroi-Gourhan*, pp. 493–505, Paris; A. Colomer *et al.*, 1990.

17 J. Courtin, 1974.

18 N. Mills, 1983; J. Courtin, 1974.

19 B. Bagolini, 1992, 'Aspects occidentaux dans le Néolithique de l'Italie septentrionale. Les Vases à Bouche Carrée et la culture de Chassey-Lagozza', in J. Guilaine and X. Gutherz (eds.), *Autour de Jean Arnal*, pp. 139–45, Montpellier; L. Barfield, 1971.

20 L. Barfield and A. Broglio, 1976, 'Die neolithische Siedlung von Fimon-Molino Casarotto', *Archaeologia Austriaca* 13, 137–57; B. Bagolini, 1980, *Il Trentino nella preistoria del mondo alpino*, Trento.

21 L. Barfield, 1985; E. Anati, 1981; F. Fedele, 1990; P. Biagi *et al.*, 1984.

22 P. Kalb, 1989; R. J. Harrison, 1994.

23 K. Spindler, 1981; A. do Paço and E. Sangmeister, 1956; H. N. Savory, 1972; E. Sangmeister and H. Schubart, 1981.

24 R. Chapman, 1990; C. Mathers, 1994.

25 J. F. Cherry, 1990; J. Lewthwaite, 1983.

26 E.g. M. Cipolloni Sampò, 1982b; R. Skeates, 1994.

27 G. Barker, 1981; G. Cremonesi, 1965; A. Cazella and M. Moscoloni, 1988, 'Le facies eneolitico delle Marche', *Rassegna di Archeologia* 7, 362–70; R. R. Holloway, 1973; 1975.

28 E.g. M. Cipolloni Sampò, 1982b; S. Stoddart *et al.*, 1993.

29 E.g. R. J. Harrison, 1994.

30 R. Chapman, 1990; R. Chapman *et al.*, 1991; A. Gilman, 1981; 1987; A. Gilman and J. B. Thornes, 1985; C. Mathers, 1984; 1994.

31 D. Geddes, 1983, and site references; J. Courtin, 1974; P. Rowley-Conwy, 1992; G. Barker, 1981.

32 K. Spindler, 1994.

33 J. Vaquer, 1990; A. Colomer *et al.*, 1990.

34 R. Chapman, 1990; F. Gusi and C. Olaria, 1991, *El poblado neo-eneolítico de Terrera Ventura (Tabernas, Almería)*, Madrid.

35 H.-P. Uerpmann, 1991, 'Die Domestikation des Pferdes im Chalkolithikum West- und Mitteleuropas', *Madrider Mitteilungen* 31, 109–53.

36 P. Biagi *et al.*, 1984.

37 J. Courtin, 1974; R. Chapman, 1990; L. Barfield, 1971.

38 R. Chapman, 1990; J. Lewthwaite, 1982.

39 R. R. Holloway, 1975. R. D. Whitehouse, 1992, is among those who are cautious.

40 N. Mills, 1983; J.-L. Vernet, 1990, 'L'évolution des garrigues', in A. Colomer *et al.*, 1990, pp. 35–8; A. Colomer *et al.*, 1990; J. Lewthwaite, 1982.

41 M. O. Rodrigues Ariza and J.-L. Vernet, 1991, 'Premiers resultats paléoecologiques de l'establissement chalcolithique de Los Millares (Santa Fé de Mondujar, Almeria, Espagne) d'après l'analyse anthracologique de l'establissement', in W. H. Waldren, J. A. Ensenyat and R. C. Kennard (eds.), *IInd Deya international conference of prehistory*, pp. 1–16, Oxford.

42 A. C. Stevenson and R. J. Harrison, 1992, 'Ancient forests in Spain: a model for land-use and dry forest management in south-west Spain from 4000 BC to 1900 AD', *Proceedings of the Prehistoric Society* 58, 227–47.

43 J. Lewthwaite, 1982.

44 E.g. H. H. Lamb, 1971, 'Climates and circulation regimes developed over the northern hemisphere since the last Ice Age', *Palaeogeography, Palaeoclimatology, Palaeoecology* 10, 125–62; M. Magny, 1993; O. Bar-Yosef and R. S. Kra (eds.), 1994, *Late Quaternary chronology and paleoclimates of the eastern Mediterranean,* Tucson.

45 M. Almagro and A. Arribas, 1963, *El poblado y la necrópolis megaliticos de Los Millares*, Madrid.

46 R. Chapman, 1990; R. Chapman *et al.*, 1991; A. Gilman, 1981; 1987; A. Gilman and J. B. Thornes, 1985; C. Mathers, 1984; 1994.

47 M. Walker, 1984, 'The site of El Prado (Murcia) and the Copper Age of south-east Spain', in T. F. C. Blagg, R. F. J. Jones and S. J. Keay (eds.), *Papers in Iberian archaeology*, pp. 47–78, Oxford. See also, in support of greater humidity, A. Ramos, 1981, 'Interpretaciones secuenciales y culturales de la Edad del Cobre en la zona meridional de la peninsula iberica', *Cuadernos de Prehistoria de la Universidad de Granada* 6, 242–56.

48 C. Malone *et al.*, 1988.

49 G. Cremonesi, 1965; U. Rellini, 1934, *La più antica ceramica dipinta in Italia*, Rome.

50 J. Vaquer, 1990.

51 J.-L. Voruz, 1991, 'Chronologie du Néolithique d'origine méditerranéenne', in *Actes du 14e colloque interrégional sur le Néolithique*, pp. 5–33, Blois.

52 N. Mills, 1983.

53 R. Skeates, 1994; R. D. Whitehouse, 1992.

54 J. Vaquer, 1990: the source for the following descriptions.

55 A. Arribas Palau and F. Molina, 1984, 'The latest excavations of the Copper Age settlement of Los Millares, Almeria, Spain', in W. H. Waldren, R. Chapman, J. Lewthwaite and R.-C. Kennard (eds.), *The Deya conference of prehistory*, pp. 1029–50, Oxford; A. Arribas, F. Molina *et al.*, 1985, 'Informe preliminar de los resultados obtenidos durante la VI campaña de excavaciones en el poblado de Los Millares (Santa Fé de Mondujar, Almeria)', *Anuario Arqueológico de Andalucía* 1985, 245–62; A. Arribas Palau and F. Molina, 1991, 'Los Millares: nuevas perspectivas', in W. H. Waldren, J. A. Ensenyat and R. C. Kennard (eds.), *IInd Deya international conference of prehistory*, pp. 409–19, Oxford; R. Chapman, 1990.

56 See note 55.

57 R. Chapman, 1990; R. Micó, 1991.

58 R. Chapman, 1990; G. Delibes de Castro, M. Fernández-Miranda, M. D. Fernández-Posse and

C. Martín, 1991, 'Almizaraque et le bassin de Vera (Almeria, Espagne). Les origines du Chalcolithique dans le sud-est de la peninsule ibérique', *Archéologie en Languedoc* 1990/1991, 291–7.

59 C. Martín, M. Fernández-Miranda, M. D. Fernández-Posse and A. Gilman, 1993, 'The Bronze Age of La Mancha', *Antiquity* 67, 23–45.

60 H. N. Savory, 1972; A. do Paço and E. Sangmeister, 1956.

61 H. Schubart, 1970, 'Die kupferzeitliche Befestigung von Columbeira, Portugal', *Madrider Mitteilungen* 11, 59–73; V. Leisner and H. Schubart, 1966, 'Die kupferzeitliche Befestigung von Pedra do Ouro, Portugal', *Madrider Mitteilungen* 7, 9–59; C. Tavares da Silva and J. Soares, 1985, 'Monte da Tumba (Torrão). Eine befestigte Siedlung der Kupferzeit im Baixo Alentejo (Portugal)', *Madrider Mitteilungen* 26, 1–21.

62 E. Sangmeister and H. Schubart, 1981.

63 See also K. Spindler, 1969, 'Die kupferzeitliche Siedlung von Penedo, Portugal', *Madrider Mitteilungen* 10, 45–116; K. Spindler and G. Gallay, 1973, *Kupferzeitliche Siedlung und Begräbnisstatten von Matacães in Portugal*, Mainz; K. Spindler, 1981.

64 J. Lewthwaite, 1983; R. Chapman, M. van Strydonck and W. Waldren, 1993, 'Radiocarbon dating and talayots: the example of Son Ferrandell Oleza', *Antiquity* 67, 108–16.

65 L. H. Barfield, 1983, 'The Chalcolithic cemetery at Manerba del Garba', *Antiquity* 57, 116–23; L. Barfield, 1985.

66 E.g. B. Bagolini, 1980, *Il trentino nella preistoria del mondo alpino*, Trento.

67 K. Spindler, 1994.

68 E. Anati, 1981; F. Fedele, 1990.

69 L. H. Barfield, 1985, and references.

70 L. H. Barfield 1971; 1985; N. Negroni Catacchio, 1988, 'La cultura di Rinaldone', *Rassegna di Archeologia* 7, 348–62.

71 L. H. Barfield, 1985; B. Bagolini (ed.), 1985, *Archeologia a Spilamberto*, Spilamberto.

72 M. Fraccaro, 1986.

73 G. Barker, 1981; R. R. Holloway, 1973. I use the term 'tomb' subject to the same qualifications set out in chapter 7.

74 R. D. Whitehouse, 1992.

75 R. D. Whitehouse, 1992.

76 R. Skeates, 1994.

77 R. Skeates, 1994.

78 R. D. Whitehouse, 1992.

79 R. D. Whitehouse, 1992.

80 G. Costantini, 1984; J. Vaquer, 1990; E. Mahieu, 1992, 'La nécropole de Najac à Siran (Hérault). I. Réflexion sur les sépultures Chasséennes', *Gallia Préhistoire* 34, 141–69; J.-P. Daugas, 1972, 'Une fosse à inhumations néolithiques à Corent (Puy-de-Dôme)', in *Congrés préhistorique de France, XIXe session*, pp. 183–9, Paris.

81 G. Costantini, 1984. See also J. Clottes and C. Maurand, 1983, *Inventaire des mégalithes de la France. 7 – Aveyron*, Paris.

82 Y. Chevalier, 1986, 'L'architecture des dolmens du Sud de la France', in J. Guilaine and J.-P. Demoule, 1986, pp. 359–77.

83 N. Mills, 1983; H. Duday, 1986, 'Organisation et fonctionnement d'une sépulture collective néolithique', in H. Duday and C. Masset (eds.), *Anthropologie physique et archéologie*, pp. 89–104, Paris; G. Costantini, 1984; J. Courtin, 1974; J. Zammit, 1991, 'Les sépultures chalcolithiques du département de l'Aude', *Archéologie en Languedoc* 1990/1991, 149–56.

84 See chapter 8.

85 R. Chapman, 1990.

86 Compare H. N. Savory, 1968 and R. Chapman, 1990.

87 R. Chapman, 1990, and references.

88 J. Tarrús y Galter, 1992, 'Les dolmens anciens de la Catalogne', in J. Guilaine and X. Gutherz (eds.), *Autour de Jean Arnal*, pp. 271–89, Montpellier.

89 G. and V. Leisner, 1943; 1956; V. Leisner, 1965; H. N. Savory, 1968; P. Kalb, 1989; R. Chapman, 1990.

90 R. Chapman, 1990.

91 G. and V. Leisner, 1951, *Antas do Concelho de Reguengos de Monsaraz*, Lisbon.

92 E. H. Whittle and J. M. Arnaud, 1975, 'Thermoluminescent dating of Neolithic and Chalcolithic pottery from sites in central Portugal', *Archaeometry* 17, 5–24.

93 See note 63.

94 F. Criado Boado and R. Fabregas Valcarce, 1989, 'The megalithic phenomenon of northwest Spain: main trends', *Antiquity* 63, 682–96.

95 I am grateful to Richard Bradley for suggesting this kind of sequence, including in northern Europe.

96 Even the tomb XXI patterning might be the result of the 1890s excavations by Flores: R. Chapman, 1990, p. 194.

97 Ma. J. Almagro Gorbea, 1973, *El poblado y la necrópolis de El Barranquete*, Madrid.

98 Set out in most detail by R. Chapman, 1990, and in earlier papers.

99 R. Chapman, 1990, pp. 184–95; R. Micó, 1991.

100 In introducing 'mutuality', I follow H. L. Moore, 1988, *Feminism and anthropology*, Oxford; and C. Gosden, 1994.

101 C. Malone, 1985.

102 C. Malone, 1985. See also L. H. Barfield, 1988, 'The Chalcolithic of the Po plain', *Rassegna di Archeologia* 7, 411–18.

103 E.g. C. Malone, 1985; information from Robin Skeates.

104 S. Stoddart *et al.*, 1993.

105 O. W. Thorpe, S. E. Warren and L. H. Barfield, 1979, 'The sources and distribution of archaeological obsidian in northern Italy', *Preistoria Alpina* 15, 73–92.

106 M. Fraccaro, 1986.

107 J. Vaquer, 1990; M. Ricq-de Bouard, R. Compagnoni, J. Desmons and F. Fedele, 1990, 'Les roches alpines dans l'outillage poli néolithique de la France méditerranéenne', *Gallia Préhistoire* 32, 125–49.

108 W. Dijkman, 1980, 'F6. Salinelles "Vigne du Cade", Dép. Gard', in G. Weisgerber (ed.), *5000 Jahre Feuersteinbergbau*, pp. 478–9, Bochum; F. Briois, 1992, 'L'exploitation du silex en plaquettes à Salinelles (Gard). Données nouvelles sur les lieux et modes d'extraction, sur les ateliers, problèmes de diffusion', in J. Guilaine and X. Gutherz (eds.), *Autour de Jean Arnal*, pp. 219–32, Montpellier.

109 Information from Robin Skeates.

110 See earlier discussion in chapter 7.

111 C. Malone, 1985.

112 R. Skeates, 1991.

113 R. Skeates, 1995, 'Early metal use in the central Mediterranean region', *Accordia Research Papers* 4; R. Chapman, 1990. See also E. Sangmeister and M. de la Cruz Jiménez Goméz, 1994, *Zambujal: Kupferfunde aus den Grabungen 1964 bis 1973*, Mainz.

114 G. Costantini, 1991, 'Les productions métalliques du groupe des Treilles et leur répartition dans le Midi de la France', *Archéologie en Languedoc* 1990/1991, 59–66; J. Guilaine, 1991, 'Roquemengarde et les débuts de la métallurgie en France méridionale', *Archéologie en Languedoc* 1990/1991, 35–40.

115 D. C. Genick and R. G. Cremonesi, 1991. See also C. Strahm, 1991.

116 E.g. C. Renfrew and R. D. Whitehouse, 1974, 'The Copper Age of peninsular Italy and the Aegean', *Annual of the British School at Athens* 69, 343–90. Contrast C. Strahm, 1991.

117 P. Ambert, 1991, 'L'émergence de la métallurgie chalcolithique dans le Midi de la France', *Archéologie en Languedoc* 1990/1991, 51–8; P. Ambert, 1990, 'Evidence, age and technological level of prehistoric cupriferous exploitations in Cabrières-Hérault (south of France). Cabrières-Hérault. Le plus vieux centre minier métallurgique de France (2500 av. J.-C.)', *Archéologie en Languedoc* supplement, 9–12.

118 R. Chapman, 1990.

119 D. C. Genick and R. G. Cremonesi, 1991.

120 E.g. A. Gilman, 1987; R. Chapman, 1990; C. Mathers, 1994.

121 R. Skeates, 1991, 'Triton's trumpet: a Neolithic symbol in Italy', *Oxford Journal of Archaeology* 10, 17–31; H. N. Savory, 1968.

122 H. N. Savory, 1968; R. Chapman, 1990, and references.

10 The creation of new worlds

1 See discussion in chapter 2.

2 N. Bird-David, 1992, 'Beyond "the original affluent society": a culturalist reformulation', *Current Anthropology* 33, 25–47.

3 E.g. A. Whittle, 1994, 'The first farmers', in B. Cunliffe (ed.), *The Oxford illustrated prehistory of Europe*, pp. 136–66, Oxford.

4 J. Chapman and J. Müller, 1990, 'Early farmers in the Mediterranean basin: the Dalmatian evidence', *Antiquity* 64, 127–34.

5 E.g. M. Zvelebil and P. Rowley-Conwy, 1984.

6 See again I. Hodder, 1990.

7 J. Thomas, 1991, was amongst the first to re-emphasise the 'otherness' of the Neolithic world.

8 As suggested by M. Eliade, 1960, *Myths, dreams and mysteries*, London.

9 Note E. E. Evans-Pritchard, 1956, *Nuer religion*, Oxford, p. 313: 'It was Durkheim and not the savage who made society into a god.'

10 T. Madsen, 1991, 'The social structure of Early Neolithic society in south Scandinavia', in J. Lichardus (ed.), *Die Kupferzeit als historische Epoche*, pp. 489–96, Bonn; C. J. Becker, 1952, 'Skeletfundet fra Porsmose ved Naestved', *Fra Nationalmuseets Arbejdsmark* 1952, 25–30.

BIBLIOGRAPHY

Albrethsen, S. E. and Brinch Petersen, E. 1977. Excavation of a Mesolithic cemetery at Vedbaek, Denmark. *Acta Archaeologica* 47, 1–28.

Ammerman, A. J. 1985. *The Acconia survey: Neolithic settlement and the obsidian trade.* London: Institute of Archaeology, University of London.

Ammerman, A. J. and Cavalli-Sforza, L. L. 1984. *The Neolithic transition and the genetics of populations in Europe.* Princeton: Princeton University Press.

Anati, E. 1981. *Le statue-stele della Lunigiana.* Milan: Jaca.

Andersen, N. H. 1988. Sarup: two Neolithic enclosures in south-west Funen. *Journal of Danish Archaeology* 7, 93–114.

1993. Causewayed enclosures of the Funnel Beaker culture. In S. Hvass and B. Storgaard (eds.), *Digging into the past: 25 years of archaeology in Denmark*, pp. 100–3. Copenhagen and Aarhus: Royal Society of Northern Antiquaries–Jutland Archaeological Society.

Andersen, S. H. 1991. Norsminde. A 'Køkkenmødding' with Late Mesolithic and Early Neolithic occupation. *Journal of Danish Archaeology* 8, 13–40.

Andersen, S. Th. 1993. Early agriculture. In S. Hvass and B. Storgaard (eds.), *Digging into the past: 25 years of archaeology in Denmark*, pp. 88–91. Copenhagen and Aarhus: Royal Society of Northern Antiquaries–Jutland Archaeological Society.

Angelov, N. 1959. Slatnoto sakrovishe ot Hotnica. *Arkheologiya* 1, 38–46.

Angelova, I. 1982. Tell Targovishte. In H. Todorova (ed.), *Kupferzeitliche Siedlungen in Nordostbulgarien*, pp. 175–80. Munich: Beck.

Anthony, D. W. 1986. The 'Kurgan culture', Indo-European origins, and the domestication of the horse: a reconsideration. *Current Anthropology* 27, 291–313.

Anthony, D., Telegin, D. Y. and Brown, D. 1991. The origin of horseback riding. *Scientific American* 265, 44–48A.

Bailey, D. W. 1990. The living house: signifying continuity. In R. Samson (ed.), *The social archaeology of houses*, pp. 19–48. Edinburgh: Edinburgh University Press.

1993. Chronotypic tension in Bulgarian prehistory: 6500–3500 BC. *World Archaeology* 25, 204–22.

1994. Reading prehistoric figurines as individuals. *World Archaeology* 25, 321–31.

Bakels, C. C. 1978. *Four Linearbandkeramik settlements and their environment: a palaeoecological study of Sittard, Stein, Elsloo and Hienheim.* Leiden: Leiden University Press.

1987. On the adzes of the northwestern Linearbandkeramik. *Analecta Praehistorica Leidensia* 20, 53–85.

Bakker, J. A. 1979. *The TRB West Group: studies in the chronology and geography of the makers of hunebeds and Tiefstich pottery.* Amsterdam: Universiteit van Amsterdam.

1992. *The Dutch hunebedden: megalithic tombs of the Funnel Beaker culture.* Ann Arbor: Prehistory Press.

Balcer, B. 1988. The Neolithic flint industries in the Vistula and Odra basins. *Przeglad Archeologiczny* 35, 49–100.

Bánffy, E. 1991. Cult and archaeological context in middle and south-east Europe in the Neolithic and the Chalcolithic. *Antaeus* 19–20, 183–249.

Banner, J. 1956. *Die Péceler Kultur.* Budapest: Akadémiai Kiadó.

Barfield, L. 1971. *Northern Italy.* London: Thames and Hudson.

1985. Burials and boundaries in Chalcolithic Italy. In C. Malone and S. Stoddart (eds.), *Papers in Italian archaeology IV. Part ii. Prehistory,* pp. 152–76. Oxford: British Archaeological Reports.

1994. The Iceman reviewed. *Antiquity* 68, 10–26.

Barker, G. 1981. *Landscape and society: prehistoric central Italy.* London: Academic Press.

Barnett, W. K. 1990. Small-scale transport of early Neolithic pottery in the west Mediterranean. *Antiquity* 64, 859–65.

Barrett, J. C. 1994. *Fragments from antiquity: an archaeology of social life in Britain, 2900–1200 BC.* Oxford: Blackwell.

Barrett, J., Bradley, R. and Green, M. 1991. *Landscape, monuments and society: the prehistory of Cranborne Chase.* Cambridge: Cambridge University Press.

Behrens, H. 1973. *Die Jungsteinzeit im Mittlelbe-Saale-Gebiet.* Berlin: VEB Deutscher Verlag der Wissenschaften.

Behrens, H. and Schröter, E. 1980. *Siedlungen und Gräber der Trichterbecherkultur und Schnurkeramik bei Halle (Saale).* Berlin: VEB Deutscher Verlag der Wissenschaften.

Beier, H. J. 1984. *Die Grab- und Bestattungssitten der Walternienburger und Bernburger Kultur.* Halle: Martin-Luther-Universität, Halle-Wittenberg.

Bender, B. 1978. Gatherer-hunter to farmer: a social perspective. *World Archaeology* 10, 204–22.

Berciu, D. 1961. *Contributii la problemele Neoliticului in Rominia in lumina noilor cercetari.* Bucharest: Editura Academiei Republicii Populare Romine.

1966. *Cultura Hamangia.* Bucharest: Editura Academiei Republicii Populare Romine.

Biagi, P. and Nisbet, R. 1987. The earliest farming communities in northern Italy. In J. Guilaine, J. Courtin, J. Roudil and J.-L. Vernet (eds.), *Premières communautés paysannes en Méditerranée occidentale,* pp. 447–53. Paris: CNRS.

Biagi, P., Nisbet, R., Macphail, R. and Scaife, R. 1984. Early farming communities and short-range transhumance in the Cottian Alps (Chisone valley, Turin) in the late third millennium BC. In W. H. Waldren, R. Chapman, J. Lewthwaite and R. C. Kennard (eds.), *The Deya conference of prehistory,* pp. 395–413. Oxford: British Archaeological Reports.

Binder, D. (ed.) 1991. *Une économie de chasse au Néolithique ancien. La grotte Lombard à Saint-Vallier-de-Thiey (Alpes Maritimes).* Paris: CNRS.

Binder, D., Brochier, J.-E., Duday, H., Helmer, D., Marinval, P., Thiébault S. and Wattez, J. 1993. L'abri Pendimoun à Castellar (Alpes-Maritimes): nouvelles données sur le complexe culturel de la céramique imprimee méditerranéenne dans son contexte stratigraphique. *Gallia Préhistoire* 35, 177–251.

Binder, D. and Courtin, J. 1987. Nouvelles vues sur le processus de néolithisation dans le sud-est de la France. In J. Guilaine, J. Courtin, J. Roudil and J.-L. Vernet (eds.), *Premières communautés paysannes en Méditerranée occidentale,* pp. 491–99. Paris: CNRS.

Binford, L. R. 1980. Willow smoke and dogs' tails: hunter-gatherer settlement systems and archaeological site formation. *American Antiquity* 45, 4–20.

Bird-David, N. 1992. Beyond 'the hunting and gathering mode of subsistence': observations on the Nayaha and other modern hunter-gatherers. *Man* 27, 19–44.

Bleuer, E. and Hardmeyer, B. 1993. *Zürich 'Mozartstrasse'. Neolithische und bronzezeitliche Ufersiedlungen. Band 3: Die neolithische Keramik.* Egg-Zürich: Fotorotar.

Boelicke, U., von Brandt, D., Lüning, J., Stehli, P. and Zimmerman, A. 1988. *Der bandkeramische Siedlungsplatz Langweiler 8, Gemeinde Aldenhoven, Kreis Düren.* Köln: Rheinland-Verlag.

Bognár-Kutzián, I. 1963. *The Copper Age cemetery of Tiszapolgár-Basatanya.* Budapest: Akadémiai Kiadó.

1972. *The early Copper Age Tiszapolgár culture in the Carpathian basin.* Budapest: Akadémiai Kiadó.

Bogucki, P. 1988. *Forest farmers and stockherders.* Cambridge: Cambridge University Press.

Bogucki, P. and Grygiel, R. 1993. Neolithic sites in the Polish lowlands: research at Brześć Kujawski, 1933 to 1984. In P. Bogucki (ed.), *Case studies in European prehistory*, pp. 147–80. Boca Raton, Florida: CRC Press.

Bökönyi, S. 1974. *History of domestic mammals in central and eastern Europe*. Budapest: Akadémiai Kiadó.

1986. Environmental and cultural effects on the faunal assemblages of four large 4th mill. B.C. sites. *A Béri Balogh Ádám Múzeum Évkönyve* 13, 69–88.

1991. Pferde- und Schafdomestikation bzw. -haltung in der frühen Kupferzeit Eurasiens. In J. Lichardus (ed.), *Kupferzeit als historische Epoche*, pp. 549–56. Bonn: Habelt.

Bökönyi, S. (ed.) 1992. *Cultural and landscape changes in south-east Hungary. I. Reports on the Gyomaendrőd project*. Budapest: Institute of Archaeology.

Bolomey, A. 1973. The present state of knowledge of mammal exploitation during the Epipalaeolithic and the earliest Neolithic in the territory of Romania. In J. Matoski (ed.), *Domestikationsforschung und Geschichte der Haustiere*, pp. 197–203. Budapest: Akadémiai Kiadó.

Bonsall, C. (ed.) 1989. *The Mesolithic in Europe*. Edinburgh: John Donald.

Borkowski, W., Migal, W., Sałaciński, M. and Zalewski, M. 1991. Possibilities of investigating Neolithic flint economies, as exemplified by the banded flint economy. *Antiquity* 65, 607–27.

Bottema, S. 1982. Palynological investigations in Greece with special reference to pollen as an indicator of human activity. *Palaeohistoria* 24, 257–89.

Boujot, C. and Cassen, S. 1993. A pattern of evolution for the Neolithic funerary structures in the west of France. *Antiquity* 67, 477–91.

Bradley, R. 1993. *Altering the earth*. Edinburgh: Society of Antiquaries of Scotland.

Bradley, R. and Edmonds, M. 1993. *Interpreting the axe trade*. Cambridge: Cambridge University Press.

Brandt, K. H. 1967. *Studien über steinerne Äxte und Beile der jüngeren Steinzeit und der steinkupferzeit Nordwestdeutschlands*. Hildesheim: August Lax.

Broodbank, C. and Strasser, T. F. 1991. Migrant farmers and the colonization of Crete. *Antiquity* 65, 233–45.

Brown, K. A. 1991a. Settlement and social organisation in the Neolithic of the Tavoliere, Apulia. In E. Herring, R. Whitehouse and J. Wilkins (eds.), *Papers of the Fourth Conference of Italian Archaeology, 1. The archaeology of power, 1,* 9–25. London: Accordia Research Centre.

1991b. A passion for excavation. Labour requirements and possible functions for the ditches of the *villaggi trincerati* of the Tavoliere, Apulia. *Accordia Research Papers* 2, 7–30.

Brukner, B. 1988. Die Siedlung der Vinča-Gruppe auf Gomolava (Die Wohnschicht des Spätneolithikums und Frühäneolithikums – Gomolava 1a, Gomolava 1a–b und Gomolava 1b) und der Wohnhorizont des äneolithischen Humus (Gomolava II). In N. Tasić and J. Petrović (eds.), *Gomolava: Chronologie und Stratigraphie der vorgeschichtlichen und antiken Kulturen der Donauniederung und Südosteuropas*, pp. 19–38. Novi Sad: Vojvodanski Muzej.

Buchvaldek, M. 1986. *Kultura se šňůrovou keramikou ve střední Evropě*. Prague: Univerzita Karlova.

Buchvaldek, M. and Strahm, C. (eds.) 1992. *Die kontinentaleuropäischen Gruppen der Kultur mit Schnurkeramik*. Prague: Univerzita Karlova.

Burgess, C., Topping, P., Mordant, C. and Maddison, M. (eds.) 1988. *Enclosures and defences in the Neolithic of western Europe*. Oxford: British Archaeological Reports.

Cârciumaru, M. 1973. Analyse pollinique des coprolithes livrés par quelques stations archéologiques des deux bords du Danube dans la zone des Portes de Fer. *Dacia* 17, 53–60.

Cassano, S. M., Cazzella, A., Manfredini, A. and Moscolini, M. (eds.) 1987. *Coppa Nevigata e il suo territorio: testimonianze archeologiche dal VII al II millennio a. C.* Rome: Quasar.

Chapman, J. C. 1981. *The Vinča culture of south-east Europe*. Oxford: British Archaeological Reports.

Chapman, J. 1989. Demographic trends in neothermal south-east Europe. In C. Bonsall (ed.), *The Mesolithic in Europe*, pp. 500–15. Edinburgh: John Donald.

1990. Social inequality on Bulgarian tells and the Varna problem. In R. Samson (ed.), *The social archaeology of houses*, pp. 49–92. Edinburgh: Edinburgh University Press.

1991. The creation of social arenas in the Neolithic and Copper Age of S.E. Europe: the case of Varna. In P. Garwood, D. Jennings, R. Skeates and J. Toms (eds.), *Sacred and profane*, pp. 152–71. Oxford: Oxford University Committee for Archaeology.

1992. Social power in the Iron Gates Mesolithic. In J. Chapman and P. Dolukhanov (eds.), *Cultural transformations and interactions in eastern Europe*, pp. 71–121. Aldershot: Avebury.

Chapman, R. 1990. *Emerging complexity: the later prehistory of south-east Spain, Iberia and the west Mediterranean*. Cambridge: Cambridge University Press.

Chapman, R. W., Lull, V., Picazo, M. and Sanahuja, M. E. 1991. The development of complex societies in S. E. Spain: the Gatas project. In W. H. Waldren, J. A. Ensenyat and R. C. Kennard (eds.), *The IInd Deya international conference of prehistory*, pp. 239–49. Oxford: British Archaeological Reports.

Chernykh, E. N. 1992. *Ancient metallurgy in the USSR: the early metal age*. Cambridge: Cambridge University Press.

Cherry, J. F. 1990. The first colonisation of the Mediterranean islands: a review of recent research. *Journal of Mediterranean Archaeology* 3, 145–221.

Cipolloni Sampò, M. 1982a. Scavi nel villaggio neolitico di Rendina (1970–1976): relazione preliminare. *Origini* 11, 183–323.

1982b. Ambiente, economia e società dall'eneolitico all'età del bronzo in Italia. *Dialoghi di Archeologia* 4, 27–38.

Clark, J. G. D. 1954. *Excavations at Star Carr*. Cambridge: Cambridge University Press.

Clason, A. 1980. Padina and Starčevo: game, fish and cattle. *Palaeohistoria* 22, 141–73.

Cloutman, E. W. and Smith, A. G. 1988. Palaeoenvironments in the Vale of Pickering. Part 3: environmental history at Star Carr. *Proceedings of the Prehistoric Society* 54, 37–58.

Coles, B. and Coles, J. 1986. *From Sweet Track to Glastonbury*. London: Thames and Hudson.

Colomer, A., Coularou, J. and Gutherz, X. 1990. *Boussargues (Argelliers, Hérault). Un habitat ceinturé chalcolithique: les fouilles du secteur ouest*. Paris: Editions de la Maison des Sciences de l'Homme.

Comşa, E. 1987. *Neoliticul pe teritoriul româniei - consideratii*. Bucharest: Edituri Academiei Republicii Socialiste România.

1991. L'utilisation du cuivre en Roumanie pendant le néolithique moyen. In C. Eluère and J.-P. Mohen (eds.), *Découverte du métal*, pp.77–84. Paris: Picard.

Constantin, C., Coudart, A., Demoule, J.-P. and Ilett, M. 1982. The late Bandkeramik of the Aisne valley: environment and spatial organisation. *Analecta Praehistorica Leidensia* 15, 45–61.

Coppola, D. and Costantini, L. 1987. Le Néolithique ancien littoral et la diffusion des céréales dans les Pouilles durant le VIe millénaire: les sites de Fontanelle, Torre Canne et Le Macchie. In J. Guilaine, J. Courtin, J. Roudil and J.-L. Vernet (eds.), *Premières communautés paysannes en Méditerranée occidentale*, pp. 249–55. Paris: CNRS.

Costantini, G. 1984. Le Néolithique et le Chalcolithique des Grands Causses. I. Etude archéologique. *Gallia Préhistoire* 27, 121–210.

Costantini, L. 1989. Plant exploitation at Grotta dell' Uzzo, Sicily: new evidence for the transition from Mesolithic to Neolithic subsistence in southern Europe. In D. R. Harris and G. C. Hillman (eds.), *Foraging and farming: the evolution of plant exploitation*, pp. 197–206. London: Unwin Hyman.

Costantini, L., Piperno, M. and Tusa, S. 1987. La Néolithisation de la Sicile occidentale d'après les résultats des fouilles à la grotte de l'Uzzo (Trapani). In J. Guilaine, J. Courtin, J. Roudil and J.-L. Vernet (eds.), *Premières communautés paysannes en Méditerranée occidentale*, pp. 397–405. Paris: CNRS.

Coudart, A. 1989. Tradition, uniformity and variability in the architecture of the Danubian Neolithic. In J. Rulf (ed.), *Bylany seminar 1987*, pp. 199–223. Prague: Institute of Archaeology.

Courtin, J. 1974. *Le Néolithique de la Provence*. Paris: Klincksieck.

Cremonesi, R. 1965. Il villaggio di Ripoli alla luce dei recenti scavi. *Rivista di Scienze Preistoriche* 20, 85–155.

Czerniak, L. and Piontek, J. 1980. The socioeconomic system of European neolithic populations. *Current Anthropology* 21, 97–100.

Davis, J. L. 1992. Review of Aegean prehistory, I: the islands of the Aegean. *American Journal of Archaeology* 96, 699–756.

de Grooth, M. 1987. The organisation of flint tool manufacture in the Dutch Bandkeramik. *Analecta Praehistorica Leidensia* 20, 27–51.

Demoule, J.-P. and Guilaine, J. (eds.) 1986. *Le Néolithique de la France*. Paris: Picard.

Demoule, J.-P. and Perlès, C. 1993. The Greek Neolithic: a new review. *Journal of World Prehistory* 7, 355–416.

Dennell, R. 1978. *Early farming in south Bulgaria from the VI to the III millennia B.C.* Oxford: British Archaeological Reports.

Dennell, R. W. 1984. The expansion of exogenous-based economies across Europe: the Balkans and central Europe. In S. P. De Atley and F. J. Findlow, *Exploring the limits: frontiers and boundaries in prehistory*, pp. 93–116. Oxford: British Archaeological Reports.

Dergachev, V. A. 1986. *Moldaviya i sosednie teritorii v epokhu eneolita*. Kishinev: Shtiintsa.

Dergachev, V. 1989. Neolithic and Bronze Age cultural communities of the steppe zone of the USSR. *Antiquity* 63, 793–802.

Desse, J. 1987. La pêche: son rôle dans l'économie des premières sociétés néolithiques en Méditerranée occidentale. In J. Guilaine *et al.* (eds.), *Premières communautés paysannes en Mediterranée occidentale*, pp. 281–5. Paris: CNRS.

Dieckmann, D. 1990. Neue Forschungsergebnisse zur Jungsteinzeit im Hegau und in Hornstaad am Bodensee. In M. Höneisen (ed.), *Die ersten Bauern, II,* pp. 157–169. Zürich: Schweizerisches Landesmuseum.

Dohrn-Ihmig, M. 1983. Das bandkeramische Gräberfeld von Aldenhoven-Niedermerz, Kreis Düren. *Rheinische Ausgrabungen* 24, 47–189.

do Paço, A. and Sangmeister, E. 1956. Vila Nova de São Pedro. Eine befestigte Siedlung der Kupferzeit in Portugal. *Germania* 34, 211–30.

Dumitrescu, V. 1965. Căscioarele: a Late Neolithic settlement on the lower Danube. *Archaeology* 18, 34–40.

  1970. Edifice destiné au culte découvert dans la couche Boian-Spanţov de la station-tell de Căscioarele. *Dacia* 15, 5–24.

Dumitrescu, V., Bolomey, A. and Mogosanu, F. 1982. The prehistory of Romania from the earliest times to 1000 BC. *Cambridge Ancient History* III, part I, pp. 1–74. Cambridge: Cambridge University Press.

Ebbesen, K. 1993. Sacrifices to the powers of nature. In S. Hvass and B. Storgaard (eds.), *Digging into the past: 25 years of archaeology in Denmark*, pp. 122–5. Copenhagen and Aarhus: Royal Society of Northern Antiquaries–Jutland Archaeological Society.

Efstratiou, N. 1985. *A Neolithic site in the northern Sporades: Aegean relationships during the Neolithic of the 5th millennium*. Oxford: British Archaeological Reports.

Ehret, C. 1988. Language change and the material correlates of language and ethnic shift. *Antiquity* 62, 564–74.

Ehrich, R. W. and Pleslová-Štiková, E. 1968. *Homolka: an Eneolithic site in Bohemia*. Harvard and Prague: Peabody Museum and Czechoslovak Academy of Sciences.

Ellis, L. 1984. *The Cucuteni-Tripolye culture: a study in technology and the origins of complex society*. Oxford: British Archaeological Reports.

Eogan, G. 1984. *Excavations at Knowth, 1.* Dublin: Royal Irish Academy.

  1986. *Knowth*. London: Thames and Hudson.

Farruggia, J.-P., Kuper, R., Lüning, J. and Stehli, P. 1973. *Der bandkeramische Siedlungsplatz Langweiler 2, Gem. Aldenhoven, Kr. Düren*. Bonn: Rheinland-Verlag.

Fedele, F. (ed.) 1990. *L'Altopiano di Ossimo-Borno nella preistoria: ricerche 1988–90*. Breno: Edizioni del Centro.

Fischer, A. 1987. The Argus site – examination of a Mesolithic site 4–6 m below present sea level. *Mesolithic Miscellany* 8 (1), 1–4.

Fischer, U. 1991. Zur Terminologie der kupferführenden Kulturen in Mittel- und Süddeutschland. In J. Lichardus (ed.), *Die Kupferzeit als historische Epoche*, pp. 735–46. Bonn: Habelt.

Fol, A. and Lichardus, J. (eds.) 1988. *Macht, Herrschaft und Gold: das Gräberfeld von Varna und die Anfänge einer neuen europäischen Zivilisation*. Saarbrücken: Moderne Galerie des Saarland-Museums.

Fraccaro, M. 1986. *L'alba delle culture padane e il popolo preistorico di Remedello Sotto (Brescia)*. Maggio: Zanetti.

Gale, N. H., Stos-Gale, Z. A., Lilov, F., Dimitrov, M. and Todorov, T. 1991. Recent studies of eneolithic copper ores and artefacts in Bulgaria. In C. Eluère and J.-P. Mohen (eds.), *Découverte du métal*, pp. 77–84. Paris: Picard.

Gallay, A. 1990. Historique des recherches enterprises sur le nécropole mégalithique du Petit-Chasseur à Sion (Valais, Suisse). In J. Guilaine and X. Gutherz (eds.), *Autour de Jean Arnal*, pp. 335–57. Montpellier: Premières Communautés Paysannes.

Gallis, K. J. 1985. A late neolithic foundation offering from Thessaly. *Antiquity* 59, 20–4.

Geddes, D. 1980. *De la chasse au troupeau en Méditerranée occidentale: les débuts de l'élevage dan le bassin de l'Aude*. Toulouse: Ecole des Hautes Etudes en Sciences Sociales.

   1983. Neolithic transhumance in the Mediterranean Pyrenees. *World Archaeology* 15, 51–66.

   1985. Mesolithic domestic sheep in western Mediterranean Europe. *Journal of Archaeological Science* 12, 25–48.

Geddes, D., Guilaine, J., Coularou, J., Le Gall, O. and Martzluff, M. 1989. Postglacial environments, settlement and subsistence in the Pyrenees: the Balma Margineda, Andorra. In C. Bonsall (ed.), *The Mesolithic in Europe*, pp. 561–71. Edinburgh: John Donald.

Gellner, E. 1988. *Plough, sword and book: the structure of human history*. London: Collins Harvill.

Genick, D. C. and Cremonesi, R. G. 1991. Osservazioni sulle attività minerarie e metallurgiche nel Calcolitico italiano. *Archéologie en Languedoc* 1990/1991, 27–34.

Georgiev, G. I. 1961. Kulturgruppen der Jungstein- und der Kupferzeit in der Ebene von Thrazien (Südbulgarien). In J. Böhm and S. J. de Laet (eds.), *L'Europe à la fin de l'âge de la pierre*, pp. 45–100. Prague: Editions de l'Académie Tchechoslovaque des Sciences.

   1965. The Azmak mound in southern Bulgaria. *Antiquity* 39, 6–8.

Georgiev, G. I., Merpert, N. J., Katincharov, R. V. and Dimitrov, D. G. 1979. *Ezero, rannobronzovoto selishe*. Sofia: Bulgarian Academy of Sciences.

Gilman, A. 1981. The development of social stratification in Bronze Age Europe. *Current Anthropology* 22, 1–23.

   1987. Unequal development in Copper Age Iberia. In E. M. Brumfiel and T. K. Earle (eds.), *Specialization, exchange and complex societies*, pp. 22–9. Cambridge: Cambridge University Press.

Gilman, A. and Thornes, J. B. 1985. *Land-use and prehistory in south-east Spain*. London: Allen and Unwin.

Gimbutas, M. 1973. The beginning of the Bronze Age in Europe and the Indo-Europeans. *Journal of Indo-European Studies* 1, 163–214.

   1974. *The gods and goddesses of Old Europe*. London: Thames and Hudson.

   1989. *The language of the goddess*. San Francisco: Harper and Row.

   1991. *The civilization of the goddess*. San Francisco: HarperSanFrancisco.

Gimbutas, M. (ed.) 1976. *Neolithic Macedonia as reflected by excavation at Anza*. Los Angeles: Institute of Archaeology, University of California, Los Angeles.

Gimbutas, M., Winn, S. and Shimabuku, D. 1989. *Achilleion: a Neolithic settlement in Thessaly, Greece, 6400–5600 BC*. Los Angeles: Institute of Archaeology, University of California, Los Angeles.

Gosden, C. 1994. *Social being and time*. Oxford: Blackwell.

Gramsch, B. 1992. Friesack Mesolithic wetlands. In B. Coles (ed.), *The wetland revolution in prehistory*, pp. 65–72. Exeter: WARP/The Prehistoric Society.

Gramsch, B. and Kloss, K. 1989. Excavations near Friesack: an Early Mesolithic marshland site on the northern plain of central Europe. In C. Bonsall (ed.), *The Mesolithic in Europe*, pp. 313–24. Edinburgh: John Donald.

Gronenborn, D. 1990. Mesolithic–Neolithic interactions. The lithic industry of the earliest Bandkeramik culture site at Friedberg-Bruchenbrücken, Wetteraukreis (West Germany). In P. M. Vermeersch and P. van Peer (eds.), *Contributions to the Mesolithic in Europe*, pp. 173–82. Leuven: Leuven University Press.

Gross, E. 1990. Entwicklungen der neolithischen Kulturen im west- und ostschweizerischen Mittelland. In M. Höneisen (ed.), *Die ersten Bauern, I*, pp. 61–72. Zürich: Schweizerisches Landesmuseum.

Gross, E., *et al.* 1987. *Zürich 'Mozartstrasse'. Neolithische und bronzezeitliche Ufersiedlungen. I*. Zürich: Orell Füssli.

Grygiel, R. 1986. The household cluster as a fundamental social unit of the Lengyel culture in the Polish lowlands. *Prace i Materialy Muzeum Archeologicznego i Etnograficznego w Łodzi, Seria Archeologiczna* 31, 43–334.

Guilaine, J., Barbaza, M., Gasco, J., Geddes, D., Jalut, G. and Vaquer, J. 1987. L'abri du roc de Dourgne: écologie des cultures du Mésolithique et du Néolithique ancien dans une vallée montagnarde des Pyrénées de l'Est. In J. Guilaine *et al.* (eds.), *Premières communautés paysannes en Méditerranée occidentale*, pp. 545–54. Paris: CNRS.

Guilaine, J., Coularou, J., Freises, A. and Montjardin, R. (eds.) 1984. *Leucate-Corrège: habitat noyé du Néolithique cardial*. Toulouse and Sète: Centre d'Anthropologie des Sociétés Rurales and Musée Paul Valéry.

Guilaine, J., Courtin, J., Roudil, J. and Vernet, J.-L. (eds.) 1987. *Premières communautés paysannes en Méditerranée occidentale*. Paris: CNRS.

Guilaine, J., Gasco, J., Vaquer, J. and Barbaza, M. 1979. *L'abri Jean-Cros: essai d'approche d'un communauté du Néolithique ancien dans son environnement*. Toulouse: Centre d'Anthropologie des Sociétés Rurales.

Halstead, P. 1989. The economy has a normal surplus: economic stability and social change among early farming communities of Thessaly, Greece. In P. Halstead and J. O'Shea (eds.), *Bad year economics: cultural responses to risk and uncertainty*, pp. 68–80. Cambridge: Cambridge University Press.

1992. Dimini and the 'DMP': faunal remains and animal exploitation in Late Neolithic Thessaly. *Annual of the British School at Athens* 87, 29–59.

1993. *Spondylus* shell ornaments from late Neolithic Dimini, Greece: specialized manufacture or unequal accumulation? *Antiquity* 67, 603–9.

Halstead, P. and Jones, G. 1980. Early Neolithic economy in Thessaly – some evidence from excavations in Prodromos. *Anthropoloyika* 1, 93–117.

Hansen, J. M. 1991. *The palaeoethnobotany of Franchthi Cave*. Bloomington and Indianopolis: Indiana University Press.

1992. Franchthi cave and the beginnings of agriculture in Greece and the Aegean. In P. C. Anderson (ed.), *Préhistoire de l'agriculture: nouvelles approches expérimentales et ethnographiques*, pp. 231–47. Paris: CNRS.

Hansen, M. and Rostholm, H. 1993. Single graves and late Neolithic graves. In S. Hvass and B. Storgaard (eds.), *Digging into the past: 25 years of archaeology in Denmark*, pp. 116–21. Copenhagen and Aarhus: Royal Society of Northern Antiquaries and Jutland Archaeological Society.

Harbison, P. 1988. *Pre-Christian Ireland: from the first settlers to the early Celts*. London: Thames and Hudson.

Harrison, R. J. 1994. The Bronze Age in northern and northeastern Spain, 2000–800 BC. In C. Mathers and S. Stoddart (eds.), *Development and decline in the Mediterranean Bronze Age*, pp. 73–97. Sheffield: J. R. Collis Publications.

Hegedüs, K. and Makkay, J. 1987. Vésztő-Mágor. A settlement of the Tisza culture. In P. Raczky (ed.), *The Late Neolithic of the Tisza region*, pp. 85–103. Budapest/Szolnok.

Hiller, S. 1990. Neue Ausgrabungen in Karanovo. In D. Srejović and N. Tasić (eds.), *Vinča and its world: international symposium. The Danubian region from 6000 to 3000 BC*, pp. 197–206. Belgrade: Serbian Academy of Sciences.

Hiller, S. and Nikolov, V. 1989. *Tell Karanovo: Vorläufiger Ausgrabungsbericht*. Salzburg: Institut für Klassische Archäologie der Universität Salzburg.

Höckmann, O. 1982. Zur Verteilung von Männer- und Frauengräbern auf Gräberfeldern des Frühneolithikums und des älteren Mittelneolithikums. *Jahrbuch des Römisch-Germanischen Zentralmuseums* 29, 13–73.

Hodder, I. 1990. *The domestication of Europe*. Oxford: Blackwell.

1992. The domestication of Europe. In I. Hodder, *Theory and practice in archaeology*, pp. 241–53. London and New York: Routledge.

Holloway, R. R. 1973. *Buccino: the Eneolithic necropolis of S. Antonio and other prehistoric discoveries made in 1968 and 1969 by Brown University*. Rome: De Luca.

1975. Buccino: the Early Bronze Age village of Tufariello. *Journal of Field Archaeology* 2, 11–81.

Höneisen, M. (ed.) 1990. *Die ersten Bauern* (2 vols.). Zürich: Schweizerisches Landesmuseum.

Horváth, F. 1987. Hódmezővásárhely-Gorsza. A settlement of the Tisza culture. In P. Raczky (ed.), *The Late Neolithic of the Tisza region*, pp. 31–46. Budapest/Szolnok.

1989. A survey of the development of Neolithic settlement pattern and house types in the Tisza region. In S. Bökönyi (ed.), *Neolithic of southeastern Europe and its Near Eastern connections*, pp. 85–101. Budapest: Institute of Archaeology, Hungarian Academy of Sciences.

Hourmouziadis, G. 1979. *To Neolithiko Dimini*. Volos: Etairia Thessalikon Ereunon.

Hvass, S. and Storgaard, B. (eds.) 1993. *Digging into the past: 25 years of archaeology in Denmark*. Copenhagen and Aarhus: Royal Society of Northern Antiquaries and Jutland Archaeological Society.

Ingold, T. 1986. *The appropriation of nature*. Manchester: Manchester University Press.

Ingold, T., Riches, D. and Woodburn, J. 1988a. *Hunters and gatherers 1. History, evolution and social change*. Oxford: Berg.

1988b. *Hunters and gatherers 2. Property, power and ideology*. Oxford: Berg.

Ivanov, I. 1988. Die Ausgrabungen des Gräberfeldes von Varna (1972–1986). In A. Fol and J. Lichardus (eds.), *Macht, Herrschaft und Gold: das Gräberfeld von Varna und die Anfänge einer neuen europäischen Zivilisation*, pp. 49–65. Saarbrücken: Moderne Galerie des Saarland-Museums.

1989. La nécropole chalcolithique de Varna et les cités lacustres voisines. In C. Eluère (ed.), *Le premier or de l'humanité en Bulgarie 5ᵉ millénaire*, pp. 49–56. Paris: Editions de la Réunion des Musées Nationaux.

Jacobsen, T. W. 1981. The Franchthi cave and the beginnings of settled village life in Greece. *Hesperia* 50, 303–19.

Jacobsen, T. W. and Farrand, W. R. 1988. *Franchthi Cave and Paralia: maps, plans and sections*. Bloomington and Indianapolis: Indiana University Press.

Jennbert, K. 1984. *Den produktiva gåvan*. Lund: CWK Gleerup.

Jeunesse, C. 1990. Le Néolithique alsacien et ses relations avec les régions voisines. In M. Höneisen (ed.), *Die ersten Bauern, II*, pp. 177–94. Zürich: Schweizerisches Landesmuseum.

Jochim, M. A. 1990. The late Mesolithic in southwest Germany: culture change or population decline. In P. M. Vermeersch and P. van Peer (eds.), *Contributions to the Mesolithic in Europe*, pp. 183–91. Leuven: Leuven University Press.

Jones, G. D. B. 1987. *Apulia. Volume I: Neolithic settlement in the Tavoliere*. London: Society of Antiquaries.

Jørgensen, E. 1977. *Hagebrogård–Vroue–Kolkur: neolithische Gräberfelder aus nordwest-Jütland*. Copenhagen: Akademisk Forlag.

1993. Jutland stone-packing graves. In S. Hvass and B. Storgaard (eds.), *Digging into the past: 25 years of archaeology in Denmark*, pp. 112–13. Copenhagen and Aarhus: Royal Society of Northern Antiquaries and Jutland Archaeological Society.

Jovanovic, B. 1990. Die Vinča-Kultur und der Beginn der Metallnutzung auf der Balkan. In D. Srejović and N. Tasić (eds.), *Vinča and its world*, pp. 55–60. Belgrade: Serbian Academy of Sciences and Arts.

Kaiser, T. and Voytek, B. 1983. Sedentism and economic change in the Balkan Neolithic. *Journal of Anthropological Archaeology* 2, 323–53.

Kalb, P. 1989. Überlegungen zu Neolithisierung und Megalithik im Westen der Iberischen Halbinsel. *Madrider Mitteilungen* 30, 31–54.

Kalicz, N. 1970. *Clay gods: the Neolithic period and Copper Age in Hungary*. Budapest: Corvina Press.

    1985. *Kökori falu Aszódon*. Aszód: Petőfi Múzeum.

    1986. Über das spätneolithische Siedlungswesen in Ungarn. *A Béri Balogh Ádám Múzeum Évkönyve* 13, 127–38.

Kalicz, N. and Makkay, J. 1977. *Die Linienbandkeramik in der grosser Ungarischen Tiefebene*. Budapest: Akadémiai Kiadó.

Kalicz, N. and Raczky, P. 1984. Preliminary report on the 1977–82 excavations at the Neolithic and Bronze Age tell settlement at Berettyóújfalu-Herpály. Part I: Neolithic. *Acta Archaeologica Academiae Scientiarum Hungaricae* 36, 85–136.

    1987a. The Late Neolithic of the Tisza region: a survey of recent archaeological research. In P. Raczky (ed.), *The Late Neolithic of the Tisza region*, pp. 11–30. Budapest/Szolnok.

    1987b. Berettyóújfalu-Herpály. A settlement of the Herpály culture. In P. Raczky (ed.), *The Late Neolithic of the Tisza region*, pp. 105–25. Budapest/Szolnok.

Katz, S. H. and Voigt, M. M. 1990. Bread and beer: the early use of cereals in human diet. *Expedition* 28, 23–34.

Keeley, L. H. and Cahen, D. 1989. Early Neolithic forts and villages in NE Belgium: a preliminary report. *Journal of Field Archaeology* 16, 157–76.

Kent, S. 1992. The current forager controversy: real versus ideal views of hunter-gatherers. *Man* 27, 45–70.

Korek, J. 1987. Szegvár-Tűzköves. A settlement of the Tisza culture. In P. Raczky (ed.), *The Late Neolithic of the Tisza region*, pp. 47–60. Budapest/Szolnok.

Kosse, K. 1979. *Settlement ecology of the Early and Middle Neolithic Körös and Linear Pottery cultures in Hungary*. Oxford: British Archaeological Reports.

Kotsakis, K. 1981. Tria oikamata tou oikismou tou Sesklou: anaskafiki erevna. *Anthropoloyika* 2, 87–108.

    1995. The use of habitational space in Neolithic Sesklo. In J.-C. Decourt, B. Helly and K. Gallis (eds.), *La Thessalie, Colloque international d'archéologie: 15 années de recherches (1975–1990), bilans et perspectives, Lyon, 1990*, pp. 125–30. Athens: Tameio Arhaiologikon poron kai apallotrioseon.

Kozłowski, S. K. 1991. *Mesolithic in Poland: a new approach*. Warsaw: Wydawnictwa Uniwersytetu Warszawskiego.

Kreuz, A. M. 1990. *Die ersten Bauern Mitteleuropas – eine archäobotanische Untersuchung zu Umwelt und Landwirtschaft der ältesten Bandkeramik*. Leiden: Leiden University Press.

Kristiansen, K. 1991. Prehistoric migrations – the case of the Single Grave and Corded Ware cultures. *Journal of Danish Archaeology* 8, 211–25.

Kruk, J. 1980. *The Neolithic settlement of southern Poland*. Oxford: British Archaeological Reports.

Kuper, R., Löhr, H., Lüning, J., Stehli, P. and Zimmerman, A. 1977. *Der bandkeramische Siedlungsplatz Langweiler 9, Gem. Aldenhoven, Kr. Düren*. Bonn: Rheinland-Verlag.

Kyparissi-Apostolika, N. 1995. Prehistoric inhabitation in Theopetra cave, Thessaly. In J.-C. Decourt, B. Helly and K. Gallis (eds.), *La Thessalie, Colloque international d'archéologie: 15 années de recherches (1975–1990), bilans et perspectives, Lyon, 1990*, pp. 103–8. Athens: Tameio Arhaiologikon poron kai apallotrioseon.

Larsson, L. 1990. The Mesolithic of southern Scandinavia. *Journal of World Prehistory* 4, 257–309.

    1993. The Skateholm project: late Mesolithic coastal settlement in southern Sweden. In P. Bogucki (ed.), *Case studies in European prehistory*, pp. 31–62. Boca Raton, Florida: CRC Press.

Lech, J. 1980. Flint mining among the early farming communities of central Europe. *Przegląd Archeologiczny* 28, 5–55.

1982. Flint mining among the early farming communities of central Europe. Part II – the basis of research into flint workshops. *Przegląd Archeologiczny* 30, 47–80.

1989. A Danubian raw material exchange network: a case study from Bylany. In J. Rulf (ed.), *Bylany seminar 1987*, pp. 111–20. Prague: Institute of Archaeology.

Legge, A. J. and Rowley-Conwy, P. A. 1988. *Star Carr revisited. A re-analysis of the large mammals.* London: Centre for Extra-Mural Studies, Birkbeck College, University of London.

Leisner, G. and Leisner, V. 1943. *Die Megalithgräber der Iberischen Halbinsel: der Süden.* Berlin: de Gruyter.

1956. *Die Megalithgräber der Iberischen Halbinsel: der Westen 1. Lieferung.* Berlin: de Gruyter.

Leisner, V. 1965. *Die Megalithgräber der Iberischen Halbinsel: Der Westen 3. Lieferung.* Berlin: de Gruyter.

Lenneis, E. 1989. Zum Forschungstand der ältesten Bandkeramik in Österreich. *Archäologisches Korrespondenzblatt* 19, 23–36.

1991. Zu den ersten festen Wohnhäusern und Siedlungen im Raume Österreichs. *Mitteilungen der Anthropologischen Gesellschaft in Wien* 121, 121–36.

Lewthwaite, J. 1982. Acorns for the ancestors: the prehistoric exploitation of woodlands in the west Mediterranean. In M. Bell and S. Limbrey (eds.), *Archaeological aspects of woodland ecology*, pp. 217–30. Oxford: British Archaeological Reports.

1983. The Neolithic of Corsica. In C. Scarre (ed.), *The Neolithic of France*, pp.146–83. Edinburgh: Edinburgh University Press.

1986. From Menton to Mondego in three steps: application of the availability model to the transition to food production in Occitania, Mediterranean Spain and southern Portugal. *Arqueologia* 13, 95–119.

1989. Isolating the residuals: the Mesolithic basis of man–animal relationships on the Mediterranean islands. In C. Bonsall (ed.), *The Mesolithic in Europe*, pp. 541–55. Edinburgh: John Donald.

L'Helgouach, J. and Le Roux, C.-T. 1986. Morphologie et chronologie des grandes architectures de l'Ouest de la France. In J.-P. Demoule and J. Guilaine (eds.), *Le Néolithique de la France*, pp. 181–91. Paris: Picard.

Lichardus, J. 1988. Der westpontische Raum und die Anfänge der kupferzeitlichen Zivilisation. In A. Fol and J. Lichardus (eds.), *Macht, Herrschaft und Gold: das Gräberfeld von Varna und die Anfänge einer neuen europäischen Zivilisation*, pp. 79–129. Saarbrücken: Moderne Galerie des Saarland-Museums.

Lieberman, D. E. 1993. The rise and fall of seasonal mobility among hunter-gatherers. The case of the southern Levant. *Current Anthropology* 34, 599–631.

Liversage, D. 1992. *Barkaer: long barrows and settlements.* Copenhagen: Akademisk Forlag

Louwe Kooijmans, L. P. 1991. An early Bandkeramic settlement and a Roman cemetery at Geleen-Janskamperveld (Netherlands). *Notae Praehistoricae* 11, 63–5.

1993. The Mesolithic/Neolithic transformation in the lower Rhine basin. In P. Bogucki (ed.), *Case studies in European prehistory*, pp. 95–145. Boca Raton, Florida: CRC Press.

Lüning, J. 1967. Die Michelsberger Kultur. Ihre Funde in zeitlicher und räumlicher Gliederung. *Bericht der Römisch-Germanischen Kommission* 48, 1–350.

1982. Siedlung und Siedlungslandschaft in bandkeramischer und Rössener Zeit, *Offa* 39, 9–33.

1988a. Frühe Bauern in Mitteleuropa im 6. und 5. Jahrtausend v. Chr. *Jahrbuch des Römisch-Germanischen Zentralmuseums Mainz* 35, 27–93.

1988b. Zur Verbreitung und Datierung bandkeramischer Erdwerke. *Archäologisches Korrespondenzblatt* 18, 155–8.

Lüning, J., Kloos, U. and Albert, S. 1989. Westliche Nachbarn der bandkeramischen Kultur: Die Keramikgruppen La Hoguette und Limburg. *Germania* 67, 355–421.

Lüning, J. and Stehli, P. 1994. *Die Bandkeramik im Merzbachtal auf der Aldenhovener Platte.* Bonn: Habelt.

McPherron, A. and Srejović, D. 1988. *Divostin and the Neolithic of central Serbia.* Pittsburgh: Department of Anthropology, University of Pittsburgh.

Madsen, T. 1982. Settlement systems of early agricultural societies in east Jutland, Denmark: a regional study of change. *Journal of Anthropological Archaeology* 1, 197–236.

1988. Causewayed enclosures in south Scandinavia. In C. Burgess, P. Topping, C. Mordant and M. Maddison (eds.), *Enclosures and defences in the Neolithic of western Europe*, pp. 301–36. Oxford: British Archaeological Reports.

Magny, M. 1993. Une nouvelle mise en perspective des sites archéologiques lacustres: les fluctuations holocènes des lacs jurassiens et alpins. *Gallia Préhistoire* 35, 253–82.

Makkay, J. 1978. Excavations at Bicske. I. The early Neolithic – the earliest Linear Band ceramic. *Alba Regia* 16, 9–60.

1991. The most ancient gold and silver in central and S.E. Europe. In C. Eluère and J.-P. Mohen (eds.), *Découverte du métal*, pp. 119–29. Paris: Picard.

1992. Excavations at the Körös culture settlement of Endrőd-Öregszőlők 119 in 1986–1989. In S. Bökönyi (ed.), *Landscape and cultural changes in south-east Hungary. I. Reports on the Gyomaendrőd project*, pp. 121–93. Budapest: Institute of Archaeology, Hungarian Academy of Sciences.

Mallory, J. P. 1989. *In search of the Indo-Europeans*. London: Thames and Hudson.

Malone, C. 1985. Pots, prestige and ritual in Neolithic southern Italy. In C. Malone and S. Stoddart (eds.), *Papers in Italian archaeology IV. Part ii. Prehistory*, pp. 118–51. Oxford: British Archaeological Reports.

Malone, C., Stoddart, S. and Trump, D. 1988. A house for the temple builders. *Antiquity* 62, 297–301.

Manfredini, A. and Cassano, S. M. 1983. *Studi sul Neolitico del Tavoliere della Puglia: indagine territoriale in un' area-campione*. Oxford: British Archaeological Reports.

Marinescu-Bîlcu, S. 1981. *Tîrpeşti: from prehistory to history in eastern Romania*. Oxford: British Archaeological Reports.

Martí-Oliver, B. 1988. Early farming communities in Spain. *Berytus* 36, 69–86.

Mathers, C. 1984. Beyond the grave: the context and wider implications of mortuary practices in south-east Spain. In T. F. C. Blagg, R. F. J. Jones and S. J. Keay (eds.), *Papers in Iberian archaeology*, pp. 13–44. Oxford: British Archaeological Reports.

1994. Goodbye to all that? Contrasting patterns of change in the south-east Iberian Bronze Age *c.* 24/2200–600 B C. In C. Mathers and S. Stoddart (eds.), *Development and decline in the Mediterranean Bronze Age*, pp. 21–71. Sheffield: J. R. Collis Publications.

Meisenheimer, M. 1989. *Das Totenritual, geprägt durch Jenseitsvorstellungen und Gesellschaftsrealität. Theorie des Totenrituals eines kupferzeitlichen Friedhofs zu Tiszapolgár-Basatanya (Ungarn)*. Oxford: British Archaeological Reports.

Mellars, P. (ed.) 1987. *Excavations on Oronsay*. Edinburgh: Edinburgh University Press.

Micó, R. 1991. El calcolitico del sudeste peninsular. *Revista d'Arqueologia de Ponent* 1, 51–70.

Midgley, M. S. 1985. *The origin and function of the earthen long barrows of northern Europe*. Oxford: British Archaeological Reports.

1992. *TRB culture: the first farmers of the north European plain*. Edinburgh: Edinburgh University Press.

Milisauskas, S. 1986. *Early Neolithic settlement and society at Olszanica*. Ann Arbor: Museum of Anthropology, University of Michigan.

Milisauskas, S. and Kruk, J. 1993. Archaeological investigations on Neolithic and Bronze Age sites in southeastern Poland. In P. Bogucki (ed.), *Case studies in European prehistory*, pp. 63–94. Boca Raton, Florida: CRC Press.

Milliken, S. and Skeates, R. 1989. The Alimini survey: the Mesolithic–Neolithic transition in the Salento peninsula (S.E. Italy). *Bulletin of the Institute of Archaeology, London* 26, 77–98.

Mills, N. 1983. The Neolithic of southern France. In C. Scarre (ed.), *The Neolithic of France*, pp. 91–145. Edinburgh: Edinburgh University Press.

Milojčić, V. 1960. *Hauptergebnisse der deutschen Ausgrabungen in Thessalien 1953–1958*. Bonn: Rudolf Habelt.

Milojčić, V., Boessneck, J. and Hopf, M. 1962. *Die deutschen Ausgrabungen auf der Argissa-Magula in Thessalien, I: das präkeramische Neolithikum sowie die Tier- und Pflanzenreste.* Bonn: Rudolf Habelt.

Modderman, P. J. R. 1970. *Linearbandkeramik aus Elsloo und Stein.* Leiden: Leiden University Press.

1988. The Linear Pottery culture: diversity in uniformity. *Berichten van de Rijksdienst voor het Ouheidkundig Bodemonderzoek* 38, 63–139.

Mordant, C. and Mordant, D. 1992. Noyen-sur-Seine: a mesolithic waterside settlement. In B. Coles (ed.), *The wetland revolution in prehistory*, pp. 55–64. Exeter: WARP/The Prehistoric Society.

Němejcová-Pavúková, V. 1986a. Vorbericht über die Ergebnisse der systematischen Grabung in Svodín in den Jahren 1971–1983. *Slovenská Archeológia* 34, 133–73.

Němejcová-Pavúková, V. (ed.) 1986b. *Internationales Symposium über die Lengyel-Kultur.* Nitra and Vienna: Archäologisches Institut der Slowakischen Akademie der Wissenschaften in Nitra and Institut für Ur- und Frühgeschichte der Universität Wien.

Nielsen, P. O. 1993a. The Neolithic. In S. Hvass and B. Storgaard (eds.), *Digging into the past: 25 years of archaeology in Denmark*, pp. 84–8. Copenhagen and Aarhus: Royal Society of Northern Antiquaries and Jutland Archaeological Society.

1993b. Settlement. In S. Hvass and B. Storgaard (eds.), *Digging into the past: 25 years of archaeology in Denmark*, pp. 92–5. Copenhagen and Aarhus: Royal Society of Northern Antiquaries and Jutland Archaeological Society.

Nikolov, B. 1978. Développement du Chalcolithique en Bulgarie de l'ouest et du nord-ouest. *Studia Praehistorica* 1–2, 121–9.

Nikolov, V. 1992. Die Untersuchungen der frühneolithischen Siedlung Slatina (Sofia) in den Jahren 1985–1987. *Studia Praehistorica* 11–12, 68–73.

Nogaj-Chachaj, J. 1991. The stone-packed graves of the Funnel Beaker culture in Karmanovice, site 35. *Antiquity* 65, 628–39.

O'Kelly, M. J. 1982. *Newgrange.* London: Thames and Hudson.

Özdoğan, M. 1989. Neolithic cultures of northwestern Turkey. A general appraisal of the evidence and some considerations. In S. Bökönyi (ed.), *The Neolithic of southeastern Europe and its Near Eastern connections*, pp. 201–15. Budapest: Varia Archaeologica Hungarica.

Patton, M. 1993. *Statements in stone: monuments and society in Neolithic Brittany.* London: Routledge.

Păunescu, A. 1987. Le tardenoisien de l'Est et du Sud-Est de la Roumanie. *Dacia* 31, 11–19.

Pavlů, I. 1986. Neolithische Grabenanlagen in Böhmen. *A Béri Balogh Ádám Múzeum Évkönyve* 13, 255–63.

1989. Das Modell der neolithischen Siedlung in Bylany. In J. Rulf (ed.), *Bylany seminar 1987*, pp. 279–98. Prague: Institute of Archaeology.

Pavlů, I., Rulf, J. and Zápatocká, M. 1986. Theses on the Neolithic site of Bylany. *Památky Archeologické* 57, 288–412.

Pavúk, J. 1991. Lengyel-culture fortified settlements in Slovakia. *Antiquity* 65, 348–57.

Pavúk, J. (ed.) 1982. *Siedlungen der Kultur mit Linearkeramik in Europa.* Nitra: Archäologisches Institut der Slowakischen Akademie der Wissenschaften.

Pavúk, J. and Bakamska, A. 1989. Beitrag der Ausgrabung in Galabnik zur Erforschung des Neolithikums in Südosteuropa. In S. Bökönyi (ed.), *Neolithic of southeastern Europe and its Near Eastern connections*, pp. 223–31. Budapest: Institute of Archaeology, Hungarian Academy of Sciences.

Payne, S. 1975. Faunal change at Franchthi Cave from 20,000 BC to 3000 BC. In A. T. Clason (ed.), *Archaeozoological studies*, pp. 120–31. Amsterdam, Oxford and New York: North Holland Publishing Co. and American Elsevier Publishing Co.

Perlès, C. 1990a. *Les industries lithiques taillées de Franchthi (Argolide, Grèce). II. Les industries du Mésolithique et du Néolithique initial.* Bloomington and Indianapolis: Indiana University Press.

1990b. L'outillage de pierre taillée néolithique en Grèce: approvisionnement et exploitation des matières premières. *Bulletin de Correspondance Hellénique* 114, 1–42.

1992a. Systems of exchange and organisation of production in Neolithic Greece. *Journal of Mediterranean Archaeology* 5, 115–64.

1992b. In search of lithic strategies. A cognitive approach to prehistoric chipped stone assemblages. In J.-C. Gardin and C. S. Peebles (eds.), *Representations in archaeology*, pp. 223–47. Bloomington and Indianapolis: Indiana University Press.

Petrasch, J. 1990. Mittelneolithische Kreisgrabenanlagen in Mitteleuropa. *Bericht der Römisch-Germanischen Kommission* 71, 407–564.

Pétrequin, A.-M. and Pétrequin, P. 1988. *Le Néolithique des lacs: préhistoire des lacs de Chalain et de Clairvaux (4000–2000 av. J.-C.)*. Paris: Editions Errance.

Podborský, V. 1988. *Těšetice-Kyjovice 4: Rondel osady lidu s moravskou malovanou keramikou*. Brno: Purkyně Universita.

Pollmann, H.-O. 1993. *Obsidian im nordwestmediterranen Raum: seine Verbreitung und Nutzung im Neolithikum und Äneolithikum*. Oxford: Tempus Reparatum.

Price, T. D. and Gebauer, A. B. 1992. The final frontier: foragers to farmers in southern Scandinavia. In A. B. Gebauer and T. D. Price (eds.), *Transitions to agriculture in prehistory*, pp. 97–116. Madison: Prehistory Press.

Prinz, B. 1987. *Mesolithic adaptations on the lower Danube: Vlasac and the Iron Gates gorge*. Oxford: British Archaeological Reports.

Pucher, E. 1987. Viehwirtschaft und Jagd zur Zeit der ältesten Linearbandkeramik von Neckenmarkt (Burgenland) und Strögen (Niederösterreich). *Mitteilungen der Anthropologischen Gesellschaft in Wien* 117, 141–55.

Raczky, P. 1986. The cultural and chronological relations of the Tisza region during the Middle and Late Neolithic, as reflected by the excavations at Öcsöd-Kováshalom. *A Béri Balogh Ádám Múzeum Évkönyve* 13, 103–25.

1987a. Öcsöd-Kováshalom. A settlement of the Tisza culture. In P. Raczky (ed.), *The Late Neolithic of the Tisza region*, pp. 61–83. Budapest and Szolnok.

1989. Chronological framework of the Early and Middle Neolithic in the Tisza region. In S. Bökönyi (ed.), *Neolithic of southeastern Europe and its Near Eastern connections*, pp. 233–51. Budapest: Institute of Archaeology, Hungarian Academy of Sciences.

Raczky, P. (ed.) 1987b. *The Late Neolithic of the Tisza region*. Budapest and Szolnok.

Radunceva, A. 1976. *Vinitsa: eneolitno selishe i nekropol*. Sofia: Bulgarian Academy of Sciences.

1989. La société dans les Balkans à l'âge du cuivre. *Dossiers Histoire et Archéologie* 137, 46–55.

Rasmussen, L. W. 1993. Pitted Ware settlements. In S. Hvass and B. Storgaard (eds.), *Digging into the past: 25 years of archaeology in Denmark*, pp. 114–15. Copenhagen and Aarhus: Royal Society of Northern Antiquaries and Jutland Archaeological Society.

Renfrew, C. 1973. Monuments, mobilisation and social organisation in Neolithic Wessex. In C. Renfrew (ed.), *The explanation of culture change*, pp. 539–58. London: Duckworth.

1977. Space, time and polity. In J. Friedman and M. J. Rowlands (eds.), *The evolution of social systems*, pp. 89–114. London: Duckworth.

1987. *Archaeology and language*. London: Cape.

Renfrew, C. (ed.) 1990. *The prehistory of Orkney*. Edinburgh: Edinburgh University Press.

Renfrew, C., Gimbutas, M. and Elster, E. (eds.) 1986. *Excavations at Sitagroi: a prehistoric village in northeast Greece, I*. Los Angeles: Institute of Archaeology, University of California, Los Angeles.

Richards, J. 1990. *The Stonehenge environs project*. London: Historic Buildings and Monuments Commission.

Rodden, R. 1965. An Early Neolithic village in Greece. *Scientific American* 212, 82–8.

Rösch, M. 1993. Prehistoric land use as recorded in a lake-shore core at Lake Constance. *Vegetation History and Archaeobotany* 2, 213–32.

Rötting, H. 1985. Der älteste Totenplatz in Niedersachsen. In K. Wilhelmi (ed.), *Ausgrabungen in Niedersachsen, Denkmalpflege 1979–1984*, pp. 103–8. Stuttgart: Konrad Theiss.

Roussot-Larroque, J. 1989. Imported problems and home-made solutions: late foragers and pioneer farmers as seen from the west. In S. Bökönyi (ed.), *Neolithic of southeastern Europe and its Near Eastern connections*, pp. 253–71. Budapest: Institute of Archaeology, Hungarian Academy of Sciences.

Rowley-Conwy, P. 1992. Arene Candide: a small part of a larger pastoral system? *Rivista di Studi Liguri* 57, 95–116.

Rozoy, J. G. 1978. *Les derniers chasseurs: essai de synthèse sur l'Epipaléolithique en France et en Belgique*. Reims: Société Archéologique de Charleville.

Rulf, J. 1991. Die Umwelt zu Beginn des Äneolithikums in Mitteleuropa am Beispiel Böhmens. In J. Lichardus (ed.), *Kupferzeit als historische Epoche*, pp. 529–37. Bonn: Habelt.

Runnels, C. N. 1988. A prehistoric survey of Thessaly: new light on the Greek Middle Palaeolithic. *Journal of Field Archaeology* 15, 277–90.

Runnels, C. N. and van Andel, T. H. 1988. Trade and the origins of agriculture in the eastern Mediterranean. *Journal of Mediterranean Archaeology* 1, 83–109.

Sangmeister, E. and Schubart, H. 1981. *Zambujal: die Grabungen 1964 bis 1973*. Mainz: von Zabern.

Saville, A. 1990. *Hazleton North*. London: Historic Buildings and Monuments Commission.

Savory, H. N. 1968. *Spain and Portugal*. London: Thames and Hudson.

1972. The cultural sequence at Vila Nova de S. Pedro. *Madrider Mitteilungen* 13, 23–37.

Scarre, C., Switsur, R. and Mohen, J.-P. 1993. New radiocarbon dates from Bougon and the chronology of French passage-graves. *Antiquity* 67, 856–9.

Schadla-Hall, T. 1989. The Vale of Pickering in the early Mesolithic in context. In C. Bonsall (ed.), *The Mesolithic in Europe*, pp. 218–24. Edinburgh: John Donald.

Schlichtherle, H. 1990. Kulturgruppen zwischen Bodensee und Federsee. In M. Höneisen (ed.), *Die ersten Bauern, II*, pp. 135–56. Zürich: Schweizerisches Landesmuseum.

Schwellnus, W. 1983. Archäologische Untersuchungen im Rheinischen Braunkohlengebiet 1977–1981. *Rheinische Ausgrabungen* 24, 1–31.

Shackleton, J. C. and van Andel, T. H. 1985. Late Palaeolithic and Mesolithic coastlines of the western Mediterranean. *Cahiers Ligures de Préhistoire et de Protohistoire* 2, 7–19.

Shanks, M. and Tilley, C. 1982. Ideology, symbolic power and ritual communication: a reinterpretation of Neolithic mortuary practices. In I. Hodder (ed.), *Symbolic and structural archaeology*, pp. 129–54. Cambridge: Cambridge University Press.

Sharples, N. 1992. *Maiden Castle: excavations and field survey 1985–6*. London: Historic Buildings and Monuments Commission.

Shennan, S. J. 1993. Settlement and social change in central Europe, 3500–1500 BC. *Journal of World Prehistory* 7, 121–61.

Sherratt, A. G. 1981. Plough and pastoralism: aspects of the secondary products revolution. In I. Hodder, G. Isaac and N. Hammond (eds.), *Pattern of the past*, pp. 261–305. Cambridge: Cambridge University Press.

1982. Mobile resources: settlement and exchange in early agricultural Europe. In C. Renfrew and S. Shennan (eds.), *Ranking, resource and exchange*, pp. 13–26. Cambridge: Cambridge University Press.

1983. The development of Neolithic and Copper Age settlement in the Great Hungarian plain. Part II. Site survey and settlement dynamics. *Oxford Journal of Archaeology* 2, 13–41.

1987. Cups that cheered. In W. H. Waldren and R. C. Kennard (eds.), *Bell Beakers in the western Mediterranean*, pp. 81–114. Oxford: British Archaeological Reports.

1991. Sacred and profane substances: the ritual use of narcotics in later Neolithic Europe. In P. Garwood, D. Jennings, R. Skeates and J. Toms, *Sacred and profane*, pp. 50–64. Oxford: Oxford University Committee for Archaeology.

1994. The transformation of early agrarian Europe: the later Neolithic and Copper Ages 4500–2500 BC. In B. W. Cunliffe (ed.), *The Oxford Illustrated Prehistory of Europe*, pp. 167–201. Oxford: Oxford University Press.

Simmons, A. H. 1991. Humans, island colonization and Pleistocene extinctions in the Mediterranean: the view from Akrotiri *Aetokremnos*, Cyprus. *Antiquity* 65, 857–69.

Skaarup, J. 1993. Megalithic graves. In S. Hvass and B. Storgaard (eds.), *Digging into the past: 25 years of archaeology in Denmark*, pp. 104–9. Copenhagen and Aarhus: Royal Society of Northern Antiquaries and Jutland Archaeological Society.

Skeates, R. 1991. Thin-section analysis of Italian Neolithic pottery. In E. Herring, R. D. Whitehouse and J. Wilkins (eds.), *Papers of the fourth conference of Italian archaeology. Volume 3. New developments in Italian archaeology, part 1*, pp. 29–34, London: Accordia.

1994. Ritual, context and gender in Neolithic south-eastern Italy. *Journal of European Archaeology* 2, 153–67.

Soudský, B. 1962. The Neolithic site of Bylany. *Antiquity* 36, 190–200.

Soudsky, B. and Pavlů, I. 1972. The Linear Pottery culture settlement patterns in central Europe. In P. Ucko, R. Tringham and G. Dimbleby (eds.), *Man, settlement and urbanism*, pp. 317–28. London: Duckworth.

Spindler, K. 1981. *Cova da Moura*. Mainz: von Zabern.

1994. *The man in the ice*. London: Weidenfeld and Nicolson.

Srejović, D. 1972. *Europe's first monumental sculpture: new discoveries at Lepenski Vir*. London: Thames and Hudson.

1988. The Neolithic of Serbia: a review of research. In D. Srejović (ed.), *The Neolithic of Serbia: archaeological research 1948–1988*, pp. 5–19. Belgrade: Centre for Archaeological Research, Faculty of Philosophy, University of Belgrade.

Srejović, D. and Tasić, N. (eds.) 1990. *Vinča and its world*. Belgrade: Serbian Academy of Sciences and Arts.

Stehli, P. 1989. Merzbachtal – Umwelt und Geschichte einer bandkeramischen Siedlungskammer. *Germania* 67, 51–76.

Stöckli, W. E. 1990. Ein Siedlungsplatz im Neolithikum. Die neolithischen Ufersiedlungen von Twann im Kanton Bern. In M. Höneisen (ed.), *Die ersten Bauern*, *I*, pp. 307–10. Zürich: Schweizerisches Landesmuseum.

Stoddart, S., Bonanno, A., Gouder, T., Malone, C. and Trump, D. 1993. Cult in an island society: prehistoric Malta in context. *Cambridge Archaeological Journal* 3, 3–19.

Strahm, C. 1991. L'introduction de la métallurgie en Europe centrale. *Archéologie en Languedoc* 1990–1, 15–25.

1992. Die Dynamik der schnurkeramischen Entwicklung in der Schweiz und in Südwestdeutschland. In M. Buchvaldek and C. Strahm (eds.), *Die kontinentaleuropäischen Gruppen der Kultur mit Schnurkeramik*, pp. 163–77. Prague: Univerzita Karlova.

Strahm, C. and Wolf, C. 1990. Das Neolithikum der Westschweiz und die Seeufersiedlungen von Yverdon-les-Bains. In M. Höneisen (ed.), *Die ersten Bauern*, *I*, pp. 331–43. Zürich: Schweizerisches Landesmuseum.

Suter, P. J. 1987. *Zürich 'Kleiner Hafner': Tauchgrabungen 1981–1984*. Zürich: Orell Füssli.

Tagliacozzo, A. 1993. *Archeozoologia della Grotta dell' Uzzo, Sicilia*. Roma: Istituto poligrafico e zecca dello stato.

Talalay, L. E. 1991. Body imagery of the ancient Aegean. *Archaeology* 44(4), 46–9.

Telegin, D. Y. 1986. *Dereivka: a settlement and cemetery of Copper Age horse-keepers on the middle Dniepr*. Oxford: British Archaeological Reports.

Testart, A. 1982. The significance of food storage among hunter-gatherers: residence patterns, population densities, and social inequalities. *Current Anthropology* 23, 523–37.

Theocharis, D. 1973. *Neolithic Greece*. Athens: National Bank of Greece.

Thomas, J. 1987. Relations of production and social change in the Neolithic of north-west Europe. *Man* 22, 405–30.

1991. *Rethinking the Neolithic*. Cambridge: Cambridge University Press.

Thorpe, I. J. and Richards, C. C. 1984. The decline of ritual authority and the introduction of Beakers into Britain. In R. Bradley and J. Gardiner (eds.), *Neolithic studies*, pp. 67–84. Oxford: British Archaeological Reports.

Tinè, S. 1983. *Passo di Corvo e la civiltà neolitica del Tavoliere*. Genoa: Sagep.

1986. Nuovi scavi nella caverna della Arene Candide. In J.-P. Demoule and J. Guilaine (eds.), *Le Néolithique de la France*, pp. 95–111. Paris: Picard.

Todorova, H. 1978. *The Eneolithic in Bulgaria*. Oxford: British Archaeological Reports.

1981. Das Chronologiesystem von Karanovo im Lichte der neuen Forschungsergebnisse in Bulgarien. *Slovenská Archeológia* 29, 203–16.

1986. *Kamenno-mednata epoha v Bulgaria*. Sofia: Usdatelstvo nuaka u uskustvo.

1989. Ein Korrelationsversuch zwischen Klimaänderungen und prähistorischen Angaben. *Studia Praehistorica* 15, 25–8.

Todorova, H. (ed.) 1982. *Kupferzeitliche Siedlungen in Nordostbulgarien*. Munich: Beck.

Todorova, H. and Dimov, T. 1989. Ausgrabungen in Durankulak 1974–1987. In S. Bökönyi (ed.), *Neolithic of southeastern Europe and its Near Eastern connections*, pp. 291–310. Budapest: Institute of Archaeology, Hungarian Academy of Sciences.

Todorova, H., Ivanov, S., Vassilev, V., Hopf, M., Quitta, H. and Kohl, G. 1975. *Selishnata mogila pri Golyamo Delchevo*. Sofia: Bulgarskata Akademia na Naukite.

Todorova, H., Vassilev, V., Janusevic, Z., Kovaceva, M. and Valev, P. 1983. *Ovčarovo*. Sofia: Bulgarskata Akademia na Naukite.

Tringham, R. 1971. *Hunters, fishers and farmers of eastern Europe, 6000–3000 BC*. London: Hutchison University Library.

1991. Households with faces: the challenge of gender in prehistoric architectural remains. In J. M. Gero and M. W. Conkey (eds.), *Engendering archaeology: women and prehistory*, pp. 93–131. Oxford: Blackwell.

Tringham, R., Brukner, B., Kaiser, T., Borojević, K., Bukvić, L., Russell, N., Steli, P., Stevanović, M. and Voytek, B. 1992. Excavations at Opovo, 1985–7: socioeconomic change in the Balkan neolithic. *Journal of Field Archaeology* 19, 351–86.

Tringham, R., Brukner, B. and Voytek, B. 1985. The Opovo project: a study of socio-economic change in the Balkan Neolithic. *Journal of Field Archaeology* 12, 425–44.

Tringham, R. and Krstić, D. (eds.) 1990. *Selevac: a prehistoric village in Yugoslavia*. Los Angeles: Institute of Archaeology, University of California, Los Angeles.

Trnka, G. 1990. Zum Forschungsstand der mittelneolithischen Kreisgrabenanlagen in Österreich. *Jahresschrift für Mitteldeutsche Vorgeschichte* 73, 213–30.

1991. *Studien zu mittelneolithischen Kreisgrabenanlagen*. Vienna: Verlag der Österreichischen Akademie der Wissenschaften.

Tusa, S. 1985. The beginning of farming communities in Sicily: the evidence of Uzzo cave. In C. Malone and S. Stoddart (eds.), *Papers in Italian archaeology IV, Part ii, Prehistory*, pp. 61–82. Oxford: British Archaeological Reports.

van Andel, T. H., Gallis, K. and Toufexis, G. 1995. Early Neolithic farming in a Thessalian river landscape. In J. Lewin, M. G. Macklin and J. C. Woodward (eds.), *Mediterranean Quaternary river environments*, pp. 131–43. Rotterdam: Balkema.

van Andel, T. H. and Runnels, C. 1987. *Beyond the Acropolis: a rural Greek past*. Stanford: Stanford University Press.

van Andel, T. H. and Shackleton, J. C. 1982. Late Palaeolithic and Mesolithic coastlines of Greece and the Aegean. *Journal of Field Archaeology* 9, 445–54.

van Berg, P.-L. 1990. Céramique du Limbourg et néolithisation en Europe du Nord-Ouest. In D. Cahen and M. Otte (eds.), *Rubané et Cardial*, pp. 161–208. Liège: Université de Liège.

van de Velde, P. 1979. *On Bandkeramik social structure*. Leiden: Leiden University Press.

1990. Bandkeramik social inequality – a case study. *Germania* 68, 19–38.

Vang Petersen, P. 1984. Chronological and regional variation in the late Mesolithic of eastern Denmark. *Journal of Danish Archaeology* 3, 7–18.

Vaquer, J. 1990. *Le Néolithique en Languedoc occidental.* Paris: CNRS.

Vaquer, J., Geddes, D., Barbaza, M. and Erroux, J. 1986. Mesolithic plant exploitation at the Balma Abeurador (France). *Oxford Journal of Archaeology* 5, 1–18.

Veit, U. 1993. Burials within settlements of the Linienbandkeramik and Stichbandkeramik cultures of central Europe. On the social construction of death in early-Neolithic society. *Journal of European Archaeology* 1, 107–40.

Vermeersch, P. M. and van Peer, P. (eds.) 1990. *Contributions to the Mesolithic in Europe.* Leuven: Leuven University Press.

Vitelli, K. D. 1993. *Franchthi Neolithic pottery: classification and ceramic phases 1 and 2.* Bloomington and Indianapolis: Indiana University Press.

Weiner, J. 1993. Erkelenz, Stadt Erkelenz, Kreis Heinsberg. Abfall, Holzgeräte und drei Brunnenkästen. Neue Ergebnisse der Ausgrabung des bandkeramischen Holzbrunnens. *Archäologie im Rheinland 1992*, 27–32.

Whitehouse, R. D. 1986. Siticulosa Apulia revisited. *Antiquity* 60, 36–44.

    1992. *Underground religion: cult and culture in prehistoric Italy.* London: Accordia Research Centre.

Whitehouse, R. 1994. The British Museum 14C programme for Italian prehistory. In R. Skeates and R. Whitehouse (eds.), *Radiocarbon dating and Italian prehistory*, pp. 85–98. London: Accordia Research Centre.

Whittle, A. 1988. *Problems in Neolithic archaeology.* Cambridge: Cambridge University Press.

    1991. Wayland's Smithy, Oxfordshire: excavations at the Neolithic tomb in 1962–63 by R. J. C. Atkinson and S. Piggott. *Proceedings of the Prehistoric Society* 57(2), 61–101.

    1993. The Neolithic of the Avebury area: sequence, environment, settlement and monuments. *Oxford Journal of Archaeology* 12, 29–53.

Whittle, A. and Pollard, J. 1995. Windmill Hill causewayed enclosure: the harmony of symbols. In M. Edmonds and C. Richards (eds.), *Social life and social change: papers on the Neolithic of Atlantic Europe.* Glasgow: Cruithne Press.

Wijnen, M. 1982. *The early Neolithic I settlement at Sesklo: an early farming community in Thessaly, Greece.* Leiden: Leiden University Press.

Wiklak, H. 1990. Z badań nad osadnictwem fazy sarnowskiej kultury pucharów lejkowatych w Sarnowie na Kujawach. *Sprawozdani Archeologiczne* 42, 109–27.

Willms, C. 1985. Neolithischer Spondylusschmuck. Hundert Jahre Forschung. *Germania* 63, 331–43 .

Wiślański, T. (ed.) 1987. *Neolit i początki epoki brązu na ziemi Chełmińskiej.* Toruń: Instytut Archeologii i Etnografii Uniwersytetu Mikołaja Kopernika w Toruniu.

Wyss, R. 1988. Jungsteinzeitliche Bauerndörfer im Wauwilermoos – neuere Forschungs- und Grabungsergebnisse. In N. Tasić and J. Petrović (eds.), *Gomolava: Chronologie und Stratigraphie der vorgeschichtlichen und antiken Kulturen der Donauniederung und Südosteuropas*, pp. 124–44. Novi Sad: Vojvodanski Muzej.

Yoffee, N. 1990. Before Babel: a review article. *Proceedings of the Prehistoric Society* 56, 299–313.

Zalai-Gaál, I. 1988. Kösép-európai neolitikus temetők szociálarchaeológiai elemzése (Sozialarchäologische Untersuchungen des mitteleuropäischen Neolithikums aufgrund der Gräberfeldanalyse). *A Béri Balogh Ádám Múzeum Évkönyve* 14, 3–178.

Zangger, E. 1991. Prehistoric coastal environments in Greece: the vanished landscapes of Dimini Bay and Lake Lerna. *Journal of Field Archaeology* 18, 1–15.

Zilhão, 1993. The spread of agro-pastoral economies across Mediterranean Europe: a view from the far west. *Journal of Mediterranean Archaeology* 6, 5–63.

Zvelebil, M. and Dolukhanov, P. 1991. The transition to farming in eastern and northern Europe. *Journal of World Prehistory* 5, 233–78.

Zvelebil, M. and Rowley-Conwy, P. 1984. Transition to farming in northern Europe: a hunter-gatherer perspective. *Norwegian Archaeological Review* 17, 104–28.

INDEX

References to figures are in italics